THE SOCIAL STRUCTURE PERSPECTIVE	THE SOCIAL PROCESS PERSPECTIVE	THE SOCIAL CONFLICT PERSPECTIVE
Crime is acquired behavior.	Crime is socialized behavior.	Crime is socially created behavior.
Because aspects of the social environment are pathological.	Because interactions between individuals and their social environments include social processes whereby they learn to become deviant and criminal.	Because conflicts and contradictions within society create imbalances of power.
<ul><li>Pathological conditions include disorganization, strain, and culture conflict.</li><li>Individuals exposed to such conditions will acquire patterns of criminal behavior.</li></ul>	<ul><li>These social processes include differential learning, inadequate social integration, and stigmatization.</li></ul>	<ul><li>The state allows the ruling classes to define as criminal those actions/behaviors that go against their own interests.</li></ul>
<ul><li>Alter the structure of the social environment to eliminate its pathological conditions.</li><li>Improve individuals' quality of life; increase their opportunity for legitimate activities; and transform crime-prone neighborhoods and communities through a collaborative effort among law enforcement, community networks, and social service agencies.</li></ul>	<ul><li>Develop policies to counter the learning effects of social processes and to encourage positive associations, build social bonds, encourage self-control, and inhibit the damaging effects of negative labels.</li></ul>	<ul><li>Redistribute the wealth in society so as to eliminate class struggle.</li><li>Implement principles of conflict resolution and cooperative criminal justice alternatives that emphasize social equity, gender equality, equal justice for all, and an awareness of social issues when dealing with crime.</li></ul>

CRIMINOLOGY

William J. Chambliss
THE GEORGE WASHINGTON UNIVERSITY

Aida Y. Hass
MISSOURI STATE UNIVERSITY

Mc Graw Hill

Connect
Learn
Succeed™

The McGraw-Hill Companies

Mc Graw Hill
Connect
Learn
Succeed™

Published by McGraw-Hill, an imprint of The McGraw-Hill Companies, Inc., 1221 Avenue of the Americas, New York, NY 10020. Copyright © 2012. All rights reserved. Printed in the United States of America. No part of this publication may be reproduced or distributed in any form or by any means, or stored in a database or retrieval system, without the prior written consent of The McGraw-Hill Companies, Inc., including, but not limited to, in any network or other electronic storage or transmission, or broadcast for distance learning.

This book is printed on acid-free paper.

1 2 3 4 5 6 7 8 9 0 DOW/DOW 1 0 9 8 7 6 5 4 3 2 1
ISBN: 978-0-07-352797-0
MHID: 0-07-352797-1

Sponsoring Editor: *William Minick*
Marketing Manager: *Leslie Oberhuber*
Developmental Editor: *Elisa Adams*
Production Editor: *Catherine Morris*
Manuscript Editor: *Jennifer Gordon*
Design Manager: *Jeanne Schreiber*
Text Designer: *Elise Lansdon*
Cover Designer: *Kirk DouPonce*
Illustrators: *John and Judy Waller*
Photo Research Coordinator: *Alexandra Ambrose*
Photo Researcher: *Judy Mason*
Buyer: *Tandra Jorgensen*
Media Project Manager: *Jennifer Barrick*
Editorial Coordinator: *Amy Mittelman*
Composition: *Laserwords Private Limited*
Printing: *50# New Era Matte, R.R. Donnelley & Sons*

Vice President Editorial: *Michael Ryan*
Editorial Director: *William Glass*
Executive Editor: *Gina Boedeker*
Managing Development Editor: *Nancy Crochiere*

Cover: © Zsuzsanna Kilian/www.SXC.hu

Credits: The credits section for this book begins on page 447 and is considered an extension of the copyright page.

Library of Congress Cataloging-in-Publication Data
Chambliss, William J.
   Criminology : connecting theory, research, and practice / William Chambliss, Aida Hass.—1st ed.
      p. cm.
   Includes bibliographical references and index.
   ISBN-13: 978-0-07-352797-0 (alk. paper)
   ISBN-10: 0-07-352797-1 (alk. paper)
 1. Criminology. I. Hass, Aida. II. Title.
HV6025.C394 2012
364—dc23
                                                          2011029217

The Internet addresses listed in the text were accurate at the time of publication. The inclusion of a website does not indicate an endorsement by the authors or McGraw-Hill, and McGraw-Hill does not guarantee the accuracy of the information presented at these sites.

www.mhhe.com

Dedication

To Pernille Chambliss. To enjoy.

— William J. Chambliss

To my kids, Natalie and Sofie.

— Aida Y. Hass

ABOUT THE AUTHORS

William Chambliss is professor of sociology at George Washington University. He has written and edited over 25 books and numerous articles for professional journals in sociology, criminology, and law. His work integrating the study of crime with the creation and implementation of criminal law has been a central theme in his writing and research. His articles on the historical development of vagrancy laws and on the legal process as it affects different social classes and racial groups—and his efforts to introduce the study of state-organized crimes into the mainstream of social science research—have punctuated his career.

Professor Chambliss is the recipient of numerous awards and honors including a Doctorate of Laws Honoris Causa, University of Guelph, Guelph, Ontario, Canada, 1999; the 2009 Lifetime Achievement Award, Sociology of Law, American Sociological Association; the 2009 Lifetime Achievement Award, Law and Society, Society for the Study of Social Problems; the 2001 Edwin H. Sutherland Award, American Society of Criminology; the 1995 Major Achievement Award, American Society of Criminology; the 1986 Distinguished Leadership in Criminal Justice, Bruce Smith Sr. Award, Academy of Criminal Justice Sciences; and the 1985 Lifetime Achievement Award, Criminology, American Sociological Association.

Professor Chambliss is Past President of the American Society of Criminology and Past President of the Society for the Study of Social Problems. His current research covers a range of lifelong interests in international drug-control policy; class, race, gender, and criminal justice; and the history of piracy on the high seas.

Aida Hass received her doctorate from George Washington University in sociology in 1996 and has been a full-time professor at Missouri State University since 2006. Her major areas of interest are in criminology, deviance, and corrections. She taught for a number of years as an adjunct faculty at George Washington University, Catholic University, and American University and was also assistant professor at Fairmont State College for three years. Professor Hass has worked for the U.S. Department of Justice Federal Probation/ Parole Agency in the Office of Research and Evaluation, conducting program evaluation, policy implementation, and research development. Before joining Missouri State University, she conducted qualitative research for the Applied Research Center at California State University in Bakersfield on programmatic initiatives of the First 5 Kern Commission.

Professor Hass has taught Introduction to Criminal Justice; Analysis of Corrections; Community-Based Corrections; Criminology; Deviance and Control; and Youth and Delinquency. Her research interests include the development and implementation of community correctional alternatives to incarceration, the impact of the changing dynamics of sentencing and corrections on the structural operation of prisons, and the effect of prisoner reentry programs on successful integration of offenders after a period of extended incarceration.

BRIEF **CONTENTS**

CONTENTS

PART II
An Overview of Criminological Theory 102

5 Crime as Rational Behavior: Classical and Rational Choice Theories 102

6 Biological Theories: Crime Is in the Brain 124

9 Social Process Theories: Crime Is Socialized Behavior 198

10 Social Conflict Theories: Crime Is in the Conflict Inherent in Society 224

14 Crimes of the Powerful 330

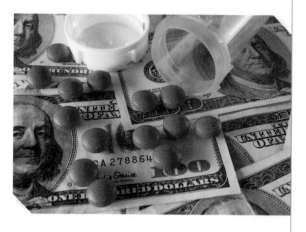

PART IV

A Look Ahead 352

15 Crime Today: Challenges Facing Criminal Justice Policy 352

16 Epilogue: The Future of Criminological Theory 373

LIST OF TABLES AND FIGURES

Figures

Tables

PREFACE

Connections among theory, research, and practice are the heart and soul of criminology. Yet students often are unaware of these connections—between scientific research and theory, between theory and practice, and between research and practice—because their textbook is not structured in a way that emphasizes them.

As a result, instead of using their critical thinking skills to understand how research and theory are linked, or how theories relate to the real world and can be applied through policy, students tend to memorize "facts," and they may never make the practical connections that provide the critical foundation in the study of criminology.

CRIMINOLOGY: CONNECTING THEORY, RESEARCH, AND PRACTICE

This book is different. It demonstrates the value of understanding the relationship among criminological theory, research, and practice in the study of crime and criminal behavior. In doing so, it better equips students to comprehend the role of criminological theory and research in the development of criminal justice policies and practices. In other words, *Criminology: Connecting Theory, Research, and Practice* supplies students with the vital connections they need to understand and succeed in criminology.

What are these connections and how do they work?

Connecting Theory to Research

Criminologists observe certain realities that characterize crime, crime trends, and criminal behavior. They study these realities and formulate theories based on their observations. They then conduct research to test various hypotheses based on those theories.

However, students need some basis for assessing the value—both empirical and theoretical—of the various theories they will encounter. Our book provides a model to do this that relies on the scientific method to describe and explain various theories within criminology. It highlights the stages of investigation in the construction of scientific theory and provides students with a way to understand the role of research in theory.

Connecting Theory and Research to Practice

Throughout the text—but particularly within the chapter-opening vignettes and the boxed features titled "Connecting Theory to Practice" and "Connecting Research to Practice"—we highlight the essential connections that show how policy is informed by theory and research. We translate the concepts articulated by criminological theory into very concrete questions that criminologists investigate through scientific research. Thus, we can show how the outcome of criminological research informs actual criminal justice practice.

We communicate to students this very important and integral connection: that theory drives research, and research dictates practices and policies. We also make an "inverse" connection: that once criminological theories have been tested through research, then policies should rest on the shoulders of sound academic theories that have proved to be valid and reliable.

Connecting Crime to Contemporary Society

One of the key themes of our narrative is that crime is both ubiquitous and embedded in the political, economic, and social relationships of modern societies. We understand crime only by analyzing the social forces that lead to criminal behavior. Crime is much more widespread than the murders, bank robberies, and drug deals our students normally envision. *Criminology: Connecting Theory, Research, and Practice* shows that it includes the criminality of corporation executives, college financial officers, professional athletes, government officials, cyberspace hackers, and purveyors of graffiti as well as street gangs and violent intimate partners.

Connecting Criminal Behavior with an Understanding of Criminal Law

It is imperative that students have a minimal understanding of how laws are created and of the basic principles of criminal law. We have found in our teaching, in fact, that students are keenly interested in obtaining at least a cursory understanding of criminal law and that this is one of the more popular reasons for non-majors to enroll in criminology classes. For all these reasons, Chapter 2 integrates the study of criminal behavior with a very brief introduction to criminal law.

This text breaks new ground in relating theory and research to practice more thoroughly and consistently than any other criminology text currently available. Instructors using this book will find their teaching challenges lessened because, for the first time, their students will see clearly how the study of criminology connects to the world they know.

FEATURES IN CRIMINOLOGY

Each chapter opens with an attention-grabbing photo and **learning objectives** phrased as questions to direct the student's focus as he or she reads. The same questions are repeated—and answered—in the chapter summary.

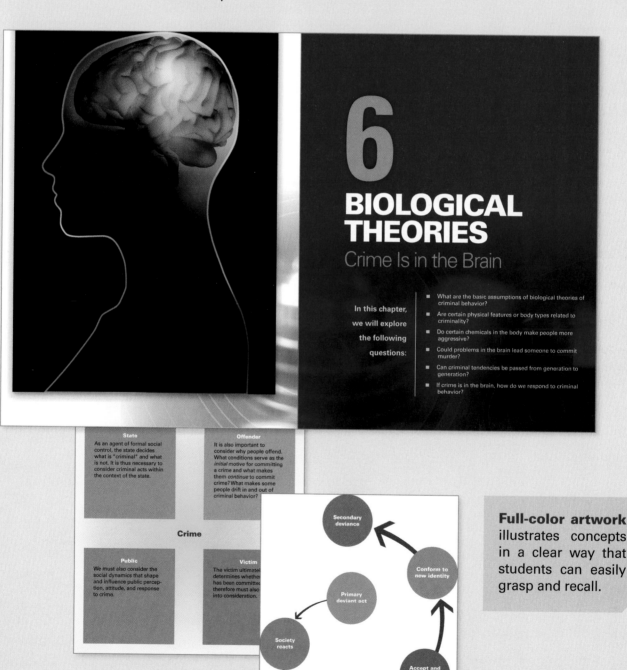

6

BIOLOGICAL THEORIES
Crime Is in the Brain

In this chapter, we will explore the following questions:

- What are the basic assumptions of biological theories of criminal behavior?
- Are certain physical features or body types related to criminality?
- Do certain chemicals in the body make people more aggressive?
- Could problems in the brain lead someone to commit murder?
- Can criminal tendencies be passed from generation to generation?
- If crime is in the brain, how do we respond to criminal behavior?

State
As an agent of formal social control, the state decides what is "criminal" and what is not. It is thus necessary to consider criminal acts within the context of the state.

Offender
It is also important to consider why people offend. What conditions serve as the *initial* motive for committing a crime and what makes them *continue* to commit crime? What makes some people drift in and out of criminal behavior?

Crime

Public
We must also consider the social dynamics that shape and influence public perception, attitude, and response to crime.

Victim
The victim ultimately determines whether has been committed therefore must also into consideration.

- Secondary deviance
- Conform to new identity
- Primary deviant act
- Society reacts
- Accept and internalize deviant label
- Deviance amplification

Full-color artwork illustrates concepts in a clear way that students can easily grasp and recall.

CONNECTING THEORY TO PRACTICE

Peer Pressure? Just Say "No"

While criminologists may not agree on the precise cause of crime and deviance, the various schools of thought can help us organize our understanding of this multifaceted social behavior and help us develop strategies at both the individual level and the societal level.

In the early 1980s, a campaign began across the United States encouraging young people to say no to a variety of vices, including taking drugs, having premarital sex, drinking alcohol, and committing violence. The campaign was largely influenced by a National Institutes of Health (NIH) theoretical research model supporting substance abuse prevention, developed by University of Houston social psychology professor Richard Evans. Evans proposed "inoculating" teens with the learning tools and skills necessary to resist peer pressure and other negative social influences.

In 1983, the campaign turned global with the founding of DARE—Drug Abuse Resistance Education, designed to discourage children from using illegal drugs, joining gangs, smoking, and drinking alcohol by teaching them to resist peer pressure, act in their own interests, and understand the adverse effects of alcohol, tobacco, and drugs.

At the heart of this and other similar programs is the focus on education to build skills and strategies to resist the temptations of getting involved in crime and delinquency. The focus of these programs lies in the underlying theoretical perspective that crime and deviance are *learned behaviors*. They are learned by interacting with individuals who engage in the behavior and by identifying with individuals who value attitudes and beliefs that support the behavior. The most suitable prevention strategies, therefore, should target those most vulnerable to education—children.[8]

Moreover, the social pressure to take drugs, join a gang, or get involved in criminal activity is also accompanied by the failure to resist such pressures. Thus, emphasis is placed on teaching children the benefits of staying in school, connecting with positive peer groups, developing positive attitudes, recognizing negative influences, and becoming aware of the risks involved in abusing drugs and alcohol. This message was graphically summarized by the unforgettable public service announcement involving a frying pan and an egg: "This is drugs" (sizzling frying pan). "This is your brain on drugs" (egg dropping in frying pan).

Social policies such as the "just say no" antidrug campaign of the 1980s are often guided by scientific studies, which can serve as the driving force or justification behind social policy development.

CONNECTING RESEARCH TO PRACTICE

Does Deterrence Work?

We all refrain from certain types of behaviors because the consequences are undesirable. We stop smoking for fear of lung cancer, skip dessert to keep those extra pounds off, come home one minute before curfew so as not to lose car privileges, and file taxes on time to avoid penalties. Unattractive consequences therefore have a deterrent effect: They stop undesirable behavior. Are certain crimes and behaviors more susceptible to deterrence than others? Does deterrence work as intended?

The relationship between crime rates and deterrent measures is often difficult to establish. Most studies rely on official statistics on crime, which, as we saw in Chapter 3, can be skewed due to reporting problems, biased police practices, and organizational and political interests. It is also difficult to measure the effects of informal social controls, such as anticrime campaigns, the fear of public exposure, and losing the respect of family and peers.

Nevertheless, research on deterrence has established that severity of punishment is indeed inversely related to the level of crime. A statewide study in Texas, conducted by the National Center for Policy Analysis, found a direct correlation between the probability of imprisonment for certain types of crime and a subsequent decline in the rate of that particular crime.[54] Murder, for example, declined 23 percent between 1993 and 1997, a time during which the probability of going to prison for murder increased 17 percent. In a study of police intervention in high-risk settings, researchers found illegal drug transactions in bars declined as police tactics such as drug raids increased.[55]

These findings, while persuasive, still do not isolate the deterrent effects of punishment alone on criminal behavior. Numerous studies show fear of punishment does not account for declines in the rate of criminal activity, which are also affected by psychological variables; environmental pressures such as poverty, unemployment, and peer influences; certain values and beliefs; and misperceptions about crime and its consequences. If the relationship between crime and punishment were that simple, capital punishment—the ultimate criminal sanction—should have the strongest deterrent effect on would-be murderers. However, while murder rates may decline shortly after a widely publicized execution, they eventually go up again to even higher levels and then back down, with no net deterrent effect. And there is little evidence of a difference in murder rates between states that impose the death penalty and those that do not.

The evidence thus suggests that relying on deterrent strategies alone is not sufficient. Since punishment does not remove the underlying cause of criminal motivations and actions, it alone will not deter them.

Some **Global Issues** boxes show the effect of cultural differences on issues ranging from the definition of crime to the role of punishment. Others highlight different ways that criminological research is conducted around the globe.

Consider This boxes attract student interest with a surprising, ambiguous, or inequitable real-world situation and ask the student, "What do you think?"

Summary tables in each of the "theory" chapters review the theories introduced and connect them with their real-world application.

TABLE 5.3
SUMMARY: The Classical and Rational Choice Perspective

Definition of Crime	Crime is rational behavior.
Why Does Crime Occur? (Theory)	■ Individuals choose to engage in criminal behavior.
	■ People make choices based on hedonistic calculations.
	■ Rational human beings act to maximize benefit and reduce cost.
	■ Crime occurs when it is a more attractive alternative than law-abiding behavior.
	■ The decision to violate the law takes into account the range of constraints and opportunities.
	■ The lifestyle of individuals contribute to both the amount and type of crime they engage in.
What Is the Solution to Crime? (Policy)	■ Make crime a less attractive alternative by increasing its cost to individuals.
	■ Deter criminals by enacting punishments that are precise and certain.

SUMMARY

How does a diseased mind affect the way we think and act?

A diseased mind alters the way in which individuals experience the social world around them. Early thoughts on the relationship between personality and criminal behavior focused on the diseased mind of the psychopath. Unable to identify with others or understand how they think and feel, psychopaths are self-centered individuals who do not feel guilt or shame, are reckless and irresponsible, are incapable of maintaining long-term relationships, and engage in ongoing antisocial, disruptive behavior.

Is criminal behavior related to a defect in personality?

Individuals suffering from antisocial personality disorder exhibit a persistent pattern of violating social norms marked with a disregard for the rights of others that begins in early adolescence and continues through adulthood. They are not concerned with right or wrong, especially when pursuing their own immediate wants and desires. They will lie, cheat, manipulate situations, become violent, and even break the law to advance their own interests.

Do crime and delinquency stem from the inability to control certain impulses?

Sigmund Freud founded the psychoanalytic perspective, a method of understanding human behavior by examining drives and impulses within the unconscious mind. His theory of human behavior centered upon the division of the human mind into three components: the id, the ego, and the superego. Under Freud's model, an inadequately developed superego will render the individual incapable of making appropriate moral judgments and therefore will be more likely to submit to the impulsive desires of the id and violate the rules.

Is crime a symptom of mental illness?

Certain types of mental illness can result in maladaptive behavior. Individuals suffering from neuroses such as phobias and compulsive disorders often experience fear and anxiety in the face of certain social stimuli, causing them to behave in unacceptable and often bizarre or disruptive ways. Individuals suffering from psychoses such as bipolar disorder and schizophrenia are unable to comprehend reality, think clearly and respond appropriately. Studies show that the presence of a psychotic disorder places individuals at a greater risk for criminal behavior.

Is crime a symptom of mental illness?

Certain types of mental illness can result in maladaptive behavior. Individuals suffering from neuroses such as phobias and compulsive disorders often experience fear and anxiety in the face of certain social stimuli, causing them to behave in unacceptable and often bizarre or disruptive ways. Individuals suffering from psychoses such as bipolar disorder and schizophrenia are unable to comprehend reality, think clearly and respond appropriately. Studies show that the presence of a psychotic disorder places individuals at a greater risk for criminal behavior.

What happens when we process information incorrectly?

The way individuals perceive their environment and appropriately judge their behaviors is the subject of cognitive theory. Cognitive processes have three major components: perception, judgment, and execution. When we have a clear understanding of environmental stimuli (perception), we are better able to evaluate choices (judgment) and are therefore more likely to make better decisions in difficult situations (execution). Distortion in cognitive processes has been used to explain a wide variety of criminal behavior such as domestic violence and rape.

Do some individuals imitate aggressive behavior?

By observing the behavior of individuals that play an important role in our lives, we learn how to think and act. This type of learning is called behavior modeling. Bandura notes that individuals become violent and aggressive through life experiences that teach them to act that way. Research studies support this claim, showing a strong correlation between exposure to violence and hostility and aggressive behavior.

How is crime rewarding to some people?

Studies show that patterns of delinquent and criminal behavior often persist because of rewards associated with them such as money, prestige, and peer approval. Human behavior therefore reflects a balance between the rewards and punishments associated with it.

If crime is in the mind, what can we do to prevent it?

According to the psychological perspective, criminal behavior is linked to the drives and motives within the human mind. Correcting inappropriate behavior therefore requires correcting faulty mental processes, through the early detection of psychological problems that may predict future criminal behavior. Once a problem has been detected, counseling or therapy helps individuals learn how to manage their disorder or minimize its impact on their behavior.

Can intelligence be related to crime?

A relationship between intelligence and crime is often proposed by linking low IQ scores to higher rates of delinquency. However, IQ is not always a measure of natural intelligence but rather reflects that IQ tests are based on the values and experiences of the U.S. white middle class.

CRITICAL THINKING QUESTIONS

1. Society sometimes reacts to crimes that are particularly difficult to comprehend by arguing that the perpetrator is insane—that no one in his or her right mind would torture and kill a child or rape an elderly woman. What types of criminal acts are the most difficult for you to understand? Can you identify a purpose or motive for the behavior? What elements make these crimes difficult to explain from the standpoint of rational choice? How can the psychological perspective help us understand "insane" behavior?

2. Psychological theories help us understand the mental processes behind human drives and motives. What role does this type of explanation play in the development of a criminal defense? What standards of responsibility do we place on individuals who suffer a mental disorder? Would it be fair to judge them by the same criteria as those who do not suffer from a mental disorder? Is someone "less guilty" because he or she is mentally ill?

End-of-chapter **summaries** repeat the focus questions that open the chapter and suggest succinct responses, helping students to review key learning outcomes.

A MESSAGE FROM **BILL CHAMBLISS**

In 1973 I published some research on the activities of two delinquent gangs that culminated in an article titled "The Saints and the Roughnecks." This piece has been widely reprinted over the years, and we have included it as an Appendix to this text. We feel that the article, which students will find easy to read, is helpful in highlighting for them the importance of research in criminology. In addition, because I have lectured on this topic to social welfare agencies and high schools where people were interested in applying the research, it provides another way to emphasize the connections among theory, research, and practice.

We feel confident that students will find this research story fascinating and come to appreciate, as the article's conclusion states, that "the impact on a person's life of labeling, stigma, and negative self-images is a powerful force in determining who we are and what we become."

CREATE

Craft your teaching resources to match the way you teach! With McGraw-Hill Create™, www.mcgrawhillcreate.com, you can easily rearrange chapters, combine material from other content sources, and quickly upload content you have written, like your course syllabus or teaching notes. Find the content you need in Create by searching through thousands of leading McGraw-Hill textbooks. Arrange your book to fit your teaching style. Create even allows you to personalize your book's appearance by selecting the cover and adding your name, school, and course information. Order a Create book and you'll receive a complimentary print review copy in 3–5 business days or a complimentary electronic review copy (eComp) via email in about one hour. Go to www.mcgrawhillcreate. com today and register. Experience how McGraw-Hill Create empowers you to teach your students your way.

COURSESMART eTEXTBOOK

This text is available as an eTextbook at www.CourseSmart.com. At CourseSmart your students can take advantage of significant savings off the cost of a print textbook, reduce their impact on the environment, and gain access to powerful web tools for learning. CourseSmart eTextbooks can be viewed online or downloaded to a computer. The eTextbooks allow students to do full text searches, add highlighting and notes, and share notes with classmates. CourseSmart has the largest selection of eTextbooks available anywhere. Visit www.CourseSmart.com to learn more and to try a sample chapter.

ACKNOWLEDGMENTS

Nothing can be more misleading than the authors' names on the front of a book, especially a textbook. It takes a host of talented and committed people to create a text. Our greatest debt is to Elisa Adams, whose diligence, talent, and brilliance shaped this book from beginning to end. Without Elisa's creative and knowledgeable editing, the project could never have come to fruition. Our editors at McGraw-Hill have also been extremely helpful and encouraging from beginning to end. We especially want to thank Katie Stevens, Nancy Crochiere, Bill Minick, Amy Mittleman, and Megan Ruggiero as well as Catherine Morris, Jennifer Gordon, and Judy Mason, for their steadfast assistance and support.

Our research assistants have not only kept us up-to-date, often they have kept us from egregious blunders. Chris Moloney, Tanya Whittle, Jeff Tiennes, Melissa Melton, Julianna Cameron, Chandra Pastel, and Tina Dirksmeyer have been a joy and an inspiration to work with.

We owe a special thanks to our loved ones—Pernille, Jeff, Natalie, and Sofie—for enduring early morning noises from our studies and solo evenings while we met deadlines and sweat blood.

And finally, many thanks for the inspiration and critical insight we received from our reviewers:

Joseph Andritzky, *Concordia University*
Ashley Blackburn, *University of North Texas*
Denise Boots, *University of South Florida–Tampa*
Marjie T. Britz, *Clemson University*
Michael Brown, *Ball State University*
Kevin Buckler, *University of Texas–Brownsville*
David C. Burlingame, *Grand Valley State University*
George Burruss, *Southern Illinois University–Carbondale*
Sally Cafasso, *Middlesex County College*
Valerie Callanan, *University of Akron*
Frank Cameron, *Quinsigamond Community College*
Susan Caringella-Macdonald, *Western Michigan University–Kalamazoo*
Brenda Chaney, *Ohio State University–Marion*
Derral Cheatwood, *University of Texas–San Antonio*
Kenneth Christopher, *Park University–Parkville*
Gregory Clark, *McNeese State University*
Linda Collier, *Delaware County Community College*
Cavit Cooley, *Mercer County Community College*
Charles Crawford, *Western Michigan University–Kalamazoo*
William R. Crawley, *Grand Valley State University*
Melissa Deller, *University of Wisconsin–Whitewater*
Vicky Dorworth, *Montgomery College–Rockville*
Yvonne Downes, *Hilbert College*
Jamie J. Fader, *State University of New York–Albany*
Joy Feria, *University of North Florida*
Richard Finn, *Western Nevada College*
David R. Foster, *University of Maryland–College Park*
Jennifer Gibbs, *University of Maryland–College Park*
Maureen Gould, *Rowan University*
Jason Hale, *County College of Morris*

Julia Hall, *Drexel University*
Virginia Grabiner, *Buffalo State College*
Carter Hay, *Florida State University–Tallahassee*
Carly Hilinski, *Grand Valley State University*
John Holland, *Butte College*
Suman Kakar, *Florida International University–Miami*
Zulfikar D. Kalam, *Miami-Dade College–North*
David Kauzlarich, *Southern Illinois University–Edwardsville*
Charles Kocher, *Cumberland County College*
Nelson Kofie, *Northern Virginia Community College–Loudoun*
Lisa Konczal, *Barry University*
Todd Krohn, *University of Georgia*
Anthony P. LaRose, *University of Tampa*
Michael Leiber, *Virginia Commonwealth University*
Samantha L. Lewis, *Miami-Dade College–Kendall*
Li Ying Li, *Metropolitan State College of Denver*
Larry Linville, *Northern Virginia Community College–Annandale*
Jennifer Lorentz, *Lindenwood University*
Mitchell Mackinem, *Claflin University*
Sean Madden, *University of Tampa*
Mary Maguire, *California State University–Sacramento*
Darren Marhanka, *Lindenwood University*
Christine Martin, *University of Illinois–Chicago*
Stacy McGoldrick, *California State Polytechnic University–Pomona*
J. Mitchell Miller, *University of South Carolina*
James Nolan, *West Virginia University–Morgantown*
Angela Ondrus, *Owens Community College*
Michael Paquette, *Middlesex County College*
Kay Kei-ho Pih, *California State University–Northridge*
Jesenia Pizarro, *Michigan State University–East Lansing*
Hillary Potter, *University of Colorado–Boulder*
Peter Puleo, *William Rainey Harper College*
Wendy Regoeczi, *Cleveland State University*
Lesley Reid, *Georgia State University*
John Reinholz, *Bryant & Stratton College*
George Rengert, *Temple University–Philadelphia*
Linda Robyn, *Northern Arizona University*
Laurie Schaffner, *University of Illinois–Chicago*
Kip Schlegel, *Indiana University–Bloomington*
Ryan Schroeder, *University of Louisville–Louisville*
Lee Slocum, *University of Missouri–St. Louis*
William Sondervan, *University of Maryland–University College*
James E. Sutton, *California State University–Chico*
Bethany Teeter, *Park University–Parkville*
Jeanie Thies, *Lindenwood University*
Tim Wadsworth, *University of Colorado–Boulder*
Eileen Weigand, *Virginia Tech*
Karen Weiss, *West Virginia University–Morgantown*
Elvira White, *Wiley College*
Kristen Williams, *Ball State University*
Robert Williams, *Mount San Antonio College*
Brad Wright, *University of Connecticut–Storrs*
Jeffrey Zack, *Fayetteville Technical Community College*
Thomas Ziesemer, *College of Central Florida*

1

CRIME, DEVIANCE, AND CRIMINOLOGY

A Brief Overview

In this chapter, we will explore the following questions:

- How do we define crime?
- What is deviance?
- When is crime deviant and when is deviant behavior criminal?
- What is criminology?
- Does the popular image of crime measure up to reality?
- How does criminology guide our study of crime?
- How does criminology influence social policy?

The stories about crime we read in the newspaper and see

on television are many and diverse, and can be viewed from widely different perspectives.

- On January 8, 2009, the Illinois House of Representatives voted to impeach the Illinois governor Milorad "Rod" R. Blagojevich for corruption and misconduct in office by a 114 to 1 vote. Blagojevich was arrested and charged in December 2008 with conspiracy to commit mail and wire fraud and bribery in connection with the alleged attempt to sell the United States Senate seat vacated by then Senator Obama to the highest bidder. On January 29, 2009, by a unanimous vote of 59 to 0 in the Illinois State Senate, Blagojevich was removed from office and permanently barred from ever holding public office again in the state of Illinois.[1] In his first trial, Blagojevich was convicted of only 1 of 23 charges against him (lying to investigators), but in a retrial, he was found guilty of 17 counts of conspiracy to commit fraud and corruption, including a conspiracy to sell Obama's Senate seat.
- In a very different setting, on May 2, 2011, Osama bin Laden, the leader of al Qaeda, an international terrorist organization, was killed by U.S. Navy SEALs in a raid on his compound in Pakistan. The raid brought an end to an international hunt for the man described by the U.S. government as "the world's most dangerous criminal." Bin Laden was the mastermind behind a series of terrorist acts on western countries including the September 11, 2011 attacks on the World Trade Center in New York and the Pentagon in Washington, DC, which killed over 3000 people. To most people in the West, there is no doubt that Osama bin Laden's acts were criminal. To bin Laden and his followers, however, he was leading a morally justifiable war against the United States and other western nations that were morally bankrupt and oppressing Muslims throughout the world.

Stories of crime, whether in Los Angeles or Little Rock, Harlem or Beverly Hills, Springfield, Illinois or Abbottabad, Pakistan, draw our attention and pique our interest. The stories range from those of thrill-seeking youth and defiant adults entangled in drugs, to sex scandals, acts of violence, abuse of power, corruption motivated by personal gain, and terrorist acts. While the stories are different, they all have one thing in common: the behaviors they describe are legally prohibited.

The study of crime has two main dimensions: a behavioral dimension that seeks to describe and explain the origins and causes of criminality, and a definitional dimension that explains why certain behaviors come to be defined as crime. When we hear about a crime story or criminal event, we want immediate answers that tell us why: why a mother kills her three children, why a priest molests a child, why a sports hero commits rape, and why a respected public servant engages in fraud. However, in order to study and account for the diversity in crime causation, we must first come to an understanding of why certain behaviors are legally prohibited.

While acts such as child abuse and political corruption meet with immediate social disapproval, there are far more behaviors that we cannot so easily or arbitrarily define as crime. In a study of the organization and growth of police bureaucracies in U.S. cities, researcher Eric Monkkonen notes that "real crime leaves an injured or dead victim, an outraged community, or inflicts some kind of human suffering."[2]

We can categorize social behavior as either conforming to the established order or contributing to social disorder. Crime control is often a means of maintaining social order. Meanwhile, the need to balance the rights of individuals against the overall protection of society is critical to the way we define certain behaviors as criminal.[3]

Individual rights are at the heart of the constitutional protections and civil liberties guaranteed to each and every U.S. citizen. We look upon the government as a sovereign protector of those rights and guarantees. The fact is, however, that we also look to the law and government to protect us from individual behaviors that threaten our sense of security. We desire order, safety, conformity, and enforcement of society's interests. We feel we have a right to be protected from acts that may threaten the integrity of our society, and we may even, in the face of peril, be willing to give up some of our personal rights in the interest of public safety or order. As a society, we do not always agree on where to draw the line between individuality and conformity. We can clearly see such disagreement in the various debates on issues such as abortion, gun control, and freedom of speech (Figure 1.1). This chapter aims to clarify how we draw the line in defining the acts of individuals as criminal.

Scholars, writers, politicians, the media, and the general public have long been fascinated with crime and punishment. This chapter introduces criminology as a systematic science, grounded in theory, whose goal is defining crime, understanding criminal behavior, and offering scientific solutions to help policymakers alleviate the problem of crime in our society. Are there elements common to all crimes? Are all crimes wrong? Are all crimes immoral? Can a mere thought or plan be a crime? Where do we draw the line in defining and limiting peoples' behavior? We turn now to the science of criminology to answer these questions.

WHAT IS CRIME?

Crime has become an integral part of U.S. popular culture. Think of prime-time television shows such as *CSI, Law & Order, The District, The Shield, The Wire, The Sopranos,* and various spin-offs that reflect the public's fascination with criminal motive, criminal intent, the apprehension of suspects, detective work, and forensics. Media coverage continues to draw our attention to the criminal acts of celebrities, athletes, and other well-known

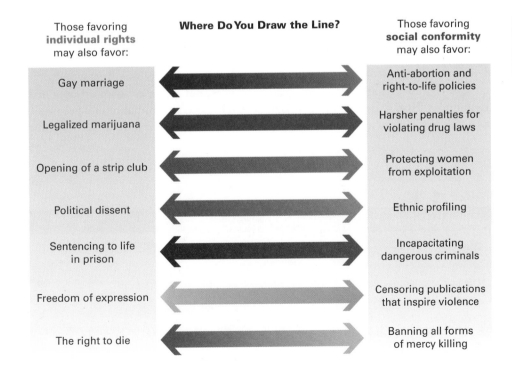

Where Do You Draw the Line?

Those favoring **individual rights** may also favor:

Those favoring **social conformity** may also favor:

Gay marriage	⟷	Anti-abortion and right-to-life policies
Legalized marijuana	⟷	Harsher penalties for violating drug laws
Opening of a strip club	⟷	Protecting women from exploitation
Political dissent	⟷	Ethnic profiling
Sentencing to life in prison	⟷	Incapacitating dangerous criminals
Freedom of expression	⟷	Censoring publications that inspire violence
The right to die	⟷	Banning all forms of mercy killing

FIGURE **1.1**
Individual Rights or Social Conformity . . . You Decide

Crime stories often receive an inordinate amount of media coverage when they involve the rich and famous, as in the 1989 murder of Jose and Kitty Menendez by their two minor children, Lyle and Erik, in an upscale Beverly Hills neighborhood. The extensive media attention of this case exemplifies sensationalism, which often misleads us into thinking that these are the only types of crimes being committed.

individuals. Self-proclaimed experts try to explain through the eyes of popular culture why Robert Downey Jr. was arrested for drug possession, Winona Ryder was convicted of shoplifting, and Mike Tyson served time for rape. Gossip, headlines, and media commentary have become the shaky foundations upon which we now build our understanding of crime and criminal behavior.

Considering the real complexity of criminal behavior, it makes sense for us to study it with a more scholarly approach.[4] To arrive at a comprehensive understanding, we turn to four perspectives—legalist, political, psychological, and sociological—that each offers a distinct approach to the meaning of crime (Table 1.1).

The Legalist Perspective

legalist perspective

View that crime is conduct that violates criminal laws of local, state, or federal government.

Within the **legalist perspective,** criminologists view crime as conduct that violates criminal laws of local, state, or federal government. For example, federal law makes it a crime to lie under oath in a court of law; this offense is called perjury. The legalist perspective assumes that without a legal definition, there would be no criminal act, no matter how deviant or offensive to society a behavior may be.[5]

The legalist definition is good as far as it goes, but it makes some unsupported assumptions. First, it assumes everyone agrees with the laws that forbid certain behaviors, such as jaywalking or euthanasia. That in turn implies that everyone shares the same

TABLE **1.1**

What Is Crime? Four Perspectives

The Legalist Perspective	Crime is behavior that violates criminal codes and statutes.
The Political Perspective	Crime is socially constructed behavior.
The Psychological Perspective	Crime is maladaptive behavior.
The Sociological Perspective	Crime is behavior that threatens the social order.

definition of morally right and wrong. We can clearly see the error in this assumption by considering all the contentious issues in our society such as gun control, the death penalty, abortion rights, and the legalization of certain drugs such as marijuana.

Moreover, the legalist definition assumes that the power to define certain behaviors as violations of the law is fair and legitimate. This implies that each person's view of right and wrong is equally reflected in the law, without the interests of any particular group outweighing another. The fact is that those with the power to define right and wrong are capable of imposing criminal definitions that reflect their own interests. Clearly, we need a definition of crime that does not rest on false assumptions. Let's examine what the political perspective has to offer.

The Political Perspective

The **political perspective** asserts that individuals with political power use their position to define illegal behavior and to establish laws governing crime. The goal of these individuals is to protect their own interests and gain control over those with less power, who may represent direct or indirect threats to their interests.[6] Thus, laws reflect not what society agrees is right and wrong but rather the views of those who have the power to define certain behaviors.

Some people argue that many laws do protect the relatively powerless against such crimes as murder, rape, and assault. However, the point of the political perspective is not that there are no such laws but rather that the primary motive behind creating laws is to serve the interests of those in power.[7] While it gives us a better understanding of the creation of legal definitions, the political perspective does not assess the role of individual behavior in determining whether certain acts are criminal; for that perspective, we turn to the psychological perspective.

political perspective
View that individuals with political power use their position to define illegal behavior and to establish laws governing crime.

The Psychological Perspective

Criminologists relying on the **psychological perspective** view crime as maladaptive behavior, or an individual's inability to be in harmony with his or her environment.[8] The environment presents stressful stimuli every day—someone cuts you off while you're driving, you get laid off from your job, you find your spouse in bed with your best friend—and the way you react and adapt to these pressures determines whether a crime will be committed. For example, if someone cuts you off on the road, you can either drive on (no crime) or chase and ram the other car (crime).

The psychological perspective, while insightful, provides a very broad definition of crime that includes overeating, alcohol abuse, and compulsive gambling. If we adhered to this definition alone, criminologists would need to understand, combat, and control a wider variety of human behavior than we normally consider criminal.

psychological perspective
View that crime is maladaptive behavior, or an individual's inability to be in harmony with his or her environment.

The Sociological Perspective

A final viewpoint on crime is the **sociological perspective.** This defines crime as any antisocial act that threatens the existing social structure or the fundamental well-being of humans.[9] Laws serve to protect human relationships, preserve individuals' well-being, and provide for their security and safety. The focus of criminological inquiry in this view is to examine *all* actions that cause harm, misfortune, and distress to others. (For a look at how crime can be perpetrated by entirely ordinary individuals, see the Crime in Global Perspective feature.)

The sociological perspective forces us to examine crime as behavior anyone can commit—first-degree murder, rape, robbery, and arson are crimes, but so are job discrimination, unsafe dumping of manufacturing waste, consumer fraud, and insider trading. This broader understanding allows us to define as criminal those actions by

sociological perspective
View that crime is any antisocial act that threatens the existing social structure or the fundamental well-being of humans.

CRIME IN GLOBAL PERSPECTIVE | Protecting Society from Ordinary People

Throughout history, armies have practiced genocide: the systematic elimination of a people or a nation. The Assyrians, Greeks, Romans, and Mongols, among others, committed genocide on a grand scale. Genocide was not even considered a crime until after World War II, however. It would never have occurred to the Romans that their acts were criminal. In fact, it was a point of pride among ancient rulers that they had eliminated an entire enemy—civilians and children as well as soldiers.

In modern times, the most infamous genocide took place in Europe during World War II when the German government under Adolf Hitler exterminated 11 million people. Six million were Jews; the remaining 5 million were Gypsies, homosexuals, communists, and others the government considered enemies of the state. One scholar describes atrocious acts committed by ordinary people:

In the very early hours of July 13, 1942, the men of Reserve Police Battalion 101 were roused from their bunks. . . . they were middle-aged family men of working and lower middle class background from Hamburg [Germany]. The Battalion had been ordered to round up the Jews living in Jozefow [Poland]. The male Jews of working age were to be separated and taken to a work camp. The remaining Jews—women, children and elderly—were to be shot on the spot by the Battalion. Between July 1942 and November 1943, these ordinary men of working and lower middle class backgrounds shot and killed some 38,000 Polish Jews.[10]

In 1948, following World War II, the United Nations Convention on the Prevention and Punishment of the Crime of Genocide created a new political reality by declaring "States would no longer have the right to be left alone" to pursue internal conflicts as they saw fit.[11] State sovereignty—the right of a nation to rule itself—would no longer shield a country from the consequences of committing genocide within its borders. The law thus intervened to protect society—not from sadists, psychopaths, or otherwise violent criminals, but from ordinary people following military orders, when their actions threatened others' lives.[12]

Whose definition of right and wrong is imposed in the controversial issue of abortion and the right to life?

individuals in positions of power that may slip through the cracks of a narrower perspective on crime.[13]

From our discussion of perspectives on crime, you might have concluded that the definition of crime is somewhat elusive. For example, why and how do we come to impose meanings and labels upon certain acts and not others? Do these meanings and labels change over time? Why do some acts elicit a stronger negative reaction, draw more attention, and require a stronger social response than others? Why does that social response vary across time, place, and individuals instead of being limited to the act itself? We can, in fact, answer these questions by looking at the relationship among crime, deviance, and social norms.

WHAT IS DEVIANCE?

When we think of criminal acts such as serial murder, rape, and child molestation, the word *deviant* seems an appropriate label. We cannot agree so easily on other acts. Underage drinking, driving above the speed limit, and betting on a football game are all illegal, yet few people would consider them deviant. By the same token, many acts that some consider deviant are not violations of criminal law; body piercing, excessive tattooing, and poor hygiene are a few examples. So, if all crime is not deviant and all deviant acts are not criminal, what then is deviant behavior, and where do the two concepts overlap? Table 1.2 provides some specific examples for us to examine.

Deviance is behavior that elicits a social reaction by violating the standards of conduct defined by society.[14] Social reactions to deviance range along a continuum from mild disapproval to arrest based on a hierarchy of **social norms** or rules of behavior that guide our everyday interactions with one another.[15]

Social norms fall into four categories (Table 1.3): folkways, mores, taboos, and laws. **Folkways** are nonbinding social conventions; they include guidelines on appropriate dress, manners, and hygiene. Western folkways suggest we shake hands with someone when first introduced. **Mores** are strong convictions about certain behaviors—rules of etiquette, matters of respect, or shared understandings of "the way things are done" in our society. We know we should stand in line at the grocery store, wait our turn to be served at a restaurant, eat with a fork at dinner, and be respectful during religious services. **Taboos** informally forbid socially offensive acts. They regulate sexual conduct, race relations, and other ethical matters. For example, in U.S. society, it is taboo for blood relatives to marry,

deviance

Behavior that elicits a social reaction by violating the standards of conduct defined by society.

social norms

Rules of behavior that guide our everyday interactions with one another.

folkways

Nonbinding social conventions, including appropriate dress, manners, and hygiene.

mores

Strong convictions about certain behaviors—rules of etiquette, matters of respect, or shared understandings of "the way things are done" in our society.

taboos

Informally forbidden socially offensive acts.

Jackie Goldberg, formerly a California state assemblywoman, and Sharon Stricker were married in San Francisco in 2008. Is this a form of deviant behavior? How does society react to gay marriages? What changes in society have influenced the public's reaction to gay marriages?

What influences our reaction to the way people look? Under what circumstances would tattoos and body piercings be considered a form of deviance?

TABLE **1.2**

Criminal, Deviant, Neither, or Both?

WHEN DO THE FOLLOWING ACTS BECOME DEVIANT? WHEN ARE THEY CRIMINAL? WHEN ARE THEY BOTH? WHAT ABOUT NEITHER?

Taking a Human Life	In the service of vigilante justice In self-defense As euthanasia During wartime In the heat of passion
Getting Married	To someone of the same sex To someone 20 years older To a blood relative
Drinking Alcohol	At 6 a.m. While driving In church At a party
Disciplining a Child	At home In public By a schoolteacher Causing bruises
Watching an X-Rated Movie	While children are present Alone at home In the theater
Engaging in Sexual Intercourse	In private In public With a same-sex partner With an underage partner Without consent With another person's spouse
Practicing a Religion	By wearing certain clothes By eating and avoiding certain foods By engaging in certain ceremonies By teaching followers to hate
Driving a Car	Without a valid license Above the speed limit Into a tree
Being Naked	At home At home with guests present At the beach In class
Not Paying Taxes	By taking allowed deductions By hiring a good accountant By making charitable donations By manipulating numbers

laws

Formal written sanctions designed to regulate behaviors society considers to require the greatest level of response and control.

although this is a common practice in other cultures around the world. **Laws** are formal written sanctions designed to regulate behaviors society considers to require the greatest level of response and control. It is in this last category of social norms—laws—that we find the overlap between crime and deviance.

The legal status of certain behaviors—and the negative societal reaction they elicit—renders them both criminal and deviant.[16] What complicates matters is that we do not all agree on the social and legal status of some behaviors. Even when we do, consensus can change from time to time and place to place. When and how does behavior become a crime?

TABLE **1.3**

Are All Rules Created Equally?

SOCIAL NORM	DEFINITION	EXAMPLE OF VIOLATION	SOCIAL REACTION	CONTINUUM OF DEVIANCE
Folkway	Nonbinding social convention	Wearing cut-off shorts to a formal wedding ceremony	Stares of disapproval or a verbal reprimand	Less deviant
More	Strong conviction about right/wrong	Talking on cell phone during a movie at the movie theater	Verbal altercation and demand to stop or be removed from the premises	
Taboo	Prohibition on socially offensive acts	Engaging in sexually explicit conduct at a public park	Verbal and/or physical confrontation; may resort to formal authority such as calling the police	
Law	Written formal decree	Walking away from a restaurant without paying	Being arrested and charged with theft	More deviant (criminal)

The definitions of both deviance and crime are subject to culturally influenced interpretation by a specific individual or group in a specific time and place. For example, commercial gambling is socially acceptable and legal in Las Vegas, Atlantic City, and on some Native American reservations, but it is outlawed in most other parts of the United States. Likewise, prostitution is morally unacceptable and illegal in nearly all states, but it is a legally regulated and acceptable behavior in parts of Nevada.

To understand the role of subjective interpretations in the way we assign definitions to behavior, consider how school officials, police, and the community responded to the actions of two different groups of delinquent boys. Although the "Saints" were more delinquent by sheer number of illegal acts than the "Roughnecks," these upper-middle-class boys were not perceived as delinquents: They were good, upstanding youths with bright futures. A Saint who got drunk in a nightclub or tavern, even if he drove around afterward in a car, was perceived as someone who had simply made a mistake. On the other hand, a lower-class boy who drank in an alley and stood intoxicated on the street corner, who stole a wallet, or who associated with someone who had committed a burglary was considered a delinquent: The Roughnecks were viewed as tough young criminals headed for trouble.[17] (For the full text of the article by Bill Chambliss reporting on his "Saints" and "Roughnecks" research study, please see the Appendix on page 383.)

Essentially, then, crime and deviance are socially constructed: They are what society says they are. With this understanding, we can develop a comprehensive understanding of crime by integrating components from the various perspectives we have discussed. **Crime** is human behavior that we interpret as violating society's norms for a specific time and place and that must be controlled and prevented by legal decree. Now let's turn to a discussion of criminology and its role in understanding crime as human behavior.

WHAT IS CRIMINOLOGY?

Throughout recorded history, people have attempted to understand, define, prevent, and punish crime and deviance. In Europe, early beliefs about criminals and social deviants were influenced by religion; those who transgressed were thought to be possessed by spirits, and the cure was to try to extract the evil forces through surgical means or physical torture.

In 1885, Italian law professor Raffaele Garofalo coined the term *criminology* to describe the study of crime as an individual act in a social context. Around the same time, French anthropologist Paul Topinard defined the field as the study of criminal body types, separate from the field of anthropology.[18] In the 1920s sociologist Edwin Sutherland described criminology as "the body of knowledge regarding delinquency and crime

crime

Human behavior interpreted as violating society's norms for a specific time and place and that must be controlled and prevented by legal decree.

criminology

The scientific study of the incidence and forms of crime and criminal behavior, their causes and consequences, and social reaction to, control of, and prevention of crime.

criminologists

Academics, researchers, and policy analysts who focus on understanding the nature and meaning of crime, patterns of criminal behavior, various causes of criminality, and society's reaction to crime.

as social phenomena. It includes within its scope the process of making laws, of breaking laws, and of reacting towards the breaking of laws."[19]

Today we define **criminology** as the scientific study of the incidence and forms of crime and criminal behavior, their causes and consequences, and social reaction to, control of, and prevention of crime. It has become an interdisciplinary study that seeks to explain (1) why some people engage in crime and others do not, (2) and why some criminals are arrested and sentenced to prison while others are not, and (3) how the characteristics of social structure account for different crime rates.

Criminologists are academics, researchers, and policy analysts who focus on understanding the nature and meaning of crime, patterns of criminal behavior, various causes of criminality, and society's reaction to crime. They examine and evaluate the origins, nature, and interpretation of criminal laws and try to find ways to alleviate crime as a social problem. Criminologists also rely on scientifically grounded theories and explanations of criminal behavior—and society's responses to it—to help us understand the experiences of victims throughout the criminal justice process. Table 1.4 summarizes the various tasks criminologists undertake.

Regardless of the specific task, criminologists are dedicated to the study of crime and criminal behavior. Who are these "criminals" that are the focus of an entire scientific discipline? We turn now to an examination of crime and criminal behavior.

THE POPULAR IMAGE OF CRIME VERSUS THE REALITY OF CRIMINAL BEHAVIOR

In the mid-1980s, high-level government officials and military personnel within the Reagan administration, while performing their jobs, hid behind political rhetoric as they sold arms to terrorist groups in Iran, diverted profits from the sales to themselves, and covered up their actions. The result was one of the nation's most embarrassing political scandals: the Iran–Contra affair.[20]

On January 6, 1994, at a practice session during the 1994 U.S. Figure Skating Championships, competitor Nancy Kerrigan was attacked and injured in a conspiracy allegedly instigated by co-competitor Tonya Harding. Harding's ex-husband Jeff Gillooly hired Shane Stant to strike Kerrigan on the knee. On February 1, Gillooly accepted a plea

TABLE **1.4**

How Do We Do Criminology?	
FIELD OF CRIMINOLOGY	**SPECIFIC TASKS**
Statistics and Research	Focus on analyzing crime data, developing methods for gathering crime information, measuring crime trends, and developing and evaluating crime prevention programs and strategies
Criminal Profiling	Study specific categories of offenses to determine the anatomy of a crime and understand the specific nature, cause, and motive of certain types of criminal behavior
Theory Development	Conduct scientific research about the causes of criminality, its beginnings, and its continuation
Law, Policy, and Social Control	Examine the evolution of law within the context of social reaction and change and its impact on criminal sanctions and crime control policies
Victimology	Highlight victims' issues, advance theories of victimization, and promote programs to support crime victims

bargain in exchange for his testimony against Harding. Harding avoided further prosecution and a possible jail sentence by pleading guilty to hindering the investigation. After conducting its own investigation, the U.S. Figure Skating Association concluded Harding knew of the attack before it happened, stripped her of her 1994 title, and banned her for life from participating in sanctioned events and from coaching.[21]

There was nothing extraordinary about Mary Kay Letourneau. She was a bright, energetic, well-dressed teacher who always showed interest in and enthusiasm for her students. She also went to prison for over seven years for the rape of 13-year-old Vili Fualaau, a former student who was 21 years her junior. After serving her time in prison, Letourneau married Fualaau, and they had two children together.[22]

Crime is committed by ordinary people—politicians, doctors, lawyers, opera singers, schoolteachers, nurses, men and women in business, car mechanics, movie stars, media figures, students, and athletes. Regardless of the crime, however, we want to know *why*. Why do politicians abuse their power, doctors and nurses kill, teachers engage in computer sex with children, people in business cheat, and professional athletes commit rape? As a society we want immediate answers that will help us understand the extraordinary behavior of apparently ordinary individuals. Not only do we want justice served, but we want to explain the apparently inexplicable acts of individuals, acts with consequences that often hit close to home.

Crime continually challenges law enforcement officials, criminal justice agents, and politicians to whom we look for protection. Close your eyes for a moment and picture "crime." What do you see happening? Who are the actors? Is someone being shot or stabbed? Do you hear screams or imagine a struggle? Is it late at night? Where does the crime take place? Are you angry or afraid? Does your response have anything to do with the image of crime we have as a society, and if so, where does that image come from?

We derive our popular image of crime from media portrayals that convince us to be afraid and to barricade ourselves behind locked doors, barred windows, and security systems. Is this fear justified? Should we be concerned about an alleged spike in violent crime that leaves us afraid in our own homes, streets, and society? We'll address these questions in more detail in Chapter 3 when we discuss patterns and trends in criminal

Who fits our perception of a criminal? When you think of crime, do you see an image of this gang-banger or do you see Martha Stewart, the successful businesswoman and popular TV host, who was convicted on four counts of obstructing justice and lying to investigators about an illegal stock sale? From where do we get these images about crime and criminals?

CONSIDER THIS...   **Cheerleaders Gone Criminal**

In March 2008, a story began to unfold about a videotape capturing a brutal attack by six assailants on a teenage girl in Polk County, Florida. The victim, a former cheerleader, was lured to the home of one of the attackers by a former friend. The footage documented six girls repeatedly taunting, punching, hitting, and pushing the girl, slamming her head into a wall, and leaving her unconscious. The six girls, all minors and also members of the cheerleading squad, took turns attacking the victim while videotaping the beating. They were jeering, shouting, and cheering in the background as the victim pleaded with them to stop, unable to defend herself. The attack was apparently prompted by comments the victim made about the girls on MySpace.

After visiting her in the emergency room, the victim's father described her as disfigured beyond recognition and suffering permanent damage to her vision and hearing. The six girls, and two boys who served

as lookouts, were arrested on charges of felony battery and false imprisonment.

While gang attacks may be fairly common in high-crime neighborhoods, this was no ordinary crime. The videotape of the attack, which the assailants were intending to proudly post on YouTube, became the center of attention on national television, played over and over on news broadcasts, talk shows, and documentary programs. The public became more and more angry, demanding the teenagers be tried as adults and given the harshest of punishments.

Why did this case draw so much media attention? Was it the brutality of the attack? The perpetrators' lack of remorse? The fact that it was captured on video? Or maybe the fact that the attackers were "good" girls?[23]

What do you think?

Several teenagers, three of them shown here waiting for booking, were charged as adults with battery and kidnapping in the March 30, 2008, attack on high school cheerleader Victoria Lindsay. They videotaped the beating and posted it on YouTube, where it went viral.

behavior. For now, we recognize the many different faces of criminals and crime victims. Yet, we tend to hear far more about peculiar or especially offensive acts of crime because they are so sensationalized by the media and public portrayal, as the Consider This feature demonstrates.

We must go beyond this misperception to a more comprehensive understanding of the many different types of crimes. The truth is that crimes reported by the media, such as murder and rape, are generally the least common crimes.[24] Studies show that although violent crimes represent 60 to 90 percent of crime news stories, they comprise only 12 percent of all crimes. Newsworthy stories emphasize the dramatic, the unusual, and the shocking, while placing less emphasis on the everyday criminal behavior of regular people who assault family members, cheat on their taxes, steal from retail stores, and abuse drugs.[25]

Trying to capture all the varieties of crime is like trying to draw a map of the world. If the map has all the details in it, it is as large as the world and worthless as a map. If it leaves out all the rivers and mountains, roads and alleys, it is compact but does not tell us enough to give us a sense of where we are or where we are going.[26] However, practicality demands that we condense our descriptions of crime so as to capture its endless varieties without being overwhelmed. To get started, Table 1.5 lists the official categories of

TABLE **1.5**

Major Categories of Crime

INTERPERSONAL VIOLENCE (CHAPTER 11)	CRIMES AGAINST PROPERTY (CHAPTER 12)	PUBLIC ORDER CRIMES (CHAPTER 13)	CRIMES OF THE POWERFUL (CHAPTER 14)	THE NEW FACE OF CRIME (CHAPTER 15)
Murder The willful (non-negligent) killing of one human being by another human being.	**Larceny** The unlawful taking away of someone's property without using force, violence, or by fraud.	**Prostitution** The unlawful engaging in sexual activities for profit.	**White-Collar Crime** Nonviolent acts involving deception, concealment, and guile committed by individuals, businesses, and corporations, for the purposes of obtaining money, avoiding loss, or gaining personal advantage.	**International Crime** Systematic practices involving the infringement of human rights, peace agreements, or other violations of international laws.
Rape The carnal knowledge of a female forcibly and against her will.	**Burglary** The unlawful entry into a building or structure to commit a theft or felony.	**Pornography** The portrayal or depiction of sexually explicit material.	**State Crime** Illegal activities by government officials to advance their political agendas or promote their own interests.	**Political Crime** Crimes committed to threaten, oppose, or challenge the government in power.
Assault The attempted commission of bodily injury to another human being. Assault can also mean putting an individual in fear of imminent bodily harm, injury, danger, or threat. An assault can therefore include threats, taunting, intimidation, and harassment; it requires no physical contact.	**Arson** The willful and malicious burning of a home, vehicle, building, or other structure or property.	**Drug Abuse** The violation of laws pertaining to the possession, use, manufacture, or sale of controlled substances.	**Organized Crime** The illegal activities of groups of individuals in the course of some type of illegal business or enterprise set up for monetary gain.	**Technology Crimes** Criminal offenses that are perpetrated using some type of network communication device such as the Internet.
Robbery The taking or attempting to take anything of value from the care, custody, or control of a person or persons by force or threat of force or violence and/or by putting the victim in fear.	**Motor Vehicle Theft** The theft or attempted theft of a motor vehicle.			
Hate Crime Crimes directed at certain individuals because of their race, sexual orientation, religion, national origin, political orientation, or physical condition.				

Source: Federal Bureau of Investigation. (2005). *Crime in the United States.* Uniform Crime Reports. Washington, DC: U.S. Department of Justice. Retrieved from http://www.fbi.gov/ucr/05cius/

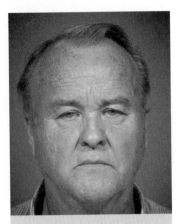

Thomas Stephen Bork stands accused of molesting five foster children. Crime stories such as this one portrayed in the media can make us angry. Criminology helps us focus on the study of criminal behavior from a neutral, scientific point of view instead of an emotional one.

criminal behavior, with a brief description of each. Only by understanding the variety of criminal behavior can we move forward with social control measures to address *all* criminal behavior.

CRIMINOLOGY AND THEORY

Crime affects the lives of many people, even those who are not direct participants in a criminal event. The perpetrator, victim, police, witnesses, family members, judge, jury, and lawyers are all touched by crime. And although we may not agree on *why* individuals engage in criminal activities, we generally have the same reaction to crime: anger and fear.[27] Our responses are often embedded in these emotions, without a true understanding of the social context of criminal behavior. Unfortunately, without this understanding, we are unlikely to develop crime-prevention strategies and solutions that will effectively address the problem.[28]

Criminology helps us think theoretically, without anger, about crime, criminal justice, and social control.[29] It guides our understanding by developing theories that elaborate on the nature, occurrence, and distribution of crime in various segments of society. In Chapter 4, we discuss how theories are constructed in greater detail. For now, we define a **theory** simply as a set of propositions that put forward a relationship between the categories of events or phenomena we are studying. For example, heredity theory is used to explain how certain traits—eye color, hair texture, height, intelligence—are passed down from biological parents to their children.

Criminological theory must account for the great diversity of crime: from petty theft to corporate fraud, simple assault to first-degree murder, campaign bribes to political assassination. It must incorporate a variety of perspectives that take into account individual, psychological, social-psychological and social-structural variables that influence the commission of crime.[30] Only then can it guide criminal investigation toward the solution of difficult cases and help us understand why some individuals break the law. See Connecting Theory to Practice to see how this perspective helps explain white-collar crime.

In the chapters to come, we will present criminological theories on the nature and origin of criminal behavior that go beyond the representation of crime in the mass media; these theories will help us gain insight into criminal events in an analytical and reflective manner. It is in this context that we recognize the significance of criminological theory in shaping the course of criminal justice policy and practice.

theory

A set of propositions that put forward a relationship between the categories of events or phenomena under study.

FIGURE **1.2**

Criminology: Connecting Theory, Research, and Practice

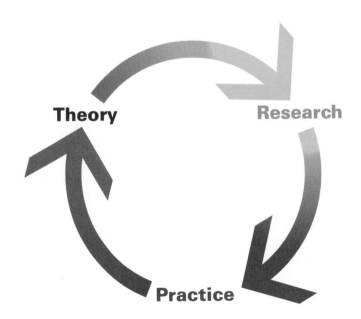

Theory   Research   Practice

How do individuals who appear to be respected members of society—who often take leadership roles in the community and perform charitable deeds—participate in illegal activities? According to the Association of Certified Fraud Examiners, over 90 percent of white-collar criminals have no prior criminal history.[31] In an interview with *Wall Street Journal* columnist Herb Greenberg, Sam E. Antar (former chief financial officer of Crazy Eddie, a New York electronics retailer that cheated investors out of millions of dollars) describes how he put on a front to protect his image:

> As criminals we built false walls of integrity around us; we walked old ladies across the street. We built wings to hospitals. We gave huge amounts of money to charity. We wanted you to trust us.[32]

Criminologist Edwin Sutherland defined white-collar crime as a criminal action committed by a person of high social status and respectability, in the course of the person's occupation. His definition put regulatory and public welfare violations by businesspeople on the same footing as criminal acts performed by those of lower social and economic standing and attached the same stigma to these white-collar crimes.

Sutherland's theories set the stage for decades of fruitful research on the nature and extent of white-collar crime and explored how the structure of modern organizations makes such acts possible. Criminology has since brought to light the acts of apparently upstanding members of the community and redefined their behavior as crime. We can now attribute white-collar offenses to larger forces, such as organizational structure and competition, and to personal factors, such as greed.[33]

Sutherland and his followers paved the way for laws targeting white-collar offenses. In fact, the Racketeer Influenced and Corrupt Organizations (RICO) Act, one of the most important of these new laws, was largely influenced by the work of Donald Cressey, a student of Sutherland. The U.S. Sentencing Commission cited Sutherland and other social science researchers as evidence of the need for standards to avoid the preferential treatment of white-collar offenders.

CRIMINOLOGICAL RESEARCH AND PUBLIC POLICY

Criminology provides the research and other tools policymakers need to make informed decisions in responding to crime.[34] Crime-control strategies grounded in evidence-based criminological research enable politicians to effectively respond to the problem of crime. However, political debates on crime-control policy are too often driven by public opinion and sensational media events. This can lead to a misguided discourse on the state of crime and the real policy choices available.

Criminology provides a more accurate representation of the nature and extent of crime, describes and explains the variables associated with criminal behavior, and evaluates the effectiveness of crime-control intervention strategies. Is violent crime increasing? Does punishment deter criminal behavior? Do individuals brought up in a deprived social environment turn to crime? Criminologists answer these questions by conducting research guided by principles of the scientific approach, which includes defining the problem, reviewing the literature, formulating a hypothesis, collecting and analyzing the data, developing a conclusion, and sharing the results (Figure 1.2). We discuss the criminological research method in detail in Chapter 4. For now, it is important to recognize the important role criminology plays in developing research studies that provide policymakers and politicians with evidence-based criminal justice strategies and interventions.[35]

Herein lies the connection between criminological research and public policy. In the 1990s, for example, a surge in school shootings prompted public concern over growing violence among youth.[36] The effects of television violence on children's behavior became the focus of deliberation in public, academic, and political arenas.[37] Studies concluded that extensive viewing of violence on television leads to an increase in aggressive and violent behavior among children—making them gradually accept violence as a means to solving problems, imitate violent behavior they observe, and become insensitive to the pain and suffering caused by violence in the real world.

Relying on expert testimony and research findings, in 1999 the Senate Judiciary Committee issued a report on media portrayals of violence, outlining national reforms aimed at reducing their effects on children.[38] The committee's policy recommendations focused on practical results, such as ensuring media companies comply with existing industry ratings systems; developing guidelines for measuring media violence and industry efforts to reduce it; allowing parents access to filtering technology to block certain types of entertainment on their televisions; criminalizing the posting of violent hate material on the Internet; and conducting further research on the effects of media violence on children and youth. Legislators relied on scientific evidence, gathered through criminological research, to create policies for controlling the impact of media violence on children and adolescents.

As technology continues to advance, debates on the effects of media violence will widen, with policymakers turning to experts to find effective solutions.[39] As described in Connecting Research to Practice, criminology continues to guide our unbiased understanding of criminal justice issues today. Only criminology can help us understand the criminal acts of ordinary individuals and what to do about their not-so-ordinary behavior.

Before we leave this chapter, let's return to the question we have touched on throughout: What defines the behavior of individuals as "not so ordinary"? We turn now to a brief description of the development of criminal law.

CRIMINOLOGY AND THE LAW

We noted earlier in this chapter that what constitutes crime changes over time and from society to society. What remains consistent is that most people accept criminal law as a given. Like the chemical composition of water, the pressure of the atmosphere, and the physics of gravity, it is just there. Criminologists, however, approach the study of criminal law by raising two very important questions: How do certain behaviors come to be defined as criminal acts, and who benefits from legally defining these behaviors as criminal acts? Two perspectives offer viewpoints on the origins and development of criminal law: the consensus view and the conflict view (Figure 1.3).

FIGURE **1.3**

Two Perspectives on Law

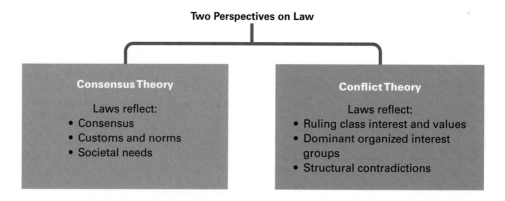

Two Perspectives on Law

Consensus Theory

Laws reflect:
• Consensus
• Customs and norms
• Societal needs

Conflict Theory

Laws reflect:
• Ruling class interest and values
• Dominant organized interest groups
• Structural contradictions

Does Increased Surveillance Reduce Crime?

We've seen them at stoplights, ATMs, and department stores—sometimes hidden and sometimes out in the open. They are designed for our protection, keeping us safe from the reckless driver and secure from the predatory thief. They are video surveillance cameras, and since September 11, 2001, they have been sparking debate about the expanded use of domestic surveillance by the Department of Defense, the FBI, and the National Security Agency, as well as the TSA (Transportation Security Administration).

Some fear the danger to individual rights and civil liberties from increased government surveillance and the use of sophisticated technology that allows facial scanning and computer-readable identification tags. These critics see such monitoring as a threat to citizens' fundamental civil rights—freedom, privacy, and anonymity.[40]

A legal debate over the right to privacy was sparked in 2010 when the FBI attached a global positioning device on a college student's car to track his movements. Yasir Afifi found out about the FBI surveillance when he took the car to a mechanic for an oil change. Puzzled, Afifi took pictures of the device and posted the photos online. A couple of days later, FBI agents showed up at his home and demanded the return of their device.[41]

Others, however, see such types of surveillance as necessary, considering the challenges faced by law enforcement in high-crime areas where gangs, violence, terrorism, and drug trafficking are prevalent. Some local politicians and police officials have turned to the federal government to sponsor video surveillance to help monitor and apprehend crime suspects.

There is very little evidence to show that video surveillance deters criminal activity, curbs violent behavior, or reduces fear of crime. Studies in Great Britain, where such monitoring is more widespread than in the United States, reported little change in crime statistics before and after the installation of video surveillance equipment. The University of Cincinnati found the installation of video cameras was an ineffective deterrent to crime; perpetrators simply shifted their criminal activity away from the view of the camera. Other research has shown that young male minorities are disproportionately targeted by video monitoring programs.

If video surveillance is a costly alternative that has not yielded the anticipated results, why do you think its use continues to expand?

The Consensus View

French sociologist Emile Durkheim noted that social conformity is achieved through sanctions that society imposes on those who choose to deviate.[42] Whether these sanctions are strict, such as the formal sanction of imprisonment, or less formal, such as social isolation, as signs of disapproval they are sufficient to coerce individuals to conform to the prevailing norms of society. Therefore, crime as a social phenomenon is behavior that society has generally agreed is harmful, undesirable, and disruptive to the smooth functioning of the culture. Thus, according to this **consensus model,** criminal law defines as criminal all behavior believed to be repulsive to all individuals in society. The law reflects the beliefs, morals, and values of mainstream society, which views certain behaviors as needing to be managed, controlled, and eliminated for the good of society as a whole, and it is therefore applied uniformly and equitably to all members.

A clear implication of Durkheim's consensus theory is that the law reflects customary practices handed down from one generation to the next. These are the values and customs that provide social cohesion for the members of society. According to this theory, the most important norms and customs passed from one generation to another are those that are codified into law.

Another implication of the consensus paradigm is the idea that laws reflect societal needs. In order for a society to maintain harmony and reproduce itself year after year, it

consensus model

View that crime is a social phenomenon; crime is behavior that is generally agreed to be harmful, undesirable, and disruptive to the smooth functioning of society.

must induce certain regularity in behavior into its members. If innovations, such as the Internet, provide opportunities for deviant acts that were not criminal before, society will respond by creating laws that define this disruptive behavior as criminal. As we shall see in the next chapter, the consensus model is frequently at odds with historical facts. Even crimes such as murder, rape, and robbery, although disapproved of, were not seen as "crimes" as we know crime today: that is, acts to be punished by the state through established criminal justice institutions.

Another critical issue for consensus theory is the proliferation in modern societies of thousands of laws on which there is little or no consensus. In the introduction to the chapter we pointed out how the "crimes" of Osama bin Laden are generally viewed in the West as among the most horrific acts of criminality imaginable. For some people in the poorer countries of the world, however, his acts were heroic attempts to liberate people from the imperial designs of the West and especially of the United States. Even on other issues such as abortion, the use of certain kinds of drugs, and sexual harassment, there is considerable disagreement about whether these acts are wrong and whether they should be considered criminal.

How do we justify the control of certain types of behavior that elicit considerable disagreement and controversy, such as gambling, prostitution, and drug use?[43] While the law claims to protect people from danger and harm, how can it do so when there is not always agreement on what we need protection from? Moreover, given there is no consensus, how do these behaviors find their way into the criminal codes and statutes? Whose view of right and wrong wins in the end? The conflict perspective offers an alternative understanding of the role of criminal law in society.

The Conflict View

conflict model

View that crime and deviance are products of unequal power relationships in society.

The **conflict model** views crime and deviance as products of unequal power relationships in society.[44] Society is made up of diverse groups of individuals—business owners, students, factory workers, engineers, clergy, teachers, and politicians—each with its own set of unique values, norms, and interests. Individuals themselves come from different classes, races, religions, and cultures. With this breadth of diversity, it is very difficult for everyone to agree about right and wrong, so conflict arises between competing groups to impose their own views on the rest of society. The groups with the greatest financial resources and political power control legislation, defining as criminal behaviors that threaten their own interests.

Crime control therefore becomes a tool of the rich and powerful to control the behavior of the less powerful, in an effort to advance their own interests and maintain their privileged position in society.[45] Conflict criminologists note that even laws forbidding crimes such as robbery and murder, which on the surface appear to be in the interests of protecting society as a whole, nevertheless are designed to maintain the overall social order by ensuring that the anger and hostility of the poor and powerless do not become directed at the wealthy and privileged.[46] Efforts to control crime are therefore primarily directed at the lower classes, who are under constant surveillance by criminal justice authorities for committing "street" crime such as theft and assault. On the other hand, the equally detrimental and sometimes more harmful acts of the upper classes—such as discrimination, environmental pollution, and political assassination—go relatively undetected and unpunished.

Criminology cannot simply accept the law as a given. It must investigate how the law came to be the way it is, why some acts are defined as criminal and others are not, what are the goals of criminal law, and what is the legal definition of a criminal act. We further explore these questions in Chapter 2.

SUMMARY

■ **How do we define crime?**	Four perspectives offer us different ideas on the nature of crime. The legalist perspective defines crime as behavior that violates criminal codes and statutes. The political perspective views crime as socially constructed behavior. The psychological perspective sees crime as maladaptive behavior. And finally, the sociological perspective defines crime as any behavior that threatens the social order. A comprehensive definition views crime as human behavior that we interpret as violating society's norms for a specific time and place and that must be controlled and prevented by legal decree.
■ **What is deviance?**	Deviance is behavior that violates society's standards of conduct or social norms, which range from folkways (nonbinding social conventions) to mores (strong convictions about certain behaviors) to taboos (socially offensive informally forbidden acts) to laws (written decrees with formal sanctions). It is in this last category of social norms—laws—that crime and deviance overlap.
■ **When is crime deviant and when is deviant behavior criminal?**	All crime is not deviant, and all deviant acts are not criminal. Because crime and deviance are both products of social interpretation, what is criminal can vary according to time, place, and individual or group. Certain types of behavior that society deems important to regulate and control through formal intervention are subject to law, the extreme form of social approval.
■ **What is criminology?**	We define criminology as the scientific study of the incidence and forms of crime and criminal behavior, its causes and consequences, as well social reaction, control, and prevention. Academics, researchers, and policy analysts who study crime, criminals, and criminal behavior are called criminologists.
■ **Does the popular image of crime measure up to reality?**	The popular image of crime is derived from media portrayals of violent criminal acts that suggest these are the most urgent and pressing social problems facing our society today. In reality, anyone can commit a crime, and crimes such as shoplifting and burglary are far more common than murder, rape, and other crimes sensationalized in the media.
■ **How does criminology guide our study of crime?**	Criminology helps us think critically about crime, criminal justice, and social control by offering various theories that expand our understanding of the nature and extent of criminal behavior.
■ **How does criminology influence social policy?**	Criminology shapes the course of crime-control policies and procedures through scientific research findings that address the complex issues related to crime and crime causation.

CRITICAL THINKING QUESTIONS

1. How far can the government go to ensure domestic peace and tranquility? What individual rights would you give up in exchange for the goal of public order and social conformity? Which would you retain under any circumstances?

2. Assuming we do not all agree on major social issues such as drug legalization, capital punishment, and gun control, how does society come up with rules and regulations that define these controversial subjects? What if your instructor allowed the class to come up with the rules defining classroom attendance, course requirements, and grading procedures? How would you reach a decision? Whose interests would become the standard of conduct?

3. If you asked your family, friends, neighbors, or co-workers to define crime, what definition would they give? What examples of criminal activities would they use? How is their description shaped by the popular image of crime? How does it measure up to the reality we know about crime?

4. Policymakers want to know whether fear of punishment will deter crime. You are the expert whose opinion will serve as the foundation for a shift in crime-control strategies for repeat offenders. Where do you begin your efforts toward gaining a scientific understanding of this subject that would effectively guide policymakers toward creating the proper legislation? What questions do you ask, and how do you go about answering them?

ADDITIONAL RESOURCES

More information on the effects of media violence on children and youth can be accessed at the National Youth Violence Prevention Resource Center website: http://www.safeyouth. gov/Pages/Home.aspx

Visit the American Civil Liberties Union (ACLU) website at http://www.aclu.org/ for further information and debates on individual rights and personal freedoms.

Further information on the various segments of the criminological enterprise can be found on the National Criminal Justice Reference Service website: http://www.ncjrs.gov/

Details about criminology's academic organizations and professional associations can be found at http://www.cybrary.info/

2

CRIME AND CRIMINAL LAW

In this chapter, we will explore the following questions:

- What are the origins of U.S. law?

- What is the difference between criminal and civil law?

- What principles determine what makes an act a crime in the United States?

- What theories explain the development of criminal law?

- How does public opinion influence the creation of criminal law?

- What role have racism and sexism played in the development of U.S. criminal law?

In the early 1900s the sale, use, and possession of marijuana,

opium, heroin, and cocaine were widespread and legal. Patent medicines laced with opium and cocaine were sold over the counter and on the streets. Little old ladies, it was said, laced their afternoon tea with opium and cocaine, and marijuana was readily available and smoked as a recreational drug.

Today the possession and sale of these drugs is a criminal act, with punishments ranging from a small fine to many years in prison depending on the drug and the particular state laws. In his classic study of antidrug laws in the United States, David Musto discovered that

> The most passionate support for legal prohibition of narcotics has been associated with fear of a given drug's effect on a specific minority. Certain drugs were dreaded because they seemed to undermine essential social restrictions, which kept these groups under control: cocaine was supposed to give blacks the strength to withstand bullets that would kill normal persons and to stimulate sexual assault. Fear that smoking opium facilitated sexual contact between Chinese and white Americans was also a factor in its total prohibition. It was believed Chicanos in the Southwest were incited to violence by smoking marihuana. Heroin was linked in the 1920's with a turbulent age-group: adolescents in reckless and promiscuous urban gangs. . . . In each instance, use of a particular drug was attributed to identifiable and threatening minority groups.[1]

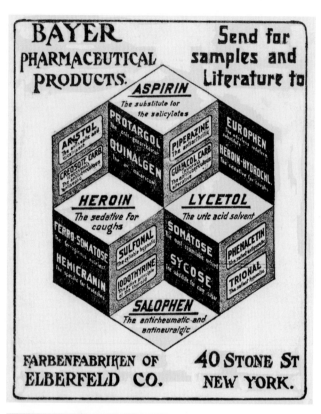

Alfred R. Lindesmith's research supported Musto's conclusion, but he found in addition that the federal bureaucracies, especially the Federal Bureau of Narcotics (forerunner to the Drug Enforcement Administration), played an important role in successfully propagandizing the dangers of marijuana, heroin, and cocaine and in lobbying for legislation to outlaw their possession and sale. Among other attempts to persuade legislators and the public of the danger of these drugs was the bureau's infamous film *Reefer Madness*.[2]

Today in the United States and Europe a reverse trend is underway. Portugal and the Netherlands have decriminalized all the major drugs, and most European countries have either lessened the punishment for drug sale and use or adopted non-enforcement policies with respect to antidrug laws.[3] In the United States there is growing sentiment that marijuana smoking should be legalized, especially for medicinal purposes. Fifteen states and the District of Columbia have legalized medical marijuana for use by patients with illnesses for which marijuana has been shown to have therapeutic value (Table 2.1). In 2010, a California referendum to legalize and tax the cultivation and sale of marijuana for recreational purposes was narrowly defeated, by a vote of 54 to 46 percent. While U.S. support for legalizing marijuana was at 12 percent in a Gallup public opinion poll in 1969, by 2001 it had climbed to 31 percent, by 2004 to 34 percent, by 2006 to 36 percent; the most recent polls show that 46 percent of people polled support the legalization of marijuana.[4]

The history of narcotics legislation raises a critical question for our understanding of crime: Why are some behaviors defined as crime while others are not? The most common answer is that a crime is an act that violates widely agreed upon cultural norms. Emile Durkheim, one of the founders of the science of sociology, put it this way: "The only common characteristic of crimes is that they consist . . . in acts universally disapproved of by members of each society."[5]

Durkheim was wrong. What constitutes a crime is often the result of the actions of a small group of people, who do not represent public opinion (including government officials), that lobby to make some acts criminal while decriminalizing others.

Laws change dramatically over time. In the 1900s the Bayer Pharmaceutical Company legally developed and advertised heroin and claimed the drug had magical curative qualities. Heroin is a derivative of opium, and today the sale or possession of opium, heroin, and other derivatives of the opium poppy is a crime punishable by a long prison sentence.

TABLE 2.1
States Where Medical Marijuana Is Legal

STATE	YEAR PASSED	POSSESSION LIMIT
Alaska	1998	1 oz usable; 6 plants (3 mature, 3 immature)
Arizona	2010	2.5 oz usable; 0–12 plants
California	1996	8 oz usable; 18 plants (6 mature, 12 immature)
Colorado	2000	2 oz usable; 6 plants (3 mature, 3 immature)
DC	2010	2 oz dried; limits on other forms to be determined
Hawaii	2000	3 oz usable; 7 plants (3 mature, 4 immature)
Maine	1999	2.5 oz usable; 6 plants
Michigan	2008	2.5 oz usable; 12 plants
Montana	2004	1 oz usable; 6 plants
Nevada	2000	1 oz usable; 7 plants (3 mature, 4 immature)
New Jersey	2010	2 oz usable
New Mexico	2007	6 oz usable; 16 plants (4 mature, 12 immature)
Oregon	1998	24 oz usable; 24 plants (6 mature, 18 immature)
Rhode Island	2006	2.5 oz usable; 12 plants
Vermont	2004	2 oz usable; 9 plants (2 mature, 7 immature)
Washington	1998	24 oz usable; 15 plants

Source: 15 legal medical marijuana states and DC: Laws, fees, and possession limits. (2011). *Procon.org.* Retrieved from http://medicalmarijuana.procon.org/view.resource. php?resourceID=000881

THE CHANGING NATURE OF LAW

Criminal laws are constantly changing. Human beings have shown an impressive ability to develop a variety of cultures that see the same or similar behaviors very differently. Some cultures value sharing and serving the community as of paramount importance, while others view individual responsibility and achievement as the highest virtue. Even within a particular culture, the history of laws is a history of change: An act that is a crime in one period is acceptable behavior in another. Until 1973, it was a criminal offense for a woman in the United States to obtain an abortion or for a physician to perform one except under certain very restrictive conditions, such as if the pregnancy were the result of rape or if it seriously threatened the mother's health. That year's U.S. Supreme Court decision in *Roe v. Wade* gave individual states the right to pass laws governing a woman's right to decide whether to have an abortion in the first trimester of pregnancy. Since then, licensed medical doctors have been able to legally perform the procedure.

The *Roe v. Wade* decision, like the laws criminalizing certain drugs, did not reflect public opinion, and indeed today, nearly 40 years after the law was passed, public opinion

TABLE **2.2**

Harris Public Opinion Poll on Abortion		
"IN GENERAL, DO YOU FAVOR OR OPPOSE . . . THE U.S. SUPREME COURT DECISION MAKING ABORTIONS UP TO THREE MONTHS OF PREGNANCY LEGAL?"		
	FAVORED RULING IN *ROE V. WADE*	OPPOSED RULING IN *ROE V. WADE*
2005	55%	40%
2004	49%	48%

Source: U.S. attitudes toward *Roe v. Wade*. (2006, May 4). *Wall Street Journal.*

is much divided over the issue. A *Los Angeles Times* poll in 2005 found that 41 percent of respondents favored making abortion illegal with few exceptions, 24 percent favored making abortion always legal, 19 percent favored making abortion legal most of the time, and 12 percent favored making abortion totally illegal.[6] A Harris poll, on the other hand, found greater support for legalizing abortion (Table 2.2). Polls are notoriously subject to misinterpretation, and results depend heavily on how the question is asked. We cannot draw definitive conclusions from these polls as to exactly how U.S. voters feel about abortion, but we can safely conclude that there is widespread disagreement over the issue, reinforcing the idea that law creation is not simply a reflection of public opinion but is in fact a complicated social process, as we will discuss later and throughout this book.

THE ORIGINS OF U.S. LAW

Our task as criminologists is to describe and explain what constitutes a criminal act and why some acts are defined as criminal while others are not. The first step is to understand the origins of U.S. criminal law.

When the American colonies gained their independence from Great Britain in 1776, the Founding Fathers adopted the legal system and most of the laws of England for the new nation, including the process by which laws were created. Under this system, the **common law,** laws are created by legislation, but their *interpretation* is left to

common law

A system in which laws are created by legislation, but their interpretation and substantive definition is left to the courts to determine.

The U.S. common law system was adopted from the British model (without the requirement that participants wear white wigs) during the formation of the United States in 1776. Common law is a legal system in which the interpretation of the law by the courts becomes the law.

In the case of *State v. Foglio* (1981), the defendant was charged with disorderly conduct resulting from the sale of tickets that permitted the holder to view a pornographic film. The trial judge dismissed the complaint because he felt that the statute, while it prohibited the sale of obscene materials, did not specifically mention the sale of tickets to live performances and was therefore ambiguous and could not be applied. The prosecutor appealed the case. The appellate court upheld the judge's dismissal of the case on the grounds that the statute was vague as to whether or not the sale of tickets to live performances was contained within the law. The court reiterated the principle that "before a man can be punished, his case must be plainly and unmistakably within the statute."

The issue of ambiguity has been addressed in many cases throughout the history of U.S. law. A landmark 1972 decision (*Papachristou v. City of Jacksonville*) has had far-reaching consequences with respect to the treatment of homeless people. Five homeless people were convicted in Jacksonville, Florida, of violating an ordinance prohibiting vagrancy, although the defense argued that the statute was too vague to be enforced. On appeal the appellate court reversed the conviction on the basis that the statute was, in fact, too vague. The court cited an earlier case (*United States v. Reese*) in which it was said, "It would certainly be dangerous if the legislature could set a net large enough to catch all possible offenders, and leave it to the courts to step inside and say who could be rightfully detained, and who should be set at large."

the courts to determine. For example, under English statutes a person who is "insane" is not responsible for his or her actions and therefore cannot commit a crime. But what constitutes "insanity"? That decision was left to the courts, which decided that a person is insane if at the time of the act he or she "did not know right from wrong." The legislature decided insanity was a defense against guilt, but the courts interpreted what insanity meant. Thus, the courts were and remain a critical element in determining what constitutes crime.

The young United States also adopted broad legal principles from Britain as well as some specific laws. The three most important general principles were legality, *mens rea* (intent), and punishment. Let's look briefly at each to understand the basis for U.S. criminal law.

The Principle of Legality

In the former Soviet Union—and in many countries today—lawmakers can pass laws that are retroactive. For example, in December they could make it a crime to have published documents critical of the government three months earlier, in September. Under English and U.S. law, retroactive rules of this sort are among the circumstances that violate the principle of legality and cannot be upheld in court. The **principle of legality** says there must be a law at the time of the act that specifically prohibits an act or requires a person to act in a certain way in order for there to be a crime. (See Connecting Theory to Practice for a closer look at the principle of legality and ambiguity in the law today.)

In 1931 in Oklahoma, a man was convicted of transporting a stolen airplane under a state statute that prohibited the transportation of stolen motor vehicles. On his appeal, the U.S. Supreme Court ruled that airplanes were not motor vehicles as defined in the statute. Thus, there was no statute prohibiting the transportation of a stolen airplane, and the conviction was overturned.[7] Needless to say the Oklahoma legislature quickly

principle of legality

In order for there to be a crime, there must be a law at the time of the act that specifically prohibits that act or that requires a person to act in a certain way.

added "airplanes" to the statute. However, since criminal laws cannot be retroactive—that is, people cannot be held accountable for acts that were not criminal at the time of their commission—the man had not committed a crime.

The Principle of Intent (*Mens Rea*)

**principle of intent
(*mens rea*)**

In order for an act to be a crime,
the person committing the act
must have intended to commit it.

The **principle of intent** or *mens rea* (Latin for "guilty mind") is fundamental to U.S. criminal law. It holds that for an act to be a crime, the person committing the act must have *intended* to commit it. This does not mean the person had to intend to commit a *crime*. People may mistakenly believe they are behaving legally, but if their act is a crime, and they intended to commit the act, then they can be held accountable for the crime. For example, a husband may believe he has the right to rape his wife. Indeed, in the not-too-distant past, statutes and court decisions gave a husband the right to rape his wife.[8] Rape laws have changed, however, and in most states it is rape if anyone (man or woman) physically forces sexual intercourse on a spouse. Therefore, whether or not someone believes he has the legal right to rape his wife, it is nonetheless against the law to do so, and a man who rapes his wife has committed a crime.

A woman in Washington, DC, chained her children to a bed in order, she said, "to protect them." She was found guilty in municipal court of violating the code that makes it a crime in the District of Columbia to "torture, cruelly beat, abuse, or otherwise willfully mistreat a child." On appeal, however, the U.S. Court of Appeals, District of Columbia, reversed the decision on the grounds that although "it was certainly unreasonable and probably dangerous to chain the children," because the "appellant chained them for their own protection, she did not 'abuse' or 'willfully mistreat' them within the meaning of the code."[9] The law requires that there must be "a combination of an evil state of mind (intent) as well as the doing of an evil act."

Over the years the courts have expanded and broadened the applicability of intent to cover a wide range of behaviors and to hold people responsible for the consequences of acts they intended to commit even if they did not intend the consequences. If two women get into an argument in a bar and one shoves the other, who then falls and hits her head on an iron plate and dies, the woman who shoved the other certainly did not intend to kill her. According to the law, however, she did intend to shove her, and this act, which is the crime of assault, makes her responsible for the person's death even though she did not intend the ultimate result. In fleeing a robbery, a robber may be chased by a policewoman who crashes her car into a light post and dies. The robber may be tried for murder under the felony murder rule even though he did not intend to kill the policewoman. The act of robbing the bank put others at risk to such a degree that the perpetrator is considered to have intended the consequences.

Notice that merely intending to commit a crime is not a crime. We discussed the case of Rod Blagojevich in Chapter 1. This former governor of Illinois had spoken emphatically to friends about how he could profit from his responsibility for appointing a U.S. senator to replace president-elect Barack Obama by selling the appointment. When Blagojevich was tried in federal court on charges of having committed a crime, however, the prosecutor failed to convince the jury that Blagojevich had taken any *action* to ensure that he would profit in any way from the appointment.

In criminal law, intention must be accompanied by an *act*. If someone simply intends to rob a bank but does not engage in any overt action toward accomplishing the robbery, there is no crime. Intent must be tied to an action. That action need not be the crime, however: *Preparing* to commit the crime is also considered part of the necessary act. If a politician plans to accept a bribe, contacts a potential briber, and arranges to meet him or her, these actions are sufficient to indicate a coincidence of intent and act and could well be found to constitute a crime. The Consider This feature offers two other examples of interpreting intention.

There is, however, an important qualification with respect to intent. Someone who suffers "diminished responsibility" cannot be assumed to have the element of intent in

CONSIDER THIS...

Interpreting *Mens Rea*

Two young men were playing Russian roulette—a game in which one bullet is placed in a revolver, and the other chambers are left empty. Each player points the gun at another and pulls the trigger, hoping, of course, that the firing pin strikes an empty chamber. When Malone, 17 at the time, pointed the gun at his friend Long, the chamber with the bullet in it fired. Long died, and Malone was convicted of manslaughter.

Malone appealed his conviction on the grounds that he did not intend to kill Long. The appellate court affirmed the conviction on the grounds that although Malone may not have intended to kill, his recklessness was such that he could anticipate the likelihood that his intended action could result in Long's death. There was, then, the necessary intent.[10]

A later case, *People v. Newton* (1973), illustrates the principle that there must be a combination of *mens rea* and voluntary action for conduct to be criminal. The defendant was convicted under a New York statute of possession of a pistol and ammunition. While clearly in possession, he argued successfully that his possession in New York was neither intended nor voluntary, because the aircraft in which he was a passenger made an unscheduled landing in that state.[11]

How might the decision in the case of *People v. Newton* have been affected if Mr. Newton's actions were believed to be part of a terrorist plot? Suppose the law enforcement agency that arrested him thought he was carrying the weapon to another destination in order to hijack the plane after it left New York. Would the court's decision have been different?

What do you think?

In order for an act to be considered a crime, it must have been perpetrated with evil intent (*mens rea*). Without the elements of intent and action, the behavior is not criminal. A player in a reckless game of Russian roulette was deemed by the courts to have evil intent.

---

his or her actions. The most important example is a person who suffers a mental illness; other exceptions are those under the influence of alcohol or drugs, those who are mentally incompetent, and those whose mental condition impairs their judgment (see the Connecting Research to Practice feature for an example of this type of impairment, brought on by the trauma of war). All may be defended against criminal charges on the grounds they had "diminished responsibility" even though they clearly intended to commit the crime.

The Principle of Punishment

Criminal law also requires that some punishment be specified in order for an act or a failure to act to be a crime. The **principle of punishment** means a statute must specify a punishment such as a fine, imprisonment, or both. A statute that simply said it is against the law to spit on the sidewalk but did not specify the punishment for violations would not be enforceable. Indeed, one of the key differences between criminal and civil law is that criminal laws must specify a punishment, whereas civil laws do not. We look at other differences next.

principle of punishment

A statute must specify the punishment for violation of the law.

U.S. soldiers' wartime experiences have often led to mental trauma on their return to civilian life. Research on these veterans has found severe symptoms of distress that have been labeled post-traumatic stress disorder (PTSD). Medical science, psychologists, and psychiatrists now generally agree that PTSD is a real and serious disorder that can dramatically affect an individual's behavior.

George Porter, a Korean War veteran, was convicted of murder in 1988. His attorney had failed to instruct the trial court as to Porter's mental condition due to PTSD. Porter was found guilty and sentenced to death. Porter appealed to the U.S. Supreme Court, arguing that his PTSD should have been taken into account in imposing the death sentence. The appeal did not question Porter's guilt but did question the sentence. The U.S. Supreme Court reversed the death sentence. In reporting the story, the *Washington Post* described the case in these terms:

> George Porter, Jr., a Korean War veteran with two Purple Hearts, pleaded guilty to the murder of a former girlfriend and her new boyfriend and was sentenced to death in 1988. The justices did not overturn the convictions but lambasted the defense lawyer's failure to introduce mitigating evidence—including military service and possible post-traumatic stress—that could have led to a reduced sentence.
>
> Had Mr. Porter's counsel been "effective," the justices wrote in the unsigned Nov. 30 opinion, the trial judge and jury would have learned about the kind of "troubled history" that the court has "declared relevant to assessing a defendant's moral culpability. . . . They would have heard about (1) Porter's heroic military service in two of the most critical—and horrific—battles of the Korean War, (2) his struggles to regain normality upon his return from war, (3) his childhood history of physical abuse, and (4) his brain abnormality, difficulty reading and writing, and limited schooling.
>
> The original lawyer for Mr. Porter either did not know of, or failed to present, any of this information. The justices concluded that the lawyer "unquestionably" failed his client . . .[12]

CRIMINAL AND CIVIL LAW

criminal law

A collection of laws that define conduct against the state and that set out the punishments for those violations.

defendant

The person or party being accused or sued in a trial.

civil law

A collection of laws dealing with disputes between individuals and organizations, as opposed to violations against the state.

plaintiff

The person or party bringing the suit to trial.

The violation of a **criminal law** in the United States is considered an act against the state or federal government. Thus, it is the government that files charges against the **defendant** or accused, and that tries the case through attorneys or attorneys general who represent the government and act as prosecutors. In **civil law** cases, a **plaintiff**—a person, organization, or government agency—brings suit against a defendant, the person being sued.

In 2009, for instance, AIG (American International Group) was tried in civil court. AIG, one of the world's largest insurers, was accused of inaccurately reporting its finances. The Securities and Exchange Commission (SEC), the government agency that regulates the banking and finance industries, charged the company's former head, Maurice R. Greenberg, with securities violations and other accounting improprieties.[13]

Greenberg, who agreed to pay the government $15 million to settle the case, could also have been charged with criminal acts, because his actions at AIG violated both criminal and civil laws (see Chapter 14 for more on white-collar crime). The government often brings civil rather than criminal charges in such cases, however, because it is easier to get a conviction in civil court. The reason is that the rules of evidence and the standard of guilt are different. In criminal court the state must show the accused is guilty "beyond a reasonable doubt," a difficult standard to meet. In civil suits it is necessary only to show "a preponderance of evidence" that the person violated civil law. Civil law also allows self-incrimination, hearsay testimony, and the damaging testimony of spouses, while criminal law is much more restrictive on all these counts. Table 2.3 outlines some of the major differences between criminal and civil law.

TABLE **2.3**

Major Differences Between Civil and Criminal Law and Procedure

U.S. CRIMINAL LAW	U.S. CIVIL LAW
Opposing parties are prosecutor and defendant.	Opposing parties are plaintiff and defendant.
Conviction culminates in a fine or imprisonment.	Responsibility requires compensation only.
Guilt *must* be established "beyond a reasonable doubt."	Responsibility (*not* guilt) is established with a "preponderance of the evidence."
Hearsay evidence is inadmissible.	Hearsay evidence is admissible.
Voluntary spousal testimony may be admissible, but the court cannot require it.	The court can require spousal testimony.

Maurice R. Greenberg, the former head of the insurance giant AIG, was found guilty of securities fraud and could have been sent to prison. Instead Greenberg paid a multimillion-dollar fine.

Another difference between civil and criminal cases is their outcomes. The well-known former football player O. J. Simpson was found not guilty in criminal court of killing his ex-wife. If convicted, Simpson would certainly have earned a lengthy prison sentence and could have faced the death penalty. Believing him to be guilty, his ex-wife's family sued him in civil court, where he was found responsible for the death of his ex-wife and ordered to pay her family millions of dollars. As pointed out above, one reason a criminal court can find a defendant not guilty but a civil court can find him or her liable is that the criteria for determining responsibility in a civil suit are less onerous than those for determining guilt in a criminal case. Criminal liability must be proved "beyond a reasonable doubt," whereas civil liability need only demonstrate that the accused "probably caused" the harm.

Although it may look and feel like punishment when, in a civil lawsuit, the defendant must pay the plaintiff or the government a sum of money, so far as the law is concerned this payment is not punishment; it is *compensation.* This is not to say that the government does not in practice use fines in civil disputes as a punishment. Indeed, the Securities and Exchange Commission (SEC), for example, "punishes" corporations by imposing fines—in some cases fines totaling hundreds of millions of dollars. No doubt the corporation views this as a punishment, and the SEC intends it to be a punishment that will hopefully deter other corporations from violating the law. In legal theory, however, the fine is compensation for the aggrieved party: In the case of SEC fines, the aggrieved party is the government and ultimately the U.S. public. Sociologically speaking, we can see that in practice there is an increasing convergence of civil and criminal law. The theoretical legal distinction is nonetheless important to recognize. Finally, the stigma of a civil conviction is much less than that of a criminal one. Research on the implementation of factory safety and health legislation found that plaintiffs consciously chose to apply civil rather than criminal penalties because there was less stigma attached to civil penalties, and civil penalties were more efficient to administer.[14]

The distinction between criminal and civil law is a starting point for criminology. It provides us with a means to develop questions, theories, and research about what constitutes a crime, even though it does not provide an ironclad distinction between acts that are criminal and those that are not.

CRIME IN EARLY ENGLAND AND ITS IMPACT ON U.S. LAW

We have noted that the leaders of the newly created United States adopted from England the common law; the general principles of legality, *mens rea,* and punishment; and the distinction between criminal and civil law, along with substantive laws prohibiting

In the 11th century, William the Conqueror of England (shown here in a panel from the *Bayeux Tapestry*) and his successors attempted to unite England under one government. Their efforts rested in part on the creation of a new, single system of criminal law that defined some offenses as crimes against the state.

embezzlement, trespass, vagrancy, murder, rape, robbery, and theft among other offenses. But how did these ideas become embedded in English law in the first place? To answer that question we briefly trace their origins in English history.

The Impact of the Norman Conquest on English Law

Before 1066, when William the Conqueror led the Norman Conquest of England, early English law treated rape and murder as disputes to be settled between aggrieved parties. For one person to kill another was " first of all an offense against the victim or his family and was therefore to be settled by suitable payment to the sufferers."[15]

These laws were not criminal laws as we know them—that is, laws defining acts as offenses against the state or society. They were what today we would call civil laws; if a man raped a woman, it was the responsibility of the woman's family—usually her father, brother, or husband since it was a patriarchal society—to demand compensation from the offender, not to seek punishment for him.

Over time, however, William and his successors extended their powers beyond simply the military in an effort to unify England under a single monarchy. Criminal law, as we know it today, was created as a singularly effective tool in accomplishing this goal. After 1066, "crime came more and more to be regarded as an offense against the King's Peace for which it was the right and duty of the state to exact punishment."[16]

Laws Against Theft

A classic analysis of the laws of theft illustrates how new criminal laws usurped English customary practices. In early England, the owner of goods was the person who had possession of them. But as commerce grew and merchants increasingly needed to hire others to transport their goods from place to place, and as the state grew more dependent on these merchants and the revenue they generated, judges began to protect the merchant's interests by making the person receiving the goods responsible for carrying out the merchant's wishes.

A critical point in the history of the law came in the carrier case, decided in England in 1473:

> *The facts are simple enough: the defendant was hired to carry certain bales to South-ampton. Instead of fulfilling his obligation, he carried the goods to another place, broke open the bales and took the contents. He was apprehended and charged with felony.*[17]

Now that ownership no longer transferred with possession, the justices had established a new law of theft, which favored the well-being of the emerging class of capitalist traders and industrialists.

An avalanche of new laws resulted from the transition from a feudalist to a capitalist economy, from the victory of capitalists over feudal landlords in a series of contests for control of the state, from capitalists' interests being represented in Parliament, and from the new social relationships resulting from the Industrial Revolution (for instance, the emergence of clerks, who took money and other negotiable instruments in the name of their employers). None of these new laws reflected traditional (customary) practices or the consensus of the people. We look next to the laws of trespass for further support that English criminal law was not a reflection of shared values, customs, or widely held norms.

Laws Against Trespass and Poaching

Under feudalism, peasants living on manorial land had the right to hunt, fish, and gather wood on the lord's property. The emergence of capitalism, however, changed the serf to a wage earner and the lord's manor to a private estate. In 1723 England passed a law making a wide range of activities punishable by death, including: poaching, wearing a disguise in an area where deer or horses were kept, damaging fish ponds, wounding or killing cattle, and gathering wood.

Despite the new laws, people continued to exercise what they considered their natural rights to hunt, fish, and gather wood in the only available space: the lord's land.[18] Since property was a "thing," it became possible to define poaching animals, fishing, and gathering wood as crimes against things, rather than as injuries to humans. The thing the poachers, fisherman, and wood gatherers were injuring was the property of the owners of the land.

> Again and again, the voices of money and power declared the sacredness of property in terms hitherto reserved for human life. Forgers, for example, were almost invariably hanged, and gentlemen knew why: "Forgery is a stab to commerce, and only to be tolerated in a commercial nation when the foul crime of murder is pardoned." In a mood of unrivaled assurance and complacency, Parliament over the [18th] century created one of the bloodiest criminal codes in Europe.[19]

Laws Against Vagrancy

Laws against vagrancy (essentially, unemployed homelessness) reflect the British monarchy's concern with protecting the interests of feudal landowners by providing an abundance of cheap labor, even as the feudal system was breaking down and the pool of available labor to work the land was being depleted. The earliest such statute, passed in the 14th century, required any able-bodied person under 60, free or slave, without land or trade or job, to work for whoever offered employment, under pain of imprisonment. In 1351 this statute was strengthened by the stipulation: "And none shall go out of the town where he dwelled in winter, to serve the summer, if he may serve in the same town."[20] These laws were "an attempt to make the vagrancy statutes a substitute for serfdom."[21]

Over their long history, vagrancy laws have been invoked for purposes that ranged from efforts to tie laborers to the land in the Middle Ages to attempts to disperse the unemployed and the homeless during the Great Depression in the United States.

Feudalism gradually disappeared, however, and the country grew increasingly dependent upon a new source of income: commerce and trade. After the turn of the 16th century, the vagrancy law's focus thus turned to prosecuting "rogues," "vagabonds," and "roadmen" who preyed upon the increasing number of merchants transporting goods from place to place.[22]

In the United States during the late 19th and early 20th centuries, vagrancy statutes were used much as they had been in early England: to create a labor force. The end of the Civil War left southern plantation owners and northern industrialists wishing to industrialize the south without an adequate workforce or a willingness to pay wages for the labor that slavery had once provided. One solution was to arrest "free Negroes" for vagrancy and then force them to labor by leasing them to landowners, mining companies, or industrialists.[23]

Until very recently in the United States, people were still arrested for vagrancy during harvest time and given the option of working as a farm laborer or being sent to jail.[24] The same statutes were also used to control "undesirables" and, in California, to limit the immigration of unemployed persons during the Great Depression.[25] Vagrancy statutes came to serve the police as a carte blanche to arrest, harass, or jail persons they found to be a nuisance or whom they suspected of being potential criminals.

As a practical matter, the long, disreputable history of vagrancy statutes in the United States ended with a 1972 Supreme Court decision declaring an ordinance in Jacksonville, Florida, unconstitutional because it was being used to arrest people on suspicion of future criminality.[26] Justice William O. Douglas said, in part:

> *Here the net is cast large, not to give the courts the power to pick and choose, but to increase the arsenal of the police. . . . Where the list of crimes is so all-inclusive and generalized as the one in this ordinance, those convicted may be punished for no more than vindicating affronts to police authority. . . . Future criminality . . . is the common justification for the presence of vagrancy statutes. . . . The Jacksonville ordinance cannot be squared with our constitutional standards and is plainly unconstitutional."*

The history of vagrancy statutes is informative in demonstrating how laws change in response to changing political, economic, and social conditions. As we shall see below, the fact that laws are not simply a reflection of customs or shared values is an important one that theories of law creation must take into account.

U.S. law is frequently referred to as "Anglo-American" law, and for good reason. While fascinating in and of itself, the history of early English laws and how these were translated into U.S. law is essential not only to understanding the origins of U.S. law, but more importantly to grasping the political, economic, and social processes that underlie law creation. The research on crime and the creation of criminal laws in England utilizing the historical record give us the facts the theories must fit. In turn, these facts constitute the basis for various theories of criminal law creation.

THEORIES OF CRIMINAL LAW CREATION

We have traced the development of the criminal law system and some of the specific laws adopted from English law by the Founding Fathers. What does this history tell us about how laws are made? To answer we turn to four major theories of criminal law creation proposed by sociologists, political scientists, and anthropologists.

Consensus Theory

The research on the origins of Anglo-American criminal law that we reviewed above does not appear to support the *consensus model* (discussed in Chapter 1), embodied in Durkheim's claim that criminal law is a codification of customary beliefs and that it reflects a consensus of the values held by "every healthy conscience." However, this does

Illustrating the difficulty of defining consensus is the fact that one person's freedom fighters are another person's terrorists. How would you describe the American Revolutionary forces?

not mean there is never any consensus among a community of people. It means that, based on our research, we cannot say it is this consensus that explains why some acts are defined as criminal while others are not.

Even when there is apparent consensus, agreement can be fragile. Most people in the United States would certainly agree there should be laws against violence, yet

> *Violence is an ambiguous term whose meaning is established through political processes. The kinds of acts that become classified as "violent" and, equally important, those which do not become so classified, vary according to who provides the definition and who has superior resources for disseminating and enforcing his decision.*[27]

Consider the politicization of aggression. In a speech on May 10, 1984, President Reagan characterized the government of Nicaragua as supporting and arming "terrorists and guerillas," and the Contras—a group fighting against the Nicaraguan government—as "freedom fighters." One person's freedom fighters are another person's terrorists and guerillas.

Even the dictum "Thou shalt not kill" is a telling example of the slippery notion of consensus.[28] Killing is not always against the law and is in fact often praised as honorable. Soldiers kill in wartime; executioners pull the switch. Governments plot and carry out executions of government leaders in peace and in war (as we will see Chapter 14).[29] *Not* to kill may itself be a crime. A soldier who refuses to kill the enemy or a citizen who refuses to serve in the military commits a crime.

The point is that what constitutes crime and deviance is the result of a political process, not a simple reflection of agreed-upon ideas of right and wrong:

> *the decision to treat deviance as a social problem is itself a political decision. . . . deviance theories [should be] about society and, therefore, politics, conflict, coercion and other such "normal" concerns. . . . There is confusion about the line beyond which "stealing" becomes "looting," "hooliganism" becomes "rioting," "vandalism" becomes "sabotage"; when do "reckless maniacs" become "freedom fighters"? Are the everyday encounters between the police and urban slum youth throughout the world somehow stripped of their political significance if what is happening is not defined as a "riot" or "disturbance"?*[30]

Societal Needs Theory

Another theory often proposed to account for the origins of criminal law, the **societal needs theory,** says law reflects the needs of society. Jerome Hall applied this theory to criminal law:

> [T]he chronological order of the principal phases of legal change is (1) a lag between the substantive law and social needs; (2) spontaneous efforts (practices) of judges, other officials, and laymen to make successful adaptations; and (3) legislation.[31]

The first question we should ask about a theory that criminal law meets social needs is, Whose needs are they? Every modern society consists of many different groups and social classes. Do they all share the same basic needs so that when a choice is made, it is good for everyone? For complex modern societies divided by class, race, ethnicity, and gender, the answer is clearly no.

Recall the laws of theft that labeled the person who broke open the bales and took the goods a criminal. These laws favored the merchant over the employee. Whether or not we agree this was a good thing, it is still true that the law made a decision in favor of the merchant and against the interests of the employee. When vagrancy laws were passed in England and the United States, creating a labor force dependent on the landowners, industrialists, or mine owners, they were defining crime in a way that favored the interests of the capitalists over the interests of the workers. "Societal needs" were nonexistent; the needs of one class of people were in conflict with the needs of another. The state chose sides, and criminal law reflects this choice.

Choices between opposing sets of interests characterize modern law creation as well. Even laws that on the surface appear to serve the needs of everyone often turn out, on closer inspection, to be fraught with special interests that conflict with the interests of significant numbers of people. In 1970, for example, legislation was passed ostensibly to curtail the growth and influence of organized crime.[32] On the surface, nothing would seem to come closer to meeting societal needs than laws designed to control organized crime. Even here, however, those who influence and write the law were making important choices about whose needs were met.

The Organized Crime Control Act of 1970 vastly increased the powers of the federal government in law enforcement, transferring to it tasks previously left to state and local governments, and giving it, for instance, the power to send an uncooperative witness to prison for an indefinite period of time.[33] The law was revolutionary and was steadfastly opposed by many groups including the New York Bar Association and the American Civil Liberties Union. Did it reflect societal needs? Like most laws, this one invariably risked the interests of some groups while protecting the interests of others.

The idea that criminal law reflects societal needs appears at first brush like indisputable common sense. Closer scrutiny and practical research suggest, however, that this commonsensical theory is not an adequate explanation of why acts are defined as criminal.

Ruling Class Theory

Faced with the failure of traditional sociological theories (consensus theory and societal needs theory), social scientists sought alternative explanations. **Ruling class theory**—suggested by the work of classical political theorists such as Machiavelli, Pareto, Marx, and Weber—says that law is simply a reflection of the interests and ideology of the ruling class. Max Weber put it this way:

> [W]ith government as an instrument or vehicle available to whomever can control or use it, opportunities for gain, whether pecuniary or political or other advantage, accrue to those who can use government.[34]

Who is most likely to use and control the government? According to Marx: "In every era the ruling ideas are the ideas of the ruling class."[35]

For both Marx and Weber the ruling class consisted of those who controlled the economic resources and political power. Thus, the theory that the ruling class also determined the content and functioning of criminal law (as well as other law) made sense. As we have seen, it is also consistent with what we know about the historical development of law.

The ruling class theory finds some support in research into the lawmaking process. Legislation requiring meatpackers to comply with federal health standards, for instance, was widely publicized as a moral campaign to protect the consumer. In fact, the legislation was sought, lobbied for, and largely written by the nation's largest meatpacking companies, to give themselves a competitive advantage over smaller ones that would struggle to bear the added costs.[36] We find similar results in research on other industries.[37]

The theory fails, however, when we try to apply it to the entire spectrum of criminal law. For instance, while in the 1800s and early 1900s it was a crime for workers to engage in strikes or boycotts or try to organize into labor unions, today it is a crime for employers and business owners to interfere with the right of labor to do so.[38] The law changed against the desires, ideals, and political organization of the ruling class.[39]

Ruling class theory argues, however, that even when laws are against the short-term interests of the ruling class (capitalists, in capitalist societies), they are essential for purposes of legitimacy—the state must *appear* to be representing everyone and occasionally passes laws against the ruling class to demonstrate its neutrality and the inherent goodness of the system. Thus, it perpetuates capitalism in the long run and serves the interests of the ruling class.[40]

The arguments of ruling class theory have some cogency, but they are nonetheless limited. Clearly some laws that apparently conflict with the interests of the ruling class are in reality designed to subtly serve those in power.[41] On the other hand, the ruling class is not one monolithic class with wholly shared interests. The history of legislation is full of examples of a divided ruling class whose factions struggle quite openly against one another for favorable laws. Immigration law in the United States is a good illustration.[42]

During the 1800s U.S. immigration laws allowed immigration from countries with a labor surplus. But as the labor market was gradually filled and the initial phase of industrialization subsided, a large unemployed urban labor force was left behind, creating militant labor movements and open rebellion. Bankers and clothing manufacturers sought restrictions on immigration to solve the problem, while the steel industry sought to keep immigration policies open to meet its continuing labor needs. Eventually the steel industry lost, and in 1921 the nation's first general law restricting immigration was passed. Can ruling class theory explain this result? It can, if we argue that the real interest of the ruling class was in restricting immigration.

That the ruling class influences vast areas of law cannot be denied. But it is not the only force responsible for law creation. What we need is a theory that recognizes both the strengths and the limitations of ruling-class influence on the legal order.

Pluralist Theory

A **pluralist theory** of lawmaking suggests that "What makes law . . . is not 'public opinion' in the abstract, but public opinion in the sense of exerted social force."[43] In other words, the passage of criminal laws inevitably favors some groups' interests. As one scholar put it: "Social values which receive the protection of the criminal law are ultimately those which are treasured by dominant interest groups."[44] The problem is that this theory does not tell us how to determine which groups are dominant and will, therefore, be able to "exert social force" to create laws. If the only measure of whether a group or social class is dominant is that it succeeds in having its laws enacted, then the theory tells us nothing about the law. On the other hand, if the theory accepts that "the possession of money almost automatically confers power in Western society,"[45] then it becomes a thinly veiled disguise for ruling class theory, which as we have seen has weaknesses of its own.

pluralist theory

A theory of lawmaking that holds that law inevitably favors some groups' interests.

Pluralist theory must also assume either that all judges represent the same interest, or that they all are influenced by the same "exerted forces." Yet much lawmaking occurs through individual decisions. Finally, some legislation, including some we examined in this chapter like the Organized Crime Control Act of 1970, reflects the political infighting of government officials over different ideologies and can be explained only by the "interest group" theory tautologically. That is, the reasoning is circular, and the theory then becomes true by definition.

Structural Contradictions Theory

Thus far, we have looked at four general theories of law creation: consensus, societal needs, ruling class, and pluralist theories (Table 2.4). Our method for evaluating these theories has been consistent with the scientific methods we outlined in Chapter 1. First, we evaluated the logical structure of each theory; then we examined the evidence to see whether it supported the claims about law creation implied by the theory. None of the theories was consistent with the greater part of the research data available on the lawmaking process.

This does not mean there is *no* evidence to support the theories. Indeed, juvenile welfare laws in Canada have been found to reflect widespread concern over juvenile welfare, as consensus theory predicts they should. And, ruling class theory is consistent with some cases of law creation, but not all.

structural contradictions theory

A theory of lawmaking that holds that law is the result of structural contradictions leading to conflicts, which create dilemmas, which legislators and judges attempt to resolve.

Thus, we propose a **structural contradictions theory** of lawmaking, which builds upon existing theory while explaining facts that other theories have failed to account for. The starting point for the theory is that every society, nation, economic system, and historical period contains within it *structural contradictions,* and that human efforts to resolve these contradictions are the moving force behind social changes, including the creation of criminal laws.

Structural contradictions can be economic, political, social, or ideological. Within capitalist systems, for instance, a basic economic contradiction exists between the private ownership of production and the public nature of the productive process: That is, it is the public that provides the labor resulting in the private production of the goods. Simply put, those who own the factory have the legal right to do almost anything they want with their property and what it produces.[46] Without workers to produce goods, however, the factory is only an expensive shell. This interdependence of owners and workers creates a contradiction: Both owners and workers want to keep everything produced by

TABLE **2.4**

Theories of Law Creation		
THEORETICAL PERSPECTIVE	**MAJOR THEORIST**	**ESSENTIAL CONCEPTS AND IDEAS**
Consensus theory	Emile Durkheim	Shared customs and values are codified into law.
Societal needs theory	Jerome Hall	Legislatures and judges create laws to meet the perceived needs of society.
Ruling class theory	Karl Marx, Max Weber	Law reflects the basic interests and ideologies of the ruling class.
Pluralist theory	Lawrence Friedman	Interest groups compete for laws in their favor.
Structural contradictions theory	William Chambliss	Structural contradictions lead to conflicts that create dilemmas, which legislators and judges attempt to resolve.

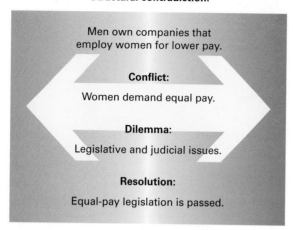

FIGURE **2.1**
A Structural Contradictions Model of Lawmaking

the combination of private property and public work. The contradiction builds conflict between workers and owners into the system. The law is an effort to resolve that conflict (Figure 2.1).[47]

The structural contradictions theory assumes it is not systems, society, or culture that creates law. It is people, responding to contradictions but bound by existing resources and constraints.[48] Repressive and exploitive law, however, generate resistance, which may yield new legislation, new interpretations of old laws, or the use of existing laws. The ruling class will win some struggles and lose some. An adequate theory of law creation must accommodate this fact.

Let's look more closely at the conflict between owners and workers. Early in its history, the United States adopted laws that overwhelmingly favored property owners. They could set inhuman conditions of labor at whatever wages they chose to pay. Slavery was legal, as was the exploitation of the labor of women and children. It was a criminal act for workers to try to organize, to strike to interrupt the work process, or to interfere with property owners' right to do anything they chose with the property or the products produced.

That these laws reflected neither consensus nor societal needs is clear from the fact that in the 19th century, workers, slaves, women, and children rebelled against them, risking beatings, imprisonment, and even death, while owners saw any concession toward fair labor practices as a first step toward "socialism, anarchy, and communism."[49] More immediately, it was a threat to profits. Since the economic elite of a society is better organized and can afford to purchase labor for the sole purpose of manipulating the state, this class is more likely to see its views reflected in law than any other class. But if ruling class theory were entirely correct, the situation would never have changed; owners would simply have replaced the uppity and recalcitrant with new immigrants or more slaves.

Instead, after much conflict, including workers' rebellions in the 1920s and 1930s, lawmakers and those who owned the economic resources had to compromise. The oppressive and exploitative conditions of work were the impetus for legal changes that benefited the workers; collective bargaining was made legal by the National Labor Relations (Wagner) Act of 1933, as were trade unions and the right to strike.[50] What had been criminal was criminal no longer.

RACISM AND SEXISM IN U.S. CRIMINAL LAW

Historically, the criminal law has played a central role in institutionalizing race and gender discrimination. When slavery was legal in the United States, it was a crime for a slave to depart from his or her "owner" without their permission.[51] Slaves were sold at

The Wagner Act of 1930 greatly improved the lives of U.S. workers, who for years had struggled against unfair and oppressive work conditions. The contradictions and conflicts in the relationships among labor, government, and business were reduced through legislation aimed at resolving the conflicts (but not the contradictions) and are an excellent example of the structural contradictions theory at work.

auctions; criminal laws made the sales legal, and any slave who refused the orders of his or her new "owner" was subject to severe criminal sanctions ranging from beatings to imprisonment.[52]

As we saw in the discussion of U.S. drug laws, these laws were originally focused on the oppression of particular ethnic groups. As recently as 2010, penalties for crack cocaine, which was thought to be most often consumed by minorities, carried much stiffer penalties than powder cocaine, which was assumed to be used more frequently by whites. There is overwhelming evidence that even today minorities are disproportionately subjected to search and seizure laws, sentenced to prison more often than whites for the same offense, and sentenced for longer periods.[53]

The Women's Movement and Criminal Law

In 1867 the U.S. Supreme Court held that a woman who had successfully completed law school and passed the bar in Illinois had no right to practice law. In 1869 the University of Edinburgh in Scotland refused to award the chemistry prize to the student with the highest marks, as was traditionally done, because that year the student with the highest marks was a woman. The controversy grew so heated that the university ultimately refused to allow women to attend. The seven women who had fought for admission went to court for satisfaction but received none. The court ruled the university had the right to discriminate against women even though it could not discriminate based on religion or race.[54]

British women in the 1800s could not serve in Parliament or city councils. By law they were not considered persons—only men were—and therefore women were not eligible for or covered by laws applied to persons. Women in the United States were denied the vote. Only when women violated the law by violently and consistently opposing the oppression and exploitation institutionalized in the law did matters change. It was not the case that the law gradually changed as customs and beliefs changed, or that the male legislators, lawyers, and judges became fairer and more tolerant as the logic of a democratic and free society for all slowly worked its magic through legal reasoning. The laws changed as women collectively, and individually, violated the existing laws and demanded equal justice.

One hundred fifty years of women's struggle for equality in law have brought changes but not equality. One authority estimates that in the United States today there are over 800 pieces of blatantly sex-discriminatory laws currently on the statute books.[55] In Wisconsin a wife can be disinherited by her husband. In most states women cannot co-sign for a loan even though the property is jointly owned. In some states a man can legally kill his wife if he finds her having sexual relations with another man. In rape cases, a woman with prior sexual experience is less likely to be believed if she claims she was raped. To some extent in Western societies, women continue to be seen in law and in practice as "property" to be owned and controlled by men.[56]

Women's rights movements and struggles effectively changed the law. As we will see through the coming chapters, however, changing the law does not guarantee that patterns of social relations will change.

Perhaps the most important change to take place in the law with respect to women in recent times occurred when, as we saw earlier in the chapter, the Supreme Court decided in *Roe v. Wade* that laws criminalizing obtaining or performing an abortion during the first trimester of pregnancy were unconstitutional.[57] Abortion laws had for years restricted a woman's right to determine her own destiny. They discriminated against the poor by making illegal abortions unaffordable and dangerous. The women's movement focused considerable attention on these laws, generating conflict between those who sought to maintain male dominance of women, even over the decision of whether to have a baby, and those who sought to give women the right to choose.

The conflict has not abated with the Supreme Court decision and will not go away soon. We can anticipate continued conflict from the contradictions inherent in the oppression of women and the struggle of those who benefit from that oppression to try to maintain their privileges and power.[58]

Throughout U.S. history, conflicts between women seeking equal rights with men have been ubiquitous. The women's movement of the 1970s and 1980s led to some fundamental changes in law, but women continue to earn lower wages than men for the same work and to struggle for equality in both public and private arenas.

The Civil Rights Movement: Racism and Criminal Law

The history of racist laws in the United States is a history of contradictions and struggles against them. To legitimize slavery as an institution, whites defined blacks as non-human while demanding that they perform human tasks: building shelters, forming communities, raising children, and working. Thus, slavery was "a system constructed on the contradiction between denying the humanity of Blacks but depending on their human qualities for the survival of the system."[59] This contradiction led to the creation of laws trying to make logical sense of what was inherently illogical. Slaves could not testify against whites, for example, because slaves were not human and only human beings had the right to appear as witnesses in court. Thus, a white abolitionist was set free during trial because the only witnesses who could have testified that he had incited the slaves on a plantation to rebel were the slaves themselves.[60]

Throughout the southern states as recently as the 1960s, it was a crime for a black person *not* to step off the sidewalk if a white person was walking past. Blacks attempting to form labor unions were arrested and fired from their jobs. Blacks could not enter white restaurants, drink from white water fountains, or use white-only toilets.

Prior to 1954 if a black child attempted to attend a white public school, the child and his or her parents were subject to arrest for violating state statutes prohibiting the integration of blacks and whites in school. In 1954 the U.S. Supreme Court decided in *Brown v. the Board of Education* that segregated schooling was unconstitutional. Since 1954, the most measurable impact of that decision has been to give legitimacy to continued racial discrimination in schooling.[61] More recent court decisions also undermine the effect the *Brown* decision might have by upholding the right of different school districts to spend vastly different amounts of money on education.

Discriminatory laws restricting the freedom of blacks were in blatant contradiction of the Constitution and of the overtly expressed values of many in the United States, yet they persisted for a hundred years after the Civil War. The contradiction between these laws and generally held values inexorably led to conflicts that were often personal, culminating in lynchings, beatings, and imprisonment for blacks who violated discriminatory laws. The laws themselves changed, however, when blacks organized, under the leadership of people like Martin Luther King Jr., and created the civil rights movement.

Like those who fought for women's suffrage, participants in the civil rights movement were often the victims of police brutality and injustice in the administration of the courts; many were sentenced to prison. Some paid with their lives. Despite a systematic attempt to suppress the movement, it culminated in a major overhaul of criminal law in which laws making it a crime for blacks to behave like whites were abolished. The practice of discrimination, however, outlived the laws, and perhaps its most blatant institutionalized form today is the differential treatment of blacks and whites in the criminal justice system.[62]

For over a hundred years following the Civil War, blacks still were not accorded the same rights as whites. Under the legal doctrine "separate but equal," in many jurisdictions schools were segregated into black and white schools from the end of the Civil War until the 1960s. This photo depicts early efforts by black children to enter white-only schools.

SUMMARY

■ **What are the origins of U.S. law?**

U.S. law is an adoption of the British common law. In addition to adopting specific laws—such as those prohibiting theft, vagrancy, murder, and trespass—the fundamental principles of legality, intent, and punishment were also adopted. Within the U.S. system, laws are created through the process of legislation but are interpreted by the courts.

What is the difference between criminal and civil law?

The violation of a criminal law in the United States is considered an act against the state or federal government. Thus, it is the government that files charges against the defendant or accused, and the government tries the case through attorneys or attorneys general who represent the government and act as prosecutors. In civil law cases, a plaintiff (person, organization, or government agency) brings suit against a defendant, the person being sued.

Several major differences separate criminal from civil law trials. In criminal law the person must be found guilty "beyond a reasonable doubt," but in civil law "a preponderance of evidence" is sufficient to determine liability. Hearsay evidence is admissible in civil but not criminal cases. A person can be required to provide evidence that shows his or her liability ("self-incrimination") in civil but not in criminal cases. Spouses may be required to testify against the defendant in civil cases but cannot be required to do so in criminal cases, though they may do so voluntarily. A final significant difference between crime and civil infractions is that a crime must carry with it a specified punishment while a civil violation does not.

What principles determine what makes an act a crime in the United States?

In the U.S. legal system, a crime cannot occur without meeting the requirements of legality, *mens rea*, and punishment. Legality means that an act must be explicitly prohibited by law in order for a person to be found responsible for a crime. Absent a law restricting some act, a crime cannot occur.

Mens rea—literally "guilty mind," otherwise known broadly as intent— indicates that a person must have intended to commit some act that has been deemed illegal. It does not matter if the person did not know his or her actions were illegal, nor does it matter if he or she did not anticipate the unfortunate consequences of the actions (such as someone's death), so long as the person committed the action knowingly and with evil intention. Thus, intent encompasses a mental state (evil mind) and some form of overt action.

Punishment indicates that a crime cannot occur without a prescribed punishment against those who commit it. Someone found guilty of a crime must be given a fine, be imprisoned, or both.

What theories explain the development of criminal law?

The most important theories that attempt to explain how criminal laws are created include consensus, societal needs, pluralist, ruling class, and structural contradiction theories. Consensus theory posits that crimes and criminal laws are defined as a result of societal consensus against a certain act or form of conduct. Societal needs theory states that criminal laws result from shared needs in an entire society and are decided by judges and legislatures. Ruling class theory argues that the law reflects the basic interests and ideologies of the ruling class. Pluralist theory holds that the competition among interest groups leads to laws favoring one over the other.

Alternatively, structural contradictions theory argues that built into the political, economic, and social relations of every historical period are contradictions that generate conflicts. These conflicts, in turn, create a dilemma for legislators and judges who ultimately make the criminal law. Efforts to resolve the conflicts are manifested in new criminal laws and the reinterpretation of existing law. The resolutions often generate further contradictions, conflicts, and dilemmas. Law creation is therefore an ongoing historical process that reflects the lives and times of people coping with institutions and practices inherited from the past.

■ **How does public opinion influence the creation of criminal law?**

Public opinion may force compromises between conflicting groups and bring about the creation of laws aimed at mitigating and resolving this conflict. Public opinion, however, is a poor predictor of what will be defined as a crime in the criminal law. As we have seen, acts that are customary practices (hunting on public grounds, for example) may become law in order to serve special interests. Furthermore, public opinion is often divided on issues of criminal law such as abortion, the legalization of marijuana, and many others.

■ **What role have racism and sexism played in the development of U.S. criminal law?**

Both the women's movement and the civil rights movement provide support for the theory of structural contradictions. The general principle that everyone in society should be treated equally contradicts the reality of unequal treatment of women and people of color. Discriminatory laws and practices—such as segregated schooling, unequal voting rights, and unequal pay for the same work—fly in the face of the equality principle. Conflicts between different groups (whites versus blacks, men versus women) result from these contradictions and create a dilemma for lawmakers: How to resolve the conflicts?

Laws emerge as attempted solutions. These laws may take the form of oppression (initially segregation laws were upheld by the U.S. Supreme Court, as were voting and job discrimination laws oppressive to women); but ongoing conflicts may force lawmakers to relieve such contradictions in the system.

CRITICAL THINKING QUESTIONS

1. Which theory of law creation do you feel most adequately explains the injustices present in society? Does your answer change based on the type of injustice you are examining—for instance, racial or sexual inequality, environmental degradation?

2. How would you explain the creation of laws that make it a crime to steal ideas (for instance, intellectual property)? Who benefits from such laws—business, the individual who lays claim to the idea, government, or some combination? What are the implications of criminalizing the theft of ideas, when those ideas generate advances in medicine or food production that could benefit all of society?

3. Recap each of the theories of law creation and provide one or two examples of a law not already mentioned that would be best explained by that theory. Do you find it easier to match laws to one specific theory than to another? Why or why not?

4. Most white-collar crimes (typically financial, health and safety, or environmental violations) are perpetrated by corporations or government agencies and are prosecuted in civil courts, despite the fact that they could be prosecuted criminally. Why do you think this is the case, and what are the consequences of finding these offenders guilty of civil infractions rather than criminal acts? Does their prosecution in civil court signal anything about how society perceives the harm stemming from these actions?

5. Suppose you were put into a position never before created, with the power to reform the U.S. legal system singlehandedly. What changes would you implement and where would you begin? Would you maintain the emphasis on defining crimes within the U.S. court system, or undertake a drastic change and allow society to define all crimes? Formulate several ideas and develop benefits and consequences for each.

ADDITIONAL RESOURCES

Learn more about the U.S. legal system and read up on a case of interest to you at the Supreme Court website http://www.supremecourt.gov/ or check out some information about state and constitutional laws and other issues at http://www.justia.com/

Find basic information and policy and legal discussions on a host of relevant women's issues—from women's rights, sexual assault, and immigration to pay imbalances and contraception—at http://womensrights.change.org/blog/category/sex

Learn more about labor struggles and keep track of corporate pay at the AFL-CIO website: http://www.aflcio.org/countdown_uiexpire.cfm?continue5/index.cfm

View information pertaining to numerous civil and human rights causes, struggles, and legal issues at the Leadership Conference: http://www.civilrights.org/

3

HOW MUCH CRIME IS THERE?

In this chapter, we will explore the following questions:

- Where do we get our information about crime?
- What picture of crime do official data sources give us?
- Is there a typical criminal?
- Are there certain crime trends or patterns of offending?
- Who are crime victims and what do they have in common?

Sociologist Ray Surette found that crime and justice topics

occupy 25 percent of all newspaper news space.[1] He also found that 13 percent of all national TV news and over 20 percent of local news was devoted to crime reporting. Doris Graber found that over 30 percent of the television programs in the United States are about crime or law enforcement.[2] In addition, shows like *60 Minutes, Nightline,* and *48 Hours* frequently focus on crime. The History Channel, MSNBC, and numerous other cable channels present lengthy documentaries about organized crime, drug smuggling, and life in U.S. prisons. Judging from the media coverage, an observer might think we live in a sea of violence from which there is no escape.

Dennis Rader, known as the BTK strangler, murdered 10 people in Sedgwick County, Kansas, between 1974 and 1991. For years, Rader taunted police and local news sources with letters describing his killings. Stories about his life and crimes flooded the media after his arrest in 2005.

Media attention is especially concentrated when a particularly heinous crime has been committed or when someone is arrested who has committed a series of violent crimes. The media had a field day, for example, when on August 18, 2005, Dennis Rader was sentenced to 10 consecutive life terms in prison after pleading guilty to 10 murders from 1974 to 1991. Sixty years old and an active member of his church congregation and a Boy Scout leader, Rader had led a double life for decades. Referring to himself as BTK for "bind, torture, and kill," he eluded police investigators during his reign of terror in Wichita, Kansas. Graphic details of Rader's murders revealed a serial killer fascinated with taking control of and torturing his victims.

It is safe to say that most people obtain their knowledge about crime from the media. People may realize that the picture they get from the Internet, TV shows, and films is not an accurate one, but there is no doubt that it has an effect on their image of the prevalence and seriousness of crime.

Sensational media coverage of crime highlights the importance of obtaining objective information about how much crime there is and the types of crime that are typical. Crimes depicted in the media (almost always violent crime and often serial killings) are extremely rare. The three crimes that account for the vast bulk of arrests in the United States are theft, driving while under the influence, and the possession or sale of illegal drugs.[3] Homicide, the subject of so much media attention, is actually one of the crimes least often committed. Not only is homicide rare, but fewer than six people in 100,000 are the victims of homicide in any given year. In fact, the homicide rate in the United States has shown a steady decline since the 1980s and is now the lowest it has been in 40 years (Table 3.1).

Declining homicide rates, however, do not make for interesting headlines—unless, of course, a politician or law enforcement official wants to claim responsibility for the decline, as did New York's Mayor Rudy Giuliani in the 1980s.

CRIMINOLOGY AND CRIME DATA

Criminology is built on two great pillars: *facts* (or data) and *theories.* The goal of criminology is to know what the facts are and then to create theories that explain the facts. Unfortunately, neither facts nor theories come to us in a package—we must discover both. In the chapters to come, we will introduce various theoretical perspectives on crime and examine their relevance in light of important facts presented in this chapter. In discovering what the facts are, we also uncover some common misconceptions, some of which derive from data gathered by organizations with a vested interest in having the facts turn out a certain way.

Most people realize that novelists, journalists, and scriptwriters promote images of crime that are tantalizing, exciting, sometimes horrifying, but inevitably misleading. What is not so well recognized is that police departments, politicians, prosecutors, and judges sometimes do the same thing. If police can convince lawmakers and the general public that crime is a serious problem that threatens everyone's well-being, they are better able to prove the importance of their work, increase their budgets, and enhance their

TABLE 3.1

U.S. Homicide Rates per 100,000 People, 1950–2008

Year	Rate
1950	4.6
1955	4.1
1960	5.1
1965	5.1
1970	7.9
1975	9.6
1980	10.2
1985	7.9
1990	9.4
1995	8.2
2000	5.5
2005	5.9
2008	5.6

Source: Federal Bureau of Investigation. (2009, September). *Uniform crime reports. Crime in the United States, 2008.* Retrieved from http://www2.fbi.gov/ucr/cius2008/index.html (accessed May 6, 2011).

working conditions. Thus, when the FBI approaches Congress in the spring to request an increase in its budget, we must view with caution the claims it makes about crime and crime rates.

Politicians and judges also share a vested interest in creating certain images of crime. If elected officials have promised to "do something about crime," it is in their interest to show a decrease in crime. Candidates running for office, on the other hand, may use the "crime problem" as a way of attacking the incumbent in an effort to win the seat. Judges who wish to convey that they are justified in being lenient on a particular offender may selectively report findings such as the offender's background, community involvement, and age to show that this type of offender deserves leniency.

One consequence of these personal motivations and interests is that the general public gets a distorted idea of what types of crime are most prevalent and *how much crime there is.* Law enforcement officials and politicians, for example, are fond of painting a picture of crime in the United States as being out of control. They underscore this idea by claiming that crime is far more prevalent in the United States than in other industrialized (especially European) societies. The fact is, however, that with the exception of murder rates, recent studies have shown that the U.S. crime rate is *lower* than in most other industrialized countries (Figure 3.1).

Fortunately, we are not dependent on the media or politicians for the facts we need to have in order to scientifically study crime. To some extent we are dependent on law enforcement agencies (the FBI and the U.S. Attorney General's Office in particular), but because these agencies provide us with considerable information about how they collect their data, we are in a position to objectively assess the data's validity.

The Uniform Crime Reports (UCR)

The FBI systematically collects data on crime from about 17,000 local, state, and federal law enforcement agencies. These data are compiled and published annually by the FBI in the **Uniform Crime Reports (UCR).** The UCR was created in 1929 on the recommendation

Uniform Crime Reports (UCR)

Published data on crime from about 17,000 local, state, and federal law enforcement agencies.

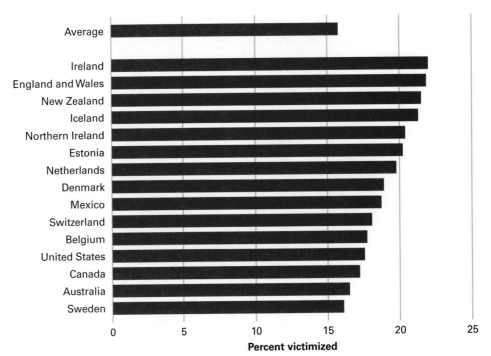

FIGURE **3.1**

**Comparative Crime
Rates in 17 Industrialized
Countries**

The overall victimization rate is the
percentage victimized once or more in
1999.

Source: Van Kesteren, J. N., Mayhew, P.,
& Nieuwbeerta, P. (2000). *Criminal
victimization in seventeen industrialized
countries: Key findings from the 2000
International Crime Victims Survey.* The
Hague: Ministry of Justice, WODC.

of the International Association of Chiefs of Police, in recognition of the need to collect reliable crime data.[4] The FBI annually publishes the UCR, which provides data on (1) crimes known to the police, (2) crimes cleared by arrest, (3) persons arrested, and (4) data on the number and employment of law enforcement personnel. While the UCR data are an important source of information about crime, it is also important to know how the data are collected and whether bias may be systematically built into the reporting.

Data Collection for the UCR

The "crimes known to the police" concentrate on what the FBI defines as **Part I offenses,** also referred to as *index crimes.* These are the crimes considered to be the most serious crimes by the FBI. Index crimes include homicide, forcible rape, robbery, aggravated assault, burglary, larceny, arson, hate crimes, and motor vehicle theft. Arrest data for crimes considered by the FBI to be less serious—such as public intoxication, drug offenses, simple assault, vagrancy, and gambling—are called **Part II offenses,** and these are also reported in the UCR. The compilation of **crimes known to the police** is based on (1) telephone calls to the police station and (2) crimes reported to or observed by police officers.

The UCR also reports the number of **crimes cleared by arrest.** A crime is considered *cleared* when police have made an arrest, or when the perpetrator is known but has not been arrested for some reason (for instance, he or she has fled the country or has died).

Problems with the UCR

The most glaring weakness of the UCR is its mobilization of bias toward certain types of crime while ignoring others. A few of the glaring omissions are corporate crime, corruption, political crimes, business violations of health and safety regulations, and terrorism (domestic and foreign). In recent years the UCR has begun reporting hate crimes, which is a slight improvement, but the omission of crimes most often committed by businesses, politicians, law enforcement agencies, and governments reinforces the public's belief that the "really serious crimes" are those most often committed by the lower classes, when it is arguably upper-class crimes that cause the most harm and are the most costly to the general public.

Part I offenses

Also called index crimes, these include homicide, forcible rape, robbery, aggravated assault, burglary, larceny, arson, hate crimes, and motor vehicle theft.

Part II offenses

Crimes considered by the FBI to be less serious—such as public intoxication, drug offenses, simple assault, vagrancy, and gambling.

crimes known to the police

A compilation of crime based on telephone calls to the police station and crimes reported to or observed by police officers.

crimes cleared by arrest

A crime is considered cleared when police have made an arrest or when the perpetrator is known but has not been arrested for some reason (for instance, the person has fled the country or has died).

Studies of how the FBI obtains crime statistics consistently show the process to be seriously biased, perhaps compromising its use for scientific purposes because the data-gathering process yields some misleading information. Little attention is given to ensuring accuracy, for example. Since the data used for determining the extent and trends of criminality are "crimes known to the police," they may reflect an unknown number of crank calls where no crime has actually been committed. There is no requirement that the call be investigated to determine whether a crime was committed, and no suspect need be arrested.

The categories used to classify acts as crime are arbitrary, inconsistent, and contradictory. "Homicide," which is usually interpreted by the media (and sometimes the FBI reports themselves) as "murder," includes "non-negligent manslaughter." Non-negligent manslaughter does not require that the perpetrator *intended* to kill someone, which is a legal requirement for murder. Non-negligent manslaughter includes "any death due to injuries received in a fight, argument, quarrel, assault, or commission of a crime."[5] The instructions also tell police departments to report a death as a homicide regardless of whether objective evidence indicates otherwise: "the findings of coroner, court, jury or prosecutor do not unfound offenses or attempts which your [police] investigations establish to be legitimate."[6]

Other categories of crime are equally confusing for scientific purposes. Burglary requires the use of force for breaking and entering in many states, but the FBI tells local police departments to report the crime of burglary if there is simply unlawful entry.[7] With the exception of homicide, attempted crimes are counted as crimes. If several people get into a fight, each person involved is counted as a separate crime of aggravated assault: The instructions from the FBI to local police departments are consciously designed to show the highest incidence of crime possible: "If a number of persons are involved in a dispute or disturbance and police investigation cannot establish the aggressors from the victims, count the number of persons assaulted as the number of offenses."[8] In general, the UCR data are highly unreliable because of inconsistent definitions of crime and the FBI's systematic effort to inflate the incidence and severity of the crimes it reports.

As early as 1931 the Wickersham Commission[9] warned that the publication of the Uniform Crime Reports was problematic:

> *Nothing can be more misleading than statistics not scientifically gathered and compiled. The uniform crime reports . . . make no suggestion as to any limitations or doubts with respect to the utility or authority of the figures presented. On the contrary they contain a graphic chart of "monthly crime trends," and along with them the bureau has released to the press statements quoting and interpreting them without qualification. It requires no great study of these reports to perceive a number of weaknesses.*[10]

Equally problematic for using the Uniform Crime Reports for scientific purposes is the degree to which crime rates are subject to political manipulation. William Selke and Harold Pepinsky report a longitudinal study of police reporting in Indianapolis demonstrating how crime rates fluctuate to suit those in political power.[11] Other researchers report a study of the crime rate in Washington, DC, when President Richard Nixon was using the city to demonstrate that his "war on crime" was effective.[12] Under pressure to reduce the crime rate, the police consistently reported the dollar amounts of larcenies as $49 (the limit at the time in that locale), which kept them from being reported as felonies and thus kept the crime rate down.

Evidence suggests the police and FBI often manipulate and poorly report crime rates, thereby limiting their utility.[13] Police departments have the discretion to define certain crimes and may record an assault on a female as an attempted rape, which the UCR then reports as a rape. This can lead to the false perception that crime rates are on the rise.[14]

Another reason reported crime is an inadequate reflection of the crime problem is underreporting by victims. Studies show that victims often fail to report their

CONSIDER THIS...   The Cost of Corporate Crime

The UCR does not include fraud as a crime, yet corporate and individual fraud are among the most costly and harmful crimes in the modern world. Fraudulent reporting by corporations costs taxpayers, employees, and individual retirees billions of dollars. The last 30 years have witnessed an almost continuous corporate crime wave.

In the 1970s and 1980s, Michael Milken was indicted for racketeering and securities fraud. Milken spent several years in prison for his crimes, which cost investors and taxpayers billions of dollars. Fraud and embezzlement in the savings and loan crisis of the 1980s cost investors over $500 million. Ten years later, fraudulent reporting of earnings by dozens of large corporations—including Enron, Rite Aid, Reliant Energy, Qwest Communications, and numerous other large corporations—cost billions of dollars and led to a wave of corporate bankruptcies. Fraudulent practices in the mortgage lending industry in 2007 and 2008 caused people to lose their jobs and their homes. Others were forced to declare bankruptcy. The U.S. government spent billions to bail out the banks and the mortgage lenders that had made loans through fraudulent practices, such as overstating the value of homes.

In the aftermath of Hurricane Katrina, which in August 2005 devastated the city of New Orleans and much of the Gulf Coast region, fraud contributed to the already widespread human misery.[18] In March 2006, Henry Edwards and Dwight Thomas pleaded guilty to stealing federal funds from the Federal Emergency Management Agency (FEMA) designed to help victims recover from the devastation of Katrina. It is estimated that fraudulent activities perpetrated by individuals against the federal government cost taxpayers billions of dollars each year. Despite the criminal nature of the FEMA fraud cases and countless other similar acts, they will go unrepresented in official crime statistics.

What do you think?

victimization to police due to fear of retaliation by the offender.[15] Mistrust of police, ignorance that a crime has been committed,[16] and apathy about the criminal event also come into play.[17] A further reporting problem with the UCR is the fact that only a small sample of criminal offenses is included—those most likely to be committed by the working class. Completely absent are data on white-collar crimes, consumer fraud, child molestation, spousal abuse, and other offenses. The Consider This feature illustrates the variability in criminal behavior we must take into account when considering descriptions and explanations of crime.

The UCR also presents the data in misleading ways. Gimmicks like a "crime clock" distort the reality of crime, while making good newspaper copy and lending law enforcement agencies considerable political clout. This influence translates into ever-increasing budgets, pay raises, and more technologically sophisticated crime-fighting equipment. It does not, however, provide policymakers or social scientists with reliable data about preventing crime or mitigating its effects. As Selke and Pepinsky conclude, "The police cannot and should not be expected to be objective about the compilation of reported crime statistics. The field is one of the few where those who are evaluated are responsible themselves for gathering their own evaluation data."[19]

UCR statistics, then, must be used with extreme caution. Organizational considerations dictate their content far more than does reality. For example, when police make an arrest, they typically charge the suspect with a number of different offenses to increase the bargaining power of the prosecutor who confronts the suspect with the charges. The charges that appear in the arrest statistics are a reflection of police activity, but a very poor reflection of the offenses actually committed. Moreover, the arrest statistics are recorded according to the **hierarchy rule,** which means that in a multiple-offense situation, when

hierarchy rule

In a multiple-offense situation, when more than one Part I offense is classified, the law enforcement agency must report the offense that is highest in the hierarchy and not the other offense(s).

TABLE **3.2**

Methodological Biases Built into the UCR Data Collection

- Corporate and white-collar crimes are not reported.

- Corruption is not reported.

- Political crimes are not reported.

- State crimes are not reported.

- Business crimes, such as fraud and the violation of health and safety regulations, are not reported.

- Reports are voluntary and vary in accuracy and completeness.

- Not all police departments submit reports.

- The FBI uses estimates in its total crime projections.

- Only one offense is counted per incident.

- Homicide includes intentional killing of another human being (murder) *and* the accidental killing of another human being through an assault, fight, argument, or quarrel.

- The decision of coroner, prosecutor, grand jury, or trial is not taken into account in counting homicides.

- Incomplete acts are lumped together with completed ones.

- Important differences exist between the FBI's definition of certain crimes and those used in different states.

- Victimless crimes are often undetected and unreported.

- Child abuse and family violence are often undetected and unreported.

more than one Part I offense is classified, the law enforcement agency must report the offense that is highest in the hierarchy and not the other offense(s).

This does not mean that UCR statistics are worthless. For example, the UCR reports the number of arrests made each year. These data will tell us with reasonable accuracy what charges the police use when they make arrests, though they cannot tell us how much crime there is or whether the rate of crime is increasing. Table 3.2 provides a summary of some of the built-in biases in the structure of the UCR.

National Incident-Based Reporting System (NIBRS)

In 1982, the Federal Bureau of Investigation and the Bureau of Justice Statistics sponsored a five-year project to revise the UCR to better suit the needs of law enforcement agencies. The goal was to provide a more comprehensive measure of crime statistics that was driven by a reporting mechanism focusing on each reported criminal event. This effort culminated in the creation of the **National Incident-Based Reporting System (NIBRS),** designed to collect data on each reported incident of crime. Under this new system, law enforcement agencies would provide the FBI an individual record for each reported crime in a single incident. The NIBRS records criminal incidents relating to 46 specific offenses, including the eight Part I crimes in the UCR. It also records arrest information about 11 lesser offenses (Table 3.3).

Besides expanding the crime categories, the NIBRS reporting system requires the collection of a much more detailed description of each criminal incident:[20]

- *Information about the offense:* Where it occurred, whether a weapon was involved, influence of drugs or alcohol on the perpetrator during the offense, and whether the offense had any gender, racial, or religious motivation behind it.

National Incident-Based Reporting System (NIBRS)

A revision of the UCR designed to provide a more comprehensive measure of crime statistics and to collect data on each reported incident of crime.

TABLE **3.3**

Offense Categories in the National Incident-Based Reporting System

GROUP A OFFENSES OFFENSES AND ARRESTS ARE REPORTED FOR THE FOLLOWING CRIMES, FOR WHICH A HIERARCHY DOES NOT APPLY:	GROUP B OFFENSES ARRESTS ARE REPORTED ONLY FOR THE FOLLOWING:
Arson	Bad checks
Assault offenses	Curfew/loitering/vagrancy
Bribery	Disorderly conduct
Burglary/breaking and entering	Driving under the influence
Counterfeiting/forgery	Drunkenness
Destruction/damage/vandalism of property	Nonviolent family offenses
Drug/narcotic offenses	Peeping Tom
Embezzlement	Runaways
Extortion/blackmail	Trespassing
Fraud offenses	All other offenses
Gambling offenses	
Homicide offenses	
Kidnapping/abduction	
Larceny/theft offenses	
Motor vehicle theft	
Pornography/obscene material	
Prostitution offenses	
Robbery	
Sex offenses, forcible	
Sex offenses, nonforcible	
Stolen property offenses	
Weapon law violations	

- *Information about the parties:* Sex, age, and race of victim and offender; any possible relationship between them; and circumstances that may have motivated the criminal incident (such as breaking a relationship).
- *Information about the property (if any):* The value of the property stolen or damaged as a result of the criminal incident.

Incident-based data provide a wide array of complex and detailed information that has a significant advantage over summary-based crime reporting systems.[21] The data collected by the NIBRS should therefore provide a more comprehensive understanding of criminal behavior patterns and more accurate crime data than the UCR.[22] Table 3.4 displays the differences between the UCR and the NIBRS.

The NIBRS provides law enforcement agencies with a valuable tool in their crime-fighting efforts by allowing for a more accurate description of when, where, and how crime takes place, as well as the characteristics of offenders and their victims. Moreover,

TABLE **3.4**

Differences Between Summary UCR Data and Incident-Based NIBRS Data

UCR	NIBRS
Aggregates monthly crime counts for 8 index crimes.	Reports each individual incident for 8 index crimes and 38 other crimes, including details on the offense, victim, offender, and property.
Counts one offense per incident according to the hierarchy rule.	Counts each offense that is committed within a single incident.
No distinction between attempted crimes and completed ones.	Distinguishes between attempted crimes and completed ones.
Defines rape as an offense against women only.	Modified definition of rape to include men as victims.
Records information about weapons use for murder, robbery, and aggravated assault only.	Records information about weapons use for all violent crimes.
Arrest counts for 8 index crimes and 21 other crimes.	Arrest details for 8 index crimes and 49 other crimes.

criminologists are provided with data on crime that is more accurate, detailed, and meaningful than that provided by the traditional UCR. The FBI plans for all state law enforcement agencies to eventually submit incident-based crime data. As of 2007, more than 6,440 law enforcement agencies from 31 states had contributed NIBRS data. The data

What information from this crime scene would be reported in the NIBRS?

from those agencies represent 25 percent of the U.S. population and 25 percent of the crime statistics collected by the UCR program.

National Crime Victimization Survey (NCVS)

National Crime Victimization Survey (NCVS)

A comprehensive survey of crime victimization within the United States.

One problem with the UCR is that many incidents of victimization go unreported to or unobserved by the police.[23] Because of this problem, the U.S. Department of Justice has sponsored the **National Crime Victimization Survey (NCVS),** a comprehensive survey of crime victimization within the United States, in order to uncover the "dark figure" of crime.[24] The first national victim survey was a pilot study conducted in 1967. The survey asked people whether they or any member of their household had been the victim of a crime. The questionnaires and sampling procedures were designed by sociologists, and the interviews were conducted by the Census Bureau. The NCVS, in the words of a leading methodologist, is "the most important innovation in criminological research in several decades."[25] The pilot study was completed in 1971, and in 1972 the NCVS began collecting and publishing its findings.

The NCVS surveys a nationally representative sample of more than 77,000 households or approximately 134,000 people. Individuals interviewed must be over the age of 12 and are asked to report their victimization experiences with certain targeted crimes, including rape, sexual assault, robbery, assault, theft, household burglary, and motor vehicle theft, during the past six months. Interview questions are designed to elicit information about

- *The victim:* Sex, age, race, ethnicity, marital status, income, and educational level; prior experience with the criminal justice system.
- *The offender:* Sex, age, race, and relationship to the victim; possibility of substance abuse.
- *The offense:* Time and place of incident, weapons involved, consequences of the crime including injury and/or economic loss.

Respondents who are victims also answer questions about their perception of the handling of their case by law enforcement officials, if the criminal incident was reported to the police. The NCVS is designed to draw adequate samples and to gather detailed data as objectively as possible. Interviewers are trained to ask questions so as to avoid leading the respondent in a certain direction. Thus, the NCVS provides a much better description of selected characteristics of criminality than do official statistics. While these surveys have their own shortcomings (which we discuss below), they are, nonetheless, quite useful for scientific purposes.

Victim survey data suggest that criminologists who questioned the reliability of official statistics generated by police departments were right to be skeptical. For decades, official crime data sources have reported a steady increase in the amount of crime. Likewise, criminologists have questioned the official data and claims of ever-increasing crime rates, which periodically spark a public and media outcry over the crime problem, which in turn has an impact on the policy and legislation developed to address criminal justice issues.[26]

Victimization surveys provide a clearer understanding of the characteristics of crime and crime victimization by (1) putting into proper perspective the actual level of crime and (2) directing attention toward the crime categories that actually lead to the most victimization, rather than focusing on popular images of stranger-precipitated and random acts of violence.[27] One of the most significant findings of the NCVS is that the rate of violent crime was steady for decades, between 1973 and 1993, and actually declined from 1993 to 2003, reaching the lowest level ever in 2005 (Figure 3.2). Moreover, property crime rates have also been declining significantly for the past three decades (Figure 3.3).

Another important finding of the NCVS is that the vast majority of crimes committed are not very serious in terms of either personal or property damage. Of the 13 million completed thefts of property in 2005, nearly 70 percent were property thefts of less than

$250.[28] Moreover, NCVS data indicate that 67.4 percent of crimes committed against individuals do not involve the use of any weapon, and that rape and sexual assault are twice as likely to be committed by a non-stranger (family, friend, relative, acquaintance) as by a stranger.[29]

The overwhelming findings of victimization surveys reveal that it is very unlikely anyone will be the victim of a crime in any given year. Over 85 percent of the respondents in the NCVS say neither they nor any member of their household was the victim of a criminal offense. Indeed, most people are unlikely to be the victim of a serious offense in their entire lifetime. The NCVS estimates the chance of an individual's becoming the victim of a violent crime is about 2.3 (about 23 crime victimizations per 1,000 persons age 12 and older).[30]

FIGURE **3.2**

Violent Crime Victimization Rates per 1,000 U.S. Population Age 12 and Over, 1973–2009

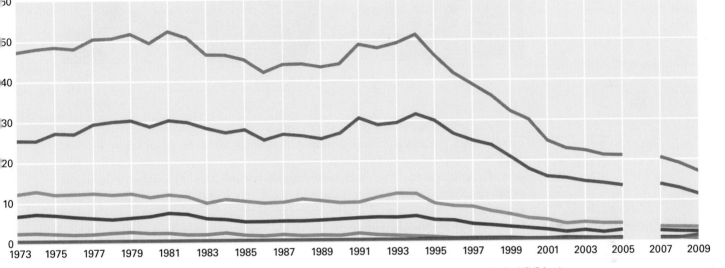

Note: There is a gap in the graph lines for 2006 because of differences in methodologies for data gathering in the NCVS for that year.

Source: Bureau of Journal Statistics, U.S. Department of Justice. *National Crime Victimization Survey, Violent Crime Trends, 1973–2009.* Retrieved from http://bjs.ojp.usdoj.gov/content/glance/tables/viortrdtab.cfm (accessed May 6, 2011)

Rates per 1,000 U.S. households

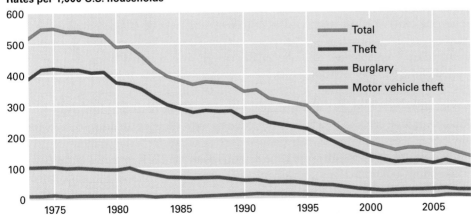

FIGURE **3.3**

Property Crime Victimization Rates per 1,000 U.S. Households, 1973–2008

Source: U.S. Department of Justice, Bureau of Justice Statistics, *National Crime Victimization Survey,* Key Facts at a Glance, 2008.

Victimization surveys help us better understand the prevalence of crimes such as domestic abuse, as opposed to the more sensationalized random acts of violence perpetrated by strangers.

Judging from the results of the victim surveys, the most likely crime of violence is a *simple assault,* an "attack without a weapon that results either in minor injury (bruises, black eye, cuts, scratches, or swelling) or an undetermined injury requiring less than two days of hospitalization."[31] While these findings do not indicate the likelihood of being the victim of a crime in one's lifetime, the evidence is very persuasive that the risk of being victimized by crime in general, and by violent crime in particular, has been exaggerated by law enforcement officials, politicians, media, and the general public.

The NCVS clearly provides us with a more accurate depiction of crime in U.S. society.[32] The random sampling of households allows for a more reliable estimate of the number of crimes actually being committed and captures detailed data about the context of the victimization and characteristics of the victim and the offender. Criminological research can better analyze criminal behavior with this clearer understanding of issues surrounding race, gender, and victimization.

Despite the reporting advantages of victimization surveys, we must nevertheless approach their findings with caution. Inaccuracy is a major drawback of self-reporting that becomes more problematic when respondents are recalling a traumatic event. Over-reporting can also occur when victims mistakenly interpret certain acts as crime, such as labeling "sexual harassment" as "sexual assault" or viewing losing an item as having that item stolen. Some victims may also report crimes that occurred before the six-month period of the NCVS.

On the other hand, the NCVS can also underestimate the amount of crime. Some victims may have forgotten about an incident or may not be aware that it was a crime. Underreporting can also be a result of the victims' unwillingness to disclose any information about their victimization, especially in the case of rape or sexual assault.[33]

Finally, the NCVS suffers the same design flaw as the UCR in that it excludes white-collar crime, political crime, corruption, and state crime. By focusing on the categories more commonly associated with "street" criminals, "the NCVS perpetuates the myth that these are the 'most important' crimes committed, a point of view that is arguable at the very least."[34]

Self-Report Surveys

One research technique developed by sociologists to reveal types of criminality ordinarily hidden from victim surveys or official statistics is the **self-report survey.** This technique asks a sample of people to indicate whether they have committed certain criminal acts in a given time period. We use the results to measure the prevalence of both recent and lifetime criminal offending among respondents.[35] Respondents are assured anonymity and are informed of the usefulness of the survey's results in social science research. These techniques are used to increase the validity of self-report surveys by encouraging participation and increasing the likelihood of respondents answering questions truthfully.

In 1946, Austin Porterfield administered a questionnaire to Texas college students and discovered that over 90 percent of the respondents admitted to committing at least one felony.[36] Another study at about the same time found similar results among 700 adults: 90 percent reported committing at least one of 49 criminal acts punishable by at least one year in prison.[37] The men in the sample admitted committing an average of 18 offenses, the women an average of 11.

Since these pioneering studies, dozens of others have confirmed their findings. High school and college youth admit to frequent occurrences of truancy, fighting, stealing, running away from home, and drinking while underage.[38] The University of Colorado, under the auspices of Delbert Elliot and his colleagues, conducts the National Youth Survey (NYS). The NYS began in 1976 and spanned 28 years; this long study has been monitoring respondents' changing attitudes, beliefs, and behaviors in delinquency, violence, drugs, and crime, among other subjects. The NYS findings also confirm earlier studies: Over 90 percent of the respondents in the survey admit to having committed some type of serious criminal offenses over the course of their lives.[39] Figure 3.4 provides a summary of data compiled by the Monitoring the Future survey, administered to high school seniors across the nation. Results once again indicate that many high school seniors have committed criminal acts.

The data consistently confirm that virtually everyone sampled in self-report surveys admits to having committed criminal acts. What has proven controversial among criminologists is how to interpret the data. On first brush there appears to be little difference by social class in the propensity to violate the law. Since the vast majority of people sentenced to prison or to juvenile institutions are from the lower classes, some interpreted the survey results to mean that the difference between lower-class and other youth was

self-report survey

A research technique developed by sociologists to reveal types of criminality ordinarily hidden from victim surveys or official statistics.

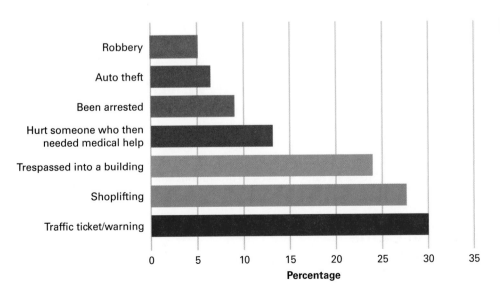

FIGURE **3.4**

Percentage of High School Seniors Reporting Criminal Involvement in Selected Activities

Source: Johnston, L. D., Bachman, J. G., & O'Malley, P. M. (2010). *Monitoring the Future: Questionnaire responses from the nation's high school seniors, 2009.* Ann Arbor, MI: Institute for Social Research.

not in the frequency or severity of their criminality, but in the biased law enforcement practices of the police.[40] Others pointed out, however, that lower-class youth committed more, and more serious, offenses than middle- or upper-class youth.[41] Raymond Michalowski comments:

> *Recent studies using national youth samples and more sophisticated questionnaires have tended to confirm both interpretations. That is, there appears to be no significant difference between lower class, working class, and middle class youth when it comes to self-reported involvement in property crimes (excluding robbery); drug offenses (either selling or using); status crimes such as truancy, runaway and underage drinking; or public disorder crimes such as carrying a concealed weapon, drunkenness, hitchhiking, and so forth. However, lower class youth appear disproportionately among those reporting a high frequency of offenses. It should be noted, however, that high frequency offenders accounted for less than 5 percent of the juveniles surveyed in each of the three social classes.*[42]

A common criticism of self-report studies is their failure to ask questions about the more serious forms of personal violence such as murder, rape, and aggravated assault.[43] Studies of college students reveal a high incidence of date rape.[44] Thomas Meyer reports that over 20 percent of college women are the victims of rape or attempted rape.[45]

Self-report studies also suffer some of the same shortcomings as victim surveys. Gauging the criminality of inner-city youth through self-reports is difficult. Most surveys are of local high schools, although recent data from national surveys reduce the shortcomings of earlier studies. In the end, of course, one of the most serious limitations is the perception of the respondent.[46] Respondents may not think their act was criminal and therefore may not report it.[47] Child abuse, sexual assault of a girlfriend or wife, rape on a date or at a party where both people were drinking—all these incidents may go unreported because the respondent does not perceive them as criminal or does not want to admit to committing a crime.

If the questionnaire does not ask about certain offenses, they will not be recorded; for example, none of the questionnaires asks about driving under the influence of alcohol. Evidence from participant observation studies indicates, however, that this may be one of the most common and most serious criminal acts committed by middle- and upper-class youth.[48] Even with the promise of anonymity, respondents may be reluctant to admit they have committed very serious offenses.[49] It seems unlikely that many would risk the possibility of being prosecuted in order to provide accurate questionnaire results. Finally, the questionnaires do not tap white-collar, corporate, and governmental crimes.

In short, although self-report studies provide yet another piece of valuable information about crime and delinquency, it is only a piece, which we must study in conjunction with many others before the picture is complete.

SOCIAL CORRELATES OF OFFENDING

Two of the most consistent findings of criminological research are that (1) the frequency of committing crime is correlated very strongly with age, and (2) women commit far fewer crimes than men. Another fairly consistent finding is that race is a correlate of crime frequency. However, just because the data indicate that these factors (age, gender, and race) are related to crime rates, we need to be cautious when considering them, as the discussion below describes.

Age and Crime

The first thing to realize about the relationship between age and crime is that criminal behavior decreases with age.[50] Criminal activities tend to peak around the age of 17 or 18 and then decline through early adulthood and aging, regardless of differences in

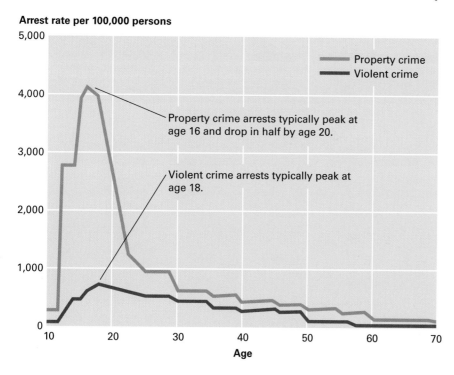

Arrest rate per 100,000 persons

Property crime arrests typically peak at age 16 and drop in half by age 20.

Violent crime arrests typically peak at age 18.

- Property crime
- Violent crime

Age

FIGURE **3.5**

Relationship Between Age and Arrest for Serious Crimes

Source: Federal Bureau of Investigation. (2005). *Uniform crime reports.* Washington, DC: U.S. Department of Justice.

race, gender, economic status, and other social variables (Figure 3.5).[51] While 13- to 17-year-olds make up about 10 percent of the population of U.S. youth, they commit about 27 percent of the UCR index crimes and account for 17 percent of arrests for all crimes.

Several explanations help account for the relationship between age and crime.[52] A study conducted by criminologist Robert Agnew accounts for the peak of criminal activity during adolescence by linking criminality to features of adolescent life in U.S. society.[53] Agnew points to several factors that seem to be in play during adolescence:

- The desire of youth to be more accountable to peers and seek their approval
- An increase in economic demands on youth
- A decrease in adult supervision
- A desire for independence and adult privileges
- The propensity to resolve problems in a criminal manner

Other studies account for the decline in criminality with age by citing the natural human life cycle, whereby individuals begin to mature and become better integrated into society as they take on conventional roles.[54] The strengthened bond to society gives individuals an increased sense of responsibility to social values and norms, making it more difficult for them to risk getting involved with crime. This pull is especially strong when individuals begin to take on the tasks of acquiring a full-time job, getting married, and having children.[55]

Race and Crime

A common and persistent trend is the disproportionate arrest rate of young black males compared to young white males.[56] While African Americans make up about 13 percent of the U.S. population, they account for over 30 percent of the arrests for UCR index crimes (Table 3.5).

In the 2008 FBI publication *Crime in the United States,* blacks constituted 39.4 percent of arrests for violent crimes and 30.1 percent of arrests for property crimes. Roland Chilton, a leading authority on the social correlates of criminal behavior, found that

What social pressures of the teenage years make youth more susceptible to becoming involved in criminal activity?

TABLE **3.5**

Comparison of Arrest Rates for Whites and Blacks, 2008

OFFENSE CHARGED	TOTAL	NUMBER OF ARRESTS		PERCENT DISTRIBUTION	
		WHITE	BLACK	WHITE	BLACK
Murder and non-negligent manslaughter	9,859	4,721	4,935	47.9	50.1
Forcible rape	16,847	10,990	5,428	65.2	32.2
Robbery	100,525	41,962	56,948	41.7	56.7
Aggravated assault	328,736	208,081	112,325	63.3	34.2
Burglary	235,407	157,252	73,960	66.8	31.4
Larceny-theft	979,145	666,360	286,844	68.1	29.3
Motor vehicle theft	74,881	44,674	28,510	59.7	38.1
Arson	10,734	8,139	2,331	75.8	21.7
Aggregate Violent Crime Data	455,967	265,754	179,636	58.3	39.4
Aggregate Property Crime Data	1,300,167	876,425	391,645	67.4	30.1

Source: Federal Bureau of Investigation. (2008). *Crime in the United States.* Washington, DC: U.S. Department of Justice.

in Boston, although the 15–19 age group constituted 7.4 percent of the population, it accounted for 32 percent of the arrests for robbery, assault, burglary, theft, and rape (Part I offenses).[57] The age group of 15–29 accounted for 59 percent of all Part I arrests in 1960 and 76 percent in 1980. Non-white males in Boston constituted less than 1 percent of the Boston population in 1960, but made up approximately 15 percent of those arrested for Part I offenses. In 1980 non-white males were 4.5 percent of the population and accounted for 33.6 percent of the arrests.

The finding that young minority males are most often arrested for crimes such as theft, burglary, assault, and robbery is consistently reported by studies relying on arrest data supplied by police and other law enforcement agencies. Moreover, data obtained by the NCVS seem to support the findings of the UCR: The proportion of offenders identified by NCVS respondents as African American is similar to the proportion of black offenders identified in UCR statistics.[58] These findings lead many to conclude that African Americans are responsible for the majority of violent criminal offenses.[59]

Again, however, we must approach these conclusions with caution. The most obvious flaw in these researches is that the underlying statistics reflect only a tiny fraction of the criminality at any point in time.[60] Completely absent from the data are white-collar and corporate crimes, police corruption, organized crime, crimes of the state, prostitution, child pornography, and assault, rape, and battery by family members against one another. Moreover, studies suggest that differences in rates of arrest between African Americans and whites can be a byproduct of police bias within the criminal justice system.[61] Police departments make decisions about where to look for crime and whether to make an arrest and generally devote a disproportionate amount of their surveillance energies to areas where non-whites live. The finding that blacks are more likely to be arrested than whites thus becomes a self-fulfilling prophecy.

Recent studies examining self-report data from the National Youth Survey suggest that racial disparities between black and white youth are smaller than actually reported in the UCR.[62] Thus, we must analyze arrest data in the context of police practices that routinely profile African Americans as suspects in certain crimes and stop them disproportionately often for routine searches, citations, and arrests without probable

The Fourth Amendment of the U.S. Constitution protects the right of individuals against unreasonable searches and seizures by police officers. The practices of law enforcement officers must strike a careful balance between that right and their duty to control crime and apprehend criminals. Achieving this balance can be a challenging task for any metropolitan police department.

In recent years, the New York City Police Department (NYPD) has come under scrutiny for engaging in practices that border on violating civil liberties. These practices are often the result of the discretion granted to police officers to stop and question individuals whom they suspect of being involved in criminal activity. According to the New York City Civil Liberties Union (NYCLU), the NYPD arrested nearly 400,000 individuals for marijuana possession between 1997 and 2007.[63] These arrests were marked by significant racial disparities between blacks and whites, with blacks accounting for over 50 percent of the arrests, while only comprising 26 percent of New York City residents during that period.

In 2006, the NYPD stopped and frisked nearly half a million individuals suspected of being involved in criminal activity. Data on these encounters indicate that almost 90 percent of the stops were of minority individuals, with blacks comprising over 50 percent. Researchers at RAND Corporation analyzed data on more than 500,000 street encounters between law enforcement officers and pedestrians to assess the degree to which the overrepresentation of minorities was due to racial bias in police practices.[64] The research produced illuminating findings, with significant implications for policy changes in police practices and procedures. RAND's report suggests that statistics on the racial disparity of police stops could be attributed to factors other than racial bias, such as the overrepresentation of blacks in high-crime areas and the higher proportion of policing in those areas.

These findings suggest the importance of research-guided policies and practices that adequately address the potential for racial bias in police procedures. An accurate measure of the scale of the problem can effectively direct law enforcement agencies, public officials, and policymakers to make small-scale changes to improve reporting and administration, as opposed to a large-scale organizational restructuring. As a result of their findings, RAND researchers made several recommendations: improve communication between police officers and potential suspects during a stop; revise police reports to capture data on the use of force; internally review areas with the largest racial disparity in stop outcomes; familiarize all officers with training pertinent to stop and frisk documentation policy; and monitor the behavior of police officers with recurrent patterns of racial disparity in their policing practices.

cause.[65] The Connecting Research to Practice feature discusses racial profiling with the New York City Police Department.

Gender and Crime

The UCR reports that men are five times as likely to be arrested for a violent crime as women, with the ratio of male to female arrests for homicide being 8 to 1. Figure 3.6 indicates that, according to UCR arrest data, men are responsible for about 81 percent of arrests for violent crimes and 63 percent of arrests for property offenses.

Moreover, victimization surveys and self-report studies also support the finding that men are disproportionately responsible for the majority of serious violent crimes. In the NCVS, respondents identify the perpetrator as a male in 86 percent of violent offenses,[66] and in a study of self-reported involvement in various criminal activities, male high school seniors report more criminality than their female counterparts (Table 3.6).

How has the changing role of women contributed to an increase in their criminal activity?

While most criminologists agree with the obvious conclusion that females are less criminal than males, there is less agreement on the reasons.[67] Early theories focused on trait differences. That is, they regarded women as weaker, more emotional and less aggressive than men, and therefore less likely to engage in criminal activities.[68] Criminologist Cesare Lombroso argued that women who did occasionally commit acts of crime were essentially exhibiting masculine characteristics not typical of most females.[69] Later studies saw hormonal differences between the two genders, linking aggressive and antisocial behavior to male sex hormones.[70]

Other studies of gender differences in crime rates look at the way socialization affects the behavior of women. A study conducted by Jean Bottcher examines gender socialization and delinquency.[71] Male behavior is a product of their socialization into an assertive, aggressive, and powerful gender role, accounting for their higher rate of involvement in delinquency and crime. In contrast, females are socialized into passive and submissive gender roles and are more likely to consider their attachment to peers and seek social approval, thereby reducing their risk of becoming involved in criminal behavior.

With the emergence of feminist criminology in the early 1970s (see Chapter 10), researchers began to explore the connection between lower rates of criminality among females and their relatively lower economic and social position. As the lifestyles and roles of women have changed, factors contributing to criminality seem to be affecting them in the same ways that they affect men.[72] Trends in crime statistics seem to support the feminist view of crime-rate differences between men and women. Data show that female criminality is increasing considerably, while male rates tend to be steady and in some instances are actually declining.[73]

FIGURE **3.6**

Gender and Arrest Rates for Violent and Property Crimes

Source: U.S. Department of Justice Federal Bureau of Investigation. (2009). *Crime in the United States:* Table 42. Retrieved from http://www2.fbi.gov/ucr/cius2009/data/table_42.html (accessed April 27, 2011). Table adapted by SOURCEBOOK staff.

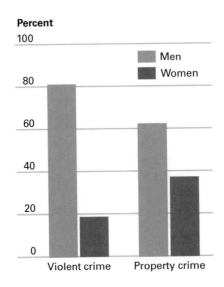

TABLE **3.6**

Percentage of Male and Female High School Seniors Admitting to at Least One Offense

DELINQUENT BEHAVIOR	MALE STUDENTS	FEMALE STUDENTS
Serious fight	15	9
Gang fight	19	13
Hurt someone badly	17	6
Used a weapon to steal	5	2
Stole less than $50	29	20
Stole more than $50	12	6
Shoplifting	28	23
Breaking and entering	28	17
Arson	4	1
Damaged school property	15	6
Approximate Weighted Number of Cases	**1110**	**1090**

Source: Johnston, L. D., Bachman, J. G., & O'Malley, P. M. (2010). *Monitoring the Future: Questionnaire responses from the nation's high school seniors, 2009.* Ann Arbor, MI: Institute for Social Research.

CRIMINAL CAREERS

The study of crime and criminal behavior reveals that the majority of offenders engage in a single act of criminality and then stop. Most criminal behavior is thus accounted for by a small group of persistent offenders who are chronic or **career criminals.** This concept was first studied in 1972 by researchers who followed a **cohort** or group of individuals with similar characteristics, of 9,945 boys from birth to age 18.[74] The study, which used police records to identify delinquents and track their criminal careers, found that about 54 percent of those identified as delinquent were repeat offenders, while 46 percent committed a single offense. Among repeat offenders, a small percentage (about 6 percent of the total cohort) were chronic offenders who were arrested more than five times and were responsible for about 52 percent of all acts of delinquency committed by the group.

The discovery that there are persistent patterns of criminal behavior has had a significant impact on criminological theory and practice. Longitudinal studies that track the behavior patterns of chronic offenders over a period of time have sparked debates about why people stop offending. A 1986 National Academy of Sciences (NAS) panel report emphasized the need to study criminal behavior over the life course of the offender.[75] **Life course criminology** emerged, drawing upon the concept of "life course": "pathways through the life span involving a sequence of culturally defined, age-graded roles and social transitions enacted over time."[76] Life course theorists examine patterns of continuity, frequency in life events, and sequences of behavior to establish a causal link between the early development of delinquency and later adult deviant behavior. The sequential continuity of antisocial behavior in different life domains throughout various stages of life, from childhood to adulthood, is regarded as a variable in the persistence of adult criminality. On the other hand, informal social bonds and attachment to primary group members—such as to family and peers—and attachments during adulthood—such as to family and co-workers—can explain the lack of adult criminality over the life span, despite early childhood tendencies to delinquent behavior.

career criminals

Persistent offenders; those who account for most criminal behavior.

cohort

A group of individuals with similar characteristics.

life course criminology

The study of criminal behavior over the life course of the offender.

CONNECTING
THEORY
TO PRACTICE

Three Strikes and You're Out:
Life Course Theories in Action

In October 1993, 12-year-old Polly Klaas was abducted at knifepoint during a slumber party at her home in Petaluma, California, and later found raped and strangled. Her assailant, Richard Allen Davis, was convicted of her murder in 1996 and received the death penalty for his crime. The case drew nationwide attention due to the fact that Davis was a paroled felon with an extensive history of violence and brutality, including arrests, charges, and convictions for crimes such as burglary, robbery, kidnapping, extortion, and sexual assault.

Public opinion shifted to a get-tough political ideology, which called for the incapacitation of repeat, chronic offenders. The outcome of these debates culminated into the passage of California's "three strikes" laws in 1994, which mandated prison terms of 25 years to life without the possibility of parole for defendants convicted of a third felony. Several states followed with similar laws, and in 1994, Congress passed federal laws enacting the same type of policy. The stated rationale behind these laws was to ensure the public's safety by automatically imposing life sentences for chronically incorrigible criminal offenders. However, the practical outcome of such policy initiatives does not take into consideration the variable effects they may have on criminal justice dynamics.

An offender convicted under this type of legislation can, in theory and in reality, be sentenced to life in prison for committing a relatively minor offense such as shoplifting, which can, in some states, be the theft of property valued at under $200. Studies have also shown that three strikes legislation disproportionately affects minority offenders, especially African Americans. The original goal of three strikes laws was to protect the public from repeat violent criminals. The reality, though, is that these policy initiatives have resulted in the long-term imprisonment of criminals with a history of petty infractions, involving theft or drugs, and an explosion in prison populations across the nation, placing an even heavier toll on correctional management and staff.[77]

Nor does a lengthy prison sentence for this category of chronic offenders decrease crime or reduce violence. Research on the impact of three strikes laws on crime found that the incapacitation of offenders at the end of their careers is not likely to have an impact on the overall crime rate.[78] Moreover, the crime rate is more likely to be a reflection of national trends in crime rather than specifically related to the application of three strikes laws.

The practical application of theory to crime-control policy and practice must be balanced against research evidence indicating the success or failure of such theoretical application. A careful assessment of three strikes laws seems to suggest that they may not be an effective crime-control strategy.

Three strikes laws are designed to incapacitate repeat violent offenders such as Richard Allen Davis (*left*), who kidnapped, assaulted, and killed 12-year-old Polly Klaas (*right*).

incapacitation

The removal of offenders from society so that they are no longer a threat to public safety.

three strikes

A policy advocating mandatory life imprisonment for offenders convicted of a third felony offense.

The study of chronic offending has also affected criminal justice policy. The goal of rehabilitating offenders has become secondary to **incapacitation,** or the removal of offenders from society so that they are no longer a threat to public safety. The logic behind these policies is that chronic life course offenders are not likely to be deterred by apprehension, punishment, and treatment. Thus, laws targeting these habitual offenders have become more focused on longer prison sentences, mandatory minimum sentences, and **three strikes** policies advocating mandatory life imprisonment for offenders convicted of a third felony offense. See the Connecting Theory to Practice Feature for more on three strikes policy implementation.

CRIME TRENDS IN THE UNITED STATES

Crime rates that are officially reported tend to focus on street crimes—what the UCR classifies as Part I or index crimes, as we discussed at the beginning of the chapter. But, as we have pointed out consistently in this chapter, such depictions of crime are misleading. Corporate crimes, white-collar crimes, corruption, and political crimes are rarely reported unless there is a major scandal. Recent years bear witness to a host of enormous losses to taxpayers and employees resulting from fraud, corruption, embezzlement, and other offenses engaged in by corporate executives and government officials. For instance, in the 1980s, the savings and loan crisis

> *was one of the worst financial disasters of the twentieth century. The estimated cost to taxpayers, not counting the interest payments on government bonds sold to finance the industry's bailout, is $150 to $175 billion. If interest over the next thirty years is added to this tab, the cost approaches $500 billion.*[79]

Between 1988 and 1992 over 646 criminal cases involving more than a thousand defendants were brought against former savings and loan officers and employees (Table 3.7). As researchers point out, these defendants had engaged in the systematic plundering of the companies they worked for at the expense of the stockholders and ultimately the taxpayers. These crimes were made possible by collusion between company officers from different institutions and government regulators who failed to oversee the business operations.[80]

The savings and loan criminality was followed in the 1990ss by massive fraud in other industries—from drug stores to telephone companies to energy providers. The most thoroughly researched corporate criminal enterprise in this period took place at Enron Corporation, which at the time of its collapse was the largest bankruptcy in U.S. history.[81]

The Enron executives committed a multitude of crimes during its brief history as one of the most profitable and successful energy companies in the world. The crime that ultimately brought the company down was *fraud,* intentionally lying for economic gain. For years Enron executives had lied to stockholders, accountants, the government, and the general public in order to increase the firm's stock value. Even when they knew that Enron had lost billions of dollars and that there was no possible way to avoid bankruptcy, the officers lied about the income of the company and its future profits, all the while taking millions of dollars in salary and bonuses for themselves. Thousands of people working for Enron who had purchased the company stock in good faith were encouraged to continue

TABLE **3.7**

Major Savings and Loans Criminal Cases, 1988–1992	
Number of cases	646
Defendants charged	1,098
Defendants convicted and sentenced	580
Defendants sentenced to prison	451
Median prison term (months)	22
Median loss per case	$ 500,000
Total losses	$8,222,398,550
Total restitution paid	$ 335,620,349
Total fines	$ 11,917,061

Source: Calavita, K., Pontell, H. N., & Tillman, R. H. (1997). *Big money crime: Fraud and politics in the savings and loan crisis.* Berkeley: University of California Press.

buying it, although ultimately it was practically worthless, and its drop in value wiped out the employees' retirement savings.

Enron was not alone in fraudulently reporting profits and earnings during the 1990s and early 2000s:

■ *Worldcom:* The giant telecommunications firm was found guilty of committing the largest accounting fraud in U.S. history. In 2000–2001, the company was telling stockholders it was profitable when its officers knew that in fact it had lost $64.5 billion. In all the company made over $74.5 billion in accounting errors.

■ *Reliant Energy:* Four current or former employees are accused by the state of California of conspiracy, fraud, and manipulating the price of electricity in California that led to a severe energy crisis in 2000 and 2001.

■ *Rite Aid:* CEO Martin Grass pleaded guilty to conspiracy to inflate company earnings in a plea bargain that included a five-year prison sentence, forfeiture of $3 million, and a $500,000 fine.

■ *Duke Energy:* Two former executives and a state utilities regulator were accused of fraudulently using bogus trades to make the company appear more profitable and raise its stock prices. The phony trades resulted in more than $50 million in fraudulent profits.

■ *Northrop Grumman:* The manufacturer is accused by the U.S. government of lying about the readiness of the B-2 Spirit or Stealth Bomber. The government is seeking $1.2 billion in damages.

■ *Microsoft:* The company was found guilty of systematically violating antitrust regulations. The firm settled by paying billions of dollars in fines and settling suits with companies ($1.3 billion with PeopleSoft) and with the European Union.

These are only a few examples of the corporate crime that has been rampant for at least the past 30 years.

The exposure of corrupt government officials also has been on the rise. Because of the paucity of data, we do not know whether the recent revelations of corruption represent an increase in these crimes or merely an increase in public awareness. The U.S. Attorney General's office reports that in a 10-year period between 1994 and 2003, it successfully prosecuted over 5,000 cases of corruption brought against public officials.[82] One of the most infamous cases of public corruption in recent years involved Representative Randy "Duke" Cunningham, congressman from California. In November 2005, Cunningham pleaded guilty to taking more than $2 million in bribes. Cunningham's crimes consisted of selling his influence as a member of Congress to obtain Defense Department contracts for companies who paid him in cash, houses, luxury yachts, and expensive vacations. Cunningham was sentenced to 10 years in prison and forced to pay $350,000 in fines.[83]

Despite their seriousness, the criminal activities of corporate executives and political officials remain relatively unnoticed by the public and are generally absent from official crime data gathered by police departments. We turn now to an examination of those types of crimes that are more visible to the public, beginning first with the category generating the most amount of attention: violent crime.

Trends in Violent Crime

As we noted earlier, the violent crime rate has been steadily decreasing since 1994, reaching the lowest level ever recorded in 2005.[84] Moreover, preliminary figures indicate that, as a whole, U.S. law enforcement agencies reported a decrease of 1.8 percent in the number of violent crimes brought to their attention in the first half of 2007 when compared with figures reported for the first six months of 2006.[85]

Some criminologists believe statistics for homicide are among the more accurate data provided by law enforcement agencies; since their consequences are difficult to hide, homicides are more likely to be reported. While this may be true, there is still ambiguity involved, since the way the UCR instructs police to report a death as a homicide—even if the coroner, the prosecutor, the jury, and the judge do not confirm that a murder took place—makes the data suspect.

Victim surveys offer another indication that police may overestimate the number of homicides. From 1967–1973 the victim surveys asked respondents whether any member of their household had been the victim of a homicide. The answer was 3.1 people per 100,000 in the population. The UCR for that year reported a homicide rate of 5.1, almost twice the rate indicated by the victim survey. It is quite possible the discrepancy is the result of consistent overreporting by the police, which could be accounted for by the reporting methods we pointed out earlier.

Despite flaws in the data-collection methods of the UCR, criminologists rely on official crime reports to examine trends in rates of criminality over the years. Crime data provided by the UCR indicate that between the mid-1960s and the late 1970s, the homicide rate in the United States nearly doubled, peaking in 1980 at 10.2 per 100,000 people and falling to 7.9 per 100,000 in 1984. It rose again in the early 1990s, reaching 9.8 per 100,000 in 1991. Between 1991 and 2010, the rate declined significantly from 9.8 to 4.9 per 100,000. Figure 3.7 provides a summary of trends in the homicide rate.

The highest percentage of homicides, 48 percent, occurs between relatives and close acquaintances. About 18 percent of the homicide victims in 2010 were strangers to the perpetrator. The relationship between victim and offender could not be determined in over one-third of the homicides. Individuals between the ages of 18 and 24 have historically had the highest rate of offending across all race and gender categories. While males commit about 90 percent of all homicides, black males between the ages of 18 and 24 have the highest rate of homicide offending. White females in all age groups have the lowest rate.

In one study, researchers combined data from police department reports, interviews with police officials filing the reports, and information from other sources.[86] They analyzed data for the period 1968–1978 and compared homicides by sex, age, race, city, region, and a host of other variables. Some of the most important findings are that (l) homicide rates show minor fluctuations from year to year and (2) between 1968 and 1978 the homicide rate rose slightly. Other data of interest from this report show that[87]

- Males are almost three times as likely to be victims of homicide as females.
- Blacks are twice as likely to be victims as whites.
- The age group 20–49 has the highest homicide victimization rate, while the elderly and the very young have the lowest. The greatest proportion of all homicides takes place between acquaintances; the lowest proportion between strangers. Surprisingly,

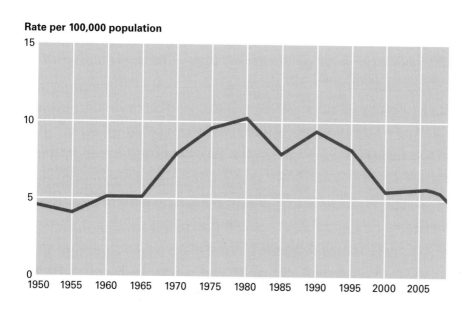

Rate per 100,000 population

FIGURE **3.7**

U.S. Homicide Rate Trends, 1950–2009

Source: Federal Bureau of Investigation. (2010). *Uniform crime reports, 2006–2009.* Retrieved from http://www.fbi.gov/about-us/cjis/ucr/ucr (accessed April 27, 2011)

56 percent of homicide victims within the family are men and 43 percent are women. In cities this ratio increases to 70 percent for male victims and 30 percent for female.

- Among victims of acquaintance homicide, 84 percent are men and 16 percent women. This pattern is the same for stranger homicides: 88 percent of victims are men, 12 percent are women.
- Over 80 percent of offenders are male.
- The age of the majority of offenders is 15–29.
- Blacks and whites commit about an equal number of homicides, but, since blacks constitute only 15 percent of the population, they are overrepresented in the category of offenders.

This research paved the way for the study of homicide as patterned according to certain sociodemographic characteristics. In the theory chapters to come, we will examine these studies in light of their development of violent crime causation models based on variables such as neighborhood characteristics, cultural norms and values, geographic region, and victim–offender relationship.

Trends in Property Crime

Property crimes make up slightly more than three-quarters (75 percent) of all crimes committed in the United States. Most property crimes involve theft of property where there is no physical contact between the perpetrator and the victim. Like violent crime rates, property crime rates have declined in recent years (see Figure 3.3). According to the National Criminal Victimization Survey the property crime rate in 2008 was 134.7 per 1,000 population. Property crime includes burglary, theft, motor vehicle theft, and arson. Theft of property is the most common with a rate of 101.8 per thousand. Most property thefts are for relatively small amounts: 58 percent of the thefts were for property valued at less than $249 and only 27 percent of the thefts were of property valued at over $250.[88]

Data provided by NCVS report a number of trends with regard to property crimes:

- In about 84 percent of all burglaries, the offender gained entry to the victim's residence or other building on the property.
- In about 79 percent of all motor vehicle theft attempts, the vehicle was stolen.
- Of 13 million completed thefts of property in 2005, 4.1 million netted less than $50, 4.7 million netted between $50 and $249, and 3.2 million netted $250 or more.
- Households in rented property experienced 192 property crimes per 1,000 households, while owner-occupied homes experienced 137 property crimes per 1,000 households.
- Households in rented property had more than twice the rate of motor vehicle theft than those in owned property.
- Urban households experienced higher overall property crime rates than suburban or rural households.
- Black males have the highest rate of victimization of property crimes.

These data indicate that property crimes, like the majority of other crime categories, fluctuate according to sociodemographic variables, such as neighborhood characteristics and location. Moreover, the total number of property crimes has declined over the past decade by about 15 percent, with the property crime rate declining by about 25 percent.

Trends in Crimes Against Women

The most serious crimes committed against women include assault, rape, and murder. Most of these crimes are perpetrated by men, consistent with the fact that *most* crimes are

Adjusted victimization rate per 1,000 persons age 12 and over

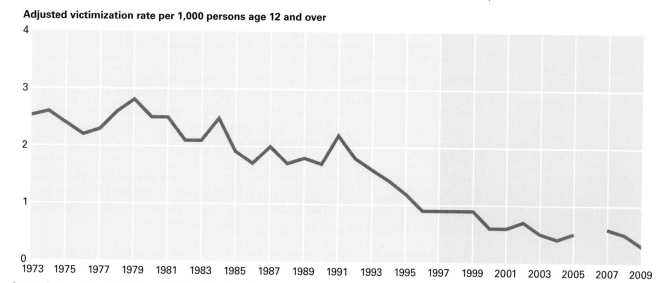

Source: Bureau of Justice Statistics. (2011, May). *National Crime Victimization Survey.* Retrieved from http://bjs.ojp. usdoj.gov/content/glance/tables/viortrdtab.cfm (accessed April 28, 2011)

Note: Includes both attempted and complete rapes. *Rape* is defined as forced sexual intercourse, including both psychological coercion and physical force. Forced sexual intercourse means penetration by the offender(s). Figure includes both rapes and attempted rapes, male as well as female victims, and both heterosexual and homosexual rape. *Attempted rape* includes verbal threats of rape.

Note: There is a gap in the graph lines for 2006 because of differences in methodologies for data gathering in the NCVS for that year.

FIGURE **3.8**

Rape Trends in the United States, 1973–2009

committed by men. The UCR provides statistics on the crime of rape, including forcible rape and attempted forcible rape. In 2009 there were an estimated 88,097 forcible rapes in the United States, which represents a rate of 28.7 per 100,000 population compared to a rate of 41.1 in 1990 (see Figure 3.8).

An analysis of data on rape and sexual assault shows the following trends:[89]

- An estimated seven of 10 female rape or sexual assault victims report the offender was an intimate partner, relative, friend, or acquaintance.
- Almost two-thirds of rapes/sexual assaults occurred from 6 p.m. to 6 a.m.
- 7 percent of all rapes/sexual assaults include the use of a weapon.
- 97.8 percent of perpetrators of rape/sexual assaults are men.
- Approximately 70 percent of rape/sexual assault offenders are over the age of 21.
- White offenders make up approximately 32.8 percent of offenders, while black offenders make up 48.5 percent.
- The lower the family income, the greater the likelihood that a woman will be the victim of a sexual assault or a rape.
- The victimization rate is highest for females between the ages of 16 and 19.
- Black females are three times more likely to become victims of rape or sexual assault than white females.

Other crimes for which women are most often the victim are incest and child sexual abuse. Data on these offenses are notoriously unreliable. Children who are the victims of incest, especially by their father or a close relative, are reluctant to report these acts to police. Families are often complicitous in a conspiracy of silence to protect both the offender and the victim in sexual assaults of any kind, since a widespread belief remains that a female who is the victim of a sexual assault is stigmatized or is even somehow guilty of encouraging the assault. Empirical data clearly demonstrate the error of these assumptions, but their prevalence nevertheless inhibits reporting and skews the data. Despite tendencies to underreporting, however, the incidence of sexual crimes is very high.

Trends in Victimization

The National Crime Victimization Survey reports that in 2005, U.S. residents age 12 and older experienced about 23 million different types of crimes: 77 percent were property crimes, 22 percent were violent crimes, and 1 percent personal thefts.[90] Moreover, for every 1,000 people age 12 or older, there occurred one rape or sexual assault, one assault with a resulting injury, and three robberies. NCVS data indicate that crime does not occur uniformly; there is a definite relationship among age, race, gender, and the risk of being the victim of a crime. More crimes are committed against men than women, against young men rather than older men, against people who live in cities, and against those in working-class areas rather than in the suburbs or upper-class areas. Although women are more likely to be victims of rape than men, the discrepancy is probably less than the data show, given the reluctance of police to arrest for male rape and of male victims to report the offense. The following is a summary of trends in victimization:

- People between 16 and 24 years old are more likely to be victimized than those of any other age group; approximately one-third of murder victims are under the age of 25. The risk of being a victim declines steadily after age 24, with people over the age of 65 accounting for the fewest incidents of victimization.
- Except for the crimes of rape and sexual assault, men are more likely to be the victims of all crimes and twice as likely to be the victims of violent crimes. In 2005, males represented 77 percent of homicide victims.
- African Americans experience a higher proportion of victimization than whites across most crime categories.
- The lower the social class, the greater the likelihood that one will be the victim of a crime, especially violent street crime that occurs in many neighborhoods where drug abuse, poverty, and social deprivation are prevalent.

Cross-Cultural Trends in Victimization

The International Crime Victimization Survey (ICVS) was created in 1989 to make cross-cultural comparisons of crime victimization, while accounting for differences in patterns of reporting crime by both victims and police practices. It also aims to create a standard measure of crime victimization to make comparisons easier. The ICVS has conducted surveys in 24 industrialized countries and 46 cities in developing countries since its inception.

What is surprising to many is that U.S. citizens are *not* the most frequent victims of crime among 17 industrialized nations studied.[91] These findings suggest that, as we pointed out earlier, the FBI, politicians, the media, and law enforcement officials exaggerate the frequency and seriousness of crime in the United States, whereas other industrialized countries do not. Some of the more revealing findings from the cross-cultural research are that

- Reported crime victimization was highest (more than 24 percent of those reporting in 1999) in Australia, England and Wales, the Netherlands, and Sweden.
- In Canada, Scotland, Denmark, Poland, Belgium, France, and the United States, between 10 and 24 percent of the respondents reported being victimized.
- Finland, Catalonia (Spain), Switzerland, Portugal, Japan, and Northern Ireland had the lowest rates of victimization (below 20 percent).

In terms of the measure of crime rate (the number of crimes experienced per 100 people), the picture is slightly different: The United States fares relatively worse on incidence rates than on prevalence rates, with incidence being the actual number of victimizations that occurred and prevalence being the per capita rate of victimizations, whereas Denmark and Canada are somewhat lower on incidence. Incidence rates are highest in England and Wales, Australia, and the Netherlands.

According to researchers, ICVS data indicate the following cross-cultural trends in patterns of crime victimization and risk:[92]

- Crime rose between 1988 and 1991, stabilized or slightly dropped in 1995, then dropped even more in 1999.
- The picture in North America differs from that in Europe. Although ICVS data suggest that crime generally rose between 1988 and 1991, crime levels in North America actually dropped in 1991, whereas in the European countries with four ICVS measures (England and Wales, Finland, and the Netherlands), crime levels were still higher in 1991 than in 1988. Compared to surveys conducted in 1991, the rate of victimization dropped more in 2000 in North America than it did in five of the seven European countries showing similar trends.
- Since 1995, property crime has fallen more consistently than violent crime across all countries.
- Risk of victimization was 60 percent higher in the more urban areas than in the less urbanized ones, with the biggest differentials being for sexual incidents and thefts of and from cars.
- Households with higher incomes were more vulnerable to individual victimization across all crime categories by about a third, compared to poorer ones, with the biggest disparity being for automobile theft.
- The risk of victimization across all ICVS crime categories was well over double for younger respondents compared to that for people aged 55 or older.
- Across all ICVS categories, individuals who went out or spent more time out of the house were at a greater risk for victimization by about 20 percent than respondents who spent more time at home.
- Individuals who were unmarried were twice as likely to be victims of contact crimes—defined as sexual assault, robbery, and assaults using force—compared to individuals in permanent relationships.
- Men were about 20 percent more at risk of victimization for robbery and assault than women.

Cross-cultural trends in crime victimization are an important source of data for criminologists, as they provide a better understanding of crime around the world. We can learn more about the phenomenon of crime by examining its social correlates in different societies, as well as the various crime-control efforts that are used to respond to it. We will take a closer look at the study of crime in different countries in Chapter 15.

SUMMARY

Where do we get our information about crime?

In this chapter, we introduced various data sources that give us a better understanding of crime-related facts. Official statistics on crime are compiled by the FBI in the annual Uniform Crime Reports (UCR), which presents data on crimes reported to law enforcement authorities by victims and data voluntarily submitted by police agencies. In the early 1980s, the FBI began to revise the UCR program by providing a more comprehensive data source that focuses on each incident in a reported crime. Under the National Incident-Based Reporting System (NIBRS), detailed information is gathered for each reported criminal incident.

What picture of crime do official data sources give us?

Unfortunately, the picture of crime painted by official crime data sources is tainted by inherent methodological flaws and biases in the reporting system and in the representation of facts by law enforcement officials. Many facts about crime fly in the face of commonly held ideas. To differentiate between scientifically reliable data and data generated for political or bureaucratic purposes, we must dispel certain myths about crime, particularly those generated by law enforcement agencies. While these agencies need not be intentionally deceptive, it is in their interests to give a report on crime that corresponds with their needs.

◼ Is there a typical criminal?

There is no typical criminal, nor is there a group of people who are particularly responsible for the majority of crime. In an effort to overcome some of the reporting flaws of official crime reports, researchers developed two alternative crime data sources: the National Crime Victimization Survey (NCVS) and the self-report survey. Both data sources are designed to gather information about criminal activity beyond what is reported to police departments. As we've seen from crime statistics compiled by these two data sources, crime cuts across race, class, gender, and most other socioeconomic and demographic variables. We can therefore glean a more accurate picture of who is the victim, who commits criminal acts, and what types of crime are committed from the more systematic and less biased researches summarized in this chapter.

◼ Are there certain crime trends or patterns of offending?

Data compiled for the UCR only focus on street crimes. As we have seen in this chapter, this depiction is, at the minimum, distorted and in many ways misleading. Despite the seriousness and prevalence of corporate crimes, white-collar crimes, corruption, and political crimes, these types of criminal activities rarely get recorded in official crime reports gathered by police departments. Public scrutiny and media attention continue to focus on the more visible types of street crimes such as murder and assault, which, according to official data sources, have been declining over the past several decades.

◼ Who are crime victims and what do they have in common?

As we have seen from data compiled by the NCVS, there is a significant relationship among age, race, gender, and the risk of being the victim of a crime. Men are more likely to be victimized than women, except for the crime of rape, which may be more of a reflection of reporting rather than actual occurrence. Moreover, data indicate that more crimes are committed against young men rather than older men. Working-class individuals who live in cities also have a greater chance of being victimized as opposed to more affluent residents of suburbs.

CRITICAL THINKING QUESTIONS

1. Close your eyes for a few moments. Now, picture a crime being committed. What is it? Describe what is happening. Who do you see? What does the perpetrator look like? Who is the victim? Where do these images come from?

2. You are watching television one evening and are deciding between two programs: one is profiling a case of corporate fraud among top executives and the other is profiling the murder of an actress by her estranged lover. Which one would you choose to watch? What factors influence your decision? Which program will likely draw the most viewers? Why?

3. Your best friend is deciding whether to rent an apartment in a major urban city close to work or live in a condo in a small town and commute every day. His decision is largely influenced by the high crime rate in the city. What can you advise him about official data on crime? How can you go about getting a better picture of the crime problem in that city to help your friend make a more informed decision?

4. Someone knocks at your door one evening and tells you she is conducting a survey for the NCVS. Would you participate? Why or why not? Which crimes do victims have the most difficulty reporting to the police? Why?

5. Someone knocks at your door one evening and tells you that she is conducting a self-report study on crime. Would you participate? Why or why not? Which crimes are you most likely to be honest about? Least honest?

ADDITIONAL RESOURCES

For more information about the consequences of adolescent victimization, visit the Office of Juvenile Justice and Delinquency Prevention (OJJDP) website at http://www.ncjrs.gov/html/ojjdp/yv_2002_2_1/contents.html

To find out more about rape and the college campus, see http://www.ncjrs.gov/pdffiles1/nij/182369.pdf

Learn more about California's three strikes law by visiting http://www.silicon-valley.com/3strikes.html

Additional Readings

Akers, R., Krohn, M., Radosevich, M., & Lanza-Kaduce. L. (1981). Social characteristics and self-reported delinquency. *Sociology of Delinquency,* 48–62.

Bachman, R., & Taylor, B. M. (1994). The measurement of family violence and rape by the redesigned National Crime Victimization Survey. *Justice Quarterly, 11,* 499–512.

Gould, L. (1969). Who defines delinquency: A comparison of self-report and officially reported indices of delinquency for three radical groups. *Social Problems, 16,* 325–336.

Gove, W. R., Hughes, M., & Geerken, M. (1985). Are Uniform Crime Reports a valid indicator of the index crimes? An affirmative answer with minor qualifications. *Criminology, 23,* 451–501.

Jensen, G., & Eve, R. (1976). Sex differences in delinquency: An examination of popular sociological explanations. *Criminology, 13,* 427–448.

Wilson, J. Q., & Herrnstein, R. (1985). *Crime and human nature* (pp. 126–147). New York: Simon & Schuster.

Wright, J. P., & Cullen, F. (2000). Juvenile involvement in occupational delinquency. *Criminology, 38,* 863–896.

4

DOING CRIMINOLOGY
Research and Theory

In this chapter, we will explore the following questions:

- How is criminology scientific?
- How do scientific theories help us understand the real world?
- What makes a theory "good"?
- What are the various research methods that help us do criminological research?
- What are the specific stages to follow when conducting scientific research?
- When do we have to consider issues of privacy and confidentiality in research?
- How does research guide criminal justice policy?

Claims about the danger to society of the widespread use

of drugs are frequently rooted in ideology. Those who want to advance their own interests and views of right and wrong associate drug use with certain lifestyles, a youth culture of rebellion, or the routine activities of lower-class individuals. Claims about drugs can also reflect the bureaucratic agendas of law enforcement agencies, politicians, legislators, and other officials seeking to advance their own needs for resources, power, visibility, and prestige. For evidence, we can look to the mid-1980s, when cocaine was replaced by its cheaper and more potent form—crack—as the preferred drug among inner-city users. This led to an all-out war on drugs by the federal government.

The reality of drug use in U.S. society has often been tainted by myths promoting an urgent need to combat its explosive growth and harmful social effects. Media, politicians, and legislators ignore historical, medical, and statistical evidence regarding the perceived threat, creating fear and panic greater than the actual social injury of drug use. One researcher notes that such drug panics share common patterns in which the drug under public scrutiny "is currently enjoying an explosive growth in popularity; is extremely addictive; and is destructive to the user or to others, threatening health or encouraging bizarre and violent behavior."[1] Very often, these drug panics are founded on questionable studies that are easily discredited upon thorough examination.

The danger is that panic can have a direct impact in shaping the law and guiding public policy.[2] The result is that we create policies built on moral opinion and political manipulation, instead of on the empirical evidence of scientific research. This was the finding in a 1990s study by Philip Jenkins of the public's reaction to the alleged explosion in use of the drug "ice," a form of methamphetamine that is smoked, and the ensuing political debates on what to do about this "epidemic."[3] Political and media representation distort the public's understanding of illicit drug use and scapegoat addiction, diverting attention away from the larger social problems (such as discrimination, poverty, and unemployment) that are potential causes of the drug use.

The value of science is its distinct way of seeing and investigating the world around us. Of course, poets, novelists, filmmakers, painters, musicians, and theologians all provide diverse ways of viewing the world and understanding our surroundings. However, science is unique in that it searches for understanding by building data and theories in a particular form. Some people believe science is about predicting and controlling events. Nothing

Colombia is the largest cocaine producer in the world. Its government, backed by the United States, employs different strategies—including manual eradication, conducted by children in this photo, and aerial spraying—to destroy coca crops. Highly concentrated and toxic chemical pesticides kill vegetation and animals, poison the waters, and spread respiratory illnesses. While the global drug markets continue to flourish, the frontline victims continue to be innocent human beings harmed in the eradication process.

could be further from the truth. The essential methods of science are to create reliable means for gathering data, to construct logically consistent theories, and to test the theories through observation.[4] The science of criminology strives to achieve these same goals.

In the first three chapters we have presented a large number of facts about crime and criminal law. But the scientific effort does not end with fact gathering. As mathematician and thinker Henri Poincaré notes, "science is built up of facts as a house is built up of stone, but an accumulation of facts is no more science than a heap of stones is a house."[5] For facts to become part of the house of science, we must understand how they are *connected:* Why is A related to B? How did it happen that X followed Y and not Z? As we shall see, our observations and theories lead us to ask many different questions about the facts. Asking these questions is a critical step in developing reliable scientific knowledge about crime.

CRIMINOLOGY AND SCIENCE

Society is fascinated with crime. The popularity of crime-related entertainment is a testimony to the public's fascination with the criminal mind, police work, and the apprehension, prosecution, and punishment of people who commit crimes. As a result of media attention, unscientific descriptions and explanations of crime abound. The child molester who engages in deviant sexual acts is depicted as weird, inhuman, and "sick"; the murderer is seen as possessed by some sort of "evil"; and the white-collar criminal is motivated solely by greed. Social policy is often driven by these simplistic, media-generated views of crime. (The Consider This feature offers a look at how the war on drugs has been promoted.) It is thus essential for us to develop sound scientific knowledge about crime if we are to avoid social policies based on prejudices and "common sense" that do not consider all the facts.

Some people argue that personal experience and common sense about the world are often fine starting points for sociological research. But they can mislead us. In the 14th century, common sense suggested the earth was flat (it looks flat), and even today many people believe that when the sun sets, it moves down in the sky. Scientific findings, however, inform us that the earth moves around the sun and gives the illusion that the sun is "setting." Facts about crime can be swayed in a similar way. As Table 4.1 shows, surveys conducted by the University of Michigan consistently demonstrate that, contrary to many people's commonsense ideas about drug use, black high school students are *less* likely to use illegal drugs than are white high school students.

CONSTRUCTING SCIENTIFIC THEORIES

Scientific theories answer questions about how and why we observe what we do, and they also reveal useful relationships in the real world. Theories explain behaviors, establish logical connections between facts, and predict the occurrence of events. They add to our understanding of the social world around us, give it meaning, and suggest solutions. The Connecting Theory to Practice feature shows how theoretical constructs can serve as the foundation of social policy development.

A good scientific theory has the following characteristics:

CONSIDER THIS...   Making the War on Drugs

The following first-person account was written especially for this text by Eric E. Sterling, J.D., and recounts his experience while assistant counsel to the House Judiciary Committee Subcommittee on Crime from 1979 to 1989. Sterling describes his work on mandatory minimum sentences for drug offenses as "the low point of my career." [6]

On June 18, 1986, Len Bias, number-two pick in the NBA draft, signed a contract with the Boston Celtics. He caught a late plane home and celebrated with his University of Maryland teammates that night. Early the next morning, after using cocaine, he suffered a cardiac arrhythmia and died. His unexpected death made national headlines.

The national leader of the Democratic Party was Speaker of the House Thomas P. ("Tip") O'Neill, Jr. from Massachusetts. During the Independence Day recess, O'Neill's constituents lamented the death of their potential sports star and the unbelievable lethality of cocaine. O'Neill heard similar reports from other representatives. He realized if the House Democrats took on the cocaine crisis and the drug problem, they could position themselves as the party of action and lay the groundwork to win control of the U.S. Senate in the election four months later.

O'Neill soon announced that the entire House would make anti-drug legislation the focus of the four weeks leading to the August recess. Every committee was included. Press releases were issued, and press conferences and subcommittee hearings occurred daily, with tales of the terrible threat of drugs and appeals from citizens and bureaucrats for solutions and programs.

The Subcommittee on Crime of the House Judiciary Committee, where I then worked, had primary jurisdiction over the penalties of the Controlled Substances Act. In the last week before the August recess, Republicans on the Subcommittee demanded a bill to raise the sentences for drug traffickers.

On Wednesday, I reported to the Subcommittee that the Drug Enforcement Administration (DEA) considered its highest-level traffickers to be those who imported or distributed hundreds of thousands of dosage units per month for at least six months. But some Subcommittee members, noting their districts did not have such large traffickers, wanted smaller quantities to trigger long sentences.

To identify appropriate lesser quantities, I consulted "Jehru" St. Valentine Brown, a narcotics detective in Washington's Metropolitan Police Department, detailed to the House Select Committee on Narcotics. Brown suggested much smaller quantities of drugs, perhaps typical of transactions of committed traffickers or managers of retail drug markets.[7] Adopting Brown's recommendations on Thursday without holding hearings or fully comprehending their meaning, the Subcommittee rushed the bill through the Judiciary Committee on Friday. Over the August recess all the House committees' work was folded together into the omnibus *Anti-Drug Abuse Act of 1986*. After hasty House and Senate action, it was signed into law by President Reagan on October 27, in time for the election.

The result is that a mandatory minimum of 10 years imprisonment (and up to life) must be imposed for a conviction involving at least 5 kilos of cocaine powder, 50 grams of cocaine base (1/100th as much cocaine), 1 kilo of heroin, 10 grams of LSD, or 1000 kilos of marijuana (or 1000 marijuana plants). A mandatory sentence of 5 years (and up to 40 years) must be imposed for only 5 grams of crack cocaine and lesser quantities of the other drugs. Given that seizures of 1 million grams of cocaine are not uncommon, these are tiny amounts. Fifty grams, now the average weight in federal crack cocaine prosecutions, is the weight of a common candy bar. Instead of focusing on high-level traffickers as Congress intended, federal agents and prosecutors are content to meet the small-quantity thresholds for the mandatory minimum sentences. Thus the overwhelming majority of federal drug offenders are minor, low-level offenders, and Black or Hispanic.

Since the Anti-Drug Abuse Act of 1986 greatly increased the penalties for the sale of drugs, the federal prison population in the United States has skyrocketed. In 1986, it was about 38,000. This was already a dramatic increase from 25,000 in 1979, a number that had been steady for decades. By spring 2011, however, it exceeded 212,000 persons, more than half of them serving drug sentences.

Should law enforcement agencies have chosen to use the small quantities and mandatory minimum sentences hastily adopted after the death of Len Bias to incarcerate mostly African-American and Hispanic drug offenders at the bottom of the distribution chain?

What do you think?

TABLE **4.1**

Illicit Drug Use by High School Seniors by Race/Ethnicity, 2009*

	MARIJUANA	COCAINE	CRACK	LSD
Lifetime Use				
White (N = 16,300)	43.3	7.3	2.5	4.0
African American (N = 3,100)	40.0	1.5	1.1	1.2
Annual Use				
White (N = 16,300)	34.3	4.4	1.4	2.6
African American (N = 3,100)	28.6	0.7	0.9	0.7

Contrary to stereotypes fueled by media reports and political statements, a larger proportion of white high school seniors use illegal drugs than black high school seniors.

*Percentages are based on 2008 and 2009 data combined to increase subgroup sample size and provide more stable estimates.

Source: Johnston, L. D., O'Malley, P. M., Bachman, J. G., & Schulenberg, J. E. (2010). *Monitoring the Future national survey results on drug use, 1975–2009. Volume I: Secondary school students* (NIH Publication No. 10-7584). Bethesda, MD: National Institute on Drug Abuse.

- *It is logically consistent.* One part of the theory does not contradict another part.
- *It is testable.* It leads to conclusions that can be refuted or supported by evidence.
- *It is valid and reliable.* It is consistent with available evidence, and it produces the same results when measured over and over.
- *It shows relationships among variables.*
- *It is objective.* It is free of personal biases.

Let's now discuss each of these qualifications and what they mean to criminology in particular. We begin with logical consistency.

Theories and Concepts Are Logically Consistent

As we learned in Chapter 1, a *theory* is a comprehensive explanation about certain phenomena or experiences based on facts that have been gathered over a period of time. For example, we can propose the theory that sleep deprivation is a major cause of poor academic performance. Our theory can be based on information gathered over time showing that students who sleep fewer hours the night before a final exam consistently score lower than students who sleep more hours.

Theories are made up of **concepts**—words, phrases, or ideas used to explain a category of individuals or a certain class of events. Concepts are the building blocks of research and theory. A concept can be as tangible as the word *poverty,* to describe a category of people living below a specific standard of economic means, or as abstract as the word *prejudice,* to describe the attitudes of certain individuals toward a specific racial or ethnic group. In order to gather accurate data and ensure that parts of the theory do not contradict one another, we need to define our concepts as precisely as possible. For a study of violent crime and social class, for example, we would need to begin with a clear definition of what violent crime and social class are. We would want to create an **operational definition,** which defines the concept in such a way that we can observe and measure it. Let's see how this works.

First, what is social class? Sociologists define social class as a person's status, derived from his or her income, wealth, education, occupation, and consumption patterns. This definition highlights the researcher's perspective that class is not just linked to income but also includes education and occupation. Highly successful drug dealers who have a high income thus would not be "upper class" unless they also met the other criteria.

concepts

Words, phrases, or ideas in a theory used to explain a category of individuals or a certain class of events.

operational definition

A definition of concepts in a theory that allows them to be observed and measured.

CONNECTING THEORY TO PRACTICE

Peer Pressure? Just Say "No"

While criminologists may not agree on the precise cause of crime and deviance, the various schools of thought can help us organize our understanding of this multifaceted social behavior and help us develop strategies at both the individual level and the societal level.

In the early 1980s, a campaign began across the United States encouraging young people to say no to a variety of vices, including taking drugs, having premarital sex, drinking alcohol, and committing violence. The campaign was largely influenced by a National Institutes of Health (NIH) theoretical research model supporting substance abuse prevention, developed by University of Houston social psychology professor Richard Evans. Evans proposed "inoculating" teens with the learning tools and skills necessary to resist peer pressure and other negative social influences.

In 1983, the campaign turned global with the founding of DARE—Drug Abuse Resistance Education, designed to discourage children from using illegal drugs, joining gangs, smoking, and drinking alcohol by teaching them to resist peer pressure, act in their own interests, and understand the adverse effects of alcohol, tobacco, and drugs.

At the heart of this and other similar programs is the focus on education to build skills and strategies to resist the temptations of getting involved in crime and delinquency. The focus of these programs lies in the underlying theoretical perspective that crime and deviance are *learned behaviors*. They are learned by interacting with individuals who engage in the behavior and by identifying with individuals who value attitudes and beliefs that support the behavior. The most suitable prevention strategies, therefore, should target those most vulnerable to education—children.[8]

Moreover, the social pressure to take drugs, join a gang, or get involved in criminal activity is also accompanied by the failure to resist such pressures. Thus, emphasis is placed on teaching children the benefits of staying in school, connecting with positive peer groups, developing positive attitudes, recognizing negative influences, and becoming aware of the risks involved in abusing drugs and alcohol. This message was graphically summarized by the unforgettable public service announcement involving a frying pan and an egg: "This is drugs" (sizzling frying pan). "This is your brain on drugs" (egg dropping in frying pan).

Social policies such as the "just say no" antidrug campaign of the 1980s are often guided by scientific studies, which can serve as the driving force or justification behind social policy development.

On the other hand, a highly successful drug dealer might have very high status in one community, such as among fellow drug dealers, and relatively low status in another, such as among legitimate business executives, thus raising interesting questions about social class for criminological research and theory.

Second, what is violent crime? The FBI uses a legal definition of crime and defines violent crime as robbery, assault, and murder. For some research purposes, this might be a perfectly adequate operational definition (especially if we are using FBI data for the study). For other purposes, however, a researcher might want a more sociological definition, such as one that considers that *all* physically harmful acts toward others are violent crimes. Grouping by legal categories (as the FBI does) is, obviously, a much narrower definition and would exclude many acts, such as the violation of workplace health and safety regulations, that lead to physical harm but are excluded from the FBI's definition.

Theories and Hypotheses Are Testable

Theories must be testable. By creating operational definitions, we can begin to deduce specific hypotheses from the theory. **Hypotheses** are ideas about the world that we derive from theories and that we can disprove when we test them against observations.

For example, we can hypothesize that children exposed to violent media are more likely to resolve disputes in a physical, aggressive manner, based on psychological theories about learning violence by imitating observed behavior. To test this hypothesis, we can have a group of children watch a cartoon that shows aggressive behavior and observe their interaction with one another. We can then compare their interaction to that of a group of children who have not watched the violent cartoon to see whether there is a difference. The results of these observations let us test the accuracy of psychological theories on the effects of media portrayals of violence on imitating behavior. Hypotheses thus enable scientists to check the accuracy of their theories.

However, good theories can never be proved to be absolutely true; otherwise, they would no longer be theories but would be facts or natural laws. That the sky is blue and not purple or orange is a fact indeed. That a child who throws a ball in the air can be assured it will always come down is a tribute to the natural law of gravity. Good theories, however, must be constructed in a way that makes it possible for us to prove them *wrong*, if indeed they *are* wrong. Karl Popper's famous **principle of falsification** holds that to be scientific, a theory must lead to testable hypotheses that can be disproved if they are wrong.[9]

Theories and Hypotheses Are Valid and Reliable

If we want to test theories and hypotheses, we need concepts and measurements that are valid and reliable. **Validity** is the extent to which a measure actually reflects the phenomenon under study. A very simple example comes from our experience of measuring academic performance. A chemistry professor administers a final exam to assess her students' understanding of the course material covered in a given semester. The test would be invalid if the questions on it did not reflect the content of the course in terms of lectures, readings, and assignments. **Reliability** refers to the extent to which a measure consistently produces the same results over and over again. Consider a bathroom scale. That scale would be highly unreliable if it gave different readings every time you stepped on it.

Suppose you want to know whether the crime rate in the United States has gone up or down. For years criminologists depended on the Uniform Crime Reports (UCR). As we saw in Chapter 3, however, these reports were known to be incomplete, subject to local political events, and sometimes manipulated for political purposes.[10] The newer annual National Crime Victimization Survey (NCVS) provides more comprehensive data, which include, among other things, how many people have been the victims of crime, crime trends, and characteristics of perpetrators. This comprehensive data make the NCVS a more valid source of information about crime.

When testing a hypothesis, researchers must make sure the findings are consistent with other studies of the same phenomenon or with the same study over time. Comparing UCR data with data from the NCVS, for example, provides a test of the reliability of both these different ways of measuring crime and crime victims. A major cause of unreliability in research is the presence of **bias,** a distortion that systematically misrepresents the true nature of what we are studying or the results of our study. Bias may creep into research through the use of inappropriate measures, for example, when survey respondents do not tell the truth. In a study on drug use, respondents were asked whether they used illegal drugs (Table 4.2). Some of the respondents were wired to a machine they

hypotheses

Ideas about the world derived from theories and that can be disproved when tested against observations.

principle of falsification

A scientific theory must lead to testable hypotheses that can be disproved if they are wrong.

validity

The extent to which a measure actually reflects the phenomenon under study.

reliability

The extent to which a measure consistently produces the same results over and over again.

bias

A distortion that systematically misrepresents the true nature of what is being studied or the results of the study.

TABLE **4.2**

How Truthful Are Respondents on Surveys?

Do you:	PERCENT ANSWERING YES	
	SUBJECTS NOT HOOKED UP TO A LIE DETECTOR	SUBJECTS TOLD THEY WERE HOOKED UP TO A LIE DETECTOR
Ever drink and drive?	17.2	30.6
Ever smoke pot?	56.9	71.0
Ever use LSD?	19.0	27.4
Ever use cocaine?	25.9	43.5
Ever use amphetamines?	19.0	38.7

Source: Tourangeau, R., Smith, T. W., & Rasinski, K. A. (1997). Motivation to report sensitive behaviors on surveys: Evidence from a bogus pipeline experiment. *Journal of Applied Social Psychology, 27*(3), 209–222.

were told was a lie detector, while others were not. The subjects who thought their truthfulness was being monitored by the "lie detector" reported higher rates of illegal drug use than the others.

Criminologists often rely on questionnaire data as a basis for testing theories. One problem that can arise is that the results may be biased because people do not tell the truth. In this study, respondents told that they were attached to a lie detector were much more likely to admit to illegal drug use than those who were not. The findings suggest that people are much more likely to tell interviewers the truth when they believe their responses can be checked.

Based on the assumption that actual drug use would be about the same for both groups, the researchers believed the subjects who were not connected to a "lie detector" were understating their actual rate of illegal drug use. They thus concluded that simply asking people about drug use would lead to biased findings because respondents would not tell the truth.

Theories Show Relationships Among Variables

variable

In a theory, a concept that can take on two or more values.

In addition to being logically consistent, testable, and valid and reliable, scientific theories also show us the relationships among specific concepts or variables. A **variable** is a concept that can take on two or more values.[11] Some familiar variables include gender (male, female, transgender), work status (employed, unemployed), and geographic location (inner city, suburbs, rural area).

We can measure variables either quantitatively or qualitatively. Crime rates, unemployment rates, and frequency of drug use are *quantitative* variables; we can attach numbers or quantities to them. *Qualitative* variables include people's attitudes towards drug use, fear of crime, and perception of dangerousness of their neighborhood. These are concepts we measure by asking people questions about their opinions, beliefs, thoughts, or feelings on a certain subject.

Establishing a relationship between two or more variables is at the very heart of criminological (and all other scientific) research. Suppose you want to find out whether there is a relationship between homicide and the level of social disorganization in a neighborhood, as Charis Kubrin did.[12] The first step is to define the two variables: violent crime and social disorganization. Kubrin used the UCR definition of homicide as both murder—the intentional taking of another person's life—and non-negligent manslaughter—causing someone's death as a result of behavior that, while intentional, was not intended to cause the person's death.

For her measure of neighborhood social disorganization, Kubrin identified a number of variables such as poverty, number of households headed by a single parent, frequency of changing residence, and so on. Her findings generally supported the theory that the higher the level of social disorganization in a neighborhood, the higher the homicide rate.

Notice that what Kubrin explored is the *correlation* between the two variables: social disorganization and homicide. **Correlation** (literally, "co-relationship") is the degree to which two or more variables are associated with one another. When two variables are correlated, we may be tempted to infer that they have a **causal relationship,** a relationship between two variables in which one is the cause of the other. However, just because two variables are correlated, we cannot assume that one causes the other. Correlation does *not* prove causation.

We can also observe an apparent correlation between two variables that is a result of a spurious relationship. A **spurious relationship** is a correlation between two or more variables that is the result of another factor not being measured.[13] In the example above, some criminologists argue that the correlation between social disorganization and violent crime is spurious, and that what causes both is a third variable, a subculture of violence.[14] We must always critically analyze criminological research to ensure that positive relationships are not spurious.

Scientific Theories Are Objective

Even if criminologists develop logical and testable theories based on good operational definitions and collect valid and reliable data, they still may have passions and biases that can color their research. For example, criminologists long ignored the criminality of women because they assumed that women rarely committed crime. Until that bias was recognized and corrected, researchers did not have an accurate picture of women and crime.

Similarly, criminologists overlooked the crimes of corporations and the state.[15] In the example above concerning the link between violence and social disorganization, if Kubrin had included the violent crimes of large corporations, the correlation she found might have disappeared. In the President's Report on Occupational Safety and Health (1972), for instance, the government estimated "the number of deaths from industrial disease at 100,000":[16]

> *numerous studies have documented . . . the fact that much or most of the carnage is the consequence of the refusal of management to pay for safety measures . . . and sometimes of management's willful defiance of existing laws.*[17]

Personal values and beliefs may endanger the researcher's **objectivity,** or ability to represent the object of study accurately without being affected by personal bias. Nineteenth-century sociologist Max Weber argued that in order for scientific research to be objective it has to be value-neutral, that is, personal beliefs and opinions should not influence the course of research. The sociologist should acknowledge personal biases and assumptions, make them explicit, and prevent them from getting in the way of observation and reporting.

How can we best achieve objectivity? First, recall the principle of falsification, which proposes that the goal of research is not to prove our ideas correct, but to find out whether they are wrong. To accomplish this, researchers must be willing to allow the data to contradict their most passionately held convictions. Theories should deepen human understanding, not prove a particular point of view.

A second way to ensure objectivity is to invite others to draw their own conclusions about our data. They can do this through **replication,** the repetition of a previous study using a different sample or population to verify or refute the original findings. The original study must spell out in detail the research methods employed, and researchers wishing to replicate a study should have access to the original materials, such as questionnaires or field notes.

Karl Popper described scientific discovery as an ongoing process of "confrontation and refutation."[18] Criminologists subject their work to this process by publishing their

correlation

The degree to which two or more variables are associated with one another.

causal relationship

A relationship between two variables in which one is the cause of the other.

spurious relationship

A correlation between two or more variables that is the result of another factor not being measured.

objectivity

Ability to represent the object of study accurately without being affected by personal bias.

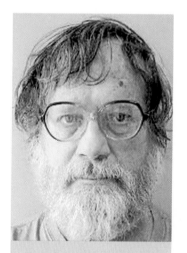

William Fox spent 20 years in the U.S. Army and served three tours in Cambodia as a Special Forces medic during the Vietnam War before being convicted of first-degree sexual assault for abusing two young girls in 1994. In 2008, Fox's neighbors panicked over an unconfirmed report that he had followed a school bus; they alerted school officials and placed fliers identifying Fox in a local deli. Fox died shortly after of natural causes. How is objectivity in research compromised by media portrayals of certain types of crimes or criminals?

replication

The repetition of a previous study using a different sample or population to verify or refute the original findings.

research strategy

A clearly thought-out plan that guides the work.

research methods

The specific techniques—such as questionnaires, experiments, or surveys—used to systematically gather data.

results in scholarly journals and other outlets. Once research has been published, other scholars read it with a critical eye, making criticisms, offering suggestions for modifications, or making supportive arguments. Then they may replicate the study in a different setting. Good scientific theories are rooted in the systematic collection and analysis of data that add to our understanding of a specific subject. Let's explore now the various methodologies used by criminologists to conduct scientific research.

CRIMINOLOGICAL RESEARCH METHODS

Criminological research requires a **research strategy,** a clearly thought-out plan that guides the work. For instance, if you want to study the relationship between poverty and crime, you must establish the level of understanding you want to achieve about the subject. Do you want to know how living in poverty can influence an individual's choice to commit crime, or do you want to assess whether involvement in criminal activity creates financial loss and hardship for an individual? Do you want to investigate long-term trends, or do you want to develop an in-depth understanding of the personal experiences of individuals? The research strategy's purpose is to fill gaps in our understanding of the social world and to obtain preliminary knowledge that will help guide our choice of **research methods**—the specific techniques—such as questionnaires, experiments, or surveys—we use for systematically gathering data.

Criminologists employ a variety of methods to learn about the social world (Table 4.3). Since each method has strengths and weaknesses, a good research strategy may use several methods. If they all yield similar findings, we are more likely to have confidence in the results.[19] The principal methods are the survey, fieldwork, experiments, and working with existing information.

TABLE **4.3**

Some Sociological Research Methods: How to Choose?	
METHOD	**WHEN APPROPRIATE**
Survey Research	To obtain basic information about a large population, conduct survey research by selecting a sample that is representative of the entire population.
Fieldwork	To obtain detailed information and when surveys are impractical (for example, when studying the day-to-day behavior of youth gangs), conduct fieldwork for relatively small samples.
	Detached Observation To stay removed from the people being studied and gather data in a way that minimizes impact on the subjects, use detached observation.
	Participant Observation To obtain firsthand knowledge of the direct experience of subjects, including a deeper understanding of their lives, use participant observation.
Experiments	To test the effect of a variable on human behavior, match experimental and control groups on relevant variables, but provide them with different experiences in the experiment.
Use of Existing Information	When direct acquisition of data is either not feasible or is not desirable (because the event studied occurred in the past or because gathering the data directly is too costly or difficult), analyze existing information.

Survey Research

A **survey** consists of administering a questionnaire or interviewing a group of people (in person or by telephone or email) to determine their characteristics, opinions, and behaviors. Surveys are common in sociological research. We can use them to test a theory or simply to gather data. The National Crime Victimization Survey is an example of survey research. It gathers data on crime victimization from a sample of 100,000 citizens and publishes the results through the Bureau of Justice Statistics.

The first step in designing a survey is to identify the population of interest. That is, who makes up the population from which the data are drawn? For the NCVS, who should we survey? All U.S. citizens? Everyone in a certain age group? People in the lower classes? Pet owners? To conduct a good study we want to clearly identify the survey population that will most effectively answer our research question. The NCVS includes people aged 12 or older in all social classes.

Once we have identified a population of interest, we usually study a **sample** of that group: a sub-set or portion of the larger population selected to represent the whole. Researchers seldom have the time or money to talk to all the members of a population, especially if it is a large one, so they sample from it. Thus, the size of the sample selected is an important consideration. Other things being equal, larger samples better represent the population than smaller ones. Ideally, a sample should reflect the composition of the population we are studying. For instance, if we want to be able to generalize research data about the population of the United States to draw conclusions about the whole population, we would need to collect correctly proportioned samples from different social classes, neighborhoods, and urban and rural areas.

With proper sampling techniques, criminologists can use relatively small (and therefore relatively inexpensive) samples to represent large populations. A well-chosen sample of 1,000 voters can represent 100 million U.S. voters with a fair degree of accuracy, enabling survey researchers to reasonably predict election outcomes.

To avoid bias in surveys, criminologists often use **random sampling** in which everyone in the population has an equal chance of being chosen for the study. Typically, researchers draw up a list of everyone in the population of interest. Then they draw names at random until they reach the desired sample size. Moreover, in constructing surveys, criminologists take care to ensure that the questions and their possible responses will capture the respondents' point of view. Poorly worded questions can produce misleading results (Figure 4.1). Through effective sampling techniques, surveys can save a great deal of time and money.

survey

A research method that consists of administering a questionnaire or interviewing a group of people to determine their characteristics, opinions, and behaviors.

sample

In a survey, a sub-set or portion of the larger population selected to represent the whole.

random sampling

In a survey, a sample of the population in which everyone has an equal chance of being chosen for the study.

Qualities of a Survey	Good Question	Poor Question
Brief	Do you believe in the death penalty?	Do you believe the death penalty should be imposed as a sanction on individuals who are convicted of first-degree murder, as opposed to life in prison?
Objective	Do you feel there should be educational programs for prison inmates?	Do you believe that violent offenders behind bars deserve to get federal funding for college education?
Simple	What are your thoughts on gun control?	What are your thoughts on gun control laws, versus the constitutional right to bear arms?
Specific	Should airport officials use profiling when screening passengers?	Should airport officials occasionally use profiling when screening passengers?

FIGURE 4.1

How to Make a Good Survey
The following questions can help you gather information about survey respondents' thoughts and opinions. What type of misleading responses can you get from the examples of poor questions?

Fieldwork

fieldwork

Also called ethnography, a research method using in-depth and often extended on-site study to describe a group or community.

Fieldwork, sometimes called *ethnography,* takes the researcher into the field where people live their lives. It uses in-depth and often extended on-site study to describe a group or community. Criminologists have employed the techniques of fieldwork to study everything from organized crime,[20] to graffiti,[21] delinquent gangs,[22] prostitution and drug use among inner-city women,[23] and a host of other criminal and delinquent behaviors.

Most fieldwork combines several different methods of gathering information. These include interviews, detached observation, and participant observation. An **interview** is a detailed conversation designed to obtain in-depth information about a person and his or her activities. In surveys, interview questions can be either open-ended, where there is no definite answer, or closed-ended, where the answer is limited to specific choices such as "agree," "disagree," and "no opinion." In fieldwork, however, questions are usually open-ended to allow the respondent to answer in his or her own words. Sometimes the interviewer prepares a detailed set of questions; at other times, the best approach is to simply have a list of broad topics to cover.

interview

A detailed conversation designed to obtain in-depth information about a person and his or her activities.

leading questions

Questions that elicit a particular response.

Good interviewers guard against influencing the respondent's answers. In particular, **leading questions,** questions that elicit a particular response, are a danger. Imagine a question on attitudes toward the environment that reads, "Do you believe poor neighborhoods, which have high incidences of violent crime, are likely to have high incidences of domestic violence?" The bias in this question is obvious: The stated association of poor neighborhoods with violent crime creates a bias in favor of a "yes" answer. Gathering accurate data depends upon asking questions that are not biased and do not bias the respondent.

detached observation

Conducting research in the field from a distance and observing without getting involved.

Sometimes the study strategy requires that researchers in the field keep a distance from the people they are studying, simply observing without getting involved.[24] The subjects may or may not know they are being observed. This approach is called **detached observation.** William Chambliss (one of this book's co-authors) employed detached observation to discover how two delinquent gangs, one middle class and one working class, conducted their "routine activities." Chambliss spent many hours observing gang members without actually being involved in what they were doing.[25] With the gang members' permission, he sat in his car with the window rolled down so he could hear

How do the techniques of field research help us better understand the structure and function of street gangs and the daily interactions and experiences of group members?

them talk and watch their behavior while they hung out on a street corner. At other times he observed them playing pool while he played at an adjoining table, or followed them in his car as they drove through the streets or sat nearby in bars and cafés to hear their conversation. Through his observations at a distance, Chambliss was able to observe in detail the kinds of delinquencies in which the gangs were engaged. He was also able to unravel some of the social processes that led to the delinquent acts and observe other people's reactions to the gang members. (For the full text of his well-known article about this research, see the Appendix on page 383.)

Detached observation is particularly useful when there is reason to believe that other forms of fieldwork might influence the behavior of the subjects being observed. It is also a useful technique for checking the validity of what the researcher has been told in interviews. A great deal of sociological information about illegal behavior has been gathered through detached observation.

One problem with detached observation, however, is that the information gathered is likely to be incomplete. Without actually talking to them, researchers cannot check their impressions against the experiences of the people they are studying. For this reason, detached observation is usually supplemented by in-depth interviews. In his study of delinquent gangs, Chambliss periodically interviewed gang members to complement his findings and check the accuracy of his detached observations.[26]

Another type of fieldwork is **participant observation,** a mixture of active participation and detached observation. Participant observation research can be dangerous. Research by Chambliss on organized crime and police corruption in Seattle exposed him to threats from the police and organized crime network members who feared he would reveal their criminal activities.[27]

Experiments

Experiments are research techniques for investigating cause and effect under controlled conditions. In a typical experiment, participants are selected who share characteristics such as age, education, social class, and experiences that are relevant to the experiment and then randomly assigned to two groups. The first, called the **experimental group,** is exposed to the independent (or experimental) variable. This is whatever the researchers hypothesize will affect the subjects' behavior. The second group is the **control group,** where subjects receive no special attention. The Crime in Global Perspective feature profiles an international experiment on the effects of violent media on children's behavior.

To study the effect of violent images in the media on viewers' tolerance of real violence, researchers showed one group of undergraduate male students sexually explicit and violent films (the experimental group), while others were shown no films at all (the control group). The students were then interviewed to determine how sympathetic they were to a woman who had been raped. The studies found that students in the experimental

participant observation

A fieldwork method that combines active participation with detached observation.

experiments

Research techniques for investigating cause and effect under controlled conditions.

experimental group

In an experiment, the group that is exposed to the independent (or experimental) variable.

control group

In an experiment, the group that receives no special attention.

Albert Bandura's theory that children can learn aggressive behavior by example, including via the media, was the subject of a famous experiment in which children were shown a video of a model punching and kicking a plastic doll. Given a similar doll a few moments later, 88 percent of the children repeated the model's violent behavior. Experiments are often used to determine causal relationships in a controlled environment.

CRIME IN GLOBAL PERSPECTIVE | A European Experiment to Study Effects of Violent Media

Sixteen-year-old José Rabadan was a passionate enthusiast of the video game *Final Fantasy VIII,* whose main character, teenager Squall Lionheart, fights his enemies using a katana, a type of Japanese sword. In April 2000, José killed his parents and sister with a katana in Murcia, Spain. It was reported that when he was arrested trying to flee to Barcelona, José's physical appearance resembled Squall's.

The effect of violent media on children and youth has become a public concern around the globe. Research on the subject is at the forefront of experimental criminology, both in the United States and in countries worldwide. While the prevalence of violence on television, the Internet, movies, and video games is indisputable, the effect of its exposure on children's behavior is still unclear.

Researchers at Utrecht University in the Netherlands developed an experimental study on the aggressive behavior in children when they actively played violent video games versus when they passively watched the games.[28] The study was premised on the idea that actually playing violent video games is more interactive and rewarding than merely watching the same violence on a screen and will therefore lead to more aggressive behavior. Game condition (active violent, passive violent, active nonviolent) was the independent variable, and aggressive behavior was the dependent variable. The study included 56 children aged 10 to 13 from the 5th and 6th grades; half were boys and half girls. The children were equally and randomly distributed across game conditions and were told the researchers were conducting a study of their skill in playing video games.

After the experiment, which took place at the children's schools, participants were given a questionnaire about their gaming habits, including such items as frequency of playing video games and familiarity with the game. They also were asked to list the names of their peers who had displayed acts of aggression such as hitting, kicking, pushing, fighting, and name calling. Analysis of the findings suggests there are significantly different effects on aggressive behavior between actively playing violent video games or watching violent video games. Specifically, in real-life play situations, boys selected to participate in the active violent game condition were more aggressive later than boys in the passive violent game condition.

This difference did not exist for girls, but the researchers note this should not be taken as evidence of no difference in effects for girls, given the small sample used in this study (28 girls). The study has strong implications for future research on the variable effects of different levels of participation in violent media in producing aggressive behavior in children.

group were less sympathetic than those in the control group. The researchers concluded that exposure to violence against women in the media increases men's tolerance of actual violence against women.[29]

Working with Existing Information

Criminologists frequently work with existing information and data gathered by other researchers, including statistical data, documentary analysis, and historical research.

Statistical data include numerical information obtained from government agencies, businesses, and other organizations that collect data for their own or others' use. The Uniform Crime Reports and the National Crime Victimization Survey are two sources of statistical data provided by the government that are invaluable for criminological research. In addition, the Bureau of Justice Statistics provides a vast amount of information about police departments, courts, and prosecutors and public defenders' offices.

Document analysis is the analysis of written materials: previous studies, newspaper reports, court records, and other forms of text produced by individuals, government agencies, private organizations, and other sources. However, because such documents are not

statistical data

Information used for research including numerical information obtained from government agencies, businesses, and other organizations.

document analysis

The analysis of written materials: previous studies, newspaper reports, court records, and other forms of text produced by individuals, government agencies, private organizations, and other sources.

always compiled with accuracy in mind, good researchers exercise caution in using them. People who keep records are often aware that others will see the records and take pains to avoid recording anything unflattering. The expert researcher looks at such materials with a critical eye, double-checking other sources for accuracy where possible. The diaries and memoirs of politicians are a good example of documents that are an invaluable source of data but that must be interpreted with great caution.

Historical research is research based on historical documents. Often such research is comparative, examining historical events in several different countries, looking for similarities and differences. Historical research in criminology often differs from the research conducted by historians. Criminologists usually identify patterns common to different times and places, whereas historians focus on a particular time and place and are less willing to draw broad generalizations from their research. One example of historical research in criminology is studies of law creation.[30]

historical research

Research based on historical documents.

Historical data requires precautions because it may be incomplete, inaccurate, or even deliberately biased. Gaps in the historical record exist, and it may be difficult or impossible to obtain crucial information. Finally, the researcher must guard against the possibility that words had different meanings in earlier times.[31]

Criminological research seldom follows a recipe that indicates exactly how to proceed. Criminologists often have to feel their way as they go, responding to the challenges that arise during research and adapting new methods to fit the circumstances. The following section provides you with a guide to the various stages of criminological research.

A STUDENT'S GUIDE TO CRIMINOLOGICAL RESEARCH

The stages of criminological research can vary, even when researchers agree about the ideal sequence to follow. The ideal process in fact includes six basic steps, according to the scientific method:[32] (1) define the problem, (2) review the literature, (3) formulate a hypothesis, (4) collect and analyze the data, (5) develop a conclusion, and (6) share the results. Figure 4.2 displays the steps of the scientific method.

Defining the Problem

The main goal of the scientific method is to answer the question we are posing at the beginning of the process, so defining the problem (or the research question) is the most important step. Defining the problem means stating, as clearly as possible, what it is we want to investigate. What exactly do we want to know?

Suppose we want to find out whether having a higher level of education reduces a person's chances of becoming involved in criminal activity. Start by narrowing down key words, definitions, and ideas. Essentially, we must *operationalize* the abstract concepts of education and crime by making them measurable, such as stating educational achievement in terms of years of schooling completed and degrees acquired. Likewise, we must narrow down our study of criminality. Are we investigating the relationship between educational achievement and violent crime, property crime, or both? Or are we going to narrow the topic even further by choosing a certain category of violent or property crime? Are we studying criminality among a certain class, age, race, or gender of individuals? Are there other social structural variables we want to examine? All these considerations must be taken into account before moving on to the next step.

FIGURE **4.2**

The Scientific Method

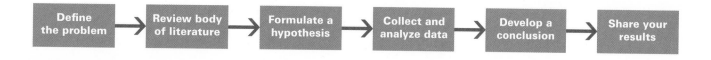

| Define the problem | → | Review body of literature | → | Formulate a hypothesis | → | Collect and analyze data | → | Develop a conclusion | → | Share your results |

Reviewing the Literature

The next step is to review the literature. This means reading and describing other scholarly studies relevant to the topic. If the topic has been researched before, we can add to our own methodology by incorporating insights that already exist in the literature. If, in fact, previous research and experiments have been conducted on the particular topic, we should be able to see what has or has not worked in the past and test our hypothesis in a different way, learning from the outcomes of past efforts.

Reviewing the information in the scientific literature will also provide a more in-depth understanding of the topic, making our research stronger, more effective, and scientifically grounded. We will be better able to assess the extent to which our research will add to the existing body of knowledge on the subject.

A literature review also alerts us to methodological problems that have been encountered by prior researchers so we can refine our own methodology. Comparing our intended research methodology with other studies also provides a context within which to compare and contrast our findings. The American Psychological Association (APA) outlines several important research issues that a thorough review of the literature can clarify (Table 4.4).

Formulating a Hypothesis

After a thorough examination of the literature, it is time to formulate a hypothesis. Think of the hypothesis as an educated guess based on prior observations. It can be part of a theory, or it can be a theory on its own. A hypothesis is therefore a speculative statement about the relationship between certain variables, made in order to draw out and test its conclusion.

A hypothesis tells us how one aspect of human behavior affects another. The direction of this relationship determines which variable under study is independent, and which is dependent (Figure 4.3). The **independent variable** is the variable that we hypothesize has caused or influenced another. The **dependent variable** is the variable we believe is caused by or influenced by the independent variable.

Recall our research topic about the relationship between educational achievement and criminality. In this study, we are interested in the effect education has on crime. Thus, educational achievement is our independent variable, and criminality our dependent variable. Correctly identifying independent and dependent variables is essential to establishing a logical consistency to the research study and to clarifying cause–effect relationships. Does the independent variable actually cause or lead to the dependent variable, or is the event connecting the two variables an existing correlation? If we find,

independent variable

The variable that is hypothesized to have caused or influenced another.

dependent variable

The variable that is hypothesized to have been caused by or influenced by the independent variable.

TABLE **4.4**

Questions Raised by a Good Literature Review

- How is the research question relevant, important, and current to the field being studied?
- Is the research using methodologies that demonstrate reliability and validity?
- Does the outcome of the investigation relate to the variables being measured?
- To what extent is the research construct compatible with testing the hypothesis?
- Is the research sample representative enough to make generalizations from the study?
- Did the study adhere to sound ethical research principles?

Source: American Psychological Association. (1983). *Publication manual* (3rd ed.). Hyattsville, MD: Author.

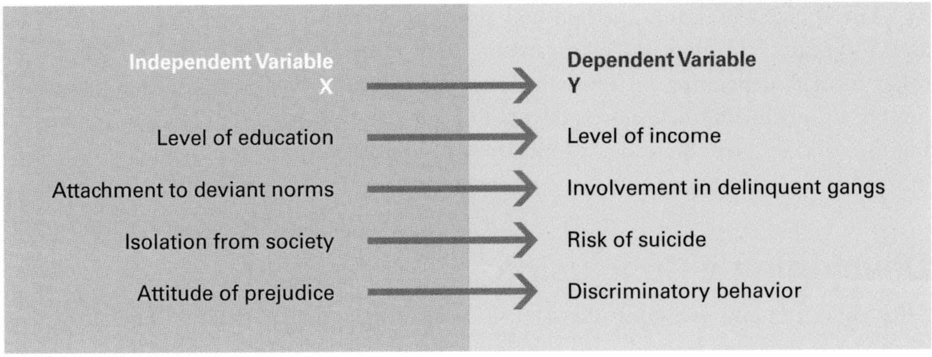

Independent Variable X		Dependent Variable Y
Level of education	→	Level of income
Attachment to deviant norms	→	Involvement in delinquent gangs
Isolation from society	→	Risk of suicide
Attitude of prejudice	→	Discriminatory behavior

FIGURE **4.3**

Examples of Causal Logic: X Leads to Y
The following hyptheses propose a correlation between the independent and dependent variables in the example.

for example, that crime goes down as educational achievement goes up, we must also consider that a third variable, such as income, may be acting as the causal link, therefore making the relationship between educational achievement and criminality only a spurious relationship.

Collecting and Analyzing Data

To begin the task of collecting data, we first select a representative sample from the population under study.[33] Ideally, social scientists conduct research studies using a random sample, in which, as we said earlier, everyone in the population under study has an equal chance of being selected. For example, if we want to examine the opinion of people in a specific city on the subject of sex offender registration, we can obtain a random sample of residents by using the city telephone directory and a computer-generated sampling technique for randomly selecting names.

Sometimes, however, we cannot obtain a truly random sample. For example, if we wanted to study the social organization of maximum security prisons, then to get a true random selection we would have to ensure that all maximum security prisons, both state and federal, had an equal chance of being selected for the study. For practical and logical reasons, this would not make sense. We would likely have to take into consideration other issues such as geographic location, access, and security.

We must also ensure the reliability and validity of the research.[34] One way to test validity is to make certain the variables selected for study are an accurate measure of the phenomena we are researching. For example, let's say we are trying to examine the effects on class participation of enforcing strict attendance policies. Is increased attendance alone a valid measure of class participation? Or, is class participation more accurately measured by an increase in questions, discussions, and comments made by students? Make sure to measure what it is we want to measure. Equally important, make certain that the research will produce results that are reliable in their measure, meaning that other researchers who replicate the study will get the same results.

After selecting a sample to study and addressing the issues of reliability and validity, we now need to determine how to collect the data based on the type of research questions and hypothesis we have proposed. Select a research method that is most suitable to gathering the data necessary to answer the question posed. The choice of research design depends on how we want to structure the research. It also may be influenced by the particular subject we are studying, the type of information we want, and personal preferences. For example, if we are interested in studying the effect of sex offender registration laws on the personal experiences of sex offenders, we may want to capture and record details about the daily hardships, obstacles, and difficulties they face by conducting in-depth interviews. This is where a good literature review can provide valuable insight.

The choice of research method will also determine how we analyze the data. Data analysis means "cleaning up" or organizing data into charts, tables, figures, graphs, or other formats depending on research design. It can also include transcribing recorded interviews, organizing field notes, or recalling information from observation. By analyzing the data, we give the reader a summary of our observations, comments on our findings, and an assessment of how our data sheds light on the question under study.

Developing a Conclusion

After collecting and analyzing the data, we should be ready to draw a conclusion that summarizes what we learned: Did the data support the original hypothesis or didn't it? Are there questions that remain unanswered? What are the benefits and advantages of the research? What are the possible flaws and shortcomings in the research? Any suggestions or recommendations for future inquiry into the subject?[35] A conclusion is like the final act or scene in a play. It ties the beginning to the end. It may not turn out the way the audience wanted or expected, but it puts the entire play in perspective.

Conclusions do not need to answer all questions raised by a particular research subject. The social world is an unstable, unpredictable environment that is very difficult to evaluate. Relationships between variables are, at the least, imperfect. A good scientific conclusion, therefore, will give the research a sense of completeness and value and not try to establish absolute principles. It does not necessarily need to prove something, but simply comment on the relevance of the results in advancing knowledge and understanding of the subject.

Sharing the Results

The development of reliable knowledge depends on researchers sharing their results with others. This can be a painful experience; methods and findings may be criticized for failing to take into account some of the many criteria for good research outlined in this chapter. Nonetheless, sharing the results is imperative.

Most criminologists publish the results of their research either in professional journals (such as *Criminology, The British Journal of Criminology,* and *Law and Society Review*) or in books. Another way of sharing the results is to present a paper at a meeting of a professional association such as the American Society of Criminology, the Society for the Study of Social Problems, or the Academy of Criminal Justice Sciences. Whatever avenue is chosen, an important part of the scientific process is letting other people know what research we are doing and its results.

The need to share the results of our work with the academic community places a responsibility on the researcher to ensure that the research does not violate any moral or ethical standards. Considering ethical issues that may affect various components of the research project is just as important as using an organized, scientific approach. We turn now to a discussion of ethics in conducting criminological research.

ETHICAL CRIMINOLOGICAL RESEARCH

Social scientific research is most often conducted on human beings. The value and integrity of criminological research therefore depend on our upholding the highest level of ethical standards and considerations. Issues of confidentiality, privacy, disclosure of research methods, and the protection of human subjects are concerns we must address at the outset of any research endeavor. The researcher's right to know must be balanced against the subject's right to privacy. The social value of gathering data and obtaining information for the purpose of advancing knowledge must be weighed against the duty and obligation of the researcher to be honest, forthright, and value-neutral.

Frank E. Hagan offers an intuitive understanding of the role of the researcher in exercising objectivity and pursuing professional integrity while engaging in scientific research.[36] Hagan suggests that criminologists adhere to a code of professional ethics that will guide them in accepting responsibility for:

- Protecting subjects from harmful procedures
- Honoring commitments to subjects by respecting mutual agreements
- Reporting research findings in an objective manner
- Preserving the privacy and confidentiality of subjects

We hold criminological research to such rigorous standards because it can and does influence public policy. The Academy of Criminal Justice Sciences (ACJS) has adopted an official code of ethics in conducting scientific research that underlies the values, ideals, and professional responsibility of criminologists in pursuit of their academic endeavors. General principles within this code of ethics call for members of the criminal justice academic and professional community to be

committed to enhancing the general well-being of society and of the individuals and groups within it . . . to avoid incompetent, unethical or unscrupulous use of criminal justice knowledge . . . [and] recognize the great potential for harm that is associated with the study of criminal justice, and . . . not knowingly place the well-being of themselves or other people in jeopardy in their professional work.[37]

Table 4.5 highlights the guidelines set forth by the ACJS as ethical standards to maintain objectivity and integrity in conducting criminological research.

Adhering to ethical standards in scientific research is essential in criminological inquiry. We turn now to a discussion of the future of criminological theory and research.

In 1971, a team of researchers at Stanford University under the direction of Dr. Philip Zimbardo conducted a mock prison experiment to determine the psychological impact of becoming a prisoner and a guard. Participants were randomly assigned the role of guard or inmate. After a few days, the experiment was terminated prematurely because of the authoritarian and abusive treatment of the "prisoners" by those adopting the role of "guards." Zimbardo's experiment has been a source of controversy for years. What ethical questions does it raise?

TABLE **4.5**

Ethical Considerations in Conducting Research

- Adhere to the highest possible technical standards in research.

- Acknowledge the limitations that may affect the validity of findings.

- In presenting research findings, do not misrepresent the findings or omit significant data.

- Do not make any commitments to respondents, individuals, groups, or organizations unless there is full intention and ability to honor them.

- Human subjects have the right to full disclosure of the purposes of the research as early as it is appropriate to the research process, and they have the right to an opportunity to have their questions answered about the purpose and usage of the research.

- Subjects of research are entitled to rights of personal confidentiality unless they are waived.

- The process of conducting criminal justice research must not expose respondents to more than minimal risk of personal harm . . . make every effort to ensure the safety and security of respondents and project staff. Informed consent should be obtained when the risks of research are greater than the risks of everyday life.

Source: Academy of Criminal Justice Sciences. (2000, March 21). *Code of ethics* III. Ethical Standards, March 21, 2000. Retrieved from http://www.acjs.org/pubs/167_671_2922.cfm

In January 2001, Aida Hass (co-author of this book) began working as a program analyst for the Court Services and Offender Supervision Agency (CSOSA) for the District of Columbia, a federal agency providing treatment and supervision services to pre-trial release, probation, and parole offenders in Washington, DC. Her role as a research specialist was to design research for evaluating programs and initiatives within the agency and make recommendations for improving its policies and practices for supervising offenders in the community.

In May 2001, Hass was directed to identify and develop an intervention that would better address the issue of re-arrest among violent and drug-related offenders. The aim was to find out how law enforcement workers can better supervise offenders in the community to make them more accountable and responsible citizens, thereby reducing their chances of getting in trouble or being re-arrested. Hass began addressing this question by developing a profile for a sample of 36 offenders (30 probationers and six parolees) under some form of community supervision who were re-arrested in October, November, and December 2000.

An analysis of the gathered demographic data revealed that the majority of offenders in the sample were young, single, African American males. They were either unemployed or underemployed, with very little education and unstable housing arrangements, making multiple moves in a short period of time. Moreover, the overwhelming majority of offenders in the sample had a history of violent behavior and drug-related offenses. Approximately 60 percent of the offenders under probation supervision had prior convictions for violent offenses, and 93 percent had prior convictions for drug-related offenses. Virtually all those under parole supervision had a violent felony conviction.

The study also examined patterns and trends in the type of re-arrest, day and time of re-arrest, and time frame of re-arrest. More than 80 percent of offenders were re-arrested for violent and drug-related offense, with almost 90 percent of offenders being re-arrested within the first year of their period of supervision, and over 50 percent within the first six months. Another significant finding was that the vast majority of offenders were re-arrested during the daytime on a weekday.[38]

This research suggested that providing offenders with a program designed to increase accountability and structure their environment and daily routine was fundamental to reducing re-arrest among violent and drug-related offenders under community supervision. As a result of the findings, CSOSA began the Day Reporting Center Program, which was designed as a one-stop place where select offenders on probation or parole supervision would report on a frequent and regular basis. The goal of the program was to provide offenders with a greater intensity of services, focusing on education, vocational training, job placement assistance, drug treatment and screening.

By increasing surveillance and providing a variety of services, the day reporting center gave offenders a greater sense of responsibility, made them more accountable for their time and activities, and provided them with the opportunity to become more successful during their period of community supervision—an achievement that will serve the ultimate goal of reducing their re-involvement in criminal activity.

LOOKING AHEAD: EVIDENCE-BASED CRIMINAL JUSTICE POLICY

As we mentioned earlier, reliable data have the power to shape and influence the course of crime-control policy. But educating policymakers and the public about scientific research findings in criminal justice issues is no easy task. Unless conclusions and suggestions for social change agree with what people already believe, they are often disregarded as irrelevant, flawed, or extremist.

This means future criminology researchers must strive to produce legitimate and consistent results that clearly support the policy changes they recommend. The goal is not to perpetuate policies that are shortsighted, ineffective, or counterproductive but rather to alleviate the problem of crime. This goal can be accomplished only if criminal justice policy initiatives are guided by a thorough review of the literature and driven by research evidence that supports the theoretical wisdom of planned changes and reforms. (The Connecting Research to Practice feature gives an example of how research can lead to tangible change.) The results of high-quality evaluative studies of criminology must be integrated into the decision-making practices of policymakers and legislators. Only then can criminal justice policy reflect the empirical evidence of what works and what does not.

Experimental criminology is one relatively new tool for reaching this goal. Experimental criminology relies on transforming subjective evidence into more reliable objective data by conducting randomized, controlled experiments in a social setting. The idea is to ensure research findings are more valid by using experimentation to create a stronger tie between causes and effects.[39]

In a randomized experimental study, researchers Lawrence Sherman and Heather Strang conducted a series of experiments to test the effects of a restorative justice program on offenders with a wide range of offenses, in different correctional settings and at various stages in the criminal justice system.[40] (Restorative justice is an approach to justice that focuses on repairing the harm committed by a criminal act; offenders are required to make direct reparations to the victims as well as to the community. We will explore this further in Chapter 10.) Experiments were designed to evaluate the impact of participating in the restorative justice program on adult offenders. Sherman and Strang's study provides evidence to support the restorative justice model as a viable component of criminal justice practice.[41]

For decades the federal government has provided funding for programs and initiatives promising to provide solutions to the problem of crime. Now more than ever, these programs are being held accountable and need demonstrable results in order to ensure continued funding. The scientific guidance of research in the field of criminology has become a valuable tool in producing evidence-based findings about what works, what does not work, and what is promising.

experimental criminology

Transforms subjective evidence into more reliable objective data by conducting randomized, controlled experiments in a social setting.

SUMMARY

■ **How is criminology scientific?**

Criminology is a science. It relies on the scientific method to study crime, crime facts, and criminal behavior. Conclusions are made based on observations that are grounded in research methods established for the collection of data and the gathering of facts. This is what differentiates the science of criminology from expressions of public opinion, media hype, and political rhetoric.

■ **How do scientific theories help us understand the real world?**

Explanations of phenomena that are arrived at through scientific methods allow us to better understand the world and to formulate theories that are based on scientific research. This is the role of criminological theory: to establish an understanding of criminal behavior that accounts for crime causation based on factual, scientific data and not on assumptions derived from misguided, biased, and distorted portrayals of individuals who violate the law.

■ **What makes a theory "good"?**	Theories that are scientifically useful—that is, logically consistent, testable, valid, and objective—are good theories. Scientific theories are systematic expressions of observations that are predictive and tentative. They must be stated in a way that makes them subject to correction, scrutiny, and revision.
■ **What are the various research methods that help us do criminological research?**	In this chapter, we have examined the various strategies that are used to conduct scientific research: surveys, fieldwork, experiments, and using existing information. Each strategy provides a unique approach to the gathering of data. The selection of a research method must take into consideration practical issues such as time, location, and availability, as well as the design of the project and the personal preference of the researcher.
■ **What are the specific stages to follow when conducting scientific research?**	An effective research study must follow the various steps of the scientific method: define the problem, conduct a thorough literature review, formulate a hypothesis, collect and analyze the data, develop a conclusion, and share the results with other individuals in the scientific community.
■ **When do we have to consider issues of privacy and confidentiality in research?**	Very often, research in the field of criminology uses human beings as the subject of inquiry. For this reason, social scientific inquiry must adhere to the highest standards of ethics in research. Protecting the privacy of research subjects must take precedence over the researcher's desire to obtain data.
■ **How does research guide criminal justice policy?**	The end product of the scientific endeavor is a reliable body of descriptions and explanations that can effectively guide criminal justice policy and practice. Yet crime and delinquency are social phenomena that continue to intrigue scientists and resist description and explanation. Still, we can draw on these guiding principles for our study of crime from the history of science.

CRITICAL THINKING QUESTIONS

1. If some people steal because they do not have enough money to buy what they want, then why do those who do have enough money to buy what they want also steal? How can you use the scientific approach to study this apparent paradox?

2. Would most people commit crime if they knew they would not get caught? Does the answer to that question change, depending on the type of crime? Would some people commit murder? What about robbery or rape? What about driving above the speed limit or cheating on taxes? How would you design a survey in which you assess the involvement of college students in certain types of criminal activities? What would their answers tell us about the fear of punishment versus the desire to obey the rules when considering the commission of different types of crime?

3. Crime makes us angry. It hurts, destroys, and often shocks our understanding of the world around us. In light of public opinion and media sensationalizing about crime-related facts, how can you be objective in conducting criminological research? How can you set aside your own personal biases to ensure the scientific accuracy of your data? Are some research methods less bias-prone than others? Why?

4. You are conducting a series of interviews with known gang members. What obstacles do you face in conducting such a research study? What steps do you take to ensure the privacy of your subjects? How can you make sure the data you gather remains anonymous? When does the scale of balance tip in favor of ethical research over the dissemination of useful information?

ADDITIONAL RESOURCES

You can learn more about ethics and social scientific research by visiting the Academy of Criminal Justice Sciences website at http://www.acjs.org/pubs/167_671_2922.cfm

To learn more about the growing field of experimental criminology, visit the Academy of Experimental Criminology website at http://www.crim.upenn.edu/aec/about.htm

The Science Buddies website has information on the scientific method (http://www.sciencebuddies.org/mentoring/project_scientific_method.shtml), variables to consider as part of your research project (http://www.sciencebuddies.org/mentoring/project_variables.shtml), and how to write a research plan (http://www.sciencebuddies.org/mentoring/project_background_research_plan.shtml).

Additional Readings

American Society of Criminology. (n.d.) *Draft code of ethics,* sec. II, para. 7, unpublished manuscript.

Barr, W. P. (1992, July 29). *Crime, poverty, and the family.* Heritage Lecture 401.

Chambliss, W. J. (1989). State-organized crime. *Criminology, 27,* 183–208.

Cohen, B. (1989). *Developing sociological knowledge: Theory and method* (2nd ed.). Chicago: Nelson-Hall.

Handon, N. R. (1968). *Patterns of discovery.* London: Cambridge University Press.

Hoover, K. R. (1992). *The elements of social scientific thinking* (5th ed.). New York: St. Martin's.

Kubrin, C. E., & Weitzer, R. (2003). New directions in social disorganization theory. *Journal of Research in Crime and Delinquency, 40,* 374–402.

Popper, K. (1963). *Conjectures and refutations: The growth of scientific knowledge.* New York: Basic Books.

Thompson, E. P. (1975). *Whigs and hunters: The origin of the Black Act.* London: Alan Lane.

van den Berghe, P. (1963). Dialectic and functionalism: Toward a theoretical synthesis. *American Sociological Review, 28,* 695–705.

Whyte, W. F. (1943). *Street corner society: The social structure of an Italian slum.* Chicago: University of Chicago Press.

Whyte, W. F. (1991). *Participatory action research.* Newbury Park, CA: Sage.

Wilson, W. J. (1987). *The truly disadvantaged: The inner city, the underclass, and public policy.* Chicago: University of Chicago Press.

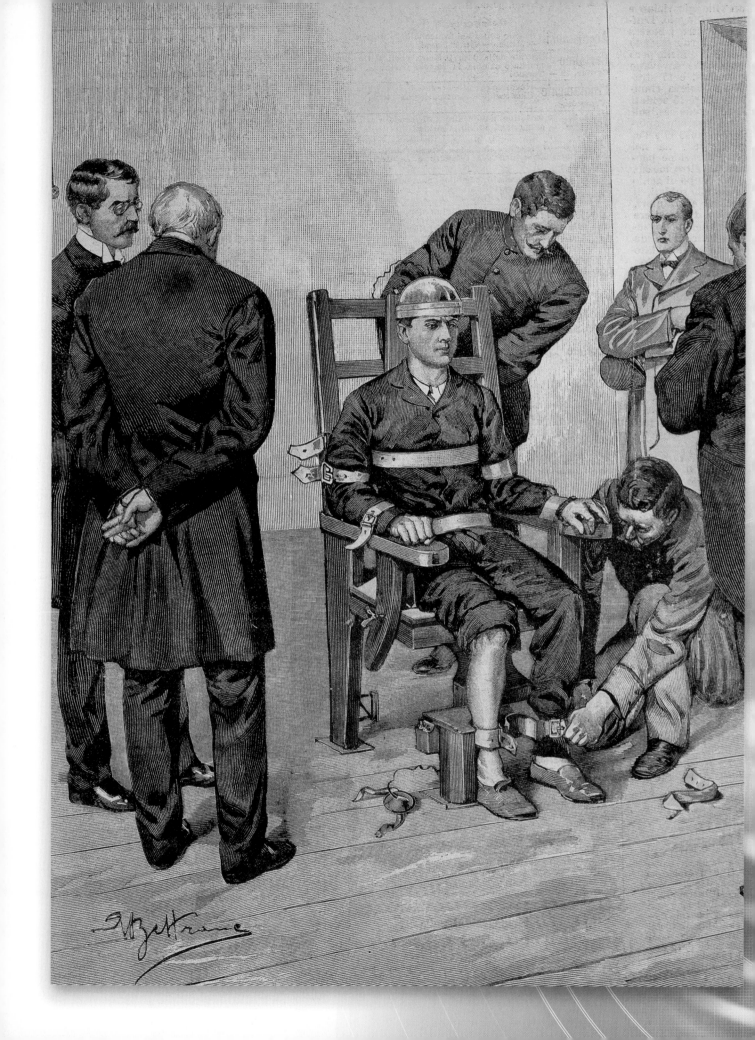

5

CRIME AS RATIONAL BEHAVIOR

Classical and Rational Choice Theories

In this chapter, we will explore the following questions:

- How did people explain criminal behavior in the past?
- In what ways did the Enlightenment change society's view of crime?
- What does classical theory tell us about why people break the law?
- Do individuals actually choose to engage in criminal activities?
- How did rational choice theory expand our understanding of crime causation?
- Does crime always make sense?
- What are the policy implications of classical and rational

Do individuals who break the law act recklessly and

impulsively, or are their actions based on reasoning and calculations of risk and yield? Harry King was a well-known "boxman"; his specialty was opening safes. He enjoyed his life of crime and accepted prison sentences when they came as "the price you pay." With money obtained by robbing grocery stores, banks, and restaurants, King would spend tens of thousands on a weekend in Las Vegas, buy his current girlfriend a house (cash down), wear expensive suits, and lavish money on friends and strangers alike. If arrested, he relied on lawyers to get him out on bail. If he had no money, he would immediately commit another "caper" to get the $10,000 or $20,000 to pay the bail bondsman's fee, compensate his lawyer, and make whatever bribes to judges and prosecutors he needed to have his case "fixed."[1]

Harry King hardly fits the popular image of a desperate and irrational criminal. On the contrary, he very carefully calculated his criminal endeavors, weighing the benefits from his thefts against the consequences of getting caught and doing time in prison. King does not blame his behavior on circumstances or his upbringing. Instead, he explains:

> *I never could blame my life on my parents. I mean, I could sit down and talk about it and say if it hadn't been for my mother I wouldn't have been a thief. . . . I can't say that . . . if you're built one way you're going to live that way . . . you know? There's nothing going to change it. It's just like why don't you go opening safes? I didn't know how to steal when I started, but I was inclined that way, or I wouldn't have done it.[2]*

Harry King's career seems to support the theory that crime is rational behavior, and therefore, in order to deter criminals, we must make the consequences of crime—punishment—outweigh its benefits.

In "Deterring Delinquents: A Rational Choice Model of Theft and Violence," researchers used data collected by the Denver Youth Survey, a study of juvenile delinquency and drug use in high-risk neighborhoods, to analyze key variables that affect rational choice and the decision to engage in acts of violent crime and theft. Their findings support a rational choice model of criminal behavior. The decision to engage in criminal acts of violence and theft is largely based on the offender's perception of the cost of the crime, such as certainty of arrest, and the potential reward of the crime, such as monetary gain or the respect of peers. The study suggests that we look at criminal behavior using the individual rational actor as the starting point and then explore the variable effects of social and structural variables such as education, peer group interaction, and opportunity that may intervene in the decision to engage in criminal behavior.[3]

As we saw in Chapter 4, theories answer questions, clarify relationships between events, and provide causal explanations for them. They tell us why or how the facts we observe are as they are. In this chapter, we begin to answer our questions about crime and its causes by looking at the theory of crime that is most closely linked to the concept of punishment in our society. We will study criminal behavior from the point of view that individuals *choose* to engage in it, and that to stop it we must influence this choice. We begin with the story of how criminological theory emerged.

Harry King was a professional thief. As a safecracker, he ranked high within the criminal hierarchy of burglars. His exploits were well planned and carefully executed—not those of your typical criminal.

EARLY EXPLANATIONS OF CRIME

Before the birth of scientific criminology, explanations of crime were based on religious concepts such as sin and evil, or utilitarianism, the idea that people calculated the relative likelihood of pleasure and pain in deciding how to act. In England as recently as the 19th century, criminal indictments accused the defendant of having been provoked by the devil and not being God-fearing.[4]

The Middle Ages and the Renaissance

Throughout history, explanations of crime and deviance centered on moral and religious ideas of good and evil. For cosmic events such as plagues, wars, and floods that bring devastation to many, and for single acts of violence that affect a few, society has sought explanations in the form of some sort of evil or the vengeful actions of angry gods.

Thus, efforts to control and prevent crime and deviance also focused on supernatural intervention to remove the evil forces residing within the individual.[5] In the Middle Ages and the Renaissance, individuals often brought loved ones believed to be tormented by some form of evil or demon to the church, hoping members of the clergy would perform an **exorcism,** a practice of prayers and rituals to literally evict the demon from the individual's body. Another attempt to control crime and deviance was surgical penetration of the skull to allow the release of evil spirits residing within the individual's mind.

Since criminal behavior was regarded as being caused by demons and other wicked spirits, the punishment of those determined to be guilty of criminal acts was seen as directed toward those evil forces and not the individual. Thus, punishments were harsh and severe, including physical torture to force confession, beatings and other forms of corporal punishment, public humiliation, and death. Religious explanations of crime and deviance dominated until the Enlightenment ushered in new methods of scientific inquiry.

The Enlightenment

The 17th- and 18th-century period of the **Enlightenment,** also known as the *Age of Reason,* was an era of inspired innovative thinking and a search for truth using philosophical reasoning.[6] European philosophers

exorcism

A practice of prayers and rituals to literally evict a demon from the individual's body.

Enlightenment

Also known as the Age of Reason, a 17th- and 18th-century period of inspired innovative thinking and a search for truth using philosophical reasoning.

Before criminology offered scientific explanations of criminal behavior, people blamed crime on evil spirits and demonic possession.

105

John Locke (*left*) was an English philosopher and physician and is widely regarded as the father of the Enlightenment. Locke questioned principles of knowledge and truth, laying the foundation for modern liberalism. Locke's writing influenced other great Enlightenment philosophers, such as Voltaire (*center*) and Jean-Jacques Rousseau (*right*).

such as Jean-Jacques Rousseau (1712–1778), Voltaire (1694–1778), and John Locke (1632–1704) challenged the prevailing social institutions of education, law, and religion on the grounds that they perpetuated ignorance and superstition while inhibiting progress. Hallmarks of the Enlightenment era include ideas about the intricate yet comprehensible nature of the universe and about how we can understand it through intellectual reasoning and scientific inquiry.

The Enlightenment had a significant impact on moral and social reform. It encouraged the use of logic, reason, fairness, and justice, leading writers and scholars to challenge existing authority as they extended the concept of human rights to include common citizens. No longer was the government or the church the ultimate source of knowledge and understanding. Fate was in the hands of each individual, with personal choices defining human destiny. As social and government institutions came under drastic reform, the practices defining crime and punishment were no exception.

PRINCIPLES OF CLASSICAL THEORY

With the Enlightenment came several new ideas about the reasons for criminal behavior, as well as how to handle the criminals themselves. Entire philosophies developed around the issues of explaining crime, as we see below.

Beccaria and the Idea of Free Will

One challenger to traditional explanations of crime was Cesare Beccaria (1738–1794), who in 1764 published his classic work, "Essay on Crimes and Punishments."[7] Rather than seeing crime as a manifestation of sin, or of demons in possession of a person's mind and soul, Beccaria looked for a more practical explanation: crime as a wrong and immoral behavior driven by personal human choices.

Beccaria noted that all individuals possess free will and are therefore capable of making rational choices and calculated decisions. They will always look out for their own benefit, which may include engaging in crime and deviance. In this proposition, Beccaria saw the relationship between crime and the law. According to Beccaria, the function of the law is to preserve the social order and curb the deviant and criminal behavior that individuals with free will and rational choice might commit in the pursuit of personal pleasure.

With both individual actors and the social order seeking to satisfy their opposing goals, a clash of interests is inevitable. However, because human behavior is rational, it is also predictable and therefore controllable by punishment. The right punishment, or even just the threat of it, is enough to control the rational decision whether to engage in criminal behavior. The question is, what punishment is right?

We can think of Beccaria's writings as a philosophy of punishment rather than as a theory of crime. Beccaria argued against the cruel and arbitrary punishments that existed during his time, maintaining that physical torture and capital punishment were uncivilized and motivated by a desire for revenge; furthermore, they did not deter crime. In Beccaria's view, then, punishment is a means to an end—crime prevention—and not an end in itself. For punishment to effectively deter crime, Beccaria argued, it must be swift, certain, and proportionate to the crime (Figure 5.1).[8] Let's see why.

We can associate punishment with a particular behavior only if the consequence is *swift,* immediately following the behavior itself. A child who breaks the family's rule by grabbing a cookie before dinner gets an immediate time-out of 10 minutes, effectively associating the time alone with the deed itself. Waiting several hours to impose the punishment weakens the link between the punishment and the behavior.

For punishment to be *certain,* the actor must believe the consequence will actually happen if the behavior takes place. Punishments that are threatened but not enforced will have little deterrent effect on an individual's behavior. (The Connecting Theory to Practice feature explores the questions of certain punishment on crime deterrence in Texas.)

Finally, punishment must be *proportionate* to the crime, not only in quantity but also in quality, meaning the consequences of criminal behavior must somehow be related to the weight or seriousness of the crime. Punishments that outweigh the harm caused by an individual's actions are not only unjust but fail to serve the goal of deterrence. Punishments must be severe enough only to outweigh the benefit or pleasure derived from engaging in the criminal act.

Beccaria also advocated equity and fairness in the treatment of those accused of a crime, urging citizens to protect one another by discouraging a vigilante type of justice. Instead, he called for a system of justice that protected the rights of the accused, presuming their innocence until the necessary requirements for guilt were established in a court of law. Beccaria's theories and proposals paved the way for many legal and social science writers who followed him, including Jeremy Bentham.

The rational behavior of criminals is portrayed in *Ocean's 13,* a Hollywood movie about a highly calculated, scrupulously thought-out heist of a casino.

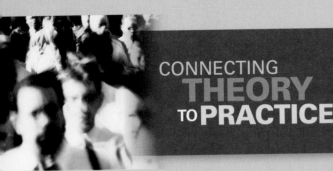
Whether you are starting a new job, shopping at a grocery store, beginning a new semester, or visiting a state park, your behavior is governed by formal and informal rules about what you can and cannot do. Rules help you understand what is expected. Without them, you would be in a state of chaos and confusion, unable to function in your environment.

Just as important to governing your behavior as is understanding the rules is *knowing* what will happen if you violate them. If you are *certain* of the consequences, you feel a level of safety and control. Imagine your boss told you that sometimes you would get paid and sometimes not, or your professor said sometimes she will grade tests and sometimes she won't. How would that make you feel about going to work every day or doing the readings for your class? You can make a rational decision about how to behave only if you truly know the outcome. Thus, the quality of punishment most closely associated with inhibiting a behavior is *certainty*.

During the 1990s, the crime rate in Texas fell to the lowest rate since 1974. Some have attributed the decline to significant changes in sentencing practices, prompted by an expansion of prisons to accommodate more offenders. Longer sentences became a certainty for violent criminals, under guidelines that required them to serve 75 percent of their sentences before release instead of 30 percent. Between 1990 and 1999, the certainty of serving time and expected sentence length for murder went up 213 percent, for rape 243 percent, and for aggravated assault 300 percent. Moreover, new crime-prevention strategies aimed at expanding the number of jail and prison beds, making it more difficult to be released on bond and limiting the use of early release, increased the probability of serving time in prison after being arrested and convicted of a crime. In fact, the ratio of prisoners to population in Texas rose 143 percent during the 1990s.

With more offenders behind bars, and with time served tripling on average, should we be surprised to see a decline in the crime rate? Is the decline a side effect of having more criminals off the street, or are the tougher punishments affecting the rational choices of potential offenders by allowing them to take certainty into account?[9]

Bentham and the Classical School

Classical School

A school of criminology that holds that people calculate the rewards and risks of their actions and decide how to act based on what they believe will bring them the most pleasure and the least pain.

The writings of the English jurist Jeremy Bentham (1784–1832) characterized what we today call the **Classical School** of criminology. The Classical School holds that people calculate the rewards and risks of their actions and decide how to act based on what they believe will bring them the most pleasure and the least pain. Let's take a closer look at the basic ideas of classical theory.

In his "Introduction to the Principles of Morals and Legislation," Bentham describes human nature as governed by the desire to maximize pleasure and minimize pain,

FIGURE **5.1**

Beccaria on Punishment— A Means to an End?

Punishment

Swift (immediately follows behavior)

Certain (will definitely happen)

Proportionate to crime (does not outweigh harm done)

Deterrence

FIGURE **5.2**

Pleasure Versus Pain: A Dilemma of Choice

a principle also called **hedonism.**[10] Inspired by Enlightenment thinking, Bentham believed all human beings are fundamentally rational and therefore will weigh the pain caused by punishment against the benefit or pleasure derived from the criminal act (Figure 5.2). Bentham therefore agreed with Beccaria that the goal of punishment should be to deter individuals from future crimes. He also agreed that in order for punishment to have a deterrent effect, it must be swift and certain and strike a careful balance by being painful enough to outweigh the rewards associated with the criminal endeavor.

In Bentham's view, human beings are in a constant dialog with themselves, weighing the possible consequences of their actions before following through with their behavior. To a large extent, we do engage in this dialog, countless times a day. Should I eat dessert, or will that ruin my diet? Should I go out with my friends, or will that not give me enough time to study for finals? Should I buy that expensive phone, or will it break my budget? The scenarios we play out in our minds are driven by our desire to increase our happiness and reduce our distress (Table 5.1).

However, because we are all different and attach different meanings to our experiences, Bentham argues that the value we associate with any given pleasure, as well as our desire to avoid pain, is governed by the sensation's intensity, duration, certainty, and immediacy.[11] *Intensity* of pleasure or pain is the degree to which an act is pleasant or painful, time and time again. *Duration* is a function of how long it lasts, and *certainty* refers to the probability it will happen. Finally, *immediacy* describes the closeness between the act and the associated pleasure or pain.

Bentham expands our understanding of how hedonism influences our rational decisions. He shows us a glimpse of the human struggle to do the right thing, while at the same time balancing the need to maximize pleasure and minimize pain.

Evaluating Classical Theory

Classical theory and the works of Beccaria and Bentham shaped the course of criminological theory for hundreds of years, and they continue to play an important role in debates about the origins of criminal behavior and the social response to it. But critics

hedonism

The principle that human nature is governed by the desire to maximize pleasure and minimize pain.

TABLE **5.1**

Calculating Pleasure Versus Pain

WHEN YOU . . .	WHAT DO YOU TAKE INTO CONSIDERATION?
Go to work late	Catching up on much-needed sleep versus getting fired
Study for a test	Getting a good grade versus missing out on a party
Drink with your friends	Staying out late and having fun versus missing class the next day and losing attendance points
Exercise	Having a healthy, lean body versus being tired and sweaty
Buy something expensive	Watching a football game on your new flat screen TV versus going into debt and not having enough money for necessities
Eat dessert	The taste of chocolate in your mouth versus the extra hour at the gym you will have to spend to burn it off
Take drugs	Getting high, partying, and gaining peer approval versus risking your health and your career if you get caught

Dorothea Puente, a notorious serial killer, was sentenced to life in prison without the possibility of parole in 1993 at the age of 64. Puente was convicted of the murders of three of the tenants who lived in her Sacramento home. She took in elderly and disabled boarders, then killed them and buried them in her backyard to collect their government checks and buy luxuries. What does classical theory suggest about the hedonistic calculations she might have failed to assess?

observed that they could not entirely account for criminal behavior, because individuals do not always weigh the costs and benefits of their actions. Classical theory approaches the study of criminal behavior from a simplistic point of view that places too much emphasis on the value of free will and personal choice in the decision to engage in crime. We can hardly imagine how situations riddled with emotions such as jealousy, anger, and rage can escalate into violence as the product of a rational calculation of pleasure and pain.[12]

Classical theory emerged during a time when society was redefining the value of punishment as a deterrent. While it made sense for the cost of crime to outweigh the benefits, classical theorists overlooked the simple fact that people do not always agree on what constitutes pleasure and pain. There is no universal formula that policymakers can employ to determine what and how much punishment is painful enough to deter crime or to make it less attractive or pleasurable.[13] For example, for an unemployed, homeless youth it may be worth the risk of spending six months in jail to steal money from a cash register at a convenience store, but those same consequences may not be worthwhile for a college student tempted to cash a stolen check.

Finally, classical theory has been criticized for its failure to take into account the wide array of variables that affect an individual's decision to engage in crime. These include innate differences in biological and psychological makeup, as well as variations in the social experiences that shape us. Some people are quick to anger while others are patient until sufficiently provoked. It was this need to identify and isolate the individual traits that create variations in criminal behavior that inspired the rise of positivist theories.

Positivism uses the scientific method to research biological, psychological, and social variables within the individual, and in his or her immediate social environment, to uncover the root causes of criminal behavior.[14] Positivist theorists focus on forces beyond the individual's control—heredity, genetics, psychological trauma, abuse, socialization, peer influences, economic deprivation—as contributing to crime and delinquency. Rejecting the notion of free will and choice, positivists argue that the only solution to the problem of crime is to address the conditions that lead to criminality. Essentially, individuals who break the law are in need of rehabilitation, as they have been victims of the circumstances that led to their involvement in crime.

We will discuss positivist theories in greater detail in chapters to come. For now, we turn to an examination of rational choice theory, which, ironically, represented a reaction against positivism and led to a resurgence of classical ideas about personal responsibility and choice.

PRINCIPLES OF RATIONAL CHOICE THEORY

In the 1970s, positivism came under attack on the grounds that it shifted responsibility for crime from the individual to experience and the social environment, placing a greater burden on society to correct those conditions. A surge of research studies showed the apparent failure of offenders to change and become rehabilitated, regardless of the interventions tried.[15] At the same time, growing public fear of crime and a movement to get tough on criminals swung the pendulum back to focus on individual choice and personal responsibility. Criminal justice policies began once again to reflect the idea that individuals were accountable for their criminal choices, and punishment became viewed as the deserved outcome of offenders' poor decisions.[16] Classical theory was reborn in the rational choice model.

Rational Choice Theory

Rational choice theory emerged in the late 1970s and early 1980s, resurrecting some of the major ideas of classical theory and its emphasis on the conscious decision to engage in criminal behavior.[17] Rational choice theory retained the Classical School's central notion of free will, but it recognized that certain circumstances may affect the exercise of personal choice. It views criminals as reasoning human beings who evaluate the total circumstances before choosing to participate in acts that violate the law, including their own *personal circumstances* (experiences, needs, wants, desires); *situational factors* (type of security barriers, efficiency of law enforcement); *risk of getting caught;* seriousness of expected punishment (such as life in prison); and *value of expected yield* (monetary gain or benefit, desired approval by a group). Thus, rational choice theorists see the decision to commit crime

positivism

A criminological approach that uses the scientific method to research biological, psychological, and social variables within the individual, and in his or her immediate social environment, to uncover the root causes of criminal behavior.

rational choice theory

A criminological approach that retains classical theory's view of free will but recognizes that circumstances may affect the exercise of personal choice.

On April 29, 1992, a jury acquitted four police officers accused in the videotaped beating of black motorist Rodney King following a high-speed pursuit. In the days following the announcement of the verdict, thousands of Los Angeles residents took to the streets in protest, rioting and looting, and committing acts of violence including assault, arson, and murder. How does rational choice theory explain mob behavior?

offense specific

Within rational choice theory, variables that are related to the offense.

offender specific

Within rational choice theory, variables that are related to the offender.

situational choice theory

A variation of rational choice theory that argues that the individual decision to engage in criminal activities is shaped by the opportunities, risks, and benefits—the situation—attached to certain types of crimes.

as influenced by two types of variables: those related to the offense, **offense specific,** and those related to the offender, **offender specific.** Table 5.2 lists a variety of questions rational choice theorists suggest an individual may contemplate in evaluating the cost and benefit of a criminal enterprise.

We are still left with a big question: What places individuals in circumstances where they make such choices? If you are running behind in paying your bills and are short on cash, do you go out and rob a bank, sell drugs, or commit a theft? What makes these options for some individuals? The following two variations of rational choice theory offer us some answers.

Situational Choice Theory

Situational choice theory argues that the individual decision to engage in criminal activities is shaped by the opportunities, risks, and benefits—the *situation*—attached to certain types of crimes.[18] Situations will vary according to time, location, personal circumstances, who is there, and what is going on.[19] These variables provide individuals with a context within which they rationally calculate the decision to violate the law. Thus, crime is not just a matter of motivation or opportunity but rather a complex interaction between the two.[20] *Motivation* is as diverse as human beings are and may "flow from temptation, bad company, idleness, or provocation."[21] *Opportunity* is equally distinct and takes into account the opportunity for financial reward, knowledge of criminal techniques, and personal experiences.

To choose to engage in certain types of criminal behavior, an individual must see the criminal enterprise as paying off despite the possible risks, like getting caught. Researchers note that individuals will continue to engage in illegal activities only if they perceive the enterprise as attractive.[22] Moreover, studies suggest the existence of a lucrative opportunity will increase the chances of an individual's deciding to act.[23] (The Consider This feature gives us an example of an unusual decision-making process.)

Can someone choose to traffic marijuana across the Mexican border into the United States without knowing the intricate mechanisms necessary to carry out this illegal activity? Can someone wake up one day disillusioned with the government, bent on destruction,

TABLE **5.2**

Rational Choice Theory: Variables in Evaluating Criminal Choice		
THINKING ABOUT COMMITTING . . .	**OFFENDER-SPECIFIC VARIABLES**	**OFFENSE-SPECIFIC VARIABLES**
Theft from a retail store	How desperate am I for money or other items of value?	How much will I benefit from this crime?
Burglarizing a home	Am I physically and mentally capable of carrying out the crime?	Do I have what I need to successfully carry out this crime: equipment, weapons, lookouts, a method of escape/getting away?
Fencing stolen property	Is there a better, more legitimate alternative I can resort to?	Will anyone be watching: occupants, neighbors, crimewatch groups?
Stealing a car	What will I do if I get caught?	How effective are the police in this neighborhood?
Committing armed robbery	Am I willing to handle the punishment that may come with this crime?	Are there other barriers such as dogs, alarms, or fences to overcome?

CONSIDER THIS...   Ivy League Call Girl

How far will people go to violate the law when a lucrative criminal opportunity presents itself? What variables are likely to influence their choices?

An unlikely offender, a college teacher with a master's degree from Yale University and a doctorate in social anthropology, found herself in desperate need of money when her boyfriend ran off after emptying her checking account. With bills to pay and rent due, she began looking for part-time work to supplement her meager salary. Her situation is not uncommon, but what is unusual is what she decided to do about it. She became a high-priced prostitute working for an escort service.

Her clients were diverse. Some were single, some married, some led fulfilling lives, and others were socially inadequate. Some were polite and courteous, others were rude and abusive. They met her at bars, in motels, in their homes, on boats, and in malls. They engaged in a variety of activities including conversation, dining at fine restaurants, attending parties, and having sex. The clients all had one thing in common: They could afford to pay $200 an hour for her services.

In a revealing first-person account, the teacher describes and explains her decisions:

They used the time in a variety of ways, and that is my usual response when someone—and someone will, inevitably, in any conversation about the profession—says something judgmental about the perceived degradation of exchanging sex for money. Because, in my experience, that doesn't make sense. You think I'm just manipulating semantics here, don't you? I'm not: Hear me out. Many people are paid by the hour, right? An employer hires a consultant, for example, on the basis of certain areas of expertise the consultant can offer. The employer—or client—pays for the consultant's time by the hour. A call girl is a consultant, using her expertise and experience in seduction and giving pleasure to fulfill a verbal contract with a client who is paying her by the hour. She is a skilled professional possessing knowledge for which there is a demand and for which the client is willing to pay her a predetermined rate.[24]

Did it make sense for this university professor to become a prostitute? Was her decision rational?

What do you think?

and instantly decide, "I am going to become a paramilitary special tactics official in a terrorist organization"?

Although these examples sound extreme, criminal opportunities are created by a knowledge of the necessary skills and techniques, an understanding of the limitations and risks, and a means of avoiding detection. Studies show training in effective criminal techniques often precedes the decision to carry out a crime.[25] Certainly, skill, knowledge, and understanding motivated Dennis Nikrasch to steal $6 million dollars from Las Vegas casinos in the late 1990s through an intricate scheme that included rigging mechanical slot machines. Investigators still wish they knew how he did it.[26]

Routine Activities Theory

Routine activities theory, the second variation of rational choice theory, argues that victim and offender lifestyles contribute to both the amount and type of crime within society.[27] The volume and distribution of certain types of predatory crimes, such as robbery, depend on three characteristics of the average U.S. lifestyle, as shown in Figure 5.3 and described below.[28]

- *Presence of motivated offenders:* A large population of individuals who are unemployed, underemployed, or idle, and who want money or other valued goods.
- *Availability of suitable targets:* Individuals, homes, vehicles, grocery stores, and convenience markets that are easily accessible and provide the goods motivated offenders want.

routine activities theory

A variation of rational choice theory that argues that victim and offender lifestyles contribute to both the amount and type of crime within society.

FIGURE **5.3**

The Three Variables of Routine Activities Theory

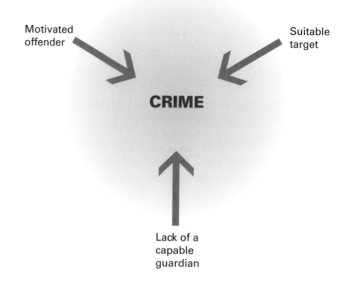

Motivated offender

Suitable target

CRIME

Lack of a capable guardian

- *Absence of capable guardians:* Individuals such as homeowners, police, and friends, and barriers, such as security alarms and locks, that can discourage the decision to engage in crime.

Routine activities theory sees criminal behavior as the dynamic interplay between opportunity and the lifestyle of both victim and offender.[29] Individuals who live in high-crime neighborhoods and do not take measures to protect themselves and their property increase their risk of victimization, while at the same time providing motivated offenders with a suitable target. Those who go to an ATM alone at night carrying expensive valuables such as jewelry increase their risk of victimization and provide motivated offenders with an easy target for perpetrating a crime.

Opportunity is also affected by the offender's lifestyle and routine activities. Individuals who live in urban communities where crime and poverty abound are more likely to learn about criminal opportunities through family, friends, peers, and their own experiences. Weapons, drugs, and a culture that tolerates violence and predatory behavior act as facilitators and may escalate a motivated offender's desire to seek a suitable target.[30]

The propositions made by rational choice theory can have a profound impact on the crime-control strategies and practices we choose, as a society. But does research support the finding that crime is rational behavior? Let's turn now to an evaluation of rational choice theories.

How do the location, hours of operation, and type of products sold make this convenience store a possible crime target?

Evaluating Rational Choice Theory

Does crime make sense? Do offenders really make active decisions to engage in criminal behavior based on a cost–benefit analysis of a criminal opportunity? The elaborate financial schemes of corporate executives, the intricate mechanisms behind technology scams, and the market analyses and profit-and-loss assessments made by international drug cartels are all testimony to the rational, calculated decisions some offenders undertake when engaging in criminal activities. The decision to commit a burglary is guided, theorists say, by careful considerations about the best house to target, patterns of vacancy established by occupants and neighbors, methods and ease of entry, type of goods inside, and means of getting out quickly.[31]

More difficult to explain, however, are the acts of violent offenders that often seem the product of desperation, poor judgment, irrational thinking, emotions, misguided beliefs, and mental instability. In 2004, Marcus Wesson shot and killed nine members of his own family in Fresno, California. In 2005 in Florida, John Evander Couey abducted and raped 9-year-old Jessica Lunsford, then murdered her by burying her alive. Are these acts of violence the calculated decisions of rational individuals who somehow benefit from their crimes? Rational choice theorists would argue they are.

Crime expert Richard Felson maintains that even violent forms of criminal behavior take on very specific meanings and motives for the offender and are not the product of some type of mental breakdown, emotional hysteria, or randomly unbalanced decisions.[32] Violent crime is a matter of personal choice, involving very intricate planning, victim selection, a clear definition of motive, an assessment of risk involved, and a level of reasoning that takes into consideration the consequences of the act.[33] Felson argues that violence, while it may appear to be the irrational behavior of deranged individuals, actually serves very specific goals:[34]

- *Violence as a means of control:* Violent offenders often perpetrate their crimes as a way of controlling the victim's life, behavior, and sense of freedom or independence. This is often the case with perpetrators of spouse abuse and domestic assault.
- *Violence as a means of revenge:* Acts of violence may be committed to punish or get back at someone for real or perceived harm done. A type of vigilante justice, violence can be used by individuals who feel they have been wronged, injured, or mistreated, where the system of justice has not intervened in an appropriate manner.
- *Violence as a means of deterrence:* Individuals may resort to violence if they feel threatened by the hostile or provocative actions of another and believe a violent response is necessary to make it cease.
- *Violence as a means of establishing reputation:* Violence can often serve to establish a certain image, prove worth, make a statement, or gain the approval of others. Teenagers seeking the approval of and membership in a street gang sometimes engage in random attacks on individuals.

Yet, we are still left with a certain uneasiness about the purely rational nature of criminal behavior. Are famous celebrities, political figures, corporate executives, superstar athletes, and military heroes rational when they sabotage their careers, jeopardize their reputations, and face legal consequences, as well as public disproval and shame, by taking drugs, stealing, lying, cheating, and committing acts of violence and abuse? Was New York Giants superstar Plaxico Burress thinking rationally when he decided to carry a concealed weapon without a permit, getting arrested after accidentally shooting himself in the thigh at a Manhattan nightclub in November 2008, almost one year after leading his team to victory in the Super Bowl?[35] Skeptics of rational choice theory argue to the contrary.

Critics say rational choice theory oversimplifies the complexity of human interaction with the social environment. Faced with certain circumstances and situations—such as peer pressure, abuse, anger, and frustration—do some individuals even have the choice to reason effectively? When 39-year-old Claire MacDonald snapped and killed her husband one evening after suffering several years of physical, emotional, and sexual abuse, jurors agreed she had no choice and acquitted her of murder charges.[36]

Moreover, rational choice theory fails to explain the impact of socialization, poverty, and social structure on crime. A study surveyed households in a small city in Virginia, in neighborhoods with low and high crime rates, to test the effect of routine activities on patterns of property crime victimization.[37] Findings indicated routine activities theory explained 28 percent of variation in crime rates and types of crime in high-crime neighborhoods, but only 11 percent of variation in low-crime neighborhoods. High-crime neighborhoods are socially disorganized and characterized by higher rates of unemployment, poverty, family disruption, and residential mobility, thus increasing the likelihood of crime and victimization. These dynamics, the researchers argue, create a larger population of motivated offenders, reduce guardianship over property and individuals, and contribute to the presence of suitable targets.

Other critics of rational choice theory argue that it does not account for certain characteristics that may influence reasoning. Individual choices, they say, are often influenced by moral judgment, personal temperament, and character, which are not related to rationality. Many individuals eschew crime to adhere to higher standards of what they view as right. By the same token, others may engage in criminal activities due to personal characteristics that make them more excitable, impulsive, and unthinking.[38] Another factor is a combination of personal characteristics and external variables, such as the influence of drugs and alcohol. A study examining the effects of alcohol and anger on cognitive functioning showed they increased aggression and diminished the ability to distinguish between success and failure, risk and reward, and cost and benefit in the decision to engage in violent behavior.[39]

Thus, a true empirical test of rational choice theory must take into account the range of human emotions, reasoning capabilities, individual psychology, and social experiences that influence the immediate decision to engage in criminal behavior. With these limitations in mind, we consider the practical implications of both classical and rational choice theories in terms of reducing crime.

PRACTICAL APPLICATION OF CLASSICAL AND RATIONAL CHOICE THEORIES

Table 5.3 summarizes the classical and rational choice theories. Together these ideas form a single perspective that focuses on the *act* of committing a crime, as opposed to other variables such as the individual's state of mind, environmental influences like peer pressure, or experiences that teach individuals deviant norms and values. The cause of crime is a rationally calculated choice between the risk and the possible benefit. The challenge for crime control, then, is how to make criminal behavior a less attractive alternative. How can we convince potential offenders that crime does *not* pay? Crime-prevention policies and procedures that rely on the classical/rational choice perspective focus on two types of intervention: situational crime control and deterrence strategies.

Situational Crime Control

situational crime prevention

A strategy for crime control that makes crime a more difficult and costly alternative.

Assuming ordinary people engage in criminal acts after assessing the costs and benefits, crime-control policies based on **situational crime prevention** attempt to make crime a more difficult and costly alternative. These policies consider the characteristics that put people and places at greater risk of being crime targets, the situations or mechanisms that allow potential offenders to prey upon these targets, and the immediate variables that can trigger criminal acts.[40]

Developed in the early 1970s, situational crime prevention began as a method of reducing crime in high-risk neighborhoods, such as public housing, by increasing

surveillance.[41] Since then, it has focused on altering the physical and social environment within which crime takes place.[42] This strategy includes

- Increasing the effort necessary to commit the crime, such as installing immobilizers in cars or adding a photo to a credit card
- Increasing the perceived risk of committing crime by forming neighborhood watch groups or improving street lighting
- Reducing the potential rewards of the criminal act, such as by placing ink tags on garments sold in retail stores

TABLE **5.3**

SUMMARY: The Classical and Rational Choice Perspective

Definition of Crime	Crime is rational behavior.
Why Does Crime Occur? (Theory)	■ Individuals choose to engage in criminal behavior. ■ People make choices based on hedonistic calculations. ■ Rational human beings act to maximize benefit and reduce cost. ■ Crime occurs when it is a more attractive alternative than law-abiding behavior. ■ The decision to violate the law takes into account the range of constraints and opportunities. ■ The lifestyle of individuals contribute to both the amount and type of crime they engage in.
What Is the Solution to Crime? (Policy)	■ Make crime a less attractive alternative by increasing its cost to individuals. ■ Deter criminals by enacting punishments that are precise and certain.

Bank officers who place an exploding dye bag with the money taken during a robbery (detonating here in a surveillance camera image) are hoping to reduce the potential reward of the crime. Is this an effective deterrence strategy?

general deterrence

A strategy for crime control that is based on people's fear of apprehension and punishment.

determinate sentencing

A type of general deterrence, this crime-control strategy mandates a fixed sentence for every type of offense.

specific deterrence

A crime-control strategy that focus on deterring particular offenders by administering punishment that is severe enough to affect rational decision making and prevent future offenses.

mandatory minimum sentences

A specific deterrence crime-control strategy requiring fixed jail terms for specified offenses.

truth in sentencing guidelines

A specific deterrence crime-control strategy requiring that offenders serve more than 80 percent of their sentence in prison before they can be released.

- Reducing situations that provoke anger and aggression by, for example, limiting the capacity of bars and nightclubs to avoid excessive crowding
- Removing rationalizations for committing crime by setting clear rules and employing clear reminders such as "*we prosecute shoplifters*"[43]

Deterrence Strategies

The second type of crime-control strategy inspired by classical and rational choice theories focuses on punishment as deterrence. Criminologists distinguish between two types of deterrence: general and specific. The idea behind **general deterrence** is that individuals will refrain from crime if they fear apprehension and punishment. In other words, the choice to commit a deviant or criminal act will be affected by the threat of punishment. Thus, society should identify which behaviors are acceptable, which are not, and what social sanctions and punishment result from the latter.[44] General deterrence is meant to reduce crime and deviance by setting standards that announce to everyone "This is what happens when you break the law."[45] Table 5.4 poses some questions about the power of deterrence.

General deterrence strategies thus focus on preventing individuals from choosing criminal activity by influencing their rational decision-making process. Random traffic stops looking for drunk drivers, police visibility in high-crime neighborhoods, special law-enforcement task forces designed to uncover drug trafficking and gang activities, and even warnings about movie copyrights and prosecution of shoplifters are all strategies to inform the public of the consequences of violating the law.

Determinate sentencing, which mandates a fixed sentence for every type of offense, is another general deterrent. If you know the punishment for trafficking drugs is a definite 10 years in prison, you may be less willing to engage in that behavior than if the punishment can range from five to 10 years. Policies that increase the visibility of crime's consequences, such as sex offender registration, are also general deterrents—in this case they are designed to make the public aware of the shame of criminal behavior and its aftermath.[46]

In contrast to general deterrence, **specific deterrence** strategies focus on deterring particular offenders by administering punishment that is severe enough to affect rational decision making and prevent future offenses.[47] The intent is to teach criminals a lesson. Stiff fines and harsh **mandatory minimum sentences,** which require jail terms for offenses like domestic abuse and driving while intoxicated, are specific deterrence policies, for example. Another is **truth in sentencing guidelines** that require offenders to serve more than 80 percent of their sentence in prison before they can be released.

Consider the specific deterrence practices of Sheriff Joe Arpaio of the Maricopa County Office in Phoenix, Arizona, who runs a jail holding roughly 8,000 inmates. Sheriff Arpaio houses offenders in tents in the Arizona desert where summer temperatures

TABLE **5.4**

Which Punishment Would Stop You From . . .
■ Stealing from your employer?
■ Sexually assaulting a date?
■ Cheating on your taxes?
■ Speeding in a residential neighborhood?
■ Lying under oath?
■ Accepting a bribe?
What characteristics of the punishment give it deterrent value?

How are these prison conditions in Maricopa County, Arizona, examples of specific deterrence strategies?

reach 120 degrees, requires chain-gang prisoners to perform community work normally worth thousands of dollars, serves two cold meals a day of food that is surplus and often rotten, and makes inmates wear pink underwear. Arpaio defends his system by arguing that he is teaching a lesson so vivid offenders will not want to come back.[48]

Another specific deterrence practice designed to divert juvenile offenders gained popularity in the 1970s when a group of inmates serving life sentences at Rahway State Prison (now East Jersey State Prison) in New Jersey began a program called Scared Straight. The program was designed to bring youth offenders inside prison walls for a guided tour and a confrontational lecture by inmates, who would give the young people a realistic and aggressive depiction of prison life, including incidents of assault, rape, and murder. For a time Scared Straight served as a model for similar programs that hoped to turn juvenile offenders and at-risk youth from their delinquent ways. While these programs were well meant, critics point to studies showing they have no deterrent value and may in some cases increase the likelihood of offending.[49] Researchers question the merit of using scare tactics as a method for deterring future criminal behavior. That leaves us with the question, how *does* deterrence work?

To be deterred from crime, potential offenders must be convinced they will get caught and suffer the legal consequences. There cannot be any hope of getting off lightly or finding a legal loophole.[50] The punishment must be imposed with certainty, so rational individuals will refrain from criminal activities.[51] When they weigh the costs and benefits of committing a crime, potential offenders take into consideration their perceived possibility of getting caught, as well as the possibility of gain from the act.[52]

Deterrence also works when would-be offenders fear formal and informal sanctions. Studies show that individuals who take into account the shame, embarrassment, and rejection by family, friends, and peers that their criminal involvement may bring are more likely to refrain from criminal activity.[53] The Connecting Research to Practice feature discusses other policies and practices designed to deter crime.

We all refrain from certain types of behaviors because the consequences are undesirable. We stop smoking for fear of lung cancer, skip dessert to keep those extra pounds off, come home one minute before curfew so as not to lose car privileges, and file taxes on time to avoid penalties. Unattractive consequences therefore have a deterrent effect: They stop undesirable behavior. Are certain crimes and behaviors more susceptible to deterrence than others? Does deterrence work as intended?

The relationship between crime rates and deterrent measures is often difficult to establish. Most studies rely on official statistics on crime, which, as we saw in Chapter 3, can be skewed due to reporting problems, biased police practices, and organizational and political interests. It is also difficult to measure the effects of informal social controls, such as anticrime campaigns, the fear of public exposure, and losing the respect of family and peers.

Nevertheless, research on deterrence has established that severity of punishment is indeed inversely related to the level of crime. A statewide study in Texas, conducted by the National Center for Policy Analysis, found a direct correlation between the probability of imprisonment for certain types of crime and a subsequent decline in the rate of that particular crime.[54] Murder, for example, declined 23 percent between 1993 and 1997, a time during which the probability of going to prison for murder increased 17 percent. In a study of police intervention in high-risk settings, researchers found illegal drug transactions in bars declined as police tactics such as drug raids increased.[55]

These findings, while persuasive, still do not isolate the deterrent effects of punishment alone on criminal behavior. Numerous studies show fear of punishment does not account for declines in the rate of criminal activity, which are also affected by psychological variables; environmental pressures such as poverty, unemployment, and peer influences; certain values and beliefs; and misperceptions about crime and its consequences. If the relationship between crime and punishment were that simple, capital punishment—the ultimate criminal sanction—should have the strongest deterrent effect on would-be murderers. However, while murder rates may decline shortly after a widely publicized execution, they eventually go up again to even higher levels and then back down, with no net deterrent effect. And there is little evidence of a difference in murder rates between states that impose the death penalty and those that do not.

The evidence thus suggests that relying on deterrent strategies alone is not sufficient. Since punishment does not remove the underlying cause of criminal motivations and actions, it alone will not deter them.

The debate about whether deterrence strategies reduce crime will continue to rest on classical and rational choice theories. We can take from these theories many practical ideas for controlling crime and making it less attractive, but they do not supply us with a complete explanation of why crime occurs or how to prevent it. In the following chapters we will address many other promising theories that tackle the problem of crime prevention.

SUMMARY

How did people explain criminal behavior in the past?

Before the science of criminology emerged, explanations of crime and deviance focused on moral and religious definitions of right and wrong. Crime and deviance were seen as the manifestation of evil and attributed to the supernatural forces of demons and spirits.

■ **In what ways did the Enlightenment change society's view of crime?**

During the Enlightenment of the 17th and 18th centuries, scholars and philosophers developed a more logical understanding of crime based on the human capacity to choose. Challenging existing authority, they focused attention on principles of fairness and justice. Writers like Cesare Beccaria sought to account for crime as a product of human reasoning, promoting the idea of punishment as a means to an end, deterrence, and not an end in and of itself.

■ **What does classical theory tell us about why people break the law?**

Classical theory, as characterized by English jurist Jeremy Bentham, argues that human beings are rational actors who weigh the potential pleasure of engaging in crime against the potential pain of apprehension and punishment. The goal of punishment in classical theory is to deter individuals from crime by influencing their perception of the associated punishment. The ability of the law to control human behavior is increased if punishment is swift, certain, and severe enough to outweigh the benefits of the crime.

■ **Do individuals actually choose to engage in criminal activities?**

According to classical theory, individuals are the product of their own free choices to do whatever they want. Thus, individuals actually choose to engage in crime and deviance of their own will, according to the hedonistic principle of maximizing pleasure and minimizing pain.

■ **How did rational choice theory expand our understanding of crime causation?**

Rational choice theory elaborates on the relationship between personal circumstances, situational factors, and risk of getting caught in a person's evaluation of the expected benefits of a criminal act. One variation, situational choice theory, places the decision to violate the law within constraints and opportunities that vary according to time, location, personal circumstances, who is there, and what is going on. Another variation, routine choice theory, proposes that lifestyle and opportunity both contribute to the amount and type of crime within society, creating variations among motivated offenders, suitable targets, and the lack of capable guardians.

■ **Does crime always make sense?**

If all offenders were like Harry King in the chapter's opening story—making rational decisions based on a calculation of the cost and benefit of their criminal activities—the answer would be yes. The truth, however, is that crime does *not* always make sense. It does not always include careful assessment of the risks or a full understanding of the benefits. While offenders often do reason about motive, goal, means, and outcome, classical and rational choice theories fail to account for variables such as socialization, personal characteristics, moral upbringing, and environment.

■ **What are the policy implications of classical and rational choice theories?**

Policies stemming from classical and rational choice theories focus on the *act* of crime and try to alter the circumstances affecting an individual's decision to engage in criminal or deviant activity. Thus, the goal of crime-control strategies is to make the criminal act a less attractive alternative to the rational individual. This is accomplished by two means: situational crime-control strategies that focus attention on the physical, social, and environmental context within which criminal opportunities arise, and deterrence strategies aimed at getting tough on crime and criminals, convincing them that crime does not pay.

CRITICAL THINKING QUESTIONS

1. The Enlightenment brought about great changes in thinking about a variety of social issues, including crime and punishment. What trends in our current social and political climate may inspire similarly new thinking about crime causation and appropriate response to criminal behavior? What ways of reasoning about crime and justice may become obsolete? Are there punishments currently in practice that we may someday regret?

2. You are an overworked, underpaid employee in the stockroom of a major grocery store chain. You are working hard to pay off student loans, yet your extra efforts, working overtime and filling in whenever other workers slack off, are hardly recognized by company executives. Your co-worker has devised a scheme to embezzle money from the store over a period of six months that will land each of you about $50,000, after paying off the necessary employees to make sure the scheme will work and reduce the risk of getting caught. Suppose for half a minute you consider going along with the plan. What dilemmas does it pose? What choices do you make? Are you thinking rationally? What makes your thinking rational? What elements of hedonism are included in your deliberations?

3. What characteristics of a college campus increase the likelihood of criminal opportunities? Who are the motivated offenders? Who and what are the suitable targets? Why is there a lack of capable guardians? What can *decrease* the likelihood of victimization in such an environment?

4. The debate about what type of criminal punishment works is endless. Where do you stand in this debate? Do you think people would reconsider their criminal actions if the punishments included cutting the hands off thieves, flogging vandals, publicly shaming perpetrators of fraud, and castrating rapists? Would potential murderers think twice if they had seen a televised execution? Why or why not? How would you defend these types of punishments in light of spontaneous crimes that occur in the heat of the moment?

ADDITIONAL RESOURCES

Learn more about the influence of the Enlightenment on the philosophy of punishment and law in the United States by visiting http://www.international.ucla.edu/euro/article.asp?parentid=29410

For more information about the Marcus Wesson story, visit http://www.rickross.com/groups/wesson.html

For more information about the John Couey story, visit http://www.foxnews.com/story/0,2933,294371,00.html

You can learn more about the positivist approach in studying criminal behavior at http://law.jrank.org/pages/777/Crime-Definition-positivistic-approach.html

Does punishment deter? Read more on this debate at the National Center for Policy Analysis website at http://www.ncpa.org/

Visit the Center for Problem-Oriented Policing website at http://www.popcenter.org/ to learn more about situational crime prevention.

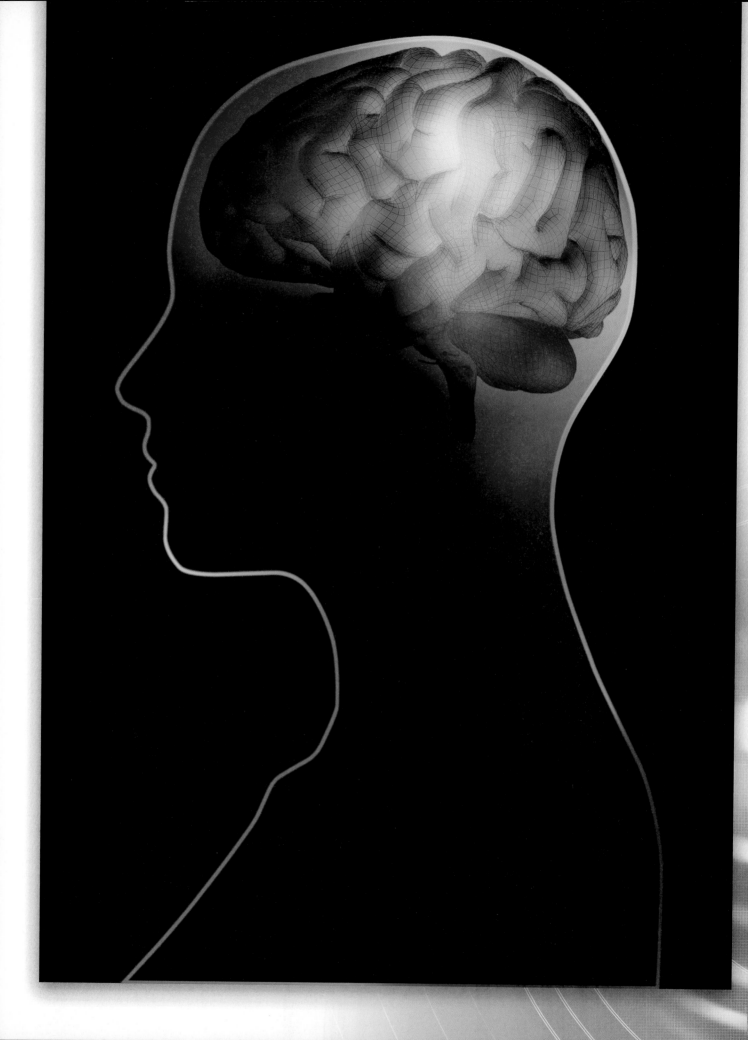

6

BIOLOGICAL THEORIES
Crime Is in the Brain

In this chapter, we will explore the following questions:

- What are the basic assumptions of biological theories of criminal behavior?

- Are certain physical features or body types related to criminality?

- Do certain chemicals in the body make people more aggressive?

- Could problems in the brain lead someone to commit murder?

- Can criminal tendencies be passed from generation to generation?

- If crime is in the brain, how do we respond to criminal behavior?

By all accounts, Daniel White, former police officer and

A notorious murder trial took place in San Francisco in 1979 when former police officer Daniel White (*left*), accused of the murders of Mayor George Moscone and Councilman Harvey Milk, was convicted of the much lesser crime of manslaughter. Although White shot both men during the day inside city hall, defense experts testified that White was not completely responsible for the murders. The jury bought the defense arguments. How could this be?

San Francisco City Councilman, was a good man and an upstanding member of the community; however, White became increasingly disgruntled at what he considered dirty politics in city hall. White's rage and frustration eventually turned deadly, and in 1979 he was sentenced in the shooting deaths of San Francisco Mayor George Moscone and fellow Councilman Harvey Milk.

The line of defense and the outcome of this case were landmarks in the field of criminology and our understanding of crime causation. White's guilt was never in question; at issue instead were his degree of responsibility and criminal intent. Based on the argument of "diminished capacity," caused by a combination of emotional and physiological variables, his defense attorneys built a case for a lesser charge than first-degree murder. Experts testified that he suffered from various symptoms of depression, compounded by the effects of consuming large amounts of refined sugar in common snack foods such as Ho Ho's and Twinkies prior to the shootings. In a pivotal moment in legal history, and what some would argue was a miscarriage of justice, jurors agreed with what became known as White's "Twinkie defense" and convicted him of voluntary manslaughter instead of the more serious charge of murder.[1]

What do we make of such explanations of violence and aggression? Is it possible that the structure and function of the human body can drive an individual to criminal behavior? Are violence and aggression waiting within us, ready to manifest as criminal behavior given the right triggers from the environment? What does the science of criminology have to say about this matter?

Studies on the biological basis of crime attempt to draw a link between traits such as impulsivity, aggression, and intelligence and criminality. Do criminals have certain common traits? Researchers note that some biological characteristics are strongly correlated with the likelihood of criminal offending.[2] These include variables such as male sex hormones, maternal smoking during pregnancy, certain brainwave patterns, and low blood sugar. A growing body of literature has found evidence of a link between low monoamine oxidase (MAO) activity and antisocial behavior.[3] MAO is an enzyme found throughout the body. These enzymes work to maintain a balance of chemicals within the brain, chemicals that affect mood and behavior. MAO activity is measured in the blood and is referred to as "platelet MAO." In a study of 483 schoolchildren around the age of 15, researchers examined the relationship among levels of MAO activity, personality, and traffic behavior. Their findings reveal that risky traffic behavior, such as drinking and driving, were strongly correlated with impulsivity and agreeableness, personality traits associated with low platelet MAO activity.[4]

This chapter examines biological perspectives in criminology, focusing on how the innate characteristics of the human body interact with forces in the environment to shape human behavior. Is it possible that we are ruled by instinct and nature, with biology and environment competing for control of our actions? Or, should we dismiss claims that reduce criminal behavior to uncontrolled, predetermined responses by the human organism? We first examine the basic premises of the biological perspective, to understand its distinct contribution to criminological theory.

MAJOR PRINCIPLES OF THE BIOLOGICAL APPROACH

The **biological perspective** on crime is built on the foundation of positivism, which presumes criminal behavior is caused by biological forces beyond an individual's control (see Chapter 5). Biological positivism rejects the notion of rational choice and free will and instead uses the scientific method to examine the basic controls of thought, behavior, and action. These are its fundamental assumptions:

- The brain controls the human mind and personality.
- The basis of human behavior is linked to a person's biological constitution.
- Differences in behavior between gender and racial groups, including differences in types and rates of criminality, are in part due to biological differences between them.
- Human behavior, including a predisposition to criminality, may be inherited. Thus, criminal tendencies can be passed down from generation to generation.
- Much of the way we behave as human beings is linked to instinctive behavioral responses similar to those of other biological organisms. Like animals, we have a desire to dominate, protect, acquire, and reproduce.
- What makes us different from other biological organisms is that our conduct, while linked to basic primitive instincts, has been disguised by modern symbolic forms of expressive behavior. A man who holds the door open for a woman or rushes to carry a heavy bag for her is practicing chivalry, a symbolic disguise for the instincts of domination and protection.
- Not all human beings are equally evolved on the developmental scale of evolution and natural selection. Those who are less evolved may behave in ways that reflect their more primitive development.
- Any comprehensive explanation of crime causation must take into account the dynamics of biology and social environment. Biology and the social environment are not mutually exclusive.

In the sections to come, we will take a close look at various competing approaches linked to specific fields within the biological and biomedical sciences, previewed in Table 6.1. We begin with an examination of early biological theories of criminal behavior.

biological perspective

In criminology, an approach built on the foundation of positivism, which presumes criminal behavior is caused by biological forces beyond an individual's control.

TABLE 6.1

Biological Perspectives on Criminal Behavior

EARLY BIOLOGICAL THEORIES	BIOCHEMICAL VARIABLES	NEUROPHYSIOLOGY	HEREDITY AND GENETICS
Criminal anthropology	Nutrition	Neurological impairment	Criminal families
Phrenology	Blood glucose	Brain chemistry	Twin studies
Atavism	Hormones	Attention deficit hyperactivity disorder (ADHD)	Adoption studies
Body type	Contaminants		Chromosomes

BIOLOGICAL ROOTS OF AGGRESSION: EARLY THEORIES

We find the earliest thoughts on the association between physical features and personality in the Greek civilization, which embraced the idea of an interconnection between mind and body.[5] Later, as discussed in Chapter 5, scientific criminology developed along with other sciences. Behavioral science first looked to biology and medicine for its framework. Not surprisingly, then, people interested in studying crime hypothesized that criminality was biologically determined. The search was on for physical and biological characteristics that would differentiate criminals from non-criminals.

Criminal anthropology proposed a relationship between physical features and criminal behavior that we can trace to the work of European anatomist and physiologist, Franz Joseph Gall (1758–1828). Gall founded the school of anatomy known as **phrenology,** which suggests that the constellation of bumps on the head indicate biological differences in the way people behave.[6] Gall's approach focused on the idea that the brain is the organ of the human mind and personality, and that particular mental functions are associated with certain regions within it. Gall believed underdevelopment of a specific brain region is associated with weakness in a particular aspect of the personality and that we can predict the development of personality and mental capacity by the underlying shape of the skull.[7]

Gall's claims were disputed by religious leaders and the scientific community alike. His research did not survive careful empirical testing, and phrenology died an early death. Seventy years later, however, the idea that criminal behavior is rooted in biological characteristics was revived by the Italian physician Cesare Lombroso.

Lombroso began his work in light of discoveries spearheaded by Charles Darwin's influential work *On the Origin of Species,* published in 1859.[8] Darwin reasoned that if species survived because of their fitness for the conditions of life, at any point in time other species would be disappearing because they were unfit. Applying this logic to humans, Lombroso hypothesized that some human beings were carrying within them biological characteristics suitable for pre-civilized peoples (aggressiveness, impulsiveness, insensitivity to pain) but unfit for contemporary society. These throwbacks to an earlier form of human being could be identified, Lombroso believed, by certain physical features that had survived the cycle of evolution. By studying the postmortem bodies of Italian prisoners, he developed a set of these characteristics, which he called "anomalies": low cranial capacity, a receding chin, long arms, insensitivity to pain, and so on (Table 6.2). Lombroso used the term **atavistic** to suggest that these individuals were inherently criminal due to their primitive biological states, which rendered them incapable of functioning according to the norms and standards of a complex society.[9]

Unfortunately, Lombroso did not look among non-criminals for the characteristics he found among prisoners. When the English prison physician Charles Goring replicated Lombroso's study in 1913, his findings did not confirm Lombroso's theory. Goring concluded criminals could be characterized by generally defective physiques and intelligence, but these differences did not support the theory of a "criminal type" with specific physical markers.[10] Failure to find any support for Lombroso's theory of atavism ultimately brought about its demise.

In the 1930s, Harvard anthropologist Ernest Hooton tried once again to establish a connection between biological features and criminality.[11] This time the research to test the theory was impressively massive. Hooton compared 14,000 prisoners and 3,000 non-prisoners on numerous physical attributes. He concluded criminals were both physically and mentally inferior to non-criminals and that these differences were inherited. Different types of offenders were also thought to differ significantly from one another. For example, Hooton thought murderers and bank robbers had different body types.

criminal anthropology

A discipline that proposes a relationship between physical features and criminal behavior.

phrenology

A school of anatomy suggesting that the constellation of bumps on the head indicate biological differences in the way people behave.

atavistic

Lombroso's term to describe inherently criminal individuals; people who, due to their primitive biological state, are incapable of functioning according to the norms and standards of a complex society.

Franz Gall founded phrenology, the study of the relationship between human physical features and criminal behavior. How do you think society reacted to this idea?

A PICTURE OF GOOD HEALTH

How do you think Lombroso was influenced by Darwin's theory of the evolution of human beings?

Hooton's research contains many shortcomings that undermine its validity. His data can tell us only about people in prison, obviously a small proportion of the total criminal population and one that is also overwhelmingly of lower socioeconomic class. Any possible generalizations are thus limited at best. Hooton's measures of inferiority also reflect his own bias rather than objectively measuring cultural or intellectual inferiority. Tattooing, eye color, low forehead, and narrow jaws are hardly evidence of inferior physical types, as he suggests. Finally, Hooton made two fundamental methodological errors: (1) He assumed that because two factors occur together, one must cause the other, and (2) he compared a large number of prisoners with a relatively small number of non-prisoners, instead of using samples that reflected their relative proportions in the population as a whole. That would necessitate drawing a non-prison sample of hundreds of thousands for a reliable comparison.

In 1949, a student of Hooton's, William Sheldon, published *Varieties of Delinquent Youth* in which he described three basic body types and their corresponding temperaments: endomorph, ectomorph, and mesomorph.[12] As detailed in Table 6.3, endomorphs are short and round, inclined to put on fat, relaxed, extroverted, and tending to prefer a comfortable and easy life. Mesomorphs are athletic, muscular, strong, and aggressive in personality. They are also assertive, seek and need vigorous physical activity, and

TABLE **6.2**

Atavistic Features of Lombroso's Primitive Man

Large jaw
Exceptionally long arms
Receding chin
Large teeth and fleshy lips
Eyes too close together or too far apart
Crooked nose
Index finger longer than the middle finger
Eyes of different hues
Attached ears that lack lobes
Excessive body hair

Source: Adapted from Lombroso, C., & Lombroso-Ferrero, G. (1911/1972). *Criminal man.* Montclair, NJ: Patterson Smith.

TABLE **6.3**

Sheldon's Three Body Types

Body type	Endomorph	Ectomorph	Mesomorph
Physical attributes	Short, round, pudgy	Lean, thin, fragile	Muscular and athletic
Temperament	Sociable and relaxed	Shy and reserved	Aggressive and assertive

Source: Adapted from Sheldon, W. (1949). *Varieties of delinquent youth.* New York: Harper and Brothers.

enjoy risk-taking behavior. Ectomorphs are lean, fragile, and slender. In temperament ectomorphs are introverted and shy with a tendency toward physical and psychosomatic disorders.

Sheldon classified 200 boys sent to a rehabilitation home in Boston and compared them with 200 college students assumed to be non-delinquent. Sheldon found the delinquent youths were decidedly more mesomorphic than non-delinquents. He argued that the mesomorph is more likely to have a higher pain threshold and be more physically aggressive and callous than either the ectomorph or the endomorph. He concluded that there is a strong correlation between body type and personality.

Another pair of Harvard criminologists, Sheldon and Eleanor Glueck, replicated Sheldon's findings. They compared 500 incarcerated delinquents aged 9 to 17 with 500 youths in the same age group who were not incarcerated and added a fourth body type to Sheldon's three: a balanced physique for boys whose bodies did not conform to any of the original categories. The Gluecks' research led them to conclude that "among the delinquents, mesomorphy is far and away the most dominant component, with ectomorphic, endomorphic and balanced types about equally represented."[13]

The studies conducted by Sheldon and the Gluecks appear to consistently find physical differences between youths officially labeled delinquent and groups not labeled delinquent. However, these findings must be approached with caution. Selecting a sample of persons labeled delinquent and comparing them to a sample of persons not so labeled does not necessarily assure us that we are comparing delinquent and non-delinquent populations. The sample college students who were compared with delinquents came from a population that often engaged in unreported delinquent and criminal acts, from illegal drinking and drug use to stealing, vandalism, and even rape. Many college students are guilty of crimes but escape the label of delinquency. But we do know, from self-report and participant observation studies, that people who are not incarcerated for crime or delinquency admit to a very high rate of delinquent and criminal acts (see Chapter 3). Thus, it is possible that what these researches are actually comparing are delinquents in institutions with delinquents *not* in institutions, and if there really is a difference in body type between the two groups, the interesting question is why institutionalized youths are more mesomorphic than non-institutionalized youths.

We can only conclude that neither mesomorphy nor any other physical or biological characteristic is correlated with crime or delinquency. Indeed, over a hundred years of research has failed to establish any physical difference between criminal and non-criminal populations, from bumps on the head to atavistic traits to body and temperament types. Should we thus abandon the biological line of inquiry completely, or can we look more deeply into the underlying principles of biological theory to understand the interrelationship of nature and nurture? Let's take a closer look at the biological perspective by examining the effects of chemical and environmental variables on human behavior.

BIOCHEMICAL VARIABLES

Early biological theories held variations in individual constitutions alone accounted for the difference between criminals and non-criminals. Recognizing the fallacy of this approach, researchers began to advance a **biosocial approach** to the study of human behavior that acknowledges the interaction between social environment and variations in individual constitutions as contributing factors in how people act and react (Figure 6.1).

Biological theories expanded our understanding of crime causation by examining the impact of biochemical, neurological, and genetic variables on human reaction to environmental stimuli.[14] Let's start with biochemical factors that affect the ability to think and behave, beginning with nutrition.

Nutrition

Criminological research has taken seriously the popular phrase "You are what you eat" and has examined the role of vitamin deficiencies, food allergies, and diet, particularly in relationship to juvenile delinquents. Evidence supports the value of a balanced diet in alleviating the symptoms of behavioral and mood disorders such as depression, hyperactivity, and aggression.[15] Too much or too little of substances such as sodium, potassium, iron, mercury, and amino acids can lead to an increase in aggression, hyperactivity, depression, memory loss, abnormal sexual behavior, and learning problems.[16] Ingesting high quantities of refined sugar, white flour, and saturated fat may also put individuals at a greater risk of developing mental disorders such as schizophrenia and dementia.[17]

Given these tentative conclusions, criminologists point to the need for further exploration into the link between diet and behavioral disorders that lead to violence and crime, and between diet and reduced aggression, irritability, impulsivity, and antisocial behavior.[18] We also need to evaluate the relationship between nutritional deficiencies and social

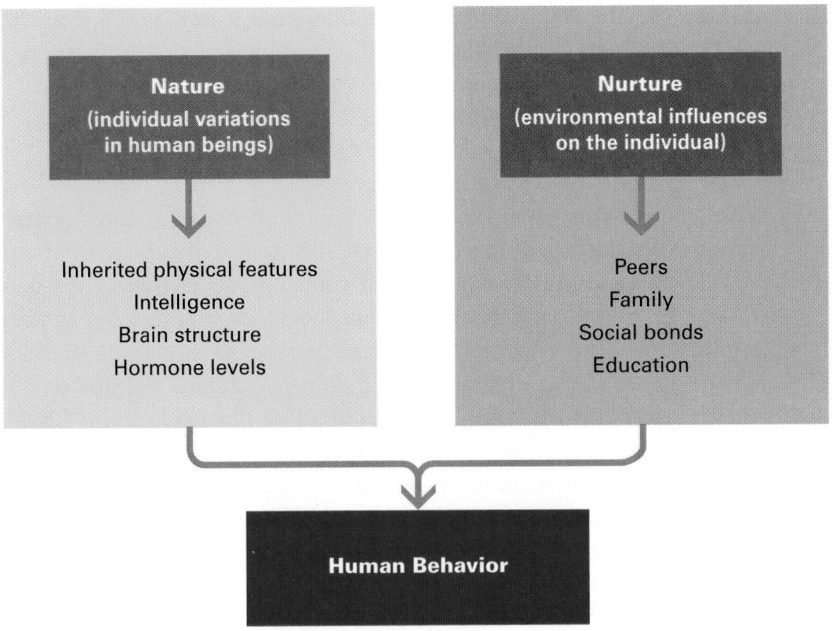

biosocial approach

A perspective on human behavior that acknowledges the interaction between social environment and variations in individual constitutions as contributing factors in how people act and react.

Nature
(individual variations in human beings)

Inherited physical features
Intelligence
Brain structure
Hormone levels

Nurture
(environmental influences on the individual)

Peers
Family
Social bonds
Education

Human Behavior

FIGURE **6.1**

How Do We Act? Nature Versus Nurture
Human behavior is influenced by variables that are attributed to our natures, such as intelligence, tolerance for pain, and levels of testosterone, and also variables attributed to our environmental and learning experiences, such as the people we interact with and where we go to school.

class. Poorer children and adolescents may be at a greater risk of inadequate nutrition given the expense of buying the varieties of food necessary for a well-balanced diet. The wide availability and relative low cost of fast food may also lead to excessive chemical additives and sugar in the diets of individuals from lower socioeconomic classes.

Blood Glucose

To date, evidence about the impact of blood glucose (sugar) on levels of behavior—especially violent, aggressive behavior—is inconclusive. Studies have examined the effects of **hypoglycemia,** a condition that occurs when blood glucose falls below the necessary level for the brain to function effectively (Figure 6.2). Hypoglycemia can be caused by too much production of the hormone insulin in the body or by inadequate diet. Individuals experiencing low blood sugar become irritable, excitable, and confused, and often lack proper judgment.[19] Several studies have linked hypoglycemia to outbursts of aggression, violence, and assault.[20] Research has also found a higher incidence of hypoglycemia in repeat violent offenders.[21]

We must also evaluate these findings in the context of their interaction with environmental variables. An individual experiencing symptoms of hypoglycemia, if untreated, may continue to exhibit signs of irritability, poor self-control, and lack of reasoning, which can affect his or her job performance, relationships, and other social circumstances.[22]

Hormones

Studies of differences between male and female rates of criminality have focused on the biological differences between the sexes, rooted in sex-based hormones. Research on the male hormone **testosterone** has not shown a consistent relationship to aggressiveness or sexual aberrations, although some studies support the finding that an elevated level of male hormones can in fact lead to aggressive behavior.[23] However, testosterone levels naturally vary daily and seasonally, making comparisons difficult. Even with some evidence suggesting a relationship between elevated levels of testosterone and behavioral measures of aggression, we cannot assume this condition alone causes criminal behavior. We must instead consider the dynamic interaction between hormonal levels and other physical and social variables.

Research on variations in female hormones as possible links to antisocial and aggressive behavior began in the early 1970s. Studies attempted to show that females are more likely to exhibit poor impulse control, anxiety, depression, and antisocial behaviors just prior to or during their menstrual cycle.[24] This condition, commonly referred to as **premenstrual syndrome (PMS),** has been used in courtrooms as a defense strategy to reduce the culpability of female offenders in criminal cases.[25] While evidence does support the theory that elevated levels of female hormones prior to and during menstruation can contribute to an increase in psychological and physical stress, there is little agreement about whether PMS is linked to criminality.

Contaminants

Research has linked long-term exposure to certain environmental pollutants such as copper and mercury to the onset of physical, mental, and behavioral disorders. Lead—in paint, water, and soil—and other environmental contaminants can affect the development, growth, and behavior of children and adolescents by causing learning and reading problems, hearing impairment, and brain damage. Exposure can even result in death.

The presence of high levels of lead inside buildings, schools, and apartments has been linked to an increase in antisocial behaviors and juvenile delinquency.[26] Researchers note a positive relationship between concentration of lead in the air and the occurrence of violent crime.[27] (The Consider This feature explores a possible link between the Clean Air Act and a drop in criminal activity.) A recent study at the University of Cincinnati that examined longitudinal data found evidence to support a direct link between prenatal and early-childhood lead exposure and an increased risk for criminal behavior later in life.[28] In the study, after age 18, individuals with elevated levels

hypoglycemia

A condition that occurs when blood glucose falls below the necessary level for the brain to function effectively.

testosterone

The male hormone; possibly linked to aggressive behavior.

premenstrual syndrome (PMS)

A biological condition wherein females are more likely to exhibit poor impulse control, anxiety, depression, and antisocial behaviors just prior to or during their menstrual cycle.

Where is this home that has been evacuated for high levels of lead toxins likely to be, and who has been affected by its contamination?

CONSIDER THIS...

A 30-Year Decline in Crime Rates: Could It Be the Clean Air Act?

Crime rates across the United States have dropped after hitting a peak in the early 1990s. According to the FBI's Uniform Crime Reports and the National Crime Victimization Survey, U.S. crime dropped to a 30-year low in 2003. Since then, researchers have been searching for an answer that explains this trend. A *New York Times* article suggests one unique reason: the removal of leaded gasoline from the market under the Clean Air Act passed by Congress.[29] The act required leaded gas to be phased out by the mid-1980s.

Studies citing the harmful effects of lead poisoning are abundant.[30] Such poisoning has been found to cause increased depression, aggression, and antisocial behavior. Research studies on the effect of lead on children link it to lower levels of intelligence and learning disabilities, as well as impulsivity and behavioral problems that last into adulthood.

Economist Jessica Reyes, proposes that the removal of leaded gasoline across the country brought blood lead levels down to a fraction of what they were previously.[31] Those who were children when leaded gasoline use peaked in 1973 reached their most crime-prone years around the same time crime topped off in the United States—the early 90s. Since then, U.S. crime rates, especially for violent crime, have been dropping steadily. Similar findings were reported in a comparison study of nine countries throughout the world, which found that dropping world crime rates were consistent with government-enforced removal of lead from consumer gasoline and paints.[32]

Could the Clean Air Act and similar remedies to remove lead and toxic substances from consumer markets have done more to lower crime rates in the United States than any criminal justice policies have in the past?

What do you think?

of lead in their blood before birth and during early childhood had higher rates of arrest for violent crimes than other individuals in the population. It is also important to note that these types of pollutants and toxins are disproportionately found in poor neighborhoods.

The evidence from these and similar studies make it clear that we need an integrated understanding of criminal behavior—one that incorporates research on specific influences

Grains Vegetables Fruits Milk Meat and Beans

FIGURE **6.2**

What Fuels Our Brain? The Food Pyramid

Glucose from carbohydrates is the fuel your brain uses to produce the energy it needs to help you think, act, and get motivated. Research findings support the conclusion that a well-balanced diet providing appropriate nutrition from the four food groups can have a positive impact on brain function and mental health.

Source: USDA Center for Nutrition Policy and Promotion, 2005.

on human behavior and their connection to environmental experiences. We turn now to a discussion of another perspective that examines the effects of brain activity on human behavior: the field of neurophysiology.

NEUROPHYSIOLOGY

Ever wonder why some people enjoy riding roller coasters, jumping out of airplanes, and wrestling wild animals? Have you noticed how some children, when reprimanded, will cower in fear, while others stand up to authority in defiance? We hear that people are "wired" differently, and that's what makes us act differently and react differently to environmental stimuli. Is there therefore something about the structure and function of some people's brain that makes them more prone to violence and aggression? This question is explored by criminologists who focus on the study of brain activity, or **neurophysiology.**[33] They work in three main areas of research: neurological impairment, brain chemistry, and attention deficit hyperactivity disorder (ADHD). Let's first take a look at the research on neurological impairment.

Neurological Impairment

Brain abnormalities are either inherited or acquired, as from poor blood flow to the brain or from a head injury or other trauma. Using **brain imaging,** scientists have been able to capture three-dimensional images of the brain. These allow us to examine the structure and function of various regions and identify tumors, lesions, and developmental deficits. Studies support the finding that individuals who exhibit antisocial behavior, aggression, and violence show significant structural and functional deficits within the prefrontal regions of the brain.[34] These brain areas affect the ability to communicate effectively, control impulses, develop social skills, and reason abstractly.

Research indicates that impairments in the regions of the brain responsible for self-control, reasoning, and problem solving have been linked to violent, aggressive behavior.[35] Criminologists note that at the core of such behavior is an underlying disregard for the rules and guidelines of moral reasoning. Evidence shows a significant number of individuals who exhibit these types of behavior suffer neurological impairment that severely affects their level of cognitive ability and understanding.[36]

Criminologists who study the brain caution that we must view structural and functional deficits as only partial contributors to criminal behavior. If we ignore the social, economic, and political components of crime causation, we reduce every criminal event to the behavior of the individual criminal, as though he or she exists separately from and is unaffected by the environment.

Brain Chemistry

Research has established a connection between the chemical composition of the brain and the development of different behaviors in response to our surroundings. (The Crime in Global Perspective features an international study examining the effect of brain chemistry on criminal behavior.) Chemical compounds within the brain called **neurotransmitters** are responsible for activating and controlling emotions, moods, drives, and other mechanisms of human response.

Some neurotransmitters, such as dopamine and serotonin, affect our ability to tolerate excitement, manage stress, and deal with anxiety. The reason some of us enjoy horror movies while others have to cover our eyes, why many of us panic when speaking in public while some actually embrace it, and why most of us stay up all night before taking an exam is that these chemical compounds vary in their level from individual to individual. The appropriate level of neurotransmitter function within the brain maintains a balanced level of excitement-seeking activity. Individuals without

neurophysiology

The study of brain activity.

brain imaging

Techniques to capture three-dimensional images of the brain.

neurotransmitters

Chemical compounds within the brain that are responsible for activating and controlling emotions, moods, drives, and other mechanisms of human response.

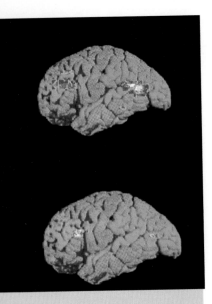

Different regions of the brain are responsible for differences in behavior. The lower image in this photo shows a normal brain; the upper one is the brain of a person suffering from depression.

CRIME IN GLOBALPERSPECTIVE

The Effects of Low Brain Serotonin on Behavior

Serotonin is a neurotransmitter manufactured by the brain that affects sleep, mood, sexual function, and appetite, among other functions of the central nervous system.[37] Medications such as Prozac and Zoloft control serotonin levels in the brain to control anxiety and depression.

In 1973, researchers tested the effects of serotonin on behaviors in rats and mice, isolating rats for four weeks and then measuring their serotonin levels.[38] When placed with mice, the rats with significantly lower serotonin rates attacked and killed them, while rats with steady serotonin rates ignored the mice, and rats with higher rates were actually friendly toward the mice. Rhesus monkeys that had poor impulse control and habitually violent behavior were also found to have low brain serotonin.

In studies at the University of Helsinki in Finland, 800 test subjects—including a group of alcoholic, impulsive, and habitually violent Finish offenders and their relatives and other male cohorts—were tested for serotonin turnover rates. The alcoholic offenders were found to have low serotonin turnover in the brain, which researchers associated with low impulse control and a history of suicide attempts. The offenders were also prone to hypoglycemic levels of blood glucose, which researchers concluded played a further role in escalating impulsive behavior into more excitable, aggressive behavior patterns.

Other international studies report similar findings, linking serotonin levels and aggressive behavior and suggesting violent offenders may need medicinal intervention. A recent study at the University of Groningen in the Netherlands found "serotonin deficiency appears to be related to pathological, violent forms of aggressiveness, but not to the normal aggressive behavior that animals and humans use to adapt to everyday survival."[39] These results seem to conclude that medicinal intervention to regulate serotonin levels will help keep aggressive offenders from engaging in future impulsive, violent crimes.

How are these two individuals—a skydiver and a gangbanger—both thrill seekers? How is their nature (their level of brain chemicals) influenced by their nurture (their social experiences, opportunities, peer interactions)?

the proper level of chemical stimulation will be unresponsive to normal levels of excitement and thrill and will seek alternative measures of stimulation within the environment.[40]

Evidence suggests abnormally low levels of neurotransmitters in the brain are associated with impulsive, aggressive responses.[41] People with abnormal levels of the neurotransmitter monoamine oxidase (MAO) tend to be more defiant of authority, impulsive, and hyperactive and are also more likely to engage in risky behavior.[42] Within this context we can see why some individuals, through their social learning experiences and available network of social contacts and means, may seek to jump out of an airplane, while others may join a gang. Once again, we can see the interaction between nature and nurture.

Attention Deficit Hyperactivity Disorder

Over the past several years we have seen a surge in diagnosis of the neurological condition known as **attention deficit hyperactivity disorder (ADHD).** Children who are merely unable to sit still, do not pay attention in school, and are easily distracted are often misdiagnosed with ADHD and inappropriately treated with stimulant medications such as Ritalin, Focalin, and Strattera. Experts in the medical community refer to this incorrect diagnosis as **socially induced hyperactivity (SIH),** a behavior that is learned and has no clear neurological basis.[43] There are three marked characteristics of a true ADHD diagnosis: poor attention skills, deficient impulse control, and hyperactivity.[44] Table 6.4 outlines some of the behavioral manifestations of these three characteristics.

The causes of ADHD are not yet fully known, although experts point to neurological damage, allergic reactions, prenatal consumption of alcohol or drugs, prolonged

attention deficit hyperactivity disorder (ADHD)

A neurological condition involving poor attention skills, deficient impulse control, and hyperactivity.

socially induced hyperactivity (SIH)

A learned behavior, without a neurological basis, of inattention and distractibility that is often incorrectly diagnosed as attention deficit hyperactivity disorder.

How do hyperactivity, distractibility, and poor attention span contribute to delinquent behavior? What role might parents, teachers, and peers play in this process?

TABLE **6.4**

How Do Those with ADHD Behave?		
POOR ATTENTION SKILLS	**DEFICIENT IMPULSE CONTROL**	**HYPERACTIVITY**
Has a hard time keeping eye contact	Interrupts peoples' conversations	Is unable to sit still for a period of time
Mind wanders during a conversation	Is very impatient	Always wants to be on the go
Gets easily bored during group play	Jumps from one thought, idea, or activity to another	Has excessive movement
Has trouble focusing on assignments, homework, tasks	Blurts out information	Has awkward, aggressive motor skills
Is easily distracted by sounds or by others	Constantly needs to be told what to do	Runs around, fidgets

Source: Adapted from Adler, L., & Florence, M. (2006). *Scattered minds: Hope and help for adults with ADHD.* London: Penguin.

exposure to environmental contaminants such as lead, and even inherited genetic tendencies.[45] ADHD is a lifelong disorder that begins in early childhood and continues through adolescence and adulthood. In the early years, it has been linked to poor academic performance, bullying, defiance of authority, and lack of response to treatment or discipline. Adolescents and adults with ADHD continue to suffer in their personal and social lives; they may have difficulties in maintaining relationships, risk-taking behavior, erratic work performance, and low self-esteem.

Research has attempted to link ADHD with the onset of delinquency among juveniles. We know children with ADHD are more likely to be suspended from school, get into fights, use drugs and alcohol, and have multiple arrests throughout their lives.[46] Early detection and treatment of ADHD symptoms is thus imperative.[47] We also know this biologically based human characteristic can be compounded by the reactions of others and the reinforcement of negative labeling.

We have seen from our look at neurophysiology and biochemistry that innate differences among individuals produce behavioral differences in violence, aggression, and criminality that are mediated by our environment and our experiences. We turn now to the unanswered question: What may individuals inherit that produces a biological predisposition to criminal behavior?

HEREDITY AND GENETICS

Does criminality run in some families, like blue eyes, curly hair, or tall stature? Are certain people predisposed to violence and aggression simply because they were born that way? How have criminologists attempted to isolate the variable effects of inheritance on crime?

Criminal Families

The exploration of criminal behavior and inherited characteristics began in the late 1800s when researchers started to study families that exhibited criminal tendencies through several generations. In the late 1800s researchers conducted the **Juke family study** traced six generations of the family to attempt to demonstrate a genetic basis for their antisocial behavior.[48] Of 709 family members identified, 76 were criminals, 128 were prostitutes, and 206 were on public welfare. However, a closer look establishes no scientific basis for any influence of inheritance. The Juke family study is inherently flawed because any claim to have found a criminal tendency in a family lineage must compare the frequency of criminality between groups of descendents *in the same family.* Herein lays the major flaw, as the Juke family lineage was compared to the descendents of Jonathan Edwards, a Puritan preacher who was a former president of Princeton University and whose descendents

Juke family study

A study that traced six generations of the family to attempt to demonstrate a genetic basis for the family's antisocial behavior.

Key

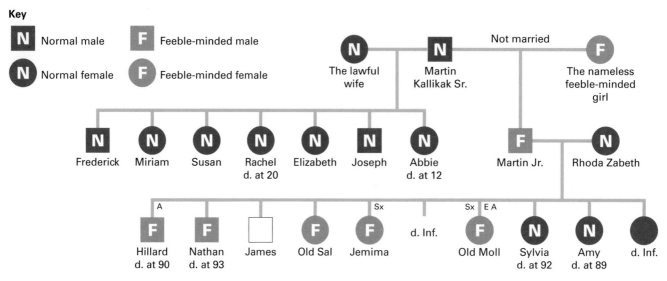

Note: "N" refers to normal and "F" refers to feebleminded.

Source: Goddard, H. H. (1912). *The Kallikak family: A study in the heredity of feeble-mindedness.* New York: Macmillan.

FIGURE **6.3**

The Kallikaks: A Family of Criminals?

Henry Goddard studied the descendents of the Kallikak family, which was divided into two lineages: a "good" one and a "bad" one. Both lineages were from a common father, Martin Kallikak Sr. a Revolutionary War soldier who had a liaison with a feebleminded barmaid that resulted in an illegitimate son, Martin Kallikak Jr. and the "bad" line of descendents. Years later, Martin Kallikak Sr. married a Quaker woman from a good family. The union between Martin Kallikak Sr. and the tavern girl resulted in generations of defective descendents who were plagued by illegitimacy, prostitution, alcoholism, epilepsy, and lechery. Kallikak's marriage to the Quaker woman yielded generations of society's finest citizens. How are Goddard's findings biased?

Kallikak family study

A study that claimed there was a genetic basis for mental deficiency or feeblemindedness that could lead to criminality.

included several United States presidents and vice presidents, successful entrepreneurs, and wealthy business owners.

An equally famous example was the **Kallikak family study** conducted in 1912.[49] Its subjects were the descendants of Martin Kallikak, who had an illicit encounter with a mentally impaired barmaid during the Revolutionary War before returning home to later marry a Quaker woman. Following the offspring of both unions, researchers found numerous paupers, criminals, alcoholics, and mentally deficient descendents from the illegitimate union, but few, if any, from the second (Figure 6.3). Ignoring all the differences in social and economic circumstances experienced by the children of these two unions (and concealing the fact that some of the photographs of the "deficient" Kallikaks were altered to make them appear moronic and shifty), the study concluded that a genetic cause of antisocial behavior had been established.

The implications of such research had a profound impact on social policy. They largely contributed to the **eugenics movement** in the 1920s and early 1930s, in which science and policy merged in an attempt to improve the human race through breeding.[50] According to this theory, individual worth and potential are genetically determined; to improve the quality of life in the United States, society needed to improve the quality of the individuals in it. Individuals, classes, races, and countries in power were obviously superior to those at the bottom of the status hierarchy, who had only their defective genes to blame.

Today we can see the weaknesses of both the family studies and the eugenics philosophy. The fact that family members inhabit similar environments as well as having similar genes makes it impossible to conclude that similar behavior is the product only of genetics and not also of the environment. But the history and impact of the eugenics movement demonstrates that theories need not be accurate to have a significant influence. The Connecting Theory to Practice feature shows how this influence can be harmful.

How, then, can we accurately explore the link between heredity and criminal behavior? We turn now to an examination of twin studies, which attempt to separate the variables of nature and nurture.

Twin Studies

While family studies have been abandoned, criminologists' efforts to identify genetic influences on crime go on. One continuing problem, however, is our inability to control

Even when theories have been discredited, practices based upon them may linger. In the early 1970s, evidence came to light that involuntary sterilizations might still be occurring in the United States, for the purpose of social control. In a 1972 federal case looking into the sterilization of two African American children in Alabama, Judge Gesell remarked:

Over the past few years, an estimated 100,000 to 150,000 low-income persons have been sterilized annually under federally funded programs. . . . there is uncontroverted evidence in the record that minors and other incompetents have been sterilized with federal funds and that an indefinite number of poor people have been improperly coerced into accepting a sterilization operation under the threat that various federally supported welfare benefits would be withdrawn unless they submitted to irreversible sterilization.[51]

Emphasizing savings in welfare payments and vague standards like "fitness for parenthood," these practices targeted the same group at risk from the earlier eugenicists—low-income minority women.[52] Physicians themselves acknowledged the common practice of performing elective hysterectomies on poor African American and Hispanic women as part of standard obstetrics and gynecology training in teaching hospitals. A rural doctor in South Carolina refused all medical treatment to his financially dependent female patients when they declined sterilization after their third child.

Only if we believed the children of minorities and the poor were destined (or predestined) to poverty, public welfare, and crime would such policies ever make any sense. Both past and present abusive practices see the poor, the illiterate, and the unemployed as the *source* of poverty, illiteracy and unemployment, instead of the more complex social conditions that deny individuals the opportunity to succeed.

---

for variations in social experiences. If we could create an experiment in which genetically identical persons grew up in different controlled environments, we might be able to distinguish genetic from environmentally produced similarities and differences in behavior. Fortunately, nature provides researchers with part of this experiment in the form of identical twins.

Monozygotic (identical) twins are the product of a single egg and sperm and therefore are 100 percent genetically alike. **Dizygotic (fraternal) twins,** on the other hand, are the product of two eggs and two sperm and have the same genetic similarity as any two siblings (approximately 50 percent).

This biological fact led researchers to look at how similarly identical twins behave, compared to fraternal twins. Since both types of twins are raised together and exposed to similar environments, greater similarity in behavior among identical twins (as opposed to fraternal twins) could be the result of greater similarity in genetic makeup.

The first study to report greater similarity in criminal behavior among identical twins was conducted in 1929. Researchers identified prisoners who had twins and then tried to determine whether the twin was also in trouble with the law. Of 13 identical pairs studied, 10 (77 percent) were *concordant;* that is, both twins were criminals, while among the 17 pairs of fraternal twins located, only two pairs (12 percent) were concordant. The study concluded that the significantly higher level of concordance for identical twins was due to heredity rather than environment.[53]

The vast majority of twin studies report greater similarity in criminal behavior for identical twins than for fraternal twins. Studies have also reported significantly greater risk for suicide among identical twins than fraternal twins.[54] Moreover, psychiatric problems such as antisocial personality and conduct disorder are more likely to exist in pairs of identical

eugenics movement

A movement in the 1920s and early 1930s in which science and policy merged in an attempt to improve the human race through breeding.

monozygotic (identical) twins

The product of a single egg and sperm; they are 100 percent genetically alike.

dizygotic (fraternal) twins

The product of two eggs and two sperm; they have the same genetic similarity as any two siblings (approximately 50 percent).

Do you think that identical twins behave similarly because they are treated similarly? How might similarity in appearance affect the way identical twins are treated versus fraternal twins?

twins than fraternal twins.[55] Identical twins are also more likely than fraternal twins to exhibit behavioral correlates of criminality such as impulsivity, aggression, and lack of emotions.[56]

However, we should not interpret these findings as conclusive evidence that inherited traits are the sole cause of the more frequent similarities in behavior among identical twins. The reason for caution is that we still cannot control for, and therefore remove as a possible factor, the environmental impacts on two different individuals who look to the outside world like the same person.[57] While most siblings grow up in the same family and have generally comparable environmental and social backgrounds, identical twins have unique experiences. Often dressed alike, treated alike, and able to confuse friends and teachers, identical twins may experience an environment significantly more similar than same-sex fraternal twins, and any similarity in their behavior may be explained by this fact rather than by genes.

Adoption Studies

Another way to examine the impact of heredity on criminal behavior is to compare adopted children with both their genetic and their rearing parents. If adopted children are more similar in behavior to their genetic (though absent) parents than to their adopted parents, it would provide support for the argument that criminal traits are inherited.

One of the largest adoption studies of its kind was conducted in Copenhagen, Denmark, where 1,145 males born between 1927 and 1941 and adopted by non-family members were compared with both biological and adopted fathers. Researchers concluded that the criminality of the adoptees' biological fathers was of greater importance in predicting their criminality than was their adoptive fathers' criminality and that the probability of criminality increased for boys whose adoptive and biological fathers were both criminal.[58]

Evidence from adoption studies seems to support a genetic basis to criminal behavior. Adopted individuals whose biological parents have criminal tendencies also engage in criminal behavior.[59] Nonetheless, while these studies are more successful than others in separating environmental and genetic influences, they too have serious problems. Children are often placed in adopted homes not in the random ways that are best suited for experimentation, but in ways authorities deem best for each child. Furthermore, the attempt to match adoptive parents with genetic parents may also reduce environmental differences between the two sets of parents.

Chromosomes

behavioral genetics

The study of the role of genetics in human behavior.

In the mid-1960s, developments in the field of **behavioral genetics,** the study of the role of genetics in human behavior, led to the identification of an anomaly in the structure of the male chromosome that seemed to link to a propensity for violence and aggression. The average person possesses 23 pairs of chromosomes, one pair of which determines the person's sex. Two X chromosomes is the common configuration for females, and an X and a Y produce a male. Occasionally, a person is born with too few or too many chromosomes, and this variation can occur in any of the 23 pairs. An extra chromosome, for example, causes Down syndrome, resulting in a total of 47. Klinefelter syndrome is a condition of certain males who possess an extra X chromosome (XXY) and appears to be related to some mild mental deficiency and mild degeneration of certain sex characteristics. Another, rarer, variation is the possession of an extra Y chromosome—**XYY syndrome**—seen in a very small number of males.

XYY syndrome

A rare chromosomal anomaly suspected of predisposing males to criminal behavior.

The link between XYY syndrome and criminal behavior was first studied in 1965, when researchers examined 197 maximum-security prisoners at an institution in Scotland for mentally disturbed patients with violent or criminal histories. Though the expected number of XYY men in the general population is 0.15 percent, the study revealed the incidence of the XYY anomaly among the prisoners to be about 3.5 percent.[60] The response to these findings was immediate. Hundreds of studies in prisons and mental hospitals followed as researchers claimed they too had found a larger-than-expected percentage of XYY men.[61] The media also focused on these reports. Richard Speck, the 1968 murderer of eight Chicago nursing students, was falsely reported as having the XYY variation. The California Center for the Study and Reduction of Violence announced in 1972 that it would begin measures to screen junior high boys for the XYY chromosome as one part of its research in the prevention of violence. A few states passed laws to screen delinquent boys for data to use in sentencing decisions, and in 1968 a group of doctors started a massive screening of newborn males at the Boston Hospital for Women.

Since then, many studies have attempted to link the genetic abnormality to a predisposition to criminal behavior.[62] They have been inconclusive, providing little evidence that males with the XYY chromosome are generally more violent than males without it. More importantly, the underlying explanation for the supposed relationship between this biological oddity and crime is based on a stereotypic and unsupported view that assumes males are innately (chromosomally) more aggressive than females. Only if we assume the single Y of the normal male causes aggression in men (and its absence explains the lack of aggression in women) could we predict an extra Y would make a man "extra male" or extra aggressive.

Behavioral genetics research will undoubtedly continue, but we must for now dismiss the notion that we have found a single cause of serious criminal behavior in the genetic code of a very small percentage of males. While certain traits may be consistent among men with XYY syndrome (Table 6.5), we can reasonably ask whether there is any actual "syndrome" here at all. Certainly, a significant number of XYY men (about 250,000 in the United States alone) lead perfectly normal and uneventful lives.

We must also weigh the influence of innate traits against that of environmental variables. Indeed, in our effort to understand human nature, it is unlikely that we will ever be able to isolate it from our everyday social interactions and learning experiences. With that in mind, we turn now to an evaluation of the biological perspective, to assess how it contributes to our understanding of the causes of crime.

EVALUATING BIOLOGICAL THEORY

The biological perspective has provided us with an array of research studies. Their basic premise is that criminality—as well as other behaviors like conformity and teamwork—is largely a product of constitutional variations and biological conditions

TABLE **6.5**

The XYY Phenomenon: What Are the Findings?

- XYY men tend to be taller than comparable XY men.
- XYY men convicted of crimes are more likely to be guilty of property offenses and less likely to have committed violent offenses than convicted XY men.
- The families of XYY inmates tend to have less history of crime or mental illness than the families of XY inmates.
- The prevalence of XYY men appears to be higher in mental and/or penal institutions than in the general population.

Source: Adapted from Are XYY males more prone to aggressive behavior than XY males? (2007). *Science Clarified: Science in dispute* (Vol. 1).

that profoundly affect our actions. Whether the studies focus on heredity, genetics, biochemical influences, or brain structure, their underlying message is the same: Human behavior, while subject to environmental stimuli and social experiences, is mediated by biological factors. We are not all the same, and we will not respond to the world in similar ways.

But these theories fall short of explaining the diversity and complexity of criminal behavior;[63] they reduce it to an uncontrolled and predetermined response. Not only is this an inaccurate depiction of crime in general, but it distorts the relationship of biology to human behavior. We *are* biological creatures, but that does not mean we are ruled by our biology, or that biology and environment compete for control of our actions.

There is, in fact, no persuasive evidence to support the conclusion that we are biologically programmed for certain types of behavior such as aggression simply because we are often aggressive. Genetic potentials do not lead to inevitable outcomes. Violence, sexism, and racism are biological only in the sense that as humans we are capable of them, just as we are biologically capable of nonviolence, equality, and justice. The fact that we are affected by gravity does not mean we must seek an explanation of crime in gravitational forces. The fact that learning relies on biochemical processes does not mean that those processes predetermine what we learn or what we will do with it.

Moreover, research methods in biological theories are fundamentally flawed.[64] The studies do not account for the scope and variety of criminal behavior, generally focusing on street crimes involving violence and aggression and failing to address the criminality of the middle and upper classes.[65] Small sample sizes, sampling bias, flawed statistical procedures, and lack of generalizability make it difficult to draw any reliable connection between biological explanations and criminal behavior.

Finally, a major concern about the biological perspective on crime is its implications for how we treat those who violate the law. If we determine that behavior is entirely controlled by the brain, we need to shift our focus to prevention; instead of responding to criminal behavior after it has occurred, we must try to identify those at risk for committing crime before it happens. The potential for class, sex, and race bias here is profound.[66] It is a short leap to the assumption that some individuals are biologically inferior and that we are justified in treating them in an inhumane manner.[67] Although these problems make it difficult for us to conceive of any potential benefit we may derive in terms of social policy, nonetheless we turn now to the practical implications of biological theories of criminology.

PRACTICAL APPLICATION OF BIOLOGICAL THEORY

Table 6.6 summarizes the biological approach to the study of crime and crime causation. For the biological theorist, the starting point for the study of crime is the individual, and his or her physical or genetic codes are the ultimate components of analysis. The characteristics of society are the sum of the characteristics of its individual members. Crime and even war, the most organized form of aggression, are the product of clusters of hostile, aggressive individuals. Economics, politics, culture, and social relations are all reduced to the sum total of the individuals and their biological makeup. Some would argue that this form of analysis is **reductionism,** the attempt to study the whole (society) by reducing every event to the behavior of its parts (people), as if the parts exist separately from and are unaffected by the whole.

What then can we say of the policy implications of the biological approach? Do we abandon its potential contribution to the domain of criminal justice practice? The science of criminology suggests otherwise, because to do so would be to ignore a major aspect of human behavior that relies on our innate biological drives and predispositions,

reductionism

The attempt to study the whole (society) by reducing every event to the behavior of its parts (people), as if the parts exist separately from and are unaffected by the whole.

TABLE **6.6**

SUMMARY: The Biological Perspective	
Definition of Crime	Criminal behavior is an instinctive response to environmental stimuli.
Why Does Crime Occur? (Theory)	Because the brain is the organ of human behavior, any disturbance of the brain structure or function (neurological impairment, chemical imbalances, exposure to toxins, genetic defects) will result in a disturbance of behavior.
What Is the Solution to Crime? (Policy)	■ Monitor infants and children to address potentially harmful developmental conditions. ■ Identify symptoms of behavioral disorders in children and adolescents through neurological examination. ■ Intervene on behalf of individuals identified with behavioral disorders by altering or modifying their social environments to reduce violence-inducing experiences.

those components of our being that make us unique as individuals, different from one another.[68]

In order for criminology to be an effective science, we must recognize that variations in human behavior are a complex interplay between individuals and their social, political, and economic environments.[69] What makes each person unique in his or her response to the surrounding environment? This is the starting point of the biological approach's explanation for criminal behavior.

Policies guided by biological theory try to alter human behavior by implementing the medical model of identification, prevention, and treatment. Several strategies have been suggested for the early diagnosis and treatment of potentially harmful conditions that can have long-term effects on physical and social development:[70]

■ Implementing screening clinics for the early identification of neurological disorders and other harmful conditions. This strategy includes pre- and postnatal care of pregnant women and their newborn children, especially those identified as at risk for exposure to environmental variables that can be violence-inducing, such as alcoholism, drugs, abuse, and criminality among other family members.

■ Monitoring children in the early stages of development to screen and test for the possibility of learning disabilities, hypoglycemia, lead exposure, ADHD, and other conditions that result in behavioral changes and conduct disorders.

■ Intervening early in the lives of children identified with behavioral and conduct disorders to minimize their exposure to environmental variables that may heighten the effects of their biological condition. This may include drug-based treatment, behavior modification therapy, school-based intervention, educational enrichment programs, and family counseling.

■ Supporting research on the origins of aggressive behavior that integrates the role of environmental variables. Further study of the link between sensory stimulation and the need for excitement can help criminal justice professionals develop youth programs that replace criminal activities (gang membership, taking drugs, getting into fights) with afterschool competitive sports, rock climbing, hiking, and other exciting sports and activities. (See the Connecting Research to Practice feature for an example.)

The biological perspective reminds us to consider the individual in our study of crime, along with the dynamics of social structure and the impact of environmental variables. In this chapter, we focused on those unique characteristics that originate with the human brain. In the next chapter we turn to an examination of another component of individual variation—the human mind.

For over 60 years, Outward Bound has been giving at-risk youth an alternative to delinquency through an adventurous outdoors sports and education program. The program targets endangered teens who are consistently making bad choices as a result of negative influences in their lives. By taking them on expeditions into the wilderness to participate in challenging sports and activities, the program aims to help them realize their positive potential and develop responsibility, leadership, effective decision-making skills, and a dedication to service. Outward Bound currently works with over 70,000 teachers and students throughout the world each year.[71]

According to an annual evaluation conducted by the Florida Department of Juvenile Justice (FDJJ), Outward Bound has consistently kept 67 percent of females and 62 percent of males crime-free for at least one year through 2002–2004. In 2006, the FDJJ ranked STEP, a program within Outward Bound, as the fourth most effective low-cost program of 16 programs in the state. Another Outward Bound program, FINS, was found to have an 83 percent success rate, ranking 5 percent above the statewide average.

Other research into outdoor education programs has come back with mixed reviews. A study on outdoor education conducted at the University of New Hampshire reported a small to moderate impact in areas such as self-esteem, behavior issues, and teamwork—the typically measured outcomes of these kinds of programs.[72] Citing a report that considered 96 studies of over 12,000 participants in adventure education and Outward Bound programs, researchers found both immediate and long-term positive effects after an 18-month follow-up. This is of particular interest because the value and impact of most other educational programs decline over time following the program's completion, giving Outward Bound a distinct advantage.

Studies do show, however, that outcomes may vary according to differences in participants and programs. More research is needed to find out just how effective outdoor education programs are overall.

SUMMARY

- **What are the basic assumptions of biological theories of criminal behavior?**

Biological theories assume human behavior is intricately linked to our biological constitution, with the brain being the central control for personality. Thus, these theories suggest a predisposition to criminality may be inherited, and criminal tendencies can be passed down from generation to generation. Finally, the biological perspective argues that those who are less fully evolved may behave in ways that reflect their more primitive state of development.

- **Are certain physical features or body types related to criminality?**

Lombroso's theory of atavism suggests that criminals are primitive human beings, identified by a set of physical anomalies such as low cranial capacity and insensitivity to pain. Other criminologists such as Sheldon and the Gluecks conducted studies to correlate body type with delinquency. Early studies of physical features and criminal body types have been widely criticized and ultimately dismissed for their fundamentally flawed research designs and sampling procedures.

■ **Do certain chemicals in the body make people more aggressive?**

Theories stemming from biochemistry focus on aspects of nutrition, blood glucose, hormones, and contaminants as factors in human behavior. Research on the impact of nutrition has shown that changes in diet can alleviate the symptoms of a variety of behavioral and mood disorders and patterns of behavior such as aggression, hyperactivity, depression, memory loss, abnormal sexual behavior, and learning disorders.

Several studies have linked hypoglycemia or low blood sugar to outbursts of aggression, violence, and assault. Research data have, however, found no consistent relationship between varying levels of the male hormone testosterone and criminal behavior. An elevated level of female hormones prior to and during menstruation, known as premenstrual syndrome (PMS), has been shown to increase psychological and physical stress among women, which may affect their behavior and cognitive reasoning capacity. Finally, evidence suggests that early exposure to certain environmental contaminants such as lead is linked to an increase in risk for criminal behavior later in life.

■ **Could problems in the brain lead someone to commit murder?**

Studies focusing on the structure and function of the brain focus on three main areas: neurological impairment, brain chemistry, and attention deficit hyperactivity disorder. Studies support the finding that individuals who exhibit antisocial behavior, aggression, and violence show significant structural and functional deficits within certain regions of the brain. Evidence also links abnormally low levels of neurotransmitters in the brain with impulsive, aggressive responses to certain environmental stimuli. Finally, research on the lifelong disorder ADHD has attempted to link this physiological condition with the onset of delinquency among juveniles. Children with ADHD are more likely to be suspended from school, get into fights, use drugs and alcohol, and have multiple arrests throughout their lives.

■ **Can criminal tendencies be passed from generation to generation?**

Criminological research has had tremendous difficulty separating the variable effects of heredity on human behavior from the effects of environmental factors. Studies of criminal families have largely been discredited as methodologically flawed and racist in their policy implications. The vast majority of twin studies report greater similarity in criminal behavior for identical twins than for fraternal twins. However, we must view these findings with caution because we cannot control for the similarity of twins' environmental experiences. Adoption studies seem to support the finding that adopted individuals whose biological parents have criminal tendencies also become involved in criminal behavior. These studies are more successful in separating environmental and genetic influences, but they too suffer some problems, including fewer environmental differences between adoptive and genetic parents than we might expect due to efforts to match biological and adoptive parents' characteristics. Studies attempting to link the genetic abnormality known as XYY syndrome to a predisposition to criminal behavior in males have been inconclusive.

■ **If crime is in the brain, how do we respond to criminal behavior?**

Crime-prevention strategies from the biological perspective are designed to identify and treat harmful conditions that can have long-term effects on physical and social development. They include screening for the early identification of neurological disorders and other harmful conditions;

monitoring children for learning disabilities, hypoglycemia, lead exposure, ADHD, and other conditions; minimizing exposure to environmental variables among children identified with behavioral disorders; and finally, supporting research that integrates the role of environmental variables in the onset of violence and crime.

CRITICAL THINKING QUESTIONS

1. Let's say you are interested in studying the body types of male criminals convicted of violent crimes. You develop a scale from 1 to 10 that ranks individuals on objective physical measures, with 1 being the least muscular, and 10 the most. You administer this scale on a sample of maximum security prisoners across the United States and find that about 75 percent of your sample rank above a 7. What conclusions do you draw? Do your findings support a biological theory of criminal behavior? What other variables would you take into consideration? What are the implications of your findings?

2. Economists have attempted to link the decline in crime rates during the 1990s to a rise in abortions resulting from the 1973 ruling in *Roe v. Wade,* legalizing abortion. The argument is based on the assumption that the majority of abortions occurred among lower-class, poor, unwed teenagers, who, if they did carry their infants to term, would have produced a class of potential criminals. What do you think about this argument? How can the science of criminology shed light on it? What do scientific research methods tell us about the simultaneous occurrence of two unrelated phenomena?

3. Researchers who combine the fields of biology and sociology argue that biological traits may predispose individuals to certain patterns of behavior, but environmental factors influence the nature and extent of their influence. If this is true, what can we do to help children diagnosed with ADHD? What components of their social environment need to be modified to limit the detrimental effects of their biological condition?

ADDITIONAL RESOURCES

To read more about the various regions of the brain as control centers for pleasure, pain, emotions, and reactions, and phrenological mapping, visit http://www.phrenology.com/index.html

Learn more about the relationship between diet and its impact on behavior at http://faculty.washington.edu/chudler/nutr.html

For additional information on the effects of hormones on stress and aggression, visit the American Psychological Association website at http://www.apa.org/monitor/nov04/hormones.html

Get a variety of literature, resources, and publications about ADHD from the National Institute of Mental Health: http://www.nimh.nih.gov/health/publications/attention-deficit-hyperactivity-disorder-teens-fact-sheet/attention-deficit-hyperactivity-disorder.shtml

More details about brain-imaging techniques and research can be found at http://archives.drugabuse.gov/NIDA_notes/NNvol15N3/Brain.html

Born criminal or product of environment? Read more about this debate by visiting http://library.thinkquest.org/C007405/

7

PSYCHOLOGICAL THEORIES

Crime Is in the Mind

In this chapter, we will explore the following questions:

- How does a diseased mind affect the way we think and act?
- Is criminal behavior related to a defect in personality?
- Do crime and delinquency stem from the inability to control certain impulses?
- Is crime a symptom of mental illness?
- What happens when we process information incorrectly?
- Do some individuals imitate aggressive behavior?
- How is crime rewarding to some people?
- If crime is in the mind, what can we do to prevent it?
- Can intelligence be related to crime?

Is it possible that components of our personality affect the

way we think, how we react, and the way we treat others? If so, what life experiences shape the development of our minds? What aspects of growth and development affect the mental processes that determine personality?

Criminological research has a long history of associating components of human behavior with certain personality characteristics. In a study analyzing the offending behaviors and personalities of three serial rapists, researchers found evidence to link the structure of an offender's personality to the methods and behaviors of the criminal act.[1] Components of personality—such as impulsivity, agreeableness, conscientiousness, self-confidence, and sensation seeking—were found to be directly correlated to the motive behind the rape, the selection of the victim, and the method of operation, producing three distinct patterns of offending.

These results suggest that in the identification, diagnosis, and treatment of rapists and other sex offenders we must take into account the integral link between personality traits and patterns of offending.[2] The findings can also play an important role in crime prevention and in law enforcement's investigation of complaints and apprehension of criminal suspects.[3]

On May 27, 1991, in the early morning hours, police officers were dispatched to an old neighborhood in a Milwaukee suburb after witnesses reported seeing a young Asian teen running naked, frightened, and bleeding. Police officers arriving on the scene were met by 31-year-old Jeffrey Dahmer, a white male, who told them it was just a lover's quarrel and that there was nothing wrong. Police escorted the boy back to Dahmer's apartment. Dahmer later strangled the boy and dismembered his body, keeping parts of it to eat and saving his skull as a trophy. One year later, Dahmer was convicted of the murders of 15 young men.[4]

What police did not know when they were called to the scene in 1991 was that Dahmer was on probation for a prior sexual offense—sexually assaulting a 13-year-old boy, a pattern of behavior that marked an integral component of Dahmer's personality and a link to his progressive acts of violence, assault, and murder. His killing spree spanned more than a decade and included a ritual of luring unsuspecting victims, mostly Asians and African Americans, into his apartment, drugging them, engaging in sexual acts, sometimes torturing them, and then killing them, usually by strangulation.

For years, the acts of Jeffrey Dahmer confounded human understanding and became the subject matter of crime stories in both academic literature and the media. All painted the same picture of a monster, a fiend, and a psychopath. However accurate these labels may be, they do not tell us much about the mind of a serial killer like Jeffrey Dahmer. How can we understand such uncommon acts? What light can the science of criminology shed?

In this chapter, we explore the various explanations of criminal behavior that stem from the psychological perspective. Is crime an uncontrolled or symbolic expression of basic human urges? Does criminality stem from disturbances in childhood relationships that are necessary for the adequate development of inhibitions?

MAJOR PRINCIPLES OF THE PSYCHOLOGICAL APPROACH

We often turn to the field of psychology for answers when explosive acts of violence are committed by individuals who by all indications have led seemingly normal lives.[5] However, the psychological perspective in criminology is not concerned with how we collectively arrive at definitions of normal and abnormal behavior; there is a general assumption within the field that normalcy is defined by social consensus. That is, we as a society can reach general agreement about which behaviors fall within the realm of the typical and which fall outside it.

Our starting point for understanding the cause of criminal behavior from the psychological perspective is the individual actor. The primary component within individuals that guides behavior is the personality, that element of our being that dictates, motivates, and drives our mind.[6] Various explanations tell us how inappropriate, dysfunctional, or abnormal mental processes can affect the personality and create disruptive, deviant, and criminal behavior patterns. What are these defective mental processes and how do they come about?

The mind is complex, with the ability to perceive, reason, believe, imagine, create, and engage in a variety of other mental processes. With this complexity, there are various sources of disturbances to the mental processes of the mind. These sources are distinct, yet all equally important in providing us with an understanding of their impact on human behavior. In this chapter, we identify four sources of defective mental processes: a pathological personality, maladaptation, faulty cognitive processes, and inappropriate learning and conditioning. Table 7.1 provides a summary of these distinct approaches to the understanding of crime causation. As we explore these approaches, we will also evaluate their merit in explaining criminal behavior.

PATHOLOGICAL PERSONALITY: THE PSYCHOPATH

The term **psychopath** found its way into the clinical literature in the early 1940s with the publication of *The Mask of Sanity,* which describes individuals with this type of personality as incapable of experiencing genuine emotions.[7] Psychopathic individuals are described as fully comprehending their social environments and often seeming on the surface to be genuine, sincere, and even intelligent. There is nothing remarkable about their appearance or demeanor. They can be polite, carry on a conversation, and even seem happy and content.

Inside, however, psychopaths lack the ability to identify with or understand how others think and feel. Consequently, they are self-centered, shallow, and detached from others. Their lack of affect or emotions dominates their personality. With prolonged interaction, especially on an interpersonal level, it becomes clear these individuals are chronic liars, do not feel guilt or shame, are reckless and irresponsible, are incapable of maintaining long-term relationships, and engage in ongoing antisocial and disruptive behavior.[8]

psychopath

An individual who lacks the ability to identify with or understand how others think and feel; is self-centered, shallow, and detached; is often a chronic liar, feels no shame or guilt, is reckless and irresponsible, is incapable of maintaining relationships, and engages in antisocial and disruptive behavior.

TABLE **7.1**

Psychological Perspectives on Criminal Behavior			
PATHOLOGICAL PERSONALITY	**MALADAPTATION**	**COGNITIVE THEORY**	**BEHAVIORISM**
The psychopath	Psychoanalysis: id, ego, superego	Social perception and the processing of information	Modeling and imitation
Antisocial personality disorder	Mental disease: Neurosis		Stimulus–response conditioning
	Mental disease: Psychosis		

Notorious serial killer Charles Manson was believed by many to be a psychopath. Friendly and charming, he was also capable of committing horrific acts of brutality without guilt or remorse.

Not all psychopaths evolve into criminals. However, psychopathic criminals are viewed by experts as perversely cruel, committing their acts without any regard to the consequences to their victims.[9] Whether it is brutality in the form of torture and rape, or scamming an elderly woman out of her life savings, there is a wanton disregard for the pain and suffering they are causing their victim.

Experts disagree about the origins of the psychopathic personality. Some studies suggest that environmental variables such as traumatic childhood experiences of neglect, violence, and abuse can play a role in the development of psychopathic traits.[10] Research on inmates with psychopathic personality traits shows that these offenders display a significantly lower rate of accuracy in identifying facial affect than the control group, indicating that they are incapable of identifying certain emotions.[11] Other studies point to the evolution of inherited neurological defects in the brain as the origin of psychopathy. These deficits are primarily in the *amygdale,* the part of the brain associated with emotional learning and reaction, and the *prefrontal cortex,* associated with impulse control, reasoning, and the ability to adapt.[12]

The term *psychopathy* was abandoned by the American Psychiatric Association (APA) in the late 1960s and replaced by **antisocial personality disorder (APD).**[13] Table 7.2 lists the behavioral characteristics of individuals with APD, including a persistent pattern of violating social norms and a disregard for the rights of others that begins in early adolescence and continues through adulthood. APD is a chronic mental illness in which an individual's perception of the social world, including ways of thinking and reacting to others, is dysfunctional.[14] Individuals with APD will lie, cheat, manipulate situations, become violent, and even break the law in the selfish pursuit of their own immediate wants and desires. It is not surprising that many individuals with APD come into contact with the criminal justice system at some point in their life. Studies of inmate populations reveal that the overwhelming majority of offenders classified with a mental disorder suffer from APD. Researchers also note that individuals diagnosed with APD exhibit both high rates of criminality and repeat patterns of chronic offending.[15]

Researchers who study pathological personalities have found that personality traits such as a consistent failure to abide by social norms, a disregard for the feelings of others, and a lack of remorse for harmful actions predispose individuals to delinquency and crime. We turn now to a discussion of other forms of mental disorders that also put people at odds with society, categories of mental illness that manifest in forms of maladaptive behavior.

antisocial personality disorder (APD)

The current term for psychopathy.

MALADAPTATION

How do we respond to circumstances in our social environment? For example, if you have been standing in line for a long time and someone cuts right in front of you, how do you react? Do you get angry and frustrated? How do you manage your anger? Do you politely indicate you are first or push the person out of the way?

The ways in which we react to and manage certain frustrations, disappointments, and hostile situations are all forms of *adaptation.* We learn to act and react in ways that make us better suited to our social environments. Unlike small children, who may first encounter the concept of sharing at preschool or a daycare facility, we do not forcibly take something we want from someone, and we do not bite or hit another when the person refuses

TABLE **7.2**

Signs and Symptoms of Antisocial Personality Disorder

- Disregard for right and wrong
- Persistent lying or deceit
- Using charm or wit to manipulate others
- Recurring difficulties with the law
- Repeatedly violating the rights of others
- Child abuse or neglect
- Intimidation of others
- Aggressive or violent behavior
- Lack of remorse about harming others
- Impulsive behavior
- Agitation
- Poor or abusive relationships
- Irresponsible work behavior

Source: Mayo Foundation for Medical Education and Research. (2009). *Antisocial personality disorder.* Retrieved from http://www.mayoclinic.com/health/antisocial-personality-disorder/DS00829

What skills must children develop in order to adapt to this type of structured environment? What happens if they do not develop these skills?

maladaptation

An inappropriate way of coping with the social environment.

psychoanalytic perspective

A method of understanding human behavior by examining drives and impulses within the unconscious mind.

id

In psychoanalytic theory, the part of personality that seeks instant gratification for immediate need and wants.

ego

In psychoanalytic theory, the part of personality that takes into consideration the reality of situations; the ego guides behavior within the boundaries of what is socially acceptable.

superego

In psychoanalytic theory, the part of the personality that judges the appropriateness of behavior in a given situation; also known as conscience.

to give it to us. That would represent **maladaptation,** an inappropriate way of coping with the social environment. Why do some individuals exhibit maladaptive behavior?

Psychoanalysis

Modern explanations of the origins of disturbances in patterns of behavior are rooted in the works of Sigmund Freud (1856–1939). Freud founded the **psychoanalytic perspective,** a method of understanding human behavior by examining drives and impulses within the unconscious mind.[16] His theory divided the human mind into three components: the id, the ego, and the superego (Figure 7.1).

According to Freud, we are born with the **id,** that part of our personality that seeks instant gratification for our immediate need and wants. The id represents our biological drives for comfort, shelter, food, and sex. It does not consider the feelings of others or the reality of the situation when seeking pleasure or satisfying desire. When a baby gets hungry, he will shriek in protest, regardless of whether he is waking the whole house in the middle of the night or sitting in a quiet church service.

Over the next few years, a baby begins to learn that wishes cannot always be granted immediately. The second part of the personality, the **ego,** takes into consideration the reality of situations. The ego creates a sense of balance for the unlimited desires of the id by guiding behavior within the boundaries of what is socially acceptable. A 4-year-old child who is hungry will consider that mom is cooking dinner, so there is no need to cry or have a tantrum. Instead of acting upon the impulsive and selfish desires of the id for instant gratification, the child may ask for a small snack and then simply wait for the appropriate time to eat.

The appropriateness of our behavior in a given situation is judged by the **superego,** that aspect of personality that develops around the age of 5 or 6 and is the result of the morals and values instilled by parents, teachers, and other significant individuals. The superego is often referred to as our conscience. It is that aspect of personality that determines right and wrong, the watchful eye of the mind that will keep our behavior in line whether we think others will find out about it or not. Suppose the child who wants a snack sneaks into the kitchen to get one anyway after mom has refused. In this situation, a properly developed superego will urge the ego to stop, because the behavior is inappropriate.

A poorly developed superego can be the result of different variables, including inappropriate socialization, unhappy experiences in childhood, and a weak ego damaged by a traumatic event. (See Consider This for an extreme example of such a trauma.) Under Freud's model, an inadequate superego will render the individual incapable of making

FIGURE **7.1**

Freud: One Personality, Three Parts

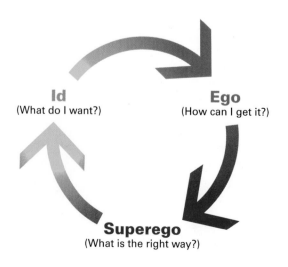

Id
(What do I want?)

Ego
(How can I get it?)

Superego
(What is the right way?)

CONSIDER THIS...

24 Years of Rape, Abuse, and Imprisonment

In 2008, the world was shocked and outraged when 73-year-old Austrian Josef Fritzl was arrested for the crimes of murder by neglect, enslavement, deprivation of liberty, multiple counts of rape and incest, and coercion.[17] Fritzl was accused of locking his then 18-year-old daughter Elisabeth in a windowless cellar in August 1984. Over the next 24 years, he held her captive, raping her and fathering seven children with her; one child died of respiratory problems a few months after he was born. Fritzl had refused to seek medical attention for the infant. Three of her children were raised by Fritzl and his wife Rosemarie in the home upstairs. The other three were locked up in the basement with their mother. A jury took just four hours to find Fritzl guilty on all charges. He was sentenced to life imprisonment.

The trial may have been over quickly, and Fritzl is now paying for his crimes, but the psychological impact on his victims cannot be easily erased. Elisabeth Fritzl and her children are seeking psychiatric care in a secret location in Austria. Some of the children are trying to get used to seeing sunlight for the first time and adjusting to walking in rooms with ceilings higher than 5 feet 6 inches—the height of the underground cellar. Austrian officials have had to provide them all with new identities and enforce a countrywide no-fly zone over their new location. Elisabeth and her children have to learn how to live again physically, psychologically, and emotionally.

Not even the victims can imagine what the long-term effects of their years of abuse and neglect will

Elisabeth Fritzl was imprisoned for 24 years by her father, shown here, who raped and abused her and fathered her seven children. How could the experience of years of rape and abuse affect an individual's personality?

be. Experts note that "time does not heal all wounds. Elizabeth and her three children have been traumatized beyond belief, in ways that most of us cannot comprehend and never will."[18]

Psychoanalytic theory maintains that an individual's personality can be damaged by traumatic experiences in childhood. With this understanding, can we predict the long-term effects this ordeal might have on the victims? Are there interventions we could recommend to try to avoid the onset of antisocial behavior in them?

What do you think?

---

appropriate moral judgments. Thus, in the struggle between the instinctive needs of individuals and the obstacles presented by social norms, the ego will submit to the unlimited desires of the id, without any consideration of the boundaries set forth by conventional society. An individual driven by a desire for the comforts and pleasures of material goods may decide to steal in order to get what he or she wants. The ego will present the reality of the situation: I don't have enough money, my job doesn't pay well, getting an education will take too long, selling drugs is a bit risky, stealing is quick and easy, and so on. Without a properly developed superego, the individual is likely to act instinctively to meet immediate needs, with little consideration of the consequences of the behavior or the wrongfulness of the act.

In a healthy individual, the ego has the challenging task of balancing the reality of the situation with the wants and needs of the id, while staying within the boundaries of acceptable behavior as defined by the superego. A disturbance in the development of these three components of personality will create a conflict that can manifest as criminal

neurosis

A form of mental illness manifested by behavior expressing fear, tension, anxiety, and emotional distress.

phobia

An irrational fear.

kleptomania

An obsessive compulsion to steal.

psychosis

A major form of mental illness manifested by the inability to comprehend reality, think clearly, and respond appropriately.

The name Jared Lee Loughner did not mean much until January 8, 2011, when Loughner opened fire at a Safeway grocery store in Casas Adobes, just north of Tucson, Arizona. He has been charged with killing six people, including a federal judge, and critically wounding Arizona Congresswoman Gabrielle Giffords, his apparent target. Speculation about the motives behind the 22-year-old's actions revealed reports of mental illness. Other claims were made about his abuse of drugs and antigovernment sentiments. This crime, like many others, opens up the debate about the relative roles of individual psychological factors and other social variables in the causation of crime.

behavior, a form of maladaptation that balances desires with available choices. We turn now to a form of maladaptation resulting from personality disturbances created by mental illness.

Neurosis

A **neurosis** is a form of mental illness manifested by behavior expressing fear, tension, anxiety, and emotional distress.[19] Individuals who suffer from neurosis are well in touch with reality. In fact, they recognize the symptoms of their disorder but simply cannot help themselves. They adapt to their environment in ways inconsistent with the norms and standards of acceptable behavior, so their actions often seem unreasonable, bizarre, disruptive, and inexplicable. Some examples of neuroses include depression, acute or chronic anxiety and panic attacks, irrational fears or **phobias,** and obsessive-compulsive tendencies.

Neurotic individuals develop behaviors to manage and cope with their disorders. Someone with an irrational fear of heights may avoid taking the elevator or traveling by airplane. This can be a very disruptive form of adaptation if it interferes with that person's job or choice of where to live, go on vacation, and the like, but if the alternative will create an unbearable state of panic and anxiety, it is not an option. While most neuroses do not lead to criminal behavior, some can. Individuals suffering from **kleptomania,** the obsessive compulsion to steal, may shoplift items despite their lack of financial need.

Many individuals with neurosis will go through life without any major disturbance in their social interactions and adapt to conventional social norms and roles. Their patterns of maladaptive behavior will in all likelihood go unnoticed by most of those who come into contact with them. The situation is very different, however, when someone suffers from a psychosis.

Psychosis and Other Major Mental Disorders

A **psychosis** is a major form of mental illness manifested by the inability to comprehend reality, think clearly, and respond appropriately.[20] Symptoms of psychosis include disorganized and confused thoughts, extreme and unfounded paranoia, mistaken perceptions, hallucinations, and social withdrawal. Individuals may hear voices that command them to do certain things or think they are a spy for the federal government or believe they need to carry out the work of the devil. They are unaware of their faulty thought processes and their distortion of reality, which makes it very difficult for them to function properly in society and often disrupts every aspect of life, including the ability to work, maintain meaningful relationships, and carry out responsibilities.[21]

In addition to psychoses, there are other major mental disorders that can seriously affect an individual's behavior. Table 7.3 provides a brief overview of various psychoses and some major mental disorders and their corresponding behavioral components.

The association between crime and psychotic disorders has been researched extensively. Studies show that offenders committing violent crimes often suffer from mental illness, and the presence of a psychotic disorder places individuals at a greater risk for criminal behavior.[22] Delinquents also have higher rates of clinically diagnosed psychotic disorders than adolescents in the general population.[23] In a study of over 79,000 offenders incarcerated between September 1, 2006, and August 31, 2007, researchers found inmates diagnosed with major psychotic disorders such as bipolar disorder and schizophrenia had a significantly higher rate of recidivism over the six-year study period. Prisoners with major psychiatric illnesses were more likely to have had multiple prior incarcerations than inmates not so diagnosed.[24]

We must interpret these research findings with some caution. The presence of mental illness alone does not establish a causal link between the psychosis and the criminal behavior; there may be intervening social variables. For example, mentally ill individuals may be more susceptible to weakened social ties, unemployment, poverty, and low

TABLE **7.3**

Psychoses and Major Mental Disorders

DISORDER	CHARACTERISTICS
Schizophrenia	■ Distorted sense of reality ■ No logical relationship between thoughts and feelings ■ Delusional thoughts and ideas ■ Hallucinations in the form of hearing voices or seeing visions
Bipolar Disorder	■ An elevated manic mood marked by irrational behavior such as an increase in spending and risk-taking behavior, feelings of grandiosity, and tendency toward extravagance ■ Manic phase is followed by a period of depression, feelings of guilt, worthlessness, and loss of hope
Psychotic Depression	■ Feelings of extreme sadness, failure, hopelessness, or rejection ■ Feelings are inconsistent with environmental variables; instead, they originate from untrue or unfounded thoughts ■ Thoughts of persecution, paranoid fears of illness, and self-blame for uncontrollable circumstances
Schizoaffective Disorder	■ Symptoms of both schizophrenia and a mood disorder, such as depression or bipolar disorder ■ Unable to distinguish between the real world and what is imagined ■ Cannot establish concrete thoughts
Dissociative Identity Disorder	■ Have two or more distinct personalities that are often in conflict with one another ■ Incapable of accounting for gaps in time and experiences ■ Changes in personality often associated with a stressful event or emotional experience

Source: Sadock, B., & Sadock, V. (2002). *Synopsis of psychiatry.* Philadelphia: Lippincott Williams & Wilkins

educational achievement, any of which may increase their likelihood of involvement in criminal activity.[25] Moreover, the behavior and demeanor of mentally ill individuals may make them more likely to be confrontational when approached by law enforcement officers, inflating their rate of arrest in crime statistics.[26]

Criminal behavior associated with the presence of a neurotic or psychotic condition is marked by unconscious turmoil that results in disturbances to the personality. We turn now to another explanation of criminal behavior—that it results from faulty cognitive processes.

COGNITIVE THEORY

Suppose your grades are slipping in one of your classes, you are put on academic probation, and you are in danger of losing your financial aid if you do not bring up your grades. One of your classmates works as a student assistant to the professor in the class where you are having difficulty. When you tell her of your predicament, she says she is willing to help you out by getting you a copy of the next exam. What do you do in this situation? How do you perceive the option to cheat? Which variables come into play in your solution to this problem?

The branch of psychology that studies the mental processes of understanding, perceiving, interpreting, and manipulating information is **cognitive theory.**[27] Cognitive processes have three major components: perception, judgment, and execution (Figure 7.2). *Perception* is the process of accumulating data when we seek out, recognize, understand, and recall certain stimuli and information. *Judgment* is the process of organizing and evaluating that information to make a decision. *Execution* is simply acting on the decision.

According to cognitive theory, individuals who properly process information by having a clear understanding of environmental stimuli and who better evaluate choices are more likely to make better decisions in difficult situations. The opposite is also true. Suppose someone is facing financial hardship after being laid off from work during difficult economic times. Cognitive processes will begin to take place when the individual realizes bills are piling up, foreclosure on the family home is imminent, and childcare expenses continue to mount. What to do? An individual who processes information appropriately is more likely to explore a range of options that may include getting a loan to pay off bills, refinancing the mortgage to reduce monthly payments, and temporarily taking a lower-paying job to make ends meet. An individual who processes information inappropriately may see criminal activity as a suitable means to meet immediate financial needs. This error in cognitive processing can result from a number of factors including lack of development of appropriate moral reasoning, personal values that emphasize survival over adherence to social norms, and faulty calculation of the long-term consequences.[28]

Distortion in cognitive processes has been used to explain a wide variety of criminal behavior such as domestic violence and rape. Research on the behavior patterns of child molesters has found that the perpetrators perceive children as desiring sexual contact with adults, believe sexual contact is beneficial to the child, feel entitled to sexual activity with the child, and feel a need to control their social environment, which they see as dangerous and threatening.[29]

cognitive theory

The branch of psychology that studies the mental processes of understanding, perceiving, interpreting, and manipulating information.

FIGURE **7.2**

Cognitive Processes in the Decision to Cheat

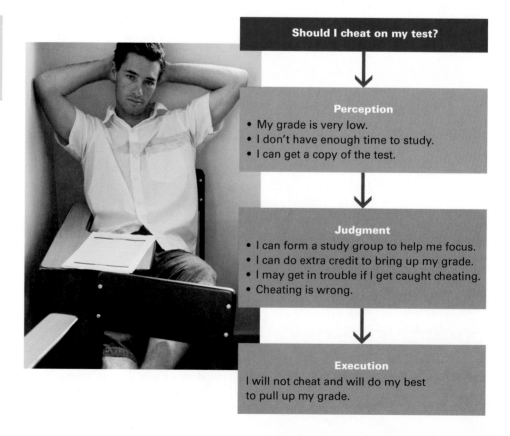

Should I cheat on my test?

Perception
- My grade is very low.
- I don't have enough time to study.
- I can get a copy of the test.

Judgment
- I can form a study group to help me focus.
- I can do extra credit to bring up my grade.
- I may get in trouble if I get caught cheating.
- Cheating is wrong.

Execution
I will not cheat and will do my best to pull up my grade.

Treatment interventions for sexual offenders are designed to prevent attacks from recurring by emphasizing the control of deviant arousal patterns and correcting cognitive distortions.[30]

In 2002, researchers Barry Maletzky and Cynthia Steinhauser published a 25-year followup on 7,275 sex offenders treated with behavior modification in a northeastern U.S. clinic.[31] The patients included child molesters, pedophiles, rapists, and exhibitionists. These are some of the behavior modification techniques used to alter their thoughts and reactions to certain stimuli:

- *Aversive conditioning:* A negative stimulus (such as an offensive odor) is paired with the onset of sexual arousal in an offending scenario (such as child pornography).
- *Plethysmographic biofeedback:* The plethysmograph measures volume changes of the penis. This allows the offender to reduce arousal to deviant thoughts or images using objective evidence from visual cues that indicate when arousal is increasing or decreasing.
- *Aversive behavior rehearsal:* This technique is used primarily for the crime of exhibitionism. Offenders are required to perform an actual offense before therapeutic staff who are instructed not to respond, and the offender becomes conditioned not to be aroused by the offending behavior.
- *Masturbatory reconditioning:* Sexual fantasy plays a major part in patterns of sexual offending. In this technique, offenders are reconditioned to change

the themes of their sexual fantasies by becoming aroused to consensual, nondeviant sexual scenarios.

- *Vicarious sensitization:* Stimuli such as a video can make an offender more cognitively aware of negative effects on the victim of a sexual crime.
- *Relapse prevention:* Identifying thoughts or events that trigger offending behavior may inhibit patterns of offending before they begin.
- *Cognitive restructuring:* Group therapy is used to discuss and correct thinking errors offenders make to rationalize, minimize, or justify their actions. All offenders do not share the same distortions and can therefore recognize the errors in one another's thinking in a group setting.

Treatments were administered at the clinic on an outpatient basis. Telephone follow-up interviews were given over the course of the study between 1973 and 1997. Police records were also reviewed, and, in some cases, plethysmographs were checked.

Overall, the treatments appeared generally effective over the time period. According to Maletzky and Steinhauser's data, the rate of reoffending for those who did not prematurely drop out of treatment was 1.7 percent of 5,606 participants, versus 8.1 percent of the 1,669 participants who did quit early.

The benefits of cognitive behavior treatment for sexual offenders have been well documented in the empirical literature.[32] Researchers also note that behavioral modification treatments are most effective when customized to individual offenders and their circumstances.

Various behavior modification treatments attempt to undo errors in cognitive thinking. The Connecting Theory to Practice feature discusses cognitive behavior treatment for sex offenders. We turn now to another form of disturbance to personality—those that develop through learning experiences.

BEHAVIORISM

Much of what we do is the result of learning. What we watch on television, the way our parents handle problems, and the reactions we get from others all serve as learning experiences from which we develop our various patterns of behavior. **Behavior theory** says that human actions are derived from learning experiences that include observing others and getting reinforcement for certain behaviors.[33] Let's first turn to the concept of observation and see how it affects our learning.

behavior theory

The branch of psychology that holds that human actions are derived from learning experiences that include observing others and getting reinforcement for certain behaviors.

Modeling

Children learn from their parents all the time. Without the input of any lecturing, instructing, or admonishing, a child will learn what to think and how to act, just by watching the behavior of mom and dad. For example, a child may grow up in a home where parents make derogatory statements about certain racial groups, participate in racist rallies and meetings, and forbid their children to have friends who are minorities. Such experiences can lead the child to grow up with similar attitudes and behavior patterns. This type of learning is called **behavior modeling,** learning by watching, listening, and copying what we see and hear.

behavior modeling

Learning by watching, listening, and copying what we see and hear.

Prominent theorist Albert Bandura noted that individuals become violent and aggressive through life experiences that teach them to act that way.[34] These experiences can be very personal, such as being physically abused as a child or growing up in a neighborhood where assault and homicide were common occurrences, or less personal, like viewing violent interactions in films or television and playing video games (see Connecting Research to Practice). For example, a child who watches his mom being slapped by his dad when dinner is not ready may in turn slap his classmate at daycare when he does not get the toy he wants immediately. Table 7.4 summarizes the various sources from which we model our behavior.

Research studies show a strong correlation between exposure to violence and hostility and aggressive behavior.[39] Children who see repeated patterns of abuse at home are more likely to exhibit aggressive tendencies throughout their lives and more likely to be abusive in their own relationships.[40] Moreover, studies on the effects of violent video games show a positive relationship between playing these games and having hostile thoughts, acting aggressively, and engaging in delinquency.[41] Children who are exposed to violent content in video games become more aggressive than their counterparts who have less exposure, even when controlling for how aggressive the children are at the beginning of the research study.

Violent television content has also been controversial. In 2001, 12-year-old Lionel Tate, who weighed 170 pounds, was charged with murder in the beating death of his 6-year-old cousin Tiffany. Young Lionel claimed it was an accident; he did not mean to kill his cousin. He was imitating the pro wrestling moves he had been watching and

Even though this child is actually playing, what is the role of the social learning mechanism of modeling here?

Curbing Media Violence: Lessons Learned from Research

Media technology has exploded during the 20th century. Today, it is estimated that over 98 percent of U.S. homes own televisions, VCR or DVD players, and/or video game and computer equipment of some kind. With this unprecedented expansion, the debate about the influence of violent media images on behavior has grown.[35]

The National Television Violence Study analyzed three seasons of television programming between 1994 and 1997 and found two of every three shows contained some form of violence, with viewers watching an average of six violent acts during each hour of television.[36] The empirical literature shows overwhelming evidence of the link between media violence and aggression. Psychologists have performed hundreds of studies testing the effects of media violence and aggressive behavior; over 1,000 have substantiated a causal connection.

In response, the media have developed several mechanisms to warn people about the content they will be watching. The Motion Picture Association of America (MPAA) reviews and rates each movie based on how most parents would respond to it. Upon review and a group discussion and vote, the film is given its rating. Violent content is one of the main factors the MPAA board must consider when viewing any film.

Video games are given similar ratings by the Entertainment Software Rating Board (ESRB) so consumers can make informed decisions about their software purchases.[37] Computer and video games with the "mature" rating may contain "intense violence" and/or "blood and gore," and most stores and other outlets are not allowed to sell them to anyone under 18 without a parent's or legal guardian's consent.

In 1999, the Federal Communications Commission (FCC) announced it would begin requiring television manufacturers to install V-chips into their product (the V stands for "violence").[38] Parents program the chip with a code to block certain television shows based on their content as set forth by FCC programming ratings. As of January 1, 2000, all television sets 13 inches or larger sold in the United States must include a V-chip. According to a 2003 study on V-chip usage, only 27 percent of all parents in the research sample who owned the V-chip actually used it. Those who did not use it cited difficulty in understanding how to program it and the inability to get it to work properly.

Another study conducted in 2004 found similar results. Of 1,001 parents of children between the ages of 2 and 7, only 15 percent had used the V-chip. Some stated they were not even aware that their television sets had the device. In April 2007, the FCC released a report on the use of V-chip technology, citing the need to make parents more aware of the device and its usage through education.

TABLE 7.4

Whom Do We Observe? Family, Peers, Co-Workers, Environment, Mass Media

POSITIVE ROLE MODELING	NEGATIVE ROLE MODELING
Sharing	Apathy
Cooperation	Verbal abuse
Peaceful conflict resolution	Hostility
Honesty	Aggressive conflict resolution
Accepting responsibility	Manipulation
Caring for the feelings of others	Deception
Respecting authority	Blaming others
Working hard	Praising violence
	Rebellion

What impact might this event have on the behavior of observers?

thought it would be all right to body-slam her—that she would get up and walk away unhurt, just like they do on television.[42]

Researchers note that the observation of violence, hostility, and aggression leads us to model those patterns of behavior, communicating to us that this is an acceptable way of interacting. Moreover, prolonged exposure to violence desensitizes us to its emotional impact. If we see someone getting slapped, punched, beaten, or killed over and over again, whether at home, in our neighborhood, or on television, it becomes an almost ordinary event.[43] Modeling of aggressive, violent behavior also occurs and is likely to persist and be repeated if the outcome of the encounter is positively reinforced, such as by showing it to be acceptable or making the aggressor a hero. Let's look at the effects of positive and negative reinforcement on modeling.

Stimulus–Response Conditioning

Behavior theory is based on the assumption that actions are learned and maintained by the results or consequences they produce.[44] Thus, behavior is more likely to persist the more it is rewarded. Think for a moment about someone starting a new diet and exercise program. How long will the person continue that program if it does not produce the intended consequences of losing weight or having a healthier body?

Behavior can be reinforced in direct or indirect ways (Figure 7.3). *Direct reinforcement* occurs when the behavior itself is rewarding. When you exercise and eat well, you feel better and your body is healthier. It also occurs when the behavior is praised by another; for example, someone notices you working out at the gym and says you're looking great. *Indirect reinforcement* occurs when you see someone else's behavior producing positive

How do you think this dog learned to obey his owner's command? Did the treat have anything to do with it?

A College Education

Direct Reinforcement
- Expands your mind
- Allows you to make new friends
- Increases your opportunity for a better career
- Is praised by your family
- Is socially accepted

Indirect Reinforcement
- Is emphasized as important in school
- Was the reason your parents are successful
- Is portrayed positively in the media
- Has been a tradition in your family
- Gave your sibling a sense of identity

FIGURE **7.3**

Direct and Indirect Reinforcement

results. When you attend your 20th high school reunion and that chubby kid that every-one picked on is now lean and physically fit, you may decide to follow his diet and exercise regimen.

Patterns of delinquent and criminal behavior, too, often persist because of rewards associated with them.[45] Reinforcement and punishment also influence the extent to which an individual exhibits a behavior that has been learned. Studies of gang affiliation and membership indicate that individuals join a gang to gain a sense of respect, belonging, and acceptance. Behaviors such as assault, robbery, vandalism, and homicide are not only accepted but praised as demonstrations of loyalty to the norms and values of the gang. These rewards for criminal acts further reinforce the gang member's reputation for violence and sense of group identity.[46] Research on the effects of rewarding and punishing violence in video games shows those individuals who played games where violence is praised or rewarded exhibit more hostile thinking and aggressive behavior than individuals who play games where violence is punished.[47]

Human behavior, according to the behavioral perspective, is thus a response to the environment. The presence or absence of a behavior in the future depends on the balance between the rewards and punishments associated with it now. A child who jokes around in class and receives praise and admiration from peers may continue to be the class clown, despite being punished by the teacher. The reward associated with the behavior is greater than the punishment. Violence, aggression, and criminal behavior can be rewarded in many ways. The association between criminal activities and the rewards of excitement, thrill, money, praise, and group membership will increase the individual's participation in these activities, despite the risks of punishment and social disapproval.

While all this makes sense, behavioral theory does not account for the role cognitive variables play in the way we interpret outcomes as positive or negative. Why is the approval of peers, for example, more rewarding to some individuals than the approval of parents, or vice versa? Why does someone resort to gang membership as a source of unity and belonging, as opposed to joining an athletic team or school club? In fact, the psychological perspective in general says very little about the effects of social structures on personality, modeling, and behavior. How then does the paradigm of psychology add to our understanding of criminal behavior? Before we evaluate the contribution of psychological theories to the field of criminology, we must first examine the relationship between intelligence and crime.

INTELLIGENCE AND CRIME

While the development of intelligence testing and IQ scores is relatively recent, the assumption that intelligence and crime are interrelated has a long history. As early as 1913, researchers concluded that mental inferiority differentiated the law breaker from the law abider.[48] We cannot discuss the relationship between intelligence and crime in a vacuum, however. To give it some context, we look briefly at the history of the concept of intelligence in general—a history plagued by problems of definition and measurement and by the infusion of racism and classism.

The biological paradigm introduced us to the measurement of physical characteristics, such as body size and skull shape, in order to differentiate between different types of people. This technique declined in popularity when psychological testing was introduced. In 1904, French psychologist Alfred Binet (1857–1911) developed a method of identifying children whose poor school performance suggested the need for special education. He did this by developing numerous tests that ranged in level of difficulty, to each of which he assigned an age level. The difference between the child's mental age (the age associated with the last tasks performed successfully) and the child's chronological age was termed the subject's intelligence quotient (IQ). Binet never claimed that this score represented *inborn intelligence:* The number was simply an average of many scores.

IQ tests became popularized in the United States in 1916 by researchers at Stanford University, who revised the test and gave it a new name—the Stanford-Binet test. By that time, the meaning of IQ scores had changed. The score came to represent intelligence—a single quantifiable entity that was both fixed and inherited. Since smart and successful people seemed to produce equally successful children, it was assumed that intelligence must be inherited, and since IQ scores were predictive of this same success, IQ scores must represent intelligence.[49]

Some of the earliest studies of the relationship between intelligence and crime examined IQ test scores of incarcerated offenders. These studies found the scores of prisoners and juvenile delinquents to be low and concluded that low intelligence was a cause of crime. This research has been criticized for various reasons. First, the prisoners were not representative of all criminals but were only the select few who were caught, convicted, and incarcerated. Second, these conclusions were reported before the test scores of prisoners could be compared with those of the general public.

The argument that IQ is related to criminality became popular again in the late 1970s among criminologists. Travis Hirschi and Michael J. Hindelang reviewed research on the relationship between IQ and juvenile delinquency, using both official and self-reported data. Even when controlling for social class and race variables, they found that low IQ is an important determinant of delinquency.[50] More recent studies have found that the IQ scores of African Americans are between 10 and 15 points lower than the scores of whites and conclude that this lower level of innate intelligence explains their higher rate of criminality.[51] This conclusion, however, is built upon an incorrect foundation.

First, we must approach the relationship among IQ, intelligence, and crime with caution.[52] Instead of proof that intelligence exists, high IQ scores and later success may both be the product of high socioeconomic status. Children in the upper classes are more likely to be successful in the adult world. They are also more likely to have the academic background that increases IQ scores. That is not sufficient proof that these children are more intelligent than their poorer counterparts. The same is true for differences in IQ scores between whites and blacks and between different ethnic and immigrant groups. The differences in score do not indicate that whites are more intelligent than African Americans or Latino immigrants but rather reflect school achievement and familiarity with the white middle-class cultural values and experiences that the tests have been found to reflect.[53]

The assumption that criminals are mentally inferior would logically lead us to research only a limited range of criminals: the street junkie, the unemployed mugger, the delinquent drop-out. One could not credibly explain corporate crime, state crime, political corruption, or organized crime by reason of mental inferiority. The variable of intelligence narrows the definition of crime and criminals. Upper-class crime is simply outside that definition, and once again we have a theory that studies the behavior of one class while ignoring similar behaviors by people in other classes.

EVALUATING PSYCHOLOGICAL THEORIES

In many ways the psychological perspective provides us with an understanding of crime that fills a void in the literature. It helps us comprehend behaviors that environmental variables alone cannot explain. Psychological theories have paved the way toward an understanding of the role of personality in shaping human behavior, as well as the influence of role models on learning and the effects of rewards on its persistence. Now, when we read headlines about an ordinary mother like Andrea Yates, who drowned her five children, we may be able to develop a scientific understanding of what she was thinking when she committed this horrific act. We may be able to understand the faulty thought processes created by her mental illness and the delusions that compelled her to kill her children to save them from growing up and becoming agents of the devil.[54]

How can psychological theories help us understand why Andrea Yates, mother of five and a nurse by profession, drowned her five children one by one on June 20, 2001?

Despite these contributions, psychological theories of criminal behavior have been criticized on several grounds. One major shortcoming is their reliance on research conducted on criminals and delinquents within a clinical or institutional setting and rarely in their homes, on the streets, or in their neighborhood.[55] This approach overlooks the influence that jail, detention, or a mental hospital may have on an individual's mental state and thought processes.[56]

Critics have charged that the psychoanalytic approach is fundamentally flawed, relying on empirical evidence that is based on unconscious memories triggered during therapy.[57] These memories can often be the result of prompting or suggestions made by the clinician, rather than objective data. Moreover, to say that certain unconscious memories from early traumatic childhood experiences are later expressed through behavioral symptoms and disturbed personality traits adds little to our scientific understanding of crime and delinquency. That is, if someone exhibits symptoms of antisocial behavior, low self-esteem, or other negative disposition, then are we to assume the person must have experienced some trauma during childhood? This prediction is difficult to make with any true empirical accuracy.

Moreover, psychological theories attribute variations in human behavior to differences in personality, without accounting for social conditions such as poverty, lack of opportunity, and cultural differences that influence how individuals see the world around them and react to different situations.[58] Thus, these theories fail to explain variations in crime rates among different groups. Why do men commit far more crimes than women? Are men more likely to suffer mental illness then women, or is the difference more a product of how the two genders are socialized?[59] With their emphasis on an individual level of explanation, psychological theories also fail to account for changes in crime trends over time. It is very difficult to argue that criminal behavior declined during certain time periods because people were more mentally balanced.

This brings us to the final criticism of psychological theory. By what standards are we measuring normality?[60] Psychological theories interpret behavior based on the assumption that we arrive at the definition of normal by social consensus. But social structure plays a role in imposing labels and legal definitions on the behavior of certain individuals. As we discussed in Chapter 2, whether we define behaviors as normal or abnormal, legal or criminal depends on who has the power to define, not on what the majority thinks. We cannot assume that because someone does something others consider abnormal there is anything wrong or different about that individual's personality.

Moreover, many individuals who are not diagnosed with a psychological disorder violate the norms of society and engage in horrible acts of violence and crime.[61] (See Crime in Global Perspective for an example of this.) Psychological theories rely on the assumption that individuals commit crime because they have some type of personality or mental problem; cure these individuals and the crime problem will go away. With a cautious eye on this reasoning, we turn now to a brief overview of crime-control strategies offered by the psychological perspective.

PRACTICAL APPLICATION OF PSYCHOLOGICAL THEORIES

Table 7.5 summarizes the psychological approach to the study of crime and crime causation. For the psychologist, crime-control strategies based on the psychological perspective focus on two techniques: (1) identifying and treating emotional problems and conflicts before they manifest as criminal behavior, and (2) treating

CRIME IN GLOBAL PERSPECTIVE | The Abu Ghraib Prison Guards

In 2004, photographs were released showing the graphic acts of torture and abuse perpetrated by U.S. soldiers at the Abu Ghraib military war prison in Iraq.[62] The world was shocked and horrified at the evidence of physical, psychological, and sexual abuse of prisoners that included forced nudity, torture, rape, assault, humiliation, and homicide.

The U.S. military has a rigorous screening process in place for those who want to enlist.[63] It includes criminal and financial background checks, physical and mental aptitude testing, and extensive screenings for drug and alcohol abuse history, chronic sexual disease history, and moral character. After these tests, the military still holds the right to refuse service enlistment to anyone with questionable character, behavior or personality issues, or a conscientious objection to war.

So how is it that at least six members of the 372nd Military Police Company perpetrated such atrocious crimes against the prisoners detained at the Iraqi Abu Ghraib military war prison? By all accounts, these soldiers were put through a rigorous testing process to make sure they would never perpetrate these kinds of heinous acts. Still, they *did*.

Behavioral assessments alone cannot determine the risk for potential future criminal behavior.[64] Many other individual factors can contribute to whether a person is prone to deviance and/or violence. To assess risk based solely on one set of factors is to turn a blind eye to many other potential causes and, ultimately, to other potential treatments and crime-prevention measures. While psychological testing can be a useful tool in evaluating potential criminals, it should not be the only tool we rely upon, a lesson painfully learned at Abu Ghraib.

individuals who have already violated the law and are suffering some type of psychological disturbance.[65]

Predicting Criminality Before It Occurs

Policies that try to predict future criminal behavior do so by identifying risk factors such as early childhood aggression, truancy in school, and teenage alcohol and drug abuse as indicators.[66] Policymakers rely on studies showing children who display early signs of aggression and disruptive behavior are likely to persist in these patterns of behavior as adults.[67]

TABLE **7.5**

SUMMARY: The Psychological Perspective	
Definition of Crime	Crime is purposeful behavior that is a response to certain felt needs.
Why Does Crime Occur? (Theory)	Because the personality controls motivation and all aspects of human behavior, any disturbance of the mental processes affecting personality (personality disorder, mental illnesses, errors in cognitive development, inappropriate modeling) will result in a disturbance of behavior.
What Is the Solution to Crime? (Policy)	■ Early detection of behavior symptoms of psychological problems that may be predictive of future criminal behavior. ■ Therapeutic intervention and treatment of individuals identified with a psychological disorder to correct the faulty thought process or minimize its impact on behavior.

Programs to identify early warning signs of interpersonal conflicts, anger, depression, substance abuse, and other symptoms of psychological problems are meant to help us identify a condition and intervene with therapy and counseling to avoid its escalation into violence and crime.[68] When a problem is suspected, parents, teachers, school-based clinicians, employers, and social welfare and juvenile justice agencies are encouraged and often required to make a referral to individual or group counseling, substance abuse treatment, mental health assessment, or family therapy.[69]

We can divide strong predictors of future involvement in criminal activities into two categories: *family factors,* such as coercive or inconsistent parenting techniques, and *child factors,* such as hyperactivity and conduct disorder.[70] Within each category, **static factors** are experiences in the past that cannot be reversed or altered. **Dynamic factors** are capable of changing over time with treatment or counseling. Table 7.6 summarizes these factors.

The task of predicting criminal behavior is only one step to take in the direction of crime prevention, according to the psychological perspective. A variety of programs, which we look at next, are designed to intervene on the behalf of individuals who have already become engaged in criminal activity.

static factors

Predictors of future involvement in criminal activities are experiences in the past that cannot be reversed or altered.

dynamic factors

Predictors of future involvement in criminal activities that are capable of changing over time with treatment or counseling.

Responding to Criminality After It Occurs

Psychological theories say behavior, including criminal behavior, originates within the mind.[71] Correcting inappropriate behavior therefore focuses on correcting faulty mental processes. Psychologically based treatment practices operate at several levels, including school-based counselors, private clinicians, and mental health practitioners in institutional settings such as mental hospitals or prisons. Interventions range from individual counseling to behavior modification therapy.

According to the literature, criminal behavior is often connected to deep-rooted, unconscious hostilities and anxieties that, if left in the hidden mind, will interfere with any effort at rehabilitation.[72] Mental health experts often work with offenders through counseling sessions to uncover repressed memories from traumatic childhood experiences that may be driving their delinquent or criminal behavior. Critics note, however, that it is

TABLE **7.6**

Behavior Predictors of Future Criminality

FAMILY FACTORS	CHILD FACTORS
Static Risk	
Parental involvement in criminal activity	Age of onset of delinquency
Complications during pregnancy	Age of onset of alcohol and drug use
Dynamic Risk	
Parental mental health	Lack of self-control
Parental management	Developmental delay
Family structure	Aggression
Adverse family environment	School-related problems such as truancy
	Involvement with alcohol and drugs
	Experiences of abuse and maltreatment

Source: Leschied, A., Chiodo, D., Nowicki, E., & Rodger, S. (2008). Childhood predictors of adult criminality: A meta-analysis drawn from the prospective longitudinal literature. *Canadian Journal of Criminology and Criminal Justice, 50:4.*

often difficult to find objective evidence that demonstrates the authenticity of repressed memories that come back through therapy.[73]

Other programs focus on treatment methods aimed at correcting how people process information. Individuals who are easily excited and quick to become hostile and aggressive need to learn how to manage frustrating situations by approaching them as problem-solving experiences. When someone cuts in front of you in a long line, you can look at that situation in two very different ways: On the one hand, you can take it as an insult, challenge, or form of disrespect that sends you into a quick moment of anger that may affect how you react; on the other hand, you might see that person's actions as simply accidental or maybe the person does not understand the norm of waiting in line.

Cognitive behavioral therapy programs are made up of two major components: cognitive skills training and cognitive restructuring. **Cognitive skills training** helps offenders become more effective problem-solvers by teaching them how to cope with anger, resist peer pressure, respect the feelings of others, exert better self-control, accurately assess the consequences of behavior, and understand moral reasoning.[74] Techniques such as role play, listening to others talk, and following instructions during an exercise are often employed in a group setting. **Cognitive restructuring** focuses on changing faulty thought processes called criminal thinking errors.[75] These errors may include rationalizing deviant and criminal behavior and lacking appreciation for the crime's consequences on the victim.

Some correctional programs require that offenders come face to face with their victims, to hear how their behavior has affected their lives.[76] Research studies indicate that cognitive behavioral therapy programs have had positive results in reducing delinquent and criminal activities among juveniles and adults.[77]

Practices stemming from the psychological perspective on criminal behavior can also focus on "unlearning" faulty patterns of behavior.[78] We have seen in this chapter that much of what we do stems from what we observe others doing, and that certain behavior patterns we model persist because of the rewards they produce. One technique to correct a faulty connection between inappropriate behavior and a rewarding result is **aversion therapy,**[79] which pairs a stimulus that brings pleasure with an unpleasant response. For example, a child molester may be allowed to look at a sexual image of a child while simultaneously receiving a mild electric shock. This conditioning is repeated several times until the pedophile no longer associates the image with pleasure, but rather with disapproval or dislike. While this method may produce the desired results, the conditioning may be short-lived or become reversed once again.

Many group homes for juvenile delinquents use an intervention called **token economics.**[80] Program participants earn tokens or points for good behavior like following directions and attending class, and likewise lose them for inappropriate behavior such as disrespecting authority or fighting. Tokens can be used to buy items from a store, watch television, or get a weekend pass to go home. Earning them is therefore associated with positive rewards and becomes an incentive to increase the frequency of desirable behavior.[81]

While these techniques are effective in gaining compliance and reducing problem behavior in an institutional setting, researchers caution about their limitations in the real world. Ordinary compliant behavior does not always produce the immediate rewards of points and tokens in the social environment. A juvenile who earned tokens for attending class at the group home will probably not get the same type of reward for going to school. How will this environmental change affect the thinking and behavior of the individual? Will he or she continue to go to school? Indeed, our thoughts and actions are intertwined, yet they are both inherently connected to aspects of the social environment. In what ways does the social environment affect the way we think and act? We turn to an exploration of this question in the next chapter.

cognitive behavioral therapy

A program to correct how people process information involving cognitive skills training and cognitive restructuring.

cognitive skills training

A technique of cognitive behavior therapy that helps offenders become more effective problem-solvers by teaching them how to cope with anger, resist peer pressure, respect the feelings of others, exert better self-control, accurately assess the consequences of behavior, and understand moral reasoning.

cognitive restructuring

A technique of cognitive behavior therapy that focuses on changing faulty thought processes or criminal thinking errors.

aversion therapy

A psychological technique for unlearning faulty patterns of behavior by pairing a stimulus that brings pleasure with an unpleasant response.

token economics

An intervention used in many group homes for juvenile delinquents awarding tokens or points for good behavior and subtracting them for inappropriate behavior.

SUMMARY

■ **How does a diseased mind affect the way we think and act?**	A diseased mind alters the way in which individuals experience the social world around them. Early thoughts on the relationship between personality and criminal behavior focused on the diseased mind of the psychopath. Unable to identify with others or understand how they think and feel, psychopaths are self-centered individuals who do not feel guilt or shame, are reckless and irresponsible, are incapable of maintaining long-term relationships, and engage in ongoing antisocial, disruptive behavior.
■ **Is criminal behavior related to a defect in personality?**	Individuals suffering from antisocial personality disorder exhibit a persistent pattern of violating social norms marked with a disregard for the rights of others that begins in early adolescence and continues through adulthood. They are not concerned with right or wrong, especially when pursuing their own immediate wants and desires. They will lie, cheat, manipulate situations, become violent, and even break the law to advance their own interests.
■ **Do crime and delinquency stem from the inability to control certain impulses?**	Sigmund Freud founded the psychoanalytic perspective, a method of understanding human behavior by examining drives and impulses within the unconscious mind. His theory of human behavior centered upon the division of the human mind into three components: the id, the ego, and the superego. Under Freud's model, an inadequately developed superego will render the individual incapable of making appropriate moral judgments and therefore will be more likely to submit to the impulsive desires of the id and violate the rules.
■ **Is crime a symptom of mental illness?**	Certain types of mental illness can result in maladaptive behavior. Individuals suffering from neuroses such as phobias and compulsive disorders often experience fear and anxiety in the face of certain social stimuli, causing them to behave in unacceptable and often bizarre or disruptive ways. Individuals suffering from psychoses such as bipolar disorder and schizophrenia are unable to comprehend reality, think clearly and respond appropriately. Studies show that the presence of a psychotic disorder places individuals at a greater risk for criminal behavior.
■ **Is crime a symptom of mental illness?**	Certain types of mental illness can result in maladaptive behavior. Individuals suffering from neuroses such as phobias and compulsive disorders often experience fear and anxiety in the face of certain social stimuli, causing them to behave in unacceptable and often bizarre or disruptive ways. Individuals suffering from psychoses such as bipolar disorder and schizophrenia are unable to comprehend reality, think clearly and respond appropriately. Studies show that the presence of a psychotic disorder places individuals at a greater risk for criminal behavior.

■ **What happens when we process information incorrectly?**

The way individuals perceive their environment and appropriately judge their behaviors is the subject of cognitive theory. Cognitive processes have three major components: perception, judgment, and execution. When we have a clear understanding of environmental stimuli (perception), we are better able to evaluate choices (judgment) and are therefore more likely to make better decisions in difficult situations (execution). Distortion in cognitive processes has been used to explain a wide variety of criminal behavior such as domestic violence and rape.

■ **Do some individuals imitate aggressive behavior?**

By observing the behavior of individuals that play an important role in our lives, we learn how to think and act. This type of learning is called behavior modeling. Bandura notes that individuals become violent and aggressive through life experiences that teach them to act that way. Research studies support this claim, showing a strong correlation between exposure to violence and hostility and aggressive behavior.

■ **How is crime rewarding to some people?**

Studies show that patterns of delinquent and criminal behavior often persist because of rewards associated with them such as money, prestige, and peer approval. Human behavior therefore reflects a balance between the rewards and punishments associated with it.

■ **If crime is in the mind, what can we do to prevent it?**

According to the psychological perspective, criminal behavior is linked to the drives and motives within the human mind. Correcting inappropriate behavior therefore requires correcting faulty mental processes, through the early detection of psychological problems that may predict future criminal behavior. Once a problem has been detected, counseling or therapy helps individuals learn how to manage their disorder or minimize its impact on their behavior.

■ **Can intelligence be related to crime?**

A relationship between intelligence and crime is often proposed by linking low IQ scores to higher rates of delinquency. However, IQ is not always a measure of natural intelligence but rather reflects that IQ tests are based on the values and experiences of the U.S. white middle class.

CRITICAL THINKING QUESTIONS

1. Society sometimes reacts to crimes that are particularly difficult to comprehend by arguing that the perpetrator is insane—that no one in his or her right mind would torture and kill a child or rape an elderly woman. What types of criminal acts are the most difficult for you to understand? Can you identify a purpose or motive for the behavior? What elements make these crimes difficult to explain from the standpoint of rational choice? How can the psychological perspective help us understand "insane" behavior?

2. Psychological theories help us understand the mental processes behind human drives and motives. What role does this type of explanation play in the development of a criminal defense? What standards of responsibility do we place on individuals who suffer a mental disorder? Would it be fair to judge them by the same criteria as those who do not suffer from a mental disorder? Is someone "less guilty" because he or she is mentally ill?

3. How do you think information about the mental health status of a suspect or offender should affect the decision of law enforcement officials in handling a particular case? In what ways could such information be helpful? What obstacles or detriments may it pose?

4. Do individuals adapt to their environment, or does the environment affect the way in which individuals adapt? Why do some people cope with stress, conflict, and trauma in positive ways—such as joining a support group, picking up a hobby, or getting counseling—while others engage in maladaptive behaviors—such as turning to drugs or alcohol or becoming hostile and abusive? Could the environmental experiences of these two types of individuals have been different? What different environmental factors affect the way we manage and adapt to certain difficult situations and experiences?

ADDITIONAL RESOURCES

Learn more about the crimes of Jeffrey Dahmer by visiting http://www.biography.com/articles/Jeffrey-Dahmer-9264755

Visit the Mayo Clinic website at http://www.mayoclinic.com/health/antisocial-personality-disorder/DS00829 to get more information on the signs and symptoms of antisocial personality disorder.

Additional information on the treatment of obsessive-compulsive disorders can be found at http://www.psychologytoday.com/conditions/obsessive-compulsive-disorder

Research on the relationship between childhood psychiatric disorders and adult criminality can be found at http://ajp.psychiatryonline.org/cgi/content/full/164/11/1668

Read more about the field of forensic psychiatry by visiting the *Forensic Psychiatry Resources on the Web* at http://njms2.umdnj.edu/psyevnts/forensic.html

8

SOCIAL STRUCTURE THEORIES

Crime Is in the Structure of Society

In this chapter, we will explore the following questions:

- How do criminologists explain trends and variations in criminal behavior?
- Where does the sociological approach search for the cause of crime?
- What is the social structure and how does it affect our behavior?
- Are certain places more conducive to crime than others?
- Can certain types of frustrations lead to crime?
- Do all subcultures go against the dominant norms of society?
- If crime is acquired behavior, what can we change about the social structure to prevent it?

When Tai Yang was 10 years old, he got hold of his father's gun

and accidentally shot himself in the chest; he was fortunate to survive. By age 15, he was a member of the Asian Bloods gang and had shot someone he thought was a rival gang member. On May 10, 2009, at approximately 1:30 a.m., 20-year-old Tai was beaten to death outside a bar in St. Paul, Minnesota, only 13 days after being released from prison for a gang-related shooting. Witnesses described the scene as a chaotic melee of violence and confusion.[1]

How can we explain the variations in type and distribution of criminal behavior from place to place, individual to individual, and group to group? Why is it that four of five offenders are male, that males are more likely to be victims of violent crime than females, that urban communities experience higher rates of crime, that minorities are arrested at a disproportionate rate, and that theft is the most common category of crime?[2] What is it about the social environment that creates trends and variations in the distribution and content of criminality? The makeup of a community or neighborhood, the availability of jobs, and the individual's cultural background, desire for wealth and success, and access to education are all dynamics that affect behavior.

According to a 2001 research report on youth violence by the surgeon general of the United States, most youth violence begins in early adolescence; 30 to 40 percent of male youth and 15 to 30 percent of female youth report having committed a serious violent crime by the age of 17. The study describes certain "pathways" to violence that include both personal characteristics and environmental conditions that place children at risk for the onset of deviant behavior. Personal characteristics—such as gender, aggression, attitudes toward school, and drug use—interplay with environmental conditions—such as ties to delinquent peers, involvement with a gang, socioeconomic status, and poverty—to produce violent behavior. These results suggest we should direct intervention and prevention efforts at the immediate environment of at-risk youth—family, school, peer group, neighborhood, and community—in order to identify those variables and conditions contributing to the onset of criminal behavior.[3]

Criminologists explain trends and variations in criminal behavior by analyzing how social forces influence human behavior. Biological and psychological traditions examine criminal behavior by looking at the specific traits that make criminals different from noncriminals. In this chapter, we examine theories that search for the origins of criminal behavior *outside* the individual, collectively known as **sociological theories.**[4] What is the sociological approach, and what aspects of society do we study in our search for a better understanding of crime and its origins?

Tai Yang was beaten to death outside this bar in St. Paul, Minnesota. What aspects of the social environment may have contributed to the fight that broke out that night?

THE SOCIOLOGICAL PERSPECTIVE

Have you ever looked at pictures of your parents when they were your age and wondered how they ever survived without iPods, laptops, and text messaging? Now imagine your grandparents at your age, and think how they must have been dazzled by the first computer, color television, and microwave ovens. Our social environment is constantly changing, and we must adapt to the emergence of new technology, different ways of thinking, and changing expectations for the roles we play.

sociological theories

Theories that search for the origins of criminal behavior outside the individual.

As we discussed in Chapter 1, the *sociological perspective* explains patterns in human behavior by examining those aspects of society that affect the way people think, act, and react. What happens when there are more people than jobs? How does a single mother who barely makes ends meet afford to take care of her children? When a teenager runs away from his abusive, dysfunctional family, where does he go and whom will he turn to on the streets? How does a person survive in a neighborhood where gunshots are fired every day? Does marriage affect people in different ways?

Sociologist Emile Durkheim helped develop the sociological approach.[5] Durkheim studied many aspects of society such as religion, education, crime, and suicide. He focused on describing how different parts of society functioned to make society "work." According to Durkheim, all aspects of society serve a specific function that contributes to the order of social life, and even to crime. Crime is an objective indication of what is wrong and immoral in society. It lets us know what needs to change, the ways in which rules and regulations should be established, and how we should move toward becoming a better—more ordered—society.[6]

Crime is a social fact; it exists outside the individual traits and variations in human thought and action. We find the starting point for the study of crime, therefore, not within the individual, but rather within the society in which the individual lives—a society made up of groups, organizations, and institutions. Crime develops from the various dynamics, relationships, and interactions that take place within the social environment. By studying these, we can develop a more comprehensive understanding of the characteristics of criminal behavior, estimate trends and rates of criminal activities, and question the larger social forces affecting criminal choices.

ONE PERSPECTIVE, THREE APPROACHES

While all sociological theories share a common theme in the study of crime, we can divide the sociological perspective into three distinct approaches: social structure, social process, and social conflict. Let's look at what makes each approach unique and different from the others.

How might the social forces of economic depression and unemployment affect the behavior of these individuals applying for a job opening?

social structure approach

An approach to criminology that looks for the origins of crime within the immediate environment.

The **social structure approach** looks for the origins of crime within the immediate environment. What holds society together and what breaks it apart? What social and economic conditions are people exposed to on a daily basis? The social structure approach examines conditions of life such as poverty, deprivation, frustration, lack of opportunity to succeed, and deviant cultural values and analyzes their influence on the development of criminal behavior.[7] We will examine this perspective in more detail in this chapter.

The *social process approach* sees crime as the product of the various interactions that take place between individuals and the social environment.[8] Problems within society do not alone cause crime: It is the way we react to and deal with these problems that forms the starting point for the study of criminal behavior. Crime is the outcome of inappropriate or faulty social processes that contribute to crime. We will examine this approach in greater detail in the next chapter.

Finally, the *social conflict approach* to the study of crime examines the fundamental distribution of wealth and power within society. It sees the law as a mechanism of social control in which society's dominant classes—those with the most wealth and political power—are able to coerce the rest into compliance. Power relationships in society determine who has the influence to create the law, which acts will be defined as crime, and which individuals will be treated as criminals.[9] We will talk more about conflict theory in Chapter 10. For now, let's take a closer look at the social structure approach.

MAJOR PRINCIPLES OF SOCIAL STRUCTURE THEORIES

Social structure theories search for the cause of criminal behavior in the immediate conditions of society. With a quick glance at the world around us, we can easily see major differences in the people's environments: Some are poor, some are rich; some drop out of high school, and others have college educations; some live in the city, others in suburban neighborhoods; some have high-paying jobs, and others struggle to make ends meet. The social structure approach looks at these variations in the economic and social environments and highlights those that contribute to socioeconomic disadvantage.[10] They include poverty, lack of educational opportunities, limited employment options, poor or deteriorated neighborhoods and housing, dysfunctional family conditions, social injustices, and exposure to conflicting value systems.

According to the social structure approach, the root cause of crime can be found in these formal and informal structures of society.[11] While individuals are responsible for their own actions and should be held accountable for them, in this view the social environment creates certain conditions of imbalance, discord, and chaos that provide the causal link from which criminal behavior occurs.[12]

social disorganization theory

An approach to criminology that links high rates of crime to the social and economic conditions of urban communities.

Thus, in order to understand crime, we must direct our attention to the environmental forces driving individuals toward criminal activity. According to the social structure approach, crime is an acquired pattern of behavior: Individuals are a product of their social environment and the conditions that limit and impose upon their opportunities, experiences, choices, and ways of thinking.

TABLE **8.1**

Social Structure Theories of Criminal Behavior

SOCIAL DISORGANIZATION	STRAIN THEORY	CULTURE CONFLICT
Chicago School	Anomie	Subcultures
Environmental criminology	General strain	Differential opportunity
		Drift

Within the social structure approach, there are three major theoretical perspectives: social disorganization, strain theory, and culture conflict (Table 8.1). While each offers a unique understanding of the specific aspects of the environment that contribute to crime and delinquency, they all share a common understanding of criminal behavior as largely a phenomena of the socially and economically disadvantaged members of society. We turn now to a discussion of these theories, beginning with social disorganization.

SOCIAL DISORGANIZATION THEORY

Some criminologists link high rates of crime to the social and economic conditions of urban communities. They point to the disordered nature of certain neighborhoods where overcrowding, increased transience, the presence of business and retail stores alongside residences, and lack of cohesion contribute to a deteriorating social life.[13] This approach to the study of crime is known as **social disorganization theory.**

Under these conditions, the social structure begins to collapse. The environment is failing to provide the necessary elements of a healthy community, such as adequate education, proper housing, meaningful employment, access to healthcare, and a positive family life. Some of the groundbreaking studies of social disorganization theory are found in the tradition known as the **Chicago School.**

What aspects of the social environment may contribute to the high rate of crime found in this urban community?

The Chicago School

Between the 1920s and 1940s, criminological research was dominated by the University of Chicago, where the works of Robert Park and Ernest Burgess began an ecological approach to the study of crime.[14] **Social ecology** is a method of analysis that studies how the environment adapts to the human interactions and natural resources within it.

Park and Burgess aimed to explain the distribution of crime rates by thinking of cities as made up of **concentric zones,** identified by the rate and incidence of certain social characteristics within the city such as immigration, residential mobility, housing structure, and family income (Figure 8.1). Park and Burgess used this model to explain why crime was concentrated in certain parts of inner-city zones where the structure is weak and disorganized due to high rates of poverty and unemployment, rapid social change, competition for limited resources, and conflict between different cultural values.[15] These conditions produce personal and group interactions marked by strained relationships, deteriorating values, lack of family solidarity, and community fear. Individuals living under such conditions, which become a breeding ground for criminal activity, are exposed to **social pathology** and turn to deviant behavior and crime.

The concentric zone model was used by researchers Clifford Shaw and Henry McKay to study juvenile arrest rates in Chicago.[16] Shaw and McKay were interested in studying how crime and delinquency were normal responses to social, economic, and cultural characteristics of certain communities. Using official data spanning three distinct time periods marked by high rates of immigration (1900–1906, 1917–1923, and 1927–1933), they illustrated the distribution of delinquency rates among juveniles within different ecological environments. Rates of juvenile delinquency remained stable over time and corresponded to certain inner-city urban zones, despite changes in immigrant populations (for example, from German to Italian). Areas farther from these zones had lower rates of crime and delinquency.

These findings support the theory that crime is a characteristic of ecological conditions within the social environment of urban communities, rather than a consequence of individuals' characteristics. It is in the structure of neighborhoods within the inner

Chicago School

Groundbreaking studies of social disorganization theory coming out of the University of Chicago between the 1920s and the 1940s.

social ecology

A method of analysis that studies how the environment adapts to the human interactions and natural resources within it.

concentric zones

A concept within social ecology analysis that explains the distribution of crime rates by envisioning cities as being made up of areas of social characteristics, such as immigration, residential mobility, housing structure, and family income.

social pathology

Social conditions marked by strained relationships, deteriorating values, lack of family solidarity, and community fear; such conditions become a breeding ground for criminal activity.

Source: http://www.crimetheory.com/Soc1/Chic1.htm

FIGURE **8.1**

A Concentric Zone Model

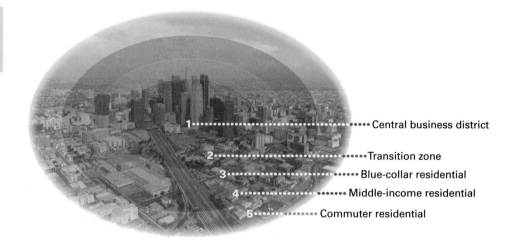

1 ••••••••••••••••••••••• Central business district

2 ••••••••••••••••••••••• Transition zone

3 ••••••••••••••••••••• Blue-collar residential

4 ••••••••••••••••••• Middle-income residential

5 •••••••••••••• Commuter residential

city where deviant norms and values, impoverished lifestyles, unemployment, cultural conflict—all the elements of social disorganization—perpetuate criminal behavior.

Shaw and McKay laid the foundation for the development of social disorganization theory in a theoretical movement that spanned over seven decades of research. We turn now to a brief look at the legacy of the Chicago School in the field of environmental criminology.

Environmental Criminology

Are certain places more prone to criminal activity than others? If so, what is it about these places that make them crime magnets? These questions are the subject of contemporary criminological research, which draws a link between criminal behavior and the geographic location and physical features of specific neighborhoods.[17] (See Connecting Research to Practice for a study of crime, disorder, and the impact of collective efficacy.)

When we observe children playing in a bounce house, we can see that this type of environment makes them more hyper, playful, and active. But consider the effect of the children's playing on the bounce house itself. How many children can this structure hold before it collapses? If they do not remove their shoes, will the fabric tear? The effect of various interactions on the social structure is considered by social ecologists.

Social disorganization theory has focused on location and neighborhood-specific aspects as they relate to criminal activity. Structurally disorganized neighborhoods lack the formal and informal controls needed to prevent crime and delinquency. Public order crimes such as public intoxication, graffiti, and vandalism are an invitation to potential offenders; these crimes signal that residents in the neighborhood are apathetic about their community and will not intervene on the behalf of victims, question strangers, or call the police when suspecting a crime.[18]

In a long-term National Institute of Justice study, researchers repeatedly examined the effect of neighborhood disorder in Chicago communities as a pathway to predatory criminal behavior.[19] The study proposed that both crime and disorder stem from structural characteristics specific to certain neighborhoods. These include concentrated poverty, unemployment, residential mobility, high population density, and the absence of social resources. Using a method known as *systematic social observation,* researchers videotaped blocks of over 23,000 streets in 196 neighborhoods with different racial, ethnic, social, and economic compositions. What were they looking for? Signs of disorder, recorded and measured by visual cues such as trash and litter on the streets, graffiti, abandoned cars, syringes, loitering, people intoxicated or consuming alcohol on the street, evidence of gang membership such as young people in groups, and observed drug transactions.

Findings suggest that disorder and crime both stem from similar structural characteristics of certain neighborhoods. While bearing no direct causal link, disorder and crime are inherently connected in that they both reduce *collective efficacy,* which is the cohesion among neighborhood residents in combination with shared expectations for informal social control of public space.[20] Collective efficacy is a significant deterrent to crime and disorder in neighborhoods and communities. When there is no collective efficacy, rates of violence and the amounts of disorder are high, even after controlling for sociodemographic characteristics.

These findings suggest that policies aimed at reducing community disorder *indirectly* reduce crime by increasing neighborhood stability and enhancing collective efficacy. Tough law enforcement practices and procedures to "clean up the streets" by eliminating violence and disorder are often insufficient without a comprehensive understanding of the link between crime, disorder, and collective efficacy.

During the mid-1980s, studies in **environmental criminology** emerged to highlight the importance of deteriorated conditions within communities as contributing to high rates of criminal activity.[21] Environmental criminologists analyze the immediate context within which criminal behavior occurs in order to understand how environmental variables, potential offenders, and targeted victims interact. Within this approach, there are three basic premises:[22]

■ Criminal behavior is significantly influenced by the immediate nature of the environment in which it occurs.

■ The distribution and pattern of criminal activity is not random but vary according to time, place, and situation. Certain times, places, and situations facilitate criminal opportunities.[23]

■ Understanding the role of environmental variables in the pattern and distribution of criminal activity is essential to controlling and preventing crime.

The basic premise behind the study of crime and environmental variables is that disorganized neighborhoods send a message to would-be criminals that this is a vulnerable target for crime because we, as a community, either do not care, are afraid, or also are involved in criminal activity.[24] Researchers have identified five components that help to predict the likelihood of a criminal event—space, time, the offender, the victim, and social control (Table 8.2).

environmental criminology

Analysis of the immediate context within which criminal behavior occurs in order to understand how environmental variables, potential offenders, and targeted victims interact.

TABLE **8.2**

Anatomy of Dangerous Persons, Places, and Situations

TYPE OF VARIABLE	CHARACTERISTICS
Space	Presence of blind spots due to excessive trees, shrubs, bushes
	Rundown or abandoned buildings and apartments
	Bars on windows, broken windows, boarded-up windows
	Dirty, littered parks and other public spaces
	Excessive graffiti on public buildings
	Poor street lighting
Time	Businesses open late/all night
	Increased nighttime activities, especially on weekends
Offender	Network links to other offenders
	Lack of financial resources
	Unemployed
	Have nothing to lose
	Triggering event prompts frustration, anger
Target/Victim	Large numbers of single-parent families
	Regularized/predictable patterns of movement
	Loss of trust in social institutions such as law enforcement, government, and education
	Little sense of community
	High degree of residential instability
	Fear of crime
	High rates of unemployment
Social Control	Lack of informal surveillance by family, peers, neighbors due to weak social ties
	Limited social control efforts by schools, recreation centers, and churches due to atmosphere of fear and mistrust
	Absence of sufficient formal social control resources (law enforcement)

Source: Wortley, R., & Mazerolle, L. (2008). *Environmental criminology and crime analysis.* UK: Willan Publishing.

Environmental criminology thus helps us gain a better understanding of patterns and trends in crime. This in turn becomes a useful tool in the development of policies and interventions that target specific crime-prone situations. Studies have shown that changing or altering certain temporal or spatial patterns, such as putting in a street light in a dark neighborhood, can have a significant impact on reducing criminal activity.[25]

Places sustain criminal activity because of the structure of their environment. People may come and go, but crime rates will always remain high. This is the basic idea behind social disorganization theory and environmental criminology. At the end of this chapter, we will examine the merits of this theory. Another approach to the study of criminal behavior focuses on the specific mechanisms whereby individuals react and adjust to the structure of their environment. Let's now look at strain theory.

STRAIN THEORY

In 1938, Robert Merton, arguing against the idea that criminality was the result of variations in individual traits, proposed that conditions within the social structure create situations to which criminal activity is the response.[26] Merton's **strain theory** grew out of this argument. What are these strained situations and why is crime a response to them?

Anomie

Merton was interested in why rates of deviant behavior differed among different societies and between certain groups within the same society.[27] He argued that the key lies in **anomie,** a state of normlessness and confusion that leads to strain. Anomie results from the discrepancy between the cultural norms that define success in life (goals) and the legitimate and appropriate ways to achieve it (means).[28]

Think for a moment about how we define success in our society. Perhaps you envision a nice home and car. What about fancy clothes or a flat-screen television? How about the latest cell phone and electronic gadget? Whatever the case, through various institutions like family, education, and media, our culture constantly bombards us with messages of success that revolve around the acquisition of material goods. People from all walks of life feel pressured to keep up, get ahead, and stay on top of things. But how? The

strain theory

A social structure theory that argues that crime is a response to conditions of strain in society.

anomie

A state of normlessness and confusion that leads to strain.

How does society define success for us? What happens when we cannot all shop in Beverly Hills?

culturally accepted means is through education, hard work, and perseverance. The problem however, is that the access to these avenues is not equally distributed to all members of society, even though the message of achievement and success is spelled out loud and clear . . . to everyone.[29] How do people deal with this apparent dilemma?

Anomie leads to frustration and resentment, to which people react in different ways. Many will continue to run the rat race their entire lives, working hard to pursue the American dream and hoping to one day pay off their debts, buy a nice car, and own their own home. These individuals are *conformists*. Some who are *ritualists* may simply give up, settling for a minimum-wage job just to make ends meet. Others, recognizing their limited opportunities, will become *innovators*, turning to other avenues such as stealing or selling drugs to get what they want. Table 8.3 describes the various adaptations people make to the discrepancy between culturally desired goals and legitimate means of achieving them.

Merton's theory helps us understand how the strain between culturally defined success and the legitimate means of achieving it leads to deviant behavior patterns. Once again, the roots of crime lie within the social structure and not within individuals or their unique qualities. But what about individuals who commit criminal acts despite their access to legitimate avenues of success—Ivy League thieves, millionaire murderers, or well-educated bank robbers? What about the variety of crimes committed by successful business owners and corporate executives who have all the necessary means to achieve the American dream? (See the Consider This feature for a closer look at one incidence of such a crime.) We turn now to a discussion of general strain for a possible explanation.

general strain theory (GST)

A broader concept of strain theory maintaining that various sources of strain and frustration exist within the social structure that are not the result of economic failure.

General Strain

In 1992, Robert Agnew broadened anomie theory by developing the concept of general strain. **General strain theory (GST)** maintains that various sources of strain and frustration exist within the social structure that are not the result of economic

TABLE **8.3**

Ways of Adapting to a Frustrating Social Structure

CULTURALLY DESIRED GOALS	LEGITIMATE MEANS	ADAPTATION	WHO AM I?
Accepted	Accepted	*Conformity*	I am ambitious, motivated, and hardworking. I go to school to get an education so that I can get ahead in the workforce and make more money so that I can afford to travel, buy the things that I want, and live the American dream.
Accepted	Rejected	*Innovation*	I live in an inner-city deteriorated neighborhood with my mom and five siblings. I dropped out of school to get a job and help my mom with finances. I turned to drug trafficking, which makes a lot more money and gives me a better life.
Rejected	Accepted	*Ritualism*	I work at a factory from 9 to 5. I gave up on achieving success a long time ago. I'm just happy to have a job to make ends meet. I'll probably never own a home or drive a car that runs well. These are the facts, and there's nothing I can do to change them.
Rejected	Rejected	*Retreatism*	I have given up on life in general. I just don't care anymore about anyone or anything. I spend most of my days drunk and high on drugs. I peddle for money to buy food and drugs and live on the street.
Rejected *but* substituted	Rejected *but* substituted	*Rebellion*	I am dissatisfied with the way society is structured so I'm going to change things my way. I am a political activist whose goal is to achieve social justice and egalitarianism.

CONSIDER THIS... Living the American Dream?

Bernard Lawrence "Bernie" Madoff is an American success story. Born in 1938 in the borough of Queens, New York, Madoff lived a modest life as a plumber. Through hard work and perseverance, he graduated from high school and college, and in 1960, he founded the Wall Street firm Bernard L. Madoff Investment Securities LLC (BMIS). Madoff began as a small, penny stock trader with the $5,000 he earned working as a lifeguard and installer of sprinkler systems. With help from his accountant father-in-law, the company grew enough to compete with other investment companies on the New York Stock Exchange floor, developing innovative computer software that helped create what eventually became known as the NASDAQ.

Through the 1970s, Madoff and his family lived in a beautiful ranch house in a New York suburb. By 1981, Madoff owned an oceanfront residence in Montauk,

with his primary residence a penthouse apartment in Manhattan's wealthy Upper East Side. He owned another home in France and docked a 55-foot fishing boat on the French Riviera; he also maintained a mansion in Palm Beach, Florida, where he was a member of the Palm Beach Country Club. According to income tax returns, in 2009 Madoff and his wife were worth about $126 million, and the value of his business interest in Bernard L. Madoff Investment Securities LLC was estimated at $700 million.

However, on December 11, 2008, Madoff was arrested and charged with securities fraud.[30] He pleaded guilty in what was soon revealed as the largest investor fraud scandal ever committed by a single person, with an estimated loss to investors of almost $65 billion.[31] On June 29, 2009, Madoff was sentenced to 150 years in federal prison, with billions of dollars in restitution to be paid to his victims. What could have driven him to commit the acts to which he has pleaded guilty?

What do you think?

failure.[32] Individuals who experience certain types of strain, especially if repeated over time, may cope by turning to delinquency and crime.[33] According to Agnew, there are three types of strain: failure to achieve positively valued stimuli, loss of positively valued stimuli, and presence of negative stimuli (Figure 8.2). In practical terms these may include losing a loved one, getting fired, ending a relationship, feeling pressure to perform on the job, or being discriminated against.

Strain and frustration can create hurt and disappointment in some, while others become angry and resentful. Feelings of injustice can lead to a desire for revenge, which some may use to rationalize criminal activities. Studies show individuals who experience racial discrimination have higher rates of violent crime.[34] Those who blame others for their own misfortunes may turn to delinquency and crime. Consider the following events in the life of a real teenager:

> *A 14-year-old boy lives with his mother and her alcoholic boyfriend; his father left them several years earlier. His mother is diagnosed with cancer and spends her last days in great pain in the hospital. One Saturday morning, the hospital calls and tells the boy to rush over, as his mother is dying. On the way, the mother's boyfriend insists on stopping at the liquor store to buy some alcohol. The boy begs him not to, but he does so anyway; his mother dies 10 minutes before they arrive, and he never says goodbye. The boyfriend is uncaring, and the boy runs away from home. He spends a year or so moving from one foster home to another. He becomes angry, hurt, and resentful. He turns to drugs and alcohol to find some relief from his pain. He begins to steal to support his habits.*

Some people accept responsibility for their negative circumstances and actively seek to change them in a positive manner. They often have a positive outlook on life, are emotionally strong, communicate effectively, have positive social support systems, and

General Strain

Failure to achieve positively valued stimuli	Loss of positively valued stimuli	Presentation of negative stimuli
Money	Death	Adverse economic conditions
Achievement	Divorce	Abuse
Respect	Theft of a valued object	Neglect
Power	Getting fired	Hostile relationships
Autonomy		

FIGURE 8.2

Sources of Strain: What Hurts?

are financially capable.[35] Someone who has been discriminated against and has good financial resources is more likely to hire an attorney to right the wrong than to resort to violence for revenge. But others—because of lack of financial resources, negative experiences, lower tolerance for frustration, lack of ability to handle stress in a legitimate way, or personal relationships and social support networks—use crime and delinquency to cope with strain.

What are these value systems and how are they acquired? We examine this question through a discussion of culture conflict theory.

CULTURE CONFLICT THEORY

If you found a hundred dollar bill on the floor of a grocery store, would you keep it or turn it in? Let's say you are taking a test and your classmate is cheating; would you tell the instructor? How do you feel about legalizing marijuana? Is prostitution a criminal act? Do you believe people deserve the right to marry someone of the same sex? If your class took an opinion poll on each of these issues, our guess is there would be more disagreement than consensus. We are all different in some way, and our ideas and opinions will often disagree.

culture conflict theory

A social structure theory that maintains that the root cause of crime is the clash of values between different cultures producing different beliefs about what is acceptable and unacceptable behavior.

Culture conflict theory emerged in the works of Thorsten Sellin, who argued that we find the root cause of criminal behavior in the clash of those values by which we decide what is acceptable and unacceptable behavior.[36] Cultural diversity is particularly common

How do you suppose the differences in cultures found here can affect the ways people think and act?

CRIME IN GLOBAL PERSPECTIVE | Murder for the Sake of Honor

Imagine that a father murders his own daughters by shooting them and then burying them alive. This tradition was recently enacted in a remote village of Jafarabad, a district of Pakistan. The three victims were teenage girls between 16 and 18 years old whose crime was tarnishing the family honor by wishing to marry someone of their own choosing.[37]

An *honor killing* such as this is an act of murder in which "a woman is killed for her actual or perceived immoral behavior."[38] Such behavior can include being unfaithful in marriage, refusing to submit to an arranged marriage, wearing makeup or short skirts, asking for a divorce, flirting with or receiving phone calls from men, and not having dinner prepared on time. In some cultures, a woman raped by a man is also accused of committing an immoral act that brings shame to the honor of the family and perhaps the wider community. If her execution is considered deserved, it is usually carried out by one or more of her family members.

Honor killings result from a tradition that sees murder as justified when an individual has brought shame to the family name, a dishonor that can be removed only by killing the offender. In the Turkish province of Sanliurfa, one young woman was publicly executed by having her throat slit in the town square. Apparently a love song had been dedicated to her over the radio. Within such traditions, cultural norms become intertwined with deviant behavior, and crime becomes a matter of social definition.[39]

---

in modern, industrialized society, especially within inner-city communities. According to culture conflict theory, this vast diversity produces a clash in values because different people are socialized in different ways. Thus, **conduct norms,** those rules of acceptable behavior we learn early in life, will vary. Consider an Armenian in his 80s who visits his grandson in the United States for the first time to attend his wedding. The elderly man accompanies his grandson to the local grocery store, where he repeatedly picks up different types of fruits and tastes them. He explains his behavior by fervently defending his right to taste the merchandise to see whether it is good before buying it, arguing with a store employee that this is the normal practice in his own country.

The law exists to ensure that all people adhere to a common set of rules about right and wrong. For Sellin, however, the law's definitions of right and wrong are based on middle-class values—values that are not equally shared by all members of society. Crime, therefore exists because there is disagreement over what is acceptable behavior. Consider, for example, cultures where people commit murder in the name of family honor and tradition (see Crime in Global Perspective, for example). Sellin argues that the more diverse society becomes, the more likely there will be conflict and disagreement and, therefore, the more likely there will be increases in deviance and crime. The question is, Why and how do some individuals adhere to norms and values that support criminal behavior? We turn now to a brief look at the concept of delinquent subcultures.

conduct norms

Rules of acceptable behavior we learn early in life.

Subcultures

In 1958, Walter B. Miller developed a theory of delinquent behavior that attributes crime to a lower-class culture.[40] Miller studied gangs in Massachusetts for three years, observing that urban youth learn values conducive to criminal activity from their exposure to a lower-class **subculture,** a group within the larger social culture that has a distinct set of norms and a unique pattern of behavior. The dominant values of mainstream, middle-class society—working hard, getting an education, and abiding by the rules—become less meaningful among the urban poor who are exposed to the daily hardships of deteriorated living conditions, economic struggle, and limited resources.[41] It is very difficult

subculture

A group within the larger social culture that has a distinct set of norms and a unique pattern of behavior.

focal concerns

Values and behaviors that emerge to meet the specific conditions of the environment and that may result in deviant activities and violence.

delinquent subculture

A subculture that emerges among youth who have a common need to resolve similar problems and who engage in delinquent activities as a means of compensating for their lack of legitimate opportunities within the dominant social structure.

reaction formation

A rejection of the mainstream culture and hostility toward its norms and values.

subculture of violence

Theory that violent behavior is not evenly distributed within the social structure; rather, it is a learned pattern of behavior and an adaptation to environmental stimuli—anger, frustration, conflict, or provocation.

to convince an urban youth to stay in school and aim for college when his immediate problem is surviving the day without getting shot.

According to Miller, members of the lower class have different **focal concerns,** values and behaviors that emerge to meet the specific conditions of the environment and that may result in deviant activities and violence. Table 8.4 illustrates these concerns for these members of the lower class. The concern with toughness, for example, may lead to fighting in order to gain respect, whereas a concern with autonomy can justify disobedience or disregard for the law.

A theory of **delinquent subcultures** was articulated by Albert Cohen in his 1955 publication of *Delinquent Boys*.[42] In this now-classic study, Cohen examines the delinquent activities of youth, arguing that a delinquent subculture emerges from the common need to resolve similar problems. Lower-class youth engage in delinquent activities as a means of compensating for their lack of legitimate opportunities within the dominant social structure. They often feel rejected by parents, teachers, and society in general. They are well aware of their failure and of the relative impossibility of achieving anything close to the American dream. Thus, in a process Cohen refers to as **reaction formation,** lower-class youth reject the mainstream culture and develop hostility toward its norms and values.

Consequently, their disadvantaged social and economic position makes them vulnerable to joining gangs and participating in nonconformist, lawless behavior.[43] These youth adhere to the norms and values of a delinquent subculture, one that emphasizes negative, spiteful, destructive, and generally "hell-raising" behavior—values directly opposed to the dominant culture. Essentially, society at large is the enemy, and all acts that go against its norms—whether theft, vandalism, or assault—are positively valued and desirable forms of behavior.

In 1967, Franco Ferracuti and Marvin Wolfgang elaborated on the concept of culture conflict and crime by developing the **subculture of violence** theory.[44] Wolfgang and Ferracuti observed that violent behavior is not evenly distributed within the social

TABLE **8.4**

Focal Concerns: What Do the Urban Poor Worry About?

CONCERN	CONTEXT
Trouble	Getting in and out of trouble is a main concern of the lower-class subculture; fighting, handling conflicts and disputes with aggression, drinking, and running into cops are all a part of the daily routine.
Toughness	Value is placed on being tough, both physically and in attitude. Masculinity is equated with fighting prowess, strength, and athletic capability.
Smartness	Lower-class members equate smartness with being savvy or streetwise, outwitting the opponent at any contest, game, or transaction. Gambling, con games, and outwitting police become survival techniques.
Excitement	The definition of excitement within the lower-class subculture centers upon the available activities that can deliver a "high" or "rush." Participating in a driveby shooting, taking drugs, and being in a high-speed police chase, are all considered forms of excitement.
Fate	The outlook of individuals from the lower class is connected to the concepts of destiny, luck, and inevitability. This type of attitude encourages risk-taking behavior as there is some higher power that is always in control of the outcome of events.
Autonomy	The independence from all sources of authority is a major concern of the lower-class subculture. Adherence to rules, being coerced, and being controlled by others are all signs of weakness.

Source: Miller, W. B. (1958). Lower class culture as a generating milieu of gang delinquency. *Journal of Social Issues, 14,* 5–19.

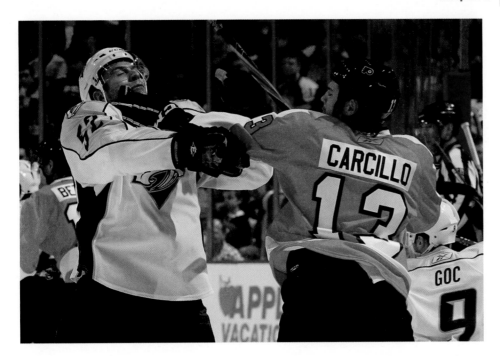

structure; rather, for some individuals it is a learned pattern of behavior and an adaptation to certain environmental stimuli—anger, frustration, conflict, or provocation.

In a study of 588 criminal homicides in Philadelphia, researchers found non-white males aged 20 to 24 committed homicide at a rate of 92 per 100,000, compared to 3.4 for white males aged 20 to 24.[45] They concluded that violence is most prevalent among a homogeneous group within the larger urban community, because in this subculture's value system, violence is an acceptable means of behavior in a variety of circumstances.[46]

The basic premise of subculture of violence theory is that some individuals within certain groups—such as males, African Americans, and southerners—regard violence as a normative, acceptable, and even required means of upholding values such as honor, masculinity, and courage. Research shows violence is often a means of gaining status and approval among peers.[47] Thus, it becomes a tradition and an expectation within circumstances the group defines, and nonviolence is a rejection of the group's norms with negative consequences such as exclusion or ostracism.

Subculture of violence theory does not explain why violence becomes part of the normative structure for certain groups of individuals. Could it be that some individuals resort to violence and criminal activity simply because the opportunity presents itself to them, over and over again, and therefore the violent response becomes embedded as regular, ordinary, or routine? We explore this question by looking at differential opportunity.

Differential Opportunity

We can probably agree with some certainty that most people would not know how to organize a drug-trafficking operation, join the underground nicotine market, connect with international terrorists, or set up a methamphetamine lab. And even if life becomes difficult and education and a good career seem unattainable, typically these illegitimate avenues are not readily available to most people.

Researchers Richard Cloward and Lloyd Ohlin noted that Merton's strain theory was correct in its observation that legitimate opportunities for success were not evenly distributed within the social structure.[48] However, the distribution of crime and delinquency also depend on the presence of illegitimate opportunities.[49] Indeed, frustration and strain contributed to the evolution of delinquent and violent subcultures; but it is variable access to illegitimate opportunities that contributes to the development of crime and delinquency, hence the term **differential opportunity.**[50]

differential opportunity

The variable access to illegitimate opportunities that contributes to the development of crime and delinquency.

On September 22, 1961, President John F. Kennedy made battling juvenile delinquency a national priority by signing the Juvenile Delinquency and Youth Offenses Control Act, stating that

> The future of our country depends upon our younger people who will occupy positions of responsibility and leadership in the coming days. Yet for 11 years juvenile delinquency has been increasing. No city or state in our country has been immune. This is a matter of national concern and requires national action.[51]

This legislation made the federal government a more active participant in assisting local and state governments to control and prevent juvenile delinquency at its very source—the community. The resulting Mobilization for Youth Program began the organization of neighborhood councils to correct conditions leading to poor education, poor health, idleness, despair, and ultimately juvenile delinquency. This national effort and its pilot projects began what came to be called *community action.*

Community action agencies were established across the United States to continue and expand the work begun by President Kennedy.[52] With the goal of eliminating social conditions that contributed to delinquency and crime, these agencies provided many needed programs and services within disadvantaged communities. They expanded opportunities for job training and access to education and promoted economic development, community healthcare delivery centers, legal services, youth recreational and mentoring programs, senior citizen centers, and other innovative practices.

Adopting Cloward and Ohlin's ideas on dealing with juvenile delinquency, the initiatives begun by the Kennedy administration were indeed an effort at providing disadvantaged youth with resources to combat the effects of poverty, unemployment, and deteriorated living conditions and empowering communities into action. However, they were also a direct challenge to the unbalanced distribution of resources within the United States.

Cloward and Ohlin developed a typology of three different delinquent subcultures: criminal, conflict, and retreatist:

- *Criminal subcultures:* These gangs are predominantly present in longstanding, steady neighborhood environments where adolescent offenders have close access to adult criminals who teach them the successful path of criminal enterprise, including the necessary skills and techniques, the proper criminal associates and friendships, and even the right lawyers, politicians, and corrupt police with whom to connect. Criminal activities are generally organized and well planned and often include extortion, fraud, theft, and other income-generating illegal activities.

- *Conflict subcultures:* Within this subculture, status is derived from engaging in violent activities. Unstable, disorganized neighborhood communities provide little access to legitimate opportunities for success and few opportunities for illegitimate activities. There is little or no network of criminal enterprise between adults and delinquent youth, and therefore adolescents turn to the random and disorganized acts of teen gangs that include fighting, assault, vandalism, and arson. Violence is a means of survival and gaining respect.

- *Retreatist subcultures:* Some youth who face blocked access to legitimate opportunities are not tough enough to survive within the conflict subculture and do not have the knowledge of criminal enterprise prevalent in the criminal subculture. They gain peer approval by remaining in a continuous state of oblivion or a drug-induced high, adopting a disorganized lifestyle marked by hustling through prostitution, pimping, drug selling, and petty theft.

Cloward and Ohlin brought together the concepts of subculture and social disorganization to explain emerging and adaptive patterns of delinquent behavior. Their theory had significant impact on social policy and the creation of programs meant to increase educational and employment opportunities for disadvantaged youth (see Connecting Theory to Practice).

Differential opportunity theory also raised some very important issues not brought to light by other culture conflict theories. For Cloward and Ohlin, participants in deviant subcultures were still members of the larger culture, and their beliefs and values were not always counter to the dominant value system within society. Given that these individuals know right from wrong and understand the value of conventional behavior, how do they justify their criminal actions? How do they explain their loyalty to norms that go against those of mainstream society? For one answer, we turn to research on the concept of delinquency and drift.

Drift

The concept of justifying criminal behavior was articulated by Gresham Sykes and David Matza in their 1957 publication "Techniques of Neutralization: A Theory of Delinquency."[53] **Techniques of neutralization** are rationalizations people use to justify their criminal acts (Figure 8.3).

techniques of neutralization

Rationalizations people use to justify their criminal acts.

Sykes and Matza note there is a difference between a *delinquent subculture* and a *subculture of delinquency*. A delinquent subculture sets up its own moral system that completely replaces the dominant social system of beliefs and values. The subculture of delinquency exists when individuals form groups whose members share common values and beliefs that do not necessarily agree with the dominant culture, yet retain certain elements of it. These can include various groups and organizations that are protesting against war, embracing sexual freedom, and defying the establishment.[54] Thus, when individuals adhere to a subculture of delinquency, they must develop various rationalizations to justify their deviant acts that are inconsistent with some of the values and beliefs of the larger dominant culture to which they also adhere.

In his 1964 publication *Delinquency and Drift*, Matza suggested that individuals **drift** from conventional, law-abiding behavior to delinquent and criminal behavior by gradually altering their way of thinking and reacting to their acts using neutralization techniques.[55] A necessary condition of drift is the experience of injustice and despair within the social environment, which creates a disconnect with society and diminished loyalty to its values. An inner-city youth who is failing in school, repeatedly demeaned by his parents, and bullied by his peers may become lonely and isolated. When a criminal opportunity presents itself, such youths may justify acts such as spray-painting graffiti,

drift

A process by which individuals shift from conventional, law-abiding behavior to delinquent and criminal behavior by gradually altering their way of thinking and reacting to their acts using neutralization techniques.

Condemning the condemner
"Police are corrupt."

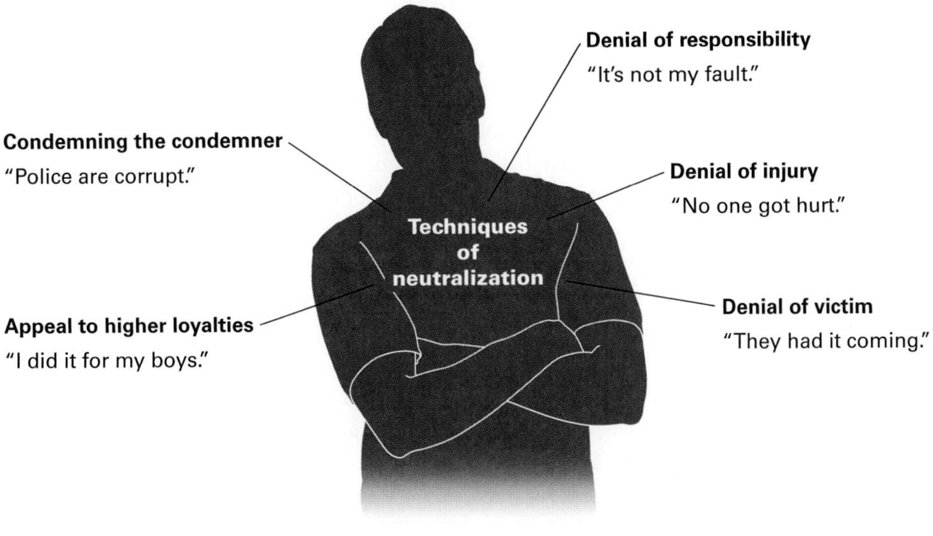

Denial of responsibility
"It's not my fault."

Denial of injury
"No one got hurt."

Techniques of neutralization

Denial of victim
"They had it coming."

Appeal to higher loyalties
"I did it for my boys."

FIGURE **8.3**
Techniques of Neutralization

When given the opportunity to choose between right and wrong, such as whether to shoplift or not, how do individuals who choose to do wrong justify their actions?

robbing a convenience store, or selling drugs by neutralizing their loyalty to the dominant value system and regarding their actions as convenient, appropriate, and right given their situation, thereby reducing their feelings of guilt.[56]

Research studies find support for Sykes and Matza's contentions.[57] Neutralization techniques are highly correlated with involvement in gang activities.[58] Moreover, youth engaged in delinquent acts use techniques of neutralization to protect their self-concept, especially when they are more attached to their parents.[59] In a study of 27 male offenders who had committed violent crimes, the subjects used a series of justifications for the harm they caused the victim, believing the victim either provoked the act or deserved the harm, or the act was not intended or blameworthy.[60]

While these studies confirm the basic premises set forth by Sykes and Matza, we would still like to know how the individual pondering criminal choices interacts with the social environment to make a decision. Consider individuals who share similar adverse experiences and negative conditions within the social structure: Why do some rationalize their drift into a delinquent subculture while others do not engage in criminal activities at all? We will explore this dilemma in our next chapter on social process theories. For now, we turn to an evaluation of the social structure approach and its merits in explaining crime and delinquency.

EVALUATING SOCIAL STRUCTURE THEORIES

The root cause of criminal behavior, according to the social structure approach, lies in the conditions of the social environment that produce poverty, inequality, and injustice. Within this perspective, we identified three distinct approaches to the study of crime: social disorganization, strain, and culture conflict. Each provided us with a unique understanding of the problems within the social structure that contribute to patterns of crime and delinquency. To ensure we have a critical understanding of each theory, we now look at their various shortcomings.

Social disorganization theory provides us with an ecological approach to the study of crime that emphasizes ills within the social environment assumed to be the cause of crime and delinquency. Some, however, would argue to the contrary—that it is the presence of violence, fear, and crime that lead to the deterioration of neighborhoods and the presence of high rates of poverty and unemployment.[61] It is in fact very difficult to distinguish whether crime and delinquency are *symptoms* of social disorganization or actual *components* of it. This problem reveals the flaw in social disorganization theory: We cannot isolate aspects of social disorganization as sources of crime and delinquency when crime and delinquency are basic components of social disorganization; the consequence of a phenomenon cannot also be its cause.

The ecological approach of social disorganization theory uses crime statistics as evidence that some places are more crime-prone due to the structure of their social environment. However, as we saw in our discussion of bias in official crime statistics in Chapter 3, high reported rates of crime in these areas may simply reflect increased police visibility and activity.[62] Researchers note this presence also leads to an overestimation of criminal behavior among certain racial and ethnic minorities.[63]

Social disorganization theory also fails to account for the presence of criminal activities within affluent neighborhoods. Murder, rape, robbery, assault, and drug use clearly occur in areas *not* characterized by social disorganization. How do we account for crimes such as securities fraud, identity theft, and embezzlement that are committed more frequently by individuals from well-established communities and social environments? Clearly, social disorganization theory does not adequately account for this variety of criminal behavior.

The concept of strain has also been widely criticized as an oversimplified explanation of crime that focuses on a disjunction between aspiration and opportunity. Empirical evidence suggests strain is not always consistent with delinquent behavior.[64] Moreover, if crime were merely a consequence of economic deprivation, then only the economically deprived should become criminal. If matters were that simple, we could solve the problem of crime and delinquency by giving everyone equal access to legitimate means of achieving success. How then do we explain the criminal behavior of individuals who are not economically disadvantaged? The flaw in strain theory is its narrow focus on limited economic opportunity, with little attention to other influences such as poor socialization or a psychiatric disorder.

Moreover, we know that not all individuals who experience strain and frustration adapt by engaging in criminal acts. Some individuals adapt to the disjunction between goals and means by rejecting the goals set forth by society, yet reluctantly accepting the means in the adaptation, which Merton identified as ritualism. Why do individuals adapt to strain in different ways? Merton never answers this question. Thus, strain theory fails to account for variations in crime and delinquency among individuals with common socioeconomic characteristics; it does not explain the subjective effects of the intensity or frequency of strain or individual differences in coping strategies.[65]

The final group of theories we discussed in this chapter came to us from the culture conflict approach, based on the assumption that crime is a reflection of norms and values in conflict with the dominant social structure. This method of analysis fails to recognize one very important fact: Definitions of right and wrong are subject to social interpretation and therefore cannot be used as a standard to measure crime and delinquency. In a classic critique of cultural deviance theory, Ruth Kornhauser explains:

> *In cultural deviance models, there is no such thing as deviance in the ordinary meaning of that word. If conformity is defined as obedience to the norms of one's own culture and deviance as violation of those norms, then human beings apparently lack the capacity for deviance. Except for the idiot and the insane, we cannot know what they are about, the universal experience of mankind is conformity to the norms of the groups into which they have been socialized, and to which they owe allegiance. People never violate the norms of their own groups, only the norms of other groups. What appears to be deviance is simply a label applied by an outgroup to the conforming behavior endorsed in one's own subculture.*[66]

Saying rates of crime and delinquency are higher among those whose norms emphasize violence and toughness is like saying those who are successful work hard, and working hard therefore explains their success. This type of circular reasoning merely describes; it does not explain the behavior itself. Why do some people work hard for years to achieve success while others are unable to delay their immediate needs for money and other desired goods? The culture conflict approach also neglects variables like self-control that may prevent involvement in criminal behavior.[67]

Finally, culture conflict theories have been criticized for bias against certain racial and ethnic groups. To say we find violent subcultures more often among African American youth, for example, and that this is why crime is higher in areas that are predominantly African American is not only biased but also fails to recognize the structural barriers within the social environment that create inherent inequalities for certain groups. We discuss these barriers in greater detail in Chapter 10.

Despite their shortcomings, social structure theories have had a significant influence on the development of social policies that acknowledge the role of environmental variables in the development of crime and delinquency. We turn now to a discussion of the policy implications of social structure theories to assess their impact on crime-control programs and strategies.

PRACTICAL APPLICATION OF SOCIAL STRUCTURE THEORIES

Table 8.5 provides a summary of the social structure approach to the study of crime and crime control. The social structure paradigm in criminology has influenced a variety of intervention strategies aimed at combating the effects of environment on behavior and life experiences,

TABLE **8.5**

SUMMARY: The Social Structure Perspective	
Definition of Crime	Crime is acquired behavior.
Why Does Crime Occur? (Theory)	Because aspects of the social environment are pathological due to disorganization, strain, and culture conflict, individuals exposed to such conditions will acquire patterns of criminal behavior.
What Is the Solution to Crime? (Policy)	■ Alter the structure of the social environment to eliminate its pathological conditions. ■ Improve individuals' quality of life, increase their opportunity for legitimate activities, and transform crime-prone neighborhoods and communities through a collaborative effort among law enforcement, community networks, and social service agencies.

including the war on poverty during the 1960s and the Weed and Seed programs in the early 1990s. The legacy of social structure theory began during the 1930s when Clifford Shaw attempted to put theory into practice by establishing the Chicago Area Project.

Chicago Area Project

In the 1930s, the Chicago Area Project (CAP) was founded by sociologist Clifford Shaw to address the problem of juvenile delinquency in some of the poorest communities in Chicago.[68] Its central goal was to assist neighborhoods in organizing their communities by making residents more aware of criminal activity, improving the physical environment and quality of life within their community, and creating positive role models for youth.

The CAP aimed at strengthening communities by doing three things:

1. Developing academic educational and recreational programs designed to provide underprivileged youth with the opportunity to participate in positive and structured activities, sports, academic enrichment, employment training, and mentoring programs.

2. Mobilizing citizens to take pride in their neighborhoods and participate in efforts at cleaning up parks, picking up trash, renovating rundown buildings, removing graffiti, and improving the overall appearance of their community—all to encourage residents to collaborate in solving common problems.

3. Intervening on behalf of troubled teens who had already become part of the juvenile justice system in order to connect them to the proper community agencies and resources to improve their social environment and provide them with alternatives to drug abuse, gang involvement, and truancy.

The CAP continues to serve the members of its community today, with over 40 affiliate organizations, partners, and special projects throughout the city of Chicago.[69] Its core ideas are modeled in programs across the country, including public housing tenant boards, neighborhood watch groups, community action programs, and youth initiatives. These programs are driven by urban planning, self-sustenance, community improvement, and alternatives to crime and delinquency. We turn now to a national initiative that also rests upon the foundations of social structure theories—the war on poverty.

War on Poverty

In 1964, President Lyndon B. Johnson declared a "war on poverty" in his first State of the Union address, declaring poverty a priority in the public policy arena.[70] For the next decade, the federal government, in collaboration with state and local governments, non-profit organizations, and other citizen action groups, created a series of legislative acts aimed at improving the welfare of citizens across the United States. These are some of the strategies developed by the war on poverty:

- Economic Opportunity Act (1964)
- Job Corps
- Volunteers in Service to America (VISTA)
- Upward Bound
- Head Start
- Legal services
- Neighborhood Youth Corps
- Community action program (CAP)
- College work-study program
- Neighborhood development centers
- Small business loan programs
- Rural programs
- Migrant worker programs

- Remedial education projects
- Local healthcare centers
- Food Stamp Act (1964)
- Elementary and Secondary Education Act (1965)
- Higher Education Act (1965)
- Social Security amendments creating Medicare/Medicaid (1965)
- Creation of the Department of Housing and Urban Development (1965)
- Model Cities Act (1966)
- Fair Housing Act (1968)
- Urban renewal projects

The philosophy behind the war on poverty and its initiatives rested on decades of research about the detrimental effects of poverty on individuals, and the need for social reform to counter the effects of deteriorated living conditions. Legislators recognized the need for massive social reform to reach generations of poverty-stricken individuals who embraced values and behaviors that kept them in a cycle of poverty.[71] They were heavily influenced by the Chicago School and drew upon the research and premises of opportunity theory, emphasizing systematic change in urban ghetto communities to help eliminate criminal opportunity structures.

Weed and Seed

Another national policy initiative resting on the theoretical foundation of the social structure approach is the Weed and Seed program. In 1991, the U.S. Department of Justice initiated this innovative program aimed at preventing and controlling violent crime, drug abuse, and gang activities in targeted neighborhoods by combining law enforcement efforts with community revitalization.[72] The program employs a strategy of "weeding" out violent criminals and drug traffickers and "seeding" communities with much-needed social services and neighborhood restoration programs. This strategy is used to accomplish three goals:

1. Develop a comprehensive strategy to control and prevent violent crime, drug trafficking, and gang activity through the collaborative efforts of law enforcement and the prosecutor's office.

2. Coordinate existing community resources and build new initiatives to restore communities and provide intervention, treatment, and prevention of violent crime and drug abuse.

3. Use a community-oriented policing approach to mobilize neighborhood citizens to assist law enforcement in identifying violent offenders, gang members, and drug traffickers.

An evaluation of Weed and Seed programs in various jurisdictions shows a persistent pattern of long-term decrease in criminal activity in targeted communities.[73] More research needs to be conducted to account for differences in results across jurisdictions.

Today, Weed and Seed initiatives are implemented in over 150 communities across the United States, integrating law enforcement and community action to improve the structure of urban environments and reduce criminal activity. These programs are based on findings that crime-control efforts must address the underlying factors making some communities susceptible to high levels of crime.[74]

Indeed, social action is essential to changing environment. In the following chapter, we explore the concept of social action further in a discussion of social process theories.

SUMMARY

How do criminologists explain trends and variations in criminal behavior?

Criminologists explain trends and variations in criminal behavior by examining the effects of the social structure, the socialization process, and conflicts inherent to social institutions on patterns of human behavior.

Where does the sociological approach search for the cause of crime?

The sociological perspective explains patterns in human behavior by examining those aspects of society that affect the way people think, act, and react. Thus, this approach looks for the causes of crime *outside* the individual.

What is the social structure and how does it affect our behavior?

The social structure is the foundation upon which society is built. It includes the social and economic conditions to which people are exposed on a daily basis. Harsh conditions such as poverty, deprivation, frustration, the lack of opportunity to succeed, and deviant cultural values can influence the way people think and act.

Are certain places more conducive to crime than others?

Social disorganization theory argues that crime is a characteristic of ecological conditions within the social environment of urban communities, rather than a consequence of the distinct qualities of types of individuals. It is the structure of neighborhoods within the inner city—where deviant norms and values, impoverished lifestyles, unemployment, culture conflict—characteristics of social disorganization—that perpetuates criminal behavior. Thus, some places draw more criminal behavior because of their geographic location and physical features.

Can certain types of frustrations lead to crime?

According to strain theory, variations in the structure of society creates anomie, or strain due to the discrepancy between the cultural norms that define success in life and the legitimate and appropriate ways to achieve success. Anomie leads to frustration and resentment, to which people react in different ways. Some adapt by accepting the culturally defined goals but rejecting the legitimate means. This adaptation is referred to as innovation and often includes criminal and deviant activities such as stealing or selling drugs.

Do all subcultures go against the dominant norms of society?

Culture conflict theory finds the root cause of criminal behavior in the clash of values about what is right and what is wrong. Subcultures are groups within the larger society that have a distinct set of norms and a unique pattern of behavior. Not all subcultures go against the dominant norms of society. However, deviant subcultures emerge among urban youth who learn values conducive to criminal activity from their exposure to a lower-class subculture. Moreover, individuals adhering to a subculture of violence regard violent behavior as a normative, acceptable, and even required means of upholding certain values such as honor, masculinity, and courage, and they rationalize their behavior accordingly.

■ **If crime is acquired behavior, what can we change about the social structure to prevent it?**	The solution to crime, according to social structure theories, is social policies and programs that alter social-environment variables contributing to the development of crime and delinquency. Crime-control strategies influenced by this theory have focused on interventions that improve individuals' quality of life and enhance the neighborhoods and communities in which they live.

CRITICAL THINKING QUESTIONS

1. Imagine a society where no one is very wealthy or very poor. All homes have the same value and cars the same price. Everyone has a job that is equally rewarded, and there is no unemployment. Would such an environment lead to criminal activity? If so, what types of crimes would be committed and how would we explain their cause?

2. Have you ever thought about the expression the "black sheep of the family"? What does that phrase mean? How do we account for individuals who deviate from social norms despite being raised in a positive, nurturing, and pro-social environment?

3. How would you describe the social structure of the neighborhood in which you grew up? Which of its aspects contributed to the way people acted and the dynamics of its group behavior? Were delinquency and crime a problem in your neighborhood? Why or why not?

4. We live in a society where the value of entertainment far exceeds the value of saving lives. How does this make you feel? How do you overcome feelings of strain and frustration to avoid *retreatism* and *rebellion?* What keeps us going as *ritualists* and *conformists?* When and why do some cross the line to *innovation?*

ADDITIONAL RESOURCES

Learn more about Emile Durkheim and the foundations of sociological theory by visiting http://www.faculty.rsu.edu/~felwell/Theorists/Durkheim/index.htm

You can get more information about the study of the environment as related to human interactions at the Institute for Social Ecology website: http://www.social-ecology.org/

Visit Environment Criminology Research at http://geographicprofiling.com/?s= geographic+profiling for additional facts on this field of study.

For an excellent study on urban subcultures, see *Code of the Street: Decency, Violence, and the Moral Life of the Inner City* by Elijah Anderson, referenced at http://www.amazon. com/Code-Street-Decency-Violence-Moral/dp/0393320782

Read more about the programs and initiatives of the Chicago Area Project by visiting http://www.chicagoareaproject.org/

9

SOCIAL PROCESS THEORIES

Crime Is Socialized Behavior

In this chapter, we will explore the following questions:

- What is the social process approach?

- How are we socialized?

- Do individuals learn to become criminal? If so, who are their teachers?

- What do social learning, social control, and labeling theories tell us about the specific mechanisms by which individuals learn crime?

- Does the social process approach tell us everything we need to know about crime?

- How do social process theories guide our understanding of criminal justice policy?

The images of students running away in a panic on April 20,

1999, at Columbine High School in Jefferson County, Colorado, leave us with an array of questions about apparently inexplicable violence. Columbine students Eric Harris and Dylan Klebold went on a shooting rampage that day, killing 12 students and a teacher and wounding 24 others, before turning their weapons on themselves. The attack remains one of the deadliest high school shootings in U.S. history. Why did Harris and Klebold do it? Were they alienated from family and peers, social isolates who lacked the appropriate bond to society? Did they act upon a self-image imposed upon them by their social environment? Did they have a long-term predisposition to commit their crime, or was it an explosive act precipitated by something that triggered a gruesome response to social pressure?

The deadly violence unleashed by two armed students at Columbine High School raised questions about the shooters' motives that criminologists still seek to answer.

Now, contrast this image with that of John Ford, a former state senator, arrested May 26, 2005, on charges of bribery and threatening to kill a witness during an FBI sting operation targeting bribery and corruption among high-level political officials. In a videotape recording, Ford is seen meeting with an undercover FBI agent representing a phony company called E-Cycle and accepting $10,000 in exchange for his support in securing the company a state contract. In other conversations, Ford is reported to have threatened to kill anyone who turned him in (FBI agents reported uncovering two guns in his Memphis office). On August 28, 2007, Ford was sentenced to 66 months in federal prison for accepting bribes totaling $55,000. He also faces corruption charges in Nashville for accepting bribes totaling over $800,000 from contractors doing business in the state. What questions do Senator Ford's actions raise in our minds? How could a respected government official do such a thing? Why would someone risk career and reputation to engage in this type of activity? What breakdown in self-control could justify such actions?

Criminologists often face the daunting task of explaining a variety of criminal events. In many circumstances the search for the cause leads to the usual suspects: poverty, drugs, unemployment, social inequality, criminal subcultures, and mental illness. However, none of these was an issue for Klebold, Harris, or Ford.

In a research study conducted by Ronald Akers and Adam Silverman, a social learning model is used to explain terrorism as a form of violence, arguing that the exposure of individuals to propaganda that favors radical militant ideologies justifies, rationalizes, and excuses their deviant attitudes and actions.[1] Akers and Silverman argue that the socialization of individuals into deviant attitudes and beliefs that support violence serves to define and justify their behavior as morally right, appropriate, and acceptable.[2] Let's look now at the social interactions that take place as part of the learning process and how they may contribute to crime and delinquency.

MAJOR PRINCIPLES OF THE SOCIAL PROCESS APPROACH

This chapter introduces a way of understanding crime that goes beyond the theories we have presented thus far. At one end of the spectrum, in the chapters on biological and psychological theories of crime, we saw that 200 years of research have failed to discover significant personality, biological, anatomical, or psychological traits common to individuals who engage in criminal behavior. In fact, we found that criminal behavior is not a characteristic of individuals, but rather a legal category created by lawmakers who define particular types of behavior as criminal.[3] In Chapter 8, we looked at the other extreme,

social process theory

In criminology, the view that everyone has the potential to commit criminal acts as a consequence of social learning, social ties or bonds, labeling, and other social processes.

socialization

The process through which people learn the skills, knowledge, values, motives, and roles of the groups to which they belong or the communities in which they live.

which seeks the cause of crime in the "pathologies" of society. These theories focus on problems such as poverty, unemployment, and injustice and portray the criminal as a product of his or her social environment. Yet most people who live in poverty do not make crime a part of their way of life, and many of the most harmful crimes—such as white-collar crimes, war crimes, and genocide—are committed by people of privilege (see Chapter 14).

Criminology came of age when it abandoned both biological-personality theories and societal pathology theory. Criminologists then turned to an examination of the *social processes* that led to patterns of criminality in different social groups. These offer us an explanation of criminal behavior that transcends time, place, setting, and individual characteristics and looks at the often-overlooked quality of human interactions.

Social process theory maintains that criminality is not an innate human characteristic. Instead, everyone has the potential to commit criminal acts, as a consequence of social learning, social ties or bonds, labeling, and other social processes. In other words, *crime is socialized behavior.* Social process theories differ on the precise mechanisms, but they all agree that crime is learned in the process of lifelong interactions between individuals and their social environments.

Socialization is the process through which people learn the skills, knowledge, values, motives, and roles of the groups to which they belong or the communities in which they live.[4] It is "the medium for transforming newcomers into bona fide members of a group."[5] Socialization shapes our behavior and is one reason that simply living in a violent neighborhood does not by itself produce violent individuals. Criminologists therefore focus a great deal of their research on the **agents of socialization,** that is, the groups and individuals who are the main influences on the process of socialization.[6] They include the family, peer groups, media, educational and religious institutions, and authority figures.

The effect of socialization on crime is clear. We can be socialized to *conform* to generally held values and norms, or to *violate* them. The question is, what makes the difference?

Criminologists' efforts to answer this question have generated three major theories in criminology: social learning, social control, and labeling. We will look at each in some detail in this chapter, but briefly, **social learning theory** maintains that we learn criminal behavior in the same way we learn any other behavior: We acquire the norms, values, and patterns of behaviors conducive to crime. **Social control theory** focuses on the interaction between an individual's personality and his or her social environment, through which the person forms, or fails to form, the appropriate bonds to society. **Labeling theory** says that deviance is not a type of behavior but rather a name or label by which society makes certain behaviors undesirable. Table 9.1 provides a summary of these three social process

agents of socialization

The groups and individuals who are the main influences on the process of socialization.

social learning theory

In criminology, the view that we learn criminal behavior in the same way we learn any other behavior: We acquire the norms, values, and patterns of behaviors conducive to crime.

social control theory

In criminology, the view that focuses on the interaction between an individual's personality and his or her social environment, through which the person forms, or fails to form, the appropriate bonds to society.

labeling theory

In criminology, the view that deviance is not a type of behavior but rather a name or label by which society makes certain behaviors undesirable; also called societal reaction theory.

TABLE **9.1**

Social Process Theories

Socialization Process Involved in Learning Criminal Behavior	SOCIAL LEARNING THEORY	SOCIAL CONTROL THEORY	LABELING THEORY
	Differential Learning	Integration	Stigmatization
	Association	Social containment	Primary deviance
	Reinforcement	Social bonds	Secondary deviance
	Identification		

THE FAMILY CIRCUS®   **By Bil Keane**

© 1998 Bil Keane, Inc.
Dist. by Cowles Synd., Inc.

"That's the DOLL aisle, Daddy.
Somebody might see us!"

Family Circus © 1998 by Bill Keane, Inc.
Distributed by King Features 12/15/98.

differential association

In social learning theory, the idea that criminal behavior results from having more contact with individuals who hold attitudes favorable to criminal behavior than with individuals who hold attitudes that discourage it.

theories and presents the various processes involved in learning criminal behavior, which we will discuss below.

SOCIAL LEARNING THEORY

The perspectives we discuss in this part of the chapter focus on the processes involved in learning criminal behavior. The modeling, imitating, and adopting of criminal behavior patterns is discussed in the context of three learning components: differential association, differential reinforcement, and differential identification. We turn first to the concept of differential association.

Differential Association

One of the earliest and most influential social learning theorists was Edwin Sutherland. Sutherland noted that other explanations of criminality, focusing on individual traits and socioeconomic variables such as poverty and unemployment, fail to recognize one very important fact: All significant aspects of human behavior are learned. 7 The key to understanding criminality, Sutherland believed, is to examine individuals' various learning experiences that put them into contact with values, attitudes, and beliefs that favor criminal behavior.

Sutherland's starting point was to see society not as a harmonious collection of people who agree on what behavior is right, but rather as different groups and social classes with very different beliefs about right and wrong. From there it is logical to argue, as Sutherland did, that people are exposed to a variety of behavior patterns, some labeled criminal and some not. This led Sutherland to the general principle of **differential association:** Criminal behavior results from having more contact with individuals who hold attitudes favorable to criminal behavior than with individuals who hold attitudes that discourage it. In Sutherland's words:

The classroom is a major learning environment for children and adolescents. What other social environments are also sources of modeling, imitating, and adopting certain behaviors?

Criminal behavior is learned in association with those who define such behavior favorably and in isolation from those who definite it unfavorably . . . . a person in an appropriate situation engages in such criminal behavior if, and only if, the weight of the favorable definitions exceeds the weight of the unfavorable definitions.[8]

We can think of this theory as proposing a balance between associations with attitudes favorable and those with attitudes unfavorable to the violation of criminal law. The scale will tip toward the side that weighs more (Figure 9.1).

Sutherland died in 1950, but his work was continued by Donald Cressey. Both Sutherland and Cressey highlighted **differential learning** as the socialization mechanism whereby we learn criminal behavior. The basic principles of the differential learning process are as follows:[9]

- *Criminal behavior is learned.* Criminality is a byproduct of socialization and not caused by any innate characteristic within the individual. It is not something we are born with or acquire from the environment. Crime is a function of learning processes that can affect anyone at any time.
- *A person learns criminal behavior by interacting with others.* Learning criminality is an interactive process in which we must associate with other individuals who serve as the "counselors" or "mentors" of our criminal behavior.
- *A person learns criminal behavior through a process of communication within intimate personal groups.* Our relationships with family, friends, and peers are the primary mechanisms by which we learn and become socialized, and therefore their influence far outweighs the effects of other forms of communication such as radio, television, video games, and the Internet.
- *Learning criminal behavior means acquiring the techniques of committing the crime, as well as the associated motives, drives, rationalizations, and attitudes.* Learning means understanding, not just simple imitation. The novice criminal must learn not only how to commit specific crimes, but also how to react to violating the law, the proper language associated with the specific acts, and ways to rationalize the behaviors in which he or she is engaging.
- *A person's behavior is motivated by whether he or she views legal codes as favorable or unfavorable.* Learning criminality is a violation of society's norms, and therefore

differential learning

In social learning theory, the socialization mechanism whereby we learn criminal behavior.

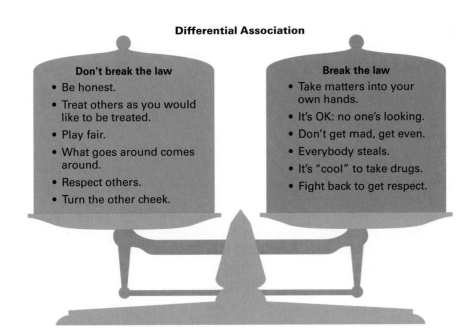

Differential Association

Don't break the law	Break the law
• Be honest.	• Take matters into your own hands.
• Treat others as you would like to be treated.	• It's OK: no one's looking.
• Play fair.	• Don't get mad, get even.
• What goes around comes around.	• Everybody steals.
• Respect others.	• It's "cool" to take drugs.
• Turn the other cheek.	• Fight back to get respect.

FIGURE **9.1**

To Break or Not to Break the Law: Pro-Criminal Versus Anti-Criminal Attitudes

individuals experience what Sutherland calls culture conflict: being exposed to a variety of opposing definitions about what is right and wrong.

■ *A person learns to become criminal when he or she perceives the consequences of violating the law as more favorable than unfavorable.* Here, according to Sutherland, is the key to becoming a law violator. In an intimate group setting, the individual is constantly bombarded with thoughts and ideas about emulating the criminal behavior, while at the same time isolated from thoughts and ideas that affirm the virtues of upholding the law.

■ *Differential associations may vary in frequency, duration, priority, and intensity.* Sutherland defined *priority* in terms of how early in life the associations occur; *duration* describes how long the associations last; *frequency* is how often they occur; and *intensity* refers to the amount of prestige attributed to the person or persons from whom the learning occurs.

■ *The process of learning criminal behavior relies on the same mechanisms that are involved in any other learning process.* It involves interacting with the instructor, observing, listening, understanding, practicing, imitating, following directions, and so on. Learning criminality is a process just like learning how to read, bake a cake, or ride a bicycle.

■ *General needs and values do not explain criminal behavior, because non-criminal behavior expresses those same needs and values.* Personal frustrations or desire for money or material goods cannot be primary motives of criminality because these same drives also prompt people to get a job, work hard, and save. Instead, we learn criminality through a process of socialization and association with individuals who foster criminal attitudes and behaviors.

Differential association theory well satisfies several criteria of good scientific theory. It explains a wide range of behaviors in a single, straightforward way, and it is very general and seeks to account for all criminal behavior. Because we can look at real events and experiences to see whether the theory is correct, we can verify it by experiment.

We then must consider whether the theory fits the facts we know about crime and criminal behavior. Research suggests it does:

■ Children who associate with aggressive peers are more likely to engage in aggressive behavior themselves. One study examined the behavior of 118 second-graders who participated in a six-week summer school program that paired moderately aggressive children with nonaggressive peers. It found that aggressive children had lower levels of disruptive behavior when their teammate was not aggressive, regardless of whether the teammate was a friend. Moreover, the highest level of aggressive behavior occurred in pairs of aggressive teammates who were friends.[10]

■ A study conducted on undergraduate college students showed that individuals who engage in deviant behaviors are also likely to agree with norms, values, and attitudes that support their acts.[11]

■ Parents engaged in criminal activities are likely to produce children who continue the same patterns of criminality. Research using a three-generation study design supported the finding that there is continuity in patterns of antisocial behavior passed down from generation to generation.[12]

■ A study conducted on 1,492 youths between the ages of 18 and 24 used questionnaires to explore subjects' attitudes toward deviance and also the attitudes of their peers. The study revealed that having delinquent friends who support criminal attitudes is strongly related to the development of a long-term criminal career.[13]

Differential association theory succeeded in moving sociological theory away from a view of criminality as a function of personality, neighborhood, or class. But it does have some weaknesses. It proposes that exposure to long-term crime-inducing stimuli causes people to commit criminal acts, but it does not take into account short-term triggers that prompt individuals to commit crimes impulsively or opportunistically. It also does not explain why some individuals who have never come into contact with criminal associations also commit crimes, or why others, even when surrounded by norms, values, and definitions favorable to rule violation, are able to resist and abide by the standards of conventional society.

Differential Reinforcement

Recognizing the limitations in the theory of differential association, social scientists tried to fill the gaps. Robert Burgess and Ronald L. Akers published an article outlining their *differential association-reinforcement theory* of criminal behavior.[14] They drew upon concepts of psychology to argue that criminal behavior, like any other learned behavior, is a function of social and environmental rewards and punishments. They emphasized the idea that we are more likely to repeat behavior that results in a reward and less likely to repeat behavior that results in punishment. Essentially, Burgess and Akers built on Sutherland's original theory of differential association by adding the psychological component of **differential reinforcement,** whereby individuals learn to define their behavior according to the rewards or punishments attached to it. Thus, the behavior that results in a greater reward will more likely persist over the behavior that results in a lesser reward, whether that behavior is deviant, criminal, or both.[15]

For example, teenagers who join a street gang whose members value stealing, fighting, and getting high on drugs, will be encouraged to engage in these activities, as they are positively rewarded by the group members themselves. According to Akers, therefore, individuals engage in behaviors and activities that are positively rewarded by the groups with whom they most intimately interact and identify, whether they are criminal or deviant groups, church groups, peer groups, school groups, or others.

While promising, Burgess and Akers's theory suffers some of the same pitfalls as does Sutherland's original theory of differential association. For one thing, it generally neglects the role of opportunity in criminal behavior by assuming that individuals who learn to become criminal must have interacted with other individuals who engage in such behavior. Nor does the theory explain why some individuals manage to escape the effects of seeing deviant behavior positively reinforced and choose instead to conform to law-abiding behavior. On the flip side, how do some individuals engage in criminal acts when they have never had criminal contacts?

Finally, the theory cannot be proven false.[16] By definition, behavior is strengthened by reinforcement. If a behavior is repeated, then the experience was reinforcing. If the behavior is *not* repeated, then the experience was *not* reinforcing. We have no independent measure of whether a particular experience of behavior is reinforcing. The logic of the definition is infallible, and, therefore, it is also inadmissible as scientific explanation no matter what empirical research reveals.

Differential Identification

Daniel Glaser added to social learning theory the concept of **differential identification.**[17] Glaser argued that the degree to which individuals symbolically identify with criminal or non-criminal behavior patterns determines whether they will commit criminal acts, and not the frequency or intensity of their associations.[18] Differential identification thus focused attention on an individual's susceptibility to environmental pressures. It maintained that the learning of criminality through differential association is mediated, or modified, by individual factors that intervene between social contact and criminal behavior. The individual becomes an active participant in the learning process, making a voluntary, subjective choice to identify with criminals or non-criminals, whichever he or she desires to copy.

How are these teens influenced by the "teachings" of one another? What values, norms, techniques, and rationalizations are being communicated here?

differential reinforcement

In social learning theory, the process whereby individuals learn to define their behavior according to the rewards or punishments attached to it.

differential identification

In social learning theory, the degree to which individuals symbolically identify with criminal or non-criminal behavior patterns is what determines whether they will commit criminal acts.

For example, certain groups in high school that are perceived to be the most popular will influence the behavior of other students who admire them and may copy their style of dress or join their clubs in order to become more like them. Glaser refers to these groups as **reference groups,** composed of those whom we most admire, respect, and emulate. While this argument has the merit of linking criminal behavior theory to an impressive body of social psychological theory, it still leaves unclear why some individuals admire or favor criminal groups over other types of reference groups.

reference groups

In social learning theory, groups composed of those whom we most admire, respect, and emulate.

SOCIAL CONTROL THEORY

Coming at the problem from the opposite angle is *social control theory,* which tries to explain why people *don't* commit crime, rather than why they *do.* Since, as we have seen, virtually everyone commits crime, the question might seem a bit silly. Nonetheless, if we assume there is always something to be gained by committing criminal acts, but some people nonetheless refrain from doing so, then the question makes sense.

Social control theory examines the element of socialization that builds our mechanisms of social control and allows us to refrain from engaging in indulgent, norm-violating behavior. It directs us to understanding conformity, rather than deviance, on the grounds that the root cause of deviant behavior is the absence of those social controls that allow most individuals to manage their passions and impulses and obey the rules of society. Social control theorists assume all people have the potential to deviate from the norms of society—to drink under age, cheat on their taxes, and drive above the speed limit—and therefore, we must understand criminal behavior in the context of the social relationships, values, and beliefs that tie individuals to society, limiting their chances of becoming involved in crime.[19] We turn now to an examination of *social integration,* the process by which we develop social bonds with conventional society and internalize a sense of responsibility to abiding by the rules, simply because we have a greater stake in it.

Containment

Walter C. Reckless observed that prevalent sociological theories did not explain how individuals who face social pressures to commit crime also fail to resist such pressures. He developed a theory to answer this question that he called **containment theory.**[20]

According to containment theory, individuals must become socialized to resist the "pushes" and "pulls" imposed upon them by individual and environmental factors.[21] Pushes include various aspects of our experiences and personal characteristics that make us more vulnerable to committing a crime. These may include a biological predisposition to aggression, psychological maladjustment, membership in negative peer groups, and exposure to a deviant subculture, or the experience of strain or deprivation.[22] Pulls signify the perceived rewards of engaging in criminal acts such as financial gain, sexual gratification, or peer approval.[23] So, for example, we might be tempted to rob a bank because we are hanging out with a group of peers who are encouraging the behavior (push), and we also want the immediate financial rewards associated with the crime (pull). Social containment is therefore a barrier or obstacle that neutralizes the effects of pushes and pulls. According to Reckless, containment is both external and internal (Figure 9.2).

External containment represents "the holding power of the group,"[24] or the "watchful eyes" around us that we take into consideration before we decide to engage in certain acts. External containments set our limits and boundaries by continually reassuring us someone or something is evaluating our decision to act in certain ways. Reckless describes external containment as society, state, tribe, village, family, or any group that can keep the individual's behavior within accepted norms.[25] For example, if you believe your partner will disapprove of your cheating on your income taxes, you will be motivated not to do it.

containment theory

In social control theory, the view that individuals who commit crime have failed to resist the social pressures, the "pushes" and "pulls," that non-criminals are able to resist.

external containment

In social control theory, the idea that there is someone or something evaluating our decisions to act in certain ways.

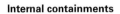

External containments

- My girlfriend might leave me.
- My parents will be disappointed.
- I will never be able to show my face again at school.
- I may get kicked off the football team.
- What if I get caught?

Internal containments

- This goes against everything I believe.
- I should know better.
- This is not how I was raised.
- Someone might get hurt.
- How can I live with myself?

FIGURE 9.2

What Should I Do? Internal Versus External Containments

Conversely, **internal containment** is the ability of the person to follow expected norms and to direct him- or herself.[26] Internal containment comes from within us, and we develop it by being successfully socialized into the approved norms, values, and standards of society. It is our desire for socially approved goals, a commitment to the beliefs of society, a healthy and positive self-image, and the ability to manage strain and frustration. No longer do we need to look our shoulder to walk the straight and narrow path; rather, we search within ourselves to resist the temptations of crime, no matter how much gain they seem to offer. According to Reckless, internal containment is much stronger than external; as our social relations become less personal, as our society becomes "more diverse and alienated," as people live farther and for longer times "away from a home base," the self becomes increasingly important as an agent of control.[27]

Social control mechanisms, both external and internal, undoubtedly do inhibit some crime. We all have observed containment theory's two general standards of conduct in action: *I do not steal cars because it is wrong, I cannot act that way,* or *I'm better than that* (internal containment), or *I do not steal cars because I will get caught, I will lose the approval of significant individuals,* or *I will lose my position in society* (external containment). However, social control theory does not provide all the answers we seek.

Social Bonds

In his 1969 publication *Causes of Delinquency,* Travis Hirschi proposed that it is not the number or quality of their associations that keeps people from committing criminal acts. Rather, it is their close interpersonal attachments to people who disapprove of criminality.[28] Our successful integration into society includes the development of these **social bonds,** or ties between individuals and conventional social groups within society, such as friends, family, teachers, co-workers, neighbors, and church members.[29] On the other hand, weak social bonds with members of the law-abiding community will increase the likelihood that a person will get involved in criminal behavior. Thus, while we are all vulnerable to engaging in criminal behavior, it is our fear of damaging our relationships with individuals to whom we are bonded that keeps us from doing so.[30]

internal containment

In social control theory, the idea that our behavior is guided by our desire for socially approved goals, a commitment to the beliefs of society, a healthy and positive self-image, and the ability to manage strain and frustration.

social bonds

In social control theory, ties between individuals and conventional social groups within society, such as friends, family, teachers, co-workers, neighbors, and church members.

Hirschi proposed four components of the social bond (Figure 9.3):

- *Attachment* is a person's shared interests with others in society. Hirschi emphasized the importance of attachment to family, especially to parents, as essential to this element of the social bond. Other important attachments are those to peers and to school.
- *Commitment* is the amount of effort and energy an individual puts into conventional activities with others in society. Commitment values hard work, education, and personal success and working toward these goals by, for instance, going to school or having a job.
- *Involvement* describes how an individual spends his or her time in conventional activities. Idleness encourages deviation toward criminal behavior, while actively participating in sports, school clubs, community organizations and events, and religious groups leaves little opportunity for lawbreaking.
- *Belief* is sharing with members of society an understanding of moral values such as honesty, equity, social responsibility, and respect.

Social bond theory appears consistent with the experiences of many people who commit crimes. In fact, the chief merit of control theory may be its proposition that individuals engaging in crime and delinquency are generally detached from conventional society, with weak social bonds. Research findings seem to support this basic proposition:

- Attachment to family, peers, and school has been found to be a major variable in the ability of children and adolescents to develop positive affection, respect for authority, and the social skills necessary to manage stress and avoid alienation. A study on the interrelationship of family and peer experiences in predicting adolescent problem behaviors was conducted on an 18-year longitudinal sample using 198 adolescents from both traditional and nontraditional families. The study found that the most powerful predictors of teen drug use and delinquent behavior were similar behaviors by peers.[31]
- Commitment to educational achievement has been linked to a decrease in the likelihood of youth becoming involved in illegal drinking, drugs, and other forms of delinquency, and an increase in the likelihood of attending school. Children with lower academic performance committed more, and more serious, crimes, and re-offended more frequently than children with higher academic performances.[32]
- Studies conducted on afterschool programs available to teens have consistently shown that kids involved in sports, supervised activities, school clubs, and other school-sponsored events are less likely to engage in illegal activities than kids who

FIGURE **9.3**

Elements of the Social Bond: Successful Social Bonds Equals Conformity

Social Bond

Attachment	Commitment	Involvement	Belief
Family	Future goals	Afterschool activities	Fairness
Friends	Education	Clubs/teams	Honesty
Peers	Career	Community events	Morality

are not involved in such programs. Analyses of the National Education Longitudinal Study of 1988 suggest that regular participation in extracurricular activities from 8th to 12th grade predicts academic accomplishments, as well as pro-social behaviors in young adulthood.[33]

■ A belief in society's moral values has also been linked to the likelihood of refraining from criminal activity. The more likely a person is to value honesty, morality, and ethical behavior, the less likely that person will behave in manners inconsistent with those beliefs.[34]

While control theory will continue to hold its place as a prominent perspective in criminological literature, it falls short of answering some very important practical questions. For example, how do we account for the fact that many offenders have strong attachment to family, friends, co-workers and peers, yet nevertheless risk damaging this social bond to engage in criminal activities? Many crimes have been committed by people described as "very close" to their family. Indeed, they are not at all the loners detached from society that social bond theory describes. Moreover, research indicates that individuals committed to success and achievement, but unable to obtain them through conventional means, often engage in criminal activities to reach their goals. (See the Consider This feature for such an example.) Another shortcoming of social bond theory is the fact that many criminals, while actively violating the law, will acknowledge their belief in society's general principles of morality and even express remorse for their actions.

Thus, while lack of social control may pave the way for the onset of criminality, there must be other forces in play that account for persistent patterns of deviant behavior. We turn now to an examination of these dynamics.

LABELING THEORY

Sex offenders are among the most despised criminal offenders. Many people believe they are dangerous predators who cannot be rehabilitated and want to see them locked up forever. Highly publicized sex crimes have led all 50 states to pass central registration

On August 4, 1974, Richard Nixon resigned his office as president of the United States after being implicated in the notorious Watergate scandal, involving key government officials in his administration engaging in acts of conspiracy, burglary, and illegal wiretapping. How does social control theory fall short of explaining this type of criminal behavior committed by such well-integrated members of society?

How does the constant bombardment with negative labels influence one's self-image? Do laws that require sex offenders to publicly declare their criminal activities serve to reinforce their deviant identity?

CONSIDER THIS...

Commitment to Social Norms and Breaking the Law: Enron

In 1999, Enron Corporation was one of the largest companies selling gas and electricity in the United States. Behind the profits, however, were suspect corporate strategies and irregular accounting procedures that treaded on the boundaries of fraud.

As early as 1996, Andrew Fastow, the chief financial officer (CFO) of Enron, began creating off-book business entities the firm used to avoid paying taxes and create the illusion that Enron was making huge profits each quarter, when it was actually losing money.[35] Corporate executives and other Enron insiders were trading millions of dollars of Enron stock, making huge profits for themselves at the expense of company workers, stockholders, and investors.

The distortion and manipulation of accounts could not be sustained and finally led the company's finances into a downward spiral. Enron filed for bankruptcy on December 2, 2001. When the scope of its top managers' wrongdoing was revealed, the value of the company's stock shares dropped down to pennies. Kenneth Lay, the former chairman of the board and chief executive officer, and Jeffrey Skilling, the former chief operating officer and chief executive officer, went on trial for their part in the Enron scandal in January 2006. They were indicted on 53 criminal counts including insider trading, securities fraud, money laundering, wire fraud, bank fraud, conspiracy, and making false statements. Both were found guilty, and on October 23, 2006, Skilling was sentenced to over 24 years and in federal prison and ordered to make restitution of Enron's squandered pension funds, in the amount of $26 million. Lay died of a heart attack that summer, before he could serve any time. Fastow pleaded guilty to two counts of fraud for his role in the accounting scandal and, on December 26, 2006, was sentenced to six years in prison, followed by two years of probation.[36]

How can criminological theory account for individuals like Fastow, Lay, and Skilling, who appear to be engaging in conventional activities, who adhere to the values and norms of society, and who have developed social bonds and networks of attachment to family, friends, peers, and business associates, yet who go beyond the boundaries of social control to violate the law? How do the basic tenets of social control theory hold up to the observable facts in this case? Has emphasis on profit become so integral to the fabric of U.S. financial institutions that it can jeopardize and even neutralize the controlling effect of social bonds and attachments?

What do you think?

laws requiring convicted sex offenders to register with the state or local law enforcement agency, which in turn disseminates the information to the public. These laws focus on controlling released sex offenders at the expense of their individual rights. The emphasis seems to have shifted from solving and punishing crimes to identifying dangerous people and depriving them of their liberty before they can do harm.[37]

The requirement that sex offenders must fulfill registration and notification laws has the net effect of branding them with a deviant label for life, preventing them from ever being able to properly function as members of society, make new friends, hold a job, develop a relationship, or just start over. One researcher notes that sex offender registration results in the offender's rejection by the community, threats, harassment, shame, isolation, and feelings of hopelessness that are difficult to overcome.[38] Many people respond to this situation by saying "they deserve it" or "society must be defended." However, the idea behind labeling theory suggests this may not be the case.

In the 1960s, Howard Becker built upon the sociological theories of Frank Tannenbaum, Edwin Lemert, and Alfred R. Lindesmith, applying their ideas and research methodologies to the study of deviant behavior among jazz musicians. In *Outsiders: Studies in the Sociology of Deviance*,[39] Becker called for criminology to recognize the basic fact that deviance or crime is a label attached to people by those with the power to do so, rather than a characteristic of the person. According to Becker, social groups create deviance by making the rules; breaking those rules constitutes deviance. Those rules are applied to particular people, who are then labeled "outsiders." To Becker, the deviance is not the quality of the action itself but is a consequence of the application of the rules by others.[40]

This perspective came to be known as *labeling* or *societal reaction theory* and led criminologists to examine the process by which laws are made and by which people are labeled deviant. Most importantly, it resurrected Edwin Sutherland's idea that criminology was not just the study of criminal behavior but also the study of why acts get defined as criminal and what kinds of acts are punished.

Clarence Schrag summarized the basic propositions of the labeling perspective as follows:[41]

- No act is inherently criminal. It is the law that makes an act a crime.
- Criminal definitions are enforced in the interest of powerful groups by their official representatives, including the police, courts, correctional institutions, and other administrative bodies.
- People do not become criminal by violating the law. Instead, they are designated as criminal by the reactions of authorities who confer upon them the status of outcast and deprive them of some social and political privileges.
- Only a few people are caught violating the law, although many may be equally guilty.
- Criminal sanctions vary according to characteristics of the offender, and for any given offense they tend to be most frequent and most severe among males, the young, the unemployed or underemployed, the poorly educated members of the lower classes, members of minority groups, transients, and residents of deteriorated urban areas.
- The criminal justice system is built on a stereotyped conception of the criminal as a pariah—a willful wrongdoer who is morally bad and deserving of the community's condemnation.
- Individuals labeled criminal begin to view authorities and society in general as the enemy, and their subsequent behavior is an outcome of this negative interaction.

In this sense, no act is objectively deviant or criminal until it is receives the subjective definition by society as such. Hence, no individual is deviant or criminal until reacted to and symbolically labeled as such by society.

These reactions and definitions are shaped by individuals—called "moral entrepreneurs" by Becker—who determine the content of the criminal law and impose sanctions according to their standards of right and wrong.[42] Moreover, labeling theory notes that criminal law is applied differently, to the benefit of those with social and economic power in society. The likelihood of an individual's being charged and prosecuted has more to do with his or her socioeconomic standing than with the person's actions Labeling theory also concludes that police, courts, and corrections officers are not only biased and selective in their application of negative labels, but actually perpetuate criminality by imposing a deviant identity upon the individuals they are supposed to treat or correct.

Primary and Secondary Deviance

Labeling theory represents the first attempt to distinguish between primary and secondary deviance.[43] According to Edwin Lemert, **primary deviance** refers to an offender's original act of violating the law. This violation can occur for many reasons—to meet an immediate need, adhere to a subculture, deal with frustration, or respond to deviant association. Primary deviance can go relatively unnoticed. We can find out that the president of the United States smoked marijuana in his youth, a famous ballplayer was convicted of assault, or an admired movie star used to be a thief. Because the behaviors were somehow excused, dismissed, or quickly forgotten, they had little impact on the future of the individual. However, if the event came to the attention of agents of social control (such

primary deviance

In labeling theory, an offender's original act of violating the law.

secondary deviance

In labeling theory, the continued pattern of offending based on an individual's adjustment to society's negative social reaction.

as police) who applied a negative label to the behavior *and* to the individual, its consequences would undoubtedly determine the course of the person's future.

Secondary deviance is the continued pattern of offending based on an individual's adjustment to society's negative social reaction.[44] Understanding secondary deviance is the key to understanding why some individuals refrain from engaging in future acts of criminality, while others react to the negative label attached to them by continuing on the path of recurrent deviance (Figure 9.4). When primary deviants learn, accept, and internalize a deviant self-concept bestowed on them by society, they develop behavior patterns that live up to their new expected role. Secondary deviance thus becomes a self-fulfilling prophecy that results from being *stigmatized*.[45]

Stigmatization

For better or for worse, our behavior as human beings is to a great extent controlled by the reactions of others. Throughout our lives, we are showered with a variety of symbolic labels that help us define who we are. We are "athletic," "talented," "smart," "pretty," "a troublemaker," "bad," or "antisocial" according to parents, siblings, teachers, friends, and peers. In fact, these are not mere descriptions that come and go without leaving their mark. Rather, such labels confirm and define our identity and bestow upon us a variety of attitudes and behaviors consistent with them.

stigmatization

In labeling theory, occurs when a negative label applied to an individual has an enduring effect on that person's self-identity.

Stigmatization occurs when a negative label applied to an individual has an enduring effect on that person's self-identity. The perception of an individual as a social deviant will

FIGURE **9.4**

Secondary Deviance: How Does It Occur?

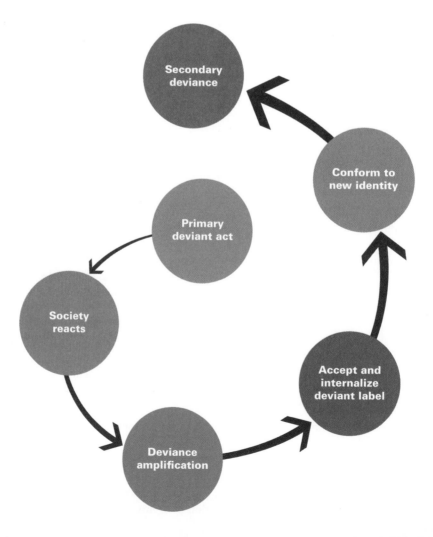

negatively affect his or her treatment at home, school, work, and other social contexts.[46] The stigmatized individual will turn to others similarly labeled for support, friendship, and interaction, which reinforces a new personality, attitudes, and actions consistent with criminal behavior. Stigmatized individuals will come to interact and identify with other outcasts and social pariahs who affirm, approve, and facilitate their behavior. Figure 9.5 summarizes this interactive process of labeling.

Moreover, research suggests the application of a negative label can create **deviance amplification,** whereby the activity labeled as deviant is amplified by the spiraling effect of negative social reaction.[47] The social deviant becomes isolated from society and reacts by becoming more actively deviant. The increase in deviant activity draws further disapproval from society, and the whole process is perpetuated.

Labeling theory constituted a fundamental challenge to the prevailing models of the time. If we accept the labeling school of thought, we cannot keep looking for the causes of criminal behavior in the individual offender. Instead we must look to the system of justice

deviance amplification

In labeling theory, the process by which the activity labeled as deviant is amplified by the spiraling effect of negative social reaction.

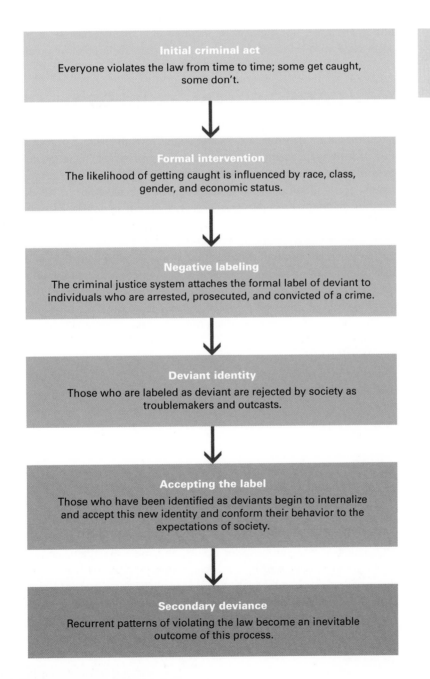

Initial criminal act
Everyone violates the law from time to time; some get caught, some don't.

Formal intervention
The likelihood of getting caught is influenced by race, class, gender, and economic status.

Negative labeling
The criminal justice system attaches the formal label of deviant to individuals who are arrested, prosecuted, and convicted of a crime.

Deviant identity
Those who are labeled as deviant are rejected by society as troublemakers and outcasts.

Accepting the label
Those who have been identified as deviants begin to internalize and accept this new identity and conform their behavior to the expectations of society.

Secondary deviance
Recurrent patterns of violating the law become an inevitable outcome of this process.

FIGURE **9.5**
The Process of Labeling

that defines acts as criminal and labels some people criminal and not others. We have already encountered the concept of discretion (arrest bias, reporting errors, and politically motivated data reports) throughout the criminal justice process in Chapter 3. According to labeling theory, the way this discretion is used proves that deviant labels are applied to those who are powerless and unable to defend themselves.[48]

Labeling theory forces us to consider the context within which criminal acts take place, with research studies putting a greater burden on society for the perpetuation of crime and deviance. (See Connecting Research to Practice for a look at the impact of stigmatization on youth.) Nevertheless, it has been criticized on several points. First, it fails to explain the original act of violating the law. Why does the primary deviance occur? Second, labeling theory relies on the notion that recurrent patterns of deviant behavior are primarily caused by the offender's acceptance of a deviant self-image. Many criminals and delinquents do not claim to have a deviant identity.[49]

Finally, labeling theory has been criticized for its unequivocal contention that the criminal justice system perpetuates crime and deviance. It is unreasonable to argue that formal intervention will *always* lead to more crime, while lack of formal intervention will *always* lead to less crime. Community sanctioning, informal processing, restorative justice, and other nonstigmatizing methods of correction have been attempted time and again yet have failed to produce the outcome that labeling theory predicts.

EVALUATING SOCIAL PROCESS THEORIES

Despite their shortcomings, social process theories have brought us closer to understanding crime within the context of socialization. If we understand human behavior as a function of structure, context, interaction, and interpretation, social process theories provide us with a clear picture of the many causes of crime. We must incorporate the effect that family, peers, education, societal reaction, and role have on the development of human behavior and not rely on personal traits or environmental variables alone to explain crime. The multifaceted views we find in social process theories help explain a wide variety of deviant behaviors across all class structures.

Research has also found social process theories to be consistent with some basic facts: that people move in and out of delinquency and crime as youths and adults, that almost everyone commits some criminality at different times in their lives, and that often this is a transitory event. But social process theories share the same fundamental flaw as earlier theories: They fail to recognize that crime is politically defined behavior embedded in the structure of society.

The harshest lesson for any scientist to learn is that not all questions can be scientifically answered. We must develop our science in different directions if we are to overcome the shortcomings of conventional approaches to crime. In the next chapter we turn to yet another approach to the study of crime and criminality, but first let's briefly examine the policy implications of social process explanations of crime and delinquency.

PRACTICAL APPLICATION OF SOCIAL PROCESS THEORIES

We have outlined the three levels of the social process approach to the study of criminal behavior. Table 9.2 summarizes the social process perspective's definition of crime, explanation of why the behavior occurs, and solutions offered in terms of prevention. Public policies influenced by the social process approach advocate programs to counter the socialization of individuals into deviant behavior patterns. These policies have the goal of encouraging positive associations, building pro-social bonds, encouraging self-control, and providing alternatives to formal sanctioning. We will focus on three policies that highlight how the social process perspective has shaped criminal justice policy: youth mentoring initiatives, Head Start, and diversion.

In the 1970s William Chambliss conducted a research study of two delinquent gangs—the Saints and the Roughnecks.[50] The Saints were a group of eight promising young men from "good," white, upper-middle-class families. They were active in school affairs, received good grades, and played on athletic teams. At the same time, they were some of the most delinquent boys at Hannibal High. However, their techniques for covering truancy were so successful that teachers did not even realize that the boys were absent from school much of the time.

The local police also saw the Saints as good boys who were among the leaders of the youth in the community. On rare occasions when they were stopped in town for speeding or running a stop sign, the Saints were always polite, contrite, and pleaded for mercy. Although constantly occupied with truancy, drinking, wild driving, petty theft, and vandalism, none of them was officially arrested for any misdeed during the two years they were observed.

Although their rate of delinquency was about equal to that of the Saints, the Roughnecks were constantly in trouble with the police, who suspected that they were engaged in criminal activities. They knew this in part from catching them but also from the circumstantial evidence; most of all, the police shared the view of the community in general that this was a bad bunch of boys. Because the Roughnecks were constantly involved with the police, teachers also saw the boys as heading for trouble.

What was the cause of this disparity in treatment between the Saints and the Roughnecks, and what was the result? Why did the community, the school, and the police react to the Saints as though they were good, upstanding, non-delinquent youths with bright futures but to the Roughnecks as though they were tough, young criminals who were headed for trouble? Why did the Saints and the Roughnecks in fact have quite different careers after high school, which, by and large, lived up to (or down to) the expectations of the community?

The community responded to the Roughnecks as boys in trouble, and the boys agreed with that perception. Once their pattern of deviance was reinforced, the boys acquired an image of themselves as deviants, selecting friends who affirmed that self-image. As that self-conception became more firmly entrenched, they also became willing to try new and more extreme deviances. With their growing alienation came freer expression of disrespect and hostility for representatives of the legitimate society. This disrespect increased the community's negativism, perpetuating the entire process of commitment to deviance.

The discovery, processing, and punishment of some kinds of criminality and not others means that visible, poor, non-mobile, outspoken, undiplomatic "tough" kids like the Roughnecks will be noticed, whether their actions are seriously delinquent or not. Their noticeable deviance and the reaction to it will have been so reinforced by police and community that their lives will be effectively channeled into careers consistent with the self-image they developed in adolescence. Other kids—like the Saints, who establish a reputation for being bright, reasonably polite, and involved in respectable activities, who are mobile and moneyed—will be invisible when they engage in delinquent activities. When it is time to leave adolescence, most will follow the expected path, settling into the ways of the middle class.

This study makes a very important finding: Labeling, stigma, and negative self-images are powerful forces in determining who we are and what we become. The practical implication of the study on the Saints and the Roughnecks guides us in the direction of labeling theory's emphasis on secondary deviance as a product of social reaction.

The inescapable lesson from "The Saints and the Roughnecks" is that the less formal intervention by the criminal justice system in the minor crimes of juveniles, the better off they, and society, will be.

*To read the full text of the article, see the Appendix on page 383.

Youth Mentoring Initiatives

Youth mentoring initiatives replace the law-and-order model characteristic of crime-prone neighborhoods, drawing upon community resources to provide at-risk youth constructive alternatives to criminal activity. These programs operate on the premise that reaching out to troubled teens through nurturing, mentoring, and education will reverse the detrimental experiences and negative social influences that led to their involvement in crime and

TABLE **9.2**

SUMMARY: The Social Process Perspective

Definition of Crime	Crime is socialized behavior.
Why Does Crime Occur? (Theory)	Interactions between individuals and their social environments include social processes whereby individuals learn to become deviant and criminal. These social processes are ■ Social learning theory (differential learning) ■ Social control theory (inadequate social integration) ■ Labeling theory (stigmatization)
What Is the Solution to Crime? (Policy)	Develop policies to encourage noncriminal associations, to build social bonds, to encourage self-control, and to inhibit the damaging effects of deviant labels.

break the cycle of delinquency and violence. They focus primarily on youth identified by family members, schools, or government agencies as at risk for becoming involved in delinquency and crime.

In 1997, a collaborative effort between local faith-based institutions and juvenile justice and law enforcement organizations in 15 cities laid the foundation for the National Faith-Based Initiative for High-Risk Youth; the program provided vulnerable teens with a productive alternative to delinquency and violence by matching them with mentors according to skills, needs, and interests.[51] The goal was to offer the opportunity for learning positive social skills in order to better handle conflict, improve educational outcomes, and reduce the likelihood of substance abuse, teen pregnancy, and truancy.

The Youth and Congregations in Partnership (YCP) is an example of a youth mentoring program. Established in 1997 by District Attorney Charles Hynes, in Brooklyn, New York, the YCP is a community-based alternative to incarceration that offers youth offenders a second chance to benefit from the help and care of a volunteer mentor from the faith community.[52] Program participants between the ages of 13 and 22 are referred to the Kings County (Brooklyn) District Attorney's Office by the courts, social service agencies, and other organizations for troubled youth. The program continues to operate today on the premise that these young people are amenable to rehabilitation in an enriched social environment that encourages positive support and learning. By providing troubled teens with positive role models to offer support and friendship, and someone who accepts, understands, and respects them, the program aims to develop their self-worth, accountability, and respect for others.[53] Classes help teens learn anger management and conflict resolution skills and techniques, recover from substance abuse, and receive mental health counseling. The program also provides educational support, career counseling, and recreational development.

Head Start

Mounting evidence suggests that early childhood experiences are paramount in the social and developmental growth of children.[54] One of the best-known social policy initiatives aimed at strengthening the socialization process of low-income children is Head Start, which, drawing from social control theory, emphasizes developing pro-social bonds early in life.

Head Start is a federally mandated program created in 1965 as part of President Lyndon Johnson's war on poverty. It focuses on providing comprehensive services to assist preschool children from low-income families to increase their attachment to conventional norms and values and to solidify their bonds to society. Administered by nonprofit organizations and local schools, Head Start services are designed to help end the cycle of social and economic disadvantage by providing a program that serves the physical, emotional, and psychological needs of young children. Programming focuses on four major areas of growth: education, health and nutrition, social services, and cognitive development. Parental involvement is an essential component.

The educational element of Head Start emphasizes acquiring the intellectual skills necessary to become successful in school, with special attention to the development of math and reading skills. The health and nutrition component emphasizes the identification and prevention of health-related problems early in life. Resources are offered to participating families to provide children with immunization, medical treatment, dental hygiene, mental health counseling, and nutritional services. Families are taught the skills necessary to ensure the safety of their children and reduce the risk of injury. Moreover, the Head Start program is mandated to conduct an initial screening to identify developmental, sensory, or behavioral problems in the child, to better provide appropriate community services.

Head Start is now also available to the parents of preschoolers enrolled in the program. By attending classes that improve parenting skills, promote literacy, reduce domestic violence, promote health and nutrition, and identify community outreach resources and social service agencies, parents take on a more active and supportive role in their child's preparation for school and general well-being.

Federally funded programs such as Head Start are founded upon the premise that the early experiences of children are essential to their development and socialization.

Diversion

A final policy offshoot of social process theory's perspective on the negative effects of labeling is diversion. Diversion programs are designed to prevent youth and adult offenders from being formally processed through the criminal justice system. In 1967, when the labeling perspective was raising serious questions about secondary deviance and social reaction, the President's Commission on Law Enforcement and the Administration of Justice report called for the creation of youth services bureaus to develop alternative sanctioning within local communities.

The goal of diversion is to reduce the need for formal sanctioning by the criminal justice system as a solution to the social problem of crime.[55] It assumes that formal processing—including arrest, trial, and incarceration—may actually produce more harm than good by stigmatizing first-time offenders for relatively minor violations of the law. Diversion programs therefore provide remedial actions for youth and adult offenders within the informal context and setting of the community.

The diversion process usually assembles a panel of experts who determine offenders' eligibility and amenability to diversion on a case-by-case basis. Offenders must successfully complete the diversion program requirements, which often focus on some element of rehabilitation, including substance abuse treatment, outpatient mental health screening and evaluation, educational and vocational training, anger management training, and a variety of other services tailored to fit the specific needs of the offender. A diversion agreement may also include some form of restitution, where the judge orders the offender to make a monetary payment to the victim for the harm resulting from the offense.[56] Restitution can also be a court order to do some type of service to the community as a form of repayment for crimes committed. For example, a youth who has been caught spray-painting graffiti in a public place can be ordered to spend a certain amount of hours doing volunteer work within the community such as picking up trash at a park, cleaning up a church, or working at a shelter in lieu of receiving a formal court-ordered sentence.

And now we turn back to the puzzling question that began this chapter: Why did Eric Harris and Dylan Klebold go on a shooting rampage at Columbine High School in April of 1999? How can the social process perspective shed some light on their acts of violence and retaliation? On the surface, Harris and Klebold appeared to be two average, intelligent kids from good homes whose adult members were by all accounts highly regarded members of the community. As the investigation into their crime got deeper, however, a picture formed of a troubled pair of teenagers, angry at the world and out for revenge.

Police investigations centered on the discovery of a website created by Harris, where he expresses hostility toward Littleton residents, with his anger directed mostly at teachers and students from Columbine High School. He claims to want revenge against those who angered, irritated, or annoyed him over the years, and his desire for revenge is expressed in terms of blowing up the city and shooting everyone he can.[57] Harris and Klebold even posted the results of their experimentation with pipe bombs on the website. Many teachers claimed that Harris and Klebold had shown various signs of disturbing behavior, and although they reported their concerns, the authorities could take no action as no crime had actually been committed. Even more bizarre is their parents' claim that they were never informed of their sons' anger, rage, and antisocial behavior. Harris's parents were also never aware of the complaints about their son to police, made by the parents of another student at Columbine who was apparently threatened by him.

Harris and Klebold were the products of the negative effects of strained relationships, alienation from family, school, and peers, and the feeling of rejection and isolation by members of society. This was no small-scale plot for getting back at a few individuals who wronged them. Their plans for revenge were much grander than that. In a note left by Harris, he blames their deadly scheme on the parents, teachers, and students of Columbine High.[58] He points the finger at students for their rejection, ridicule, and non-acceptance of individuals who are "different."[59] In turn, parents and teachers are blamed for making the students behave that way and not teaching them any better. Harris and Klebold were acting upon their rage and anger with nothing to lose and revenge as the only force driving their behavior. A journal chronicling their plot stated their intention to kill as many people as possible, with Columbine being just the beginning of their lethal rampage that would leave a path of deadly destruction throughout the community of Littleton.[60]

The extent of the wrongs the teenage boys perceived to be done to them was clearly the foundation that served to trigger their rampage. At the heart of this perception are their feelings of being wronged and rejected by members of society who essentially labeled and treated them like outcasts. They turned to each other as a means of affirming their antagonistic attitudes, as their attachments to conventional norms, values, activities, and relationships had been strained, if not entirely severed, over the years.

Moreover, Harris and Klebold developed associations that made it possible to carry out their plans. Police investigations revealed that a close friend of Klebold was responsible for purchasing the weapons used in the attacks. Robyn K. Anderson was an 18-year-old student and close friend of Klebold at Columbine High. Although Anderson made the purchase, she had no knowledge of their plans to use the weapons in the massacre.[61] Police also believe that Harris and Klebold had used the Internet to learn the techniques of making pipe bombs and other explosive devices and to find out where to purchase materials.

Policy changes stemming from the analysis of events relating to the Columbine shooting have focused attention on the need for preventive strategies, rather than imposing restrictions and control mechanisms such as limiting access to school property, reducing student gatherings, operating metal detectors, and installing security cameras in schools. Instead, initiatives have been developed to identify students who have been socialized into deviant behavior patterns and provide them with programs and services designed to encourage and promote academic success, appropriate conflict management, and mental and emotional enhancement. (See the Connecting Theory to Practice feature for an example of these policy changes.)

Reacting to School Violence

The Columbine tragedy illustrates the need to integrate community resources to prevent school violence by embracing key sectors within the social domain of youth. These sectors include the school, mental health and social service agencies, juvenile justice components, and law enforcement.

The U.S. Departments of Justice and Education, along with the American Institutes for Research, have developed specific policy guidelines to address the problem of school violence. These recommendations involve three levels of policy response:[62]

- *Tier 1: Build a schoolwide foundation for all children.* To accomplish this task, which helps schools develop strategies to improve academic performance and behavior of students, these components are required: modeling of caring, supportive, and respectful behavior by school teachers and staff; developing programs that reinforce adequate conflict resolution skills; initiating learning techniques that are both child and family focused; and collaborating with community agencies to create the most effective and engaging curricula.

- *Tier 2: Intervene early for some children.* Early identification of students at risk for severe academic or behavioral difficulties requires the training of teachers, counselors, and other staff to recognize early warning signs of potential problems and to act upon those signs by making appropriate referrals. Early intervention includes the creation of services and support mechanisms that address risk factors and build protective measures for them; this involves developing interventions such as anger management training, structured afterschool programs, mentoring support, group and family counseling, educational enhancement, and tutoring.

- *Tier 3: Provide intensive interventions for a few children.* Some children require intensive intervention. These intensive measures are specifically tailored to the student's needs, strengths, and weaknesses. This tier involves a planning process that includes the child and family, social service agencies, and school staff to create a unique set of school and community services, customized for that child and family.

Services are provided to children identified as experiencing significant emotional and behavioral problems. Intensive intervention programs include day treatment programs, which provide students and families with intensive mental health and special education services; multisystemic therapy, focusing on the child and his or her family, the peer context, school/vocational performance, and neighborhood/community supports; or treatment foster care, an intensive, family-focused intervention for children whose delinquency or emotional problems are so serious and so chronic that they are no longer permitted to live at home.

The key to such policy measures is to provide strategies and plans to reduce behavioral problems that may escalate into acts of violence by providing children with access to the services they need, to enhance and enrich their socialization experiences. The value of early intervention and preventative approaches is demonstrated in the empirical literature. However, these policies must be balanced against the detrimental effects of profiling and labeling students as potential troublemakers. Warning signs and checklists must be approached with caution to identify children who are socially withdrawn, feeling rejected or isolated, and performing below their academic level; the goal is to avoid unfairly labeling children who are simply not reflecting some desirable image.

SUMMARY

- ## What is the social process approach?

The social process approach suggests that criminal behavior is a function of the various interactions that take place between individuals and their social environments. These interactions are seen as the core of socialization and form the foundation upon which all aspects of human behavior are learned.

Inadequate socialization is therefore the key to understanding criminality. From this perspective, any person—regardless of age, race, gender, or socioeconomic class—has the potential to deviate from the law. The specific mechanisms of social learning will dictate the course of behavioral choices that individuals make in various situations.

How are we socialized?

Socialization occurs from the moment we are born. It is a lifelong process whereby we learn how to live and interact with others on a daily basis. By communicating with individuals who are close to us—classmates, friends, family, and peers—we learn the various norms, rules, beliefs, and values that govern our behavior. Through these interactions, we learn the complex meanings and shared understandings of our culture, which guide and shape the roles we play in society.

Do individuals learn to become criminal? If so, who are their teachers?

Our socialization can have a positive or negative impact on our lives. Agents of socialization can transmit deviant norms, beliefs, and values, and therefore play a critical role in determining the outcome of our behavior, by teaching individuals to embrace attitudes and behaviors that support crime and delinquency.

What do social learning, social control, and labeling theories tell us about the specific mechanisms by which individuals learn crime?

Social process theories explore three distinct social processes by which individuals are socialized to criminal behavior: differential learning, inadequate social integration, and stigmatization.

Social learning theory stresses the mechanisms involved in learning criminality through differential associations with individuals who favor definitions of crime over definitions that emphasize law-abiding behavior, the differential reinforcement of rewards and punishments, and the differential identification with criminal versus non-criminal reference groups.

Social control theory analyzes human behavior from the aspect of those mechanisms of internal and external constraints that are created by the social bonds that exist between individuals and conventional society. The positive integration of individuals into society forms the basis for social control that inhibits criminal behavior. On the contrary, weak social bonds create a lack of integration, which in turn allows individuals to behave in antisocial ways.

Labeling theory finds the cause of criminal behavior in the negative reactions by society to the behavior of some individuals. Formal negative labels such as "delinquent" or "criminal" are attached to individuals and serve to isolate them from mainstream society. Their apparent rejection from society has a spiraling effect whereby the individuals come to internalize the negative label and become stigmatized, identifying with the new deviant identity and behaving in ways that are consistent with the expectations of that label.

Does the social process approach tell us everything we need to know about crime?

Social process theories have been criticized for focusing too much attention on aspects of social learning, while ignoring people's individual variations and neglecting the influence of social-structural variables that contribute to crime and delinquency. Not all individuals exposed to deviant social learning processes will develop patterns of criminal behavior, and some become deviant who have not been so exposed. Differential association theory therefore fails to explain why some individuals who are surrounded by deviant norms and values continue to hold on to conventional attitudes and behaviors.

Social control theories have also been criticized on similar grounds. Attributing crime and delinquency to the absence of those social bonds or socialization processes that encourage law-abiding behavior does not tell us very much about why some individuals who do have conventional ties and attachments to society nevertheless break the law.

Moreover, the labeling approach, while shedding some light on the emergence of continued patterns of criminal behavior, tell us little about the original cause of primary deviance. There is also lack of empirical support for the claim made by labeling theory that contact with the criminal justice system alone serves to perpetuate criminality. If that were true, then career criminals who generally escape formal sanctions would desist from their criminal activities.

| ■ **How do social process theories guide our understanding of criminal justice policy?** | Despite its shortcomings, the social process perspective has served as the cornerstone for the development of criminal justice policy. Social process theories have guided policy in the direction of enhancing the learning experiences of individuals to increase their self-control and promote the their positive integration into society by encouraging healthy social bonds. The basic ideologies behind this perspective have laid the groundwork for policies and practices that emphasize an improvement in teaching positive values, the mentoring of youth to encourage control and accountability, and the re-orientation of criminal justice toward community intervention as a response to crime and delinquency. |

CRITICAL THINKING QUESTIONS

1. Do you think negative labels cause crime or does getting involved in criminal behavior result in the negative label? In either case, how can an individual escape the spiraling effects of internalizing a deviant status? What labels have significant people in your life attached to you? How did these labels affect the image you had of yourself, your identity, and your behavior?

2. How much of our behavior is really socialized? Is most of what we do learned behavior or is it instinctive? Try to remember what activities you engaged in last weekend? Besides, sleeping, breathing, and occasionally sneezing, is there much else we can attribute to nature or is most of it a product of our nurture?

3. What type of social bonds do you experience? Have your attachment, commitment, involvement, and belief in conventional activities and groups contributed to your positive integration into society? How could things have been different in the absence of these pro-social bonds?

4. Why do we refrain from engaging in particular types of criminal activities, such as rape, assault, and murder? Why do we try to drive the speed limit, pay our taxes, and avoid parking in a handicapped parking space? What mechanisms of social control govern our behavior in these examples? Are they internal or external containments? Do different types of containment prevent different types of crime?

ADDITIONAL RESOURCES

For more information on the Head Start initiative, visit http://www.acf.hhs.gov/programs/ohs/

The following website highlights the process of deviance amplification: http://www.sociologyindex.com/amplification_of_deviance.htm

Details on diversion programs can be obtained at http://www.ncjrs.gov/html/ojjdp/9909-3/div.html

For more information on the Columbine shootings, refer to the following website: http://www.disastercenter.com/killers.html

More statistics on school violence can be found in the National School Safety Center Report, http://www.schoolsafety.us/

For the full report, "Safeguarding Our Children: An Action Guide," see http://www.ed.gov/admins/lead/safety/actguide/action_guide.pdf

Additional Readings

Akers, R. L. (1998). *Social learning and social structure: A general theory of crime and deviance.* Boston: Northeastern University Press.

Blank, S., & Davie, F. (2004). *Faith in their futures: The youth and congregations in partnership program of the Kings County.* New York: District Attorney's Office, National Faith-Based Field Report Series.

Bynum, J. E., & Thompson, W. E. (1996). The family and juvenile delinquency. *Juvenile Delinquency, 3,* 430.

Hasaballa, A. (2001). *The social organization of the modern prison.* New York: Edwin Mellen Press.

Matsueda, R. L., & Anderson, K. (1998). The dynamics of delinquent peers and delinquent behavior. *Criminology, 36,* 269–308.

Rosecrance, J. (1988). Whistle blowing in probation departments. *Journal of Criminal Justice, 16,* 99–109.

Sutherland, E. H. (1949). *White collar crime.* New York: Dryden.

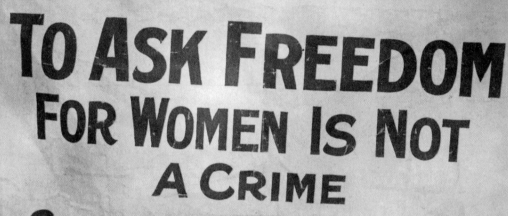

10

SOCIAL CONFLICT THEORIES

Crime Is in the Conflict Inherent in Society

In this chapter, we will explore the following questions:

- How does conflict theory describe the social order?
- What is the relationship among power, politics, and the economy?
- Does conflict lead to crime?
- Is it possible that the criminal justice system perpetuates human suffering?
- Why is there a huge gap in crime statistics between men and women?
- What causes contradictions in the social structure?
- Can radical criminology offer a peaceful solution to crime?

In March of 1991, Rodney King, an African American male

in his mid-20s, along with two passengers, entered a freeway in the San Fernando Valley area of Los Angeles. It was about midnight when a California highway patrol car began pursuing King's speeding vehicle. A freeway chase ensued between the police and King, who, according to later reports, refused to stop because he feared getting a DUI, which would have been a violation of his parole conditions.

King eventually exited the freeway into a residential neighborhood where police cornered his vehicle. Several Los Angeles Police Department officers arrived at the scene. The three men were ordered to exit the vehicle and get down on the ground. King's two passengers complied and were taken into custody without incident. After initially remaining in the car, King finally came out but was described as acting "bizarre" (probably from being intoxicated). When officers attempted to restrain and handcuff him, he became agitated and resisted. King was shot with a taser, which knocked him to the ground.

He was subsequently beaten several times with police batons and repeatedly stomped and kicked by police officers while he was on the ground. The incident, which lasted over a minute and a half and left King with cuts, bruises, and several broken bones, was captured on video by a nearby private citizen. Following the incident, four officers were charged with using excessive force. On April 29, 1992, a jury acquitted three of the officers on all charges and was hung on one of the charges for the fourth.[1]

The news of their acquittal sparked one of the longest and most devastating riots in U.S. history. Angry citizens took to the streets—looting, setting fires, destroying property, assaulting, and protesting what they considered an unfair, biased verdict. At the end of the almost weeklong rampage, over 50 individuals were dead and more than 2,380 injured; property damage amounted to nearly $1 billion.[2]

Commentators, political activists, scholars, and ordinary citizens have since debated the reaction to the acquittal of the police officers in the King case. Was it an outcry against racism and bias inherent in the criminal justice system?[3] Would the outcome have been different if Rodney King were white? What if the jury had not consisted of 11 whites and 1 person of Filipino descent? Was there an inherent bias in the LAPD against certain types of suspects? Do law enforcement practices include a certain level of racial profiling?

In a study of racial profiling, researchers at George Washington University examined these issues. Using data from a national survey, they found nearly 75 percent of African American men between 18 and 34 said they were victims of profiling.[4] Moreover, research studies have found a strong link between police use of force and certain neighborhood contexts where larger minority-group representation, lower socioeconomic status, and increased conflict create the perception that more drastic interventions are needed.[5]

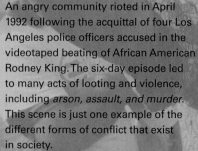

An angry community rioted in April 1992 following the acquittal of four Los Angeles police officers accused in the videotaped beating of African American Rodney King. The six-day episode led to many acts of looting and violence, including *arson, assault, and murder*. This scene is just one example of the different forms of conflict that exist in society.

A study found officers are significantly more likely to use force during citizen encounters in disadvantaged neighborhoods, even taking into account individual factors such as the suspect's resistance.[6]

What do such findings suggest about our perception of criminal behavior? Do the law and various agents of social control operate in the interests of justice and equity? Or are they an instrument of bias and oppression? We turn to the conflict perspective in this chapter for an exploration of these questions.

MAJOR PRINCIPLES OF THE SOCIAL CONFLICT APPROACH

In this chapter, we will take a look at the third major sociological approach to the study of crime—social conflict. Recall from Chapter 8 that the **social conflict approach** examines the fundamental distribution of wealth and power within society. The Rodney King incident and ensuing riots are an example of one of the many levels of conflict inherent to society. Conflict occurs between adversaries, family members, citizens and police, religious groups, political opponents, and various other groups. It can be a source of unrest and destruction, but it can also be the impetus for social change.

A theory of criminal behavior that purports to explain all criminality must account for the incidence of the entire range of criminal acts. White-collar, corporate, state-organized, and political crimes are widespread. Mass political movements also lead to vast amounts of criminal behavior. The American revolutionaries who terrorized the British were criminals by the law of the land, as were the workers who fought for their right to collectively bargain and strike, and the women in Western societies who for centuries have committed criminal acts in the course of opposing oppressive and discriminatory laws that prevented them from voting or inheriting property. They are joined by the students who violate trespass and other laws while demonstrating against war or apartheid, the farmers who mobilize civil disobedience, and the civil rights activists who protest segregated schools, buses, housing, and restaurants.

We cannot casually dismiss these criminal actions while focusing on mugging, burglary, and assault. Indeed, we can explore the possible connections among varieties of criminality only by seeking the links between social class, crime, and the need for social control. We must now approach our understanding of crime—such as burglary, robbery, arson, and assault—as an expression of outrage against greater social ills and injustices.

The data and observations we have used in evaluating theories of crime in the last few chapters show that we must somehow integrate the political nature of criminal law with the social character of criminal behavior. This will help us understand why the official crime rate for certain types of crime is higher for some classes and groups of people than it is for others, why black under-class males have a higher official crime rate for burglary, assault, and robbery while white upper-class males have a higher official crime rate for corporate, political, and white-collar crimes, and why white male college students are rarely arrested for rape despite the fact that 20 percent of female college students experience date rape on college campuses.

Criminologists who view crime as an outcome of social and economic contention are known as *conflict theorists*. They try to explain crime by understanding the social, political, and economic structure of society and the role this structure plays in the distribution of power. Conflict theory (also called *social conflict theory*) argues that the root cause of crime is the social conflict created by the unequal distribution of wealth and power in society. According to this approach, the political and economic structure of society allows the

social conflict approach

An approach to criminology that examines the fundamental distribution of wealth and power within society; law is a mechanism of social control that the dominant classes use to coerce the rest into compliance; crime is defined by those in power.

CRIME IN GLOBAL PERSPECTIVE | Defining Who Is Criminal in Pakistan

Set in Lahore, Pakistan, the novel *Moth Smoke* is a realistic portrayal of how the wealthy yet corrupt members of the ruling classes within this society are able to insulate themselves from the very laws that bind the subordinate classes.[8] The story describes the life experiences of Darashikoh "Daru" Shezad. Daru is a young banker who despite his education lacks the connections to become a part of the elitist class. His life takes a downward spiral when he gets fired from his job in Lahore for being late to work and keeping a wealthy customer waiting. When he tries to get a job at another bank, he is told there are enough applicants with more wealth and power than the salaries being offered, who are hired out of respect and to gain their families' business.

Desperate, Daru turns to drugs, alcohol, and robbery. When he first holds a gun in his hand, he experiences an overwhelming sense of power. For the first time he feels in control of his life rather than a victim of his vagrant status. For a short while, Daru is reunited with Ozi, a childhood friend who is a part of the upper echelon of Pakistani society. However, their friendship crumbles under the strain caused by Daru's declining social status as well as his attraction to Ozi's wife Mumtaz. Daru's life becomes filled with disillusion as he not only goes on trial for a murder committed during a robbery but is also framed for a hit-and-run crime committed by his friend Ozi, who is able to escape sanction due to his privileged status.

Moth Smoke describes how the ruling classes within Pakistani society are able to create laws, escape punishment, get good jobs, accumulate wealth, and perpetuate their privileged status. The rest of society is forced to obey their rules, accept lower-class status, and serve as scapegoats for the wealthy, perpetuating their subordinate positions. The story of Daru describes how the criminal justice system in Pakistan operates as a tool of oppression. It reinforces the ruling class' privileged status while keeping the lower class under its control.[9]

criminal justice system to operate in favor of those who have the power to define the law.[7] Moreover, the wealthy and privileged use the law as a tool to control the less advantaged members of society who threaten their position, by defining their acts as criminal. The Crime in Global Perspective feature examines this phenomenon in Pakistan.

How do the social, political, and economic structures of society create social conflict that allows these dynamics to occur? What is the relationship between group power and the shaping of criminal law? How does a capitalist economic structure influence crime rates? What role does the criminal justice system play in perpetuating criminal behavior? The various branches of conflict theory (Table 10.1) attempt to answer these questions. We turn now to a closer look at the emergence of conflict theory for a better understanding of the origins of crime.

THE EMERGENCE OF CONFLICT THEORIES

The origins of conflict criminological theory date back to World War II and have often been described as a reaction to mass changes taking place around the world in both the political arena and the economy.[10] The civil rights movement in the United States showed us people struggling for their rightful place in society, with breaking the law and going to prison as the only means of exercising their rights.

Aware that not all crime was contained in the violence and property offenses of urban ghetto youths, criminologists had to recognize that the legal system did not always express the values and norms of the community.[11] Two different forms of conflict theory emerged: a functional conflict approach and a power conflict approach (Figure 10.1). Let's look at what makes each one unique.

TABLE **10.1**

Social Conflict Theories of Criminal Behavior			
RADICAL THEORIES	**CONTEMPORARY RADICAL THEORIES**	**FEMINIST THEORIES**	**STRUCTURAL CONTRADICTIONS THEORY**
Marx and Engels	Left realism	Marxist feminism	Contradictions and conflicts
Willem Bonger	Peacemaking criminology	Radical feminism	Crime in capitalist societies
Raymond Michalowski		Multiracial feminism	Political-economic forces
Dawn Rothe		Liberal feminism	

Functional Conflict Theory

Functional conflict theory views society as consisting of different groups of individuals who have very different goals and interests in life. Think about the advertisements you see on television. One moment, you see a commercial about a weight-loss product, and the very next ad is promoting a delicious calorie-rich dessert. During a football game, you will see countless commercials for beer, and during prom season or homecoming, you will see a plethora of public service ads warning about the dangers of drunk driving. Why is that? These messages reflect the natural human diversity in our society and the need to meet the different goals and interests that are a function of it.

According to functional conflict theory, this diversity also puts people in conflict with one another. Different groups continually seek to achieve their own goals—through lobbying, media, and petitions—and to hinder the efforts of their opponents. Functional conflict theorists see this process as a system of checks and balances that gives society stability while at the same time nurturing the underlying forces for social change.[12]

Theorists George Vold and Austin Turk took on the challenge of applying functional conflict theory to criminology[13] Vold described society as "held together in a shifting

functional conflict theory

In criminology, the view that crime results as a consequence of the disagreement between different interest groups over the definition of law.

How did the violation of criminal laws during the civil rights movement affect our understanding and definition of crime? Who are the criminals in this photo?

FIGURE **10.1**
**Functional Conflict Versus
Power Conflict**

Functional Conflict Theory	Ideas common to both theories	Power Conflict Theory
Conflict is a source of checks and balances and impetus for social change.	Society consists of different interest groups.	Not all groups in conflict are equally powerful.
Crime is a result of disagreement over the definition of law.	Groups compete to advance their own interests.	Crime is the result of the ability of groups in power to impose the law on the powerless groups.

but dynamic equilibrium of opposing group interests and efforts."[14] According to Vold, groups with the authority to define the law will impose definitions that represent their own interests. Thus, crime is a consequence of a disagreement between different interest groups over the definition of law. Turk echoed this idea when he described social order as "an always tenuous approximation of an order, more a temporary resolution of conflicting notions about right and wrong and of incompatible desires."[15] Turk saw criminal behavior as that occurs in the course of interaction that takes place between individuals, whereby crime is a label imposed by some individuals on others. Therefore, no act is inherently criminal. The question that remained unanswered, however, was *how* some groups achieved the power to impose definitions on others.

While the functional conflict perspective articulates the nature of group conflict in society, it mistakenly treats all conflict as equal. It views conflicts arising from differences in culture, for example, as similar to those arising from structural variations in power, such as between classes or genders. So it is power conflict theory instead that highlights the connection between group conflict and the distribution of economic, social, and political resources.

Power Conflict Theory

Power conflict theory is an elaboration of Max Weber's sociology of law as applied to criminology.[16] The starting point for this perspective is the recognition that not all groups in conflict are equally powerful and that the task for sociological understanding is to

power conflict theory

In criminology, the view that elaborates Max Weber's sociology of law: Crime results as a consequence of the unequal distribution of power in society, as one group is able to force its will on others.

Society includes groups and individuals with opposing points of view: Opposition can unite, divide, or bring about social change.

explain which groups are able to force their will on other groups. In 1938, researcher and scholar Thorsten Sellin observed that the cultures brought from Europe in massive waves of immigration in the late 1800s were repressed by the dominant culture of the United States, just as the cultures the fascists defined as "alien" were decimated in the name of "law" and "progress" because one group had the power to use the law to the detriment of others.[17] In contrast to Vold and Turk, Sellin believed it is not sufficient to merely point out that conflict and power struggles are ubiquitous in human social relations; we must go on to describe and explain who wins and who loses in the struggle.

Power conflict theory aims to develop a radical vision for structuring society in the direction of equity and justice, rather than building upon the existing differentials in power distribution. A body of other research on law and crime (which we look at below) supported the power conflict approach and contributed to the ongoing search for criminological theories that better fit the reality of the times. Thus, conflict criminology has undergone several phases in the ensuing years. We turn now to a discussion of the specific components of this radical approach in criminological theory.

RADICAL CRIMINOLOGICAL THEORIES

Over the years, the conflict approach has developed under various names such as "radical," "critical," "Marxist," and "the new criminology." To avoid confusion, we will use the term **radical theory** to refer to all the theories within this tradition, which basically originate with the propositions made by Marx and Engels.[18]

Karl Marx and Friedrich Engels on Capitalism

Karl Marx and Friedrich Engels are considered the founders of modern socialism.[19] Their many writings span a variety of topics that present a complex analysis of society and history in terms of class relations.

Marx and Engels's philosophy centered upon the nature and organization of labor in society and how this determines the course of human relations. Marxist theory begins with the observation that every human group faces the same fundamental problem: how to organize its labor.[20] Unless they convert the natural environment to usable products—food, shelter, clothing—human beings cannot survive. There are an infinite number of ways people may organize their labor. In Marxist theory, the way they choose is called the **mode of production.** The mode of production may allow each member to seek, hoard, and consume everything he or she acquires. Or a group might organize the production and distribution of products equally among all the members regardless of how much each person contributes to acquiring them. Groups of people may take most of the production for themselves and redistribute only enough to keep those who produce alive. If there is an unlimited supply of people producing, they can organize the distribution so some people consume all and others die for lack of food, shelter, and clothing. Every historical era contains examples of how human groups organize the acquisition and distribution of the products of labor. Most, but not all, societies have created modes of production that result in social classes with different shares of the goods.

radical theory

A term to refer to all the criminological theories within the tradition founded by Marx and Engels.

mode of production

In Marxist theory, the way that people choose to organize their labor.

Great thinkers Karl Marx and Friedrich Engels laid the groundwork for the development of radical criminological theories.

proletariat

In Marxist theory, the working class or the laborers.

bourgeoisie

In Marxist theory, the capitalists or the class who owns the means of production—the land, the factories, the businesses, or the enterprises.

According to Marx and Engels, the uneven division of labor in society is the central feature of capitalism, where labor itself becomes a valuable commodity.[21] The working class or **proletariat** sell their labor to the **bourgeoisie,** the capitalists or the class of individuals who own the means of production—land, factory, business, or enterprise. The proletariat greatly outnumbers the bourgeoisie. Under capitalism, people are compensated with less than the value of the commodity they are producing in order for the wealthy capitalists to make a *profit.* If this were not the case, commodities would be priced too high for consumers to purchase. Can you imagine paying even more than $4 for a cup of coffee?

Marx believed the long-term effect of capitalism is to produce a capitalist class that is rich and powerful and a working class that is impoverished and relatively powerless. Thus, one of the problems facing every society with an unequal distribution of wealth and power is that those social classes receiving more of the products will strive to retain their privileged position, while those who receive less will strive to increase their share. This simple and obvious fact bestows on every class society a fundamental contradiction: the need to maintain class relations that inevitably produce antagonisms and conflicts between the classes. The people with the control over a greater proportion of the resources generally also have access to more effective tools of physical coercion. One solution, then, is for the upper class to implement the continuation of the unequal distribution of goods by force. A more clever way to organize people to accept an unequal distribution of goods, however, is to convince them that this is the right and proper way for the world to be ordered.

The law therefore becomes the principal source of both legitimation and coercion. It is the law that maintains inequality in the distribution of the products of a people's labor. The law defines the rights, duties, and responsibilities people have to one another and to various institutions within society.

One facet of the law central to maintaining existing social relations, including inequality, is the definition of some acts as criminal and the punishment of people who engage in those acts. Thus, in the Marxist tradition, law in capitalist societies is a reflection of class struggle that attempts to maintain both the institutions that facilitate the accumulation of capital and a relative level of social peace. Crime, on the other hand, is a reaction of the oppressed working class to the disadvantaged conditions under which capitalism forces them to live.[22] It is a mechanism by which the worker compensates for being exploited, deprived, and living in distress and despair. Crime can also be a symbol or expression of rebellion and hostility toward the ruling classes of society.[23]

Figure 10.2 highlights the various components of Marx and Engels's views on capitalism. The two did not elaborate too much on crime and the law. However, they laid the foundation upon which other theorists built their research on the relationship between crime, law, and the economy.

Willem Bonger on Economic Culture

In 1916, Dutch criminologist Willem Bonger published a classic work titled *Crime and Economic Conditions*[24] that began from the Marxist position outlined above. Bonger applied this perspective to crime and theorized that crime varied depending on the degree to which a society was structured around capitalist or communist modes of production. More than anything else, the capitalist mode of production relies on competition to make a profit. In the struggle for survival, not everyone will come out on top; someone must win and someone must lose, and the winner wins at the expense of the loser. A neighborhood deli must compete for customers with the deli that just opened down the street. In order to get more business and increase its profit, each deli must develop strategies to "steal" customers from the other.

egoism

In Bonger's theory, the prevailing personality type produced by capitalism; one that strives for self-attainment and that places only secondary importance on providing support or aid to one's neighbors.

According to Bonger, the prevailing personality type produced by capitalism is what he calls **egoism**—a personality that strives for self-attainment and that places only secondary importance on providing support or aid to one's neighbors.[25] The resulting emphasis on profit and greed make people less likely to abide by the law in their effort to gain economic advantage, even if their actions may hurt someone along the way. More importantly, Bonger argued that in an economic system based on capitalist principles, those who ultimately gain control of the means of production are those who behave in the most egoistic fashion. Bonger believed that in societies whose economies are built primarily on socialism, crime rates are very low. The emphasis on equality and sharing produces **altruism,** or the sacrifice of self to help others, and competition is replaced by cooperation and the desire for peace and harmony among different groups in society.

In support of his theory Bonger presents a summary of the existing anthropological data comparing societies with different modes of production. Bonger's studies found that preindustrial capitalistic societies without exception had ongoing problems of deviance, crime, and violence. By contrast, communistic societies revealed a consistent tendency to be harmonious, relatively free of conflict, crime, violence, and disruptive forces.[26] Subsequent research surveying hundreds of later anthropological studies also supports Bonger's proposition that societies based on equality and sharing manifest a much lower incidence of conflict and crime than do societies based on acquisitiveness and personal accumulation.[27]

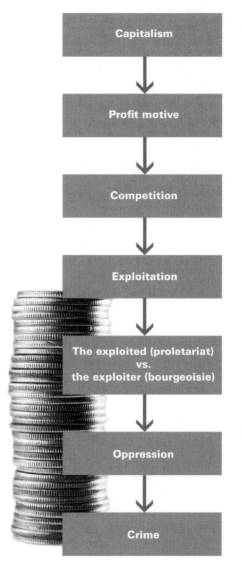

FIGURE 10.2

Marx and Engels: The Cycle of Capitalism

Capitalism → Profit motive → Competition → Exploitation → The exploited (proletariat) vs. the exploiter (bourgeoisie) → Oppression → Crime

altruism

In Bonger's theory, an emphasis on equality and sharing or the sacrifice of self to help others; in contrast to egoism, competition is replaced by cooperation and the desire for peace and harmony among different groups in society.

Sales and other tactics retail stores use to attract customers are characteristic of economic competition to increase merchandise sales and make a profit. The winner of this competition, according to Bonger, is the one who makes the most profits.

Bonger argued that crime was inherent in capitalist economies. The potential to break the law is characteristic of all individuals in a capitalist economy, regardless of their social or economic status. However, Bonger argued that although the economically advantaged commit crimes, they do not suffer the same legal consequences as do the economically disadvantaged, because the law is designed to control the poor in the interest of the wealthy. How and why is the law designed to favor the ruling classes of society? The work of William Chambliss provides an answer.

William Chambliss on Law and Politics

Hundreds, even thousands, of local, state, and federal laws are passed each year—some out of the specific need or interest of a particular individual or group. This was the case when the federal government enacted Megan's Law, requiring all states to develop procedures for notifying residents about sex offenders living in their neighborhoods. (See Consider This for more about Megan's Law.) Some laws emerge because a group of individuals lobby for the specific interests of a significant segment of society, such as those in favor of gun control. Still others simply develop out of legislative debates that represent the views of individual lawmakers and congressional committees. Regardless of origin, laws emerge from conflict-ridden situations that arise between different groups within society.[28]

The process of law creation is complex, but we highlight one area here—its relationship to power. A prominent study by William Chambliss and Robert Seidman sees the connection between law and power as the key to understanding the origin of criminal

TABLE **10.2**

Class Interest, Class Conflict, the Law, and Crime

PROPOSITION	OBSERVATION
Complex societies consist of a variety of groups that live under different conditions and have different life experiences.	People live in different environments that range from urban ghettos to suburbs to high-rise apartments in Beverly Hills.
The conditions under which we live affect our values and norms.	People have different concerns such as survival, making ends meet, buying a new car, getting a promotion, attending college. These different concerns lead to diversity in values and norms.
Complex societies are thus composed of a very different and often conflicting set of values and norms.	People do not agree about, for instance, lying or cheating to get ahead versus maintaining honesty and integrity, or establishing a reputation by being tough versus gaining respect by being respectful.
The likelihood that the law will reflect our norms and values is not evenly distributed in society but is instead related to our political and economic position.	The AARP (American Association of Retired Persons) is one of the most powerful lobby groups in the United States; those 65 and older are also the largest group of voters.
The higher a group's political and economic status within society, the greater the likelihood its norms, values, and interests will be reflected in the law.	The NRA (National Rifle Association) is one of the most politically and economically advantaged interest groups in the United States; its views are more likely to be represented in the legislature than the views of gun control advocates.

Source: Adapted from Chambliss, W. J., & Seidman, R. T. (1971). *Law, order, and power.* Reading, MA: Addison-Wesley.

Megan's Law: A Powerful Voice

In the summer of 1994, Jesse K. Timmendequas lured 7-year-old Megan Nicole Kanka into his New Jersey home by telling her he wanted to show her his puppy. Once she entered her neighbor's house, he sexually assaulted and murdered her. Timmendequas had previously been convicted of raping a 5-year-old girl and had also attempted to sexually assault another 7-year-old girl. Why did his neighbors not know about this?

Grief-stricken and angry, Megan's family started lobbying for stricter laws regarding registration of sexual offenders. Only three months later New Jersey signed what became nationally known as Megan's Law. This legislation required the active notification of residents about the presence of registered sexual offenders who live in their neighborhoods. Active notification requires police to go door-to-door informing residents of an offender's presence and/or sending out letters alerting neighbors.

The Kankas, along with other parents whose children were murdered by repeat offenders, then lobbied federal lawmakers to pass a federal version of Megan's Law. In May 1996, the federal government did so, enacting a law requiring law enforcement departments within each state to develop policies regarding the release of information about registered sex offenders to communities. Moreover, individuals convicted of sexual crimes against children are required to notify local law enforcement of any change of address or employment after they are released from prison. However, the effectiveness of Megan's Law has been questioned, and many are convinced that the registration is counterproductive.[29]

The parents who lobbied for Megan's Law had lived a nightmare many parents fear. Their personal experiences and suffering allowed them to attract the attention of media as well as lawmakers. This gave them the power they needed to get such laws passed on a state and federal level. Does our society allow all victims of crime to lobby successfully to get such laws passed?

What do you think?

---

behavior.[30] In stratified societies, where social status depends on economic privilege and political authority, the dominant groups must enforce the norms and rules of conduct most likely to guarantee their advantaged positions. Those in power are able to do this through the criminal law.

History shows that in adjudicating disputes between classes, the state will usually be persuaded by the interests and actions of the dominant economic class. Thus, what makes the behavior of some individuals "criminal" is the state's ability to enforce the will of the dominant classes through the coercive but legitimate power of the law.[31] In an analysis of the development of vagrancy law in England in the mid-1300s, Chambliss shows how wealthy landowners benefited from its passage, which forced would-be beggars to accept low-wage jobs as serfs instead of committing what the law had made a criminal act.[32]

When you came home past your curfew in high school, what made your behavior "criminal" was the ability of your parents (the dominant class in your house and the one that defined the rules) to enforce their definition of a curfew on you, the subordinate member of the household. Similarly, for Chambliss, crime is rooted in social conditions that empower the wealthy to define as criminal those acts that go against their own interests. At the same time, the government, law enforcement, and the criminal justice system as a whole perpetuate criminal activity by providing a distorted sense of the reality of crime as primarily a problem of poor, urban minority youth.[33] This not only deflects attention from the harmful and dangerous crimes committed by the rich and privileged, but also endlessly expands crime-control strategies—building more prisons, hiring more police, and making tougher laws—that continue to fail while diverting resources away from education, social services, and healthcare.[34] Table 10.2 summarizes the propositions offered by Chambliss and Seidman.

Thousands of people are killed or injured each year in post-collision fires caused by defective designs in auto fuel systems. This car killed the three young girls who were inside. Manufacturers continue to produce these vehicles, avoiding newer, safer designs that are not as cost effective. Why aren't these carmakers held accountable for the resulting injuries and loss of life?

left realism

A contemporary theory of radical criminology that argues that crime has a profound impact on criminals, victims, and society in general; the focus should be on the consequences of street crime on its victims, who often share the same backgrounds as their criminal perpetrators.

relative deprivation

In left realism theory, the idea that the most probable source of criminal behavior is the individual feeling deprived relative to others in similar social groups.

Chambliss laid the foundation for a critical approach to the study of crime, one that emphasizes the reality of crime as manipulated by the vested interests of politicians, media, law enforcement, and prison industries.[35] Essentially, criminal law perpetuates the existing social and economic order. Contemporary radical theories emerged to build upon these concepts, taking a more practical approach to the study of crime. We turn now to an exploration of these theories.

CONTEMPORARY RADICAL THEORIES

Radical criminological theories contend that crime and the criminal justice system are products of, and are affected by, capitalism. Capitalist societies are riddled with conflicts and contradictions that create a disharmony in social relations. Essentially the criminal law serves as a tool by which those with political power and economic advantage can coerce the poor into compliance by engaging in certain patterns of behavior that maintain the status quo. What are these behaviors and how do they maintain the status quo? Let's take a closer look at the theories, beginning with left realism.

Left Realism

Left realism emerged in the 1980s partly in reaction to radical criminology's failure to provide a practical understanding of street crime and its portrayal of criminals as political dissenters reacting to the alienation caused by capitalism.[36] Left realism provides us with a more concrete approach. According this perspective, crime has a profound impact on criminals, victims, and society in general, and we should focus our attention on the consequences of street crime on its victims, who often share the same backgrounds as their criminal perpetrators.[37]

Prominent theorist Jock Young, a major contributor to the development of left realist thought, argued that the most probable source of criminal behavior is **relative deprivation,** feeling deprived relative to similar social groups around you. Relative deprivation occurs when people become disillusioned due to the experience of social inequality and injustice. Criminal behavior becomes a means by which individuals tip the scale toward fairness and justice, in the absence of real solutions for being degraded and exploited. We see this in the criminal acts of rioters reacting to the perceived injustice of the Rodney King verdict discussed earlier in this chapter.

Moreover, we should view the criminal justice system not simply as an agent of oppression in the hands of the powerful, but rather as a mechanism by which both victim and offender can achieve social justice. For left realists, the causes of crime lie in the social forces that perpetuate deprivation and social conflict and impose social and economic hardships on some individuals. Thus, crime-control strategies should focus on a unified, cooperative effort between law enforcement and the public.[38] The Connecting Research to Practice feature discusses the emergence of community policing and some findings on its successful implementation as a crime-control strategy.

Left realist theory does a good job of unifying structure and action. Crime is a dynamic process that includes actions committed by an offender, the impact of those actions on the victim, formal reaction by the state, and informal reaction by society (Figure 10.3). We will discuss the impact of left realism on applied research and policy development in sections to come. For now, we turn to a discussion of peacemaking criminology, which also has a profound impact on the direction of criminal justice policy and practice.

CONNECTING RESEARCH TO PRACTICE

Community Policing—A Good Partnership?

Community policing is an approach to crime control that builds a partnership between law enforcement and the community so that they can together address the neighborhood conditions that create fear, tension, and social disorder. Unlike other strategies, community policing encourages police officers to become a part of the communities they are policing—for example by having more police on foot patrol and establishing smaller substations in high-crime areas.

The community policing approach aims at reducing the adversarial side of the relationship between residents and police. Its goal is to form collaborative partnerships between law enforcement officers and the individuals, businesses, and organizations they serve, creating a team effort to keep communities safe. It changes the role of police officers from mere enforcers of the law to supportive community members who solve crime problems, participate in neighborhood safety meetings, and serve their communities.

Currently 12,000 police departments nationwide have adopted community policing strategies.[39] Over the years, research findings have found a positive influence on residential communities throughout the United States.[40] There is less fear of crime, and improved communication between residents and law enforcement lets police be better informed about the problems and concerns of the neighborhoods they are patrolling. Residents, in turn, are more informed about the specific steps the police force is taking to address their concerns, are more confident in the police, and feel their community is a better place to live.

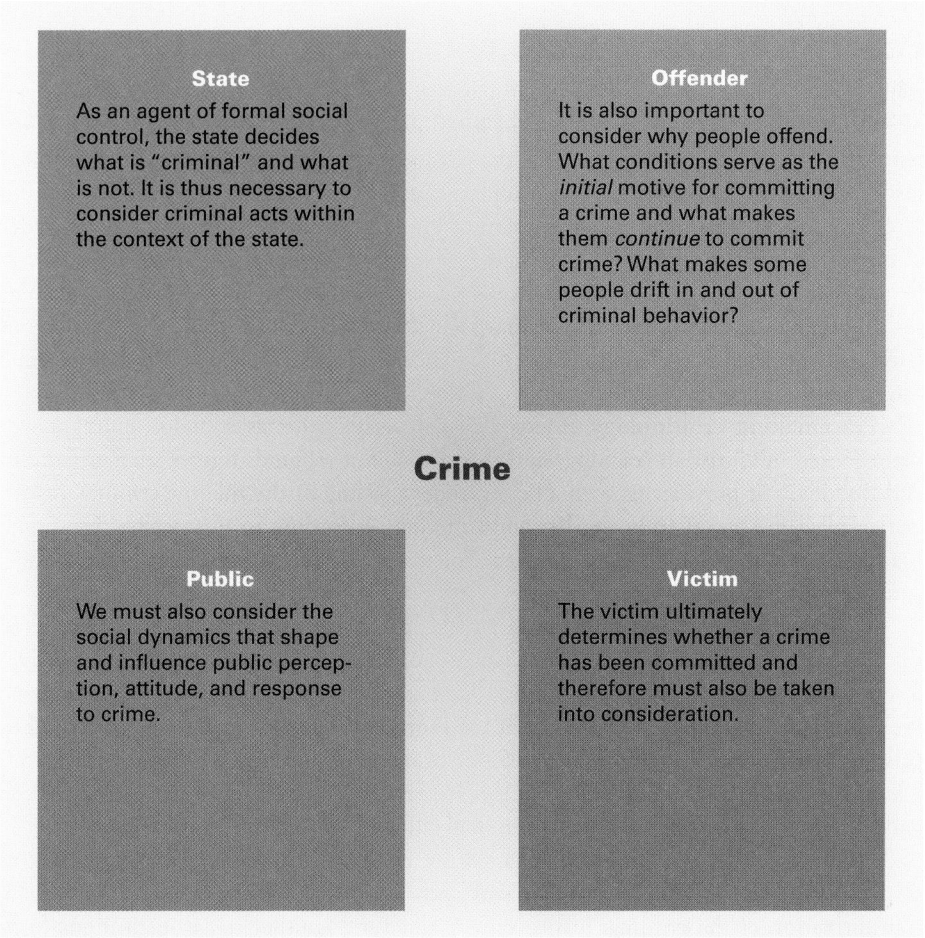
State
As an agent of formal social control, the state decides what is "criminal" and what is not. It is thus necessary to consider criminal acts within the context of the state.
Offender
It is also important to consider why people offend. What conditions serve as the *initial* motive for committing a crime and what makes them *continue* to commit crime? What makes some people drift in and out of criminal behavior?
Crime
Public
We must also consider the social dynamics that shape and influence public perception, attitude, and response to crime.
Victim
The victim ultimately determines whether a crime has been committed and therefore must also be taken into consideration.

FIGURE 10.3

The Square of Crime

When examining a crime, we must consider the four following aspects: the state, the offender, the public, and the victim.

tudies have repeatedly shown that individuals from all social classes commit crime. However, society's disadvantaged classes experience higher rates of arrest, criminal charges, and convictions, spend more time in prison, and are more often denied parole. This apparent bias within the criminal justice system has led to the publication of works such as *The Rich Get Richer and the Poor Get Prison*.[41] Here, author Jeffrey Reiman illustrates conflict theory's argument that the criminal justice system is used as a means to keep disadvantaged classes in society from gaining social and political power.

Reiman argues that the rhetoric surrounding crime suggests members of the lower class are responsible for most criminal acts, in spite of the fact that wealthy white-collar criminals and powerful corporations commit many of the most devastating and harmful criminal activities. Yet media, politicians, and social propaganda continue to reinforce and exploit the idea that young, inner-city, urban minorities should be feared the most.[42]

Moreover, Reiman notes that the processes of law formation, police arrest, judgments, and sentences are all misguided. Instead of addressing the most dangerous or harmful crimes, the criminal justice system still focuses on criminalizing the poor. This emphasis diverts valuable resources away from social programs that can address the poverty, unemployment, discrimination, and inequality disadvantaged groups face, in turn sustaining a socioeconomic system that perpetuates crime and violence and a growing distrust of the criminal justice process.

Peacemaking Criminology

John Doe is accused of trafficking marijuana across the border from Mexico, a federal offense. His court indictment reads, the *United States v. John Doe,* implying, even if unintentionally, that John Doe has become the adversary of the entire country. Our criminal justice system is an adversarial one, from the beginning moments of investigation and arrest, throughout the trial process and sentencing. The accused is up against the upholder of the law, in a battle where who wins and who loses often depends on variables that may be unrelated to the facts or circumstances surrounding the case. These variables, such as the offender's socioeconomic class, often overshadow the interests of achieving justice and fair treatment. (See Connecting Theory to Practice for a closer look at how socioeconomic class can influence judicial rulings.)

peacemaking criminology

A contemporary theory of radical criminology, rooted in Christianity and Eastern religions, that crime is a form of suffering, a means by which people react to conditions of hardship, injustice, and oppression.

Peacemaking criminology emerged in the early 1990s as a philosophical movement rooted in Christian teachings and the ideology of religious figures such as Gandhi and Buddha.[43] It provides us with a better understanding of the role the criminal justice system plays in perpetuating conflict and suffering. According to this perspective, crime is a form of suffering, a means by which people react to conditions of hardship, injustice, and oppression.

To make matters worse, the adversarial nature of the criminal justice process adds to this suffering. Consider, for example, a single mother of three small children whose live-in boyfriend is arrested for manufacturing methamphetamines in her basement. Imagine the profound hardship on her children if the mother were also arrested and sentenced to prison. What good would come of this? Some would say this punishment would teach her a lesson. But at whose expense? Could this lesson worsen the continuing cycle of crime and suffering to which her three children may fall victim?

Peacemaking criminologists emphasize the need to treat crime and crime-control strategies as social issues involving citizens and criminal justice agents. They call for a transformation of the criminal justice system and various other social institutions from ones that add to human suffering and misery to ones that focus on forgiveness, repair, and healing. We will elaborate on the policy implications of peacemaking criminology later in this chapter. For now, we turn to an examination of feminist theories for another critical examination of crime and justice.

FEMINIST THEORIES

Until the 1970s, criminological theory and research focused almost exclusively on male criminality. One of the most profound developments in the understanding of crime causation was the emergence of **feminist theories.** Feminist perspectives in criminology directed our attention to the role of gender and gender relations in ordering social life.[44] With the development of research on the criminal behavior of women and girls, we are now in a better position to develop social policies that address the specific needs of female offenders, understand the dynamics of female victimization, and elaborate on the huge gap in crime rates between males and females.

Types of Feminist Theories

Various branches of feminist criminology have emerged over the years. While each has its unique approach, they all include gender stratification—the unequal access to wealth, power, and prestige on the basis of sex—as an integral component in the study of crime.

Marxist Feminist Theory

Marxist feminist theory sees the capitalist economic structure as the source of gender inequality. According to this perspective, the division of labor in capitalist society has traditionally allowed men to adopt a primary role within economic production. A historical look at the development of capitalism reveals that men were the primary workers in farms, factories, and other labor markets, forcing women to become economically dependent on men. Moreover, changes in the social and economic position of women—such as the rise in divorce, an increase in female-headed households, and the concentration of women in low-paying jobs—has contributed to women's involvement in criminal activity, especially property crimes, to compensate for their disadvantaged position in society.[45]

Radical Feminist Theory

Radical feminist theory examines the role of patriarchy in the exploitation of women by men. Patriarchy exists mainly because women are physically smaller and in most cases weaker than men, and because women are the child bearers, which makes them dependent on men for help during their childbearing years. The role of men in the structure of the household allows them to dominate women in many ways, including through violence, aggression, and sexuality. Radical feminist theory explains violent female crime as a product of the violence women experience from men. Moreover, the exploitation of women by men can lead to other forms of deviant behavior, especially in young girls, such as running away, using alcohol, and turning to drugs or prostitution.[46]

Socialist Feminist Theory

Socialist feminist theory encompasses ideas from Marxist and radical feminist perspectives by emphasizing the importance of both capitalism and patriarchy on the subordination of women in society.[47] The economic and social organization of gender roles affects the life experiences of women and their opportunities in society. This in turn has a direct impact on both the amount and types of crimes they commit. According to socialist feminist theory, the distribution of power created by the economic and social order diverts women into offenses such as shoplifting and prostitution, while men are responsible for the majority of violent street crimes such as assault and homicide.[48]

This statue is a symbol of our justice system's embodiment of fairness and equity in the treatment of those accused of a crime. Has the concept of "blind justice" closed our eyes to injustices that have an oppressive effect on the accused? Should true justice also incorporate the circumstances and status of the offender?

feminist theories

Views of criminology that direct attention to the role of gender and gender relations in ordering social life.

Multiracial Feminist Theory

Another feminist framework emphasizes the consideration of race, in addition to economic and social class, as an important variable in the study of women and crime.[49] *Multiracial* or *multicultural feminist theory* examines the disadvantaged conditions of African American women who experience subordination not only because of gender and class, but also due to race. The interconnection of these three variables helps us understand why African American women have higher rates of criminality than white women.[50]

Liberal Feminist Theory

Liberal feminist theory emphasizes the role of gender role socialization in patterns of criminal behavior. Men are socialized to adopt roles that increase their opportunities within society, while women are socialized to believe they have certain limitations,[51] which in turn affects the manner in which women engage in criminal activities.[52] When the socialization of men and women becomes less diverse, according to this view, the genders become more similar—occupying economically lucrative positions, getting a college education, heading a household, and being politically active—and the crime rate of men and women should also become more similar.

As we saw in Chapter 3, however, this has not been an accurate prediction. While the rate of female criminality has increased at a much greater rate than that of men, a huge gap in criminality continues to exist between the genders, especially with regard to violent crime. We will discuss this controversy in greater detail in the sections to come.

How does the subordinate status of females in the work place influence the gender gap in crime rates between men and women?

Feminist Theory on the Victimization of Women

The emergence of feminist theories in the 1970s brought about significant changes in our understanding of violent crimes against women. These theories examined the role of inequality in the victimization of women, as well as the effect of such crimes as rape and sexual assault on the emotional and behavioral development of female victims. In a classic study on the relationship between rape and inequality, researchers Julia and Herman Schwendinger suggest rape is a consequence of female powerlessness under capitalist development.[53] Women constitute a reserve labor force that elevates men to a position of political and economic domination, rendering women powerless and men able to take advantage of their powerlessness to act violently toward them.

The Schwendingers support their argument in part with survey data from four non-industrialized societies that show that rape is not universal and that it is linked to the economic system. Their data demonstrated that the emergence of exploitive modes of production either created or increased the prevalence of sexual inequality, violence against women, and rape. Recent research has focused on the role of patriarchy in creating a culture where the exploitive treatment of women is regarded as socially acceptable;[54] violence against women is a product of social conditions that create gender inequality and leave women relatively powerless.

A growing body of feminist literature has also directed attention to the role of victimization in the onset of delinquency among juvenile girls. Studies show that delinquent girls and young women are disproportionately victims of domestic assault, rape, and incest prior to their offending.[55] Moreover, the vast majority of females in prison have been the victims of violence and sexual abuse.[56] Childhood sexual abuse is also significantly correlated with female offending behavior.[57]

The victimization girls and young women experience serves as a catalyst for finding an escape, and turning to the streets opens the door for a variety of delinquent and criminal behaviors such as prostitution and drugs. Researchers note that gender-specific differences in victimization between male and female delinquents are an important variable in the treatment of female offenders by the juvenile and adult systems of justice and the development of gender-responsive programming and approaches to female criminality.[58]

Feminist Theory on Female Criminality and the Gender Gap in Crime Rates

Early on, feminist theorists such as Freda Adler[59] and Rita J. Simon[60] speculated about why a gender gap exists in the rate of criminality between men and women, especially with regard to violent crime. Even as the gender socialization of men and of women has grown more similar over the years, the gender ratio in crime statistics has remained about the same, with men committing far more crimes than women. What could explain this gap?

How has the changing role of women in the workforce affected the type of crimes they commit?

Criminological research in this area has focused on two broad categories of explanation.[61] One line of study has explored the role of gender stratification within crime networks. Despite changes in gender role socialization, femininity is still associated with being nurturing and cooperative and masculinity with being aggressive and protective. Research shows these attitudes also exist within the criminal world of offenders. A study of female gang members shows girls are reluctant to fight rival gang members unless absolutely necessary, and this reluctance is due to their understanding of female gender roles. The gang members referred to themselves as "ladies," not "dudes."[62]

Another area of research explores the impact of family class structure on the gender distribution of delinquency and crime. **Power control theory** distinguishes two types of family structures: *patriarchal,* where the father usually works outside the home, and the mother is responsible for taking of the children; and *egalitarian,* where both parents work outside the home, and children receive less care and nurturing from their mothers.[63] Within a patriarchal family structure, boys are encouraged to be "real men," adopting attitudes that encourage aggressive, macho behavior, while girls are encouraged to be "lady-like," acting in a cooperative, submissive manner. Within egalitarian households, sons and daughters are treated more similarly, and expectations about their behavior are the same. Power control theory suggests that gender differences in criminality are more characteristic of patriarchal than egalitarian households. Research has produced mixed results, with some studies finding that gender differences in delinquency are *not* higher in patriarchal families[64] and others that female criminality is higher in households characterized by a more egalitarian structure.[65]

power control theory

In feminist theory, the view that gender differences in criminality are more characteristic of patriarchal than egalitarian households.

With these and many other research studies on female offenders, feminist theory brought a distinct awareness of the role of gender to the analysis of criminal behavior and to our understanding of how gender relations shape the dynamics of crime and criminal justice.[66] We turn now to another critical perspective that also highlights inequality: conflict and contradiction within society.

STRUCTURAL CONTRADICTIONS THEORY

The various structural analyses of crime and criminal law we've looked at so far have provided us with a theoretical framework that accepts that criminality is widely distributed in the social structure and that different types of criminality characterize different social classes or groups. It avoids the errors in other explanations of crime by not seeking to explain individual adaptations but rather linking characteristics of the social structure with differences in crime rates and the distribution of crime.

One thing missing from these theories, however, is a description of the specific characteristics of social structures that can explain how laws and criminal behaviors are produced. For this we turn to an analysis of the social structure and the various *contradictions* inherent to different forms of political, economic, and social relations.

As we discussed in Chapter 2, *structural contradictions theory* seeks to answer questions about why criminal behavior exists, why it is distributed as it is, and why it varies from place to place and from one historical period to another. We do not seek to answer why Jessica steals and Bob makes airplanes; why one politician accepts bribes and another does not; or why one manager violates health and safety regulations and another promotes the rules. Instead, we seek to understand the larger relationship between crime and social structure.

Contradictions and Conflicts

A contradiction exists in a given set of social relationships (political, economic, ideological) when these relationships simultaneously maintain the status quo and produce the conditions necessary to transform it (Figure 10.4). The owner of a coffee shop must make a profit in order to pay the rent for his store. In order to make a profit, he must increase coffee sales. Too much increase, however, means that customers will stop buying their coffee at his shop. An alternative would be to decrease the wages of his employees who are actually selling the coffee and running the shop. Workers become dissatisfied, complain, do not have enough money to buy what they need to live a good life, and seek some type of change. These contradictions inevitably lead to conflicts between groups, classes, and strata. Workers go on strike; women demonstrate against unequal pay; farmers march on Washington; small landowners take up arms against agribusiness; religious cults barricade themselves against federal agents.

Every historical era has its own unique contradictions and conflicts. The most important derive from the way the social, economic, and political relations are organized. How people make a living, the work they do, the way they organize their labor to produce the things that are necessary for survival, how they distribute the results of their labor and organize power relations—these are the most basic characteristics of any human group.

FIGURE **10.4**

Conflicts, Contradictions, Dilemmas, and Resolutions

Source: Adapted from Chambliss, W. J., & Zatz, M. S. (Eds.). (1993). *Making law: The state, the law, and structural contradictions* (p. 11). Bloomington: Indiana University Press.

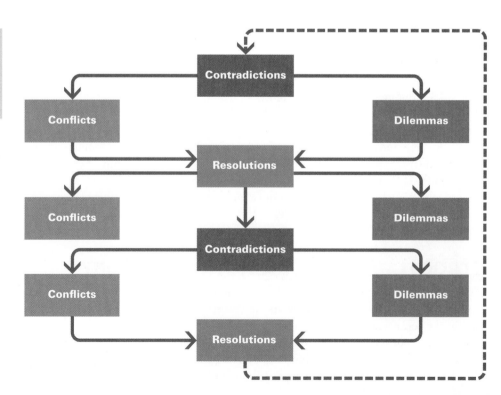

According to structural contradictions theory, the types, amount, and distribution of crime in a particular time and place depend on the existing contradictions, the conflicts that develop as people respond to them, and the mechanisms institutionalized for handling the conflicts and dilemmas the contradictions produce. Workers are paid less or laid off because of downsizing, yet they still have to make their mortgage payment. A business owner must charge more for retail merchandise because the cost of production has gone up, yet it is the same lower-paid or unemployed workers who must pay the higher prices for the merchandise they want. Criminal laws emerge, change, and develop as people attempt to respond to conflicts generated by contradictions in the political and economic organization of their world.

Crime in Capitalist Societies

The capitalist economy depends upon the production and consumption of commodities by large numbers of people. Thus, it presents a twofold problem: how to make people work to produce the commodities, and how to make people desire them. Some commodities are essential for survival—food, clothing, shelter. If the only means of obtaining these essentials is to work for someone who owns them, people will generally choose to work rather than starve or freeze to death. But capitalism does not depend on the production and consumption of necessities alone. It depends on the production and consumption of goods and services that have little or nothing to do with survival. Thus, for capitalism to develop, people must be motivated to work in order to purchase commodities that are not essential.

There are many ways people are taught to want nonessentials: advertising; being socialized to believe that acquiring such commodities bestows status and personal integrity on the owner; fearing that property must be accumulated to stave off the possibility of falling below the level of consumption necessary for survival. Creating the desire to consume, however, simultaneously creates the seeds of discontent and the possibility that people will discover ways to increase consumption without working. If, instead of spending eight hours at a boring, tedious, and sometimes dangerous occupation, people can obtain the money necessary for purchasing commodities by theft, fraud, trickery, or bribery, then some will choose that option. In an effort to avoid this possibility, those who own the means of production and those who manage the state pass laws making such acts illegal. In this way they try to reduce the attractiveness of alternative routes to consumption.

Other forces push people to discover alternative ways of accumulating capital. Not everyone has an equal opportunity to consume the products they are taught to want. In capitalist economies there are vast differences in the wages people receive and the wealth they can accumulate. Some jobs pay only enough for survival. This social structure paradoxically requires that the vast majority of people spend most of their lives working at tasks they find unsatisfactory, in order that a large enough population of consumers can fuel the engines of capitalist production and consumption.

People must work for wages in order to have the power to consume, and they must consume in order for the economy to survive. This, too, creates its own contradictions. There is only one source of profit for the capitalist: the difference between what the capitalist pays the worker and the price for which the capitalist sells the product of that worker's labor. If the worker is paid the full amount for which the product is sold, then there is no profit, and the economic system comes to a grinding halt. Without an accumulation of surplus capital to re-invest, the economy collapses. If, on the other hand, the worker is not paid enough to survive, the population is decimated, and there is no one to purchase the commodities produced. Thus, a fundamental *contradiction of wages, profits, and consumption* explains a large part of the history of modern capitalism. Workers seek higher wages and owners seek to pay the minimum amount.

From the point of view of crime, the conflicts culminate in criminal behavior on the part of both workers and owners. Owners cut corners (violate health and safety

Structural contradictions theory helps us understand strikes and protests as outcomes of the conflicts and dilemmas that arise between workers and management. These protestors are demonstrating against the Wisconsin legislature's plan to limit collective bargaining in that state.

regulations, illegally deal in the stock market, ignore Securities and Exchange regulations); workers steal from employers, supplement their wages by selling illegal drugs, illegally strike and organize, and join illegal political groups. The state sits squarely in the midst of the contradiction: Although generally influenced more by owners than workers, it cannot allow the ongoing conflict to destroy either capitalism or democracy. It responds by passing laws to keep workers from disrupting production or stealing property and to keep owners from disregarding the health and safety of workers and consumers. It also prohibits economic activities that undermine the state's own interests (such as avoiding taxes by laundering money through overseas banks) or that give one group of capitalists an advantage over another (such as insider trading).

Capitalism also fosters a fundamental *contradiction of wages and labor supply*. The owners pursuing the logic of capitalist economies will strive to pay workers as little as possible. It is not possible, however, to pay nothing, unless an overabundance of labor, as in slave labor, allows for workers to be used up and replaced by others flowing in. In advanced industrial societies much of the needed labor requires skills that take time to learn. However, if there is full employment under capitalism, workers have an advantage in the struggle for increased shares of profits with owners. If there is a reserve labor force—that is, if a significant proportion of the labor force is unemployed or underemployed—then when the demands of labor threaten the profits of the owners, the owners can turn to the reserve army to replace the workers. The reserve army, however, forms an underclass that cannot consume but nonetheless is socialized into a system in which consumption is the necessary condition for happiness. Criminal behavior offers a solution for the underclass: What they cannot earn legitimately they can earn illegally.

EVALUATING SOCIAL CONFLICT THEORIES

Critics of radical criminology accuse this perspective of being more a commentary on the unbalanced state of capitalist society than a theoretical understanding of crime causation.[67] They argue that radical criminology assumes crime exists predominantly under capitalist economic modes of production and would virtually disappear under socialism. This assumption, however, neglects to explain relatively low crime rates in capitalist societies, such as Japan, and the conflicts and struggles within oppressive socialist and communist nations, such as China.

Critics also fault radical criminology for overemphasizing class relations in the development of criminal behavior, neglecting many other variables that should be factored in.[68] Crime in general is condemned by society, even by the socially isolated and exploited members of the working class. Thus, it is incorrect to say criminal behavior is a means of protesting the unfair distribution of wealth and power in society. Defenders of radical theory note that these criticisms are directed at Marxist traditions and do not apply to the many branches of radical theory that have developed since and that take a more structural and practical approach.

Feminist criminology has been criticized as more descriptive than empirical, focusing too much attention on the victimization of women and their subordinate status in society rather than developing a theoretical understanding of female criminality.[69] Other critics note that feminist theory has failed to develop an adequate understanding of the continued gender gap in crime statistics.[70] Moreover, there seems to be a contradiction in the basic premise of feminist theory relative to the conflict perspective in general. If power relations shape the course of criminal behavior, then why do men, who invariably have more power than women, commit more crimes?[71] Despite these criticisms, we cannot neglect the valuable contribution of feminist theory in bringing gender to the forefront in the study of crime and criminal justice and developing a feminist orientation in criminology.

PRACTICAL APPLICATION OF SOCIAL CONFLICT THEORIES

At the core of the various theories within the conflict perspective is the notion that conflict is inherent to society and is a major driving force behind criminal behavior. The sources of conflict vary, but conflict theories generally focus on the unequal distribution of social, political, and economic power. Table 10.3 summarizes conflict theory's contribution to the definition and cause of crime, as well as the approach to its resolution.

Policy implications of social conflict theories can fall under various extremes. At one end of the spectrum, reducing conflict and crime can call for the radical restructuring of society, to eliminate the competition and greed that exist under capitalism and replace them with a more equitable distribution of wealth and power. Some conflict theorists, however, recognize the need for more practical solutions, such as increasing public

TABLE **10.3**

SUMMARY: The Social Conflict Perspective	
Definition of Crime	Crime is socially created behavior.
Why Does Crime Occur? (Theory)	Conflicts and contradictions within society create imbalances of power, and the state allows the ruling classes to define as criminal those actions/behaviors that go against their own interests.
What Is the Solution to Crime? (Policy)	■ Redistribute the wealth in society so as to eliminate class struggle. ■ Implement principles of conflict resolution and cooperative criminal justice alternatives that emphasize social equity, gender equality, equal justice for all, and an awareness of social issues when dealing with crime.

awareness of criminal justice issues—for example, the consequences of crime on both victims and offenders, the role of gender socialization in female criminality, and the recognition of structural contradictions in the development of social policies.

The most successful application of conflict theory comes to us from the principles of peacemaking criminology and its call for the resolution of conflict through the development of programs that emphasize repair and reconciliation within the criminal justice system. Criminologists embracing this concept point to the failure of harsh penalties such as imprisonment in reducing crime within society.[72] What then is the alternative?

Crime-control strategies have historically and traditionally focused on developing coercive forms of punishment designed to inhibit potential criminal behavior.[73] These have not only failed to reduce crime but have also produced a class of alienated individuals unlikely to ever become integrated into society as productive, law-abiding citizens. An alternative approach to offender rehabilitation is known as restorative justice.

What Is Restorative Justice?

restorative justice

An ideological model of justice that brings together the offender, the victim, the community, and the criminal justice system in responding to delinquency and crime.

Restorative justice is an ideological model of justice that brings together the offender, the victim, the community, and the criminal justice system in responding to delinquency and crime.[74] The restorative justice movement began in Canada in 1974 when a court ordered two juveniles who robbed and vandalized 21 homes in Ontario to visit and make a personal apology to each victim, as well as pay for the damages. During the late 1970s and early 1980s the restorative justice philosophy was first embraced in the United States by the juvenile courts, as a method of informally processing first-time, nonviolent juvenile offenders.[75]

Since the 1990s, restorative justice practices began to spread throughout the court system as a sentencing alternative designed to allow offenders to repair the harm caused by their criminal acts and provide a forum for bringing equity and justice to all individuals affected by the crime. The restorative justice model offers offenders a learning experience that both increases their sense of responsibility and makes them more accountable for their acts. It thus makes community reintegration a more practical option than making criminal choices.

Restorative justice is more than just a treatment philosophy or justice initiative; it is a working process that draws on various program guidelines and components.

How Does Restorative Justice Work?

Restorative justice is designed to give offenders a second chance at a clean record. The process begins when juvenile and adult offenders convicted of nonviolent crimes are referred by the state's attorney to participate in the program as an alternative to formal court proceedings. Offenders agree to fulfill all requirements of the program, and in exchange for their successful completion, all charges are dismissed.[76]

The restorative justice approach views crime within its social context. Thus, the various program components are designed to identify and challenge the root causes of the criminal behavior in order to break the cycle of deviance. There are three general goals: repairing harm to the victim and the community, encouraging dialog among victims, offenders, and community citizens, and transforming the role of community and government.[77] Table 10.4 provides an overview of the various practices of restorative justice as they pertain to each goal.

Over the past several years, jurisdictions across the United States have reported significant benefits of restorative justice programs, including reductions in recidivism and a high rate of programmatic success.[78] The literature paints a picture of moderate to significant

TABLE **10.4**

Restorative Justice in Action

PROGRAM GOAL	PROGRAM PRACTICE
Repair Harm	■ *Restitution:* Offenders are required to make full monetary compensation to the victim for any loss or damage caused by the criminal act. ■ *Community service:* Offenders are required to perform a set amount of volunteer hours serving nonprofit organizations within the community where the crime was committed. ■ *Letter of apology:* Offenders are required to write a formal letter of apology to their victims expressing their regret and remorse for the criminal act.
Encourage Dialog	■ *Victim impact panel:* Offenders are required to participate in a face-to-face meeting of various crime victims from the community who explain the struggle and hardship caused by crime. ■ *Victim empathy course:* Offenders are required to complete a course curriculum designed to teach them how their actions affected the lives of their victims and encourage them to respect others and accept responsibility for the consequences of their actions. ■ *Reparative board:* Volunteer members of the community are trained to become citizen participants on a reparative board. The board meets once a month and plays an active role in monitoring the progress of offenders in the program and holding them accountable.
Transform Community and Government	■ *Respect essay:* Offenders must prove to reparative board members that they understand the consequences of the crime and recognize the need to become responsible, law-abiding citizens. ■ *Prison tour:* Offenders are often required to participate in a tour of a state correctional institution. The Department of Corrections collaborates with the restorative justice program in order to provide offenders with the opportunity to see the potential consequences of criminal choices. ■ *Alternative dispute resolution:* Restorative justice programs collaborate with the courts, social service agencies, and local universities to provide offenders and crime victims with workshops and consultation meetings to mediate conflicts, discuss family issues, and encourage dialog.

Source: Hass, A., & Corno, J. (2010). Forgiveness, repair and healing: An examination of the Greene County Missouri Restorative Justice Program with implications for peacemaking criminology. *International Journal of Conflict and Reconciliation,* Winter.

success in increasing offender accountability and reintegration into the community, providing victims with the opportunity to participate in the justice process, engaging the community in ensuring the welfare of all its members, and reducing recidivism by helping offenders improve their skills and become more responsible citizens.

SUMMARY

How does conflict theory describe the social order?

Conflict theory views society as consisting of different groups that have competing goals and interests. This diversity in goals and interests creates conflict within society.

What is the relationship among power, politics, and the economy?

The social, political, and economic structures of society create imbalances between groups whereby some have more wealth and power than others. Those with more wealth and power will use their privileged positions to influence the legal system to control the acts of the less advantaged members of society, who threaten their position.

Does conflict lead to crime?

Radical conflict theory maintains that crime is an outcome of the social and economic contention between different groups within society. Thus, crime is rooted in the conflict created by the unequal distribution of wealth and power, and in social conditions that empower the wealthy to define as criminal those acts that go against their own interests.

Is it possible that the criminal justice system perpetuates human suffering?

Contemporary theories in conflict criminology argue that the criminal justice system and its various components often reinforce the cycle of oppression experienced by both victims and offenders. Instead of contributing to deprivation and conflict, the theories suggest, the criminal justice system should apply unified crime-control strategies that emphasize resolution and cooperation.

Why is there a huge gap in crime statistics between men and women?

Some criminologists explain the gap in crime statistics between men and women as a function of gender stratification in the development of criminal roles within crime networks. Others point to the impact of family class structure, either patriarchal or egalitarian, on the gender distribution of delinquency and crime.

What causes contradictions in the social structure?

Contradictions within the social structure occur when the goals, rules, and social processes create situations that produce antagonistic social relations—between political rivals, employers and employees, customers and owners, clients and service providers, corporate executives and stockholders. These contradictions inevitably lead to conflicts between groups struggling against one another at the social, political, and economic levels.

Can radical criminology offer a peaceful solution to crime?

Contemporary radical theories call for an emphasis on social justice and an awareness of the inherent relationship between crime and social conflict. Thus, solutions to crime emphasize the need to repair conflict-ridden situations and relationships. Agents of criminal justice must play a unified and cooperative role in the rehabilitation of alienated individuals and in restoration to crime victims.

CRITICAL THINKING QUESTIONS

1. Suppose you were on a jury trying the case of an individual accused of robbing a bank at gunpoint, although the gun was not loaded. The accused managed to get away with $5,000 before getting caught. He is a Hispanic male in his mid-20s who has been struggling to find a job during economically challenging times. He has no prior criminal record, except for some traffic violations and driving with a suspended license. How would your knowledge of the conflict perspective influence your perception of this case?

2. Research studies show that education within prisons is a strong correlate of successful reintegration into society upon release. Why do you think society is so opposed to providing inmates with adequate access to educational programming, especially at the postsecondary level? How would radical criminology guide our understanding of this issue and shed some light on a possible resolution?

3. Which argument is more convincing—that men commit more crime than women because of biological differences in temperament, or that men commit more crime than women because of differences in the gender roles they play in society? What social changes do you think would narrow the gender gap in crime statistics?

4. Suppose your home was vandalized by two reckless youth claiming to be "just having fun." They spray-painted your walls, ruined several of your shrubs, and broke a couple of windows. Which would you rather see: (a) the two youths go to juvenile detention for six months and pay a fine; (b) they write you a formal letter of apology, do 100 hours of community service cleaning up parks in your neighborhood, pay you for all the damage they did to your property, and attend a victim impact panel where you can tell them in person how their actions affected you. Which alternative is more popular in our society? Why do you think this is the case? How can criminology address this issue and shed some light on how to change society's view?

ADDITIONAL RESOURCES

For a critical examination of the criminal justice system visit the Critical Criminology Division of the American Society of Criminology website at http://www.critcrim.org/

Learn more about the policy implications of left realist criminology at http://www.malcolmread.co.uk/JockYoung/leftreal.htm

You can read more about gender inequality and stratification by visiting the Institute for Inequality Studies website at http://ppc.uiowa.edu/pages.php?id=191

Additional information about the restorative justice model can be found at http://www.cehd.umn.edu/ssw/rjp/

11

INTERPERSONAL CRIMES OF VIOLENCE

In this chapter, we will explore the following questions:

- What is criminal homicide?
- Why do people kill?
- What constitutes an assault?
- Does assault occur more often between strangers or acquaintances?
- Is rape a sexual act?
- Why is robbery a violent crime?
- What is the motive behind stealing by force?
- What are hate crimes?

Who is more likely to hurt us—a stranger, a co-worker,

a neighbor, a friend, or an intimate partner? On July 29, 2006, Rafael Dangond escorted his wife Lissette Ochoa from a wedding party they were attending. Dangond was apparently outraged that his wife had been dancing with some friends at the party. He pushed her into their car and proceeded to physically abuse her, beating her repeatedly for about two hours while driving around. Once at home, the violence continued. Ochoa finally managed to lock herself in a bathroom where she called her father on a cell phone. An armed Dangond knocked the door down and fired, hitting his wife in the armpit. Ochoa suffered multiple physical and emotional injuries but escaped with her life. Not all victims of such violence have been as lucky.[1]

What patterns of interaction trigger a violent attack?

Research on violence against women has proliferated in the past 20 years. The U.S. Department of Justice estimates approximately 1.3 million women and 835,000 men are physically assaulted each year by an intimate partner, and intimate partner homicides make up 40 to 50 percent of all murders of women in the United States.[2] The National Institute of Justice reports that over 60 percent of women who report being raped, physically assaulted, and/or stalked were victimized by a current or former spouse, cohabitating partner, boyfriend, or date.[3]

What social dynamics place women at greater risk of being victimized by someone with whom they are so closely connected? A study by researchers at the University of Illinois found exposure to domestic violence during childhood increased the risk of victimization of both sexual assault and domestic violence. Domestic violence victimization was also significantly related to having increased education and employment skills, more children, and clinical depression.[4] A team of researchers at the National Institute of Justice examined the risk factors associated with intimate partner violence and found that almost half of women killed by an intimate partner did not recognize the danger they were facing in the abusive relationship.[5] The implications are that we need to do more research to identify demographic, social, and environmental variables associated with intimate partner violence, and that prevention strategies should focus on teaching women how to protect themselves and to identify risk factors in an abusive relationship.

Violence can take many forms and result in varying causes and consequences ranging from financial loss to emotional and physical injury and death. Rafael Dangond's violent attack on his wife is a form of assault that takes place in a domestic or intimate setting. This chapter focuses on different types of interpersonal violent crimes including homicide, rape, robbery, assault, and hate crime. We will describe and explain these behaviors according to their legal definitions, the factors that motivate these crimes, aspects of the situation that led to them, and characteristics of the victim and the offender. In chapters to come, we will examine other forms of violent crimes such as genocide, ethnic cleansing, terrorism, corporate crimes of violence, and state-organized crimes of violence. While these categories of crime result in destruction, harm, and death, they are not considered forms of interpersonal violence. For now, we turn to the first category of interpersonal violence: homicide.

HOMICIDE

On December 5, 2007, 20-year-old Robert Hawkins, armed with an assault rifle, took aim at holiday shoppers at a mall in Omaha, Nebraska. Eyewitnesses said he fired 20 to 25 times from a store's third-floor balcony, sending panicked shoppers rushing for cover. After killing eight people and wounding five others, Hawkins turned the gun on himself. Friends later said he had been on the edge after recently losing his job at McDonald's, breaking up with his girlfriend, and being kicked out of his parents' home. Hawkins left a suicide note in which he apologized for all the trouble he had caused.

Anger, stress, pressure, and conflict were all variables that led up to this criminal event. What other factors are at work in the crime of homicide? What makes some homicides distinct from others? Let's turn now to a closer examination of this crime category by defining homicide.

Describing Homicide

Homicide is the willful killing of one human being by another. It is not always a criminal offense; homicide committed in self-defense is often deemed justifiable and therefore legal. **Murder** is an *unlawful* form of homicide, the intentional killing of one human being by another without legal justification or excuse. A murder is committed with **malice aforethought,** a depraved state of mind that shows a willful and intentional disregard for human life. Thus, criminal justice officials use the term **criminal homicide** to describe the act of murder. Murder is the most serious of all violent crimes and the only crime punishable (in some states) by death.

The law categorizes the severity of murder by looking at the degree of motive or intent. **First-degree murder** is the unlawful killing of a human being by another with malice aforethought *and* **premeditation**—planning, plotting, and deliberating before committing the act. Premeditation can be proved by the simple passage of time, or anything else that demonstrates the individual had the opportunity to think about the intent to kill and to retreat from those thoughts. The following case illustrates some of these elements of first-degree murder.

homicide

The willful killing of one human being by another.

murder

An unlawful form of homicide; the intentional killing of one human being by another without legal justification or excuse.

malice aforethought

A depraved state of mind that shows a willful and intentional disregard for human life.

criminal homicide

A term criminal justice officials use to describe the act of murder.

Outbursts of violence—such as the December 2007 shooting at this Omaha, Nebraska, mall—are often spontaneous actions that take the lives of several victims.

first-degree murder

The unlawful killing of a human being by another with malice aforethought and premeditation.

premeditation

Planning, plotting, and deliberating before committing the act.

second-degree murder

The unlawful killing of a human being with malice aforethought but without premeditation.

manslaughter

Criminal homicide that occurs without malice aforethought or premeditation.

voluntary or non-negligent manslaughter

The unjustified killing that arises out of an intense conflict that provoked violence or during the commission of a felony.

involuntary or negligent manslaughter

The unlawful killing of a human being by a person's own negligent disregard of his or her harmful acts.

One night while his wife Denise Amber Lee was tied up in the back seat of his Camaro, Michael Lee King borrowed a shovel, a flashlight, and a gas can from his cousin. That same evening, while driving, Janet Kowalski stopped at a light and noticed a car pull up next to her. The passenger-side window was slightly down and Kowalski heard screaming and saw a woman's hand "slapping the left passenger window like she was trying to get out."[6] Kowalski called 911 from her car and informed the police of what she had seen. Later that evening, police entered King's home to find a roll of duct tape on the kitchen counter as well as a pillow and blanket on the floor of the bedroom, along with balled-up duct tape with long strands of light brown hair. After a manhunt that included canine teams, helicopters, and dozens of officers, King was arrested near Interstate 75. The body of Denise Amber Lee was found buried off the interstate, and her husband was charged with abduction and premeditated murder. Clearly, this was a crime he had thought about and planned, making sure he had what he needed earlier that day.

Although it may sometimes be difficult to prove premeditation, the distinct features of second-degree murder make it easier to understand what premeditation means. **Second-degree murder** is the unlawful killing of a human being with malice aforethought but *not* with premeditation. It is regarded as a "crime of passion," in which no time for deliberation elapses between the thought to kill and the killing itself. Second-degree murder implies a degree of impulsiveness or provocation. This was the case in the conviction of Tari Ramirez, who stabbed his girlfriend Claire Tempongko several times in front of her two children. Jurors agreed with defense attorneys that Ramirez acted on the spur of the moment, enraged after Tempongko told him she had aborted their unborn baby.[7]

The third category of murder, **manslaughter,** is criminal homicide that occurs without malice aforethought *or* premeditation. There are two types of manslaughter: voluntary and involuntary. **Voluntary or non-negligent manslaughter** is an unjustified killing that arises out of an intense conflict that provoked the violence. Voluntary manslaughter can also occur during the commission of a felony. For example, a burglar sneaks into a building with the intent to steal. Startled by a security guard, he begins to run, knocking the guard down a flight of stairs and killing him. Without the presence of a deadly weapon that would have suggested he had intent to kill, the burglar will most likely be charged with voluntary manslaughter.

Involuntary or negligent manslaughter is the unlawful killing of another person by a person's own negligent disregard of his or her harmful acts. This category includes homicides that occur during non-felony violations, making it distinct from voluntary manslaughter. For example, a driver who is speeding through a neighborhood where children are playing and causes a fatal accident can be charged with involuntary manslaughter. Figure 11.1 provides a summary of the categories of criminal homicide.

Understanding Homicide

The many legal categories of criminal homicide are a testament to the complex relationships we recognize among cause, motive, and situation in this form of violent behavior. Research has also focused on understanding four distinct *patterns* of homicide: (1) chronic offending and the subculture of violence; (2) situational homicide; (3) serial killing; and (4) mass murder. We start by examining homicide within the context of the subculture of violence.

Chronic Offending and the Subculture of Violence

Subcultures are groups of people who share norms, values, and beliefs that differ significantly from those of the dominant culture. In the United States, the Amish—whose values forbid the use of modern technology like electricity, automobiles, and farm machinery—are a subculture, although not a criminal one. Members of fundamentalist sects of the Church of Latter Day Saints who continue to practice polygamy are another, but unlike the Amish, they embrace norms that are in violation of the law.

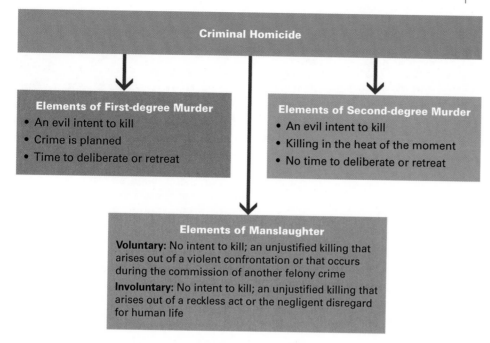

FIGURE **11.1**

Types of Criminal Homicide

As we explored in Chapter 8, subcultures exist to manage and cope with problems and situations that are not common to mainstream society. Sociologists Marvin Wolfgang and Franco Ferracuti suggest that problems unique to lower-class urban youth help create a subculture of gangs, delinquency, and violence. Among other responses, this subculture demands that its members respond violently to social situations like disputes or their reputation will be damaged.[8] A confrontation between two gangs in Tennessee illustrates the dynamic of subcultural violence.

In July 2006, violence erupted in the Opryland Mills Mall in Nashville, Tennessee. The incident, which led to the shooting of two individuals, was believed to be a dispute between rival gang members hanging out at the mall. The outburst of potentially deadly violence was typical of conflict resolution in a gang subculture, which emphasizes toughness, aggression, and brutality.[9]

Classical sociological research on urban gangs suggests a pattern of subculture norms that help explain the persistence of violence in urban areas. Researcher Albert Cohen found gang delinquency was one way that lower-class youth responded to shared problems associated with being poor and being constantly judged (in school, for example) by white middle-class standards that contradicted their experiences and opportunities.[10]

In an extensive participant observation study of low-income black Philadelphia neighborhoods, Elijah Anderson discovered the dominant culture to which most residents belonged was what he called a culture of "decent people": Adults and youth alike embraced the dominant nonviolent, law-abiding culture of U.S. society. But alongside the "decent people" culture there existed a subculture of "the street." Street families

> *often show a lack of consideration for other people and have a rather superficial sense of family and community. . . . the seeming intractability of their situation, caused in large part by the lack of well-paying jobs and the persistence of racial discrimination, has engendered deep-seated resentment and anger in many of the poorest blacks, especially young people.[11]*

The "code of the street" is the result of this resentment and anger, and of alienation from the institutions of the larger society, especially the police. In poor urban neighborhoods the police are seen as oppressors representing the interests and values of white society. Equally important, residents feel they cannot depend on police to settle disputes or come to the aid of victims of violence. Individuals must therefore protect themselves by demanding respect and, if offended, seeking vengeance.[12]

CONNECTING THEORY TO PRACTICE

Public Policy and the Subculture of Violence

Criminological studies have shown that higher rates of interpersonal violence are reported among certain ethnic and racial groups, and within certain geographic locations such as the inner city and the South and West.[13] The subculture of violence theory posits that some individuals adhere to the values, norms, and attitudes of a street subculture and therefore turn to violence, assault, and homicide as a means of resolving conflicts. The public policy implications for intervention and prevention are that we need to change the social values of high-risk populations to counteract the negative effects of their prevailing street subculture. Programs of the U.S. Department of Justice, Office of Juvenile Justice and Delinquency Prevention (OJJDP) attempt to do just that.

OJJDP programs target youth most at risk for truancy, gang activity, alcohol and drug abuse, and involvement in the criminal justice system, providing education and literacy resources, substance abuse counseling, housing, and preparation for the workforce. Another OJJDP policy initiative focuses on reducing youth gangs in targeted neighborhoods, suppressing gang crime and violence, and reintegrating known gang members into non-gang lifestyles. The model uses a five-pronged approach, emphasizing the following variables:

- *Primary prevention* targets the entire population in high-crime, high-risk communities. The key component is a one-stop resource center for prenatal and infant care, afterschool activities, truancy and dropout prevention, and job programs.
- *Secondary prevention* identifies young children (ages 7–14) at high risk and, drawing on the resources of schools, community-based organizations, and faith-based groups, intervenes with appropriate services before early problem behaviors turn into serious delinquency and gang involvement.
- *Intervention* targets active gang members, close associates, families, and gang members returning from confinement with aggressive outreach and recruitment activity to help youth make positive choices.
- *Suppression* focuses on identifying the most dangerous and influential gang members and removing them from the community.
- *Reentry* targets serious offenders returning to the community after confinement and provides appropriate services and monitoring. Of particular interest are "displaced" gang members who may attempt to reassert their former roles.

These programs have shown positive results in reducing crime and gang-related activities and in making significant improvements in the physical appearance of neighborhoods and public housing.

The contributions of subculture of violence and other theories help us understand why homicide becomes a way of life in certain neighborhoods, for certain people, and in certain situations, guiding the direction of policy development strategies. (See the Connecting Theory to Practice feature for more on the subculture of violence.)

Violent environments, violent role models, and violent attitudes and belief systems are the breeding ground for a violent mode of response. Whether the cause is defending oneself, avenging a drug deal gone bad, defending someone's honor, getting respect, settling an argument, or obtaining an expensive pair of shoes, violence is the answer.[14]

Criminologists have identified four stages in the development of chronic violent offending (Table 11.1). The first stage, *brutalization*, describes the cumulative and prolonged exposure to violence as a means of communication and conflict resolution. As the individual progresses to the stages of *belligerency, violent performance,* and *violent personality*, the predominant means by which to achieve one's goals becomes the

TABLE **11.1**

Stages of Chronic Offending

STAGE	DESCRIPTION
Brutalization	Offenders are forced at an early age to submit to authority through coercion; they are taught by others to resort to violence to achieve their goals and are often witness to the brutalization of others.
Belligerency	Offenders internalize the idea that violence is the only means to get what they want and are thus convinced it is an acceptable response in dealing with others.
Violent Performance	Offenders commit violent acts upon individuals in order to seriously injure the victim.
Violent Personality	The use of violence is reinforced as the offender comes to be defined by others as a violent person, conferring upon him or her a sense of power.

Source: Athens, L. H. (1989). *The creation of dangerous violent criminals.* New York: Routledge.

exertion of force upon others, with violent acts becoming purposeful attempts to injure whoever gets in the way, ultimately conferring a sense of power upon the individual perpetrator.

While the escalation of violence is understandable in the context of these stages, it is far less clear why homicide sometimes occurs without them. Let's take a look now at the types of homicide that arise out of a specific type of interaction or situation.

Situational Homicide

As we noted in Chapter 3, most homicides arise from interpersonal conflicts or hostilities between an offender and victim who are acquaintances, relatives, or friends. Thus, we can best understand some patterns of homicide within the situation, or context, of the victim–offender relationship.

Dwayne Smith and Robert Nash distinguished between two classifications of homicide: primary and non-primary.[15] **Primary or expressive homicides** are the most common and occur between family members, friends, and acquaintances. They are called expressive because they usually spring from some type of interpersonal conflict or dispute based on jealousy, hatred, anger, rage, or frustration. Love triangles, financial disagreements, and domestic disputes are situational contexts within which expressive homicide often takes place.[16]

Non-primary or instrumental homicides occur during the course of another crime, or in the pursuit of some other valued goal. They are less common, and usually the victims and offenders have no prior relationship—circumstance brings them together, and killing is not the offender's primary motive. An incident that begins as a robbery but in which the victim presents a great deal of resistance may turn deadly when the offender panics, for example. These types of homicide are called *instrumental,* because the violence is a means to an end such as obtaining money, eluding the police, eliminating a witness, or getting away from a botched rape.[17]

Studies have examined the relationship between homicide rates and the presence of firearms. Researchers note that disputes often escalate into violence, and the availability of a gun often influences whether the outcome is deadly.[18] Cities, states, and regions where there are more guns have elevated rates of homicide, especially firearm homicide.[19] Other countries report similar trends. The Crime in Global Perspective feature discusses international trends in homicide rates and firearm ownership.

primary or expressive homicide

A killing that usually springs from interpersonal conflict, such as jealousy, hatred, anger, rage, or frustration.

non-primary homicide or instrumental homicide

A killing that occurs during the course of another crime or in the pursuit of some other valued goal; the killing is not the offender's primary motive.

CRIME IN GLOBAL PERSPECTIVE | International Trends in Homicide Rates and Gun Ownership

According to multiple surveys on gun ownership, approximately 53 million U.S. households contain at least one firearm, and there are 60–80 million adult gun owners in the United States.[20] In contrast, Australia, Canada, and Japan have enacted strict gun control laws banning most private firearm ownership. In Great Britain, when sixteen children were killed by a gunman who opened fire at Dunblane Primary School in 1996, parents and outraged citizens called upon Parliament to radically reform gun laws. Within months, private gun ownership had been all but outlawed. For the year ending in September 2008, Great Britain reported a total of 53 gun-related homicides.[21] The following chart shows the number of firearm deaths per 100,000 people against the percentage of households in each country in which guns are privately owned.

Despite many school shootings in the United States, debate rages between those for and against gun control laws. Many people feel private gun ownership is protected by the Second Amendment to the U.S. Constitution and that it is the criminals who illegally own guns who perpetrate gun violence. They say social and cultural factors other than gun ownership influence violent crime rates in other countries. Meanwhile, according to the Centers for Disease Control, the rate of death by firearm in the United States is eight times higher than in comparable developed nations (see table).[22]

Studies have shown that people living in houses containing privately held firearms are more susceptible to violence, particularly violence involving guns.[23] Based on all the evidence, private ownership of firearms does at the very least seem to have a direct relationship with homicide rates. Those who support gun control laws call for massive gun law reform across the United States.

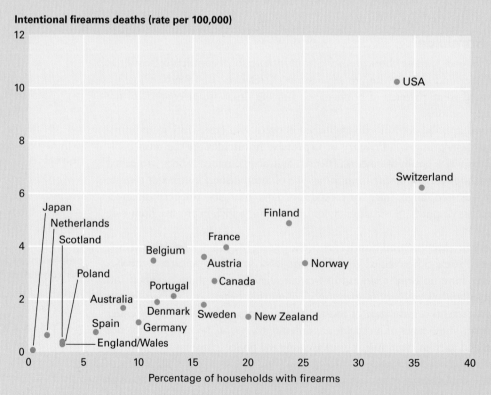

Intentional firearms deaths (rate per 100,000)

X-axis: Percentage of households with firearms

Sources: Global firearm deaths. (2005). Toronto: Small Arms/Firearms Education and Research Network.

CRIME IN
GLOBALPERSPECTIVE | (Continued)

Gun Deaths per 100,000 Population*

	HOMICIDE	SUICIDE	OTHER (INCLUDING ACCIDENT)
USA (2001)	3.98	5.92	0.36
Italy (1997)	0.81	1.1	0.07
Switzerland (1998)	0.50	5.8	0.10
Canada (2002)	0.4	2.0	0.04
Finland (2003)	0.35	4.45	0.10
Australia (2001)	0.24	1.34	0.10
France (2001)	0.21	3.4	0.49
England/Wales (2002)	0.15	0.2	0.03
Scotland (2002)	0.06	0.2	0.02
Japan (2002)	0.02	0.04	0

*Data are for the year indicated.

Source: Data from Cukier, W., & Sidel, V. W. (2006). *The global gun epidemic.* Westport, CT: Praeger Security International.

Serial Murder

Popular U.S. culture is fascinated with notorious serial killers. Entertainment media, literature, and films portray the dark shadows of crimes that bring shock, fear, and confusion to neighborhoods and police departments across the country. **Serial murder** is the killing of several individuals in at least three separate events.

The most common stereotype of a serial murderer is of a shady, low-life, bloodthirsty individual. However, many such killers have been well educated, charismatic, and attractive—like Ted Bundy, who in the 1970s killed what may have been dozens of young women across the United States. While their true profile runs the gamut of physical, social, and psychological traits, all serial killers are particularly adept at leading a double life, putting up a front of normalcy that shields them from suspicion and makes them even more difficult to apprehend.[24]

The popular image of serial murder is riddled with misconceptions about both the crime and the offender. The idea that serial killers are psychotic or antisocial, that they are an imminent threat, and that they are somehow lashing out at individuals in a cry for help all run counter to what we know. Researchers have identified various myths surrounding the crime of serial murder and perceptions of serial killers.[25] The following statements dispel some of these myths:

- Serial murder is not occurring at epidemic proportions.
- Serial killers do not have a distinct appearance.

serial murder

The killing of several individuals in at least three separate events.

Ted Bundy is a notorious U.S. serial killer who confessed to the murder of 30 women between 1974 and 1978. He graduated in 1972 with a degree in psychology from the University of Washington. By all accounts, Bundy was a sweet-talking, charming, handsome young man who had been accepted to law school—not the person we typically think of when we hear the term "serial killer."

- In most cases, serial killers are sane; they know the difference between right and wrong.
- Serial killers are generally not sociopaths incapable of abiding by the norms of society.
- Serial killers are not primarily motivated by pornography.
- Traumatic childhoods are not at the root of most serial killers' problems.
- Identifying serial killers before they strike is not always a straightforward task.
- Most serial killers are not sexual sadists.
- Victim selection is not always based on family resemblance.
- While serial killers thrive on the attention they get and on the cat-and-mouse chase with law enforcement, they do not want to be apprehended.

In reality serial killers can be anyone: young or old, male or female, of diverse ethnic background, operating alone or with a partner, from any walk of life. Researchers have developed typologies of serial murderers based on their pattern of offending and motive.[26] Criminologists recognize that differences exist within each category of serial murder. Nevertheless, they find a general similarity in the repetitive crime patterns of serial killers with regard to the types of victims selected, the motivation for the crime, and the method of carrying out the murder.[27] Table 11.2 provides a summary of the different categories of serial killer, with specific examples of each type.

Despite making up a very small proportion of the overall homicide statistics, serial murders receive an inordinate amount of attention in the media. We turn now to another pattern of homicide that is also fairly uncommon: mass murder.

Mass Murder

The U.S. Bureau of Justice Statistics defines **mass murder** as the killing of three or more individuals in a single event. Mass murders are uniquely shocking because of

TABLE 11.2

Four Types of Serial Killers Based on Motive

MOTIVE	EXAMPLE
Visionary/Missionary Serial Killer Feels compelled to kill based on hearing voices or having visions, or is on a mission to rid the world of evil	*Joseph Kallinger,* who died in 1996, constantly heard voices from a floating head that followed him around and stated that God told him to kill young boys; he was arrested and sentenced to 40 years in prison for robbery plus a life sentence for the murder of Maria Fasching. In prison Joe had expressed his desire to kill every person on earth and often told people he would become God after he died.
Comfort Serial Killer Is motivated by financial or material gain; the killing is secondary to the primary motive of personal gain	*Dorothea Puente,* a sweet-looking little old lady, was sentenced to life in prison without the possibility of parole in 1993 at the age of 64. Puente was convicted of the murders of three of the tenants who lived in her Sacramento home. She took in elderly and disabled boarders, then killed them and buried them in her backyard to collect their government checks to buy luxuries.
Thrill-Motivated Serial Killer *Hedonistic:* Is motivated by excitement and pleasure derived from inflicting pain upon the victim	On February 25, 2005, *Dennis Rader* (also discussed in Chapter 3) was arrested and charged with killing 10 people in Sedgwick County, Kansas. Known as the notorious BTK killer (for bind, torture, and kill), Radar described what occurred when he killed/attempted to kill each of his victims. He told the judge he committed these murders because he wanted to satisfy sexual fantasies.
Thrill-Motivated Serial Killer *Power:* Seeks to exercise authority, often playing cat-and-mouse games with victim	*Charles Cullen* attended Mountainside School of Nursing in New Jersey. He got a job at St. Barnabas Medical Center in Livingston, NJ. In 2003, Cullen admitted to police that he had murdered as many as 45 patients during his 16 years of working at various hospitals in New Jersey and Pennsylvania. He was sentenced to 18 life sentences in March 2006 for killing 13 patients and attempting to kill two others by lethal injection.

Source: Information from Hickey, E. W. (2005). *Serial murderers and their victims.* Belmont, CA: Wadsworth.

the number of victims; these events make people feel vulnerable as traditionally safe places—such as restaurants, schools, or office buildings—erupt in spontaneous violence. Mass murderers are also unique offenders in that they are easily apprehended or stopped; most commit suicide, are shot down by law enforcement officers, or stay at the scene of the crime until caught.[28] Victims can be randomly selected or be part of a target group.

Mass murders vary in motive, degree of planning, and victim–offender relationship.[29] Criminologists have identified four distinct categories, as shown in Table 11.3 with examples from case profiles.

Data on mass murderers is difficult to gather since most perpetrators commit suicide at the scene of the crime. Research shows, however, that most are not insane.[30] Instead, most mass murders are the result of the accumulation of anger, rage, and frustration. Factors like personal failure, social ridicule, isolation, and loss can all contribute to a culmination in mass murder. Whether a disgruntled employee, frustrated student, or political dissenter, the mass murderer wants to send out a message, make a point, or be heard, with devastating consequences.

Despite their rare occurrence, mass murder cases inspire countless news stories, documentaries, and entire Hollywood productions. We turn now to a form of interpersonal violence that stirs very little public attention, yet is far more common than mass murder or any other category of homicide: the crime of assault.

mass murder

The killing of three or more individuals in a single event.

TABLE **11.3**
Four Types of Mass Murderers Based on Motive

MOTIVE	EXAMPLE
Revenge Murderer wants to get even with a particular individual or a category of people such as women, racial or ethnic minorities, or religious groups	*Marc Lépine* entered an engineering school in Montreal on December 6, 1989, and separated women from men in a classroom. He murdered 14 women students and wounded 10 women and 4 men before killing himself. He left behind a letter blaming feminists for ruining his life and a list of 19 women he wanted to kill.
Love Murderer wants to "save" loved ones from some type of threat or imminent danger	*Andrea Yates,* convicted of first-degree murder for the 2001 drowning of her children in the bathtub, was sentenced to life in prison with the possibility of parole after 40 years. Yates drowned each of her five children, covered them with a sheet, and then called her husband and told him to come home. Yates claimed her children were bad, and she was trying to save them from going to hell. She was found to suffer a recurring severe case of postpartum psychosis, and in 2006 was found not guilty by reason of insanity.
Profit/Personal Gain Murderer seeks some material outcome or benefit	In January 1948 *Sadamichi Hirasawa* went to a branch of the Teigin Bank at Shiina in Tokyo. He said he was a public health official and gave all 16 people there a pill and a few drops of liquid that was later found to be a cyanide solution. While everyone was incapacitated, Hirasawa took all the money available at the bank. Ten of the 16 victims died at the scene and 2 died at the hospital. Hirasawa was sentenced to death but died of natural causes in a prison hospital in 1987.
Terror Murderer intends to create fear and panic or send a message or warning to society	In January 1971 *Charles Manson, Patricia Krenwinkel, Susan Atkins,* and *Leslie Van Houten* were each found guilty of murder and conspiracy to commit murder and were sentenced to death for the killing of five people, including pregnant actress Sharon Tate. The Charles Manson "family" were inspired by Manson's doomsday ideology to attack high-profile celebrities in an effort to gain attention for his beliefs.

Source: Information from Fox, J. A., & Levin, J. (1996). *Overkill: Mass murder and serial killing exposed.* New York: Plenum.

ASSAULT

assault

The attempted commission of bodily injury to another human being.

Assault is the attempted commission of bodily injury to another human being. Assault can also mean putting an individual in fear of imminent bodily harm, injury, danger, or threat. An assault can therefore include threats, taunting, intimidation, and harassment; it requires no physical contact.

Describing Assault

battery

Unwanted, nonconsensual physical contact.

Many people confuse assault with the crime of **battery,** defined as unwanted, nonconsensual physical contact. According to the FBI, assault with battery is the most common violent crime in the United States. For the sake of simplicity, we will consider the category of criminal assault to include assault *and* battery of the victim.

Criminal assault is a complex pattern of behavior to investigate because it has the potential to escalate to homicide.[31] Offenders who commit certain categories of assault are regarded as having the potential for lethal violence.[32] There are two categories of assault: aggravated and simple. **Aggravated assault** is the attempt to commit, or the commission of, serious bodily harm or injury upon an individual. It usually includes the use of some type of weapon or deadly force that can cause grave injury or death. A person can be convicted of aggravated assault even for an act that results in no physical harm, such as holding someone at gunpoint. **Simple assault** is the attempt to commit, or the commission of, less serious physical injury and usually does not include the use of a weapon.

aggravated assault

The attempt to commit, or the commission of, serious bodily harm or injury upon an individual; usually involves some type of weapon or deadly force.

simple assault

The attempt to commit, or the commission of, less serious physical injury; usually does not include the use of a weapon.

The number of assaults is much higher than the number of homicides in the United States, according to the Bureau of Justice Statistics. The profile of the typical offender in aggravated assault is African American, male, 15 to 34 years old, of lower socioeconomic status, with a prior history of arrest for other crimes.[33] The majority of offenders were victims of or witnesses to violence in their childhoods. They commit aggravated assault on strangers and acquaintances alike, usually in the victim's home or on a street nearby, or at a friend's or neighbor's home. Victims of simple assaults, on the other hand, are more likely to be acquaintances. Most assaults follow a pattern of spontaneous violence triggered by an argument or altercation.[34]

stalking

Any unwanted contact between two individuals that communicates a threat or places the victim in fear or distress.

In recent years, stalking has become regarded as a step in the continuum of violence that can lead to a more serious, even deadly encounter between victim and offender. **Stalking** includes any unwanted contact between two individuals that communicates a threat or places the victim in fear or distress. Patterns of stalking can include behaviors such as following someone, repeatedly watching the person, making unwanted phone calls, and sending unwanted letters or messages. A national study conducted by the U.S. Department of Justice suggests an urgent need for a more widespread understanding of and response to this crime.[35]

Understanding Assault

How do patterns of violence emerge between individuals? Is the continuum of violence more likely to escalate between strangers or acquaintances? We turn now to an examination of assault that distinguishes between two categories: assault between strangers and assault between acquaintances.

Assault Between Strangers

Assaults that occur between strangers tend to fall into two categories of violence, mentioned before in our discussion of homicide: *instrumental* and *expressive*.[36] An instrumental assault occurs as a means toward achieving an end and is usually preceded by some degree of planning, such as in a robbery in which the offender becomes familiar with the store in advance and prepares for the crime by assessing the type of force necessary.

The other type of assault between strangers is a more spontaneous act of violence; it is called "expressive" because it usually includes an escalation of emotions in an argument or a slight that ends up in a violent confrontation. It often occurs in an everyday setting such as a bar, restaurant, or sporting event where people find themselves in conflict with strangers.

Assault Between Acquaintances

Patterns of violence between acquaintances are much more difficult to study because victims are reluctant to report a crime committed by someone they know or live with. For years, criminology lagged behind in researching the type of violence that occurs within the intimate setting of the family. The first study to compile national data on family violence was conducted in 1975 by researchers at the University of New Hampshire. The National Family Violence Survey (NFVS) was conducted on a representative sample of 2,146 families. The second NFVSF was conducted in 1985 on a representative sample of 4,032 families.[37] Using a scale to measure the context of disagreements and how they are resolved, the 1985 study concluded that the rate of violence between spouses was 161 per 1,000 couples, a rate slightly lower than in the 1975 survey.[38] Next we examine two patterns of violence within the intimate setting of a family: Intimate partner assault and child maltreatment.

Intimate Partner Assault

The Office on Violence Against Women (OVW), part of the U.S. Department of Justice, defines **domestic violence** very broadly as a pattern of abusive behavior in any relationship that is used by one partner to gain or maintain power and control over another intimate partner. The OVW definition includes behavior that is coercive, manipulative, intimidating, and harassing, as well as behavior that is violent. **Intimate partner violence** is a more restrictive definition that criminologists use when they study spouse abuse or domestic violence. (Table 11.4 shows the major types of domestic violence.)

More than 9 of 10 victims of domestic violence are women; more than 9 of 10 perpetrators are men.[39] This does not mean men are never victims of violence and abuse at the hand of their female partners, but female violence against men is rare compared to male violence against women.[40] Domestic violence occurs in all racial and ethnic groups, cuts across all socioeconomic classes, and is a global issue that is the subject of a great deal of research and policymaking.[41]

Domestic violence is a behavioral pattern that emerges over time and continues to have long-term negative effects beyond the specific outburst of violence. In a classic research study, Lenore Walker examined its impact on 1,500 battered women.[42] She found the overwhelming majority described a similar cycle of behavior in their interaction with their intimate partners, which she referred to as the *cycle of violence.* She identified three stages within this cycle, as shown in Figure 11.2.

The *tension-building phase* begins with the normal or routine interactions between intimate partners. A breakdown in communication leads to the building of tension, anxiety, and fear in resolving conflicts and arguments and dealing with everyday matters of disappointment, disagreement, and life stresses. Tensions continue to escalate as the relationship becomes characterized by the abuser's desire for power and control in dealing with the situation, leaving the victim in continuous fear of causing an outburst.

In the *acting-out phase,* an explosive incident occurs in which the abusive partner begins to dominate his/her victim by verbally assaulting, threatening, hitting, or attacking.

domestic violence

A pattern of abusive behavior in a relationship that is used by one partner to gain or maintain power and control over another partner.

intimate partner violence

A pattern of abusive and/or violent behavior between spouses or domestic partners.

TABLE **11.4**

Categories of Domestic Violence

TYPE OF VIOLENCE	DESCRIPTION
Physical Abuse	Hitting, slapping, shoving, grabbing, pinching, biting, hair pulling, etc. Physical abuse also includes denying a partner medical care or forcing alcohol and/or drug use.
Sexual Abuse	Coercing or attempting to coerce any sexual contact or behavior without consent. Sexual abuse includes, but is not limited to, marital rape, attacks on sexual parts of the body, forcing sex after physical violence has occurred, or treating someone in a sexually demeaning manner.
Emotional Abuse	Undermining an individual's sense of self-worth and/or self-esteem. This may include, but is not limited to, constant criticism, name-calling, or damaging one's relationship with his or her children.
Economic Abuse	Making or attempting to make an individual financially dependent by maintaining total control over financial resources, withholding someone's access to money, or forbidding attendance at school or employment.
Psychological Abuse	Causing fear by intimidation; threatening physical harm to self, partner, children, or partner's family or friends; destroying pets and property; and forcing isolation from family, friends, or school and/or work.

Sources: National Domestic Violence Hotline; National Center for Victims of Crime; WomensLaw.org

FIGURE **11.2**

The Cycle of Violence

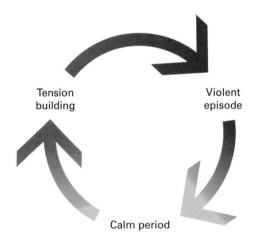

It may appear to be a loss of control over emotions, but in reality the abusive partner is beginning to take control of the victim in an effort to dominate the situation, the immediate environment, and the outcome. The victim is left hurt, betrayed, confused, and afraid.

The final phase, the *honeymoon phase,* is characterized by remorse, apology, and the apparent end of violence. This stage is the abuser's attempt to "make it up" to the victim. It may include showering the partner with love and affection or just withdrawing from violent behavior. The batterer will do anything to gain the approval and forgiveness of the victim, in an attempt to reestablish trust and security. The promise to never act out again and get help gives the victim hope that things will get better and reaffirms the intimate partner relationship. When violence escalates over time and without intervention, this stage becomes progressively shorter and may disappear completely.

Let's turn now to a closer look at the second form of violence that occurs within an intimate family setting—child maltreatment—to see whether there are patterns of similarity between it and domestic violence.

Child Maltreatment

The term **child maltreatment** describes any act or failure to act on the part of a parent or caretaker that results in the emotional harm, physical injury, sexual exploitation, or death of a minor child, or puts the minor child at risk of imminent danger.[43] The Child Abuse Prevention and Treatment Act (CAPTA) provides states with guidelines for defining child maltreatment in order to ensure they do all that is necessary to protect the well-being of the child. Most states incorporate within their definitions these different forms of child maltreatment:[44]

- *Physical abuse:* Physical abuse is the physical injury to a child that results from the non-accidental infliction of harm without reasonable explanation. It can include burning a child or hitting, punching, kicking, or beating with hands, belt, stick, or other object. It can also include actions that put a child at great risk of physical harm or injury, such as Michael Jackson's dangling his baby from a hotel balcony before crowds of observers.

- *Neglect:* Although not all neglect qualifies as a violent crime, some forms of child neglect clearly are. Withholding of adequate food, clothing, shelter, medical care, or supervision can lead to violent consequences for the child due to adults' failure to assume their responsibilities.[45]

- *Sexual abuse:* The CAPTA definition of child sexual abuse includes the employment, use, persuasion, inducement, enticement, or coercion of any child to engage in, or assist any other person to engage in, any sexually explicit conduct or simulation of such conduct for the purpose of producing a visual depiction of such conduct; or the rape, and in cases of caretaker or interfamilial relationships, statutory rape, molestation, prostitution, or other form of sexual exploitation of children, or incest with children.[46]

- *Emotional abuse:* Most definitions of emotional abuse to a child incorporate elements of parents' or caretakers' behavior that cause or can cause serious mental injury including depression, anxiety, withdrawal, and aggression. Often, emotional abuse is associated with traumatizing forms of punishment such as locking a child in the closet or using verbally abusive or derogatory language.[47]

The U.S. Department of Health and Human Services estimates there are 905,000 victims of child maltreatment each year, about half of them cases of neglect. The most vulnerable children are under 3 years of age. While male offenders account for the majority of child sexual abuse, females represent the majority of perpetrators in child maltreatment cases in general.[48] Other than the physical effects of abuse resulting in bodily injury and death, victims of child maltreatment endure long-term emotional trauma and often have behavioral problems in school, become involved with alcohol and drugs, are susceptible to teen pregnancy and promiscuity, and have a greater likelihood of juvenile delinquency.

child maltreatment

Any act or failure to act on the part of a parent or caretaker that results in the emotional harm, physical injury, sexual exploitation, or death of a minor child, or puts the minor child at risk of imminent danger.

In November 2002, while at a hotel in Berlin, Michael Jackson dangled his 9-month-old baby by the arm from a fourth-floor balcony as he greeted fans gathered below. Child abuse experts criticized Jackson's behavior as careless at the least, with some calling for his arrest for reckless endangerment. Did Jackson's actions constitute child maltreatment?

RAPE AND SEXUAL ASSAULT

sexual assault

The use of physical violence, threat, or intimidation to commit a sexual act on the victim.

forcible rape

Sexual intercourse with a victim by force and against the person's will; the use of force and coercion to take control over the victim.

attempted rape

The attempt to commit a rape by force or threat of force.

statutory rape

Sexual intercourse with a minor under the age of consent.

We turn now to another category of interpersonal violence that also has devastating effects on its victims. **Sexual assault** is a crime that includes the use of physical violence, threat, or intimidation to commit a sexual act on the victim. Sexual assaults contain an element of denigration in that the perpetrator often sees the victim as "deserving it" or as being inferior.

Rape is the most serious type of sexual assault. **Forcible rape** as defined by the FBI Uniform Crime Reports is "the carnal knowledge of a female by force and against her will." The UCR distinguishes between forcible rape and other types of sexual assault including **attempted rape** or the attempt to commit a rape by force or threat of force, and **statutory rape** or sexual intercourse with a minor under the age of consent (in most states the age of consent is 16; in some it is 18). In many cases, the crime is defined in terms of degrees of severity, as measured by the resulting physical and psychological injury to the victim, the relationship between the victim and offender, the number of offenders, and the age of the victim.[49] Regardless of its definition, rape is about power, not sex. It is the use of force and coercion to take control over the victim.

In the past, rape laws essentially allowed the focus of prosecution to become an attack on the victim's character, past sexual behavior, and general credibility.[50] Feminist groups and other reformers have criticized these traditional laws for the past two decades on the grounds that they place the burden of proof on the victim instead of the defendant, adding to the trauma and to victims' unwillingness to report the crime. Statutory definitions of rape have undergone revisions over the years, as part of a national effort to increase the public's awareness of the crime, offer support and social services to the victim, and aid the apprehension and prosecution of the rape offender.[51] Policy changes over the past several decades include:

- Replacing the single criminal act of rape with a series of offenses graded according to the presence or absence of aggravating circumstances, such as the presence of a weapon or resulting injury to the victim.
- Making obsolete the legal requirement that the victim must physically resist the attacker.
- Eliminating the legal requirement for victims to testify about the attack at trial.

How does society's perception of the crime of rape affect the treatment of rape victims?

■ Developing **rape shield laws** to protect the victim by restricting the defense's ability to use irrelevant evidence regarding the victim's past sexual behavior or reputation.[52]

■ Requiring the use of anonymous "Jane Doe kits," which collect forensic evidence in a numbered, sealed envelope in case the victim later decides to press charges.[53]

■ Broadening the scope and meaning of the crime of rape to include date rape, spousal rape, same-sex rape, and gang rape.

How have the dynamics of change in the legal definition of rape affected the nature, meaning and extent of this crime? Let us take a closer look at the various categories of rape.

Describing Rape and Sexual Assault

The vast majority of rapes occur between victims and offenders who have some prior relationship. Research shows that **acquaintance rape,** while the most common form of the crime, is probably the least likely to be reported to the police. Victims either are unaware a crime has been committed, mistakenly believe they have precipitated their own victimization, have been under the influence of alcohol, are too embarrassed or ashamed of the incident, or do not believe anything can be done about it.[54] Nevertheless, the emotional and psychological impact and trauma to the victim in these cases are significant and can have long-term negative consequences. We can better understand the crime of rape by identifying the various contexts within which it can take place.

Date Rape

Date rape is sexual intercourse forced on a person by an acquaintance acting as an escort during some type of social engagement. Most empirical research on date rape has focused on the social relationships of college dating. In a classic study on rape, Kent State University psychologist Mary P. Koss surveyed 7,000 college students and found one of every eight females had been compelled to have sexual intercourse through the use or threat of force.[55] Moreover, the overwhelming majority of victims, 90 percent, knew their assailants.

More recent data from a study conducted by the National Institute of Justice estimates that approximately 5 percent of college women will become the victims of a rape or an attempted rape in any given academic year.[56] A majority of these rapes go unreported, as women who are forced to have sex with someone they know and with whom they are likely to continue to interact are reluctant to report the crime to police, for fear of retaliation, shame, and the lack of sufficient evidence to prove a crime was committed.

Of growing concern on college campuses are date rape drugs, such as GHB (gamma hydroxybutyric acid) and Rohypnol ("roofies"), hypnotic drugs with powerful sedative effects. These odorless, tasteless drugs are usually added to alcohol in clubs, in bars, at fraternity parties, or on a date to sedate women with the intention of having sexual intercourse without their consent and against their will. The drugs induce drowsiness, blackout, and loss of memory. Because of its powerful side effects and widespread abuse, Rohypnol was included in the Drug-Induced Rape Prevention and Punishment Act of 1996.[57] In response to publicity by women's groups about the frequency with which these drugs are misused and their dangers, a pharmaceutical company, Hoffman-La Roche, changed the formula for Rohypnol to include a dye that turns a drink turn green if the drug is added to it.

College and university campuses have responded to the growing problem of sexual assault by both educating students about both personal safety issues and raising awareness of the sociocultural dynamics on campuses that may contribute to sexual violence and rape.[58] Researchers note the prevalence of rape on college campuses is largely the result of the social organization of college life and peer group interactions at fraternity

rape shield laws

Laws designed to protect the victim by restricting the defense's ability to use irrelevant evidence regarding the victim's past sexual behavior or reputation.

acquaintance rape

The most common type of rape in which the victim and the rapist are not strangers; the least reported type of rape.

date rape

Sexual intercourse forced on a person by an acquaintance acting as an escort during some type of social engagement.

houses, athletic events, parties, and other social gatherings conducive to sexual assault on young women.[59]

Studies also show rape on college campuses to be generally the result of several factors: sexual misconceptions by male college students about female sexual behavior; the prevalence of alcohol use among college students; and the notion of sexual conquest as a means of social approval by male peers.[60] To effectively change these dynamics, many colleges have implemented peer discussion groups, counselors, and campus programs to educate students on some of the misconceptions that can lead to sexual violence. These programs are designed to increase communication so that women, especially, will be aware of the dangers and recognize the situations in which sexual assault and rape may occur.

Spousal Rape

spousal or marital rape

Forced sexual intercourse in a marital relationship.

The recognition that **spousal or marital rape** is a crime is another byproduct of rape law reform, which expanded the common law definition of rape to include forced sexual intercourse in a marital relationship. Laws criminalizing this form of sexual assault were first passed in 1976, with Nebraska being the first state to abolish the marital exemption to rape laws. Today, spousal rape is illegal in every state. However, debates still spark over whether a man and woman entering a marital contract are fundamentally agreeing to a sexual relationship. If we believe they are, then spousal rape will continue to be a challenging crime to prove.

From a procedural standpoint, the standard of evidence required to convict a husband of spousal rape is usually higher than for any other form of rape, often requiring proof of violence or injury. In addition, punishment for spousal rape is often less severe. Many women are reluctant to report marital rape for fear of jeopardizing their marriage, losing their homes and families, suffering public humiliation and retaliation by their husbands, and not being taken seriously by authorities.

Unfortunately, victims of spousal rape suffer just as much trauma as victims of stranger rapes.[61] Research indicates that repeated sexual abuse in spousal rape is accompanied by longer-lasting trauma that results from the social stereotypes surrounding this crime, and the lack of social support to help victims overcome feelings of betrayal, guilt, shame, and fear.[62]

Gang Rape

gang rape

Forced sexual intercourse with a victim by more than one assailant.

Gang rape is the rape of a victim by more than one assailant. Offenders charged with gang rape include those who actually engage in nonconsensual sexual intercourse with the victim, as well those who use force or threat of force to facilitate the actions of others and make the victim submit. Although gang rape often occurs between victims and offenders who have some type of prior relationship, this type of rape is very different from individual acquaintance rape. Sometimes the expression of power and male sexual dominance over a woman is used as an affirmation of acceptance and membership into a group of men such as a street gang, social club, or college fraternity.[63]

Physical resistance is more difficult in a gang rape attack and often can lead to the use of excessive violence and restraint. The victim also suffers the added humiliation of knowing people stood by and failed to help or stop the rape. Men who participate in gang rape often use peer approval and the affirmation of their masculinity to justify a behavior they are not likely to engage in if acting alone.[64]

Gang rape is difficult for victims to prove, since the bond that exists among the group members often supersedes their willingness to cooperate or testify against their friends. According to research studies, rapes perpetrated by multiple assailants often take on a new meaning as a symbol of masculinity and dominance. Gang rapists often rape for the others, to prove their manhood or feel a sense of belonging with "the boys." It can be the spontaneous act of males egging one another on, or it can start out as a dare, joke, or even a rite of passage.[65] The Consider This feature illustrates some of the dynamics of gang rape in cases where college athletes are the perpetrators.

CONSIDER THIS... Do "Good Guys" Rape?

At campuses across the country, women are attacked and sexually assaulted during football games, at parties, and inside fraternity houses by groups of young men who claim to be having a good time.[66] In many cases, these attacks are perpetrated by members of the university's athletic teams, students often perceived by their peers as beyond reproach and looked upon fondly by the academic and social community.[67]

In the 1980s researcher Mary Koss studied 7,000 students at 32 universities across the country. She found that 1 of 12 male college students admitted committing acts that state statutes legally define as rape or attempted rape, but only 1 of every 100 admitted actually committing rape or attempted rape. Koss notes this denial of criminal behavior is largely due to a lack of understanding of the social and legal consequences of their actions, along with the scapegoating of women as "sluts" or "whores" who "deserve" or "ask for it," to absolve assailants' feelings of guilt or responsibility.[68]

Studies also show justification of rape can be heightened by the unique culture of university athletes. Participation in an all-male group or activity such as a sports team can often insulate men from feelings of guilt and responsibility for treating a woman with disrespect and brutality.[69] Male bonding is a primary element in gang rapes, connecting aggression with sexuality and fueling each group member's sense of power and dominance, especially in front of his "brothers." Moreover, the attention and special privilege granted to many collegiate athletes can often allow them to feel they are above the law, in too bright a light to be dimmed by a single victim's accusation.

How can we condone a culture that seems to overlook or underplay the prevalence of rape by supposedly "good guys"? How can criminology advance the understanding of acquaintance rape among college students?

What do you think?

Same-Sex Rape

For many years, the definition of common law rape was limited to the sexual assault of a female by a male offender. Only recently has publicity increased our awareness of **same-sex rape,** or sexual violence and abuse perpetrated by men against men and women against women.[70] In same-sex rape, neither the perpetrator nor the victim is always gay or lesbian.

Same-sex rape follows the same pattern as heterosexual rape. It is an attempt to control, dominate, and overpower the victim, forcing him or her to submit to sexual acts using fear, threat, intimidation, and violence. Survivors of same-sex rape go through the same emotional turmoil as do survivors of opposite-sex rape. However, they also have to deal with the additional stereotypes held by society that an individual cannot be raped by somebody of the same sex. As well, victims of same-sex rape must face the trauma of remaining silent for fear that others will see their victimization in a negative homophobic light.[71] In some instances, offenders will use this fear to persist in their pattern of abuse, under the threat of exposing the victim's real or supposed sexual orientation to family, friends, peers, and co-workers.[72]

same-sex rape

Sexual violence and abuse perpetrated by men against men and women against women.

Understanding Rape and Sexual Assault

Criminologists consider rape a violent form of coercive behavior, not an expression of sexual desire. Several researchers have attempted to develop a typology of rapists according to the motivation of the offender and the meaning attached to their crime.

Nicholas Groth conducted one of the first systematic efforts to study patterns of rape and identified three motivations: power, anger, and sadism.[73] In his analysis of

348 convicted rapists serving time in prison, Groth found that over half the offenders (55 percent) reported they raped their victims to dominate and exert control over the women; he called this category of offense *power rape.* Groth noted that the power rapist does not set out to hurt the victim, in contrast to the offender in *anger rape,* who impulsively assaults his victim as a means of releasing anger or hostility. Anger rapists made up about 40 percent of Groth's sample and usually carried out their attacks in a brutal, violent manner. The last category of rape, *sadistic rape,* was only 5 percent of Groth's sample; it was primarily motivated by an erotic expression of power and anger. In sadistic rape the male offender derived sexual pleasure from the torture of the victim and the exertion of power and dominance.

Several other typologies have emerged to expand upon the work of Groth. Robert Hazelwood and Ann Burgess offer a similar categorization based on motivation that classifies rape offenders into four types.[74] The *power-assertive rapist* spends a great deal of effort planning his crime and even seduces his victim. The rape is an expression of masculine power and often includes the use of a great deal of force or violence to overpower the victim. The *power-reassurance rapist* acts out of a general sense of sexual inadequacy. He usually attacks victims who are strangers, often after a period of stalking them, and often attempts to continue contact with them after the attack in a socially inappropriate expression of sexuality. The *anger-retaliatory rapist* attacks his victim by surprise and somewhat spontaneously, using direct physical force and carrying out the attack as an expression of anger and hostility. The attack becomes a source of release to the perpetrator, since the victim is often the source of his rage or a symbolic representation of it. Finally, the *anger-excitation rapist* usually takes time to plan and execute his attack, usually on a stranger. The primary motive is to inflict pain and to humiliate and degrade the victim. The offender gains sexual stimulation from hurting the victim and therefore often uses forms of torture for gratification, sometimes recording these activities.

An alternative typology—based on motivation, victim selection, style of attack, and degree of violence—is offered by Dennis Stevens from research conducted on 61 incarcerated serial rapists.[75] *Lust rapists,* the largest category in the sample, are predatory rapists who generally do not use violence and select their victim based on availability. *Righteous rapists* contend the victim bears primary responsibility for the sexual encounter and view their own behavior as based on victim consent. *Peer rapists* blame their actions on associating with "bad company" and membership in groups that define rape as acceptable behavior. This is often the case in gang rapes. *Fantasy rapists* are motivated by thoughts and ideas from their past that often include violent scenarios they want to carry out, in which the sexual act is secondary. For rapists motivated by *control and anger,* rape is secondary to the violence expressed during the attack. Finally, *supremacy rapists* are primarily motivated by the satisfaction gained from inflicting pain and suffering on the victim. Control and anger rapists and supremacy rapists are the most violent of all types of rapists.

A survey of the literature indicates that the crime of rape includes a cognitive component, whereby perpetrators justify the crime according to their perception and interpretation of the situation and their attitude toward the victim. Offenders use the following themes to minimize their offense and promote denial:[76]

- *Women are seductresses.* They entice men through their sexuality.
- *"No" means "yes."* While women may protest a man's sexual advances, they really want them.
- *Women like it.* Most women eventually give in to the forced sexual intercourse, relax, and enjoy it.
- *Only bad girls get raped.* Nice girls avoid circumstances that can lead to a rape.
- *Rape is not really a crime.* It is a minor wrongdoing based on a misunderstanding.

Many of these justifications are an extension of various myths regarding the context of sexual violence, and they reflect social and cultural biases about the role of women in society. Studies on the myths surrounding the crime of rape confirm that many people believe women bring false charges of rape to get back at men, that women draw attention to themselves by wearing suggestive clothing and engaging in certain activities, and that women secretly want to be raped but simply say no so as not to appear promiscuous.[77] These myths have the compound effect of minimizing the perceived trauma and injury to the victim and diffusing responsibility for the crime from the offender to the victim; they also undermine efforts to prosecute offenders and to shield the victim from further humiliation and scrutiny by the criminal justice system.

The social and emotional stigma associated with the crime of rape take something away from the victim that is very difficult to restore. We turn now to another category of violent crime that involves a different aspect of taking: the violent crime of robbery.

ROBBERY

The Uniform Crime Reports define **robbery** as "the taking or attempting to take anything of value from the care, custody, or control of a person or persons by force or threat of force or violence and/or by putting the victim in fear." The ultimate goal of the robber is to take something of value, but in the view of the criminal justice system, robbery is not about the value of the stolen items. It is considered a violent crime because it includes a face-to-face confrontation between victim and offender in which the victim's life is placed in jeopardy. Thus, the severity of punishment is usually related to the amount of force used during the robbery.[78]

Robberies are more likely than any other type of violent crime to include the use of a weapon, especially firearms. According to the UCR, a firearm is used in 42.2 percent of all robberies. Moreover, robberies are more likely than other crimes to include multiple assailants, as well as victims and offenders who are strangers. Stranger attacks more commonly occur in public locations, implicate multiple offenders, include weapons, and often result in greater physical harm to the victims than acts by offenders known to them.[79] The group nature of robbery is best illustrated in the typical robbery of a bank or convenience store, in which one or two people may enter the targeted place and another waits outside as lookout or drives a getaway car.

As in most violent crimes, in robbery the majority of offenders arrested are disproportionately young African American males. These data may be somewhat misleading, though, since only about 25 percent of offenses known to the police result in an arrest.[80] The National Crime Victimization Survey (NCVS) indicates about 50 percent of robberies are reported to police, with men less likely to report being robbed than women.[81]

Most robbers are not specialists who engage in robbery as their sole criminal activity. The majority are amateurs who practice a variety of criminal behaviors ranging from theft and burglary to fraud.[82] However, especially among repeat offenders, robbery has some potential to escalate in violence over time. Research indicates that the typical robbery is a spontaneous violent attack that occurs as an opportunity presents itself, with little planning and no thought about how to avoid getting caught.[83] The exception is the professional robbery, committed by a person as a source of livelihood. Professional robbers carry out their crimes using a great deal of planning, including the rational decision to select a particular target, the choice of a time to commit the crime, the anticipation of possible resistance, and the plan for escape.[84]

robbery

The act of taking or attempting to take anything of value from the care, custody, or control of a person by force or threat of force.

Since robbers select victims who are vulnerable and most likely to produce a better yield, automated teller machines (ATMs) in isolated, poorly lit places, and at night, make a quick and relatively easy target.

Describing Robbery

institutional robbery

A robbery that occurs in a commercial setting.

personal robbery

A robbery that occurs in a residential setting or on the street; a street robbery is also known as a mugging.

Robberies that occur in commercial settings—such as banks, gas stations, pawnshops, and jewelry, liquor, and other retail stores—are **institutional robberies.**[85] Commercial outlets like these are preferred targets for their easy access and availability of quick cash.[86] Often, businesses in remote areas and poorer neighborhoods are at greater risk, due to their low level of customer activity and insufficient security.

The overwhelming majority of robberies are **personal robberies,** occurring in a residential setting or on the street; street robberies are commonly referred to as *muggings.* A street robbery by a single assailant will often include the use of a weapon, usually a gun. In a street robbery by multiple assailants, the attackers usually overpower the victim in order to take his or her possessions by force. The majority of street robberies occur on an individual's way to his or her car, in parking lots, at or near an ATM, on subways, and in train stations. Robbers select victims who are more vulnerable and most likely to produce a better "yield."[87] A study conducted by criminologist Jody Miller found that robbers choose victims they perceive as likely to offer the least resistance.[88]

Personal robberies also occur in residences. Least prevalent of all robberies are home invasions, in which armed robbers force their way into someone's home, restrain the occupants, and proceed to take their personal belongings and ransack the residence. Homes selected for invasion are often located in a neighborhood that is socially disorganized, where security measures are least effective and there are few precautions.[89]

Understanding Robbery

Studies indicate that financial need is the stated motive of the majority of all convicted offenders.[90] Robberies motivated by financial gain usually occur either to meet the offender's immediate need for cash or to support a certain type of lifestyle. In a classic study conducted by researcher Floyd Feeney, a robber describes his financial need in this way:

> I needed the money for food. I tried welfare. I tried to borrow money from all the people that I could borrow from. . . . I didn't have any sources of money. I was just flat broke. I was getting it out of savings and borrowing money from my mother, but I was getting kind of run out because she was starting to need more. . . . I didn't even think about how much I wanted to get. I just felt that anything I got would help.[91]

Robbers often see their takings as quick, easy money to pay off a debt, buy food, make a rent payment, or purchase drugs. Such robberies are often associated with a particular criminal lifestyle that values lawless, reckless behavior and a street culture inhospitable to conventional means of generating stable, legitimate sources of income. Research conducted by Bruce Jacobs and Richard Wright at the University of Missouri examined the motivation and decision-making patterns of 86 active robbers in St. Louis. They found that engaging in a robbery is often associated with the values, beliefs, and behaviors of a street culture.[92]

Robbery can also spring from motives other than money. Jacobs and Wright found the majority of street robbers' activities were characterized by a "quest for excitement and sensory stimulation." For example, robberies related to drugs are sometimes a response to the violation of the informal rules or social norms of a street subculture. Researchers note there are three types of such offenses. *Market offenses* are often related to the drug trade itself, while *status-based offenses* have more to do with a challenge to character or position, such as a threat to honor. Finally, robbery can be a means for retaliation against *personalistic offenses* such as a sexual assault.[93] Table 11.5 provides a summary of these three types of violations.

With this pattern of offending, robbery becomes a symbol of revenge and retaliation. The intent is to send a message to the perpetrator of the harm in a moralistic attempt to right a wrong. We turn now to a form of interpersonal violence that also represents an emotionally charged attempt to send out a message: hate crime.

TABLE **11.5**

Robbery as a Response to Norm Violations Within the Street Subculture	
TYPE OF VIOLATION	**DESCRIPTION**
Market-Related Offenses	Emerge when there are disputes between street rivals, partners in trade, or generalized predators
Status-Based Offenses	Occur when aspects of the individual's character and personality have been challenged, disrespected, or offended
Personalistic Offenses	Result from incidents where an individual was personally harmed, injured, or violated; where the incident creates a challenge to personal autonomy and belief in justice

Source: Jacobs, B. A., & Wright, R. (2006). Street justice: Retaliation in the criminal underworld. *British Journal of Sociology, 58,* 506–507.

HATE CRIMES

The crimes we have discussed so far—murder, assault, rape, and robbery—are acts of interpersonal violence that for the most part target individuals without consideration of their race, ethnic background, or other physical characteristic. Interpersonal violence takes on a different meaning when the crime is motivated by bias. Crimes targeting a specific category of individuals, and motivated by a bias against physical or social characteristics unique to this group, are **hate crimes.**

On January 27, 2008, detailed charges were brought against 37-year-old Ivaylo Ivanov for spray-painting swastikas at 23 different locations, including private homes and synagogues, and circulating flyers that read "Kill All Jews." Police had confiscated an array of deadly homemade pipe bombs, rifles, and handguns from Ivanov's Brooklyn Heights apartment when he was arrested on January 20, 2008. Ivanov was indicted on over 100 counts of criminal mischief, including charges of criminal weapons possession and aggravated harassment in connection with a bias crime.

hate crime

A crime targeting a specific category of individuals and motivated by a bias against physical or social characteristics unique to this group.

Should this type of expression be considered a form of criminal behavior?

Key:

■ 0–10	■ 41–50
■ 11–20	■ 51–60
■ 21–30	■ 61–70
■ 31–40	■ 71–80

The Distribution of Hate Groups by State

Source: Southern Poverty Law Center

The Southern Poverty Law Center identified and counted 888 active hate groups throughout the United States in 2007, mapping their distribution by state (see map). These groups are identified by their practices and beliefs toward a particular group or class of individuals that are offensive, harmful, and derogatory. They engage in hate activities such as holding rallies and marches and distributing publications that support their ideologies. They also engage in criminal acts.

Hate crimes may take several forms and often include physical assault; property damage; arson; vandalism in the form of offensive graffiti; verbal threats, slights, insults, or harassment; and rape and murder. Because they are designed to cause fear and intimidation to an entire social group or class of individuals, hate crimes may have a greater general impact on society than crimes directed at specific individuals.

In 1990, the UCR began collecting data on specific categories of hate crimes, with the passage of the Hate Crime Statistics Act of 1990 (HCSA). The HCSA requires the FBI to collect data from law enforcement agencies across the country on crimes motivated by prejudice or bias based on race, religion, sexual orientation, or ethnicity. In 1994, Congress passed the Violent Crime Control and Law Enforcement Act of 1994, which included the collection of data on hate crimes motivated by bias against people with disabilities. Since 1992, the FBI has published an annual report titled *Hate Crime Statistics*.

In 2006, a total of 2,105 law enforcement agencies across the United States reported 7,722 crimes motivated by bias against a race, religion, disability, ethnicity, or sexual orientation.[94] Of the single-bias incidents, 51.8 percent were racially motivated, 18.9 percent were motivated by bias against religion, 15.5 percent accounted for bias based on sexual orientation, 12.7 percent were motivated by bias against ethnicity or national origin, and 1 percent were motivated by bias against disability. Of the crimes reported in 2006, 60 percent were categorized as crimes against persons, 39.6 percent against property, and 0.4 percent against society or the public order. *Hate Crime Statistics* has played a central role

Since the passage of the federal Violent Crime Control and Law Enforcement Act in 1994, public debates have questioned whether hate crime laws infringe on the constitutional right to free speech. Proponents of hate crime legislation argue that it is necessary to protect minority groups from acts of violence motivated by bias, and that increased sentences protect the rights of the innocent to be free of fear, threat, and intimidation. Moreover, hate crimes affect not only the individual targeted, but the community in which the crime occurred, disturbing its peace and creating fear and panic among those who share the victim's traits.

Opponents argue hate crime laws are unnecessary since the acts they define are already criminal violations punished by law. Adding additional penalties if the offender is also found guilty of bias toward the victim is essentially an attempt to suppress dissension and personal preference and to foster certain views of morality. For example, a minister preaching a sermon on the vices of homosexual marriage can be accused of a crime because the speech discriminates against gays and lesbians. Thus, while claiming to promote tolerance, hate crime laws can become an imminent threat to freedom of thought and speech.

What do criminological studies reveal about the need to both protect freedom of speech and identify crimes motivated by bias? Research conducted by Gregory Herek and others suggest hateful speech can have a traumatic impact on the individual to whom it is directed.[95] It should be seen as a form of terrorism that creates fear and panic by inciting violence and therefore should be considered by law as constituting a unique category of victimization. A study by Robert Boeckmann and Jeffrey Liew found that minority groups feel hate speech should be more severely punished than some forms of property crimes.[96] Other studies reveal that nearly 80 percent of U.S. adults support the passage of legislation aimed at curtailing hate crime.[97]

Despite these and similar findings, the door remains open for criminologists to explore the true impact of hate crime legislation on freedom of speech, and the benefits it may have in reducing bias-motivated crimes.

in increasing public awareness and our understanding of hate crimes. It has also inspired researchers to study groups often targeted for their personal characteristics, preferences, and lifestyles.

Hate crimes play a unique role in the development of criminal justice policy. This is especially true when debates are sparked about the First Amendment protection of free speech versus the control of hateful propaganda embedded in the ideology and teaching of certain groups. The Connecting Research to Practice feature illustrates one perspective on this debate.

SUMMARY

■ **What is criminal homicide?**

The category of crimes we call homicide is complex and diverse. Criminal homicide is the unlawful and intentional killing of one human being by another and includes first- and second-degree murder, as well as voluntary and involuntary manslaughter. First-degree murder requires premeditation (the offender has thought out the crime) and malice aforethought (the offender forms the intent to harm). Second-degree murder only requires malice aforethought. Voluntary manslaughter is the unlawful killing of another person while committing a felony without any intention to kill the victim. Involuntary manslaughter is an unlawful death resulting from the negligence or careless acts of the offender.

■ **Why do people kill?**

Many homicide offenders are chronic, violent offenders who adhere to a subculture of violence. Other patterns of homicide are situational, unique to a specific relationship or type of interaction between victim and offender. These homicides can be expressive, arising from interpersonal conflict or dispute, or instrumental, serving as a means to an end, such as obtaining money.

Homicides can also fall into the categories of serial murder (the killing of three or more individuals in separate events) and mass murder (the killing of three or more individuals in a single event). While serial killers do not fit a particular typology of criminal offender, criminologists have categorized this crime according to motivation, selection of victim, method of killing, and the expected benefit of the crime. Patterns of mass murder are quite distinct from serial murder. Researchers have attempted to differentiate mass murders according to the relationship between victim and offender, the degree of spontaneity, and the motivation.

■ **What constitutes an assault?**

In its broadest sense, an assault is an attempt to commit physical harm to another human being. No physical contact has to occur; an individual can commit the crime of assault by simply putting someone in fear of injury, harm, or danger through threats, intimidation, or harassment. When physical contact does occur, the crime is assault with battery. Assaults are also categorized by the degree of injury or harm to the victim, and therefore the law distinguishes between simple and aggravated assault.

■ **Does assault occur more often between strangers or acquaintances?**

Assaultive behavior is much more common within the intimate setting of a family and includes intimate partner assault and child maltreatment. Intimate partner assault, also referred to as domestic violence, is abusive behavior including coercion, manipulation, intimidation, and violence upon a spouse or intimate partner. It is a means by which one partner attempts to maintain power and control over the other through some form of physical, emotional, sexual, economic, or psychological abuse.

We defined child maltreatment as any act or failure to act on the part of a parent or caretaker, which results in the emotional harm, physical injury, sexual exploitation, or death of a minor child, or puts the minor child at risk of imminent danger. Most states include physical abuse, neglect, emotional abuse, and sexual abuse in their definitions.

■ **Is rape a sexual act?**

In this chapter, we distinguished between forcible rape, defined by the FBI Uniform Crime Reports as "the carnal knowledge of a female forcibly and against her will"; attempted rape, the attempt to commit sexual intercourse by force or threat of force; and statutory rape, sexual intercourse with a minor under the age of consent, which varies from state to state. States have developed legal categories that broaden the meaning of rape to include date rape, spousal rape, same-sex rape, and gang rape. Contrary to popular beliefs and images about the crime of rape and rape victims, the majority of rapes occur between victims and offenders who know each other, hence the term *acquaintance rape.*

Despite its many different motives, characteristics, and meaning, criminologists agree rape is a violent form of coercive behavior, not an expression of sexual desire. Offenders fall into various categories centering on their need to express power, anger, retaliation, and sadistic desires. Other studies have developed typologies based on motivation, victim selection, style of attack, and degree of violence.

■ **Why is robbery a violent crime?**

Robbery is considered a violent crime because it is a face-to-face confrontation in which the offender uses force or the threat of force to take something of value from the immediate possession or control of the victim. For this reason, the legal consequences of committing robbery are related to the amount of force used during the crime, rather than to the value of what was taken.

■ **What is the motive behind stealing by force?**

Economic gain is the main motivation behind most robberies. Stealing by force from a vulnerable target is often seen by offenders as a quick and easy way to get money to meet some immediate financial need, whether it is to buy food, pay rent, or purchase drugs. Studies have also found robbery to be associated with other motives such as retaliation within the street subculture.

■ **What are hate crimes?**

Hate crimes can take on several forms such as murder, rape, and assault but also destruction of property and arson. They are unique, however, in being motivated by a bias against physical or social characteristics unique to a group or individual. Often, hate crimes are an attempt to create fear and intimidate an entire social group or category of individuals.

CRITICAL THINKING QUESTIONS

1. What categories of criminal homicide elicit the most public and media attention? Are certain types easier to understand than others? Which are the most difficult to comprehend? What makes them so difficult? How does our understanding of the different types of criminal homicide guide policies directed at the social control of this form of interpersonal violence?

2. How is an assault between strangers different from an assault between acquaintances? If you were the victim of an assault, would you be more likely to report it to the police if the perpetrator were a stranger or an acquaintance? If it makes a difference, why does it? How can the field of criminology increase public awareness of domestic violence?

3. If your neighbor were raped by your best friend, what would you do? Would you gather more information about the victim, her behavior, and her past, rather

than question your best friend's integrity? Why or why not? Why is it hard for us to believe that ordinary individuals can commit rape? Why don't we worry about who the victim was, her past, or her reputation in a case of robbery? Why don't we wonder what the victim was wearing when the crime is murder?

4. When does a theft constitute a robbery? What specific elements make robbery a form of interpersonal violence? Does the victim have to be afraid or intimidated in order for a robbery to occur? Can you think of any interactions between a victim and offender that include a theft but that do not constitute a robbery?

5. How does the tension between individual rights and public order (see Chapter 1) influence the adoption of policies forbidding certain types of speech? When does freedom of expression fall under constitutional protection, and when is it subject to control as hate crime?

ADDITIONAL RESOURCES

The role of crime typologies in criminological research is further discussed at http://law. jrank.org/pages/2217/Typologies-Criminal-Behavior.html

Additional resources for victims of sexual assault can be found at the National Center for Victims of Crime website at http://www.ncvc.org/ncvc/main.aspx?dbID=DB_FAQ: RapeShieldLaws927

For more information about date rape drugs, visit http://www.womenshealth.gov/ faq/date-rape-drugs.cfm

The U.S. Department of Justice, Office on Violence Against Women provides a variety of resources on the incidence, cost, impact, and prevention of domestic violence. You can access this information by visiting http://www.ovw.usdoj.gov/

More details about the Child Abuse Prevention and Treatment Act and programs to prevent and treat child abuse can be found at http://laws.adoption.com/statutes/ child-abuse-prevention-and-treatment-act-capta-of-1974.html

A detailed description of the Hate Crime Statistics Act (28 U.S.C. § 534) can be found at http://www2.fbi.gov/ucr/hc2009/hatecrimestatistics.html

12

CRIMES AGAINST PROPERTY

In this chapter, we will explore the following questions:

- How do we categorize larceny theft?
- Why do people steal?
- In what ways is burglary different from robbery?
- What are the characteristics of burglary?
- Who steals cars and why do they do it?
- Are all fire-setters the same?

Have you ever thought about taking something that does

not belong to you? Could it have been something little, like a stick of gum, or something big, like an expensive watch? Were you at your friend's house, at the grocery store, or in a building where you didn't belong? Crimes against property take on a variety of forms. They range from the professional practices of career thieves to the opportunistic or careless behavior of first-time offenders. They can make history or go relatively unnoticed. For research purposes, criminologists categorize the property crimes of larceny, burglary, motor vehicle theft, and arson by their success or failure, as well as by the offender's level of skill, degree of planning, and method of execution.[1]

On the evening of March 18, 1990, a group of thieves made history when they broke into the Isabella Stewart Gardner Museum in Boston, Massachusetts, and stole 13 paintings estimated at $500 million, the largest art theft ever to be committed in the United States. The perpetrators, wearing police uniforms, identified themselves to museum security officers as Boston police who were responding to a call about a disturbance on the museum grounds. Once they gained access to the museum, the thieves abducted the security personnel, restrained them with duct tape and handcuffs, and kept them secure in the basement area of the museum. Video surveillance was removed and taken by the offenders before leaving the museum. To this day, none of the paintings has been recovered. These thieves were no amateurs; they were professionals who made a

This Vermeer painting, *The Concert,* was one of the masterpieces stolen from the Isabella Stewart Gardner Museum in Boston, a heist that totaled nearly $500 million in stolen artwork.

living out of stealing. How common is this pattern of theft, and how do professional thieves differ from amateurs?

One classic study of the career paths of professional thieves examined the lives and perspectives of over 50 habitual property offenders.[2] Professional thieves identify with a criminal lifestyle and are committed to crime as a way of earning a living. Theirs is a calculated decision made in the context of desperation for money, the need to support a drug habit, or the desire to live a lavish lifestyle. They know the possible consequences—arrest, jail time—and accept them as part of the job. More often than not, professionals specialize in particular forms of theft such as confidence tricks, safecracking, burglary, shoplifting, check forgery, or fraud.[3] They identify with their own subculture, which has a social hierarchy, shared unique language, and ethical code.[4] Professional thieves view their work with pride and see theft as a legitimate enterprise. They compartmentalize their profession according to the degree of specialization, complexity, and training necessary to carry it out and typically begin early in life, learning how to steal and apprenticing with an older, more experienced thief to learn the trade.[5]

Studies indicate professional theft is rare compared to other types of property crime. While we cannot estimate the incidence rate with any accuracy, only a handful of inmates in federal and state penitentiaries at any given time are professional thieves. We might suspect this is a testament to their ability to stay out of prison, and perhaps it is. However, reports of professional theft in cities throughout the United States and Europe, and the only occasional discovery of professional thieves, all suggest the incidence is small.[6] Most theft arrests are of people between 16 and 25, who will likely not have developed the skills and experience to qualify as professional thieves, which is further support for the conclusion that professional theft does not account for large amounts of crime.

In this chapter, we explore the unlawful taking and the unlawful destruction of property. Let's turn now to a discussion of larceny.

LARCENY

Larceny theft is "the unlawful taking, carrying, leading, or riding away of property from the possession or constructive possession of another."[7] The "immediate possession" part of this definition comes from the common law definition of theft created by English judges to describe the taking of someone else's property for use without the owner's permission (see Chapter 2).[8] This type of illegal possession implied trespassing upon another's land with the intent to steal. In later years, however, the courts needed also to account for theft by deception or trickery. Thus, we use the term **constructive possession** to define "the condition in which a person does not have physical custody or possession, but is in a position to exercise dominion or control over a thing."[9] As long as the money deposited in the bank is in the possession of its employees, for example, any mishandling of it comprises theft, because it is reasonable to assume the money is still the property of the persons who made the deposit and entrusted it to the bank.

States distinguish between **grand larceny,** the theft of an item or merchandise of significant value, and **petit (petty) larceny,** the theft of property of little value. The line is drawn differently according to each state's criminal codes and can vary widely. In New York, grand larceny is the theft of goods valued in excess of $1,000. In Virginia, theft of an item with a value of at least $200 is grand larceny.

Grand larceny is a felony crime meriting a high monetary fine and imprisonment of more than one year. Petty larceny, more common than grand, is a misdemeanor offense usually handled more leniently, with a lower monetary fine and/or less than one year in jail. The overwhelming majority of property theft (over 80 percent) is of property worth less than $250.[10]

larceny theft

The unlawful taking, carrying, leading, or riding away of property from the possession or constructive possession of another.

constructive possession

The condition in which a person does not have physical custody or possession but is in a position to exercise dominion or control over a thing.

grand larceny

The theft of an item or merchandise of significant value.

petit (petty) larceny

The theft of property of little value.

FIGURE **12.1**

**How Do People Steal?
Reported Larceny Offenses
by Type**

Source: U.S. Department of Justice,
Federal Bureau of Investigation, Criminal
Justice Information Services Division,
Crime in the United States, 2009.

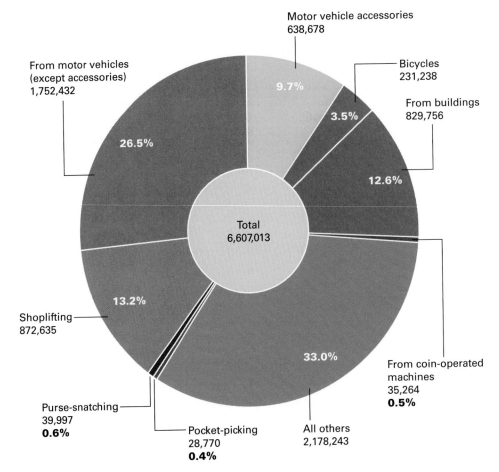

According to data gathered by the National Crime Victimization Survey (NCVS), larceny is the most frequent property offense. In the sections to come, we will take a closer look at specific forms of larceny theft in greater detail, in an effort to understand the different categories of theft, the various methods by which individuals steal, and the motives behind their crimes. Figure 12.1 shows the breakdown of different larceny types reported to police.

Describing Larceny

Why do people steal? How can individuals justify taking something that does not belong to them, cheating the rightful owner? Larceny is one of the few categories of criminal behavior to which criminologists try to attach a rational motive, perhaps because people readily understand that everyone needs material goods so there must be a reason for taking them.[11]

However, it seems that thieves apply reasoning to the specific decisions they make about the crime, rather than to the decision to commit it in the first place. For example, a thief may evaluate a store's security system or note its hours of operation. But we must also understand the crime of larceny within the social context of the offender's character and experiences, in order to grasp whether the goal is **expressive gain,** such as thrill or peer approval, or **instrumental gain,** such as to meet a need or support a lavish lifestyle. Contrast, for example, the thefts committed by Lucy, a successful Detroit businesswoman and mother of three, who admittedly stole for the thrill and high that it gave her, with the thefts of the millionaire shoplifter, who stole goods from various stores and returned the items for cash with fake receipts, accumulating enough money over the years to wear designer clothes, stay at luxury hotels, and dine in the top restaurants.[12]

expressive gain

Motivation for larceny, such as stealing for a thrill or to gain peer approval.

instrumental gain

Motivation for larceny, such as to meet a need or support a lavish lifestyle.

The crime of larceny is largely motivated by individual traits such as intelligence and personality; situational factors such as financial need, peer pressure and drug dependency; and contextual variables such as opportunity and the availability of a vulnerable victim.[13] These variables also affect the specific type of larceny that an offender commits.

Understanding Larceny

We explore the dynamics behind larceny further by taking a closer look at the specific categories, beginning with shoplifting.

Shoplifting

The term **shoplifting** describes the theft of merchandise from a retail store. Shoplifters commonly steal items such as jewelry, clothes, cosmetics, accessories, electronics, and small appliances they can easily conceal on their bodies—in pockets, under clothing, or in a purse. While there is no typical profile of a shoplifter, a University of Florida study challenges popular stereotypes of shoplifters being females, arguing that men are more likely to steal than women.[14] Moreover, people who steal from stores come from diverse backgrounds and can be of any age, ethnic group, race, and socioeconomic background.[15] The popular idea that shoplifters suffer from some type of mental disorder—kleptomania—that makes them compulsively steal is a myth. It is also untrue that shoplifters steal out of desperation or a need to survive. Most can actually afford to pay for the items they are stealing.

One groundbreaking study found the overwhelming majority of shoplifters were amateur or casual thieves who simply steal items for their own personal use. This category of shoplifters, commonly referred to as **snitches** by thieves, are generally law-abiding citizens who are not associated with a criminal lifestyle. A small minority of shoplifters are professional thieves or **boosters,** who make part of their living by stealing merchandise they can easily resell to pawnshops or fences.[16]

Shoplifting appears to be pervasive among juvenile offenders. Research findings indicate that two-thirds of juveniles admit to have shoplifted at some point in their life.[17] Some young people view shoplifting as an expected part of adolescence. A Finnish study concluded that shoplifting is a form of deviant behavior among teens who give in to temptation under the effects of weakened ties to social control.[18] They are usually motivated by peer pressure, lack of money, defiance or challenge to authority, and the excitement of getting away with it.

Regardless of the offender's characteristics and motive, shoplifting is a serious crime that costs retailers billions of dollars a year. According to the 19th Annual Retail Theft Survey conducted by Hayes International Consulting Firm on 23 major retail stores, 463,682 shoplifters were apprehended in 2006 for stealing nearly $60 million in goods. Table 12.1 provides a summary of the findings.

Credit Card Fraud

Another form of larceny is credit card fraud, which occurs when someone illegally accesses data associated with someone else's credit card, either by physically stealing the card from a wallet or purse, or accessing the credit card number during a legitimate transaction between a customer and merchant. The growth of online shopping has also contributed to security breaches in credit card databases, allowing thieves to illegally access customer accounts and use information to make unauthorized purchases.[19]

In 2008, a computer hacker gained access to data from Heartland Payment Systems involving over 600 banking institutions. The security breach was described as one of the biggest ever, compromising credit card information on over 100 million customers.[20]

If some people steal out of need and some for the rush, how might the presence of this video surveillance equipment affect a shoplifter's decision to steal?

shoplifting

The theft of merchandise from a retail store.

snitches

Amateur or casual shoplifters who steal items for their own personal use.

boosters

Shoplifters who are professional thieves who make their living by stealing merchandise they can easily resell to pawnshops or fences.

TABLE **12.1**

Shoplifting Trends in 2006: Incident and Cost at 23 Major Retailers		
TIME FRAME	COST	INCIDENTS
Annually	$11.22–$14.96 billion	224.4–299.2 million
Daily (365 days)	$30,739,700–$40,986,300	614,795–819,726
Hourly (24)	$1,280,821–$1,707,762	25,616–34,155
Per minute (60)	$21,347–$28,463	426.9–569.3

Source: Jack L. Hayes International. (2008). *Theft surveys.* Retrieved from http://www.hayesinternational.com/thft_srvys.html

check duplication or counterfeiting

Creating bogus financial documents with sophisticated desktop publishing software, or by altering a real check using solvents to remove or change information.

forgery

Falsely altering a document, usually a check, and presenting it for cash or payment using false identification.

If this bank teller took some of the money in the cash drawers, why would that type of stealing be considered embezzlement?

This form of credit card fraud is more costly because of the large amount of information compromised. It can also be more difficult to detect, because a perpetrator might hold a compromised account for several weeks before using it. Physical theft of a credit card holds greater risk for the thief, because the victim is likely to quickly discover the theft and immediately report and cancel the missing card.

Check Fraud

One of the biggest challenges to businesses and financial institutions is a category of larceny that includes the fraudulent use of checks. Individuals and gangs often carry out **check duplication,** also called **counterfeiting,** by creating bogus financial documents with sophisticated desktop publishing software, or by altering real checks using solvents such as bleach or acetone to remove or change the information.[21]

Forgery usually follows a purse snatching or pick-pocketing in which the thief steals a check, alters it, and presents it for cash or payment at a retail store using false identification. The crime of check forgery includes altering the payee, increasing the value of the check, altering the account number, and forging the signature of the legitimate check holder.[22] The majority of check forgers are amateur criminals who respond to an immediate cash flow crisis by committing a criminal act. The law usually requires that the person presenting the check know it is forged, proving intent to defraud or steal through deception, and that the forgery results in or has the possibility of resulting in loss to someone else.

Embezzlement

Embezzlement is a unique form of larceny that violates the trust of an employer when the property stolen is in the rightful possession of the perpetrator, who has the permission or consent of the owner.[23] A bank teller is entrusted with money that belongs to the bank's customers, for instance; any violation of that trust in order to commit theft is embezzlement. The crime can be a sophisticated theft of a large sum planned for months or years, or it can be repeated thefts of small amounts over time.

In one common type of embezzlement, employees underreport company income and pocket the difference. In 2005, for example, several managers from Aramark Corporation, an international food service company, were implicated in an embezzlement scheme to underreport revenues from vending machines at various customer sites. The amount taken from each machine was small, but over time the total was significant.

Embezzlement schemes are often uncovered through financial audits. Table 12.2 provides a summary of personal and organizational indicators businesses use to detect the fraudulent activities of employees. We will take another look at this crime in Chapter 14.

embezzlement

A unique form of larceny that violates the trust of an employer; the property stolen is in the rightful possession of the perpetrator, who has the permission or consent of the owner.

False Pretenses or Fraud

In a larceny perpetrated by **false pretenses or fraud,** the perpetrator uses lies and deception to trick the victim out of his or her money or property, usually by misrepresenting the nature, value, or characteristics of the merchandise.[24] The offender must know the information is false and intend to defraud. Suppose a baseball card trader offers an original autographed Babe Ruth card to a collector who later discovers the signature is not authentic. The merchant who sold the card must be shown to know it was a fake and to have sold it with intent to deceive in order for a charge of fraud to be valid.

Nondisclosure of information can also constitute false pretense. A landowner selling property as commercially zoned who has prior knowledge that it will be converted to agricultural purposes, significantly decreasing its value, is guilty of false pretense. Concealing facts that should be disclosed is a form of fraudulent misrepresentation, because the information could have been an important factor in the buyer's decision.

false pretense or fraud

A form of larceny in which the perpetrator uses lies and deception to trick the victim out of money or property, usually by misrepresenting the nature, value, or characteristics of merchandise.

Confidence Games

Confidence games, also known as *cons, scams,* and *swindles,* are schemes devised to trick or cheat unsuspecting victims out of their money by gaining their trust. Anybody can fall prey to an experienced con artist. The essential component of a con game is to gain

confidence games

Also known as cons, scams, and swindles, schemes devised to trick or cheat unsuspecting victims out of their money by gaining their trust.

TABLE **12.2**

Possible Indicators of Embezzlement
Individual
■ Financial troubles, loss of income
■ Sudden change in financial situations/unexplained wealth
■ Declining trend in performance of job
■ Change in mood or personality
■ Deviation from work-related policies and procedures
■ Interests in outside or competing businesses
■ Variations in work attendance/hours/vacation time
Organizational
■ Poor internal management
■ High rate of employee turnover
■ Out of balance accounts
■ Missing/out of sequence documents
■ Inconsistent billing practices
■ Customer complaints about monetary discrepancies

Source: Linker, S. A. (2006). Embezzlement: What? Who? Why? How? Detection!! Prevention!! *It's All About Money.* M & K Rosenfarb. Retrieved from http://www.envoynews.com/rwcpas/e_article000514029. cfm?x=b11,0,w

Televangelist Jim Bakker
and his wife Tammy Faye
operated a nonprofit religious organization called
Praise the Lord (PTL) that
eventually became its
own television network in
the late 1970s, with over
12 million viewers. Con-
tributions solicited from
dedicated supporters and
compassionate viewers to
advance the mission and
activities of the PTL organization were estimated to
exceed $1 million a week.
The couple lived a lavish
and extravagant lifestyle.
In 1988, Jim Bakker was
indicted on 24 counts of
conspiracy and fraud for
personal gain. How is
this case an example of a
confidence game?

phishing

A high-tech scam wherein identity
thieves posing as legitimate
financial institutions, government
agencies, or retail stores solicit
personal information from
unsuspecting customers via the
telephone or through e-mail.

the confidence of the "mark" or target in order to get him or her to buy into the scheme, which is often built around the victim's particular vulnerability.

Some schemes such as the one perpetrated by televangelists Jim and Tammy Faye Bakker are designed to prey upon the weak, naïve, trusting, and compassionate.[25] (See Consider This for more on religious cons.) Other types take advantage of individuals who are themselves greedy and dishonest. Nigerian letter scams work this way. Blinded by their own greed, victims are sucked in by the promise of millions of dollars from a supposedly wealthy Nigerian official trying to move large sums of money from his homeland. All the victim has to do is pay several thousand dollars in bribes up front, and millions will later be transferred into his or her account, of which the victim will get to keep a large percentage. After paying his or her portion, however, the victim never hears from the wealthy foreigner again.[26]

Modern technology has allowed confidence games to take on new power, as widespread use of the Internet and telemarketing enterprises have led to the growth of high-tech frauds that are costly and difficult to detect. One common technique is known as **phishing,** wherein identity thieves posing as legitimate financial institutions, government agencies, or retail stores solicit personal information such as Social Security numbers or bank account numbers from unsuspecting customers via the telephone or through e-mail.

Different types of common confidence games have developed over the years. Here are some examples.

Romance Fraud   In this type of scheme, the perpetrator takes advantage of a widow or other lonely victim and enters his or her life as a friend and lover with the goal of cultivating a romantic relationship. Having gained the victim's absolute trust, perhaps with the promise of commitment and marriage in return for help meeting some financial hardship, the con artist then drains the victim financially, often leaving him or her penniless. Romance fraud has spread to Internet dating as well.

A group of convicts and complicit prison guards of the Louisiana State Penitentiary in Angola, Louisiana, perpetrated their own version of romance fraud when they found a way to bilk lonely men and women out of thousands of dollars through a phony personals ad scam. When single people responded to the ads, letters would immediately be sent back that included a photo and requested money. The FBI got wise to the setup, and

Religious Confidence Games: The Ideal Scam?

The successful execution of a confidence game depends almost exclusively on the con artist's ability to deceive a vulnerable victim or victims, often by invoking their own moral values and beliefs to spur them to action. Having gained the victim's commitment to the specific cause, the criminal must ensure it continues, no matter how much money and resources he or she demands in exchange for promised benefits and rewards.

Religious confidence games that rely on the promise of divine intervention and supernatural powers for driving a supposedly charitable cause are thus an ideal scheme.[27] The con artist is established as a moral leader who has some type of unique and special connection to a sainted being or to God, who directly charges followers with supporting the leader in order to sustain the mission. Failure to comply is seen as defiance or sin.

To be successful, however, the confidence game must also have some payoff to sustain followers over the long run, which makes religious confidence games even more attractive. Many such schemes solicit money from unsuspecting victims with the promise to use it for some charitable cause such as feeding the hungry, treating disease, or spreading the "good news" to impoverished communities around the world. Very often, these funds are difficult to track, especially by followers convinced of their leader's moral integrity, and can easily be diverted to the pockets of those running the scam.

Victims are convinced of the intrinsic rewards of being the chosen followers and will seek no other material benefit. Often these intrinsic rewards include the leader's personal intervention on behalf of dedicated members, to communicate their own personal needs to God and to carry out divine healing, deliverance from sin, and release from financial hardship or addiction. Is it possible for individuals to be that gullible? Are religious confidence games the ideal scam?

What do you think?

eventually investigators found the scheme originated with convicted murderer and Angola inmate Kirksey McCord Nix Jr.[28]

Get-Rich-Quick Schemes   Get-rich-quick schemes are quite diverse and often rely on selling fake franchises or real estate, soliciting funds for bogus inventions, selling shares of hopeless business ventures, investing in useless or faulty merchandise, and participating in phony insider gambling or stock market trades. The perpetrator hopes any victim who uncovers the swindle will be too embarrassed or too fearful of being implicated to report the loss.

This was the case in 1921 when Charles Ponzi dreamed up a scheme to cash in on foreign-to-U.S. currency exchange rates. He told investors he would purchase and trade in international mail coupons and reap them a 40 percent return in just 90 days. Ponzi received over $1 million from interested investors in less than three hours! He used the money from later investors to pay off earlier ones in order to make the scheme appear legitimate. This is where we get the term "Ponzi" scheme, still used today to describe similar get-rich-quick plans that rely on eager investors, such as the ruinous fraud operated by financier Bernard Madoff and exposed in 2008.[29]

Charity Swindles   Some swindles rely on the sympathies of the public to solicit money for some type of good cause. They can be as simple as a panhandler who displays a sign about being hungry or unemployed, or as sophisticated as the operations of television evangelists who set up nonprofit organizations and plead to viewers to help support their ministry, supposedly dedicated to hunger and disaster relief across the world.

CATCH—Care and Action Trust for Children with Handicaps—fell apart in 2002 when it was found that two women and three men running the organization had stolen over $1 million in charity funds by preying on compassionate people who thought they were helping sick children. After an investigation found accounting issues and a large amount of disguised donations, charges were brought against the group including theft, failure to pay taxes, and abuse of gift aid.[30]

extortion

The use of threats or blackmail to obtain money or something of value from someone.

Extortion **Extortion** is the use of threats or blackmail to obtain money or something of value from someone. This often happens, for example, when a married man or woman (usually a man) is seduced into a sexual encounter with the intent of photographing or filming the victim in a compromising situation and threatening him or her with exposure unless a specified amount of money is paid.

Extortion is also often perpetrated on the rich and famous, such as when former Bahamian parliament member Pleasant Bridgewater and emergency medical technician (EMT) Tarino Lightbourne allegedly conspired to extort $25 million from U.S. actors John Travolta and Kelly Preston over the death of their 16-year-old son Jett in December 2008. Jett was prone to seizures, and EMTs were called to the residence where the Travoltas were vacationing in the Bahamas after he apparently suffered a seizure that caused him to fall and hit his head on the bathtub. Travolta originally wanted to fly his son back to the United States in a private jet—which would take approximately 20 minutes—instead of waiting 45 minutes for his son to be transported to the nearest Bahamian hospital and allegedly signed a document to that effect. Bridgewater and Lightbourne, one of the EMTs responding to the scene, reportedly wanted to use this document to bribe the Travoltas, through their lawyers, in return for their silence.[31]

Purposeful Accidents A purposeful accident occurs when the perpetrator deliberately sets up the victim to have a car accident, especially to hit the perpetrator from behind, and then fakes injuries in order to collect money from the victim's insurance company. Purposeful accident schemes often require the collaboration and cooperation of a physician or chiropractor who can verify the injuries claimed and document treatment in exchange for payment.

Purposeful accident schemes usually involve the collaboration or assistance of various individuals who can corroborate the story or use their expertise to verify an accident or injury. This is seen in the case of tow truck driver Jerry Blassengale Jr. who submitted approximately two dozen fake accident and vandalism claims to 11 different insurance companies over the course of almost five years. Using phony accident reports he bought from ex-Philadelphia highway patrolman Drexel Reid Jr., in addition to dishonest drivers he recruited to report the accidents, Blassengale was able to fraudulently receive over half a million dollars from insurers. In April 2009 he was sentenced to 87 months in prison and ordered to pay his victims more than $400,000.[32]

Receiving and Fencing Stolen Property

Purchasing items and thinking we "got a steal" is very different from buying property we know is really stolen. Receiving and fencing property acquired through theft or extortion by someone else is a separate crime from actually stealing the property in question. To be convicted of a crime, the receiver must know the goods exchanged were stolen at the time they were received. The fact that the buyer paid for the property is not a valid defense. Moreover, the court assumes an element of premeditation is involved when the thief disposes of the stolen items by selling them to someone else.

professional fence

A person who earns a living by purchasing and reselling stolen merchandise to merchants who turn around and market these items to legitimate customers.

Individuals are usually well aware the goods they purchase are stolen. These items, often sold on the street, out of car trunks, or at flea markets, are often grossly discounted, are in secondhand condition or obviously used, and are unavailable for purchase through legitimate avenues (legally sold), such as weapons.

The **professional fence** earns a living by purchasing and reselling stolen merchandise to merchants who turn around and market these items to legitimate customers.[33] The public also plays an important role in the perpetuation of this form of theft. The emphasis on material goods and the rising cost of merchandise from retail stores turn individuals in the direction of always looking for a bargain. This is also facilitated by the buying and selling of goods over the convenient and anonymous avenue of the Internet.[34]

Researcher Darrell Steffensmeier conducted an in-depth study of a professional fence who purchased a variety of stolen goods from different suppliers, including burglars, shoplifters, robbers, and other criminal offenders.[35] Steffensmeier identifies several characteristics of a successful fence:

- An adequate and steady supply of available cash for all transactions
- Familiarity with the rules, norms, and procedures governing the buying and selling of stolen property
- Long-term relationships with well-known, trustworthy, and reliable suppliers
- Access to merchants such as pawnbrokers who are continuous customers
- Relationships with local law enforcement in order to avoid detection, perhaps by acting as an informant in particularly important cases or paying cash or merchandise bribes

The diverse forms of theft we have discussed so far all share one common factor—the legitimate presence of the perpetrators at the place of the theft. Whether at a grocery store, in the mall, at work, or in the basement, an alley, or a friend's house, they have a legal right to be there. We turn now to a form of theft that includes unlawful access to the place of theft: the crime of burglary.

burglary

Any unlawful entry into a structure for the purpose of committing a theft or felony.

trespassing

An unlawful entry into a structure in which the offender does not necessarily possess criminal intent.

What specific elements of this crime make it a burglary?

BURGLARY

Burglary is any unlawful entry into a structure for the purpose of committing a theft or felony. The structure can be a home, office, retail store, or some other type of building.[36] The entry can either be forced, such as kicking down a door or breaking a lock, or it can involve no force at all, such as jumping through an open window or fraudulently obtaining a key or security code. The majority of burglaries are completed without the use of forced entry (Figure 12.2).

An individual can be charged with the crime of burglary based solely on intent to commit the crime, without actually completing it. For example, if Fred breaks into a restaurant to steal cash from a safe but discovers it is empty and leaves, Fred can be charged with a burglary. Burglary can also include unlawful entry for the purpose of committing a felony, such as breaking into someone's apartment to commit an assault or rape. This is what distinguishes burglary from **trespassing,** in which the offender does not necessarily possess criminal intent. Jan may come home drunk one evening, for example, and accidentally wander into the neighbor's house without any intent to commit a theft or felony. Jan has committed trespass, not burglary.

Describing Burglary

Burglary is very different from larceny in the characteristics of offenders and situational elements of the crime. The main difference is that burglary includes illegal access to the location of the theft, whereas larceny is committed while the offender has lawful access to the place where the crime is committed. If Ray steals from a retail store during regular business hours, he is committing a larceny. If he comes back after closing and forces entry into the store for the purpose of theft, he has committed a burglary.

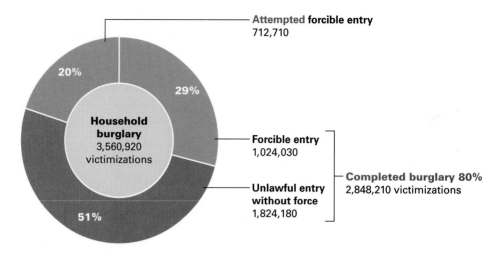

FIGURE **12.2**

How Are Burglaries Accomplished? Burglary Rates by Type of Entry

Source: Criminal victimization in the United States, 2006. (2008). National Crime Victimization Survey. Washington, DC: Bureau of Justice Statistics, U.S. Department of Justice.

Moreover, burglary is predominantly perpetrated by male offenders.[37] This trend is largely influenced by the availability of potential targets for male offenders through jobs they tend to fill, such as carpenters, television cable installers, and gardeners. Studies also show that women who commit this type of property crime do so under the coercive effects of a boyfriend or other male. Sometimes, they are unaware of what is going on until it is too late.[38]

Burglary is also distinct from robbery in being inherently evasive and nonconfrontational.[39] The majority of burglaries occur with the foreknowledge that residents will be away, buildings empty, or retail stores closed. However, the consequences of burglary on victims can be just as devastating. Their loss goes beyond the monetary value of the stolen items, since the invasive nature of burglary often leaves them with a sense of being personally violated, fearful, and apprehensive. Sometimes stolen items have sentimental value that represents an additional loss.

Even though the property crime rate in the United States is lower than in most industrialized countries, theft by burglary is a fairly prevalent crime (see Crime in Global Perspective), with studies showing 72 percent of households being victimized at least once over the course of a lifetime.[40] The number of burglaries reported to the police has been steadily declining over the past decade, however (Figure 12.3). The national burglary rate of 722.5 burglaries per 100,000 inhabitants in 2007 represents one of the lowest rates since the mid-1960s. Despite the shortcomings of UCR data discussed in Chapter 3, this trend is consistent with data gathered by victimization surveys.[41]

Police reports allow us to classify burglaries according to their location and time of day. Table 12.3 describes the four distinct categories that emerge when we do so; note how the

FIGURE **12.3**

U.S. Burglary Rates, 1988–2007

Source: Federal Bureau of Investigation. (2008). *Crime in the United States, 2007.* U.S. Department of Justice.

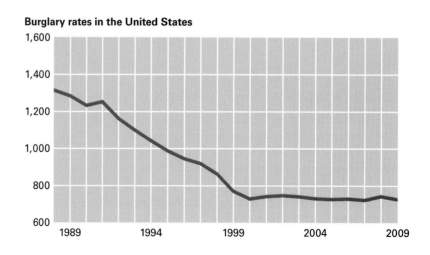

CRIME IN GLOBAL PERSPECTIVE | Burglary Trends in the United States and the United Kingdom

The property crime rate in the United States has been on a steady decline since 1990. According to the FBI's Uniform Crime Reports, arrests for burglary, larceny theft, motor vehicle theft, and arson have all decreased to the lowest number in two decades. This trend is mirrored by the Department of Justice's National Crime Victimization Survey (NCVS), which has collected crime data from U.S. households since 1973.[42] While some property crime trends such as motor vehicle theft have gone down considerably—there were nearly 60,000 fewer such thefts in 2009 than in 2008 for an 8.5 percent decrease—other property crimes such as burglary have only inched downward. Still, the overall trend in U.S. property crime rates has been a steady and continuous decline. How do these rates compare with other countries?

The United Kingdom uses similar statistical gathering methods, including the official crime data gathered by the police, as well as victim surveys such as the British Crime Survey.[43] According to their figures, property crimes are similarly declining, although the United Kingdom has a much higher rate of property crimes overall. For example, the U.S. burglary rate was 726.9 per 100,000 inhabitants for 2009; the U.K. rate was 902.4 that year.[44]

Some experts note that the difference in burglary rate between the United Kingdom and the United States is attributed to the difference in sentencing practices between the two countries for that specific crime. Suspects accused of burglary are more likely to be convicted of this crime in the United States than in the United Kingdom. Moreover, offenders convicted for the crime of burglary in England face fewer sanctions than their U.S. counterparts, such as having their prison term suspended in exchange for a period of community supervision.

Another possibility is the vastly different crime-fighting strategies employed by police in the United Kingdom as opposed to the United States. The U.S. has various well-established community-oriented policing strategies and programs, such as Neighborhood Watch and Crime Stoppers. While these programs differ from police department to police department, city to city, and state to state, their central focus is to encourage citizens to become involved with local law enforcement to help stop crime in their neighborhoods; residents become more aware of crime and crime suspects, provide police with tips to assist with investigation and apprehension, and are less reluctant to get involved with fighting crime in their neighborhood.

In contrast, the U.K. crime-fighting strategy is a national effort, including several programs: the Home Office Crime Strategy, the National Community Safety Plan, and the Prolific and Other Priority Offenders Strategy.[45] Collectively, these strategies approach crime control from the perspective of targeting the small group of offenders committing the greatest and most serious amount of crime.

rates for these categories differ. Nighttime residential and daytime commercial burglaries are considered the most serious categories, because offenders are more likely to run into residents at home at night and to encounter customers or workers in commercial settings during the day. Let's take a closer look at the crime of burglary, in order to better understand the various situational dynamics and patterns of offending that make up the four categories.

Understanding Burglary

We can best understand burglary as a combination of three components: offense specialization, offender motivation, and routine activities. Let's begin by examining offense specialization.

Offense Specialization

Studies focusing on **offense specialization** examine the degree to which burglars are highly skilled professional thieves or spontaneous, low-level criminal offenders. One study examined the criminal records of 2,000 convicted burglars and found the majority followed a pattern of repeat offending over a wide range of criminal activities, including

offense specialization

The degree to which burglars are highly skilled professional thieves or spontaneous, low-level criminal offenders.

TABLE **12.3**

Four Categories of Burglary		
	TIME OF DAY	
LOCATION	*DAYTIME*	*NIGHTTIME*
Residential	Daytime residential	Nighttime residential
Commercial	Daytime commercial	Nighttime commercial

Source: Miethe, T. D., McCorkle, R. C., & Listwan, S. (2006). *Crime profiles: The anatomy of dangerous persons, places, and situations.* Los Angeles: Roxbury.

burglary, robbery, assault, drug-related offenses, and other forms of larceny theft.[46] Thus, their burglary did not follow a pattern of specialization but rather was connected to a more general pattern of predatory behavior.

Researcher Mike Maguire offers three typologies of burglars based on the level of sophistication and planning behind the crime.[47] *Low-level burglars* are often younger offenders who commit burglary in a spontaneous, opportunistic manner. They perpetrate residential and commercial thefts by taking advantage of certain situations such as an open window, an unlocked door, or easy accessibility and are generally deterred by the presence of locks, alarms, and other security devices. They usually get away with a minimal amount of goods, since they have few connections to organized groups that can manage large quantities of stolen items. *Middle-range burglars* are a bit more sophisticated and often engage in other illegitimate pursuits such as drug use. They employ a greater degree of planning, selecting a target by weighing the risk and potential payoff, but still lack the type and level of criminal connections necessary to pull off the major, large-scale operations of high-level burglars.

High-level burglars are professional thieves who commit their crimes as a way of life. They are highly skilled in their planning, techniques, and methods of evading detection. They earn a reasonable amount of income as professional thieves, sometimes engaging in large-scale thefts at retail stores and other sellers of expensive goods such as jewelry, art, and other collectibles. On August 7, 2008, an organized gang of five was convicted in the United Kingdom after stealing $160 million worth of art and antiquities from homes in

In *Thick as Thieves,* a 2009 film about a jewel heist, Morgan Freeman plays the role of veteran crook Keith Ripley, who describes himself to the novice thief Gabriel Martin (Antonio Banderas) as "born to steal." Are most burglars professional thieves?

several counties. One of their raids had netted 300 museum-quality artworks, including a 17th-century painting worth an estimated $133 million.[48] High-level burglars often work in organized groups, with inside information about targets, surveillance, and police activity that facilitates planning.

Offender Motivation

The motivations of criminal offenders who commit burglary include a variety of instrumental and expressive rationales that have become the subject of much criminological research.[49] In the rational choice perspective, the primary goal of burglary is economic gain.[50] Studies in fact show that the most prevalent reason for residential burglary is the immediate need for cash.[51] Rather than meeting basic needs for food and shelter, however, the cash allows a certain criminal status, level of comfort, or lavish lifestyle, or it supports a gambling habit or drug addiction.[52]

Commercial burglaries often seem even more deeply driven by instrumental, rational decision processes than residential burglaries, as evidenced by professional burglars who go to great lengths in planning, strategizing, and evaluating potential risks and economic gains when selecting their targets. Criminals often choose burglary as an easier and safer means to obtain money than selling drugs or committing a robbery, both of which can result in greater penalties and more confrontation with the victim.[53]

These calculating and carefully weighed decisions seem to be the primary motivations for the majority of offenders.[54] However, a small portion of burglars identifies excitement and thrill as their motivators.[55] For them, burglary provides a level of stimulation above the ordinary activities of everyday life. The crime therefore fulfills an expressive need beyond economic gain. Some burglaries are also motivated by other expressive goals such as revenge, intoxication, and peer pressure.[56] Here, the crime takes on a new meaning associated with a riskier, more opportunistic pattern of offending.

The Environment and Routine Activities

Routine activities theory emphasizes the effects of environmental and lifestyle variables.[57] According to this approach, a burglary is made possible by three interacting components: (1) a motivated offender who wants something; (2) a suitable victim who has what the offender wants and is at the right place at the right time; and (3) the lack of a capable individual or appropriate measure to protect the targeted victim.

These dynamics help us to better understand the increase in burglaries on college campuses throughout the United States. In September 2008, police arrested 20-year-old Michael Worrell for burglarizing several residence halls at State University College at Oswego, New York. Worrell apparently entered dormitories and walked into students' unlocked rooms, stealing cell phones, laptops, iPods, and other items of value. He was not a student at the college, but he apparently knew what he wanted to steal, where he could find it, and the behavior of college students.[58]

We've seen that offenders can have a variety of motivations to commit a burglary, from instrumental goals such as material gain to expressive goals such as revenge and thrill. Moreover, they can be planners or opportunistic actors and will thus select a suitable victim for different reasons that take into consideration the following variables:

- *Knowledge and convenience:* Does the target minimize the time and effort needed to accomplish the burglary? Is the target close by and the offender possessed of the familiarity and techniques needed?
- *Barriers and obstacles:* Does the target present potential barriers such as the presence of occupants, security guards, elaborate gates, fences, and alarms? Routine activities theory argues that the lifestyle and daily activities of individuals contribute significantly to their level of vulnerability. One study found that the majority of burglaries in apartment complexes occupied predominantly by college students occurred when the students were attending class, shopping, or participating in recreational activities.[59]

CONNECTING THEORY TO PRACTICE

Burglary and Routine Activities Theory

The role of criminology in understanding crime goes beyond trying to discover why some individuals commit crime while others do not. We have learned that an array of psychological, social, and cultural variables drive offenders' constraints and opportunities, giving us a broader insight into why some individuals and some places are more likely to experience crime than others.[60]

Insights from routine activities theory allow us to predict the effect when motivated offenders and criminal opportunities exist within certain contexts. Thus, we can develop strategies to reduce specific types of crime. One major effort to reduce burglary relies on "target hardening" or crime prevention through environmental design (CPTED), to strengthen the ability of a neighborhood or community to reduce its risk as a target for burglars.[61] Steps include organizing neighborhood watch groups, educating citizens about behavior patterns that can increase the likelihood of victimization, creating barriers such as security alarms and fences, ensuring doors and windows are locked during appropriate times, and removing trees and bushes that can serve as hiding places for potential burglars.

Strategies like these—that take into consideration situational factors, the routine activities of both potential victims and offenders, and the vulnerability of potential targets—will undoubtedly have a significant impact.

- *Expected gains:* Do the potential rewards of the burglary outweigh the risks? Burglars assess the possibility that the selected target will have items of value such as computers, television sets, jewelry, and money that are easy to remove, have a high resale value, and can readily be fenced. Burglary has become a more lucrative enterprise for potential offenders as advances in technology have produced attractive, expensive, easily carried electronic items and gadgets.
- *Absence of security:* Does the burglary site lack a law enforcement officer or security guard, an alert neighbor, a neighborhood watch group, or a guard dog? Burglars may even be deterred by having lights on at night.

Routine activities theory provides us with a theoretical foundation upon which to build crime-prevention strategies geared at altering the structure of opportunity within which burglaries occur. The Connecting Theory to Practice feature discusses the policy implications of routine activity theory.

MOTOR VEHICLE THEFT

motor vehicle theft

The theft or attempted theft of a motor vehicle, including cars, trucks, buses, motorcycles, snowmobiles, and some other methods of transportation.

carjacking

Stealing a car by using force or the threat of force.

The FBI defines **motor vehicle theft** as the theft or attempted theft of a motor vehicle, which includes cars, trucks, buses, motorcycles, snowmobiles, and some other methods of transportation.[62] The theft of boats, airplanes, and construction or farming vehicles is excluded, as is taking a motor vehicle for temporary use by someone with lawful access to it. Theft of equipment or items *inside* a motor vehicle is considered larceny, not motor vehicle theft. Stealing someone's car by using force or the threat of force is also not considered motor vehicle theft but rather is a specific form of robbery known as **carjacking**.

Describing Motor Vehicle Theft

The seriousness of motor vehicle theft goes beyond the loss of property. While there is no immediate threat of danger or harm to an individual, there are long-term effects and hardships in losing such a valuable possession and going through the steps required to replace it.

The rate of motor vehicle theft has been steadily declining over the past decade; there were approximately 1.1 million motor vehicle thefts in the United States in 2007.[63] Over 58 percent of motor vehicle thefts occur at or near the victim's home, and the most commonly stolen motor vehicle is, of course, a car. It is thus understandable, considering the value of the loss, that the rate of reporting motor vehicle theft to police is high compared to other types of property crimes (Table 12.4). As with most other offense categories, the reporting percentage is higher for completed thefts (89.0 percent) than for attempted ones (48.8 percent). While the rate of victimization is fairly similar across household income, the rate of reporting increases with the level of household income.

Understanding Motor Vehicle Theft

The majority of stolen vehicles are recovered by the police or the owner, which makes it a bit puzzling to understand why the theft occurred in the first place.[64] Why do people steal motor vehicles? Who are these offenders and what is their motivation? We turn now to a closer look at the crime of motor vehicle theft, with a specific focus on four patterns of offending: joyriding, commercial theft, transportation, and the commission of other crimes.

Joyriding

Joyriding is considered an expressive act committed by teenagers, mostly boys, as a means of fulfilling a desire for fun or thrills by temporarily stealing a motor vehicle.[65] Typically, youth who engage in this type of crime are seeking excitement and peer approval.

joyriding

An expressive act committed by teenagers, mostly boys, as a means of fulfilling a desire for fun or thrills by temporarily stealing a motor vehicle.

TABLE **12.4**

Reporting Crime Victimization to the Police: How Does Motor Vehicle Theft Compare?

TYPE OF CRIME	NUMBER OF VICTIMIZATIONS	PERCENT DISTRIBUTION OF VICTIMIZATIONS REPORTED TO POLICE
Household Burglary	1,762,740	49.5
Completed	1,438,740	50.5
Forcible Entry	727,880	71.1
Unlawful Entry, No Force	710,860	39.0
Attempted Forcible Entry	324,010	45.5
Larceny	4,581,650	31.9
Completed	4,418,580	32.0
Less than $50	662,560	17.3
$50–$249	1,285,490	26.0
$250 or more	2,096,210	56.4
Amount not available	374,310	28.6
Attempted	163,080	28.5
Motor Vehicle Theft	802,690	80.9
Completed	704,840	89.0
Attempted	97,850	48.8

Source: Criminal victimization in the United States, 2006. (2008). National Crime Victimization Survey, Bureau of Justice Statistics, U.S. Department of Justice.

Why do you suppose the majority of joyriding is perpetrated by younger offenders?

They lack the skill and sophistication of professional car thieves, and therefore their motivation has little to do with financial rewards or gains from the theft. Joyriding tends to be impulsive and spontaneous, often committed by groups, with each individual sharing in the excitement and validating the careless, risky behavior of the others.[66]

Criminologists Michael Gottfredson and Travis Hirschi note that joyriding is an opportunistic crime. The typical theft is unplanned and unstructured, taking place on the spur of the moment when a juvenile or group of teens stumbles upon a car in a public street or parking lot, unlocked or with its keys easily accessible.[67] Since they do not intend to keep the car or to use it for other purposes such as stealing parts, the youths usually abandon it somewhere when it either runs out of gas, breaks down, or is crashed, or when the thrill and excitement of the moment are gone.

Commercial Theft for Profit

The vehicle least likely to be recovered is the one taken in a commercial theft and usually either resold or stripped down for parts. Selling parts separately can be a much more lucrative transaction than selling a car whole, as parts are less easy to identify as stolen, and there is a greater underworld market where organized theft rings can traffic stolen stereo systems, tires, batteries, alarms, and other parts.[68] Commercial motor vehicle thieves must therefore develop a working relationship with criminal organizations, often called "chop shops," that can break the vehicle into parts for resale to unscrupulous auto-body shops, salvage yards, and other manufacturers of motor vehicle parts.[69]

A growing trend is the trafficking of stolen vehicles, especially to overseas export rings that operate sophisticated markets and recruit highly skilled professional thieves to steal for them. Most of these groups operate in foreign countries that do not have strict standards and guidelines for verifying vehicle identification numbers (VINs), owner titles, and car registration.[70]

Transportation

Occasionally, a motor vehicle thief will steal a car, often a luxury car, as a means of personal transportation for a short period of time or a specific event or occasion. Typically, these individuals will use the car to serve their own purposes or until it becomes too risky to keep it, at which time they will abandon it, unharmed or missing whatever they can remove with ease such as a radio or GPS system. These offenders are usually novice criminals and often leave a trail of fingerprints and other items that can make it easy for law enforcement to trace the theft back to them. As theft-prevention equipment and devices have become more advanced, however, offenders in need of a quick method of transportation have often turned to carjacking instead.

Commission of Other Crimes

Some offenders who steal cars do so to obtain a quick method of transportation when committing more serious crimes such as robberies, driveby shootings, and burglaries. A stolen car reduces the chances the crime will be traced to them through identification of the vehicle they used to flee the scene.

With the exception of joyriding, most motor vehicle thefts include some degree of planning and reasoning. Reducing theft thus begins with preventive measures that deter by making it more difficult, such as locking cars, taking the keys, and not leaving valuables in plain sight.[71] Alarms, wheel clamps, and electronic tracking systems also reduce accessibility and enhance security.[72] Although they do not address the root causes of the behavior, these measure make sense as prevention strategies. We turn now to a form of property crime that is less easy to understand, and even more difficult to solve: the crime of arson.

ARSON

Arson is the willful or malicious burning or attempted burning of a home, building, motor vehicle or airplane, or other personal property. According to the UCR, 14,197 law enforcement agencies reported 64,332 arsons in 2007, a 6.7 percent decrease from arson data reported in 2006.[73]

Describing Arson

Arson is a very serious crime punished severely all over the world because it puts lives at risk and causes great damage to property.[74] In 2007, the overall average dollar loss per incident due to arson in the United States was $17,289; arsons of industrial/manufacturing structures resulted in the greatest losses, averaging $114,699 each.[75] Arsons of structures account for the majority of offenses, with vehicle fires following (Figure 12.4). Moreover, according to the U.S. Fire Administration, an estimated 295 civilian deaths occurred in 2007 from intentionally set fires. Table 12.5 provides a summary of the number of fires, deaths, and dollar losses from arsons that occurred from 1998 to 2007.

arson

The willful or malicious burning or attempted burning of a home, building, motor vehicle or airplane, or other personal property.

FIGURE **12.4**

Distribution of Arsons in 2007: Type of Structure and How Much Damage

Source: Federal Bureau of Investigation. (2008). *Crime in the United States, 2007.* U.S. Department of Justice.

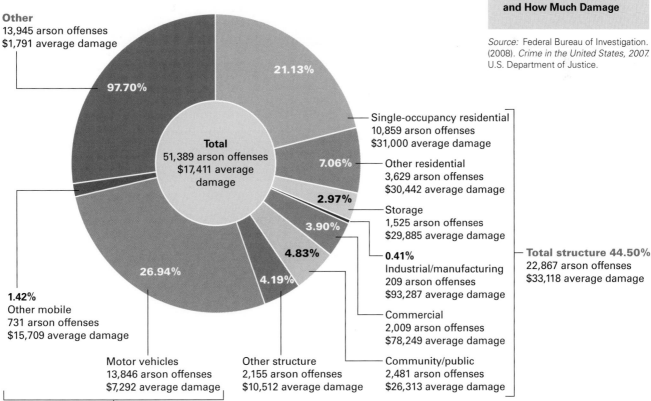

Other
13,945 arson offenses
$1,791 average damage

97.70%

21.13%

Total
51,389 arson offenses
$17,411 average damage

7.06%

2.97%

3.90%

4.83%

4.19%

26.94%

1.42%
Other mobile
731 arson offenses
$15,709 average damage

Single-occupancy residential
10,859 arson offenses
$31,000 average damage

Other residential
3,629 arson offenses
$30,442 average damage

Storage
1,525 arson offenses
$29,885 average damage

0.41%
Industrial/manufacturing
209 arson offenses
$93,287 average damage

Commercial
2,009 arson offenses
$78,249 average damage

Community/public
2,481 arson offenses
$26,313 average damage

Total structure 44.50%
22,867 arson offenses
$33,118 average damage

Motor vehicles
13,846 arson offenses
$7,292 average damage

Other structure
2,155 arson offenses
$10,512 average damage

Total mobile 28.37%
14,577 arson offenses
$7,715 average damage

Understanding Arson

Motives for arson can range from the very calculated rational decision making of profit-motivated offenders to the irrational fantasies of thrill-seeking offenders. The varied patterns of arson often make prevention strategies challenging (see the Connecting Research to Practice feature). We turn now to a discussion of the various categories of arson, in order to better understand the motivation behind this crime and the situational context within which it takes place.

Arsonists enjoy the thrill and attention that a fire can create. They like the feeling that they are responsible for the havoc and destruction, along with all the excitement.

TABLE **12.5**

Facts About Arson

YEAR	NUMBER OF FIRES	DEATHS	DOLLAR LOSS (MILLIONS)
1998	76,000	470	1,249
1999	72,000	370	1,281
2000	75,000	505	1,340
2001*	45,500	330	1,013
2002	44,500	350	919
2003	37,500	305	692
2004	36,500	320	714
2005	31,500	315	664
2006	31,000	305	755
2007	32,500	295	733

*Does not include the number of deaths, injuries, and dollar loss directly related to the events that took place on September 11, 2001.

Source: National Fire Protection Association, Overall Fire Statistics, *Fire Loss in the U.S., 2007.*

According to the Technical Working Group on Fire/Arson Scene Investigation, "the United States is one of the few countries where public authorities have statutory responsibility to investigate all fires and determine their origins and causes."[76] With nearly 21 arson fires occurring for every 100,000 people in the United States and more than 56,000 arsons in 2009, criminal justice research in this area is more important than ever.[77]

Research on arson indicates prevention requires three crucial steps: carefully investigating fires, observing conditions conducive to arson, and taking the profit out of a set fire. These principles have led to breakthroughs in arson prevention.[78]

Investigating

Arson is usually suspected only after all accidental possibilities have been ruled out, which means investigations may take longer. In 2000, the National Institute of Justice (NIJ) and the National Center for Forensic Justice (NCFS) created *Fire and Arson Scene Evidence: A Guide for Public Safety Personnel,* to clarify investigation procedures at arson scenes. It is currently being used as a training document across the country.[79]

Observing

Many security companies have installed surveillance equipment outside businesses where arson is likely to occur and have caught a number of arsonists on camera. In 2008, firefighter Michael Murphy was caught on tape lurking outside a Maryland restaurant minutes before smoke began pouring out; he was arrested on suspicion of arson.[80] Video makes for compelling evidence in a court of law and has proven to be a major factor in preventing arson-related crimes.

Taking the Profit out

Much arson is committed to cover up other crimes or to profit illegally, such as by insurance fraud.[81] Many insurance companies have programs to help stop arson committed by people trying to defraud them. Safeco Insurance, for example, has a hotline number for reporting suspected arson and will pay up to $25,000 for information leading to arson convictions in connection with fire loss to Safeco-insured property.[82] These measures are in response to a practice known as "fire brokering," in which an arsonist will seek out a dilapidated property, purchase it at low cost, then plan and commit the arson to collect an insurance payment. The most effective method for deterring arson-for-profit is to be aware of these schemes and refuse to provide policies under suspicious circumstances. Further research and improved surveillance technology will make us better prepared to prevent and deter future damage.[83]

Delinquent Fire-Setters

Delinquent fire-setters are typically younger adolescents exhibiting poor judgment and a lack of self-control.[84] They often set fires to schools or abandoned buildings and other hidden locations. Their primary motivation is mischief; their methods are fairly unsophisticated and marked by a desire to maliciously harm and rebel against authority.[85]

Pathological Fire-Setters

Pathological fire-setters have a long history of fire-setting behavior. It includes a highly sophisticated method of operation with a distinct, often ritualistic approach that leaves a path of destruction of which the arsonist becomes extremely proud.[86] Unlike most delinquent arsonists, pathological arsonists often suffer psychiatric difficulties and emotional conflicts that contribute to their fire-setting behavior. These individuals generally do not feel any remorse for their actions or the destruction they have caused. Their crime is a symptom of a generalized pattern of antisocial behavior and inability to identify with the feelings of others.[87]

Excitement-Seeking Fire-Setters

Fire setting to get a rush or thrill from its destructive power, to draw attention, or even to find sexual gratification is called excitement-seeking arson.[88] It is rarely intended to harm people or even create large-scale damage but rather serves an expressive purpose. A typical excitement-seeking fire-setter may start a fire then call for help or put it out, appearing as a hero to those around and often basking in the glory of the reaction to his or her accomplishment.

Revenge Fire-Setters

Some arsonists are motivated by a desire for revenge, or to right a wrong.[89] A girl breaks up with her boyfriend. He gets angry and sets her apartment on fire to get back at her. A contractor does some remodeling work in a customer's home and does not feel sufficiently reimbursed as agreed. He sets fire to the home to get even. This type of crime is usually carefully planned, with a very specific target. It can be a one-time event against a specific individual, or a series of fires over time to avenge a grievance or make a political statement to some type of organization such as a church or clinic, the government or military, or society in general.[90]

Instrumental Fire-Setters

Fire setting is often a secondary pattern of behavior to achieve the primary goals of material profit or personal gain. Personal gain is often the motive when arson is used to cover up a crime that has already taken place, such as burglary, motor vehicle theft, or homicide, in which the fire is an attempt to conceal fingerprints, blood stains, and other forensic evidence that can identify the offender.[91] The desire for material gain can also be a primary motive in the destruction of a property for the purpose of fraud or to collect insurance, conceal loss, or destroy documents. In both cases, instrumental arsons are very carefully planned to create a significant amount of destruction in order to achieve the intended purpose. This category of fire-setters is not likely to re-offend; once they have achieved their goal, the motive to set a fire no longer exists.

The diversity of motives behind each category of arson is indeed a testimony to the diverse nature of crimes against property. In each case, however, there is a distinct victim who suffers some form of emotional and financial loss or devastation. In the next chapter, we will turn to a category of criminal behavior where there is no such distinct victim and no clearly defined loss: the category of crimes against public order.

SUMMARY

■ **How do we categorize larceny theft?**

We divide larceny—the unlawful taking of property that belongs to someone else—into two categories, grand and petit (petty), based on the monetary value of the stolen goods. Each state draws the line between the two at a different value. Larceny crimes include purse snatching, pick-pocketing, shoplifting, stealing from motor vehicles, and embezzlement and fraud.

■ **Why do people steal?**

Larceny theft is driven by a variety of motives, ranging from the rationally calculated decision of offenders motivated by financial gain, to the impulsive choices made by offenders driven by expressive goals such as peer approval or thrill. Regardless of the motive, the nature and outcome of larceny are also linked to the offender's character, situational factors, and opportunity.

■ **In what ways is burglary different from robbery?**	Burglary is different from robbery in the characteristics of offenders and the situational elements of the crime. Burglary includes illegal access to the location of the theft, whereas robbery is committed while the offender has lawful access to the place where the crime is committed. Also, burglary is predominantly perpetrated by male offenders. Finally, burglary is also distinct from robbery in being inherently evasive and non-confrontational.
■ **What are the characteristics of burglary?**	In larceny the offender has lawful access to the place where the crime is committed, while burglary includes unlawful entry into a structure, with or without the use of force, for the purpose of committing a theft or felony. Patterns of offending include daytime residential burglary, nighttime residential burglary, daytime commercial burglary, and nighttime commercial burglary. We can best understand the elements of burglary as a combination of three variables: offense specialization, offender motivation, and routine activities.
■ **Who steals cars and why do they do it?**	Offenders steal motor vehicles for a variety of reasons: joyriding, commercial theft, transportation, and the commission of other crimes. Joyriding is the temporary theft of a car, usually by younger offenders motivated by a desire for thrill and mischievous adventure. Stealing a motor vehicle for the fun of it is very different from committing commercial theft and either reselling the car or stripping it down into parts to be sold in the black market. Some offenders steal luxury cars as a means of transportation to an event or occasion, while others use stolen vehicles as a quick means of transportation while committing a more serious crime.
■ **Are all fire-setters the same?**	The crime of arson, the willful or malicious burning or attempted burning of property, includes delinquent fire setting perpetrated by rebellious and mischievous youth, pathological fire setting where the arson represents a method of coping with some type of emotional stress or mental disorder, fire setting for excitement and revenge, and fire setting for profit or to cover up other crimes.

CRITICAL THINKING QUESTIONS

1. What characteristics differentiate the occasional from the professional thief? Can someone start as a petty thief and then turn to a career of theft? What variables may influence the likelihood of this outcome? Which deterrents would best prevent it?

2. Let's say you go into an antique store and pay top dollar for a rare item the merchant certifies as authentic. Weeks later, you discover it is merely a replica. When you go back, the merchant swears the store had no knowledge this item was not authentic. How do you resolve this dilemma? What type of theft is taking place here? Who might be implicated? Is the merchant responsible for your loss?

3. Which type of burglary should we treat more seriously, residential or commercial? Does one do more harm than the other? Should we measure the harm by the financial loss caused by the theft or by the effect on the victim? Does it matter for your answer whether entry was forced or not?

4. What are the primary differences between arsonists motivated by instrumental goals and those motivated by expressive goals? Which theoretical perspectives best explain these two patterns of fire setting? What type of criminal justice response is most appropriate for different categories of arsonists?

ADDITIONAL RESOURCES

See the U.S. Department of Justice, Office of Consumer Protection for more information on telemarketing fraud: http://www.doj.mt.gov/consumer/consumer/telemarketing.asp

Learn more about identity theft by visiting the Identity Theft Resource Center website at http://www.idtheftcenter.org/

For more information on automobile theft, contact the online auto theft information clearinghouse at http://www.auto-theft.info/index.html

Visit the U.S. Fire Administration website at http://www.usfa.dhs.gov/fireservice/subjects/arson/ for additional readings on arson and other fire-related information and statistics.

13

PUBLIC ORDER CRIMES

In this chapter, we will explore the following questions:

- Where and why do we draw the line between what is immoral and what is illegal?

- What types of drugs are illegal and why?

- Are we winning the war on drugs?

- What sexual acts do we define as prostitution?

- Why do some individuals exchange sex for money or drugs?

- When does pornography become a crime?

On December 2, 1993, billionaire Colombian drug lord Pablo

Emilio Escobar was gunned down by police in his home. Assisted by communication technology provided by the U.S. government, the Colombian police had found Escobar hiding in a middle-class neighborhood in Medellín. It was estimated that he controlled about 80 percent of the world's cocaine market. He was considered an enemy of both the Colombian and the U.S. governments.[1]

What makes a person an enemy to an entire country? Is it possible to declare war on a specific habit, lifestyle, or commodity? The U.S. government did in the early 1970s. The "war on drugs" is a political campaign begun during the Nixon administration to combat illegal drug trafficking by creating laws and policy initiatives that prohibit the production, distribution, and use of certain substances. Nixon referred to narcotics as "public enemy number one" and equated their use with a culture of crime, lawlessness, and radical anti-government sentiments.

The war on drugs took on new meaning during the early 1990s, when George H. W. Bush appointed William Bennett his drug czar, doubling annual spending on the war to $12 billion. Much of this money went to military jets designed to combat the Colombian trafficking cartels, to Navy submarines that monitored the smuggling of drugs in ships from the Caribbean, and to operatives trained to raid drug fields, ambush suspected drug lords, and capture known traffickers.[2] In the meantime, Congress adopted mandatory minimum sentencing laws that enacted severe penalties on drug users.[3]

The effect of the war on drugs, however, has been decades of costly spending and unprecedented growth in the number of people locked up for drug offenses, while the problems of drug trafficking, abuse, and addiction persist without resolution. What went wrong?

The biggest flaw in the war on drugs was policymakers' failure to rely on scientific studies that could accurately measure the effectiveness of programs and policies in reducing drug use. Studies conducted by the Drug Policy Research Center indicate that illegal drugs represent a $60 billion-a-year industry affecting about 16 million people in the United States, or 7 percent of the population over the age of 12. Response to the drug problem has generally been directed at law enforcement efforts to make it more difficult to buy, sell, use, and traffic illegal drugs. Researchers note, however, that these measures have not led to a significant reduction in the severity of the U.S. drug problem and may actually have contributed to our reluctance to focus on the treatment of drug addiction and its related social problems.[4]

public order crimes

Acts considered illegal because they violate the moral standards behind society's values and norms.

victimless crimes

Another term for public order crimes.

A Colombian antinarcotics police officer keeps watch in a poppy field near El Silencio in the former rebel safe haven in Colombia. This picture really captures a war. Who is the enemy here? How does the drug addict get caught up in this alleged war?

Unfortunately, the overwhelming evidence of the failure of "get tough" policies runs up against public sentiment that drug use is morally wrong and harmful and should be controlled through strict enforcement of punitive practices. Thus, we continue to impose harsh sentences on drug users and dealers, chase down drug lords, and combat drugs abroad, despite evidence that these efforts are ineffective in reducing the supply of drugs bought and sold on the streets.

Somehow, in the debate on public order and morality, the evidence loses its effect. In this chapter, we will take a closer look at this debate and its influence on our understanding of **public order crimes,** acts considered illegal because they violate the moral standards behind society's values and norms. We then look specifically at drug abuse, prostitution, and pornography.

CRIME VERSUS MORALITY: WHAT IS SOCIAL ORDER?

While criminal law is designed to protect society from harm and preserve peace and order, pursuing this goal becomes a questionable aim when people consent to engage in acts that have no apparent victim. For this reason, crimes against the public order have often been referred to as **victimless crimes.** Scholars note, however, that this terminology is misleading, because all criminal acts, even when the parties are in agreement, have harmful consequences on innocent people.[5]

Even if we assume crimes against the public order are not as obviously harmful as murder, rape and robbery, society has traditionally accepted the notion that certain acts should be prohibited and punished by law because they are contrary to the public's collective notion of decent and moral behavior.[6] Legal scholars note that one of the functions of criminal law is to express a collective sentiment that society disapproves of certain acts, even when these acts are not necessarily dangerous or obviously harmful to an apparent victim.[7]

Bill Slimback and Bob Sullivan are both from Whitehall, New York. In 2009, they got married in a ceremony at Moose Meadow Lodge in Waterbury, Vermont, minutes after Vermont's new law allowing same-sex marriage was passed. Vermont is one of six states (and Washington, DC) that now allow same-sex couples to marry. New York, Massachusetts, Connecticut, New Hampshire, and Iowa are the others. How does the definition of social order become redefined in this picture?

Thus, certain behaviors are outlawed because they are in direct conflict with social policy, prevailing moral standards, and current public opinion. The question, however, is by whose standards are we measuring moral behavior? Is there an objective standard of social harm we apply to certain acts and therefore deem them contrary to the public order? Is marrying an individual of one's choice, regardless of sex, a threat to moral order? Does helping a terminally ill loved one end his life harmful to society? How about smoking marijuana to ease the pain of certain types of cancer? (See Connecting Research to Practice for a discussion of this question with medical marijuana use.) While opinions vary, these acts have generally been prohibited by law. Yet, other acts that are acknowledged to be detrimental to health—such as distribution and consumption of alcohol and tobacco—are not prohibited. Who decides?

Sociologist Howard Becker calls them **moral entrepreneurs** (see Chapter 9). These are individuals who try to persuade the rest of society that their definition of a social problem and its policy resolution represents a shared consensus about what is best or the most right for the social order.[11] The **social order** consists of the various components of society—institutions, structures, customs, traditions—that preserve and maintain the normative ways of human interactions and relationships.[12] According to Becker, successful moral entrepreneurs are predominantly from the upper class and are able to effectively compete for political voice and power, generate awareness of the issue through their financial resources, and gain public support. That is why their views of morality get represented in decisions about which acts are deemed crimes against the social order and which are not.

Moral entrepreneurs include gun lobbyists, MADD (Mothers Against Drunk Driving), pro-life/pro-choice groups, and gay and lesbian rights advocates. All share the same goals: to influence lawmakers in the direction of policies that favor their cause or moral sentiment, and to control or limit certain types of behavior they consider a detriment to society, such as minors drinking alcohol. Even the women's suffrage movement in the late 1800s and early 1900s that called for voting rights for women was a group of moral entrepreneurs.

moral entrepreneurs

Becker's term for individuals, primarily from the upper class, who through their political voice and power are able to generate awareness of an issue and gain public support.

social order

The various components of society—institutions, structures, customs, traditions—that preserve and maintain the normative ways of human interactions and relationships.

Definitions of crime are influenced by moral entrepreneurs. Prior to the women's suffrage movement, women were banned from voting in political elections. What gave this relatively powerless group a voice?

What becomes defined as public order is therefore the outcome of a successful moral campaign favoring certain definitions and ideals of right, wrong, and what is best for society. We turn our attention now to a discussion of this definition, beginning with a discussion of drug use and addiction.

DRUG USE AND ADDICTION

Why do people use drugs? What makes taking drugs deviant? Is it the type of drug, the way it is purchased, or the reason it is consumed? These questions have various medical, legal, and social answers that we look at below.

Drug Taking as Deviance

In 2007, an estimated 19.9 million people in the United States aged 12 and older reported having used illicit drugs in the past month.[13] In fiscal year 2009, the national budget for drug abuse research, prevention, treatment, and enforcement exceeded $14 billion. The scope of the drug problem cuts across socioeconomic class, gender, age, and race.[14] It goes beyond our national borders and includes international traffickers, smugglers, and "public enemies." It is complex, with various intricate operations related to manufacturing, distributing, and dealing that create a variety of illegal activities by individuals, crime rings, and often corrupt law enforcement officials. Thus, there are various forms of deviance associated with drugs. Here, however, we discuss only the crime of drug abuse.

What type of feelings does riding down a raging river create in the mind? How is this effect similar to that of drugs? Why are these activities not considered deviant behaviors? Or are they considered deviant by some people?

drug

A chemical substance that affects the body's physical and psychological functioning by altering the way in which the brain sends, receives, and processes information.

drug abuse

The use of any chemical substance, whether legal or illegal, to result in the physical, mental, emotional, or behavioral impairment of an individual.

addiction

A chronic condition that causes a physical or psychological compulsion to seek the use of a drug, despite its harmful physical or social consequences.

tolerance

A physiological phenomenon in which, over time, the brain adapts to the chemical substance, and it produces less of a high; the individual needs more of the substance to experience the same effect.

What Is a Drug?

A **drug** is a chemical substance that affects the body's physical and psychological functioning by altering the way in which the brain sends, receives, and processes information. Because of this broad definition, many chemical substances are considered drugs, including legal substances such as aspirin and nicotine, and illegal substances such as cocaine and marijuana. **Drug abuse** is the use of any chemical substance, whether legal or illegal, to result in the physical, mental, emotional, or behavioral impairment of an individual.[15] An abused drug can affect the brain by either over- or under-stimulating it. However, the direct or indirect effect of nearly all abused drugs is to alter the functioning of the brain's reward system by disturbing the structure of emotions, motivation, drive, and pleasure.[16]

The brain's reaction to drugs is thus marked by a feeling of euphoria or a "high," which we otherwise derive from experiences such as scoring a touchdown, getting a good grade, being in love, riding a roller coaster, or indulging in our favorite foods. The euphoria, although short-lived, reinforces the effect of the drug, resulting in a desire to repeat the drug use in order to repeat the euphoria.[17] This cycle is what we commonly refer to as addiction.

What Is Addiction?

Addiction is a chronic condition that causes a physical or psychological compulsion to seek the use of a drug, despite its harmful physical or social consequences.[18] The addict comes to depend on the chemical substance in order to function properly. This strong dependency is what makes drug addiction so challenging to overcome.

Addiction to drugs is complicated by a physiological phenomenon known as **tolerance.** Tolerance builds over time when the brain adapts to the chemical substance, and it produces less of a high. The drug abuser begins to need more and more of the substance in order to enjoy the same pleasurable effects.[19]

The effects of drugs are powerful, creating changes in regions of the brain responsible for reasoning, judgment, cognition, and behavior control.[20] Thus, drugs can have a profound effect on the life of an individual in terms of health, daily functioning, interaction with others, and connection to the social world. For this reason, drug abuse falls under the category of public order crime.

Why Are Some Drugs Illegal?

The *deviant* nature of drug taking is seldom related to the chemical composition of any specific drug—meaning any drug can be abused. However, debates over the *legal* status of drugs have centered upon fundamental distinctions, such as type of drug, public perception of how it is used, and characteristics of users.[21] For example, morphine is commonly given to patients after major surgery to help them tolerate postoperative pain. Yet it is a controlled substance whose use is illegal if not under the control of a physician. Alcohol, on the other hand, is not now a controlled substance and can be consumed by adults in any quantity, despite its addictive qualities and harmful effects on the body when abused.[22] During the Prohibition era of 1919–1933, however, the manufacture, sale, and use of alcohol were deemed criminal.

Moreover, even when a drug is legal, the manner in which it is obtained and used can give it a criminal status. Such is the case when individuals abuse prescription painkillers. According to the Centers for Disease Control, teenage abuse of prescription drugs is on the rise, with over 20 percent of teenagers reporting having taken a prescription drug without a legitimate doctor's prescription.[23] Whether a particular drug is criminal is therefore socially created; it varies from time to time and place to place, as public perception and moral sentiment dictate the course of social control policies.

The use of chemical substances for medicinal or religious purposes has been associated with a wide variety of cultures throughout history.[24] Opium is regarded as one of the earliest drugs to be discovered; its use has been dated back to the Stone Age, several thousand years BCE. Derivatives of opium such as morphine and heroin were introduced later by merchants and traders and became widespread throughout Europe, Asia, and the United States in the 1800s. In 1858, cocaine was extracted from coca leaves and was thought to be a cure for certain ailments.[25] By the turn of the century, medicine peddlers were providing highly addictive chemical substances to millions in the United States, many of them middle-class women, and creating a new social problem that needed immediate attention.

Concern over the increase in addiction and the growing public perception of a link between cocaine and crime led to the passage of the federal **Harrison Act** of 1914, designed to regulate and control the manufacture, production, and distribution of cocaine and opiate drugs. Similar concerns drew public attention in the mid-1930s when marijuana use became associated with certain types of deviant subcultures, leading to the passage of the **Marijuana Tax Act** of 1937, which placed a $100-an-ounce tax on the drug, and the **Boggs Act** in 1951, which brought about criminal sanctions for its possession and distribution.

The cumulative effect of these and subsequent laws aimed at controlling drugs was to create a social class of deviants, who were now defined as criminal instead of addicted, and to pave the way for the underground drug market to flourish through organized criminal networks of distributors and traffickers.

Categories of Drugs

Researchers have traditionally classified drugs into categories according to their chemical composition and how they alter the structure and function of the brain. Of course, certain drugs are more popular than others, according to their accessibility and frequency of use. We can see from Figure 13.1 that marijuana is the most widely used illicit drug among teenagers who report themselves to be drug users, and alcohol is the most frequently used legal substance, although its use by minors is in itself illegal.

We divide illegal drugs into five broad categories: narcotics, depressants, stimulants, hallucinogens, and cannabis. **Narcotics** are highly addictive drugs that can be smoked, injected, sniffed, or taken orally. They are often used to relieve pain and produce relaxation and include morphine, codeine, heroin, and opium. **Depressants** are taken orally to relieve tension and anxiety. They produce a state of calmness and relaxation but can also impair judgment and interfere with motor coordination. They have a high potential

Harrison Act

A 1914 law designed to regulate and control the manufacture, production, and distribution of cocaine and opiate drugs.

Marijuana Tax Act

A 1937 law that placed a $100-an-ounce tax on the drug.

Boggs Act

A 1951 law that placed criminal sanctions on the possession and distribution of marijuana.

narcotics

Highly addictive drugs often used to relieve pain and produce relaxation; they include morphine, codeine, heroin, and opium.

depressants

Potentially addictive drugs taken to relieve tension and anxiety; they include barbitures and tranquilizers.

Source: Monitoring the Future Study, 2008. Institute for Social Research, Ann Arbor, MI.

FIGURE **13.1**

Drugs of Choice Among High School Seniors in 2010, Based on Annual Prevalence

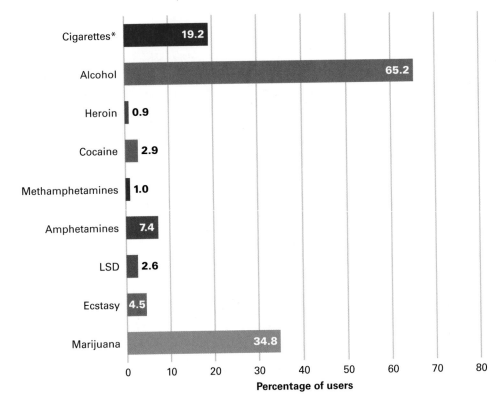

*30-day use for cigarettes.

Note: These categories are not mutually exclusive; 12th graders may report using more than one of the listed drugs.

stimulants

Drugs to heighten alertness and reduce fatigue, with a high degree a psychological dependence; they include amphetamines, cocaine, crack, and methamphetamines.

hallucinogens

Drugs that create profound mind-altering changes and distortions in feelings and perception, often producing a state of confusion and hallucination; they include PCP, LSD, and Ecstasy.

cannabis

Drugs that produce feelings of euphoria and relaxation, derived from the hemp plant; they include marijuana and hashish.

for addiction because they build tolerance. Examples of depressants include barbiturates and tranquilizers. **Stimulants** can be sniffed, smoked, injected, or taken orally to heighten alertness and reduce fatigue. They include amphetamines, cocaine, crack, and methamphetamines or "ice." They have a high degree of psychological dependence and often produce physiological changes in the body such as elevated blood pressure, blurry vision, and irregular heartbeat. **Hallucinogens** include PCP ("angel dust"), LSD ("acid"), and the drug Ecstasy. They have no known medical use and create profound mind-altering changes and distortions in feelings and perception, often producing a state of confusion and hallucination that can lead to violence and aggression. **Cannabis** is derived from the hemp plant, which yields marijuana and hashish. These drugs are generally ingested by smoking and produce feelings of euphoria and relaxation. Some studies show that prolonged use can damage the lungs and respiratory system, as can cigarette smoking.[26] The degree of physiological dependence is generally unknown. Table 13.1 provides a summary of these five major drug categories.

Trends and Patterns in Drug Use

According to the National Survey on Drug Use and Health (NSDUH), drug use among teenagers has been declining since 2001 (Figure 13.2). Every year, the Institute of Social Science Research (ISR) conducts a self-report survey of drug abuse among over 50,000 8th-, 10th-, and 12th-graders across the United States. Data reveal that while drugs are readily available and a significant percentage of teenagers have experimented with them before graduating from high school, drug use today is at lower levels than two decades ago.[27] Alcohol abuse, however, has not experienced the same decline; studies show the number of youth who begin drinking at an early age has increased over 30 percent since the mid-1970s.[28]

TABLE **13.1**

Categories of Drugs

NARCOTICS			
DRUG	**DEPENDENCE PHYSICAL/ PSYCHOLOGICAL**	**HOW USED**	**DURATION (HOURS)**
Opium	High/High	Oral, smoked	3–6
Morphine	High/High	Oral, smoked, injected	3–6
Codeine	Moderate/Moderate	Oral, injected	3–6
Heroin	High/High	Smoked, injected, sniffed	3–6
Hydromorphone	High/High	Oral, injected	3–6
Meperidine	High/High	Oral, injected	3–6
Methadone	High/High	Oral, injected	12–24

DEPRESSANTS			
DRUG	**DEPENDENCE PHYSICAL/ PSYCHOLOGICAL**	**HOW USED**	**DURATION (HOURS)**
Barbiturates	High/moderate	Oral	1–16
Methaqualone	High/High	Oral	4–8
Tranquilizers	High/High	Oral	4–8
Chloral hydrate	Moderate/Moderate	Oral	5–8
Glutethimide	High/Moderate	Oral	4–8

STIMULANTS			
DRUG	**DEPENDENCE PHYSICAL/ PSYCHOLOGICAL**	**HOW USED**	**DURATION (HOURS)**
Cocaine	Possible/High	Sniffed, smoked, injected	1–2
Amphetamines	Possible/High	Oral, injected	2–4
Methamphetamine	Possible/High	Oral, injected	2–4
Phenmetrazine	Possible/High	Oral, injected	2–4
Methylphenidate	Possible/Moderate	Oral, injected	2–4
Other stimulants	Possible/High	Oral, injected	2–4
Ice	High/High	Smoked, oral injected, inhaled	4–14

HALLUCINOGENS			
DRUG	**DEPENDENCE PHYSICAL/ PSYCHOLOGICAL**	**HOW USED**	**DURATION (HOURS)**
PCP	Unknown/High	Smoked, oral	Up to days injected
LSD (acid)	None/Unknown	Oral	8–12 hrs.
Mescaline, peyote	None/Unknown	Oral, injected	8–12 hrs.
Psilocybin	None/Unknown	Oral, injected, smoked, sniffed	Variable
Designer drugs (Ecstasy)	Unknown/Unknown	Oral, injected, smoked	Variable

(*continued*)

TABLE **13.1** (continued)

Categories of Drugs

CANNABIS			
DRUG	DEPENDENCE PHYSICAL/ PSYCHOLOGICAL	HOW USED	DURATION (HOURS)
Marijuana	Unknown/Moderate	Smoked, oral pot, grass	2–4
Tetrahydrocannabinol	Unknown/Moderate	Smoked, oral	2–4
Hashish	Unknown/Moderate	Smoked, oral	2–4
Hashish oil	Unknown/Moderate	Smoked, oral	2–4

Source: U.S. Department of Labor, America in Jeopardy: The Young Employee and Drugs in the Workplace Trainer's Manual, Appendix B Drug Category Profiles.

One variable that continues to concern policymakers and researchers is the connection between drug abuse and crime. There are three possibilities: (1) Individuals who abuse drugs and alcohol are more likely to commit crime; (2) individuals commit crime in order to obtain illegal drugs or support a drug habit; and (3) the distribution and trafficking of drugs is a source of criminal activity.

The research literature abounds with studies that persistently find a link between substance abuse and violent crime, with individuals who use drugs being more likely to engage in violent behavior.[29] According to the Department of Health and Human Services, adolescents who use at least one illicit drug are twice as likely to engage in violent behavior as adolescents who do not use drugs at all.[30] Studies have also found that a significant number of individuals arrested for domestic assault, homicide, and other violent crimes test positive for at least one illegal drug (Table 13.2).[31]

Moreover, surveys indicate that an overwhelming majority of prisoners have a history of substance abuse.[32] According to a nationally representative survey of state correctional agencies, nearly 8 million adult offenders are involved in drugs.[33] The substance abuse or dependence rates of offenders are more than four times those of the general population, with about half of all state and federal prisoners meeting the diagnostic criteria.[34]

With the growing number of drug varieties and markets and innovations in the manufacture and distribution of illegal substances, the criminal drug network has become more violent, aggressive, and complex.[35] Drug trafficking has become a divided industry

FIGURE **13.2**

Trends in Drug Use: 1991–2008

Source: 2009 White House Drug Policy, National Drug Control Report, Monitoring the Future's National Survey of 8th, 10th, and 12th Grade Students.

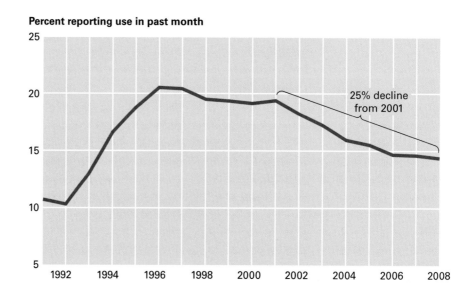

Percent reporting use in past month

25% decline from 2001

TABLE **13.2**

Illicit Drug Use and Prior Arrests		
ILLICIT DRUG	**PRIOR ARREST (PERCENT)**	**NO PRIOR ARREST (PERCENT)**
Marijuana	46.5	10.0
Cocaine	24.8	2.4
Crack cocaine	11.8	0.6
Hallucinogens	11.0	1.5
Methamphetamines	6.5	0.5
Heroin	4.3	0.1
Nonmedical Use of Any Prescription Drug	28.8	5.7

Source: *Illicit drug use among persons arrested for serious crimes.* (2005, December 16). National Survey on Drug Use and Health. Office of Applied Sciences, Substance Abuse, and Mental Health Services Administration. Retrieved from http://www.oas.samhsa.gov/2k5/arrests/arrests.htm

that has found its way into street gangs, provoked turf battles, and sanctioned the settling of differences through violence and bloodshed. International drug trafficking has also become embedded in governments across the globe, including political corruption among high-level officials and assassinations of those who refuse to comply.[36] Indeed, trends and patterns in drug use and violence are a global phenomenon. The phenomenon exists, however, because there is demand. We return to the question, Why do people use drugs?

Understanding Drug Abuse

Our individual traits and experiences do not only affect the many variables associated with drug abuse and addiction. Very often, they also both affect and reflect the drug of choice, the particular life of the drug user, and the outcome of his or her involvement in criminal activity.

Individual variables include genetic factors that predispose some individuals toward substance abuse. Studies have shown that children of alcoholic parents are more likely to develop substance abuse problems than children of nonalcoholic parents, even after controlling for environmental variables that influence the relationship between parent and child.[37] Other studies suggest that substance abuse may be linked to psychological disorders, such as antisocial personality, and to psychotic disorders, such as schizophrenia.[38] In many cases, drugs are a means of dealing with traumatic emotional experiences that lead to anxiety and depression. Researchers caution, however, that these studies do not diminish the role of socialization in the abuse of alcohol and drugs.[39]

Studies of environmental influences in the onset of alcohol and drug abuse look at whether drug use is part of a lifestyle or subculture within the inner city. (See Chapter 8 on social structure theories.) Evidence suggests it tends to be higher in neighborhoods where deteriorated living conditions, high crime rates, and limited legitimate opportunities force youth to turn to the drug subculture for peer approval, as a method of coping with feelings of alienation and rejection, and as a way to earn a living.[40]

Patterns of drug use among inner-city residents are most visible to law enforcement—a fact reflected in the higher arrest trends for drug-related offenses in these areas than on college campuses across the country.[41] It is also the inner city in which most drug enforcement policies and practices emerge and where the debate on treatment versus social control continues.

What individual and environmental variables contribute to drug abuse and addiction?

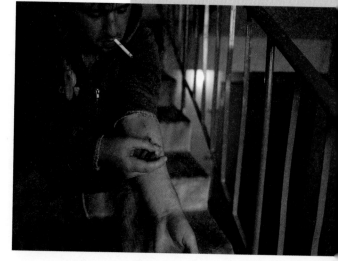

What Do We Do About Drug Abuse?

Central to the discussion of what to do about drug abuse and addiction is the question whether certain types of drugs should be legalized or decriminalized, particularly marijuana. A substantial body of literature shows that marijuana use is no more dangerous to health than cigarettes or alcohol.[42] The most widely used illicit drug, marijuana is also not generally perceived by the public as deviant, nor is it associated with a criminal lifestyle as is crack cocaine, for example.[43]

Drug policy experts note that removing the criminal component of drug use will dismantle the underground drug economy, which is a significant source of violence and organized criminal activity (discussed in Chapter 14).[44] Moreover, the legalization of restricted drugs would allow for government control of sale and distribution, therefore reducing the high price, which often leads to a variety of criminal activities to support the expensive habit.

Critics note, however, that restricted substances, whether marijuana or crack, are mind-altering drugs that have a significant impact on the physical and psychological functioning of individuals and that pose serious risks to health. Moreover, the legalization of drugs will only escalate the problems of abuse and addiction, making drugs more readily accessible to a greater number of people. This has been the case throughout history and in different societies when the availability of drugs such as narcotics preceded epidemics of drug use and addiction.[45]

For many years, drug control policies and practices focused primarily on expanding law enforcement efforts to manage drug traffickers and punish drug users. The war on drugs launched during the 1980s succeeded in arresting and incarcerating an unprecedented number of drug offenders, with drug-related convictions accounting for nearly 85 percent of the increase in federal prison inmates from 1985 to 1995 (Figure 13.3).

Despite massive local, national, and international efforts and spending on patrolling borders, eradicating crops, and sting operations to arrest drug smugglers and dealers, drugs continue to be readily available and widely used by youth and adults throughout the country, with the associated problems of overdose, addiction, drug-related crimes, and the spread of disease.[46] Critics of the war on drugs note that U.S. drug policy has been misguided in its emphasis on the arrest and incarceration of anyone associated with illegal drugs and that this strategy is too idealistic and subject to political rhetoric and manipulation.[47] Moreover, it is simplistic, failing to recognize the social and public health issues related to drug abuse and addiction. Connecting Theory to Practice discusses a theoretical

Methadone is a narcotic similar to morphine. It is used in outpatient clinics to reduce the symptoms associated with treating heroin addiction.

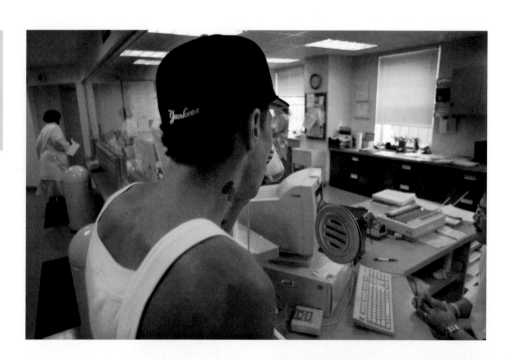

The goal of antidrug policy and legislation is to eliminate the trafficking, sale, distribution, and abuse of all illegal drugs. How to accomplish this overwhelming task, however, has been the subject of much debate. Proponents of drug prohibition call for a strict ban and punitive enforcement. Advocates of decriminalization favor legislation that either regulates or reduces penalties for the use or possession of certain drugs such as marijuana. Legalization is the outright removal of any form of legal restriction on the use or possession of drugs.

Regardless of these divisions, drug control policies must be based on an approach that accounts for the fact that strict laws enacting harsh penalties for drug offenders have largely failed to reduce the market for drugs. The idea behind strict laws and harsh sentencing is that offenders will be less likely to make the *choice* to use or sell drugs if the punishment is so great it is not worth the risk. The problem with using this theory to guide drug policy is that

it assumes drug abuse is a rational decision, based on hedonistic calculations of pros and cons (see Chapter 5's discussion of rational choice theory). It fails to recognize the emotional, psychological, and physiological components of drug use and addiction and the social and psychological variables that can influence the onset of abuse.[48] "Get tough" policies do not have the intended effect of decreasing drug abuse because they ignore the irrational nature of drug use as a form of the thrill-seeking, often self-destructive behavior pattern.[49]

A more practical approach to drug control should integrate law enforcement with education, especially for at-risk youth, about the devastating effects of drugs. Moreover, preventive measures must recognize the role of psychology and social variables in the onset of drug abuse, and holistic treatment programs should be available as an alternative to punitive measures for drug offenders.

flaw in the "get tough" approach to drug control policies. So, if the war on drugs is a losing battle, what could be the alternative?

An alternative drug control strategy, introduced in the mid-1990s by President Bill Clinton, accepted that criminal laws and sanctions alone could not solve the complicated issues and problems related to drug abuse and addiction. A national effort began to advance a model of drug control that focused on drug education programs as well as treatment interventions. This model recognizes the underlying economic and social variables associated with drug use and relies on research findings to support intervention strategies.

Thousands of drug prisoners

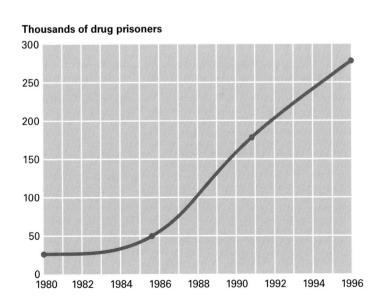

FIGURE 13.3

Consequences of a War: Incarceration for Drug Arrests, 1980–1996

Source: US Department of Justice; Bureau of Justice Statistics, Trends in US Correctional Populations, 1995. National Institute on Drug Abuse. Data from the Drug Abuse Warning Network (DAWN): Annual Medical Examiner Data, 1981–1991; Substance Abuse and Mental Health Services Administration. Data from the Drug Abuse Warning Network (DAWN): Annual Medical Examiner Data, 1992–1997.

Since 1996, drug use among teens has been declining; the period between 2002 and 2008 saw a significant drop of 25 percent.[50] Today, the antidrug strategy focuses on combining law enforcement efforts, treatment programs, and prevention to achieve three major goals: stop initiation, reduce drug abuse and addiction, and disrupt the market for illegal drugs. The goal of stopping initiation is achieved through national drug prevention efforts designed to deter drug use, especially by youth. These efforts include such initiatives as the National Youth Anti-Drug Media Campaign, state-level prescription drug monitoring programs, and community-based coalitions that implement random drug testing programs in schools and workplaces to promote safe, drug-free environments.

Treatment is prioritized as part of the goal to reduce drug abuse and addiction. It begins with the early identification of substance abuse problems through programs such as Screening and Brief Intervention and Access to Recovery. These encourage individuals to recognize their substance abuse issues through screening in a healthcare setting, in order to stop the behavior pattern before it becomes even more problematic. An outgrowth of the treatment priority has been the emergence of drug courts, which allow drug abusers who have come into contact with the criminal justice system the opportunity to participate in a drug treatment programs while remaining under community supervision.

The third goal, to disrupt the market for illegal drugs, focuses on reducing the supply of drugs by enhancing law enforcement efforts at the federal, state, and local level. Moreover, international cooperative agreements have been set up with governments such as Colombia and Mexico to protect shared borders from drug traffickers. The long-term success of these and other social control measures to reduce drug abuse will require a continued investment in policies and programs that combine prevention, treatment, and law enforcement efforts both globally and at home, until social reaction redefines what it is we are trying to control. We turn now to an examination of prostitution, another area in which the question of public order has been the subject of debate.

PROSTITUTION

prostitution

The nonmarital consensual exchange of sexual acts for material gain.

Prostitution can most broadly be defined as the nonmarital consensual exchange of sexual acts for material gain. The sexual acts can range from sexual intercourse to any other behavior from which the client derives sexual gratification. We traditionally think of prostitutes as women whose clients are men. However, individuals engaging in acts of prostitution can be male or female, and their clients can be same or opposite sex. Although the research literature on male prostitution is very limited, studies suggest that the social dynamics of male prostitution are not significantly different from those of female prostitution.

Suppose a man and a woman meet at a bar and agree to go out to dinner and then have sex. If the man pays for dinner, is the woman engaging in prostitution? What distinguishes prostitution from consensual sexual acts is an accompanying economic transaction. Something of economic value is gained by providing the sexual act, such as money, drugs, or material goods. If the stipulation for having sex was that the man would pay for dinner, then this *could* be considered a prostitution transaction. Some may be shocked by this conclusion. However, it is this example that represents the gray area when it comes to defining sexually deviant behavior. It also illustrates the difficulty of determining the incidence of prostitution.

How Common Is Prostitution?

Experts estimate that between 100,000 and 500,000 prostitutes operate in the United States in any given year.[51] According to the Uniform Crime Reports, there were 75,000 arrests for prostitution in 2008.[52] Arrest rates for prostitution have declined over the years. Some argue that this drop is largely due to the fact that the crime has become less visible to law enforcement. The widespread use of technology has allowed prostitution to go "cyber," with sexual exchanges being made via web camera. Moreover, the use of the Internet has made it easier to hide prostitution transactions.[53] This does not mean

CONSIDER THIS... Politicians and Prostitutes

The Emperors Club VIP was an international prostitution ring that provided expensive prostitutes to wealthy clients in New York, Washington, Los Angeles, Miami, London, and Paris. Women could be "ordered" online by the hour (for prices reaching $5,500 per hour) or the day (over $31,000).

On February 13, 2008, New York's governor Eliot Spitzer ordered a prostitute from the Emperors Club, unaware that federal agents were monitoring the club as part of a sting operation. His solicitation quickly became front-page news.[54]

Spitzer, who was 48 and had been governor for only a year and a half, had been elected in part for his reputation of being tough on corruption, earned as a result of his rigorous monitoring of Wall Street as the state's attorney general. Often referred to as "Mr. Clean," he was active in prosecuting 18 people on charges of promoting prostitution. With the scandal, he was forced to apologize to his family and the public.[55] Soon after, he had to resign from office.

Why would this governor, husband, and father of three teenage daughters pay for sex with a high-priced call girl?

What do you think?

the actual incidence of prostitution has gone down, just the arrest data. As we noted in Chapter 3, this is one of the pitfalls of relying on official data sources on crime. We only know who gets caught; we do not know everyone who commits the crime. And who gets caught, whether prostitute or customer, may sometimes surprise us (see the Consider This feature).

Others argue that the actual *incidence* of prostitution has gone down, because fewer clients are willing to engage in sexual acts with a prostitute given the widely known risks of sexually transmitted diseases and AIDS.[56] Moreover, as expressions of sexuality have become more liberal and legal opportunities for sex more readily available over the past couple of decades, individuals have become less inclined to seek the services of a prostitute.

Notwithstanding declining arrest rates for prostitution in the United States, the sex tourism industry has grown.[57] **Sex tourism** is an industry wherein clients, usually men from wealthier countries, travel abroad to places where young people, usually girls, are readily available for sex, either through need or through force. The sex industry in these countries is either legal or is not well regulated. Locations considered hot spots for sex tourism include Bangkok, Amsterdam, Jamaica, and Kenya.

sex tourism

An industry wherein clients, usually men from wealthier countries, travel abroad to places where young people, usually girls, are readily available for sex, either through need or through force.

Types of Prostitutes

Individuals who engage in prostitution come from a variety of backgrounds, have a variety of reasons for getting involved in this pattern of behavior, and operate by different methods. While each category of prostitute that we describe below seems to be unique, they are not in fact mutually exclusive.

Skeezers

Skeezers are women who engage in prostitution in exchange for drugs, most commonly crack cocaine. Research suggests a significant association with age; women 25 or younger are more likely to exchange sex for crack than women older than 25.[58] Moreover, skeezers tend to be poor minority women from inner cities, who have been socially and economically marginalized by poverty and addiction.[59] Most use sex as a means of supporting their addiction.[60]

Streetwalkers

Streetwalkers are prostitutes who walk the street soliciting sexual activity from customers. Often easily identifiable by their flashy revealing clothes, high heels, and elaborate makeup, they may be independent entrepreneurs, or they may be controlled by a pimp for whom they work.[61] Many times streetwalkers congregate in particular areas known as red light districts.

Often addicts or homeless, impoverished runaways, streetwalkers are described in the literature as the lowest form of prostitution.[62] They are also much more likely to be arrested and are at greater risk of suffering violence.[63] Streetwalkers are the lowest paid prostitutes in the profession, and few ever climb out of this category of prostitution into other types.

Bar Girls and Dancers

Women who work at a bar under the guise of being a hostess or dancer but are also expected to provide sexual entertainment to customers are called bar girls and dancers. Patterns of prostitution vary among them.[64] Some provide short-term individual entertainment, such as lap dancing, to many different customers on a given night. Others may have long-term or returning clients with whom they spend an entire evening or whom they accompany home. Many young women enter into this type of prostitution believing they are being hired for a legitimate job as a dancer, singer, or entertainer and find out later that sexual activity is an expectation.

In a growing trend, bar girls at "juicy bars" (commonly found near military bases)[65] entice male customers into buying them expensive drinks, usually watered-down alcoholic fruit beverages, with the promise of an exciting evening of sexual pleasure that does not always materialize. These bar girls often get a commission on the drinks they sell and may be pushed by the bar owner to engage in further sexual acts with the customer depending on how much money they generate.

Call Girls and Escorts

Call girls and escorts are usually middle-class females living a fairly lavish lifestyle and charging wealthy clients hundreds or thousands of dollars per night. In this more organized and professional form of prostitution, they often work for private companies that claim to provide escort services for both male and female clients. Clients are often checked out to make sure they are legitimate "upstanding" customers willing and able to pay top dollar. They can call and "order" a girl to come to a home or hotel room and provide a private striptease or provocative dancing and fulfill sexual fantasies. Some call girls establish a clientele and entertain them in their own homes or apartments.

Indentured Sex Slaves

Sexual slavery occurs when an individual must prostitute herself to pay off some type of debt, often to a drug dealer or a pimp from whom she is trying to get away. Sexual slavery operations are sometimes controlled by organized crime rings or gangs.[66] Thousands of young women and teenagers are smuggled into the United States and other countries every year, predominantly from southeast Asia and eastern Europe.[67] Often from poor families, they are promised a better life and a job good enough to send money to their families back home. In reality, they find themselves forced into prostitution to pay for their own home and food.

Factors Leading to Prostitution

Some individuals engage in prostitution voluntarily, having weighed the pros and cons and made a choice of their own free will. Others work out of necessity to support an addiction or pay a debt, or just to survive in particular circumstances.[68] In any case, a question still remains: Why would an individual engage in sexual activity for economic gain?

Studies identify several pathways and factors that can attract, precipitate, or predispose a person to prostitution.[69] *Attracting variables* lead an individual to consider prostitution as a form of financial support. One such variable can be a false image, like the one portrayed by Julia Roberts in the film *Pretty Woman,* where prostitution is associated with glamour and excitement and the possibility of meeting the man of your dreams who will take you away from it all and spoil you with gifts and an expensive lifestyle.

Precipitating factors are circumstances or experiences that can place certain vulnerable men and women at risk of turning to prostitution.[70] These are often sudden changes such as running away from home or being kicked out of the house by a boyfriend. Research shows that a majority of young girls turn to prostitution after running away from abusive or dysfunctional families and relationships.[71] Turning to the streets, they are often recruited into prostitution by a pimp or others already in the business.

Finally, *predisposing factors* increase the chances or likelihood of an individual turning to prostitution.[72] These include economic hardship, low education, drug abuse, and homelessness. Many prostitutes enter the sex trade at an early age, with a history of sexual exploitation and abuse.[73] They are also the most likely to experience similar patterns of abuse as adults, often by pimps and customers, finding themselves caught up in a cycle of alcohol and drug abuse, violence, and risk of disease.[74]

While these variables paint a picture of prostitution as predominantly occupied by individuals from dysfunctional backgrounds—runaway teens, victims of sexual abuse, and homeless drug addicts—researchers note that it often reflects studies of streetwalkers and not the other categories of prostitutes, which can be occupied by middle-class men and women who turn to the sex-for-profit industry as a lucrative means of economic gain. In the more liberal attitude toward sexuality that has

How do visibility and bias play a role in arrests for prostitution? Does the frequency of arrest for this type of prostitute affect our interpretation of prostitution as a threat to the public order?

brothel

A house run by a madam who recruits and trains young women as prostitutes.

emerged over the years, the exchange of money for sex is seen as an acceptable form of instant gratification in a controlled environment, without the commitment and expectations of a long-term relationship.[75] Despite these changing mores, the U.S. government continues to challenge the notion of prostitution as a socially acceptable behavior, and it continues to be illegal everywhere except in **brothels**—houses run by a madam who recruits and trains young women as prostitutes—in various counties of Nevada.

What Do We Do About Prostitution?

The debate over the illegal status of prostitution presents conflicting views on the government's ability to regulate sexual activity that occurs in private between two consenting adults.[76] At the core of these arguments is whether or not prostitution presents a threat to the public order. Some feminist theorists argue that prostitution is degrading to women and a further example of men's exploitation of women. Prostitution promotes the view of women as objects, which facilitates violence against women and renders them powerless against the conditions of poverty, drugs, and abuse that may have led to their entry into prostitution. Moreover, prostitution is linked to other forms of criminal activity such as the abduction and trafficking of young women, sex slavery, and organized crime.[77] The social control of prostitution is therefore necessary for the public good. This social control should also extend to the pursuit of criminal charges against the clients. Studies show that prostitution is emotionally and physically harmful to women, and therefore the individual who buys sex should also be charged with a crime.[78]

Some scholars note, however, that the criminalization of prostitution is a violation of an individual's right to privacy and actually represents the subjugation of women by the imposition of primarily male-created laws governing their behavior.[79] According to this perspective, whether an individual chooses to engage in consensual sexual activity for pleasure or for a monetary exchange is a matter of personal choice not to be regulated by government interference. In addition, making prostitution illegal exacerbates the problems associated with it, imposing legal sanctions on women who are already suffering from abuse and addiction. Researchers note that prostitutes who work in areas where it is legal actually feel more safe and protected and are less vulnerable to disease and exploitation.[80]

Despite arguments supporting the decriminalization of prostitution, there seems to be a general consensus, at least among lawmakers, that the public order crime of prostitution, in its various types and forms, should continue to be prohibited by the law. A more difficult task is the definition and control of pornography, which directly challenges constitutional rights.

PORNOGRAPHY

A Supreme Court justice once said, "I can't define pornography . . . but I know it when I see it."[81] What is pornography and how do we describe it? It is subject to interpretation that may vary from individual to individual and culture to culture.

What Is Pornography?

pornography

Any depicted or verbal material that is sexually explicit and is *primarily* designed to incite sexual arousal in those who seek it out.

Pornography can be defined as any depicted or verbal material that is sexually explicit and is *primarily* designed to incite sexual arousal in those who seek it out. Including books, magazines, films, and computer images, pornography is a billion-dollar industry that spans the international market. The widespread use of pornography has been facilitated by the development of new technologies that have allowed nude and provocative pictures

How do cultural norms about dress influence the definition of pornography?

to be quickly transmitted through Internet social-networking sites or via cell phones, now known as *sexting.*[82]

Of course, what is considered sexually explicit varies by cultural context. In some countries in the Middle East, the sight of a woman's ankles is considered sexually explicit and is forbidden in public. In some African villages, it is common for females to wear clothing that exposes their breasts due to the hot climate. These differences may affect the ways in which people judge what is and what is not sexually explicit. In U.S. culture, one type of sexually explicit material portrays men or women either posing nude or engaging in voluntary sexual acts such as oral or anal sex. Another type portrays sexual acts that are violent or coercive in nature, such as people being tied up, tortured, penetrated vaginally or anally by objects, or being humiliated or raped. Some people might define the first type of material described as pornographic, while others might consider only the second type pornography.

Implicit in the definition of pornography is the idea that it is objectionable material. Is all pornography considered bad or harmful? Or only a certain type or category? Without engaging in a moral debate, it would be very difficult to answer these questions. We can however, gain a better understanding of the debate by looking more closely at the context within which pornography takes place.

Is Pornography Illegal?

Certain types of pornographic material have been deemed harmful, morally reprehensible, and detrimental to the well-being of society. One of these is **child pornography,** which depicts children in sexually explicit positions or engaging in sexual acts. Child pornography is widely regarded as harmful and exploitive; studies show long-term emotional damage to child victims.[83] Referred to as "kiddie porn," this type of pornography has become an international phenomenon (see Crime in Global Perspective feature).

Some types of pornography are considered forms of **obscenity** and can be criminalized. In *Miller v. California* (1973) the courts ruled that obscene material appeals to the "prurient interest in sex, depicts sexual conduct in a patently offensive manner, and lacks

child pornography

Pornographic material that depicts children in sexually explicit positions or engaging in sexual acts.

obscenity

Material that appeals to a prurient interest in sex, depicts sexual conduct in a patently offensive manner, and lacks serious literary, artistic, political, or scientific value; not protected by the First Amendment because it lacks any social importance.

CRIME IN GLOBAL PERSPECTIVE | Protecting Children Worldwide

Over the past decade, child pornography has become more accessible than ever. According to some studies, between 2004 and 2006 there were over 1.9 million reports of illegal pornography on the Internet, 50 percent concerning child pornography and another 19 percent reporting other child-related content.[84] Child pornography is often distributed through the pedophile rings—individuals from different countries who communicate to collect and disseminate sexually explicit images of children for personal gratification. Advances in media and Internet technology have facilitated this type of communication and made it even more difficult to detect the source, causing serious concern among international agencies in the business of protecting children from this type of abuse.[85]

In response, almost every country has created a taskforce to focus solely on combating this problem on the Internet. The U.S. Department of Justice is responsible for monitoring child pornography both on the national and international levels. A number of other countries are also fighting this particular crime on a global level, and a number of organizations have been created to coordinate and facilitate the reporting of websites that contain child pornography.

In 1999, the International Association of Internet Hotlines (INHOPE) was founded. INHOPE represents Internet hotlines around the world, providing support and assistance in responding to tips and reports about illegal or questionable content found on the Internet.[86] INHOPE also maintains a worldwide network of hotlines to increase awareness, provide technical support and expertise in response to reports of illegal content, and educate policymakers on best practices for combating child pornography at the international level.

serious literary, artistic, political, or scientific value."[87] The Supreme Court also ruled that obscene materials completely lack social importance and so are not protected by the First Amendment.[88] Here the Court not only attempted to define obscenity but also set forth standards by which material could be judged obscene, by (1) determining whether the average person applying contemporary community standards would find that the material generally appeals to the prurient interest; (2) deciding whether the work depicts or describes in a patently offensive way sexual conduct that is specifically defined by the state's laws; and (3) determining whether the work, taken as a whole, lacks serious literary, artistic, political, or scientific value.[89] Moreover, in *Pope v. Illinois,* in order to ensure uniformity in the interpretation of obscenity, the Supreme Court ruled that material should be considered obscene by using "objective national standards."[90]

The definition of obscenity is therefore the central issue in the enforcement of laws prohibiting certain pornographic materials.

Is Pornography Harmful?

Feminist theorists have extensively researched the harmful effects of pornography on women;[91] some have argued that pornography in any form is degrading and exploitive, as it depicts women in a sexually subordinate status.[92] Researchers also note that some of the acts shown in pornographic materials—such as the double penetration of women or the penetration of women by large objects—are both physically and psychologically harmful.[93] Moreover, the widespread dissemination of pornographic material objectifies the human body and allows men to justify the treatment of women as objects.[94] Does this mean that there could be a relationship between pornography and sexual violence against women?

A growing body of literature examines the effects of viewing pornography, especially violent pornography, on perpetuating and reinforcing sexual assault.[95] While studies have not been able to establish a direct cause–effect relationship between viewing pornography and sexual assault, research suggests that pornography contributes to attitudes and patterns of behavior that are exploitive and abusive to women.[96] Pornography very often portrays individuals as either willing participants who enjoy being dominated and subordinated, or forced participants engaging in brutal acts of violence and degradation.[97] Pornography may serve to reinforce coercive behavior in individuals inclined toward violence and sexual aggression because of their individual traits or sociocultural upbringing.[98] Moreover, researchers note that pornography plays a factor in the misperception among men that women like, enjoy, and fantasize about violent sexual acts.[99]

What Do We Do About Pornography?

If studies confirm pornography as at least contributing to attitudes and behaviors that foster the degradation and mistreatment of women, then why is there not a general ban on the production and distribution of sexually explicit magazines, books, movies, and websites? The answer lies in the First Amendment's protection of free speech and expression. This becomes an even more complex matter when we consider the vast use of the Internet as a medium for the distribution of pornographic materials. However, one area where there is no question with regard to constitutional protection is child pornography, which is clearly forbidden and illegal.[100] However, other forms of pornography are not as easily prohibited. The restriction on pornographic materials is thus limited to what is considered obscene.[101]

Despite past court rulings, the debate about pornography will continue to put those advocating freedom of speech against those favoring stricter control of sexually explicit material, with advances in technology raising ever-more complicated issues related to computer-generated images.[102] The question about how much the government can influence the definition of public order will therefore continue to be in the forefront of criminological discourse.[103]

SUMMARY

■ **Where and why do we draw the line between what is immoral and what is illegal?**	Society favors formally controlling certain acts contrary to the public's collective sentiment about what is decent and moral behavior. These acts are called public order crimes and are often the outcome of collective campaigning by moral entrepreneurs who promote certain ideas of what is for the social good.
■ **What types of drugs are illegal and why?**	The deviant nature of drug taking is not specifically related to the chemical composition of the drug itself, but rather has more to do with the public's perception of who uses the drug and the need for its social control, which very often defines the drug's illicit status. Whether a particular drug is deviant, criminal, or both is therefore socially created and varies according to moral sentiment.
■ **Are we winning the war on drugs?**	Scholars note that efforts to reduce drug abuse and addiction that focus exclusively on the arrest and incarceration of drug users and dealers are misguided and destined to fail because they do not recognize the social and public health issues related to drug abuse and addiction. Successful strategies must integrate components of law enforcement, treatment, and prevention.

■ **What sexual acts do we define as prostitution?**

Prostitution is a diverse behavior pattern. Prostitutes come from a variety of backgrounds, have different reasons and different methods for engaging in the behavior, and different understandings of that behavior. Prostitution has one common, legal variable: It involves sexual acts that are exchanged for monetary gain.

■ **Why do some individuals exchange sex for money or drugs?**

Some do it as a financially lucrative exchange. Others do it out of necessity to support an addiction or pay off a debt, or just to survive particular circumstances. Some prostitutes are forced or coerced into the behavior.

■ **When does pornography become a crime?**

Forms of sexually explicit materials that are forbidden by law include child pornography and those deemed to be obscene.

CRITICAL THINKING QUESTIONS

1. Why is prostitution legal in parts of Nevada and not legal in any other states? How far should the government go in legislating moral behavior? Are there any behaviors currently considered to be illegal that you feel should not be subject to control by the law? What are these behaviors and who is keeping them on the books?

2. What guidelines should be used to define what constitutes obscenity? Given the empirical evidence in support of the correlation between pornography and violence against women, should all forms of pornography be considered illegal? Why or why not?

3. Do you think the moral climate is changing in the direction of legalizing certain drugs? How do you feel about this issue? What are the pros and cons in the debate on the legal regulation of certain types of drugs such as marijuana?

ADDITIONAL RESOURCES

You can learn more about international efforts to stop the trafficking of women and children by visiting the United Nations Educational, Scientific, and Cultural Organization (UNESCO) website at http://www.unescobkk.org/index.php?id=1022

Research on pornography as a catalyst to violence against women can be found at http://www.dianarussell.com/index.html

Find more facts, figures, and trends on drug use and drug control policies at http://www.whitehousedrugpolicy.gov/publications/policy/ndcs09/2009ndcs.pdf

Find more about drug courts and other problem-solving efforts at http://www.ndci.org/publications/publication-resources/painting-current-picture

14

CRIMES OF THE POWERFUL

In August 2009, former Democratic congressman William

Jefferson was convicted on 11 counts of corruption, including bribery, wire fraud, racketeering, and money laundering. Jefferson had used his power and influence to secure business deals in Africa in exchange for what prosecutors said was nearly $500,000 in bribes and was, they charged, prepared to take more. Jefferson was known to store thousands of dollars in cash in his freezer; FBI agents investigating the case had found $90,000 hidden in frozen pie crusts and wrapped in foil.

On November 13, 2009, Jefferson was sentenced to 13 years in prison, the longest sentence ever imposed on a congressman.[1] His actions were not only criminal but also a violation of ethical standards and a breach of the public's trust. Public officials are supposed to represent the interest of their constituents. Congressman Jefferson used his position to advance his own interests and those of his family. Yet, some would argue that using your position to achieve personal wealth is a common dynamic in society. What, then, is corruption?

Researchers note that corruption is a widespread global phenomenon that profoundly affects the economy and significantly reduces and undermines the rule of law. In the United States, it is estimated that nearly $1 trillion in bribes changes hands each year. In a systematic study of corruption, researcher Dennis Thompson notes that political corruption goes beyond the greed and actions of individuals to the institutional policies, practices, and procedures associated with the office.[2] Academic researchers and scholars warn that corruption is a multifaceted problem; it is not associated with any single political or economic variable, but rather is linked to factors that facilitate a conducive environment.[3]

On November 13, 2009, William Jefferson, Louisiana's first African American congressman, was not on his way to a political debate in the U.S. Capitol. Instead, he was arriving at the U.S. District Court in Alexandria, Virginia, for sentencing in his bribery case. What factors contribute to this type of political corruption?

What factors facilitate an environment of vice, deception, exploitation, and corruption? In this chapter we focus on crimes committed by individuals we do not typically think of as criminal. These are political officials, military personnel, businessmen and businesswomen, bankers, doctors, lawyers, shop owners, retailers, corporate executives, and a variety of others. They all have one thing in common: They use their position of power and authority to break the law in order to advance their own interest for financial gain, recognition, and business advancement. We will focus on three broad categories: white-collar crime, government and state crime, and organized crime. Let's turn now to a discussion of white-collar crime.

CRIMES IN THE SUITES: WHITE-COLLAR CRIME

Criminologist Edwin Sutherland (see Chapter 9) referred to "white-collar crime" as the illegal acts of high-status, respectable individuals in the course of their occupation.[4] Sutherland noted that these individuals used their positions in enterprise for personal gain, disregarding the rule of law. Contemporary criminologists use the term **white-collar crime** to collectively describe the acts of individuals perpetrated during the course of their work where deception, concealment, and breach of trust are used to obtain money and gain privilege, or to avoid losing money or privilege.[5]

White-collar crime does not involve acts of violence or coercion, although its effects on victims can often be very costly. White-collar crime can be perpetrated by a single individual or a group of people. Likewise, victims can be individuals, corporations, or the general public (Figure 14.1). For the sake of organization, we will divide white-collar crime into three categories: corporate or organizational crime, occupational crime, and client fraud.[6]

white-collar crime

Acts of an individual perpetrated during the course of the person's work where deception, concealment, and breach of trust are used to obtain money and gain privilege, or to avoid losing money or privilege.

Corporate or Organizational Crime

Corporate or organizational crime describes the acts of individuals who occupy positions of power within institutions who willfully and knowingly break the law to advance their own interests and for their own benefit or the benefit of their business or enterprise.[7] For many years, the acts of these individuals—respectable executives, upstanding corporate leaders, and billionaire businessmen and businesswomen—remained relatively unnoticed. Their acts were not as obviously harmful to society as murder, rape, and robbery. However, a surge in corporate crimes during the 1990s turned the tide of criminal prosecution, which began to crack down on the actions of corporations that violate criminal codes.[8]

Acts within this category of white-collar crime are quite diverse (Figure 14.2). Linking them, however, is that they are all committed by individuals within corporate entities acting in the interest of their organization. The acts are socially harmful and include crimes against employees, crimes against the environment, and crimes against the general public. We look at each of these.

Crimes Against Employees

In January 2006, an explosion in the Sago Mine in Sago, West Virginia, trapped 13 employees for two days; 12 of them died. Reports indicated that the Sago Mine had over 200 reports of safety violations in the previous year.[9] The **Occupational Safety and Health Act** of 1970 was designed to create and enforce federal standards to ensure that companies are providing their employees with safe and healthy working conditions.[10]

FIGURE 14.1

Victims of White-Collar Crime by Offense Type

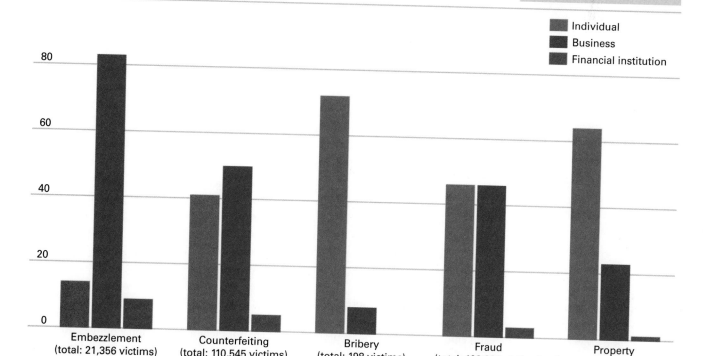

Percent of total victims for each crime

Legend: Individual, Business, Financial institution

- Embezzlement (total: 21,356 victims)
- Counterfeiting (total: 110,545 victims)
- Bribery (total: 198 victims)
- Fraud (total: 103,993 victims)
- Property (total: 4,069,324 victims)

Source: U.S. Department of Justice, Federal Bureau of Investigation, Criminal Justice Information Services Division. Barnett, Cynthia. *The Measurement of White-Collar Crime Using Uniform Crime Reporting (UCR) Data.* Retrieved from www.fbi.gov/ucr/whitecollarforweb.pdf on March 19, 2010. National Criminal Justice Reference Service (NCJRS) Library.

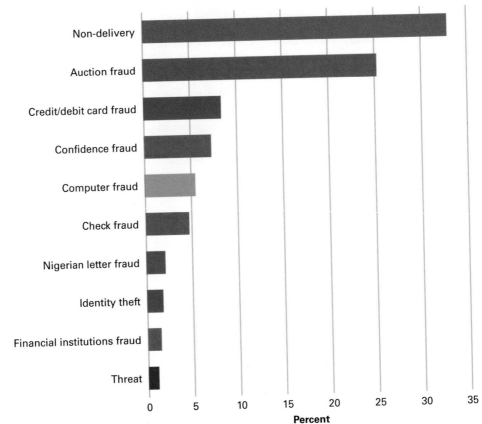

FIGURE **14.2**

**2009 Top 10 Fraud
Complaints by Type**

Source: 2009 Annual Report. (2010).
National White Collar Crime Center.

corporate or organizational crime

Acts of individuals who occupy positions of power within institutions and who willfully and knowingly break the law to advance their own interests and for their own benefit or the benefit of their business or enterprise.

Occupational Safety and Health Act (OSHA)

A 1970 law designed to create and enforce federal standards to ensure that companies are providing their employees with safe and healthy working conditions.

international environmental laws

Laws to monitor and enforce global standards protecting the environment across national borders.

Standards developed under the act are set forth by the Occupational Safety and Health Administration (OSHA), which makes guidelines and provisions regarding the proper use of hazardous chemicals; the maintenance of equipment and machinery; the inspection of vehicles, sanitation standards, and a variety of other codes ensuring safe and healthy work environments. According to OSHA, there were 3.7 million cases reported of workplace injuries and illnesses among private-industry employers in 2008, representing a slight decline from 4 million cases reported in 2007.[11] To keep costs down and increase their profits, corporations often cut corners and ignore or fail to correct safety and health violations. They are willing to do so because the fine they risk incurring is often less costly than correcting a violation. However, the purposeful negligence of OSHA safety standards can result in criminal sanctions.

Crimes Against the Environment

In 1988, the U.S. government gave the Environmental Protection Agency (EPA) the authority to prosecute violations of environmental statutes resulting in harm to our nation's air, water, public land, and wildlife. These include the negligent and willful dumping of toxic wastes in oceans and on land, oil spills by freighters, the use of illegally obtained chemicals that damage the ozone layer, and the mishandling of hazardous materials such as asbestos that expose people, often in poor areas, to serious injury, illness, and death.[12]

Because of the widespread and devastating consequences of crimes against the environment, **international environmental laws** have been developed over the years to monitor and enforce global standards protecting the environment across national borders. Recognition of the precious and finite nature of the earth's natural resources has expanded the role of criminology in developing research and strategies to regulate and prevent harm to the earth.[13]

The 1990s ushered in an era of grave concern over the earth's natural resources. Nations worldwide began to reevaluate their exploitation of metals and fossil fuels, excessive production of waste, and depletion of land, air, and water resources. A growing body of literature demonstrated the impact of environmental degradation on the quality of life and health, especially among the poor.[14]

National policies emerged to promote the use of abundant resources over scarce ones, to reduce or eliminate waste of resources such as forests, and to increase recycling of materials such as glass and aluminum. Researchers focused on strategies to reduce the harmful effects of pollution and sustain natural resources.[15] In the late 1990s, the Office of Research and Development (ORD) of the U.S. Environmental Protection Agency provided a long-term strategic plan to expand the scientific study of the environment.[16] The plan included providing research data and technical support to government agencies, organizational entities, corporations, and the general public; increasing awareness of wasteful practices; managing ecological resources; and understanding the health hazards of pollution. The research on risk assessment and risk management identified four areas of priority:

- Contaminated sites—groundwater
- Contaminated sites—soil or vadose, the unsaturated zone of the earth
- Emissions from waste combustion facilities
- Active waste management facilities

The progress made by the ORD represents the first research-driven policies and practices to systematically identify and manage risks to the environment.

It has also expanded the role of the federal government in monitoring environmental harm. (See Connecting Research to Practice for more about dealing with environmental threats.)

Crimes Against the Public

Corporations commit a variety of crimes that involve deceiving the public in order to increase their own profits by providing misleading information about a product or service. This is known as **false claims advertising.** Sometimes it is a fine line between the aggressive marketing of a product and the fraudulent and purposeful deception of consumers to increase sales and meet stockholders' expectations. Drug manufacturing companies, for example, have been accused by the Food and Drug Administration (FDA) of making false claims about the effects of certain medicines in their efforts to promote them to the pharmaceutical industry.[17]

Corporations also manipulate free market competition by conspiring with their own competitors to maintain high prices for a particular commodity, a practice known as **price fixing.** This is strictly forbidden by law and can result in criminal sanctions that include both a fine and a prison sentence. While it is a common practice for businesses to adjust prices to meet supply and demand, it is illegal for them to conspire to set and control those prices in order to stifle competition. Distinguishing between the two purposes, however, can be an arduous task for investigators.[18] A better understanding of the dynamics in each industry may help control widespread shifting of prices for high-demand commodities such as gasoline.

false claims advertising

Crimes committed by corporations that involve deceiving the public in order to increase their own profits by providing misleading information about a product or service.

price fixing

Crime committed by corporations involving manipulating free market competition by conspiring with competitors to maintain high prices for a particular commodity.

SOUTH GATE MEAT CO.

In the summer of 2009, the U.S. Department of Agriculture ordered the largest recall of ground beef in U.S. history. What corporate actions might contribute to the emergence of such crises? How does the science of criminology expand to the food service industry to help us understand and control such a threat to the public?

occupational crime

Crime that is distinct from corporate crime in that it involves the illegal acts of individuals to promote their *own* interests, rather than the interests of the organization.

pilferage

The systematic theft of small amounts of company property over an extended period of time.

Occupational Crime

Occupational crime is distinct from corporate crime in that it involves the illegal acts of individuals to promote their *own* interests, rather than the interest of the organization.[19] We will look at two particular forms of fraud within this category of white-collar crime: embezzlement and chiseling.

Embezzlement

Very often, perpetrators of occupational crime use their positions of employment to steal company property or funds entrusted to their care. This is a form of occupational crime known as *embezzlement*. The major difference between traditional theft, discussed in Chapter 12, and embezzlement is the manner in which the property is stolen: When a theft is committed, the perpetrator did not have legal possession of the stolen money or goods; when embezzlement takes place, the perpetrator *does* have legal possession of the money or item but misappropriates it for his or her own benefit. For example, the individual who walks into a convenience store, sees the cash register open, and takes a $20 bill has committed larceny theft. However, the employee who works the cash register and takes a $20 bill at the end of the day has embezzled company property. Embezzlement can be a great deal more complicated than taking $20 from the cash register. It often includes elaborate schemes to alter records, interfere with bookkeeping, or manipulate accounts.

The systematic theft of fairly small amounts of company property over an extended period of time, referred to as **pilferage,** is very common and can cost companies hundreds of thousands of dollars a year. Nevertheless, employees continue to steal from their employers, justifying their actions with a variety of rationales. Some believe they are being mistreated with regard to compensation and promotion, so they are entitled to compensate by stealing. Others do it because of the easy accessibility of the funds. Still others are motivated by financial reasons—either out of personal greed or due to economic hardship.

Chiseling

Another type of occupational crime that consists of the regular cheating of a company or organization, its consumers, or both is **chiseling.** Chiseling can be very difficult to detect and prove, because victims have often put their trust in someone they know nothing about.

Consider what happens if your car breaks down. You go to an auto mechanic who tells you several parts need to be replaced. Without knowledge of auto mechanics, you have to trust that what the mechanic is telling you is correct. Similarly, medical professionals engage in chiseling when they recommend treatments and procedures that are not a medical necessity. Thus, chiselers can be individuals who cheat their customers to increase the profits of their business or practice. They can also be employees who are cheating their customers and employers by pocketing the profits for themselves, such as would be the case if the mechanic in the example above created bogus repairs without the shop owner's knowledge and kept the profits.

Other examples of chiseling include retailers who advertise and sell as genuine expensive merchandise such as sports memorabilia, handbags, shoes, and watches that are actually replicas. The Internet has made this type of transaction more prevalent and created the need for an aggressive approach to control. Several websites have been created to monitor such sales and increase consumer awareness of fraudulent merchants.[20]

Technology has also facilitated a significant amount of chiseling in the stock market.[21] Some stockbrokers engage in **churning,** the repeated and excessive buying and selling of stocks owned by investors for the sole purpose of generating a commission on each trade.[22] In the end, the trades result in a loss of funds for the investor. **Front running** is another form of stock market fraud wherein brokerage companies purchase large quantities of a certain stock at a low cost, before advising their investors to buy the stock at a higher price. Churning and front running both violate laws governing securities exchange, which are monitored and enforced by the U.S. Securities and Exchange Commission (SEC). In November 2009, as a result of enforcement efforts and legal proceedings, the SEC distributed approximately $2 billion to injured investors, the largest compensation paid in a single calendar year.[23]

chiseling
An occupational crime that consists of the regular cheating of a company or organization, its consumers, or both.

churning
A crime in which stockbrokers repeatedly and excessively buy and sell stocks owned by investors for the sole purpose of generating a commission on each trade.

front running
A crime in which brokerage companies purchase large quantities of a certain stock at a low cost, before advising their investors to buy the stock at a higher price.

A great deal of client fraud is perpetrated by and through the healthcare industry. The National Health Care Anti-Fraud Association (NHCAA) estimates that about 3 percent of all healthcare spending, or $68 billion, is lost to fraud each year.

buildup

A common type of claim abuse wherein a legitimate claim is inflated by unnecessary treatments or medical interventions.

tax evasion

A crime in which the taxpayer, a client of the government, deliberately fails to pay appropriate taxes on earned income by using deception and fraud, such as underreporting or failing to report taxable income.

Client Fraud

At the other end of the spectrum of white-collar crime are the fraudulent activities of clients against companies providing such services as healthcare and automobile insurance. *Healthcare fraud* can be perpetrated in many different ways. Physicians often engage in fraud when they accept payment for services that are supposed to be free of charge, bill insurance companies for multiple visits that did not actually take place, receive kickbacks for patient referrals, and overcharge for medical procedures and services.[24] It is estimated that about 80 percent of healthcare fraud is committed by medical providers.[25] Pharmaceutical companies also engage in fraud when they cheat public and private insurance companies by failing to pay appropriate rebates for certain drugs, improperly classifying drugs to charge higher prices, and making illegal kickbacks to physicians in order to get them to prescribe certain drugs.[26]

False claims are also a concern for the automobile insurance industry. According to a study by the Insurance Research Council, fraudulent claims account for over $10 billion in excess payment to clients of automobile insurance companies.[27] Clients make two types of fraudulent claims. One type misrepresents the actual facts surrounding the loss, such as claiming to have a back or neck injury resulting from an accident when no such injury exists, or claiming an expensive bag or piece of equipment was stolen during an automobile theft when it actually was not. A more common type of claim abuse is **buildup**, wherein a legitimate claim is inflated by unnecessary treatments or medical interventions. In either case, the loss to insurance companies is vast, raising the cost of auto insurance for all clients.

Also included in this category of white-collar crime is **tax evasion** in which the taxpayer, a client of the government, deliberately fails to pay appropriate taxes on earned income by using deception and fraud, such as underreporting or failing to report taxable income. Tax evasion can be a challenging area of white-collar crime, for both law enforcement and criminological research. The amount in question may not always indicate criminal intent, and the difficulty thus lies in separating careless errors in tax preparation from the deliberate intention to avoid paying taxes.

The most serious federal tax crime is **willful tax evasion**, a felony crime that carries a five-year maximum prison sentence and a maximum fine of $250,000.[28] The government must prove three key elements to convict an individual of willful tax evasion: (1) an existing tax deficiency, (2) a willful intent to evade taxes, and (3) an affirmative act of evasion or affirmative attempt to evade.[29] Affirmative acts of evasion—such as making false entries, creating a double set of accounting records, and shredding documents and records—distinguish willful tax evasion from the lesser misdemeanor crime of **passive neglect**, the delay or failure to pay taxes when they are due, something most of us have probably done from time to time. In either case, the government, whether state or federal, is the victim of this type of activity. We turn now to a different category of crime in which the government, along with its agents and representatives, is the perpetrator, not the victim.

CRIMES IN THE CORRIDORS: GOVERNMENT, POLITICS, AND STATE CRIME

When we think of crime, we typically conjure up images of a murderer or rapist or mugger. We typically do not think of government leaders, military officers, and politicians as dangerous people. Nevertheless, influential people in positions of power often inflict far more social harm than traditional street criminals.[30] (The Crime in Global Perspective

CRIME IN GLOBAL PERSPECTIVE | Crimes Against Humanity

By Lynda Marie Robyn, Associate Professor, Northern Arizona University

Nowhere in the United States are government crimes more evident than on the Navajo Nation in northeastern Arizona. The Hopi people first occupied land where Arizona, Utah, Colorado, and New Mexico meet, an area known today as the Four Corners. In 1934 Congress decided to set aside a large portion of land in Arizona for the Navajo and "other such Indians as may already be located thereon." In effect, the U.S. government created a situation that would cause conflict over land between the Navajo and the Hopi village of Moenkopi, which was already in this area.

To prevent one tribe from taking unfair advantage of the other during land negotiations, Robert Bennett, commissioner of Indian Affairs, instituted a ban on any type of development in the area. The ban took effect in 1966 and left thousands of Navajos living in third-world conditions for over 40 years, because under it they could not build or repair their homes (even to fix leaking roofs or broken windows), take care of the roads, or ensure adequate schools or health facilities. Even though the Navajo Nation produces most of the energy for the Southwest, the ban also meant no electric lines could reach homes in the so-called Bennett Freeze area. There were no gas lines for heat, and no water lines for indoor plumbing or any type of sanitation. People have either hauled in water fit for human consumption or drunk from the same wells as their livestock. But these wells have been contaminated by companies that have mined and processed uranium ore, leaving huge toxic tailings in piles polluting streams and underground aquifers, with no obligation to clean up the devastation left behind.[31]

People living on the reservation also used sand and crushed rock from old uranium mines to make concrete slabs for floors in hogans and ovens, not knowing these materials were radioactive. Exposure to uranium is lethal, and new evidence shows gastric cancer rates rose 50 percent during the 1990s among Navajo in two New Mexico counties with uranium sites. Uranium has also been linked to reproductive cancers, and a sharp increase in breast, ovarian, and other cancers has been recorded among teenage girls. Cancer rates 17 times the national average were found in the entire Navajo Nation.[32]

The creation of reservations forced the Navajo off their ancestral lands to live in abysmal conditions on the reservation, while the Bennett Freeze, by preventing the construction of any life-saving infrastructure, contributed to hundreds of cancer deaths. Who will pay for this needless suffering?

President Obama lifted the Bennett Freeze in May 2009.[33] Though it will take time and work to make infrastructure repairs, thousands of tribal members are now eligible for federal compensation for health problems caused by past uranium exposure. Recently, with renewed interest in uranium on the reservation, mining companies have filed mining claims and promised jobs, safe working conditions, and environmental prudence. We can hope past mistakes will never be repeated.

feature examines crimes against the Navajo Nation, showing the enduring hardship of governmental crime.) In the late 1980s, criminological research expanded its study of traditional street crimes and white-collar crimes to include crimes committed by governments and their representatives and leaders. Among the topics about which we now know considerably more than we did 20 years ago is the abuse of power and privilege by political officials and state-organized violence.

Abuse of Power and Institutional Privilege

A citizen elected or appointed to a political office must use his or her position of power and institutional privileges for the public good. Often, however, in the struggle to reach office as well as to maintain power, officials cross ethical lines—from making a few promises along the campaign trail to accepting bribes from influential supporters. This is what happened in the case of Representative Jefferson presented at the opening of this chapter.[34] It is what happens when politicians and government officials abuse their positions of power and privilege to engage in corruption, bribery, and extortion (Table 14.1).

willful tax evasion

A serious federal tax crime; a felony that must be proved by (1) an existing tax deficiency, (2) a willful intent to evade taxes, and (3) an affirmative act of evasion or affirmative attempt to evade.

passive neglect

A misdemeanor crime involving the delay or failure to pay taxes when they are due.

TABLE **14.1**

Corruption in Government by State

STATE	PUBLIC CORRUPTION CONVICTIONS 1998–2007	POPULATION 2007	CORRUPTION- RATE CONVICTIONS PER 100,000
Alabama	252	4,627,851	5.4
Alaska	51	683,478	7.5
Arizona	140	6,338,755	2.2
Arkansas	80	2,834,797	2.8
California	547	36,553,215	1.5
Colorado	77	4,861,515	1.6
Connecticut	111	3,502,309	3.2
Delaware	44	864,764	5.1
Florida	824	18,251,243	4.5
Georgia	163	9,544,750	1.7
Hawaii	51	1,283,388	4
Idaho	38	1,449,402	2.5
Illinois	502	12,852,548	3.9
Indiana	123	6,345,289	1.9
Iowa	35	2,988,046	1.2
Kansas	38	2,775,997	1.4
Kentucky	242	4,241,474	5.7
Louisiana	332	4,293,204	7.7
Maine	25	1,317,207	1.9
Maryland	148	5,618,344	2.6
Massachusetts	188	6,449,755	2.9
Michigan	215	10,071,822	2.1
Minnesota	66	5,197,621	1.3
Mississippi	212	2,918,785	7.3
Missouri	158	5,878,415	2.7
Montana	59	959,861	6.2
Nebraska	12	1,774,471	0.7
Nevada	46	2,565,382	1.8
New Hampshire	14	1,315,828	1.1
New Jersey	418	8,685,920	4.8
New Mexico	30	1,969,915	1.5
New York	704	19,297,729	3.6
North Carolina	179	9,061,032	2

(*continued*)

TABLE **14.1** (continued)

Corruption in Government by State

STATE	PUBLIC CORRUPTION CONVICTIONS 1998–2007	POPULATION 2007	CORRUPTION-RATE CONVICTIONS PER 100,000
North Dakota	53	639,715	8.3
Ohio	547	11,466,917	4.8
Oklahoma	107	3,617,316	3
Oregon	36	3,747,455	1
Pennsylvania	555	12,432,792	4.5
Rhode Island	26	1,057,832	2.5
South Carolina	73	4,407,709	1.9
South Dakota	41	796,214	5.1
Tennessee	244	6,156,719	4
Texas	565	23,094,380	2.4
Utah	38	2,465,330	1.4
Vermont	13	621,254	2.1
Virginia	303	7,712,091	3.9
Washington	99	6,468,424	1.5
West Virginia	74	1,812,035	4.1
Wisconsin	122	5,601,640	2.1
Wyoming	14	522,830	2.7

Source: Thomassie, J., & Hatch, J. (2008, December 11). State corruption. *USA Today.* Data from the U.S. Department of Justice and the U.S. Census Bureau. Retrieved April 27, 2011.

In December 2009, Tom Corbett, then the attorney general for Pennsylvania, had the unpleasant task of holding a news conference regarding three state legislators accused of misdirecting staff salaries and office time toward Democratic campaigns in House elections.

political corruption

The misuse of entrusted power by political officials to maintain privilege and reap personal gain.

influence peddling

A form of political corruption wherein government leaders use their influence for favors, financial gain, or material advantage, such as by accepting large campaign contributions in exchange for the awarding of government contracts.

bribery

An illegal financial exchange wherein a government official accepts a direct payment in exchange for official government action, such as gaining votes, sponsoring legislation, and appropriating government funds to private contractors.

Corruption

We broadly define **political corruption** as the misuse of entrusted power by political officials to maintain privilege and reap personal gain.[35] **Influence peddling** is a form of corruption that occurs when government leaders use their influence for favors, financial gain, or material advantage, such as by accepting large campaign contributions in exchange for the awarding of government contracts. Using a public office to hire relatives, giving preferential treatment to certain interest groups, misdirecting state resources, and making expensive and lavish trips and purchases on government accounts are all examples of political corruption.

Bribery

Sometimes the abuse of power and institutional privilege can include the more serious illegal financial exchange called **bribery.** Bribery occurs when a government official accepts a direct payment in exchange for official government action, such as gaining votes, sponsoring legislation, and appropriating government funds to private contractors.[36] As we discussed in Chapter 3, former congressman Randy "Duke" Cunningham was a powerful California Republican whose military service and expertise landed him on the defense appropriations subcommittee, a position that holds a tremendous influence over the U.S. military budget. In November 2005, however, Cunningham admitted to abusing this position when he pleaded guilty to accepting $2.4 million in bribes from military contractors in exchange for pressuring the Pentagon to buy their products and services.

Extortion

State representatives and government officials often abuse their positions of power to force or coerce individuals into providing them with some type of financial reward or material gain. This type of abuse, discussed in Chapter 12, is known as *extortion*. Withholding legislation, failing to renew a contract or issue a permit, and threatening to close down a business due to lack of compliance with financial demands are all examples of extortion. Such was the case in the conviction of former New Jersey state senator Joseph Coniglio on six counts of fraud and extortion for taking over $1 million in public funding to Hackensack University Medical Center. The money was given to him under the guise of a high-paying consulting job, when, in fact, it was an exchange for his support of the funding.[37]

State Crimes of Violence

One of the most challenging topics in criminological study are large-scale, organized acts of violence committed by governments at the domestic and international level. These crimes flout the rule of law and threaten the very peace and stability of the land. They often occur in times of political unrest, military conflict, and domestic strife.

genocide

The systematic destruction of a particular national, religious, ethnic, racial, or political group.

Genocide

Throughout history, **genocide**—the systematic destruction of a particular national, religious, ethnic, racial or political group—has been practiced by societies around the world.[38] It was a point of pride among ancient rulers to have eliminated an entire enemy—civilians and children as well as soldiers.

The practice of genocide was not considered a crime until after World War II, when the need to monitor and prevent it, as well as to bring to justice its perpetrators, was highlighted in the 1948 *United Nations Convention on the Prevention and Punishment of the Crime of Genocide;* this document made it a crime to "commit genocide, plan or conspire to commit genocide, incite or cause other people to commit genocide or be complicit or involved in any act of genocide."[39] This agreement among UN members created a potentially powerful new political reality by declaring that "States would no longer have the right to be left alone" to pursue internal conflicts as they saw fit. State sovereignty would no longer shield a country from the consequences of committing genocide within its borders.

Genocide has devastating and destructive consequences. Acts of genocide include torturing members of a targeted group, eliminating them through mass killing, imposing harsh conditions intended to bring about physical deterioration and eventual death, forcing sterilization to prevent future births, and removing the group by transfer or migration, such as the forced relocation of Native American groups onto federally owned reservations during the 19th century. Genocide has attracted much international attention in recent years, with former United Nations Secretary General Kofi Annan outlining a five-point action plan for its prevention in 2004.[40]

Criminologists and researchers seeking to understand this form of collective violence against a particular group of people have identified various political climates and social environments that increase the likelihood of genocide, such as governments that are authoritarian in which only one person or group has all the power, countries plagued by civil war and strife, and states with political leaders heavily engaged in vice and corruption.[41] Under these conditions, national leaders use genocide as a mechanism of social control to eliminate threats, spread fear among potential enemies and dissenters, acquire wealth and maintain status, or implement a particular belief or ideology.[42] They must inspire and recruit a large portion of the population to participate in and carry out their task.

These leaders often do this by establishing a "genocidal mentality" in order to dehumanize the potential victims. For instance, Rwanda's Hutus called their Tutsi targets "cockroaches." Radio broadcasts imploring Hutus to "kill cockroaches" fostered mass killing.[43] (The Connecting Theory to Practice box examines the process of dehumanization in genocide.) Modern media have made the process of disseminating dehumanizing propaganda even easier. The establishment of institutions and organizations that justify and carry out the atrocities is a key component of the spread of genocide. From academia to the government to the military, the leadership mobilizes organizations in its power to destroy those defined as "others."

Predictably, governments are reluctant to label mass murders as "genocide" because under United Nations rules, doing so requires them to intervene. It was partly a fear of incurring such an obligation, as well as a desire to protect its sovereign decision-making powers, that underpinned the decades-long delay in the U.S. ratification of the Convention under the Reagan administration in 1988. Governments thus resort to calling genocide "civil war," "ethnic conflict," or a "manifestation of age-old hatreds"—none of which carry an obligation to intervene.

An estimated 800,000 men, women, and children were killed in the 1994 Rwanda massacre led by political leaders of the Hutu-dominated government.

CONNECTING THEORY TO PRACTICE

The Role of Dehumanization in Mass Killing

Ethnic conflict between Hutu crop growers and Tutsi herdsmen was a fact of life in the Rwandan villages in the tropical heart of the African continent. Although the Hutus vastly outnumbered the Tutsi, the Tutsi occupied the more prestigious, privileged, and advantaged positions in government and society. As the Hutu population became more alienated socially and politically, a revolution ensued, and by the late 1950s the Hutu had gained control, exiling many of the Tutsi and taking away their land and property. Civil war ensued for decades. After a brief ceasefire in 1993, conflict broke out again when on April 6, 1994, a plane carrying Rwanda's president (a Hutu) was shot down—an act the Tutsis were accused of plotting. Anti-Tutsi sentiment began to grow and spread among Hutu civilians. Getting even became a national agenda, and Hutu citizens began to believe it was their duty to avenge the death of their leader by wiping out the Tutsi. From April to June 1994, an estimated 800,000 Rwandans were slaughtered, most of them Tutsis.

How could such a large-scale act of genocide happen, and in such a short span of time?[44] How could so many people (including community and government leaders) engage in the beating, hacking, and killing of innocent men, women, and children who were their everyday friends, neighbors, and co-workers? How does the impetus for genocide spread?

Researchers note that participants in genocide are manipulated into accepting a dehumanized image of their victims by the widespread dissemination of hate propaganda.[45] In the years before the genocide in Rwanda, for example, political debates, demonstrations and rallies, speeches by government officials, and broadcasts on radical radio stations filled the air with what official reports describe as "vicious, pornographic, inflammatory rhetoric designed to demonize and dehumanize all Tutsi." The Tutsi became the enemy, a threat to the very existence of Hutus and not to be spared, and the motivation of every good Hutu was to eradicate them all. Thus, Tutsi men, women, and children alike became objects, not humans, making it easier to commit unthinkable acts of torture, rape, and murder.

Many scholars would agree that when it comes to genocide, perpetrators are socially constructed, made to hate, and made to kill.

Military Rape

In the mid-1990s, scholars began to examine the role of rape as a strategic military policy of war that serves specific objectives.[46] They note that this use of rape has become an "orchestrated combat tool," and not just a traditional mechanism of plunder and power.[47] The wars in Yugoslavia in the early 1990s drew the world's attention to the systematic use of rape by Serbian soldiers against Bosnian, Croatian, and Kosovo women, which brought public and legal scrutiny to this pressing issue.[48] What is the role of this form of crime in military conflicts? What motivates state-backed military soldiers to engage in the sexual assault of civilian women during war?

During wartime, civilian women are often targeted for political and strategic purposes. In former Yugoslavia, for example, as a key strategy in the campaign to "ethnically cleanse" the part of the country claimed by Serbs, Serbian soldiers raided villages of the non-Serbian population, taking men into detention centers and leaving women in towns controlled by enemy forces to be raped, beaten, and tortured.[49]

Rape in war is also a means of cultural assault on a community. Women are often the keepers of culture, passing on stories, traditions, and cultural artifacts to children, who will carry those to future generations. Amnesty International (2004) reports that "Around the world, women have long been attributed the role of transmitters of culture and symbols of nation or community. Violence directed against women is often considered an attack against the values of 'honor' of a society and therefore a particularly potent

344

tool of war."[50] It may also be a way of physically destroying a community or group, as the brutality of many war rapes can leave women unable to bear children. On the other hand, researchers note that the systematic raping of women by military soldiers is also a method of social control. Impregnating women through rape perpetuates the attacking groups' own ethnicity, while destroying the enemy's.[51]

In this section, we have seen how the collective actions of governments and their representative organizations can lead to violent crimes against citizens. These actions are the result of conscious decisions by powerful and influential political figures, using their legitimate authority to coerce compliance in destructive acts. We turn now to a different form of coercion based on *illegitimate* authority derived from a reputation for brutality, crime, and violence.

THE ILLEGAL SERVICE INDUSTRY: GUNS, DRUGS, MONEY, AND PEOPLE

In the annals of crime, everything—from sheep to wool, wine, gold, drugs, military weapons, books, people, and even ideas—has been prohibited at some time in history. The paradox of prohibition, however, is that the commodity made illegal will continue to be in great demand by certain segments of the public. This demand will inevitably create the desire on the part of some group to distribute the prohibited goods. The control, organization, and distribution of illegal goods and services, on a national and international scale, is what we refer to as **organized crime**.[52] What constitutes *organized* crime?

organized crime

The control, organization, and distribution of illegal goods and services on a national and international scale.

The Organization of Organized Crime

At the heart of our study of organized criminal behavior is an understanding of its connection to the larger social structure. Organized crime relies on the cooperation of a network of individuals who have a mutually beneficial relationship. Corrupt politicians, dishonest judges, deceitful bankers, crooked law enforcement officers, and a breakdown of the legal system protect, sustain, and facilitate organized criminal activities.[53]

Knowing who belongs to criminal networks and how they differ from one another helps criminologists better understand organized crime and guides law enforcement strategies and policies to combat it. The public also needs to grasp the reality of organized crime and the diverse activities it encompasses, beyond the glamorized images generated by popular films.

Researchers have developed various typologies of organized criminal networks based on their structural organization. Five different types of networks have been identified (Table 14.2).[54]

In addition to differing in structure, criminal groups may change their characteristics and operations over time and according to supply and demand. This variability in turn influences the nature and characteristics of organized crime.

Characteristics of Organized Crime

Organized crime requires the secret and often rapid movement of goods, money, people, and drugs, and adherence to established mechanisms for dictating rules, settling disputes, dividing territories, and controlling markets.[55] Leaders must buy or force the allegiance and cooperation of many people. This often means permeating the legitimate business world to control certain markets and industries, such as occurred with the infiltration of labor unions by major organized crime networks during the 1950s.[56] Some people are born into organized crime and enter the "family business" as part of their socialization. Others are recruited to participate. Regardless of how participants enter the illegal service industry, the price of refusal or betrayal is violence and murder.

TABLE **14.2**

Organized Crime Networks

TYPE OF NETWORK	OPERATIONAL STRUCTURE
Standard Hierarchy	■ Clearly defined with a single leader ■ A specific name is often linked to a social or ethnic identity ■ Strong system of internal discipline ■ Operates within and controls a clearly defined territory ■ Violence is embedded in most activities
Regional Hierarchy	■ Operates under a single central leader, but its regional organizations have a degree of autonomy ■ Often share an ethnic and social identity ■ Operates under the control of the central group to engage in multiple activities and help spread their influence ■ Internal discipline is high and violence is a part of most dealings
Clustered Hierarchy	■ Consists of a set of criminal groups with an established system of coordinating and controlling illicit activities ■ A core group acts as the central or oversight body, with clusters branching off into relatively autonomous groups, each with an identity of its own ■ Clusters often control divided markets ■ The potential for competition between groups and disruption of activity is high, making clustered hierarchies somewhat rare
Core Group	■ A small, tight, structured group of individuals conduct a criminal enterprise ■ The distribution of power is flat, with activities divided evenly among core group members ■ Internal discipline is maintained by virtue of the small number of members and limited number of criminal activities ■ Core groups usually have very little social or ethnic identity
Criminal Network	■ Loosely connected networks of individuals ■ Engages in ongoing criminal transactions ■ Are often built around individuals with particular characteristics, skills, or connections ■ Characterized by shifting alliances, with members providing their services to different components and "middlemen" serving as the connecting link between them and the central figures through which most connections operate

Source: Results of a pilot survey of forty selected organized criminal groups in sixteen countries. (2002, September 2002). Global Program Against Transnational Organized Crime, United Nations Office on Drugs and Crime.

In a 2002 study, the United Nations Office on Drugs and Crime surveyed 40 organized crime groups in 16 different countries.[57] The following were identified as key characteristics of organized crime:

■ Organized crime is the sustained and systematic coordination of illegal activities.
■ Criminal activities revolve around the organization and provision of illegal goods and services for economic gain, such as drugs, gambling, pornography, prostitution, loan sharking (lending money to pay debts at illegal interest rates), human trafficking, and weapons trafficking.

Images of organized crime have fascinated the public throughout history. This fascination is captured in the 1972 film *The Godfather,* which chronicled the battles fought between fictional rival mob families in New York. How does Hollywood continue to glamorize our image of organized crime?

- Most organized crime groups engage in one particular type of criminal activity.
- The majority of organized crime groups have a classical hierarchical structure with 20 to 50 members and participants.
- Violence, intimidation, corruption, and fraud are key elements in sustaining organized crime activities.
- The majority of crime groups operate in multiple countries.
- Organized crime activities penetrate the legitimate economy in order to launder illegal profits through legal businesses.

From this overview, we see that what makes organized crime a unique category of criminal behavior is the ability of ethnically diverse groups of individuals to both cooperate and compete for the control and distribution of goods and services in various geographic locations. It sounds like the operation of global corporations in the business industry. The only difference, however, is that the goods and services in demand are

CONSIDER THIS...

The Making of Organized Crime

Because organized crime is embedded within the social structure, institutional factors such as political unrest, civil struggle, and the decline of authoritarian government can compromise the rule of law, making a society particularly vulnerable and paving the way for widespread corruption. A case study in Afghanistan illustrates the making of organized crime.

The war in Afghanistan began in 2001 when, in response to the September 11 terrorist attacks, the United States and allies such as Great Britain launched a military offensive to disband and overthrow the Taliban and al Qaeda terrorist groups. This offensive marked the beginning of an ongoing counterinsurgency by Taliban forces to survive and rebuild. In the struggle between allied forces and the Taliban, several changes within the social, political, and economic structure took place. A decline in authoritarian rule, the transition to democracy, and a shift toward a market-based economic structure led to a power vacuum that shook the foundation of key government institutions. Moreover, in the aftermath of the conflict, the capacity of police to enforce the rule of law became severely compromised, as resources were hampered by civil struggle and attacks by Taliban forces.

As society adjusts to rapid change, organized criminal groups—including drug lords, terrorists, and corrupt government officials—take advantage of weak legal and political institutions, and their organized criminal activity flourishes. Researchers have identified six trends that demonstrate the escalation of organized crime:[58]

- A decline in the number of smaller criminal operators (individuals, loose networks, or small groups) and the appearance of a limited number of larger and more powerful ones.
- The identification by law enforcement officials of clear organized criminal groups as opposed to just the naming of individual "smugglers" or "traffickers."
- Evidence of close and mutually beneficial associations among government, business, and criminal enterprises, including elements of the state or business being held in criminal hands.
- The exclusion from criminal markets of new operators or groups and the forced exit of others.
- The emergence of responses to increasingly vigorous law enforcement, such as higher levels of secrecy in the operation of criminal markets.
- The development of well-organized mechanisms of criminal protection that is well understood and coordinated by key players in the criminal markets.

The weakened state institutions in post-conflict Afghanistan has made it fertile ground for the rapid growth of organized criminal markets, with their strong connections to corruption in law enforcement and government.[59] How does this connection influence the reliability of data on the nature and extent of the organized crime problem in Afghanistan?

What do you think?

Racketeer Influenced and Corrupt Organization Act (RICO)

A 1970 law intended to limit and control organized criminal activities by creating new categories of offenses.

racketeering

The organized operation of an illegal business by a structured group for the purpose of making a profit.

illegal, and the illegitimate operation often involves the use of violence and coercion to negotiate transactions.

Criminologists recognize the difficulty in monitoring and controlling organized crime because of the secretive and protective manner by which it is conducted, and the interconnection between the legitimate world of business, government, and politics and the illegitimate world of vice and corruption. The Consider This feature further examines how organized crime gained a foothold in Afghanistan.

Until the 1970s, federal and state governments did very little in terms of developing strategies to combat organized crime. In 1970, however, Congress passed the Organized Crime Control Act, which created the **Racketeer Influenced and Corrupt Organization Act (RICO).** The intention of the RICO Act was to limit and control organized criminal activities by creating new categories of offenses in **racketeering,** the organized operation of an illegal business by a structured group for the purpose of making a profit. Under RICO, being engaged in two or more activities prohibited by 24 federal statutes and 8 state statutes—including such crimes as murder, kidnapping, arson, robbery, extortion, bribery, prostitution, and fraud—constitutes racketeering. The goal of RICO was to disband the core of organized criminal enterprise by making it illegal to

- Use income derived from racketeering activity or the illegal collection of debt
- Acquire interest in a business or enterprise through a pattern of racketeering activity
- Conduct the affairs of an enterprise through a pattern of racketeering activity
- Conspire to commit any of the offenses listed above

An individual convicted of racketeering could be fined up to $25,000 and serve 20 years in prison. The accused could also forfeit to the federal government any and all property related to the racketeering violations.

RICO paved the way for the investigation of organized crime by focusing attention on aggregate acts of criminal enterprise rather than individual or isolated incidents of crime.[60] However, RICO laws have also been a great source of controversy, and they continue to stir up legal debates decades after their passage. Ambiguity lies in the application of the phrases *enterprise* and *pattern of racketeering*. The original intention behind RICO was to target organized crime. However, a broad interpretation of the law would argue that it can be applied to all forms of white-collar crime and can also define an enterprise by reference to patterns of racketeering. This ambiguity has been the source of controversy in cases where legitimate businesses have been subject to forfeiture because of patterns of illegal activities by the owner in the course of its operation.[61]

SUMMARY

What kinds of crimes are committed by the rich and powerful?

Crimes committed by the rich and powerful fall into three broad categories: white-collar crime, state or government crime, and organized crime. One common thread these categories share is the use and abuse of position, influence, power, and trust to gain personal advantage. Even without the overt use of violence, acts of deception and guile have harmful results on the public.

In what context does white-collar crime occur?

White-collar crime is perpetrated by individuals who use their positions in business and enterprise for personal gain by engaging in acts of deception in the context of their work.

How do government officials abuse their positions?

Individuals elected or appointed to political office do not always uphold the oath to act in the best interest of the public. Government officials abuse their position of public trust when they use their influence for personal gain by accepting bribes or engaging in corruption and extortion.

Do political figures engage in acts of violence?

Throughout history, political figures and their government representatives have endorsed and engaged in acts of violence against certain groups in society, including genocide and military rape, during times of conflict, war, and civil unrest.

When does crime become "organized"?

Criminal acts such as murder, drug trafficking, prostitution, and money laundering become organized when they are conducted and controlled in a systematic way by groups of individuals on a national and international scale. Criminal behavior is organized when the crime relies on the cooperation of a network of individuals who have a mutually beneficial relationship.

CRITICAL THINKING QUESTIONS

1. Which corporate criminal activities receive the most attention in the media: crimes against the environment, crimes against employees, or crimes against the public? Why do you think this is the case? Does each distinct category create the same amount of social harm?

2. Why is embezzlement often considered a more serious crime than just theft? Should the seriousness of embezzlement be related to the amount or value of what was stolen, or to the degree of breach in trust? Do particular types of jobs or positions make employees more susceptible to the temptation to embezzle company funds? What conditions may lead an employee to commit such an act?

3. How do we draw the line between the overt act of chiseling and the expert opinion or recommendation of a professional? How can we as untrained amateurs make the determination that a certified or licensed authority is fraudulently recommending a medical procedure, selling an antique, or installing new auto parts?

4. Is it ever acceptable for a public official to use his or her position of power and privilege to gain personal advantage? What if gaining personal advantage also meant the public would gain something? If an official used his or her position to influence hiring decisions, distributions of contracts, or purchases of equipment that were beneficial to the public *and* to the official, is the official committing an abuse of power?

5. If you were appointed to a law enforcement advisory board to develop a strategic taskforce for controlling organized crime rings in key U.S. cities, how would you approach this assignment? What would be the main focus of your strategies? How would you identify organized crime? In what ways would you approach this project differently from fighting isolated acts of crime and violence?

ADDITIONAL RESOURCES

Learn more about white-collar crime by visiting the National White Collar Crime Center at http://www.nw3c.org/

More information is available about corporate fraud and abuse at the Center for Corporate Policy website at http://www.corporatepolicy.org/issues/crimedata.htm

Read about the FBI's ongoing efforts to monitor public corruption by visiting http://www.fbi.gov/hq/cid/pubcorrupt/pubcorrupt.htm

Additional reading on the prosecution of criminal enterprises can be found at http://www.lectlaw.com/files/cri18.htm

15

CRIME TODAY
Challenges Facing Criminal Justice Policy

In this chapter, we will explore the following questions:

- How can we benefit from the study of crime in different parts of the world?

- What types of criminal activities violate the laws of more than one country?

- Are certain behaviors governed by international laws?

- In what ways has technology contributed to crime?

- Does the science of criminology offer strategies for dealing with crime in modern society?

In March 2009, the International Criminal Court (ICC) issued

a warrant for the arrest of the president of Sudan, Omar Hassan al-Bashir, on criminal charges of war crimes and crimes against humanity. The warrant was based on evidence that al-Bashir was responsible for intentional and strategic attacks on segments of the civilian population of Darfur, in the Sudan, including acts of pillage, torture, rape, and genocide. This historic event marked the first warrant of arrest issued to a president or head of state currently in office. It also marked the beginning of international jurisdiction in the prosecution and control of war crimes.[1]

Do certain types of criminal activities transcend national borders? The warrant for al-Bashir's arrest says yes: Faced with such crimes, different societies will unite in their prevention and control. These are generally criminal acts that jeopardize the interests of all humankind by threatening the peace and security of citizens.

The goals of this chapter are to introduce criminological issues of global concern and to give an overview of international strategies for the prevention of crime. By relying on cross-cultural research, the international criminal justice community can collaborate to protect the public order without jeopardizing the rights of individuals. As we discussed in Chapter 1, striking a balance between these two goals is not an easy task within the boundaries of our own society. How much more difficult that task becomes when crossing over to other societies, with their own definitions of individuals' rights and public order! This is the mission of comparative criminology, to which we now turn.

globalization

A process that eases interaction and integration among the people, corporations, and political systems of different countries.

COMPARATIVE CRIMINOLOGY

The 21st century has brought vast changes in the way people communicate and exchange goods and services. These changes are the result of **globalization,** a process that eases interaction and integration among the people, corporations, and political systems of different countries. Globalization is driven by international trade and

Student supporters of Sudanese President Omar Hassan al-Bashir protest against the arrest warrant issued against him by the International Criminal Court, a permanent court that has international jurisdiction for the trials of those accused of the most serious crimes of global concern. What are these crimes and what makes them so serious?

investment made possible through advances in communication technology, especially the Internet. It has profound effects on culture, the environment, and politics, as well as on the daily lives of individuals around the world.[2]

One effect of globalization on the field of criminology is the emergence of globalized crime networks that operate across national borders.[3] This trend has led to a renaissance in the study of comparative criminology.

What Is Comparative Criminology?

Comparative criminology is the systematic study of crime and crime-control policies and practices in different cultures and societies around the world.[4] The benefit of this approach is that with it we can identify common variables within criminological theory, better understand cross-national patterns of criminal behavior, and integrate new aspects of social control policies and practices that may be unfamiliar to us.[5]

The idea that sharing information among countries and cultures can help us both understand criminal behavior and develop crime-control policies is not new.[6] Criminologists have long recognized the need for comparative data in the evolution of criminological thought and practice. But with globalization this need became urgent. Testing our own theories and ideas in multiple sociocultural environments was only made possible, however, with the evolution of criminology as a reliable scientific discipline. And comparative research and analysis came into existence only when international crime data and statistics on a variety of criminal justice topics emerged in the latter half of the 20th century. With the ease of access to international trends in criminal justice information, criminologists today are in a better position to pursue comparative criminological research.

How Do We Conduct Comparative Criminology?

The task of comparative research is to find trends and patterns in criminal behavior and crime-control practices at a cross-national level, as well as to examine criminological theories in diverse cultural contexts. To accomplish this, comparative criminological researchers must have comprehensive knowledge of the social, political, and economic structure of the country or countries they are studying, including the cultural norms, value systems, and legal codes that comprise the social order and guide daily interactions. Research data they gather from other countries must be of the highest quality and integrity, and it must be compatible with other statistical reports in terms of data-gathering techniques, legal definitions, and crime measurement.[7]

Much comparative criminological research relies on data sources that compile crime statistics at an international level. One such data source is prepared by the **International Criminal Police Organization,** or **INTERPOL,** an international police organization that publishes crime data from 188 participating countries.[8] Another data source is the **United Nations Surveys on Crime Trends and the Operations of Criminal Justice Systems (CTS),** which provides statistics on crime, crime trends, and criminal justice operations at the international level.[9] These are considered official crime data sources and must be approached with the same cautions as apply to U.S. official crime data sources, discussed in Chapter 3. Another valuable data source for comparative research is the **International Crime Victims Survey (ICVS)** (also discussed in Chapter 3). The ICVS surveys households in different countries on their experiences with crime and police response, as well as matters related to crime prevention and safety.[10] When we compare official data sources

comparative criminology

The systematic study of crime and crime-control policies and practices in different cultures and societies around the world.

International Criminal Police Organization (INTERPOL)

An international police organization; a valuable resource for comparative criminal justice research.

United Nations Surveys on Crime Trends and the Operations of Criminal Justice Systems

A data source that provides statistics on crime, crime trends, and criminal justice operations at the international level.

International Crime Victims Survey (ICVS)

A survey of households in different countries on their experiences with crime and police response, as well as matters related to crime prevention and safety.

鐵達尼號】金獎導演 革新影史鉅作

超越想像 新世界

阿凡達

AVATAR

12.17 晚場起 革新數位3D & **IMAX** 3D 全球同步 磅礡上映

Globalization affects many aspects of social interaction. It enables people around the world to connect faster and allows money, goods, and information to flow easily. What impact does globalization have on crime and crime-control efforts within our own borders?

meta-level studies

A type of research used in comparative criminology relying on the comparison of criminological issues in various countries.

parallel research studies

A type of research used in comparative criminology focusing on a comparison and contrast analysis of criminal justice components in two different countries.

with the ICVS, trends in victimization are similar, although the ICVS shows slightly higher rates over time.[11]

Comparative criminologists focus on three different types of research studies.[12] **Meta-level studies** rely on the comparison of criminological issues in various countries. This type of research analyzes certain variables that may represent common trends in different societies—for example, the relationship of poverty to property crime trends in several countries or the relationship between modernization and domestic violence trends in different societies. In a comparative study of American and Canadian crime rates, for example, researchers studied the effects of residential segregation of the poor in large metropolitan cities and the availability of firearms on patterns of homicide, robbery, burglary, and car theft. Their findings challenge the notion that differences in values, culture, and political views between the two countries are responsible for the gap in crime rates.[13]

Parallel research studies usually focus on a comparison and contrast analysis of criminal justice components in two different countries. They may shed light on criminal justice policies and practices dealing with common crime and criminal justice problems such as drug trafficking, terrorism, racial profiling, and prison overcrowding. A recent comparative analysis examined the issue of prosecutorial discretion by comparing criminal court proceedings in Italy, the Netherlands, and the United States. The study highlights the importance of developing uniform criteria in the decision to initiate criminal action against an offender.[14]

Finally, a third research approach within comparative criminology is the use of **single-case studies** that describe and analyze diverse criminal justice issues within a single country, often from a historical standpoint and as they relate to social, economic, and political changes over time. In a study of violence and abuse of women in Nigeria, researchers attribute the ineffective enforcement of laws preventing rape and torture to the decentralized nature of the Nigerian legal system; in addition, violence against women is embedded in the cultural institutions designed to maintain peace and social control.[15]

All three data sources have become increasingly available and are producing valid cross-national crime data. These methods of comparative research are now leading to groundbreaking studies in crime and delinquency.[16]

What Do We Learn from Comparative Criminology?

We can learn a lot from the study of crime on a global level.[17] One tremendous benefit is the ability it gives us to validate criminological theories in different social environments.[18] For example, how does social disorganization affect human interaction in the urban communities of Copenhagen? What structural correlates affect juvenile delinquency in the different cultures of southeast Asia? What role do routine activities play in victimization in Canada?

Testing hypotheses in different cultural and national contexts allows criminologists to further refine theories and make them more informative and generalizable. It also makes them more reliable for informing criminal justice policy and research. (See Connecting Theory to Practice for a look at the application of labeling theory in China.)

Comparative criminology sheds light on what other nations have tried in dealing with issues such as human trafficking, insider trading, child abuse, and the legalization of

THEORY
TO PRACTICE

Shame, Shame: An Application of Labeling Theory

Though cultures vary in many ways, each has developed a consistent set of ideals or norms of expected behavior. When an individual acts against societal norms, the punishment represents the collective majority's moral reaction. That reaction often includes assigning deviant status to the individual, or labeling. Social reaction to crime is an integral component of labeling theory as we have seen in Chapter 9.[19]

While U.S. society goes to extreme measures to avoid labeling juveniles, the Chinese have embraced labeling theory as a means to prevent and reduce juvenile delinquency and rehabilitate youthful offenders. Because in Chinese culture violating societal norms is seen as undesirable and disgraceful, the Chinese believe juveniles will resist delinquent behavior to avoid being shamed. The two cultures differ most in the personal reaction to the deviant label. In U.S. society, individuals labeled "deviant" come to internalize the label and see deviant status as part of their identity. They often start reoffending in a self-fulfilling prophecy.

Chinese culture is very dependent on social groups and bonds with family, friends, peers, and neighbors as the primary basis for interaction, and even for the basic necessities of life. Moreover, social conformity is a key element of Chinese culture. Those who act selfishly by seeking personal satisfaction through criminal acts are scorned, labeled, and eventually cast out of their original social group. Mass public trials and public announcements of judicial rulings are a significant threat to social bonds. Individuals labeled "deviant" in the Chinese culture will do everything in their power to shed the status of criminal in order to remain accepted members of society.

Social control measures for preventing delinquency among Chinese youth begin with shaming methods of punishment. However, shaming becomes more effective when combined with efforts at reintegrating offenders back into the community so as not to create a permanent and terminal sense of alienation.[20]

drugs.[21] Comparative criminologists analyze the policies and practices implemented by law enforcement agencies, the courts, and corrections. Comparative research on the methods and approaches different communities use in responding to crime is a valuable tool in developing the most effective crime-control mechanisms. We can learn, for example, about how the city of São Paulo, Brazil, experienced an 80 percent decline in homicides by establishing a 10-point action plan that included the creation of a municipal security department to map criminal activity, the development and integration of police forces in the city, the mandated closure of bars between 11 p.m. and 6 a.m., and the institution of an array of social, educational, and environmental policies aimed at mentoring youth, reducing violence, and increasing support to schools.[22]

Finally, comparative criminology helps us identify common issues in criminal justice such as urban violence and disorder, drug abuse, gangs, terrorist threats, child pornography, stock market fraud, and piracy—a necessary step to developing collaborative efforts to control criminal activities that transcend physical barriers, legal definitions, and cultural norms. It increases our universal understanding of criminal justice by exploring the connections among crimes in different societies. In 2008, the International Center for the Prevention of Crime published the first "International Report on Crime Prevention and Community Safety," accompanied by the "International Compendium of Crime Prevention Practices to Inspire Action Across the World." Through collaborative research endeavors between university researchers, experts, and law enforcement organizations from various countries across the globe, the reports provide an international overview of the main problems linked to crime, safety, and victimization, as well as the criminal justice prevention measures that are undertaken to address them. Topics such as the safety of women, the safety of children in schools, and the safety of public spaces are highlighted as matters of global concern; integrated, participative initiatives are outlined that focus on

single-case studies

A type of research used in comparative criminology describing and analyzing diverse criminal justice issues within a single country, often from a historical standpoint and as they relate to social, economic, and political changes over time.

In this photo, police officers kick and beat a student after demonstrators refused to keep back during a May 2009 protest in front of the presidential palace in Jakarta, Indonesia. The student protestors were demanding that former Indonesian president Suharto be put on trial for corruption. From studying police violence in other cultures, what can we learn about the formal use of force to disband peaceful protestors?

prevention networks at local, national, and international levels, as well as the systematic use of tools such as crime mapping to support crime prevention.[23]

CRIMES REACHING BEYOND NATIONAL BORDERS

Comparative research in criminology has increased our awareness that the challenge of crime control is not unique to our own society but rather is a common dilemma across the globe. It only makes sense that countries collaborate to share information and development of programs to combat crime, especially transnational and international criminal activities. We look at these two crime categories next.

Transnational Crime

transnational crime

Illegal activities that cross national borders.

The National Institute of Justice has defined **transnational crime** as the criminal activities of individuals and groups who commit illegal activities that cross national borders. Transnational crimes are typically perpetrated by organized criminal groups that use violence, bribery, and corruption to carry out their illegal enterprises. Studies show these groups are most successful in countries characterized by weak political structure and civil unrest, often undermining government leadership and adding to the disruption in peace.[24] As well, advances in information technology and ease of travel have facilitated the growth of transnational criminal activity, making this a problem in various countries around the world, including the United States.[25] We will discuss five major categories of transnational crimes: intellectual property crimes, cyber crimes, money laundering, illegal trafficking, and terrorism.

Intellectual Property Crimes

Intellectual property crimes include the theft of trade secrets and trademarks and the violation of copyrights and patents, very often by selling counterfeit or illegally manufactured computer software, movies, music, books, and other commodities. Illegally manufactured products are mostly circulated in foreign markets and compete with the products of the rightful business owners, disrupting their industries and undermining legitimate commerce. East and southeast Asia and Latin America are major markets for the manufacture and distribution of counterfeit merchandise.[26]

In 2000, an intellectual property crime unit was added to INTERPOL and mandated to collaborate with international government units, cross-border private-sector industries, and patent-protection entities to monitor and enforce intellectual property laws. One of its strategies has been the creation of an international intellectual property database that serves as a depository for information about transnational intellectual property crime within the private sector.[27]

The National Intellectual Property Law Enforcement Coordination Council (NIPLECC) consists of a group of seven government officials: the U.S. coordinator for international intellectual property enforcement; the director of the U.S. Patent and Trademark Office; the assistant attorney general (Criminal Division); the undersecretary of state for economics, business, and agricultural affairs; the deputy U.S. trade representative; the commissioner of customs; and the undersecretary of commerce for international trade. The register of copyrights also consults with the NIPLECC, coordinating both domestic and international activities in the enforcement of **intellectual property laws,** or laws designed to protect the patents or copyrights applied to products, ideas, inventions, and artistic creations.[28] A recent NIPLECC report highlights the importance of cross-border enforcement of intellectual property laws noting the profound impact on public health, safety, and the international economy when intellectual property rights are compromised. Moreover, international cooperation will prove to be the most effective way to combat the manufacture and distribution of counterfeit and pirated products.

Cyber Crimes

Our growing reliance on digital technology to manage, store, and disseminate highly sensitive material has led to a variety of **cyber crimes,** or the theft, misuse, and disruption of computer-based data systems. The illegal infiltration of computer systems by hackers threatens the security of personal data and information from government agencies, financial institutions, and private industry. Cyber crimes are perpetrated by computer hackers with a variety of motives, including identity theft, industrial spying, and revenge by disgruntled employees.[29] In most cases, hackers compromise data, create chaos and confusion, and steal information.

In 2009, President Obama elevated concerns over cyber security to the forefront by naming the first White House cyber security coordinator. This was part of the president's coordinated effort to address growing concern over Internet safety and the associated threat to national security and economic well-being.[30] The coordinator will implement various strategies and initiatives that include[31]

- A public outreach and education program that would emphasize and improve science education in the United States.
- A stronger partnership among the U.S. government, its allies, and the private sector to monitor and secure digital assets.
- An effective information sharing and incident response capability both within the government and the privately owned infrastructure.
- Research and development to ensure security and reliability in future generations of information technology.

In 2008, INTERPOL, an international police organization that facilitates cross-border police collaboration, sponsored a two-day conference that brought together law enforcement officials from around the world to discuss homicide and sexual offense cases. This international forum allowed police officers to compare data, learn new investigative techniques, and become informed on best practices in handling serial homicide and sexual offense cases.

intellectual property laws

Laws designed to protect the patents or copyrights applied to products, ideas, inventions, and artistic creations.

cyber crime

The theft, misuse, and disruption of computer-based data systems.

Money Laundering

International banks and financial institutions are often used to conceal the origins of money from illegal enterprises such as gambling, drug trafficking, and fraud. After all, an individual who owns a small, rundown grocery store in downtown Manhattan that also operates as a front for a methamphetamine lab will have a hard time explaining a yearly profit of $100,000 beyond the sales of the grocery store. Organized crime groups thus "launder" money to hide their illegal enterprises behind legitimate businesses, making it very difficult for law enforcement to identify and trace their activities.

In a typical money-laundering scheme, the perpetrator will transfer money obtained from illegal activities through several financial institutions in order to obscure its origin. The money will eventually be funneled into a legitimate business in order to disguise how it was obtained and make it more difficult to detect. The extent of global money laundering is estimated at about $1 trillion annually, a large portion of which represents illegal proceeds from drug trafficking.[32]

Illegal Trafficking

Children in India participate in a rally protesting the international trafficking of children. While child trafficking is a crime under international law, there is no comprehensive law against it in India, making these children more vulnerable to human trafficking crime networks.

The illegal trafficking of drugs, humans, and weapons creates a substantial threat to the social, political, and economic stability of countries around the world. According to the United Nations, international criminal organizations are the source of most illicit drugs smuggled into the United States, providing a global black market for the manufacture and distribution of substances such as cocaine, heroin, and methamphetamine.[33] The illegal trafficking of drugs presents a great challenge to crime-control efforts, because some primary countries of origin are riddled with corruption at all levels of government (see Crime in Global Perspective).

CRIME IN GLOBAL PERSPECTIVE | Vice President or Drug Trafficker?

In 2006, the U.S. government estimated that 94 percent of the world's opium came from the southeast Asian poppy—specifically from Afghanistan and Pakistan. Most of the heroin produced in these regions is distributed in the European and Asian drug markets. In recent years, however, the illegal drug trafficking of Afghan government officials has placed a significant strain on the relationship between the United States and Afghanistan.[34]

Drug trafficking warlords in Afghanistan had taken advantage of the disruption in power resulting from the aftermath of the 9/11 attack on the United States to infiltrate the government and seize power. As a result, the illegal drug industry became intertwined with military power and government leadership. One former Afghan official, Muhammad Qasim Fahim (Marshal Fahim), was particularly worrisome to the U.S. government.[35] The CIA had evidence of Fahim's involvement in narcotics trafficking, and the United States refused to grant travel visas to Fahim and threatened to audit his finances—and the finances of other potential government officials suspected of corruption—as well as impose other sanctions if Fahim did take office.

In late 2003, President Bush began to initiate measures for the removal of warlords from powerful government positions in Afghanistan, measures collectively referred to by the Bush administration as its "warlord strategy." Fahim remained the defense minister in Afghanistan until 2004 and was Hamid Karzai's running mate as vice president until Karzai dropped him during the presidential elections that year. This was a result of the pressure placed on the Afghan government by the United States to remove known warlords from power. Karzai went on to become the first democratically elected leader in Afghanistan and was officially sworn in as president of the Islamic Republic of Afghanistan on December 7, 2004.

As Afghan government officials prepared for another presidential election, President Karzai, in his bid for reelection, once again surrounded himself with warlords, including his former running mate Marshal Fahim, whom he named his running mate in the 2009 reelection. Karzai's actions were in direct defiance to the United Nations' urgent request to select someone else without Fahim's questionable history.[36]

Karzai's actions generated criticism and dissent from the international community. With his reelection in 2009, and Fahim now serving as vice president, it will be up to the United States to revisit its foreign policies and diplomatic communications with Afghanistan.

Human trafficking (also discussed in Chapter 14) is the movement of people from one place to another using force, fraud, or deception, with the goal of exploiting them for material or financial benefit.[37] Approximately 700,000 women and children are moved across international borders by trafficking rings each year.[38] The victims are usually poor, vulnerable, and desperate individuals from developing countries who are looking for a better life and are promised legitimate work in a rich society. Instead, they find forced servitude, slavelike labor, prostitution, sexual exploitation, and the removal of their organs for transplant.[39] The United Nations Convention Against Transnational Organized Crime, adopted in November 2000, is the primary mechanism for the global monitoring, control, and punishment of human trafficking operations.[40] The goals of the convention are to recognize the seriousness and global nature of the illegal trafficking of persons and to enhance the collaboration of law enforcement agencies around the world in the development of policies and practices to combat this form of transnational crime.

The United Nations Protocol Against the Illicit Manufacturing of and Trafficking in Firearms, Their Parts and Components and Ammunition was adopted in May 2001. The primary goal of this resolution is "to promote, facilitate and strengthen cooperation among States Parties in order to prevent, combat and eradicate the illicit manufacturing of and trafficking in firearms, their parts and components and ammunition."[41] The black market transfer of arms has been a growing global concern since the early 1990s; it includes the trafficking of nuclear materials, assault rifles, spare parts for large weapons,

human trafficking

The movement of people from one place to another using force, fraud, or deception with the goal of exploiting them for material or financial benefit.

ammunition, and anti-air/tank weapons, usually to countries under United Nations restrictions or sanctions. The implications for international security and foreign policy of illegal traffic in arms are profound; these weapons and the money made from their sale support the activities and operatives of paramilitary groups, combatants, insurgents, and terrorist organizations around the world.[42]

Terrorism

terrorism

Premeditated, politically motivated violence designed to spread fear and perpetrated against civilians by subnational groups or clandestine agents.

No single crime garners a larger share of news coverage around the world today than terrorism. While there are different ways of defining the term, **terrorism** means premeditated, politically motivated violence designed to spread fear and perpetrated against civilians by subnational groups or clandestine agents.[43]

Terrorist acts include threats made by vigilante groups and extremists who are either seeking to maintain the status quo or trying to bring about radical social and political change. We have seen many of these acts in the past—ranging from the arson and vandalism of abortion clinics that began in the early 1970s, to the 1995 attack on a federal building in Oklahoma City. While terrorism is not a new phenomenon, transnational terrorism, where radical groups from one or more nations organize acts of violence against the citizens of another country has in recent years become a matter of global concern.

Although the most widely recognized terrorist group is al Qaeda, others include the Abu Nidal Organization (ANO) that fought the Soviets in Afghanistan, the Palestinian Islamic Jihad, Lebanon's Hezbollah, the Palestinian Hamas, and Egypt's al-Gama'a al-Islamiyya. These and other terrorist groups, according to the National Consortium for the Study of Terrorism and Responses to Terrorism (START), have been responsible for approximately 79,000 terrorist incidents between 1970 and 2004.[44]

To qualify as a terrorist act under START's criteria, an incident must

- Intend to coerce, intimidate, or convey some message to a larger audience beyond the immediate victims.
- Be aimed at attaining a political, social, religious, or economic goal.
- Occur outside the context of legitimate warfare.
- Be outside the scope of humanitarian law.

The global rage over transnational terrorism took on new meaning after September 11, 2001, when terrorists hijacked four airplanes and crashed two of them into the World Trade Center in New York and another into the Pentagon outside Washington, DC.

This photo depicts the aftermath of a coordinated terrorist attack on several key hotels, restaurants, and other attractions in the affluent sectors of Mumbai, the commercial capital of India. Authorities blame terrorist militants for the bombings, which injured at least 300 people and killed 100 others in November 2008. According to analysts, this attack was highly coordinated and strategically focused, targeting the tourism industry to spread fear among Western business travelers and tourists.

A fourth plane, apparently intended for the White House, crashed in a field in Pennsylvania after passengers fought with the hijackers. Today more than ever, through international satellite television networks and Internet videos, millions of people are able to watch hijackings, torture, missile firings, executions, and suicide bombings. This global threat to security will continue to be at the forefront of law enforcement and strategic military planning worldwide in the ongoing assessment of threat and the development of counterterrorist operations. Our success in this endeavor will largely depend on the ability of international organizations, regional institutions, and local governments to implement coordinated strategies that rely on a collaborative understanding of this type of criminal activity.

International Crime

While terrorism receives global attention as one of the most challenging transnational crimes, certain other criminal offenses designated as gross violations of human interests are governed by international laws.[45] These offenses are collectively referred to as **international crime.** The International Law Commission describes the following "crimes against the peace and security of mankind":[46]

- *Crime of aggression:* An individual who, as leader or organizer, actively participates in or orders the planning, preparation, initiation, or waging of aggression committed by a state.
- *Crime of genocide:* Any act committed with intent to destroy, in whole or in part, a national, ethnic, racial, or religious group.
- *Crimes against humanity:* Particularly repulsive offenses constituting a serious attack on human dignity or grave humiliation or a degradation of one or more human beings. These crimes are not isolated or sporadic events, but are part either of a government policy or of a wide systematic practice of atrocities tolerated or condoned by a government, including murder, extermination, torture, rape, and political, racial, or religious persecution and human rights violations.
- *Crimes against United Nations and associated personnel:* Crimes committed intentionally and in a systematic manner or on a large scale against United Nations and associated personnel involved in a UN operation with a view to preventing or impeding that operation from fulfilling its mandate, including murder, kidnapping, and attack upon the official premises.
- *War crimes:* A systematic or large-scale violation of international humanitarian law, including willful killing, torture, or inhuman treatment; willfully causing great suffering or serious injury to body or health; extensive destruction and appropriation of property not justified by military necessity; compelling a prisoner of war or other protected person to serve in the forces of a hostile power; willfully depriving a prisoner of war or other protected person of the rights of fair and regular trial; unlawful deportation, transfer, or confinement of protected persons; taking of hostages; making the civilian population or individual civilians the object of attack; and using methods or means of warfare not justified by military necessity with the intent to cause widespread, long-term, and severe damage to the natural environment and thereby gravely prejudice the health or survival of the population.

Recognizing the need to hold accountable the most serious perpetrators of international crime, leaders from around the world convened a diplomatic conference in Rome in the summer of 1998. The treaty that came out of that meeting came to be known as the **Rome Statute,** and it established the first **International Criminal Court (ICC).** It was not until July 2002, however, that the court took full force when the number of states required to ratify the treaty reached 60. As of July 2009, 110 countries have ratified the Rome Statute of the International Criminal Court.

international crime

Offenses designated as gross violations of human interests; crimes against the peace and security of humankind and as such governed by international law.

Rome Statute

The 1998 treaty that established the International Criminal Court; entered into force in 2002.

International Criminal Court (ICC)

Established in 1998 and entered into force in 2002, a permanent tribunal to prosecute individuals for genocide, crimes against humanity, and war crimes.

Technology has dramatically facilitated the theft of information. In an age where storing paper documents is a thing of the past, confidential files containing personal data, financial and medical records, and other sensitive materials are now available to hackers at the touch of a button.

identity theft

The illegal collection of another individual's personal information for fraudulent purposes.

hacking

A technology-assisted criminal offense that involves the unauthorized access and use of computer databases and network software systems to steal data.

spying

A technology-assisted criminal offense that involves the illegal monitoring of computer systems.

viruses

A technology-assisted criminal offense that involves introducing programs into computers, often via e-mail, that corrupt or destroy computers, software, and networks.

The magnitude and scope of international crime has increasingly become the subject of criminological research.[47] At the heart of this dialog is a discussion of the complex role of technology.

THE ROLE OF TECHNOLOGY IN FACILITATING CRIME

We are constantly flooded with opportunities to partake in new technology. Whatever the latest hi-tech innovation is, whether it tickles our musical fancy or connects us to the world around us, its cumulative effect is always the same—allowing us to process, access, and store information faster, more easily, more efficiently, and in less space. While technology is designed to make life more convenient, bringing the three-dimensional world right to our fingertips, it can also create an array of complications for law enforcement and criminology.

One outcome of technology is criminals' new ability to target thousands of victims in various places over a relatively short period of time, compromising the financial infrastructure of banks, businesses, and government.[48] One of the fastest-growing trends in crime, and one that has certainly been facilitated by the growth in technology, is **identity theft**—the illegal collection of another individual's personal information for fraudulent purposes, described by the U.S. Department of Justice as the defining crime of the information age, with an estimated 9 million or more incidents each year.[49] Identity theft allows criminals to steal funds, create fraudulent documents to obtain loans, and elude the police. The expansion of technology also enables criminals to better organize, profit from, and conceal illegal drug trafficking, prostitution, pornography, and other criminal enterprises at the national and international level, using online financial transactions to hide and launder illicit gains.[50]

Over the years, criminologists have attempted to shed some light on the growing trend in crimes facilitated through the use of technology.[51] Studies note that the rise in crimes using technology coincides with the age of the computer and the expanded use of the Internet. The following typology identifies patterns of technology-assisted criminal offenses:[52]

- *Offending related to the integrity of technology:* Examples include **hacking,** the unauthorized access and use of computer databases and network software systems to steal data; **spying,** the illegal monitoring of computer systems; and the spread of **viruses,** programs introduced into computers, often via e-mail, that corrupt or destroy computers, software, and networks.

- *Offending assisted by technology:* This category includes a wide variety of criminal offenses in which technology facilitates the illegal acquisition or exchange of money and goods. For example, as we have noted, some criminals set up illegal bank accounts via the Internet to facilitate the laundering of "dirty" money. Others use the Internet to engage in theft, counterfeiting, or securities fraud. Organized crime groups also use technology to create databases that facilitate the trafficking and distribution of drugs, weapons, and other transactions in support of their criminal enterprises.

- *Offending that focuses on content:* Crimes in this category use technology such as chat rooms as a resource for disseminating pornography, soliciting sex from children, gambling, and inciting hate, violence, and terrorism. (The Consider This feature examines the problem of soliciting terrorism via the Internet.)

Advances in technology have indeed expanded the scope and magnitude of criminal behavior, transforming crime into a global phenomenon. This has made the detection of criminal activities difficult and the apprehension of suspects a daunting task. However,

CONSIDER THIS...

Using the Internet to Solicit Terrorism

Exploitation of the Internet is all but inevitable thanks to the huge number of unmonitored sites and transactions and numerous opportunities for hacking, identity theft, and the spread of viruses. One of the newest criminal applications of the Internet is the use of websites and chat rooms to plan and coordinate terrorist attacks across national borders. More than ever, extreme terrorist organizations are turning to the Internet to recruit, train, and indoctrinate members and solicit funds to carry out attacks, all with little threat of detection.

One chilling example was the July 5, 2005, attack on a London bus system that killed 52 people. The terrorists responsible for the attacks had relied heavily on Internet sites geared toward terrorism to plan and carry out their attack. More recently, three men were arrested in Great Britain for using a chat room to motivate a global conspiracy against non-believers.[53] Holy war was the main topic of a site hosted by one of the men. This site was visited by almost 45 doctors who were planning an attack on U.S. grounds using car bombs and grenades.

The United Kingdom had the authority to pursue and apprehend the men behind this potential attack as a result of the new Terrorism Act of 2006.[54] This act strictly prohibits the publication of any work that may be interpreted as encouragement, training, and preparation of terrorism. While British civil rights activists were angered by the ratification of the Terrorism Act, claiming it violates citizens' right to freedom of speech, in the end the threat to human life and safety proved more important.

The United Kingdom has stepped up its fight against Internet terrorism beyond its borders, while the U.S. Patriot Act, passed shortly after September 11, 2001, focuses solely on terrorism that affects U.S. citizens and facilities. The Terrorism Act strictly prohibits the publication or dissemination of even so much as language that instigates, induces, or provokes terrorist acts, whereas the Patriot Act only *encourages* e-mail providers and Internet service providers to monitor the content of their services.

Besides creating new offenses relating to the sale, distribution, and transmission of terrorist publications, it also extends the authority of law enforcement by allowing the police to hold terrorist suspects from 14 days to 28 days without filing formal charges. Moreover, the act grants the home secretary greater powers to ban groups that glorify terrorism and to prevent restricted groups from using other organizations as fronts for their continued operation.

Society as a whole is racing to pass enforceable antiterrorism legislation before another human life is loss or threatened.[55] The Terrorism Act is a step in that direction. Nevertheless, monitoring all forms of online communication will continue to be a challenge, aside from the task of screening the content of all chat rooms and e-mail.

What do you think?

the growth of technology has also guided the direction of law enforcement and crime control in investigating crimes and improving public safety.[56] Scientific advances in imaging systems, for example, have increased the speed and accuracy of the detection of concealed weapons at security checkpoints.[57] Enhanced recordkeeping and identification systems, advances in information sharing, crime-solving innovations, and the speed of data transmission are all byproducts of the age of technology that have improved crime-control policies and practices worldwide.

MODERN RESPONSES TO MODERN PROBLEMS

With the expansion of technology and an increase in globalization, the prevalence of international and transnational criminal activity has posed a threat to the national and international security and stability of countries across the world. The widespread smuggling of contraband, the illegal traffic of humans, the host of fraudulent schemes, and the

Although legislators may give much attention to the possible effects of a law on society *before* it is passed, sometimes such research is an afterthought when we find a law is hindering more than it helps. Consider the residency restrictions for sex offenders passed by many states and local communities. While these laws have effectively removed sex offenders from neighborhoods within 500 to 2,500 feet of schools, churches, beaches, and parks, in many communities they have also severely limited offenders' housing opportunities.

As sex offenders reintegrate into society after being released from prison, many have little to no money and must find a home in compliance with restriction laws specific to their community. Such homes can be few and far between, or even nonexistent. While not all of New Jersey's cities subscribe to residency restrictions, for instance, many offenders in the state were found living in the exclusion areas because the only alternatives were the outskirts of towns, where much of the land is farmland or natural reserves.

Technology has played a large part in the analysis of residency laws. The main tool is Geographic Information Systems (GIS) mapping.[58] This software allows researchers to analyze and interpret the impact of sex offender residency laws within the area being mapped by comparing exclusions zones to the available housing in a community. Legislators can then use this data to determine whether or not affordable housing is available for sex offenders within approved areas, and to evaluate their suitability in terms of access to transportation to and from treatment facilities. More states are considering residency restrictions, and GIS technology can help determine their feasibility.[59]

intricate development of organized crime networks have changed the scope and meaning of criminal justice enforcement. The Connecting Research to Practice feature elaborates on the connection among technology, research, and law enforcement.

In 1995, in response to the urgent threat posed by the globalization of crime, President Bill Clinton issued a directive ordering agencies of the executive branch of government to prioritize resources devoted to combating this threat, improve internal coordination, collaborate with other governments to develop a global response, and aggressively and creatively use all legal means available to combat international crime.[60] During a speech at the United Nations, President Clinton described the threat as follows:

> *The nation's critical infrastructure systems—such as energy, banking, and telecommunications—are increasingly based on commercial information technologies, and, for economic and operational reasons, are increasingly interconnected. As a result, these systems are vulnerable to increasingly varied threats and are at a heightened risk of catastrophic failure. The range of potential adversaries that may seek to attack U.S. infrastructure systems is broad and growing. Disgruntled employees, disaffected individuals or groups, organized crime groups, domestic and international terrorists, and hostile nations are all potential sources of attack. [International criminals] jeopardize the global trend toward peace and freedom, undermine fragile new democracies, sap the strength from developing countries, [and] threaten our efforts to build a safer, more prosperous world.[61]*

**International Crime
Control Strategy (ICCS)**

An action plan with broadly defined goals and objectives for a coordinated, forceful, and enduring federal response to global crime threats.

Since the 1995 presidential directive, various initiatives have focused crime control on comprehensive strategies dealing with the threat of transnational and international criminal activities. One outcome was the development and implementation of the **International Crime Control Strategy (ICCS),** an action plan describing a far-reaching strategy with broadly defined goals and objectives that serves as an outline for a coordinated, forceful, and enduring federal response to global crime threats.

Since the 2001 terrorist attacks on the World Trade Center and the Pentagon, the focus of American domestic and international policies has shifted substantially toward the investigation and prosecution of terrorism and terrorist organizations. This shift in priorities has resulted in the reorientation of both domestic and international law enforcement activities and the funds to support them. Nowhere is the switch in crime-fighting priorities more noticeable than in the Department of Justice's own statement of goals for fiscal year 2010, which cites "combating terrorism," domestically and internationally, as the agency's number-one goal, ahead of domestic law and order.[62] Table 15.1 lists the goals and objectives of the ICCS.

TABLE **15.1**

Global Crime Concern: What Are We Doing About It?

INTERNATIONAL CRIME-CONTROL GOALS	HOW WILL THESE GOALS BE ACHIEVED?
DOJ Goal 2010: Prevent Terrorism and Promote the Nation's Security	■ Prevent, disrupt, and defeat terrorist operations before they occur. ■ Implement a three-pronged approach (intelligence, operations, and integration) to support global counterterrorism activities that attack the enemy and diminish its key resources and support. ■ Attack the infrastructure by which terrorists travel internationally by targeting smuggling organizations and strengthening worldwide enforcement mechanisms. ■ Improve host-nation law enforcement agencies that are on the frontlines of terrorism in an effort to control indigenous crime and reduce the proliferation of related transnational crime. ■ Prepare foreign counterparts to cooperate more fully and effectively with the United States in combating terrorism and related transnational crime. ■ Assist foreign partners to ensure international judicial cooperation. ■ Cultivate new partnerships to further the organization's mission to prevent transnational crime and terrorism. ■ Improve the skills of foreign prosecutors, investigators, and judges; encourage legislative and justice sector reform in countries with inadequate laws; and promote the rule of law and regard for human rights. ■ Deny safe havens to criminal organizations involved in drug-related terrorist activities. ■ Investigate and prosecute drug-trafficking organizations that use the profits of drug trafficking to finance international terrorism. ■ Use international partnerships to negotiate and enter into extradition treaties. ■ Focus racketeering-influenced crime organization methods and charges on the United States-based terrorist infrastructure.
ICCS Goal 1: Extend the First Line of Defense Beyond U.S. Borders	■ Prevent acts of international crime planned abroad, including terrorist acts, before they occur. ■ Use all available laws to prosecute select criminal acts committed abroad. ■ Intensify activities of law enforcement, diplomatic, and consular personnel abroad.
ICCS Goal 2: Protect U.S. Borders by Attacking Smuggling and Smuggling-Related Crimes	■ Enhance our land border inspection, detection, and monitoring capabilities through a greater resource commitment, further coordination of federal agency efforts, and increased cooperation with the private sector. ■ Improve the effectiveness of maritime and air smuggling interdiction efforts in the transit zone.

(continued)

TABLE **15.1**   (continued)

Global Crime Concern: What Are We Doing About It?

INTERNATIONAL CRIME-CONTROL GOALS	HOW WILL THESE GOALS BE ACHIEVED?
	■ Seek new, stiffer criminal penalties for smuggling activities. ■ Target enforcement and prosecutorial resources more effectively against smuggling crimes and organizations.
ICCS Goal 3: Deny Safe Haven to International Criminals	■ Negotiate new international agreements to create a seamless web for the prompt location, arrest, and extradition of international fugitives. ■ Implement strengthened immigration laws that prevent international criminals from entering the United States and provide for their prompt expulsion when appropriate. ■ Promote increased cooperation with foreign law enforcement authorities to provide rapid, mutual access to witnesses, records, and other evidence.
ICCS Goal 4: Counter International Financial Crime	■ Combat money laundering by denying criminals access to financial institutions and by strengthening enforcement efforts to reduce inbound and outbound movement of criminal proceeds. ■ Seize the assets of international criminals through aggressive use of forfeiture laws. ■ Enhance bilateral and multilateral cooperation against all financial crime by working with foreign governments to establish or update enforcement tools and implement multilateral anti-money laundering standards. ■ Target offshore centers of international fraud, counterfeiting, electronic access device schemes, and other financial crimes.
ICCS Goal 5: Prevent Criminal Exploitation of International Trade	■ Interdict illegal technology exports through improved detection, increased cooperation with the private sector, and heightened sanctions. ■ Prevent unfair and predatory trade practices in violation of U.S. criminal law. ■ Protect intellectual property rights by enhancing foreign and domestic law enforcement efforts to curtail the flow of counterfeit and pirated goods, and by educating consumers. ■ Counter industrial theft and economic espionage of U.S. trade secrets through increased prosecution of offenders. ■ Enforce import restrictions on certain harmful substances, dangerous organisms, and protected species.
ICCS Goal 6: Respond to Emerging International Crime Threats	■ Disrupt new activities of international organized crime groups. ■ Enhance intelligence efforts against criminal enterprises to provide timely warning of changes in their organizations and methods. ■ Reduce trafficking in human beings and crimes against children. ■ Increase enforcement efforts against high-tech and computer-related crime. ■ Continue identifying and countering the vulnerabilities of critical infrastructures and new technologies in telecommunications, financial transactions, and other high-tech areas.

(continued)

TABLE **15.1** (continued)

Global Crime Concern: What Are We Doing About It?

INTERNATIONAL CRIME-CONTROL GOALS	HOW WILL THESE GOALS BE ACHIEVED?
ICCS Goal 7: Foster International Cooperation and the Rule of Law	■ Establish international standards, goals, and objectives to combat international crime by using bilateral, multilateral, regional, and global mechanisms, and by actively encouraging compliance. ■ Improve bilateral cooperation with foreign governments and law enforcement authorities through increased collaboration, training, and technical assistance. ■ Strengthen the rule of law as the foundation for democratic government and free markets in order to reduce societies' vulnerability to criminal exploitation.
ICCS Goal 8: Optimize the Full Range of U.S. Efforts	■ Enhance executive branch policy and operational coordination mechanisms to assess the risks of criminal threats and to integrate strategies, goals, and objectives to combat those threats. ■ Mobilize and incorporate the private sector into U.S. government efforts. ■ Develop measures of effectiveness to assess progress over time.

Sources: U.S. Department of Justice. (2010). *Stewards of the American dream: FY 2007–FY 2012 strategic plan:* 17–40.

The worldwide expansion of criminal networks has created a critical need for law enforcement agencies around the globe to enhance crime-control measures to create a coordinated effort in the attack on transnational and international crime threats. Leading agencies in the United States—including the Departments of Justice, State, Treasury, Homeland Security, Defense, and Commerce—are developing programs and initiatives that are built upon the foundation of cooperation from foreign governments.[63] It is up to criminologists to integrate this trend into the theoretical understanding of criminal behavior, as well as assess its implication for criminal justice research, policy, and practice within our own borders and beyond.

SUMMARY

■ **How can we benefit from the study of crime in different parts of the world?**

By studying crime in different parts of the world, criminologists are better able to identify common variables within criminological theory and test concepts and ideas under multiple sociocultural environments. Moreover, using comparative data to understand cross-national patterns of criminal behavior can effectively direct law enforcement policies and practices.

■ **What types of criminal activities violate the laws of more than one country?**

Criminal activities that violate the laws of multiple countries and cross national borders are known as transnational crimes. Criminal groups use violence, bribery, and corruption to engage in criminal activities involving the theft of intellectual property, cyber crimes, money laundering, illegal trafficking, and terrorism.

■ **Are certain behaviors governed by international laws?**	Gross violations of human interest are considered crimes against the peace and security of humankind and are therefore governed by international laws. These acts are collectively referred to as international crime and include genocide, war crimes, and crimes against humanity.
■ **In what ways has technology contributed to crime?**	Advances in technology, especially the use of computers and the Internet, have made quick and easy access to information almost universal and have transformed crime into a global phenomenon. Crimes like malicious hacking, online pornography, and identity theft compromise the integrity of computer networks and use technology itself as a resource in the commission of crime.
■ **Does the science of criminology offer strategies for dealing with crime in modern society?**	With the globalization of crime and the expansion of criminal networks around the world, the science of criminology must continue to engage in research endeavors that represent a collaborative and cooperative effort between governments and law enforcement agencies around the world in the attack on transnational and international crime threats.

CRITICAL THINKING QUESTIONS

1. What particular transnational crime do you think is the most urgent threat to the United States? Why? What makes this crime a global problem? What aspects of it could we better understand by using comparative data from other countries?

2. What role has technology played in providing more criminal opportunities? In what ways has technology affected traditional crimes such as theft, burglary, and child abuse? How can advances in surveillance and detection technologies be used to control these and other types of crimes?

3. In what ways does the use of technology in crime control challenge the balance between individual rights and public order? In what circumstances, if any, can the use of technology to fight crime justify the compromising of personal freedoms?

4. How do violations of international laws present a direct threat to U.S. national security? What role does the science of criminology play in guiding the effective understanding of this threat and in bringing to justice perpetrators of international crimes?

ADDITIONAL RESOURCES

Learn more about the field of comparative criminology by visiting the International Centre for Comparative Criminological Research (ICCCR) website at http://www.open.ac.uk/icccr/

For more information on the structure and organization of INTERPOL, visit http://www.interpol.int/public/icpo/default.asp

Visit the United Nations Surveys on Crime Trends and the Operations of Criminal Justice Systems (CTS) website at http://www.unodc.org/unodc/en/data-and-analysis/United-Nations-Surveys-on-Crime-Trends-and-the-Operations-of-Criminal-Justice-Systems.html for more information on the compiling and comparing of international crime statistics.

Read more about facts and figures on transnational criminal organizations by visiting the United Nations Office on Drugs and Crime website at http://www.unodc.org/

Research on the use of video surveillance technology as a crime-fighting strategy is available at http://www.chs.ubc.ca/archives/files/Crime%20Prevention%20Effects%20of%20Closed%20Circuit%20Television%20a%20systematic%20review.pdf

POLICE
ANTI-CRIME
COMMUNITY
TEAM

16

EPILOGUE: THE FUTURE OF CRIMINOLOGICAL THEORY

In this chapter, we will explore the following questions:

- How do we arrive at a comprehensive definition of crime?
- What will be the role of criminological theory in solving crime today and in the future?
- Should crime-control strategies be driven by theory, reality, or both?
- In what ways will criminological research have an impact on social policy?

Within society, one variable has remained a constant feature

of social interaction: the entanglement of individual traits with environmental circumstances. A toddler with poor impulse control pulls her classmate's hair to get back a toy; a college athlete with low ethical standards cheats on an exam in order to maintain his scholarship; an urban mother with limited financial means and no social support network shoplifts to make ends meet; a corporate executive is swayed by board members to fix prices in order to maintain profits. Examples of flawed human interactions are diverse and endless. Some are common occurrences that have become embedded in the way people handle conflict and strife. Others shock us and leave us with unanswered questions.

Such was the case when Amy Bishop methodically opened fire on her university colleagues during a faculty meeting in February 2010, killing three and stopping only after her gun jammed. The Harvard-trained biology professor at the University of Alabama at Huntsville had been upset at being denied tenure, which would force her to look for work elsewhere. Records indicate she had episodes of violence in her past, including an incident, officially labeled an accident, in which she shot and killed her brother in 1986. Bishop was also questioned in regard to a pipe bomb that was sent to one of her colleagues at Children's Hospital in Boston.[1]

The attack by Bishop is riddled with questions. What individual characteristics define her mental and emotional state? What social correlates contributed to the strain and frustration leading up to the shooting? Why were measures not taken to investigate Bishop's questionable past? How did the structural dynamics of the tenure process affect the hostile interaction that took place between her and her colleagues? In this final chapter, we look back and reflect on the various paradigms in theoretical criminology that have guided our discussions of crime causation, criminological research, and policy development.

THE DEFINITION OF CRIME: A PRACTICAL SYNTHESIS

The task of criminology has traditionally revolved around explaining why some people commit crime while others do not. This question was sufficient for an understanding of crime until the 1960s ushered in an era of civil disobedience, antiwar demonstrations,

On February 13, 2010, university professor Amy Bishop was arrested and charged with capital murder in the shooting deaths of three of her colleagues at the University of Alabama, Huntsville. The biology professor opened fire during a faculty meeting, pointing her gun at the heads of her victims and shooting them one by one. What could have possibly gone wrong during this normally routine interaction between co-workers?

marijuana and cocaine use by the middle class, corruption among political leaders, and criminal violations by leading corporations.[2] At that point, criminologists became more concerned with the changing definition of criminal behavior, with patterns and trends in arrest statistics, and with the distribution of different types of crimes among women and men, ethnic and racial groups, as well as social classes.

We began this text at the heart of criminology, with a study of the lawmaking process, and discovered that many acts come to be defined as criminal because of the interplay among power, politics, and economic conditions.[3] We also learned that because certain acts were defined as crimes, those arrested, prosecuted, sentenced, and confined were not necessarily the ones posing the greatest threat to law enforcement agencies but instead were those whom society *defined* as the greatest threat.[4] They were also usually the poorest and most vulnerable. For a long time, our definition of crime ignored the acts of white-collar offenders, government officials, and organized criminals.

The definition of crime as behavior unique to certain individuals and their personal experiences led to a plethora of theoretical frameworks that searched for the origin of criminal behavior within the individual. Such individual-level analyses led to biological theories, which searched for abnormalities within the structure and function of the brain, as well as psychological theories that explored the human mind and identified weaknesses and pathological traits within the personality.[5]

Some sociological theories found the origin of crime within the conflicts and strains that make up the daily lives of individuals, while others proposed that criminality was a normal response for some people because they learned crime from their peers, parents, or subculture or had differential opportunities to achieve status, wealth, and power.[6] Labeling theory argued that everyone committed initial acts of crime or primary deviance, but some were labeled deviant by their peers, community, or themselves, and their self-image changed to reflect the labels attached to them. This collective level of analysis forced us to explore the role of social reaction in the perpetuation of crime and deviance.[7]

With this understanding, conflict theories directed our attention to different forms of inequality within the social structure, which helped us understand why some people are labeled criminal while others are not.[8] Through this revelation, we were able to see that a comprehensive understanding of the nature and meaning of crime had to go beyond the definition of individual acts of deviant behavior.

In order to effectively guide criminal justice policy and practice, criminological theory must therefore approach the study of crime through the shining light of cultural, political, and economic influences on the development of criminal laws, the distortion of the crime problem, and the prediction of criminal behavior. The challenge for criminology is to link the study of crime with political and economic forces shaping our institutions and our social relations. The most promising leads today employ the methodology of the dialectic and an integrated theoretical approach.

THE NEW CRIMINOLOGY: INTEGRATING THEORIES

We have seen throughout our journey in this text that, in order to understand the dynamics of criminal behavior and crime causation, criminology must be driven by a desire to study, explain, and solve the crime problem and not be misguided by political rhetoric, media distortion, and unfounded public fear over escalating crime rates. We must also acknowledge the cultural and structural characteristics of society that shape

The many faces of deviance and criminal behavior in mainstream society are constantly defining the nature and meaning of crime and crime causation. Acts of deviance and crime committed by college students in different contexts do not always fit the molds of differential associations or violent subcultures.

social interactions and define the nature of our communities.[9] Moreover, a scientific criminology, whether Marxist or behaviorist, must commit itself to understanding the full gamut of criminality by explaining the entire range of phenomena called crime, as well as the political, economic, and social forces leading to differences in crime rates across different historical periods and between different countries in the same period.[10]

The study of crime causation from the separate perspectives of biology, psychology, and sociology has for years created a divide between what we think people are like and how we think they behave. Increasingly, criminologists are recognizing the need to integrate a variety of views, acknowledge that each is at least partially correct, and recognize that they offer greater insight when taken together. Contemporary criminological theory is thus marked by an interdisciplinary approach. It goes beyond the effort to change individuals and instead seeks to understand the underlying components of social structure that shape human behavior.[11] Criminologists are abandoning the schisms that have traditionally divided theoretical development in favor of a more pragmatic approach that integrates the various paradigms.[12] In doing this, we are putting human behavior within a context—recognizing not only that people are different and unique in their ways of thinking, processing information, and reacting, but that their circumstances, conditions, and experiences are also diverse.

We have seen from our discussion of comparative criminology in Chapter 15 that human behavior is not tied to any particular society, group, or individual. Through the study of crime in various parts of the world, criminology has evolved to study crime as a product of interactions between people, in which individual motivations are intertwined in social organization and structural relationships. In order to better understand crime today and in the future, we need multidimensional models of crime causation that combine, link, and synthesize various theoretical constructs.[13]

By integrating components of various theories, we can make sense of the different types of crimes that span the interpersonal, organizational, and structural levels of society, advancing away from cause–effect relationships that focus on narrow explanations of particular types of crime. Just because events happen at the same time, we cannot assume the relationship between them will be constant every time or even over time. We can see, for example, that anomie and strain can be primary sources of frustration leading to white-collar crime, but more so within corporate subcultures that neutralize moral obligation and thereby threaten social bonds.[14] Moreover, when we consider why some people conform to societal norms and expectations while others do not, we also need to consider that social conformity is a bigger motivation for self-control in cultures where nonconformity is shameful.[15]

Theoretical criminology has laid the foundation for the study of crime for the past several centuries. From the founders of the discipline, we have discerned various ideas about the nature of crime, the origins of legal definition, and the pursuit of social control. The different perspectives on crime have traditionally proposed diverse, often conflicting sets of underlying assumptions about the definition of crime and the origin of criminal behavior. As we move forward toward an integrated, solutions-oriented approach to combating the social problems leading to crime, we will continue to rely on theoretical foundations that rest on the shoulders of scientifically based research methods.

Stephen and Robert Spahalski shared more than genetic identity. These twin brothers both led a life of crime, including being convicted of murder. Most twins have very similar physical and personality characteristics, but how might their various experiences in life shape the course of their behavior? What does this influence tell us about the interplay between individual characteristics and social environment in the study of criminal behavior?

CRIMINOLOGY'S IMPACT ON SOCIAL POLICY: HOW DO WE REDUCE CRIME?

Our search for reliable knowledge about the origins of crime must be embedded in the social realities that surround us. The fact is, street crimes such as robbery and assault are more common in poor, urban communities; white-collar crime reflects a value system in which cooperation and community are stifled by competition and power; political corruption is embedded in the structure of government; and globalization has redefined the nature of organized crime. We must therefore pursue crime-reducing solutions that are rooted in these and other realities revealed to us through criminological research.

Undoubtedly, criminal behavior is a matter of public concern. It is a social harm committed against an individual, a community, and society as a whole. We even build our

More than ever, technology has allowed the spread of information at a rapid pace and to a greater number of people. The FBI has been utilizing digital billboards to help capture elusive criminals since 2007. FBI officials indicate that at least 40 cases have been solved as a direct result of this crime-fighting strategy.

Many local police depart-
ments sponsor annual
"Santa Cop" programs
that match children in need
with a police officer for a
day of shopping during
Christmas (shown here
is the program in action
in Cicero, New York). The
children are of different
ages, up to the 7th grade,
and have experienced
some type of physical
or emotional trauma or
personal struggle. The programs, often partnerships
with area businesses and
individual donors, dem-
onstrate how agents of
criminal justice can reach
out to the community and
contribute in a way that
builds partnership, trust,
and mutual respect.

criminal court cases based on that premise when we say "*People v. John Doe*" or "*State v. Jane Doe.*" Indeed, reacting to crime is an age-old phenomenon, from ancient witch-hunts and public hangings to neighborhood watches and community action groups of today. What has changed over the years is that due process and civil liberties have affected our reaction to crime and criminals, and the manner in which we implement different techniques of fighting crime, as we discussed in Chapter 15.

Crime-control strategies must go beyond funneling more lawbreakers into the prisons, since this has proven the most costly and least effective method of reducing crime over the years.[16] We must address the question of crime prevention at its cultural and structural roots. Crime prevention occurs through two major models of intervention. At the primary level, crime-control strategies focus on conditions within the social environment that are known to be associated with high rates of crime. At the secondary level, crime-control strategies identify behavior patterns, relationships, and situations that increase the likelihood of criminal behavior. Let's look at some major new developments at each level.

Primary Prevention Strategies: Targeting Risk

A hallmark contribution of criminological theories over the past several decades is the development of scientifically based methods of identifying individuals at risk of delinquency and crime and intervening in their lives at the earliest possible stage.[17] This is often referred to as **risk factor analysis** in the prevention of crime and delinquency.[18] The analysis of risk approaches the study of crime with an understanding of the sociodemographic distribution of criminal behavior. The defining and measuring of risk factors is grounded in research-based evidence on the distribution of crime among different segments of the population. Risk factor analysis recognizes that delinquency is high among youth from dysfunctional families, street crime is more common in densely populated urban communities, and sexual violence is fairly high on college campuses throughout the country.

Criminology has served as a cornerstone for risk factor analysis research and the implementation of policies shaping crime prevention.[19] Individual- and community-level solutions can now be based on an understanding of the multiple risk factors associated with child development, social relationships, and structural disadvantage.[20] Initiatives for

risk factor analysis

In criminology, scientifically based methods of identifying individuals at risk of delinquency and crime and intervention at the earliest possible stage.

early intervention, for example, have been based on five principal components that have direct theoretical relevance to various biological, psychological, and social structure theories of criminal behavior:

1. Expanding pre- and postnatal healthcare to identify early any neurological impairments associated with behavioral problems.

2. Providing a comprehensive array of services to high-risk children and their families, including preschool enrichment programs, parenting classes, and in-home counseling.

3. Allowing parents to be gainfully employed by providing quality, affordable childcare and flexible work schedules.

4. Improving the quality of education within school systems plagued by the dysfunctions of urban deterioration.

5. Establishing social support networks for victims of crime in order to break the cycle of violence and abuse.

Risk factor analysis has indeed paved the way for understanding the social context within which crime takes place. However, there is still some disconnect between the variables identified and targeted within risk reduction programs and the broader social structure.[21] In order to bridge this gap, criminological theory has to provide crime-control policymakers with some guidance on the connection between social problems and risk assessment, where risk is an identified variable but does not alone drive programs and initiatives.[22] Changes in individual behavior must be connected to changes within the larger social-structural context of organizations and institutions. Who we are and the different experiences that we encounter span the life course as we transition through different phases of maturity that bring us into contact with different social, cognitive, emotional, and physical experiences.[23] Targeting risk factors related to offending must take into account these variations.

Secondary Prevention Strategies: Targeting Development

Researchers have identified a model of prevention based on the concept that interventions aimed at multiple risk factors and over a long period of time are more likely to have positive results.[24] This model is known as **developmental pathways.** By analyzing the way in which different life experiences contribute to change at the individual level, as well as change within the social environment around the individual, the developmental pathways model invests in strategies and programs that target multiple risk factors at various crucial points of transition throughout life, from birth, to preschool, throughout the school years and adolescence, and into the adult experiences of higher education and employment. This approach is guided by six major principles:[25]

1. Interventions in one context (such as the home) interact with, complement, and support interventions in other contexts (such as school).

2. Relationships, trust, and cooperation between staff and clients are valued equally with evidence about what works.

3. Better individual outcomes are achieved through the enrichment of all relevant developmental settings. Child-oriented programs are best integrated with family support initiatives and programs introduced through appropriate systems such as schools, childcare and family health centers, or community groups.

4. Intervention effects are more effective if they coincide with life transitions (such as birth and starting school or high school), when people are both vulnerable and receptive to help.

developmental pathways

A model of prevention based on the concept that interventions aimed at multiple risk factors and over a long period of time are more likely to have positive results.

5. A continuum of age-appropriate programs and resources can enhance developmental pathways over time.

6. Well-integrated programs and practices are best achieved by building partnerships between organizations, institutions, and agencies relevant to child and family well-being.

The developmental pathways model focuses our attention on the cultural and structural roots of crime as they contribute to individual risk. Under this approach, we acknowledge that risk is a symptom of the failure of social structures to initiate and support an individual's proper social development.[26] Through our understanding of criminological theory, we are able to identify key elements that contribute to this failure:

- The lack of employment or underemployment that leaves people bound to poverty and its associated social conditions.
- Segregated, densely populated public housing that contributes to deteriorated neighborhoods, weak social institutions, and high crime rates.
- The inherent suspicion and distrust in urban communities where social bonds are weak, community ties are fragile, and individuals are alienated.
- Socialization into roles in which the virtues of cooperation and respect are secondary to advancement, greed, and economic success.
- Structural inequalities that are embedded in the traditional roles of men and women, contributing to social subordination.

Crime-prevention measures must therefore go beyond the assessment of individual risk factors to helping communities create a structure within which we can combine individual intervention strategies with the right resources, opportunities, and social processes. Would we ask a child to go get a drink of water without giving that child directions for turning on the water source, providing that child with a cup, and making sure the water source is actually working?

Criminal justice policies and practices must rely on mutually beneficial relationships within the community to address social concerns, as well as to raise public trust in law enforcement.[27] The role of criminology is to guide criminal justice to make a long-term commitment to programs and services embedded in the structure of local communities.[28] Researchers have identified the most successful initiatives as those that

- Create a network of support that links home, school, and community agencies.[29]
- Encourage community members to take a stake in the well-being of their neighborhoods and streets, incorporating principles of situational crime prevention such as increasing lighting in streets, cleaning up parks, maintaining properties, creating neighborhood watch groups, reporting suspicious activity, and collaborating with law enforcement.[30]
- Invest in community resources and diversion programs that aim at reintegrating offenders into society as opposed to incarceration.[31]
- Expand upon the paradigm of community-oriented policing and direct police activities to crime "hot spots."[32] Studies show that concentrating police activities in areas that are at greater risk of crime and disorder can reduce criminal activities.[33]
- Undertake to increase public trust in law enforcement by removing elements of discrimination and profiling.[34]
- Recognize the role of structural disadvantage, inequalities, and contradictions in the development of criminal behavior.[35]

Criminologists around the world are engaging in groundbreaking research every day to guide criminal justice policy toward an effective solution to criminal behavior. Will they ever solve the problem of crime in society? Probably not. We can only hope that their research is guided by evidence-based criminological theories that analyze and explain crime as it relates to the social structure, as a phenomena that encompasses people in all social classes, races, historical time periods, and personal circumstances. It is this message we hope we have conveyed to you as a student of criminology. It is this message we hope you can carry to criminal justice administrators, policymakers, and legislators.

SUMMARY

- **How do we arrive at a comprehensive definition of crime?**

  Any comprehensive definition of crime must capture the various acts of criminal behavior in light of the cultural, political, and economic influences on the development of criminal laws, the distortion of the crime problem, and the prediction of criminal behavior.

- **What will be the role of criminological theory in solving crime today and in the future?**

  The role of criminological theory in crime control is to pursue and communicate an understanding of crime through research-driven policies and practices that are embedded in the social and cultural realities of criminal behavior.

- **Should crime-control strategies be driven by theory, reality, or both?**

  The reality of crime control is that people want to feel safer at home and on the street, and this is what tends to drive policies in the direction of funneling more lawbreakers through the criminal justice system. However, this reality does not address what we know about crime and its relationship to the larger social structure. It is the role of criminology to bridge the gap between theory and reality by guiding crime-control policy in a holistic direction of understanding social problems.

- **In what ways will criminological research have an impact on social policy?**

  Criminological research will continue to search for integrated crime-prevention solutions that are embedded in the structure of local communities and that rely on mutually beneficial relationships within the community to address social concerns as well as raise public trust in law enforcement.

CRITICAL THINKING QUESTIONS

1. How do components of various criminological paradigms work together to help us develop a better understanding of crime in society?

2. What types of scientific studies of criminal behavior can be conducted to illustrate an integrated theoretical approach to understanding crime causation?

3. In what ways can crime-control policies become better informed by taking into account both individual differences in human traits as well as variations in environmental experiences?

ADDITIONAL RESOURCES

Learn more about the emerging role of technology in fighting crime at the Department of Justice "Technology to Fight Crime" website at http://www.ojp.usdoj.gov/programs/technology.htm

A global perspective on holistic approaches to crime prevention can be found at http://www.spf.gov.sg/stats/stats2010_approach.htm

Read more about the challenges of the risk factor paradigm and youth crime-prevention programs at http://www.griffith.edu.au/__data/assets/pdf_file/0005/197978/beyondrisk.pdf

For additional information on the "Santa Cop" program, see the Wilmington Police Recreation Association website at http://www.wilmingtonpoliceofficers.org/Programs.html

APPENDIX

The Saints and the Roughnecks
William J. Chambliss

Foreword

In 1973 I published the results of research I conducted through observations and interviews with two delinquent gangs in a paper titled "The Saints and the Roughnecks." For its republication here, let me briefly describe how the study came about.

The research is a classic illustration of serendipity in the research process. It was my intention originally to administer questionnaires to a group of high school students to test the hypothesis that an adolescent's involvement in delinquency was correlated with his or her self-image. I obtained permission from the school administrators for the study, but prior to administering the questionnaires I decided to hang out around the school and get a feeling for the atmosphere in the school—what the science fiction writer Robert Heinlein in *Stranger in a Strange Land* called "groking." To "grok" the situation, I spent a couple of weeks visiting the school at different times, hanging around the hallways to watch the students as they came and went, sitting in the cafeteria at lunch, and watching the physical education classes on the playground. The school administrators gave me permission to do these things, else I would certainly have been arrested.

On several occasions, I noticed a group of three to five kids meeting in the hall and disappearing out of one of the back doors of the school. On the third day I discreetly followed them and saw that they jumped into a car and left the school. The next time this happened I followed them in my car. They went to a café several miles from the school. I sat in a booth next to them and listened to their conversation. What was most interesting was the relationship these kids had with the proprietor of the café: It was clearly hostile. I later discovered why: They would intentionally spill their soft drinks; they would replace the salt in the saltshaker with sugar and the sugar with salt; they would bend spoons and try to flip chewing gum onto the ceiling with their knives. I could only assume that the proprietor put up with this because they did spend a lot of money on food and drinks, and they were regular customers.

When they left the café they often went to a pool hall that was in the "poor section" of town. I followed them there and shot pool at the table next to them. Eventually I was able to make contact with one of the boys. One day when four of them had gone to the pool hall, one of the boys was not shooting pool because he did not have any money. I offered to shoot with him and to pay. He accepted the offer. I told him I was a sociologist who taught at the university and was doing research on adolescents. I told him that I noticed that he and his friends frequently left school and came to the pool hall. I asked if he and his friends would mind if I "sort of followed them just so I could observe what they were doing and occasionally ask them questions." He discussed this with his friends; I took them all to a restaurant and bought them lunch. We talked over my suggestion, and they agreed that if I wanted to hang around with them it was OK. I told them I did not really want to hang around *with* them; I just wanted to hang around *near* them and listen to what they said and watch what they did. They did not immediately understand the distinction, but over the next several weeks they got used to my sitting in the booth next to them in the café or playing pool, usually alone, at the table next to them in the pool hall. I was also able to interview them informally, and sometimes together, when I would offer to buy them lunch or occasionally when one of them would come up and ask me a question; for example, one day one asked me "What is a sociologist? Is that like a communist?" Apparently they were confusing "sociologist" with "socialist."

In the course of the next several months my rapport with the boys increased to the point that they would call me and tell me what they were going to do during the weekend: where they were likely to be (if it was a bar, the name of the bar; if at a party the place of the party). Over the next two years I spent hours following them in my car, sitting near them in cafés and bars, and interviewing them individually and collectively. This was the group that I named "the Saints" when I wrote up the results of the research.

With the help of one of the Saints I was able to get in touch with a group of working-class boys that hung around together. This group I called "the Roughnecks." I followed a similar procedure in getting to know these boys. I went to where they hung out after school (unlike the Saints, they rarely skipped school) and began talking to them. They were suspicious at first but agreed that I could hang around near them. Since they were less mobile than the Saints, it was easier to know where I could find them and to find a convenient place to sit (sometimes in my car with the window open) or stand and observe them. I was also able to interview them individually and collectively and get information about what they were doing when I was not around.

In both instances I had the distinct feeling that after a while I was simply part of the landscape in their world. Like a familiar bush, tree, or bartender, I was there, and they could be natural and open without being concerned to either impress me or to hide their normal behavior from me.

What I found was then published as "The Saints and the Roughnecks" in 1973 and is reproduced on the following pages.

The Saints

The Saints were a group of eight promising young men from "good" white upper-middle-class families. They attended Hannibal High: a moderate-size high school in a suburb near a large metropolitan area.* The Saints were active in school affairs, were enrolled in the pre-college program and received good grades. At the same time, they were some of the most delinquent boys at Hannibal High.

The teachers, their parents, and people in the community knew that these boys occasionally sowed a few wild oats. They were totally unaware, however, of the extent to which the Saints engaged in delinquency. No one realized that "sowing their wild oats" completely occupied the daily routine of these young men. The Saints were constantly occupied with truancy, drinking, wild driving, petty theft and vandalism. Yet not one was officially arrested for any misdeed during the two years I observed them.

This record was particularly surprising in light of my observations during the same two years of another gang of Hannibal High School students, six lower-class white boys I call the Roughnecks. The Roughnecks were constantly in trouble with police and community even though their rate of delinquency was about equal with that of the Saints. What was the cause of this disparity? The result? The following consideration of the activities, social class and community perceptions of both gangs may provide some answers.

The Saints from Monday to Friday

The Saints' principal daily concern was with getting out of school as early as possible. The boys managed to get out of school with minimum danger that they would be accused of playing hookey through an elaborate procedure for obtaining "legitimate" release from class. The most common procedure was for one boy to obtain the release of another by fabricating a meeting of some committee, program or recognized club. Charles might raise his hand in his 9:00 chemistry class and ask to be excused (a euphemism for going to the bathroom). Charles would go to Ed's math class and inform the teacher that Ed was needed for a 9:30 rehearsal of the drama club play. The math teacher would recognize Ed and Charles as "good students" involved in numerous school activities and would permit Ed to leave at 9:30. Charles would return to his class, and Ed would go to Tom's English class to obtain his release. Tom would engineer Charles' escape. The strategy would continue until as many of the Saints as possible were freed. After a stealthy trip to the car (which had been parked in a strategic spot), the boys were off for a day of fun.

Over the two years that I observed the Saints, this pattern was repeated nearly every day. There were variations on the theme. But in one form or another the boys used this procedure for getting out of class and then off the school grounds. Rarely did all eight of the Saints manage to leave school at the same time. The average number avoiding school on the days I observed them was five.

Having escaped from the concrete corridors the boys usually went either to a pool hall on the other (lower-class) side of town or to a cafe in the suburbs. Both places were out of the way of people the boys were likely to know (family or school officials), and both provided a source of entertainment. The pool hall entertainment was the generally rough atmosphere, the occasional hustler, the sometimes drunk proprietor and, of course, the game of pool. The cafe's entertainment was provided by the owner. The boys would "accidentally" knock a glass on the floor or spill cola on the counter not all the time, but enough to be sporting. They would also bend spoons, put salt in sugar bowls, and generally tease whoever was working in the cafe. Since the boys' business was substantial (between the horsing around and the teasing they did buy food and drinks) the owner tolerated their transgressions.

The Saints on Weekends

On weekends, the automobile was even more critical than during the week, for on weekends the Saints went to Big Town—a large city with a population of over a million, 25 miles from Hannibal. Every Friday and Saturday night most of the Saints would meet between 8:00 and 8:30 and would go into Big Town. Big Town activities included drinking heavily in taverns or nightclubs, driving drunkenly through the streets, and committing acts of vandalism and playing pranks.

By midnight on Fridays and Saturdays the Saints were usually thoroughly high, and one or two of them were often so drunk they had to be carried to the cars. Then the boys drove around town, calling obscenities to women and girls; occasionally trying (unsuccessfully so far as I could tell) to pick girls up; and driving recklessly through red lights and at high speeds with their lights out. Occasionally they played "chicken." One boy would climb out the back window of the car and across the roof to the driver's side of the car while the car was moving at high speed (between 40 and 50 miles an hour); then the driver would move over and the boy who had just crawled across the car roof would take the driver's seat.

Searching for "fair game" for a prank was the boys' principal activity after they left the tavern. The boys would drive alongside a foot patrolman and ask directions to some street. If the policeman leaned on the car in the course of answering the question, the driver would speed away, causing him to lose his balance. The Saints were careful to play this prank only in an area where they were not going to spend much time and where they could quickly disappear around a corner to avoid having their license plate number taken.

Construction sites and road repair areas were the special province of the Saints' mischief. A soon-to-be-repaired hole in the road inevitably invited the Saints to remove lanterns and wooden barricades and put them in the car, leaving the hole unprotected. The boys would find a safe vantage point and wait for an unsuspecting motorist to drive into the hole. Often, though not always, the boys would go up to the motorist and commiserate with him about the dreadful way the city protected its citizenry.

Leaving the scene of the open hole and the motorist, the boys would then go searching for an appropriate place to erect the stolen barricade. An "appropriate place" was often a spot on a highway near a curve in the road where the barricade would not be seen by an oncoming motorist. The boys would wait to watch an unsuspecting motorist attempt to stop and (usually) crash into the wooden barricade. With saintly bearing the boys might offer help and understanding.

A stolen lantern might well find its way onto the back of a police car or hang from a street lamp. Once a lantern served as a prop for a reenactment of the "midnight ride of Paul Revere" until the "play," which was taking place at 2:00 a.m. in the center of a main street of Big Town, was interrupted by a police car several blocks away. The boys ran, leaving the lanterns on the street, and managed to avoid being apprehended.

Abandoned houses, especially if they were located in out-of-the-way places, were fair game for destruction and spontaneous vandalism. The boys would break windows, remove furniture to the yard and tear it apart, urinate on the walls and scrawl obscenities inside.

Through all the pranks, drinking and reckless driving the boys managed miraculously to avoid being stopped by police. Only twice in two years was I aware that they had been stopped by a Big City policeman. Once was for speeding (which they did every time they drove whether they were drunk or sober), and the driver managed to convince the policeman that it was simply an error. The second time they were stopped they had just left a nightclub and were walking through an alley. Aaron stopped to urinate and the boys began making obscene remarks. A foot patrolman came into the alley, lectured the boys and sent them home. Before the boys got to the car one began talking in a loud voice again. The policeman, who had followed them down the alley, arrested this boy for disturbing the peace and took him to the police station where the other Saints gathered. After paying a $5.00 fine, and with the assurance that there would be no permanent record of the arrest, the boy was released.

The boys had a spirit of frivolity and fun about their escapades. They did not view what they were engaged in as "delinquency," though it surely was by any reasonable definition of that word. They simply viewed themselves as having a little fun and who, they would ask, was really hurt by it? The answer had to be no one, although this fact remains one of the most difficult things to explain about the gang's behavior. Unlikely though it seems, in two years of drinking, driving, carousing and vandalism no one was seriously injured as a result of the Saints' activities.

The Saints in School

The Saints were highly successful in school. The average grade for the group was "B" with two of the boys having close to a straight "A" average. Almost all of the boys were popular and many of them held offices in the school. One of the boys was vice-president of the student body one year. Six of the boys played on athletic teams.

At the end of their senior year, the student body selected ten seniors for special recognition as the "school wheels"; four of the ten were Saints. Teachers and school officials saw no problem with any of these boys and anticipated that they would all "make something of themselves."

How the boys managed to maintain this impression is surprising in view of their actual behavior while in school. Their technique for covering truancy was so successful that teachers did not even realize that the boys were absent from school much of the time. Occasionally, of course, the system would backfire and then the boy was on his own. A boy who was caught would be most contrite, would plead guilty and ask for mercy. He inevitably got the mercy he sought.

Cheating on examinations was rampant, even to the point of orally communicating answers, as well as looking at one another's papers. Since none of the group studied, and since they were primarily dependent on one another for help, it is surprising that grades were so high. Teachers contributed to the deception in their admitted inclination to give these boys (and presumably others like them) the benefit of the doubt. When asked how the boys did in school, and when pressed on specific examinations, teachers might admit that they were disappointed in John's performance, but would quickly add that they "knew he was capable of doing better," so John was given a higher grade than he had actually earned. How often this happened is impossible to know. During the time that I observed the group, I never saw any of the boys take homework home. Teachers must have been "understanding" very regularly.

One exception to the gang's generally good performance was Jerry, who had a "C" average in his junior year, and experienced disaster the next year and failed to graduate. Jerry had always been a little more nonchalant than the others about the liberties he took in school. Rather than wait for someone to come get him from class, he would offer his own excuse and leave. Although he probably did not miss any more classes than most of the others in the group, he did not take the requisite pains to cover his absences. Jerry was the only Saint whom I ever heard talk back to a teacher. Although teachers often called him a "cut up" or a "smart kid," they never referred to him as a troublemaker or as a kid headed for trouble. It seems likely, then, that Jerry's failure his senior year and his mediocre performance his junior year were consequences of his not playing the game the proper way (possibly because he was disturbed by his parents' divorce). His teachers regarded him as "immature" and not quite ready to get out of high school.

The Police and the Saints

The local police saw the Saints as good boys who were among the leaders of the youth in the community. Rarely, the boys might be stopped in town for speeding or for running a stop sign. When this happened the boys were always polite, contrite and pled for mercy. As in school, they received the mercy they asked for. None ever received a ticket or was taken into the precinct by the local police.

The situation in Big City, where the boys engaged in most of their delinquency, was only slightly different. The police there did not know the boys at all, although occasionally the boys were stopped by a patrolman. Once they were caught taking a lantern from a construction site. Another time they were stopped for running a stop sign, and on several occasions they were stopped for speeding. Their behavior was as before: contrite, polite and penitent. The urban police, like the local police, accepted their demeanor as sincere. More important, the urban police were convinced that these were good boys just out for a lark.

The Roughnecks

Hannibal townspeople never perceived the Saints' high level of delinquency. The Saints were good boys who just went in for an occasional prank. After all, they were well dressed, well mannered and had nice cars. The Roughnecks were a different story. Although the two gangs of boys were the same age, and both groups engaged in an equal amount of wild-oat sowing, everyone agreed that the not-so-well-dressed, not-so-well-mannered, not-so-rich boys were heading for trouble. Townspeople would say, "You can see the gang members at the drugstore night after night, leaning against the storefront (sometimes drunk) or slouching around inside buying cokes, reading magazines, and probably stealing old Mr. Wall blind. When they are outside and girls walk by, even respectable girls, these boys make suggestive remarks. Sometimes their remarks are downright lewd."

From the community's viewpoint, the real indication that these kids were in for trouble was that they were constantly involved with the police. Some of them had been picked up for stealing, mostly small stuff, of course, "but still it's stealing small stuff that leads to big time crimes. Too bad," people said. "Too bad that these boys couldn't behave like the other kids in town; stay out of trouble, be polite to adults, and look to their future."

The community's impression of the degree to which this group of six boys (ranging in age from 16 to 19) engaged in delinquency was somewhat distorted. In some ways the gang was more delinquent than the community thought; in other ways they were less.

The fighting activities of the group were fairly, readily, and accurately perceived by almost everyone. At least once a month, the boys would get into some sort of fight, although most fights were scraps between members of the group or involved only one member of the group and some peripheral hanger-on. Only three times in the period of observation did the group fight together: once against a gang from across town, once against two blacks and once against a group of boys from another school. For the first two fights the group went out "looking for trouble" and they found it both times. The third fight followed a football game and began spontaneously with an argument on the football field between one of the Roughnecks and a member of the opposition's football team.

Jack had a particular propensity for fighting and was involved in most of the brawls. He was a prime mover of the escalation of arguments into fights.

More serious than fighting, had the community been aware of it, was theft. Although almost everyone was aware that the boys occasionally stole things, they did not realize the extent of the activity. Petty stealing was a frequent event for the Roughnecks. Sometimes they stole as a group and coordinated their efforts; other times they stole in pairs. Rarely did they steal alone.

The thefts ranged from very small things like paperback books, comics and ballpoint pens to expensive items like watches. The nature of the thefts varied from time to time. The gang would go through a period of systematically lifting items from automobiles or school lockers. Types of thievery varied with the whim of the gang. Some forms of thievery were more profitable than others, but all thefts were for profit, not just thrills.

Roughnecks siphoned gasoline from cars as often as they had access to an automobile, which was not very often. Unlike the Saints, who owned their own cars, the Roughnecks would have to borrow their parents' cars, an event which occurred only eight or nine times a year. The boys claimed to have stolen cars for joy rides from time to time.

Ron committed the most serious of the group's offenses. With an associate who was never identified, Ron attempted to burglarize a gasoline station. Although this station had been robbed twice previously in the same month, Ron denied any involvement in either of the other thefts. When Ron and his accomplice approached the station, the owner was hiding in the bushes beside the station. He fired both barrels of a double-barreled shotgun at the boys. Ron was severely injured; the other boy ran away and was never caught. Though he remained in critical condition for several months, Ron finally recovered and served six months of the following year in reform school. Upon release from reform school, Ron was put back a grade in school. He dropped out of the Roughnecks and began running around with a different gang of boys. The Roughnecks considered Ron's new associates as "nerds" and they were apparently less delinquent than the Roughnecks. During the following year Ron had no more trouble with the police.

The Roughnecks, then, engaged mainly in three types of delinquency: theft, drinking and fighting. Although community members perceived that this gang of kids was delinquent, they mistakenly believed that their illegal activities were primarily drinking, fighting and being a nuisance to passersby. Drinking was limited among the gang members, although it did occur, and theft was much more prevalent than anyone realized.

Drinking would doubtless have been more prevalent had the boys had ready access to liquor. Since they rarely had automobiles at their disposal, they could not travel very far, and the bars in town would not serve them. Most of the boys had little money, and this, too, inhibited their purchase of alcohol. Their major source of liquor was a local drunk who would buy them a fifth if they would give him enough extra to buy himself a pint of whiskey or a bottle of wine.

The community's perception of their drinking as prevalent stemmed from the fact that it was the most obvious delinquency the boys engaged in. When one of the boys had been drinking, even a casual observer seeing him on the corner would suspect that he was drunk.

There was a high level of mutual distrust and dislike between the Roughnecks and the police. The boys felt very strongly that the police were unfair and corrupt. Some evidence existed that the boys were correct in their perception.

The main source of the boys' dislike for the police undoubtedly stemmed from the fact that the police would sporadically harass the group. From the standpoint of the boys, these acts of occasional enforcement of the law were whimsical and uncalled for. It made no sense that the police would come to the corner occasionally and threaten them with arrest for loitering when the night before the boys had been out siphoning gasoline from cars and the police had been nowhere in sight. To the boys, the police were stupid on the one hand, for not being where they should have been and catching the boys in a serious offense. And unfair on the other hand, for trumping up "loitering" charges against them.

From the viewpoint of the police, the situation was quite different. They knew, with all the confidence necessary to be a policeman, that these boys were engaged in criminal activities. They knew this partly from occasionally catching them, mostly from circumstantial evidence ("the boys were around when those tires were slashed"), and partly because the police shared the view of the community in general that this was a bad bunch of boys. The best the police could hope to do was to be sensitive to the fact that these boys were engaged in illegal acts and arrest them whenever there was some evidence that they had been involved. Whether or not the boys had in fact committed a particular act in a particular way was not especially important. The police had a broader view: their job was to stamp out these kids' crimes; their tactics were not as important as the end result.

Over the period that the group was under observation, each member was arrested at least once. Several of the boys were arrested a number of times and spent at least one night in jail. While most were never taken to court, two of the boys were sentenced to six months' incarceration in boys' schools.

The Roughnecks in School

The Roughnecks' behavior in school was not particularly disruptive. During school hours they did not all hang around together, but tended instead to spend most of their time with one or two other members of the gang who were their special buddies. Although every member of the gang attempted to avoid school as much as possible, they were not particularly successful and most of them attended school with surprising regularity. They considered school a burden—something to be gotten through with a minimum of conflict. If they were "bugged" by a particular teacher, it could lead to trouble. One of the boys, Al, once threatened to beat up a teacher and, according to the other boys, the teacher hid under a desk to escape him.

Teachers saw the boys the way the general community did, as heading for trouble, as being uninterested in making something of themselves. Some were also seen as being incapable of meeting the academic standards of the school. Most of the teachers expressed concern for this group of boys and were willing to pass them despite poor performance, in the belief that failing them would only aggravate the problem.

The group of boys had a grade point average just slightly above "C." No one in the group failed any of their grades, and no one had better than a "C" average. They were very consistent in their achievement or, at least, the teachers were consistent in their perception of the boys' achievement.

Two of the boys were good football players. Herb was acknowledged to be the best player in the school and Jack was almost as good. Both boys were criticized for their failure to abide by training rules, for refusing to come to practice as often as they should, and for not playing their best during practice. What they lacked in sportsmanship they made up for in skill, apparently, and played every game no matter how poorly they had performed in practice or how many practice sessions they had missed.

Two Questions

Why did the community, the school and the police react to the Saints as though they were good, upstanding, nondelinquent youths with bright futures but to the Roughnecks as though they were tough, young criminals who were headed for trouble? Why did the Roughnecks and the Saints in fact have quite different careers after high school careers which, by and large, lived up to the expectations of the community?

The most obvious explanation for the differences in the community's and law enforcement agencies' reactions to the two gangs is that one group of boys was "more delinquent" than the other. But which group *was* more delinquent? The answer to this question will determine in part how we explain the differential responses to these groups by the members of the community and, particularly, by law enforcement and school officials.

In sheer number of illegal acts, the Saints were the more delinquent. They were truant from school for at least part of the day almost every day of the week. In addition, their drinking and vandalism occurred with surprising regularity. The Roughnecks, in contrast, engaged sporadically in delinquent episodes. While these episodes were frequent, they certainly did not occur on a daily or even a weekly basis.

The difference in frequency of offenses was probably caused by the Roughnecks' inability to obtain liquor and to manipulate legitimate excuses from school. Since the Roughnecks had less money than the Saints and teachers carefully supervised their school activities, the Roughnecks' hearts may have been as black as the Saints', but their misdeeds were not nearly as frequent.

There are really no clear-cut criteria by which to measure qualitative differences in antisocial behavior. The most important dimension of the difference is generally referred to as the "seriousness" of the offenses.

If seriousness encompasses the relative economic costs of delinquent acts, then some assessment can be made. The Roughnecks probably stole an average of about $5.00 worth of goods a week. Some weeks the figure was considerably higher, but these times must be balanced against long periods when almost nothing was stolen.

The Saints were more continuously engaged in delinquency but their acts were not for the most part costly to property. Only their vandalism and occasional theft of gasoline would so qualify. Perhaps once or twice a month they would siphon a tank full of gas. The other costly items were street signs, construction lanterns and the like. All of these acts combined probably did not quite average $5.00 a week, partly because much of the stolen equipment was abandoned and presumably could be recovered. The difference in cost of stolen property between the two groups was trivial, but the Roughnecks probably had a slightly more expensive set of activities than did the Saints.

Another meaning of seriousness is the potential threat of physical harm to members of the community and to the boys themselves. The Roughnecks were more prone to physical violence; they not only welcomed an opportunity to fight, they went seeking it. In addition, they fought among themselves frequently. Although the fighting never included deadly weapons, it was still a menace, however minor, to the physical safety of those involved.

The Saints never fought. They avoided physical conflict both inside and outside the group. At the same time, though, the Saints frequently endangered their own and other people's lives. They did so almost every time they drove a car, especially if they had been drinking. Sober, their driving was risky; under the influence of alcohol it was horrendous. In addition, the Saints endangered the lives of others with their pranks. Street excavations left unmarked were a very serious hazard.

Evaluating the relative seriousness of the two gangs' activities is difficult. The community reacted as though the behavior of the Roughnecks was a problem, and they reacted as though the behavior of the Saints was not. But the members of the community were ignorant to the array of delinquent acts that characterized the Saints' behavior. Although concerned citizens were unaware of much of the Roughnecks' behavior as well, they were much better informed about the Roughnecks' involvement in delinquency than they were about the Saints'.

Visibility

Differential treatment of the two gangs resulted in part because one gang was infinitely more visible than the other. This differential visibility was a direct function of the social class of the families. The Saints had access to automobiles and were able to remove themselves from the sight of the community. Even routine decisions such as where to go to have a milk shake after school, the Saints stayed away from the mainstream of community life. Lacking transportation, the Roughnecks could not make it to the edge of town. The center of town was the only practical place for them to meet since they did not have access to automobiles and any non-central meeting place put an undue hardship on some members. Through necessity the Roughnecks congregated in a crowded area where everyone in the community passed frequently, including teachers and law enforcement officers. They could easily see the Roughnecks hanging around the drugstore.

The Roughnecks, of course, made themselves even more visible by making remarks to passersby and by occasionally getting into fights on the corner. Meanwhile, just as regularly, the Saints were either at the cafe on one edge of town or in the pool hall at the other edge of town. Without any particular realization that they were making themselves inconspicuous, the Saints were able to hide their time-wasting. Not only were they removed from the mainstream of traffic, but they were almost always inside a building.

On their escapades the Saints were also relatively invisible, since they left Hannibal and traveled to Big City. Here, too, they were mobile, roaming the city, rarely going to the same area twice.

Demeanor

To the notion of visibility must be added the difference in the responses of group members to outside intervention with their activities. If one of the Saints was confronted with an accusing policeman, even if he felt he was truly innocent of a wrongdoing, his demeanor was apologetic and penitent. A Roughneck's attitude was almost the polar opposite. When confronted with a threatening adult authority, even one who tried to be pleasant, the Roughneck's hostility and disdain were clearly observable. Sometimes he might attempt to put up a veneer of respect, but it was thin and was not accepted as sincere by the authority.

School was no different from the community at large. The Saints could manipulate the system by feigning compliance with the school norms. The availability of cars at school meant that once free from the immediate sight of the teacher, the boys could disappear rapidly. This escape was always well enough planned that no administrator or teacher was nearby when the boys left. A Roughneck who wished to escape for a few hours was in a bind. If it were possible to get free from class, downtown was still a mile away, and even if he arrived there, he was still very visible. Truancy for the Roughnecks meant almost certain detection, while the Saints enjoyed almost complete immunity from sanctions.

Bias

Community members were not aware of the transgressions of the Saints. Even if the Saints had been less discreet, their favorite delinquencies would have been perceived as less serious than those of the Roughnecks.

In the eyes of the police and school officials, a boy who drinks in an alley and stands intoxicated on the street corner, who steals a wallet from a store, or associates with someone who has committed a burglary, is a delinquent. An upper-middle class boy who gets drunk in a nightclub or tavern, even if he drives around afterwards in a car, is perceived as someone who has made a mistake. Stealing a lantern from a construction site is not perceived as a serious delinquency but shoplifting a pair of gloves from a department store is.

In other words, there is a built in class-bias in the definition of what constitutes "serious" delinquency. Just as driving under the influence is treated by law enforcement agencies with greater leniency than possession of drugs . . . so are the delinquencies of middle-class youths seen as less serious than the delinquencies of lower class youths. Why this is so is best explained by the way the law enforcement system is organized and who has the power to affect it.

The Organization of Policing

Visibility, demeanor, and bias describe the characteristics of the Saints, Roughnecks and police that account for the day-to-day operations of the police. Why do these surface variables operate as they do? Why did the police choose to disregard the Saints' delinquencies while breathing down the backs of the Roughnecks?

The answer lies in the class structure of American society and the control of legal institutions by those at the top of the class structure. Put quite simply, if the police treat middle-class delinquents (or cocaine snorting college students) the same way they treat lower-class delinquents (or black ghetto crack users) they are asking for trouble from people in power. If, on the other hand, they focus their law enforcement efforts on the lower-classes they are praised and supported by "the community": that is, the middle- and upper-class white community.

There is no conscious conspiracy to arrest and imprison the lower classes for acts less harmful, or at least no more harmful, than the crimes of the middle and upper classes. There is no community leader telling the police to look on street corners and in the ghettoes for crime. The law does not dictate that the demeanor of lower-class youth bespeaks future criminality and that of upper-middle-class youth promises future success. Rather, the decisions of the police and teachers grew from their experience; experience with irate and influential upper-middle-class parents insisting that their son's vandalism was simply a prank and their drunkenness only a momentary "sowing of wild oats"; experience with cooperative or indifferent, powerless, lower-class parents who acquiesced to the laws' definition of their son's behavior.

Role occupants in organizations are rewarded for acts that minimize strain and maximize rewards for the organization. Police who arrest poor kids for stealing bicycles or selling drugs are doing a good job and are promoted to sergeant. Police who arrest upper-middle-class kids for being truant and hanging out in pool halls create strains that no police chief wants. It does not take many encounters with irate parents and their high priced lawyers for the police to learn to ignore the drug dealing on college campuses or the vandalism of middle-class kids. It just makes organizational sense to look for crime in the ghetto and not the suburbs and to send middle-class kids home with a warning rather than arrest them and face the inevitable criticism of superiors.

Adult Careers of the Saints

The community's confidence in the potential of the Saints and the Roughnecks apparently was justified. If anything, the community members underestimated the degree to which these youngsters would turn out "good" and "bad."

Seven of the eight members of the Saints went on to college immediately after high school. Five of the boys graduated from college in four years. The sixth one finished college after two years in the army, and the seventh spent four years in the air force before returning to college and receiving a B.A. degree. Of these seven college graduates, three went on for advanced degrees. One finished law school and for awhile was active in state politics, one finished medical school and is practicing near Hannibal, and another completed a Ph.D. in history and is teaching at a small state university. The other four college graduates entered sub-managerial, managerial or executive training positions with larger firms immediately upon graduation and while changing firms from time to time three of the four remained in managerial positions throughout their careers. The fourth, Charles, went to work for the government for a period of time then quit and began selling real estate.

The only Saint who did not complete college was Jerry. Jerry failed to graduate from high school with the other Saints. During his second senior year, after the other Saints had gone on to college, Jerry began to hang around with what several teachers described as a "rough crowd." At the end of his second senior year, when he did graduate from high school, Jerry took a job as a used-car salesman, got married and quickly had a child. Although he made several abortive attempts to go to college by attending night school, ten years after he graduated from high school Jerry was unemployed and had been living on unemployment for almost a year. His wife worked as a waitress.

Adult Careers of the Roughnecks

Some of the Roughnecks lived up to community expectations, some did not. A number of them were, indeed, headed for trouble.

Jack and Herb were the athletes among the Roughnecks and their athletic prowess paid off handsomely. Both boys received unsolicited athletic scholarships to college. After Herb received his scholarship (near the end of his senior year), he did an about-face. His demeanor became very similar to that of the Saints. Although he remained a member in good standing of the Roughnecks, he stopped participating in most activities and did not hang on the corner as often. When I met him in the parking lot of a shopping center the summer after high school graduation he was dressed in a suit and tie. He came up to me and shook my hand (an unheard of gesture for him only a few months earlier), took me to his car and introduced me to his mother. Suddenly Herb was the "gentleman" the college he would be attending expected their students to be.

Jack did not change. If anything, he became more prone to fighting. He even made excuses for accepting the scholarship. He told the other gang members that the school had guaranteed him a "C" average if he would come to play football—an idea that seems far-fetched, even in this day of highly competitive recruiting.

During the summer after graduation from high school, Jack attempted suicide by jumping from a tall building. The jump would certainly have killed most people trying it, but Jack survived. He entered college in the fall and played four years of football. He and Herb graduated in four years, and both are teaching and coaching in high schools. Jack is the Vice Principal of his high school. They are married and have stable families. Jack appears to have a more prestigious position in the community than does Herb, though both are well respected and secure in their positions.

Two of the boys never finished high school. Tommy left at the end of his junior year and went to another state. That summer he was arrested and placed on probation on a manslaughter charge. Three years later he was arrested for murder; he pleaded guilty to second degree murder and served twelve years of a 30-year sentence in the state penitentiary and was released.

Al, the other boy who did not finish high school, also moved to another state in his senior year. When Al was twenty-four he was accused of murdering a man in a fight. He served fourteen years of a life sentence in a state penitentiary for first degree murder. While in prison Al got into a fight and was stabbed, as a result of which he was paralyzed from the waist down. Upon release from prison Al purchased a small grocery store which he ran successfully until his death.

Wes is a small-time gambler. He finished high school and "bummed around." After several years he made contact with a bookmaker who employed him as a runner. Later he acquired his own area and has been working it ever since. His position among the bookmakers is almost identical to the position he had in the gang; he is always around but no one is really aware of him. He makes no trouble and he does not get into any. Steady, reliable, capable of keeping his mouth closed, he plays the game by the rules, even though the game is an illegal one.

That leaves only Ron. Some of his former friends reported that they had heard he was "driving a truck up north," but I was unable to find him.

Labeling and the Self-Fulfilling Prophesy

The community responded to the Roughnecks as boys in trouble, and the boys agreed with that perception. Their pattern of deviance was reinforced, and breaking away from it became increasingly unlikely. Once the boys acquired an image of themselves as deviants, they selected new friends who affirmed that self-image. As that self-conception became more firmly entrenched, they also became willing to try new and more extreme deviances. With their growing alienation came freer expression of disrespect and hostility for representatives of the legitimate society. This disrespect increased the community's negativism, perpetuating the entire process of commitment to deviance. Lack of a commitment to deviance works the same way. In either case, the process will perpetuate itself unless some event (like a scholarship to college or a sudden failure) external to the established relationship intervenes. For two of the Roughnecks (Herb and Jack), receiving college athletic scholarships created new relations and culminated in a break with the established pattern of deviance.

For one of the Saints (Jerry), his parents' divorce and his failing to graduate from high school brought about significant changes in his interpersonal relationships. Being held back in school for a year and losing his place among the Saints had sufficient impact on Jerry. It altered his self-image and virtually assured that he would not go on to college as his peers did. Although the experiments of life rarely can be reversed, it is likely that if Jerry had not experienced the "special consideration" of his teachers that kept him from graduating with his peers that he too would have "become something" had he graduated as anticipated. For Herb and Jack outside intervention and labeling worked in the opposite way than it did for Jerry.

Selective perception and labeling—the discovery, processing and punishing of some kinds of criminality and not others—means that visible, poor, non-mobile, outspoken, undiplomatic "tough" kids will be noticed, whether their actions are seriously delinquent or not. Other kids, who establish a reputation for being bright (even though underachieving), reasonably polite and involved in respectable activities, who are mobile and moneyed, will be invisible when they deviate from sanctioned activities. They will "sow their wild oats," perhaps even wider and thicker than their lower-class cohorts, but they will not be noticed. When it is time to leave adolescence most will follow the expected path, settling into the ways of the middle class, remembering fondly the delinquent but unnoticed flings of their youth. The Roughnecks, and others like them, may turn around, too. It is more likely, however, that their noticeable deviance and the reaction to it will have been so reinforced by police and community that their lives will be effectively channeled into careers consistent with the self-image they developed in adolescence.

Afterthought

Since I published the article in 1973 I have kept in touch with some of the boys in the two gangs. Subsequent contacts and conversations have raised some interesting, if unanswered, questions about their subsequent careers. Were the patterns of deviance established in adolescence and the reaction of significant actors in the community reproduced in adulthood? As we have seen, the Saints apparently became successful, upper-middle-class adults; but were they also law abiding?

One of the Saints who became a lawyer had to leave the state in which he was practicing law because of a pending law suit alleging criminal violation of trust. The suit was dropped after he paid a substantial amount of money to the plaintiff. The law suit alleged not only a violation of trust but complicity with organized crime figures. He re-located as a lawyer to Atlantic City, New Jersey, where, one of his former classmates told me he works closely with organized crime figures. I have no way at this time of verifying this information.

Did the Saint who became a medical doctor or those who worked for corporations commit criminal acts? Did they smoke pot or snort cocaine as adults as they did in college? Were they involved in price fixing, insider trading, or tax evasion? When I interviewed them recently and raised these questions I was met only with laughter and the admission, as one put it, "well, maybe a little pot occasionally and of course tax evasion." It is impossible to say how criminal the Saints were as adults for although I have kept contact with most of them over the years, except for one, Charles, the closeness we shared when they were teenagers has eroded with time. They also can be expected to be considerably more circumspect about their adult crimes than they were about their juvenile "games."

The prophylactic of power to avoid scrutiny and detection of criminal acts and being labeled criminal that covered the Saints as adolescents may well be protecting them as adults. Those in low places, like the Roughnecks, are much more likely to be arrested and imprisoned while people in high places, like the Saints, usually avoid paying such a high price for their crimes.

The most important question this study of the Roughnecks and the Saints raises is this: How many poor, young, men—black, brown, and white—incarcerated for minor offenses, would be in college today instead of prison had they been treated by the police and the community the way the Saints were treated? How many Saints would be in prison instead of going on to college had they been treated as were the Roughnecks? We cannot answer this question for certain but the impact on a person's life of labeling, stigma, and negative self-images is a powerful force in determining who we are and what we become. One lesson is inescapable: The less the intervention in the minor crimes of juveniles the better off they and society will be.

---

*All the names in this article, including the name of the high school, are pseudonyms.

GLOSSARY

acquaintance rape The most common type of rape in which the victim and the rapist are not strangers; the least reported type of rape.

addiction A chronic condition that causes a physical or psychological compulsion to seek the use of a drug, despite its harmful physical or social consequences.

agents of socialization The groups and individuals who are the main influences on the process of socialization.

aggravated assault The attempt to commit, or the commission of, serious bodily harm or injury upon an individual; usually involves some type of weapon or deadly force.

altruism In Bonger's theory, an emphasis on equality and sharing or the **sacrifice** of self to help others; in contrast to egoism, competition is replaced by cooperation and the desire for peace and harmony among different groups in society.

anomie A state of normlessness and confusion that leads to strain.

antisocial personality disorder (APD) The current term for psychopathy.

arson The willful or malicious burning or attempted burning of a home, building, motor vehicle or airplane, or other personal property.

assault The attempted commission of bodily injury to another human being.

atavistic Lombroso's term to describe inherently criminal individuals; people who, due to their primitive biological state, are incapable of functioning according to the norms and standards of a complex society.

attempted rape The attempt to commit a rape by force or threat of force.

attention deficit hyperactivity disorder (ADHD) A neurological condition involving poor attention skills, deficient impulse control, and hyperactivity.

aversion therapy A psychological technique for unlearning faulty patterns of behavior by pairing a stimulus that brings pleasure with an unpleasant response.

battery Unwanted, nonconsensual physical contact.

behavioral genetics The study of the role of genetics in human behavior.

behavior modeling Learning by watching, listening, and copying what we see and hear.

behavior theory The branch of psychology that holds that human actions are derived from learning experiences that include observing others and getting reinforcement for certain behaviors.

bias A distortion that systematically misrepresents the true nature of what is being studied or the results of the study.

biological perspective In criminology, an approach built on the foundation of positivism, which presumes criminal behavior is caused by biological forces beyond an individual's control.

biosocial approach A perspective on human behavior that acknowledges the interaction between social environment and variations in individual constitutions as contributing factors in how people act and react.

Boggs Act A 1951 law that placed criminal sanctions on the possession and distribution of marijuana.

boosters Shoplifters who are professional thieves who make their living by stealing merchandise they can easily resell to pawnshops or fences.

bourgeoisie In Marxist theory, the capitalists or the class who owns the means of production—the land, the factories, the businesses, or the enterprises.

brain imaging Techniques to capture three-dimensional images of the brain.

bribery An illegal financial exchange wherein a government official accepts a direct payment in exchange for official government action, such as gaining votes, sponsoring legislation, and appropriating government funds to private contractors.

brothel A house run by a madam who recruits and trains young women as prostitutes.

buildup A common type of claim abuse wherein a legitimate claim is inflated by unnecessary treatments or medical interventions.

burglary Any unlawful entry into a structure for the purpose of committing a theft or felony.

cannabis Drugs that produce feelings of euphoria and relaxation, derived from the hemp plant; they include marijuana and hashish.

career criminals Persistent offenders; those who account for most criminal behavior.

causal relationship A relationship between two variables in which one is the cause of the other.

check duplication or counterfeiting Creating bogus financial documents with sophisticated desktop publishing software, or by altering a real check using solvents to remove or change information.

Chicago School Groundbreaking studies of social disorganization theory coming out of the University of Chicago between the 1920s and the 1940s.

child maltreatment Any act or failure to act on the part of a parent or caretaker that results in the emotional harm, physical injury, sexual exploitation, or death of a minor child, or puts the minor child at risk of imminent danger.

child pornography Pornographic material that depicts children in sexually explicit positions or engaging in sexual acts.

chiseling An occupational crime that consists of the regular cheating of a company or organization, its consumers, or both.

churning A crime in which stockbrokers repeatedly and excessively buy and sell stocks owned by investors for the sole purpose of generating a commission on each trade.

civil law A collection of laws dealing with disputes between individuals and organizations, as opposed to violations against the state.

Classical School A school of criminology that holds that people calculate the rewards and risks of their actions and decide how to act based on what they believe will bring them the most pleasure and the least pain.

cognitive behavioral therapy A program to correct how people process information involving cognitive skills training and cognitive restructuring.

cognitive restructuring A technique of cognitive behavioral therapy that focuses on changing faulty thought processes or criminal thinking errors.

cognitive skills training A technique of cognitive behavioral therapy that helps offenders become more effective problem-solvers by teaching them how to cope with anger, resist peer pressure, respect the feelings of others, exert better self-control, accurately assess the consequences of behavior, and understand moral reasoning.

cognitive theory The branch of psychology that studies the mental processes of understanding, perceiving, interpreting, and manipulating information.

cohort A group of individuals with similar characteristics.

collective efficacy Informal social control of public space by residents that significantly deters crime and disorder.

common law A system in which laws are created by legislation, but their interpretation and substantive definition is left to the courts to determine.

comparative criminology The systematic study of crime and crime-control policies and practices in different cultures and societies around the world.

concentric zones A concept within social ecology analysis that explains the distribution of crime rates by envisioning cities as being made up of areas of social characteristics, such as immigration, residential mobility, housing structure, and family income.

concepts Words, phrases, or ideas in a theory used to explain a category of individuals or a certain class of events.

conduct norms Rules of acceptable behavior we learn early in life.

confidence games Also known as cons, scams, and swindles, schemes devised to trick or cheat unsuspecting victims out of their money by gaining their trust.

conflict model View that crime and deviance are products of unequal power relationships in society.

consensus model View that crime is a social phenomenon; crime is behavior that is generally agreed to be harmful, undesirable, and disruptive to the smooth functioning of society.

constructive possession The condition in which a person does not have physical custody or possession but is in a position to exercise dominion or control over a thing.

containment theory In social control theory, the view that individuals who commit crime have failed to resist the social pressures, the "pushes" and "pulls," that non-criminals are able to resist.

control group In an experiment, the group that receives no special attention.

corporate or organizational crime Acts of individuals who occupy positions of power within institutions and who willfully and knowingly break the law to advance their own interests and for their own benefit or the benefit of their business or enterprise.

correlation The degree to which two or more variables are associated with one another.

crime Human behavior interpreted as violating society's norms for a specific time and place and that must be controlled and prevented by legal decree.

crimes cleared by arrest A crime is considered cleared when police have made an arrest or when the perpetrator is known but has not been arrested for some reason (for instance, the person has fled the country or has died).

crimes known to the police A compilation of crime based on telephone calls to the police station and crimes reported to or observed by police officers.

criminal anthropology A discipline that proposes a relationship between physical features and criminal behavior.

criminal homicide A term criminal justice officials use to describe the act of murder.

criminal law A collection of laws that define conduct against the state and that set out the punishments for those violations.

criminologists Academics, researchers, and policy analysts who focus on understanding the nature and meaning of crime, patterns of criminal behavior, various causes of criminality, and society's reaction to crime.

criminology The scientific study of the incidence and forms of crime and criminal behavior, their causes and consequences, and social reaction to, control of, and prevention of crime.

culture conflict theory A social structure theory that maintains that the root cause of crime is the clash of values between different cultures producing different beliefs about what is acceptable and unacceptable behavior.

cyber crime The theft, misuse, and disruption of computer-based data systems.

date rape Sexual intercourse forced on a person by an acquaintance acting as an escort during some type of social engagement.

defendant The person or party being accused or sued in a trial.

delinquent subculture A subculture that emerges among youth who have a common need to resolve similar problems and who engage in delinquent activities as a means of compensating for their lack of legitimate opportunities within the dominant social structure.

dependent variable The variable that is hypothesized to have been caused by or influenced by the independent variable.

depressants Potentially addictive drugs taken to relieve tension and anxiety; they include barbiturates and tranquilizers.

detached observation Conducting research in the field from a distance and observing without getting involved.

determinate sentencing A type of general deterrence, this crime-control strategy mandates a fixed sentence for every type of offense.

developmental pathways A model of prevention based on the concept that interventions aimed at multiple risk factors and over a long period of time are more likely to have positive results.

deviance Behavior that elicits a social reaction by violating the standards of conduct defined by society.

deviance amplification In labeling theory, the process by which the activity labeled as deviant is amplified by the spiraling effect of negative social reaction.

differential association In social learning theory, the idea that criminal behavior results from having more contact with individuals who hold attitudes favorable to criminal behavior than with individuals who hold attitudes that discourage it.

differential identification In social learning theory, the degree to which individuals symbolically identify with criminal or non-criminal behavior patterns is what determines whether they will commit criminal acts.

differential learning In social learning theory, the socialization mechanism whereby we learn criminal behavior.

differential opportunity The variable access to illegitimate opportunities that contributes to the development of crime and delinquency.

differential reinforcement In social learning theory, the process whereby individuals learn to define their behavior according to the rewards or punishments attached to it.

dizygotic (fraternal) twins The product of two eggs and two sperm; they have the same genetic similarity as any two siblings (approximately 50 percent).

document analysis The analysis of written materials: previous studies, newspaper reports, court records, and other forms of text produced by individuals, government agencies, private organizations, and other sources.

domestic violence A pattern of abusive behavior in a relationship that is used by one partner to gain or maintain power and control over another partner.

drift A process by which individuals shift from conventional, law-abiding behavior to delinquent and criminal behavior by gradually altering their way of thinking and reacting to their acts using neutralization techniques.

drug A chemical substance that affects the body's physical and psychological functioning by altering the way in which the brain sends, receives, and processes information.

drug abuse The use of any chemical substance, whether legal or illegal, to result in the physical, mental, emotional, or behavioral impairment of an individual.

dynamic factors Predictors of future involvement in criminal activities that are capable of changing over time with treatment or counseling.

ego In psychoanalytic theory, the part of personality that takes into consideration the reality of situations; the ego guides behavior within the boundaries of what is socially acceptable.

egoism In Bonger's theory, the prevailing personality type produced by capitalism; one that strives for self-attainment and that places only secondary importance on providing support or aid to one's neighbors.

embezzlement A unique form of larceny that violates the trust of an employer; the property stolen is in the rightful possession of the perpetrator, who has the permission or consent of the owner.

embezzlement An occupational crime in which perpetrators use their positions of employment to steal company property or funds entrusted to their care.

Enlightenment Also known as the Age of Reason, a 17th- and 18th-century period of inspired innovative thinking and a search for truth using philosophical reasoning.

environmental criminology Analysis of the immediate context within which criminal behavior occurs in order to understand how environmental variables, potential offenders, and targeted victims interact.

eugenics movement A movement in the 1920s and early 1930s in which science and policy merged in an attempt to improve the human race through breeding.

exorcism A practice of prayers and rituals to literally evict a demon from the individual's body.

experimental criminology Transforms subjective evidence into more reliable objective data by conducting randomized, controlled experiments in a social setting.

experimental group In an experiment, the group that is exposed to the independent (or experimental) variable.

experiments Research techniques for investigating cause and effect under controlled conditions.

expressive gain Motivation for larceny, such as stealing for a thrill or to gain peer approval.

external containment In social control theory, the idea that there is someone or something evaluating our decisions to act in certain ways.

extortion The use of threats or blackmail to obtain money or something of value from someone.

false claims advertising Crimes committed by corporations that involve deceiving the public in order to increase their own profits by providing misleading information about a product or service.

false pretense or fraud A form of larceny in which the perpetrator uses lies and deception to trick the victim out of money or property, usually by misrepresenting the nature, value, or characteristics of merchandise.

feminist theories Views of criminology that direct attention to the role of gender and gender relations in ordering social life.

fieldwork Also called ethnography, a research method using in-depth and often extended on-site study to describe a group or community.

first-degree murder The unlawful killing of a human being by another with malice aforethought and premeditation.

focal concerns Values and behaviors that emerge to meet the specific conditions of the environment and that may result in deviant activities and violence.

folkways Nonbinding social conventions, including appropriate dress, manners, and hygiene.

forcible rape Sexual intercourse with a victim by force and against the person's will; the use of force and coercion to take control over the victim.

forgery Falsely altering a document, usually a check, and presenting it for cash or payment using false identification.

front running A crime in which brokerage companies purchase large quantities of a certain stock at a low cost, before advising their investors to buy the stock at a higher price.

functional conflict theory In criminology, the view that crime results as a consequence of the disagreement between different interest groups over the definition of law.

gang rape Forced sexual intercourse with a victim by more than one assailant.

general deterrence A strategy for crime control that is based on people's fear of apprehension and punishment.

general strain theory (GST) A broader concept of strain theory maintaining that various sources of strain and frustration exist within the social structure that are not the result of economic failure.

genocide The systematic destruction of a particular national, religious, ethnic, racial, or political group,

globalization A process that eases interaction and integration among the people, corporations, and political systems of different countries.

grand larceny The theft of an item or merchandise of significant value.

hacking A technology-assisted criminal offense that involves the unauthorized access and use of computer databases and network software systems to steal data.

hallucinogens Drugs that create profound mind-altering changes and distortions in feelings and perception, often producing a state of confusion and hallucination; they include PCP, LSD, and Ecstasy.

Harrison Act A 1914 law designed to regulate and control the manufacture, production, and distribution of cocaine and opiate drugs.

hate crime A crime targeting a specific category of individuals and motivated by a bias against physical or social characteristics unique to this group.

hedonism The principle that human nature is governed by the desire to maximize pleasure and minimize pain.

hierarchy rule In a multiple-offense situation, when more than one Part I offense is classified, the law enforcement agency must report the offense that is highest in the hierarchy and not the other offense(s).

historical research Research based on historical documents.

homicide The willful killing of one human being by another.

human trafficking The movement of people from one place to another using force, fraud, or deception with the goal of exploiting them for material or financial benefit.

identity theft The illegal collection of another individual's personal information for fraudulent purposes.

incapacitation The removal of offenders from society so that they are no longer a threat to public safety.

independent variable The variable that is hypothesized to have caused or influenced another.

intellectual property laws Laws designed to protect the patents or copyrights applied to products, ideas, inventions, and artistic creations.

internal containment In social control theory, the idea that our behavior is guided by our desire for socially approved goals, a commitment to the beliefs of society, a healthy and positive self-image, and the ability to manage strain and frustration.

International Crime Control Strategy (ICCS) An action plan with broadly defined goals and objectives for a coordinated, forceful, and enduring federal response to global crime threats.

International Crime Victims Survey (ICVS) A survey of households in different countries on their experiences with crime and police response, as well as matters related to crime prevention and safety.

International Criminal Court (ICC) Established in 1998 and entered into force in 2002, a permanent tribunal to prosecute individuals for genocide, crimes against humanity, and war crimes.

International Criminal Police Organization (INTERPOL) An international police organization; a valuable resource for comparative criminal justice research.

interview A detailed conversation designed to obtain in-depth information about a person and his or her activities.

intimate partner violence A pattern of abusive and/ or violent behavior between spouses or domestic partners.

hypoglycemia A condition that occurs when blood glucose falls below the necessary level for the brain to function effectively.

hypotheses Ideas about the world derived from theories and that can be disproved when tested against observations.

id In psychoanalytic theory, the part of personality that seeks instant gratification for immediate need and wants.

influence peddling A form of political corruption wherein government leaders use their influence for favors, financial gain, or material advantage, such as by accepting large campaign contributions in exchange for the awarding of government contracts.

institutional robbery A robbery that occurs in a commercial setting.

instrumental gain Motivation for larceny, such as to meet a need or support a lavish lifestyle.

international crime Offenses designated as gross violations of human interests; crimes against the peace and security of humankind and as such governed by international law.

international environmental laws Laws to monitor and enforce global standards protecting the environment across national borders.

involuntary or negligent manslaughter The unlawful killing of a human being by a person's own negligent disregard of his or her harmful acts.

joyriding An expressive act committed by teenagers, mostly boys, as a means of fulfilling a desire for fun or thrills by temporarily stealing a motor vehicle.

Juke family study A study that traced six generations of the family to attempt to demonstrate a genetic basis for the family's antisocial behavior.

Kallikak family study A study that claimed there was a genetic basis for mental deficiency or feeblemindedness that could lead to criminality.

kleptomania An obsessive compulsion to steal.

labeling theory In criminology, the view that deviance is not a type of behavior but rather a name or label by which society makes certain behaviors undesirable; also called societal reaction theory.

larceny theft The unlawful taking, carrying, leading, or riding away of property from the possession or constructive possession of another.

laws Formal written sanctions designed to regulate behaviors society considers to require the greatest level of response and control.

leading questions Questions that elicit a particular response.

left realism A contemporary theory of radical criminology that argues that crime has a profound impact on criminals, victims, and society in general; the focus should be on the consequences of street crime on its victims, who often share the same backgrounds as their criminal perpetrators.

legalist perspective View that crime is conduct that violates criminal laws of local, state, or federal government.

life course criminology The study of criminal behavior over the life course of the offender.

maladaptation An inappropriate way of coping with the social environment.

malice aforethought A depraved state of mind that shows a willful and intentional disregard for human life.

mandatory minimum sentences A specific deterrence crime-control strategy requiring fixed jail terms for specified offenses.

Marijuana Tax Act A 1937 law that placed a $100-an-ounce tax on the drug.

mass murder The killing of three or more individuals in a single event.

meta-level studies A type of research used in comparative criminology relying on the comparison of criminological issues in various countries.

mode of production In Marxist theory, the way that people choose to organize their labor.

monozygotic (identical) twins The product of a single egg and sperm; they are 100 percent genetically alike.

moral entrepreneurs Becker's term for individuals, primarily from the upper class, who through their political voice and power are able to generate awareness of an issue and gain public support.

mores Strong convictions about certain behaviors—rules of etiquette, matters of respect, or shared understandings of "the way things are done" in our society.

motor vehicle theft The theft or attempted theft of a motor vehicle, including cars, trucks, buses, motorcycles, snowmobiles, and some other methods of transportation.

murder An unlawful form of homicide; the intentional killing of one human being by another without legal justification or excuse.

narcotics Highly addictive drugs often used to relieve pain and produce relaxation; they include morphine, codeine, heroin, and opium.

National Crime Victimization Survey (NCVS) A comprehensive survey of crime victimization within the United States.

National Incident-Based Reporting System (NIBRS) A revision of the UCR designed to provide a more comprehensive measure of crime statistics and to collect data on each reported incident of crime.

neurophysiology The study of brain activity.

neurosis A form of mental illness manifested by behavior expressing fear, tension, anxiety, and emotional distress.

neurotransmitters Chemical compounds within the brain that are responsible for activating and controlling emotions, moods, drives, and other mechanisms of human response.

non-primary homicide or instrumental homicide A killing that occurs during the course of another crime or in the pursuit of some other valued goal; the killing is not the offender's primary motive.

objectivity Ability to represent the object of study accurately without being affected by personal bias.

obscenity Material that appeals to a prurient interest in sex, depicts sexual conduct in a patently offensive manner, and lacks serious literary, artistic, political, or scientific value; not protected by the First Amendment because it lacks any social importance.

occupational crime Crime that is distinct from corporate crime in that it involves the illegal acts of individuals to promote their *own* interests, rather than the interests of the organization.

Occupational Safety and Health Act (OSHA) A 1970 law designed to create and enforce federal standards to ensure that companies are providing their employees with safe and healthy working conditions.

offender specific Within rational choice theory, variables that are related to the offender.

offense specialization The degree to which burglars are highly skilled professional thieves or spontaneous, low-level criminal offenders.

offense specific Within rational choice theory, variables that are related to the offense.

operational definition A definition of concepts in a theory that allows them to be observed and measured.

organized crime The control, organization, and distribution of illegal goods and services on a national and international scale.

parallel research studies A type of research used in comparative criminology focusing on a comparison and contrast analysis of criminal justice components in two different countries.

participant observation A fieldwork method that combines active participation with detached observation.

Part I offenses Also called index crimes, these include homicide, forcible rape, robbery, aggravated assault, burglary, larceny, arson, hate crimes, and motor vehicle theft.

Part II offenses Crimes considered by the FBI to be less serious—such as public intoxication, drug offenses, simple assault, vagrancy, and gambling.

passive neglect A misdemeanor crime involving the delay or failure to pay taxes when they are due.

peacemaking criminology A contemporary theory of radical criminology, rooted in Christianity and Eastern religions, that crime is a form of suffering, a means by which people react to conditions of hardship, injustice, and oppression.

personal robbery A robbery that occurs in a residential setting or on the street; a street robbery is also known as a mugging.

petit (petty) larceny The theft of property of little value.

phishing A high-tech scam wherein identity thieves posing as legitimate financial institutions, government agencies, or retail stores solicit personal information from unsuspecting customers via the telephone or through e-mail.

phobia An irrational fear.

phrenology A school of anatomy suggesting that the constellation of bumps on the head indicate biological differences in the way people behave.

pilferage The systematic theft of small amounts of company property over an extended period of time.

plaintiff The person or party bringing the suit to trial.

political corruption The misuse of entrusted power by political officials to maintain privilege and reap personal gain.

political perspective View that individuals with political power use their position to define illegal behavior and to establish laws governing crime.

pornography Any depicted or verbal material that is sexually explicit and is primarily designed to incite sexual arousal in those who seek it out.

positivism A criminological approach that uses the scientific method to research biological, psychological, and social variables within the individual, and in his or her immediate social environment, to uncover the root causes of criminal behavior.

power conflict theory In criminology, the view that elaborates Max Weber's sociology of law: Crime results as a consequence of the unequal distribution of power in society, as one group is able to force its will on others.

power control theory In feminist theory, the view that gender differences in criminality are more characteristic of patriarchal than egalitarian households.

premeditation Planning, plotting, and deliberating before committing the act.

premenstrual syndrome (PMS) A biological condition wherein females are more likely to exhibit poor impulse control, anxiety, depression, and antisocial behaviors just prior to or during their menstrual cycle.

price fixing Crime committed by corporations involving manipulating free market competition by conspiring with competitors to maintain high prices for a particular commodity.

primary deviance In labeling theory, an offender's original act of violating the law.

primary or expressive homicide A killing that usually springs from interpersonal conflict, such as jealousy, hatred, anger, rage, or frustration.

principle of falsification A scientific theory must lead to testable hypotheses that can be disproved if they are wrong.

principle of intent (*mens rea*) In order for an act to be a crime, the person committing the act must have intended to commit it.

principle of legality In order for there to be a crime, there must be a law at the time of the act that specifically prohibits that act or that requires a person to act in a certain way.

principle of punishment A person found guilty of violating the law must be given a fine, imprisonment, or both.

professional fence A person who earns a living by purchasing and reselling stolen merchandise to merchants who turn around and market these items to legitimate customers.

proletariat In Marxist theory, the working class or the laborers.

prostitution The nonmarital consensual exchange of sexual acts for material gain.

psychoanalytic perspective A method of understanding human behavior by examining drives and impulses within the unconscious mind.

psychological perspective View that crime is maladaptive behavior, or an individual's inability to be in harmony with his or her environment.

psychopath An individual who lacks the ability to identify with or understand how others think and feel; is self-centered, shallow, and detached; is often a chronic liar, feels no shame or guilt, is reckless and irresponsible, is incapable of maintaining relationships, and engages in antisocial and disruptive behavior.

psychosis A major form of mental illness manifested by the inability to comprehend reality, think clearly, and respond appropriately.

public order crimes Acts considered illegal because they violate the moral standards behind society's values and norms.

Racketeer Influenced and Corrupt Organization Act (RICO) A 1970 law intended to limit and control organized criminal activities by creating new categories of offenses.

racketeering The organized operation of an illegal business by a structured group for the purpose of making a profit.

radical theory A term to refer to all the criminological theories within the tradition founded by Marx and Engels.

random sampling In a survey, a sample of the population in which everyone has an equal chance of being chosen for the study.

rape shield laws Laws designed to protect the victim by restricting the defense's ability to use irrelevant evidence regarding the victim's past sexual behavior or reputation.

rational choice theory A criminological approach that retains classical theory's view of free will but recognizes that circumstances may affect the exercise of personal choice.

reaction formation A rejection of the mainstream culture and hostility toward its norms and values.

reductionism The attempt to study the whole (society) by reducing every event to the behavior of its parts (people), as if the parts exist separately from and are unaffected by the whole.

reference groups In social learning theory, groups composed of those whom we most admire, respect, and emulate.

relative deprivation In left realism theory, the idea that the most probable source of criminal behavior is the individual feeling deprived relative to others in similar social groups.

reliability The extent to which a measure consistently produces the same results over and over again.

replication The repetition of a previous study using a different sample or population to verify or refute the original findings.

research methods The specific techniques—such as questionnaires, experiments, or surveys—used to systematically gather data.

research strategy A clearly thought-out plan that guides the work.

restorative justice An ideological model of justice that brings together the offender, the victim, the community, and the criminal justice system in responding to delinquency and crime.

risk factor analysis In criminology, scientifically based methods of identifying individuals at risk of delinquency and crime and intervention at the earliest possible stage.

robbery The act of taking or attempting to take anything of value from the care, custody, or control of a person by force or threat of force.

Rome Statute The 1998 treaty that established the International Criminal Court; entered into force in 2002.

routine activities theory A variation of rational choice theory that argues that victim and offender lifestyles contribute to both the amount and type of crime within society.

ruling class theory A theory of lawmaking that holds that law is simply a reflection of the interests and ideology of the ruling class.

same-sex rape Sexual violence and abuse perpetrated by men against men and women against women.

sample In a survey, a sub-set or portion of the larger population selected to represent the whole.

secondary deviance In labeling theory, the continued pattern of offending based on an individual's adjustment to society's negative social reaction.

second-degree murder The unlawful killing of a human being with malice aforethought but without premeditation; regarded as a crime of passion.

self-report survey A research technique developed by sociologists to reveal types of criminality ordinarily hidden from victim surveys or official statistics.

serial murder The killing of several individuals in at least three separate events.

sex tourism An industry wherein clients, usually men from wealthier countries, travel abroad to places where young people, usually girls, are readily available for sex, either through need or through force.

sexual assault The use of physical violence, threat, or intimidation to commit a sexual act on the victim.

shoplifting The theft of merchandise from a retail store.

simple assault The attempt to commit, or the commission of, less serious physical injury; usually does not include the use of a weapon.

single-case studies A type of research used in comparative criminology describing and analyzing diverse criminal justice issues within a single country, often from a historical standpoint and as they relate to social, economic, and political changes over time.

situational choice theory A variation of rational choice theory that argues that the individual decision to engage in criminal activities is shaped by the opportunities, risks, and benefits—the situation—attached to certain types of crimes.

situational crime prevention A strategy for crime control that makes crime a more difficult and costly alternative.

snitches Amateur or casual shoplifters who steal items for their own personal use.

social bonds In social control theory, ties between individuals and conventional social groups within society, such as friends, family, teachers, co-workers, neighbors, and church members.

social conflict approach An approach to criminology that examines the fundamental distribution of wealth and power within society; law is a mechanism of social control that the dominant classes use to coerce the rest into compliance; crime is defined by those in power.

social control theory In criminology, the view that focuses on the interaction between an individual's personality and his or her social environment, through which the person forms, or fails to form, the appropriate bonds to society.

social disorganization theory An approach to criminology that links high rates of crime to the social and economic conditions of urban communities.

social ecology A method of analysis that studies how the environment adapts to the human interactions and natural resources within it.

socialization The process through which people learn the skills, knowledge, values, motives, and roles of the groups to which they belong or the communities in which they live.

social learning theory In criminology, the view that we learn criminal behavior in the same way we learn any other behavior: We acquire the norms, values, and patterns of behaviors conducive to crime.

socially induced hyperactivity (SIH) A learned behavior, without a neurological basis, of inattention and distractibility that is often incorrectly diagnosed as attention deficit hyperactivity disorder.

social norms Rules of behavior that guide our everyday interactions with one another.

social order The various components of society—institutions, structures, customs, traditions—that preserve and maintain the normative ways of human interactions and relationships.

social pathology Social conditions marked by strained relationships, deteriorating values, lack of family solidarity, and community fear; such conditions become a breeding ground for criminal activity,

social process theory In criminology, the view that everyone has the potential to commit criminal acts as a consequence of social learning, social ties or bonds, labeling, and other social processes.

social structure approach An approach to criminology that looks for the origins of crime within the immediate environment.

societal needs theory A theory of lawmaking that holds that law reflects the needs of society.

sociological perspective View that crime is any anti-social act that threatens the existing social structure or the fundamental well-being of humans.

sociological theories Theories that search for the origins of criminal behavior outside the individual,

specific deterrence A crime-control strategy that focuses on deterring particular offenders by administering punishment that is severe enough to affect rational decision making and prevent future offenses.

spousal or marital rape Forced sexual intercourse in a marital relationship.

spurious relationship A correlation between two or more variables that is the result of another factor not being measured.

spying A technology-assisted criminal offense that involves the illegal monitoring of computer systems.

stalking Any unwanted contact between two individuals that communicates a threat or places the victim in fear or distress.

static factors Predictors of future involvement in criminal activities are experiences in the past that cannot be reversed or altered.

statistical data Information used for research including numerical information obtained from government agencies, businesses, and other organizations.

statutory rape Sexual intercourse with a minor under the age of consent.

stigmatization In labeling theory, occurs when a negative label applied to an individual has an enduring effect on that person's self-identity.

stimulants Drugs to heighten alertness and reduce fatigue, with a high degree a psychological dependence; they include amphetamines, cocaine, crack, and methamphetamines.

strain theory A social structure theory that argues that crime is a response to conditions of strain in society.

structural contradictions theory A theory of lawmaking that holds that law is the result of structural contradictions leading to conflicts, which create dilemmas that legislators and judges attempt to resolve.

subculture A group within the larger social culture that has a distinct set of norms and a unique pattern of behavior.

subculture of violence Theory that violent behavior is not evenly distributed within the social structure; rather, it is a learned pattern of behavior and an adaptation to environmental stimuli—anger, frustration, conflict, or provocation.

superego In psychoanalytic theory, the part of the personality that judges the appropriateness of behavior in a given situation; also known as conscience.

survey A research method that consists of administering a questionnaire or interviewing a group of people to determine their characteristics, opinions, and behaviors.

taboos Informally forbidden socially offensive acts.

tax evasion A crime in which the taxpayer, a client of the government, deliberately fails to pay appropriate taxes on earned income by using deception and fraud, such as underreporting or failing to report taxable income.

techniques of neutralization Rationalizations people use to justify their criminal acts.

terrorism Premeditated, politically motivated violence designed to spread fear and perpetrated against civilians by subnational groups or clandestine agents.

testosterone The male hormone; possibly linked to aggressive behavior.

theory A set of propositions that put forward a relationship between the categories of events or phenomena under study.

three strikes A policy advocating mandatory life imprisonment for offenders convicted of a third felony offense.

token economics An intervention used in many group homes for juvenile delinquents awarding tokens or points for good behavior and subtracting them for inappropriate behavior.

tolerance A physiological phenomenon in which, over time, the brain adapts to the chemical substance, and it produces less of a high; the individual needs more of the substance to experience the same effect.

transnational crime Illegal activities that cross national borders.

trespassing An unlawful entry into a structure in which the offender does not necessarily possess criminal intent.

truth in sentencing guidelines A specific deterrence crime-control strategy requiring that offenders serve more than 80 percent of their sentence in prison before they can be released.

Uniform Crime Reports (UCR) Published data on crime from about 17,000 local, state, and federal law enforcement agencies.

United Nations Surveys on Crime Trends and the Operations of Criminal Justice Systems A data source that provides statistics on crime, crime trends, and criminal justice operations at the international level.

validity The extent to which a measure actually reflects the phenomenon under study.

variable In a theory, a concept that can take on two or more values.

victimless crimes Another term for public order crimes.

viruses A technology-assisted criminal offense that involves introducing programs into computers, often via e-mail, that corrupt or destroy computers, software, and networks.

voluntary or non-negligent manslaughter The unjustified killing that arises out of an intense conflict that provoked violence or during the commission of a felony.

white-collar crime Acts of an individual perpetrated during the course of the person's work where deception, concealment, and breach of trust are used to obtain money and gain privilege, or to avoid losing money or privilege.

willful tax evasion A serious federal tax crime; a felony that must be proved by (1) an existing tax deficiency, (2) a willful intent to evade taxes, and (3) an affirmative act of evasion or affirmative attempt to evade.

XYY syndrome A rare chromosomal anomaly suspected of predisposing males to criminal behavior.

NOTES

Chapter 1

1. Long, R., & Pearson, R. (2009, January 30). Impeached Illinois Gov. Rod Blagojevich has been removed from office. *Chicago Tribune* online. Retrieved from http://www.chicagotribune.com/news/local/chi-blagojevich-impeachment-removal,0,5791846.story.

2. Monkkonen, E. H. (2004). *Police in urban America: 1860–1920*. Cambridge, MA: Cambridge University Press.

3. Ibid.

4. Sampson, R. J. (2000). Whither the sociological study of crime? *Annual Reviews, 26*, 711–714.

5. Slapper, G. (2007, April 18). The law explored: What constitutes a crime? *Times Online*. Retrieved from http://business.timesonline.co.uk/tol/business/law/columnists/gary_slapper/article1671026.ece

6. Henry, S., & Lanier, M. (2001). *What is crime?* Lanham, MD: Rowman & Littlefield.

7. Chambliss, W. J. (2001). *Power, politics, and crime.* Boulder, CO: Westview.

8. Tucker, C. M., Vogel, D. L., Keefer, N., & Reid, A. (2002, Spring). Maladaptive behavior in African-American children: A self-regulation theory-based approach. *The Educational Forum.*

9. Tappan, P. W. (2001). Who is the criminal? In S. Henry & M. Lanier (Eds.), *What is crime?* Lanham, MD: Rowman & Littlefield.

10. Browning, C. R. (1992). *Ordinary men: Reserve Police Battalion 101 and the final solution in Poland* (pp. 1–2, 22). New York: Harper Perennial.

11. Convention on the Prevention and Punishment of the Crime of Genocide. Adopted by Resolution 260 (III)A of the United Nations General Assembly on 9 December 1948. Retrieved from http://www.hrweb.org/legal/-genocide.html

12. Power, S. (2002). *A problem from hell: America and the age of genocide.* New York: Basic Books.

13. Reiman, J. (2009). *The rich get richer and the poor get prison* (9th ed.). Upper Saddle River, NJ: Prentice Hall.

14. Clinard, M. B., & Meier, R. F. (2007). *Sociology of deviant behavior* (13th ed.). Florence, KY: Cengage.

15. Einstadter, W. J., & Henry, S. (2006). *Criminological theory: An analysis of its underlying assumptions.* Lanham, MD: Rowman & Littlefield.

16. The relationship between deviance and crime. (2009). *Justice, 2.* Retrieved from http://law.jrank.org/pages/973/Deviance-Relationship-between-deviance-crime.html

17. Chambliss, W. J. (1973). The Saints and the Roughnecks. *Society, 11*(1), 24–31.

18. Rafter, N. (2009). *The origins of criminology.* New York: Routledge-Cavendish.

19. Sutherland, E. (1924). *Principles of criminology.* Philadelphia: Lippincott.

20. Woodward, B. (1987). *Veil: The secret wars of the CIA 1981–1987.* New York: Simon and Schuster.

21. The Tonya Harding-Nancy Kerrigan Saga. (1998). Retrieved from http://www.oregonlive.com/special/tonya/index.ssf?/special/tonya/timeline.frame (accessed June 16, 2008)

22. Noe, D. (2008). Mary Kay Letourneau: The romance that was a crime. *TruTV Crime Library.* Retrieved from http://www.trutv.com/library/crime/criminal_mind/psychology/marykay_letourneau/1.html

23. 8 teens charged with attacking girl for YouTube video. FoxNews.com. Retrieved from http://www.foxnews.com/story/0,2933,347949,00.html; Cave, D. (2008, April 12). Eight teenagers charged in Internet beating have their day on the Web. *New York Times.* Retrieved from http://www.nytimes.com/2008/04/12/us/12florida.html?_r=1&scp=1&sq=eight%20florida%20teens&st=cse

24. Chiricos, T., Padgett, K., & Gertz. M. (2006). Fear, t.v. news, and the reality of crime. *Criminology, 38*(3), 755–786.

25. Marsh, I., & Melville, G. (2008). *Crime, justice and the media.* New York: Routledge.

26. Chambliss, W. J. (1988). *Exploring criminology.* New York: Macmillan.

27. Wilson, J. Q., & Kelling, G. L. (n.d.). *The police and neighborhood safety: Broken windows.* Retrieved from http://www.cptedsecurity.com/broken_windows_theory.pdf (accessed September 30, 2008)

28. Barak, G. (2007). Doing news-making criminology from within the academy. *Theoretical Criminology, 11*(2), 191–207.

29. Gilligan, J. (2001). *Preventing violence.* London: Thames and Hudson.

30. Barak, G. (1998). *Integrating criminologies.* Boston: Allyn & Bacon.

31. Association of Certified Fraud Examiners. (n.d.). *2008 report to the nation.* Retrieved from http://acfe.com/resources/publications.asp?copy=rttn

32. Greenberg, H. (2007, March 5). What 2 crooks told me over lunch. *Market Watch.* Retrieved from http://www.marketwatch.com/news/story/2-crooks-told-me-over/story.aspx?guid=%7BB3E79F2A-6F03-4079-8B93-189E2F8E8A92%7D

33. Baker, J. S. (2004, October 4). The sociological origins of white collar crime. *Legal Memorandum.* The Heritage Foundation. Retrieved from http://www.heritage.org/research/legalissues/upload/70073_1.pdf; Vaughn, D. (1992). The macro-micro connection in white-collar crime theory. In *White-collar crime revisited.* Retrieved from http://books.google.com/books?hl=en&lr=&id=Te1HNZN6ah0C&oi=fnd&pg=PA124&dq=investigating+crime+by+relying+on+criminological+theory&ots=8JDNFoC4pr&sig=5fIKjNdyYnsvInSW2UyjjtV-Qoc#PPR8,M1

34. King, R. D., & Wincup, E. (2008). *Doing research on crime and justice.* New York: Oxford University Press.

35. Sherman, L. W., Farrington, D. P., Welsh, B. C., & MacKenzie, D. L. (2006). *Evidence-based crime prevention* (Rev. ed.). New York: Routledge.

36. Fox, C., & Harding, D. J. (2005). School shootings as organizational deviance. *Sociology of Education, 78*(1), 69.

37. Judiciary Committee of the U.S. Senate. (2000). *Children, violence, and the media.* Washington, DC: Government Printing Office. Retrieved from http://judiciary.senate.gov/hearings/testimony.cfm?renderforprint=1&id=1824&wit_id=5195

38. Congressional Public Health Summit, Joint Statement on the Impact of Entertainment Violence on Children. (2000, July 26). Retrieved from http://www.aap.org/advocacy/releases/jstmtevc.htm

39. *Youth violence: A report of the surgeon general.* (n.d.). Retrieved from http://www.surgeongeneral.gov/library/youthviolence/ (accessed October 2, 2008).

40. Scholsberg, M., & Ozer, N. A. (n.d.). *Under the watchful eye.* Retrieved from http://www.aclu-sc.org/attach/w/watchful_eye.pdf (accessed June 6, 2008); Nestel, T. J. (2006, March). *Using surveillance camera systems to monitor public domains: Can abuse be prevented?* Master's thesis, Naval Postgraduate School, Monterey, CA; The effect of closed circuit television on recorded crime rates and public concern about crime in Glasgow. (1999). *Crime and Criminal Justice Research Findings,* 30, Scottish Office Central Research Unit.

41. Elias, P. (2010, October 16). Oil change reignites debate over GPS trackers. *Associated Press.* Retrieved from http://www.disclose.tv/forum/oil-change-reignites-debate-over-gps-trackers-t33848.html

42. Cotterrell, R. (1999). *Emile Durkheim: Law in a moral domain.* Edinburgh: Edinburgh University Press.

43. Tracy, S. W., & Acker, C. J. (Eds.). (2004). *Altering American consciousness: The history of alcohol and drug use in the United States, 1800–2000.* Amherst: University of Massachusetts Press.

44. Chambliss, 2001.

45. Reiman, 2009.

46. Conflict criminology in the Marxist tradition. (2006, November 30). *Conflict criminology.* Retrieved from www.drtomoconnor.com/1060/1060lect07a.htm

Chapter 2

1. Musto, D. (1973/1999). *The American disease: Origins of narcotics control* (p. 17). New York: Oxford University Press.

2. Lindesmith, A. R. (1962). *Opiates and the law.* Bloomington: Indiana University Press.

3. Greenwald, G. (2009). *Drug decriminalization in Portugal.* Washington, DC: Cato Institute.

4. Smith, P. (2010, October 28). US nearing 50% supporting marijuana legalization, poll finds. Retrieved from http://stopthedrugwar.org/chronicle/2010/oct/28/us_nearing_50_supporting_marijua

5. Durkheim, E. (1893/1933). *The division of labor in society* (p. 73). New York: Free Press.

6. Poll conducted from January 14 to January 18, 2005, by the *Los Angeles Times,* published January 22.

7. *McBoyle v. United States,* 283 U.S. 25 (1931). Cited in Hall, J., George, B. J., & Force, R. (1976). *Cases and readings on criminal law and procedure* (p. 44). Indianapolis: Bobbs-Merrill.

8. United Nations Development Fund for Women. (2003). Retrieved from http://www.cities-localgovernments.org/uclg/upload/docs/notaminute-more-endingviolenceagainstwomen.pdf; Elman, R. A. (1996). *Sexual subordination and state intervention: Comparing Sweden and the United States* (p. 90). New York: Berghahn; Geis, G. (1977). Rape-in-marriage: Law and law reform in England, the United States, and Sweden. *Adelaide Law Review, 6,* 284.

9. *Mullen v. United States,* 263 F.2d 275 (1958).

10. *Commonwealth v. Malone,* 354 Pa. 180, 47 A.2d 445 (1946).

11. *People v. Newton,* 72 Misc. 2d 646, 340 N.Y.S. 2d 77 (Sup. Ct. 1973).

12. A veteran's legal battle. Editorial. (2009, August 18). *Washington Post,* p. A18.

13. AIG asked for and received billions of dollars in a loan from the U.S. government to avoid bankruptcy and to avert a worldwide financial crisis.

14. Frank, N. (1983). From criminal to civil penalties in the history of health and service laws. *Social Problems, 30,* 532–545.

15. Morton, A. L. (1938). *A people's history of England* (p. 70). London: Lawrence & Wishart.

16. Ibid., p. 90.

17. Hall, J. (1952). *Theft, law, and society* (2nd ed., p. 4). Indianapolis: Bobbs-Merrill.

18. Thompson, E. P. (1976). *Whigs and hunters: The origin of the Black Act.* New York: Pantheon.

19. Ibid., p. 28; for an excellent parallel study of the postbellum south in the United States, see Hahn, S. (1982). Hunting, fishing and foraging: Common rights and class relations in the postbellum south. *Radical History Review, 26,* 37–62.

20. 25 Ed. 3 (1351).

21. Foote, C. (1956). Vagrancy-type law and its administration. *University of Pennsylvania Law Review, 104,* 615.

22. Chambliss, W. J. (1964). A sociological analysis of the law of vagrancy. *Social Problems, 12,* 45–69.

23. Adamson, C. R. (1983). Punishment after slavery: Southern state penal systems, 1865–1890. *Social Problems, 30,* 556–569.

24. Chambliss, 1964, p. 47.

25. *Edwards v. California,* 314 U.S. 160 (1941).

26. *Papachristou v. City of Jacksonville,* 405 U.S. 156 (1972).

27. Skolnick, J. (1969). *The politics of protest* (p. 4). New York: Simon & Schuster.

28. Shumann, K. F. (1975). *Moral consensus and killing.* Paper presented at European Group for the Study of Deviance, Amsterdam.

29. Chambliss, W. J. (1986, November 17). *State organized crime.* Presidential address at the annual meeting of the American Society of Criminology, San Diego.

30. Cohen, S. (1976). Protest, unrest and delinquency: Convergences in labels and behavior. In P. Wiles (Ed.), *The sociology of crime and delinquency: The new criminologists* (pp. 108–123). London: Barnes & Noble.

31. Hall, 1952, p. 4.

32. Chambliss, W. J., & Sbarbaro, E. (1986). *Public opinion and legislation.* Unpublished manuscript.

33. Bradley, C. M. (1984–1985). Racketeering and the federalization of crime. *American Criminal Law Review, 22,* 214–272.

34. Gerth, H. H., & Mills, C. W. (1946). *From Max Weber: Essays in sociology* (p. 66). Glencoe, IL: Free Press.

35. Marx, K. (1980). *Capital: The process of capitalist production* (Vol. 1, 3rd German ed.), S. Moore, E. Aveling, & F. Engels (Eds.). New York: Humbolt; Marx, K. (1853). Capital punishment. *New York Daily Tribune,* reprinted in T. B. Bottomore & M. Rubel (Eds.), *Karl Marx: Selected writings in sociology and social philosophy.* London: Harmondsworth, Penguin.

36. Kolko, G. (1963). *The triumph of conservatism.* New York: Free Press.

37. Braithwaite, J. (1984). *Corporate crime in the pharmaceutical industry* (p. 276). London: Routledge and Kegan Paul; Carson, W. G. O. (1974). Symbolic and instrumental dimensions of early factory legislation. In R. Hood (Ed.), *Crime, criminology, and public policy.* London: Heinemann.

38. Boyer, R. O., & Morais, H. M. (1955). *Labor's untold story.* New York: United Electrical, Radio and Machine Workers of America.

39. Harring, S. (1977). Class conflict and the suppression of tramps in Buffalo, 1982–1984. *Law and Society Review, 11,* 873–911.

40. Hunt, A. (1976). Perspectives in the sociology of law. In P. Carlen (Ed.), *The sociology of law* (pp. 33–43). Keele, Staffordshire, England: University of Keele Press.

41. Kolko, 1963.

42. Calavita, K. (1984). *U.S. immigration law and the control of labor: 1820–1924.* New York: Academic.

43. Friedman, L. (1977). *Law and society: An introduction* (p. 99). Englewood Cliffs, NJ: Prentice Hall; see also Hagan, J., & Leon, J. (1977). Rediscovering delinquency: Social history, political ideology, and the sociology of law. *American Sociological Review, 42,* 587–598.

44. Sellin, T. (1938). *Culture, conflict and crime.* New York: Social Science Research Council.

45. Blalock, H. M. (1970). *Toward a theory of minority group relations.* New York: McGraw-Hill.

46. Chambliss, W. J., & Seidman, R. B. (1982). *Law, order, and power* (Rev. ed., chap. 4). Reading, MA: Addison-Wesley.

47. Boyer & Morais, 1955.

48. Chambliss, W. J. (1979). On lawmaking. *British Journal of Law and Society, 6*(2).

49. Calavita, 1984.

50. Klare, K. (1978). "Judicial deradicalization of the Wagner Act and the origins of modern legal consciousness: 1937–1941." *Minnesota Law Review, 62,* 265–339.

51. Genovese, E. D. (1974). *Roll Jordan roll: The world the slave made.* New York: Random House.

52. Norde, G. S. (2008). *Peculiar affinity: The world the slave owners and their female slaves made.* Fairfax, VA: History4All.

53. Fagan, J., & Zimring, F. E. (Eds.). (2000). *The changing borders of juvenile justice: Waiver of adolescents to the criminal court.* Chicago: University of Chicago Press; Reiman, J. (2009). *The rich get richer and the poor get prison.* New York: Prentice Hall; Chambliss, W. J. (2001). *Power, politics, and crime.* Boulder, CO: Westview.

54. Sachs, A., & Wilson, J. H. (1978). *Sexism and law.* London: Martin Robertson.

55. Andersen, M. L., & Collins, P. H. (Eds.). (2007). *Race, class, and gender: An anthology* (6th ed.). Belmont, CA: Wadsworth.

56. Griffin, S. (1975). Rape: The all-American crime. In W. Chambliss (Ed.), *Criminal law in action* (p. 187). New York: Macmillan.

57. *Roe v. Wade,* 410 U.S. 113 (1973).

58. Carangella-Macdonald, S. (1984, November). *Marxian theory and legal change in rape: Michigan's model rape reform legislation.* Paper presented at the American Society of Criminology, Cincinnati, Ohio.

59. Genovese, E. D. (1988). *The political economy of slavery: Studies in the economy and society of the slave south.* Middletown, CT: Wesleyan University Press.

60. Ibid., p. 17.

61. Freeman, A. D. (1978). Legitimizing racial discrimination through anti-discrimination law: A critical review of Supreme Court doctrine. *Minnesota Law Review, 62,* 1049.

62. Chambliss, 2001.

Chapter 3

1. Surette, R. (1998). *Media, crime, and criminal justice* (2nd ed.). Belmont, CA: West/Wadsworth.

2. Graber, D. (1980). *Crime news and the public.* New York: Praeger.

3. Federal Bureau of Investigation. (2007, June). *Crime in the United States, 2006.* Washington, DC: U.S. Department of Justice.

4. Ibid.

5. Ibid.; see also Surette, 1998.

6. Federal Bureau of Investigation. (1984). *Uniform crime reporting handbook* (p. 6). Washington, DC: U.S. Department of Justice.

7. Seidman, D., & Couzens, M. (1974). Getting the crime rate down: Political pressure and crime reporting. *Law and Society Review, 8,* 457–493.

8. Federal Bureau of Investigation. (1981). *Uniform crime reports handbook.* Washington, DC: U.S. Department of Justice.

9. *United States Wickersham Commission.* Records, 1928–1931: Finding aid. Harvard Law School Library. Cambridge, MA.

10. Ibid.

11. Selke, W., & Pepinsky, W. (1982). The politics of police reporting in Indianapolis, 1948–78. *Law and Human Behavior, 6*(3-4), 327–342.

12. Seidman & Couzens, 1974.

13. Godfrey, B. (2008). Changing prosecution practices and their impact on *Crime* figures, 1857–1940. *British Journal of Criminology, 48*(2), 171–189.

14. O'Brien, R. (1996). Police productivity and crime rates: 1973–1992. *Criminology, 34,* 183–207.

15. Felson, R. B. G., Messner, S. F., Hoskin, A. W., & Deane, G. (2002). Reasons for reporting and not reporting domestic violence to the police. *Criminology, 40,* 617–647.

16. Fisher, B., Daigle, L., Cullen, F., & Turner, M. (2003). Reporting sexual victimization to the police and others: Results from a national-level study of college women. *Criminal Justice and Behavior, 30,* 6–39.

17. Rennison, C. M. (2000). *Criminal victimization 1999: Changes 1998–99 with trends 1993–98.* Washington, DC: Bureau of Justice Statistics, U.S. Department of Justice.

18. Lipton, E. (2006, June 14). Study finds huge fraud in the wake of hurricanes. *New York Times.* Retrieved from http://www.nytimes.com/2006/06/14/us/nationalspecial/14katrina.html

19. Selke & Pepinsky, 1982, p. 327.

20. Chilton, R., Major, V., & Propheter, S. (1998). *Victims and offenders: A new UCR supplement to present incident-based data from participating agencies.* Paper presented at annual meeting of the American Society of Criminology, Washington, DC.

21. Regoeczi, W. C., Jarvis, J., & Riedel, M. (2008). Clearing murders. *Journal of Research in Crime and Delinquency, 45*(2), 142–162; Rantala, R. (2000). *The effects of NIBRS on crime statistics.* Washington, DC: Bureau of Justice Statistics, U.S. Department of Justice.

22. Addington, L. (2004). The effect of NIBRS reporting on item missing data in murder cases. *Homicide Studies, 8,* 193–213.

23. Ibid.

24. Biderman, A. D., & Reiss Jr., A. J. (1967). On exploring the "dark figure" of crime. *Annals of the American Academy of Political and Social Science, 374,* 1–15.

25. Costner, H. L. (1967). *On methodology in the sociology of crime.* Paper presented at the annual meetings of the Pacific Sociological Association, San Diego.

26. Reiman, J. (2009). *The rich get richer and the poor get prison* (9th ed.). Upper Saddle River, NJ: Prentice Hall.

27. National Archive of Criminal Justice Data. (2007). Retrieved from www.icpsr.umich.edu/NACJD/NCVS/ (accessed December 17, 2007).

28. *National crime victimization survey, 2005.* (2006). Washington, DC: Bureau of Justice Statistics, U.S. Department of Justice.

29. Ibid.

30. Catalano, S. M. (2004). *Criminal victimization, 2003.* Washington, DC: Bureau of Justice Statistics, U.S. Department of Justice.

31. *Assault.* (n.d.). Bureau of Justice Statistics, Office of Justice Programs, U.S. Department of Justice. Retrieved from http://bjs.ojp.usdoj.gov/index.cfm?ty=tp&tid=316

32. O'Brien, R. M. (2000). Crime facts: Victim and offender data. In J. F. Sheley (Ed.), *Criminology: A contemporary handbook* (pp. 59–83). Belmont, CA: Wadsworth.

33. Allen, D. W. (2007). The reporting and underreporting of rape. *Southern Economic Journal, 73*(3), 623–641; Fisher, B. S., Cullen, F. T., & Turner, M. G. (2000). *The sexual victimization of college women.* Washington, DC: National Institute of Justice and Bureau of Justice Statistics, U.S. Department of Justice; Menard, S. (2002). Short- and long-term consequences of adolescent victimization. *Youth Violence Research Bulletin.* Washington, DC: Office of Juvenile Justice and Delinquency Prevention.

34. Simpson, S. S., Harris, A. R., & Mattson, B. A. (1995). Measuring corporate crime. In M. B. Blankenship (Ed.), *Understanding corporate criminality* (pp. 115–140). New York: Garland.

35. Elliot, D. S., Huizinga, D., & Ageton, S. S. (1985). *Explaining delinquency and drug use.* Beverly Hills, CA: Sage.

36. Porterfield, A. L. (1946). *Youth in trouble: Studies in delinquency and despair, with plans for prevention.* Fort Worth, TX: Leo Potishman Foundation.

37. Wallerstein, J. S., & Wyle, C. (1947). Our law abiding law breakers. *Probation, 25*(March/April), 107–112, 118.

38. Gutierrez, F. C., & Shoemaker D. J. (2007). Self-reported delinquency of high school students in metro Manila: Gender and social class. Retrieved from http://yas.sagepub.com/cgi/rapidpdf/0044118X07309986v1.pdf; Hindelang,

M. J., Hirschi, T., & Weis, J. G. (1981). *Measuring delinquency.* Thousand Oaks, CA: Sage.

39. Goemes, J. T., Bertrand, L. D., Paetsch, J. J. & Hornick, J. P. (2003). Self-reported delinquency among Alberta's youth: Findings from a survey of 2,001 junior and senior high school students. *Adolescence* (Spring); Snyder, H., Espiritu, R. C., Huizinga, D., Loeber, R., & Petechuk, D. (2003). Prevalence and development of child delinquency. *Child Delinquency Bulletin.* Washington, DC: Office of Juvenile Justice and Delinquency Prevention, U.S. Department of Justice.

40. Zatz, M. (1987). The changing forms of racial/ethnic biases in sentencing. *Journal of Research in Crime and Delinquency, 24,* 69–92.

41. Thornberry, T., & Krohn, M. D. (2000). The self-report method for measuring delinquency and crime. *Criminal Justice, 4,* 34–82; Gibbons, D. (1978). *Delinquent behavior* (3rd ed.). Englewood Cliffs, NJ: Prentice Hall; Tittle, C., Villamez, W. J., & Smith, D. A. (1979). The myth of social class and criminality: An empirical assessment of the empirical evidence. *American Sociological Review, 43,* 643–656.

42. Michalowski, R. J. 1984. *Order, law, and crime.* New York: Random House.

43. Wolitzky-Taylor, K. B., et al. (2008). Prevalence and correlates of dating violence in a national sample of adolescents. *Journal of the American Academy of Child & Adolescent Psychiatry, 47*(7), 755–762; Cernkovich, S. A., Giordano, P. C., & Pugh, M. D. (1985). Chronic offenders: The missing cases in self-report delinquency research. *Journal of Criminal Law and Criminology, 76,* 705–732.

44. Fisher, B., Cullen, F., & Turner, M. (2000). *The sexual victimization of college women.* Washington, DC: National Institute of Justice and Bureau of Justice Statistics, U.S. Department of Justice; Kanin, E. (1967). Reference groups and sex conduct norm violation. *Sociological Quarterly, 8,* 495–502.

45. Meyer, T. J. (1984). Date rape: A serious problem that few think about. *Chronicle of Higher Education,* 17–24.

46. Simon, L. (1995). *Validity and reliability of violent juveniles: A comparison of juvenile self-reports with adult self-reports incarcerated in adult prisons.* Paper presented at the annual meeting of the American Society of Criminology, Boston.

47. Ibid.

48. Chambliss, W. J. (1973). The Saints and the Roughnecks. *Society, 11*(1), 24–31.

49. Patton, D. (2005). An exploration of external validity of self-report amongst arrestees. *Surveillance*

and Society, 2(4), 564–580. Retrieved from http://www.surveillance-and-society.org/articles2(4)/arrestees.pdf (accessed July 14, 2008); Bridges, G. S. (1987). An empirical study of error in reports of crime and delinquency. In M. E. Wolfgang, T. P. Thornberry, & R. M. Figlio (Eds.), *From boy to man, from delinquency to crime.* Chicago: University of Chicago Press.

50. Verrill, S. (2008). *The age crime relationship: A function of differential association, variable-interval reinforcement, and extinction.* Paper presented at the annual American Society of Criminology meeting, November, Los Angeles; Steffensmeier, D., & Allan, E. (2000). Looking for patterns: Gender, age, and crime. In J. F. Sheley (Ed.), *Criminology: A contemporary handbook.* Belmont, CA: Wadsworth.

51. Steffensmeier, D., & Streifel, C. (1991). Age, gender, and crime across three historical periods: 1935, 1960, and 1985. *Social Forces, 69*, 869–894.

52. Brame, R. & Piquero, A. R. (2003). Selective attrition and the age-crime relationship. *Journal of Quantitative Criminology 19*(2), 107–127; Hirschi, T., & Gottfredson, M. (1983). Age and the explanation of crime. *American Journal of Sociology, 89*, 552–584; Wilson, M., & Daly, M. (1997). Life expectancy, economic inequality, homicide, and reproductive timing in Chicago neighborhoods. *British Journal of Medicine, 314*, 1271–1274; Steffensmeier & Allan.

53. Agnew, R. (2003). An integrated theory of the adolescent peak in offending. *Youth & Society, 34*, 263–302.

54. Mulvey, E., & LaRosa, J. (1986). Delinquency cessation and adolescent development: Preliminary data. *American Journal of Orthopsychiatry, 56*, 212–224.

55. Laub, J. H., & Sampson, R. J. (2003). *Shared beginnings, Divergent lives: Delinquent boys at age 70.* Cambridge, MA: Harvard University Press.

56. D'Allesio, S., & Stolzenberg, L. (2003). Race and the probability of arrest. *Social Forces, 81*(4), 1381–1397; Chilton, R. J. (1987). Race, age, gender and changes in urban arrest rates. *Gender and Society, 1*, 152–171; Hindelang, M. (1971). Age, sex, and the versatility of delinquency involvements. *Social Forces, 14*, 525–534.

57. Chilton, 1987; Hindelang, 1971.

58. Walker, S., Spohn, C., & DeLone, M. (2003). *The color of justice: Race, ethnicity, and crime in America.* Belmont, CA: Wadsworth.

59. Harris, A. R., & Shaw. J. A. W. (2000). Looking for patterns: Race, class, and crime. In J. F. Sheley (Ed.), *Criminology: A contemporary handbook.* Belmont, CA: Wadsworth; Farrington, D. P., Loeber, R., & Stouthamer-Loeber, M. (2003). How can the relationship between race and violence be explained? In D. F. Hawkins (Ed.), *Violent crime: Assessing race and ethnic differences.* Cambridge, England: Cambridge University Press.

60. Harris & Shaw, 2000.

61. Austin, R. L., & Allen, M. D. (2000). Racial disparity in arrest rates as an explanation of racial disparity in commitment to Pennsylvania's prisons. *Journal of Research in Crime and Delinquency, 37*(2), 200–220; Rushton, P. (1995). Race and crime: An international dilemma. *Society, 32*, 37–42.

62. Johnston, L. D., Bachman, J. G., & O'Malley, P. M. (2010). *Monitoring the Future: Questionnaire responses from the nation's high school seniors, 2009.* Ann Arbor, MI: Institute for Social Research.

63. New York Civil Liberties Union. (2008, April 29). *NYC marijuana possession arrests skyrocket, illustrate NYPD racial bias, new report shows.* Retrieved from http://www.nyclu.org/node/1736

64. Ridgeway, G. (2007). *Analysis of racial disparities in the New York Police Department's stop, question, and frisk practices.* Santa Monica, CA: RAND.

65. Engel, R. S., & Calnon, J. (2004). Examining the influence of drivers' characteristics during traffic stops with police: Results from a national survey. *Justice Quarterly, 21*, 49–90.

66. Greenfield, L. A., & Snell, T. (1999). *Women offenders.* Washington, DC: Bureau of Justice Statistics, U.S. Department of Justice.

67. Steffensmeir, D., & Schwartz, J. (2004). Trends in female criminality: Is crime still a man's world? In B. R. Price & N. J. Sokoloff (Eds.), *The criminal justice system and women: Offenders, prisoners, victims, and workers.* New York: McGraw-Hill.

68. Lombroso, C. (1920). *The female offender.* New York: Appleton.

69. Ibid.

70. Booth, A., & Osgood, D. W. (1993). The influence of testosterone on deviance in adulthood: Assessing and explaining the relationship. *Criminology, 31*, 93–118.

71. Bottcher, J. (2001). Social practices of gender: How gender relates to delinquency in the everyday lives of high-risk youths. *Criminology, 39*, 893–932.

72. Blackwell, B. S., & Piquero, A. R. (2005). On the relationships between gender, power control, self-control, and crime. *Journal of Criminal Justice, 33*(1), 1–17; Rowe, D., Vazsonyi, A., & Flannery, D. (1995). Sex differences in crime: Do mean and within-sex variation have similar causes? *Journal of Research in Crime and Delinquency, 32*, 84–100.

73. Steen, K., & Hunskaar, S. (2004). Gender and physical violence. *Social Science & Medicine, 59,* 567–571.

74. Wolfgang, M., Figlio, R., & Sellin, T. (1972). *Delinquency in a birth cohort.* Chicago: University of Chicago Press.

75. Blumstein, A., et al. (Eds.). (1986). *Criminal careers and career criminals.* Washington, DC: National Academy Press.

76. Sampson, R. J., & Laub, J. H. (2005). A life course view of the development of crime. *Annals of the American Academy.* Retrieved from http://www.aapss.org/uploads/Annals_Nov_2005_Sampson_Laub.pdf; Sampson, R. J., & Laub, J. H. (1993). *Crime in the making: Pathways and turning points through the life course.* Cambridge, MA: Harvard University Press; Elder Jr., G. H. (1985). Perspectives on the life-course. In G. H. Elder Jr. (Ed.), *Life-course dynamics.* Ithaca, NY: Cornell University Press.

77. Murphy, J. (2000, June 12). Are three-strikes laws fair and effective? Retrieved from http://speakout.com/activism/issue_briefs/1290b-1.html

78. Stolzenberg, L., & D'Alessio, S. (1997). "Three strikes and you're out": The impact of California's new mandatory sentencing law on serious crime rates. *Crime & Delinquency, 43*(4), 457–469.

79. Calavita, K., Pontell, H. N., & Tillman, R. (1997). *Big money crime: Fraud and politics in the savings and loan crisis* (pp. 1, 31). Berkeley: University of California Press.

80. Ibid., pp. 72–90.

81. McLean, B., & Elkind, P. (2004). *The smartest guys in the room: The amazing rise and scandalous fall of Enron.* London: Penguin.

82. U.S. Attorney General's Office. (2007). *U.S. attorney general's annual report to Congress.*

83. For more on this story, see http://articles.cnn.com/2005-11-28/politics/cunningham_1_mzm-mitchell-wade-tax-evasion?_s=PM:POLITICS

84. *National crime victimization survey, 2005,* 2006.

85. Federal Bureau of Investigation. (2007). *Crime in the United States: Preliminary semi-annual Uniform Crime Report.* Washington, DC: U.S. Department of Justice.

86. Zahn, M., & Riedel, M. (1985). *The nature and pattern of American homicide.* Washington, DC: U.S. Department of Justice.

87. Ibid.

88. FBI, *Crime in the United States,* 2007.

89. Ibid.

90. Ibid.

91. Van Kesteren, J. N., Mayhew, P., & Nieuwbeerta, P. (2000). *Criminal victimization in seventeen industrialized countries: Key findings from the 2000 International Crime Victims Survey.* The Hague: Ministry of Justice, WODC.

92. Ibid.

Chapter 4

1. Jenkins, P. (1994). The ice age: The social construction of a drug panic. *Justice Quarterly, 4,* 7–31.

2. Ibid.

3. Ibid.

4. Kuhn, T. S. (1966). *The structure of scientific revolutions.* Chicago: University of Chicago Press; Popper, K. (1959). *The logic of scientific discovery.* New York: Basic Books.

5. Quoted in Seriven, M. (1959). Explanation and prediction in evolutionary theory. *Science, 130,* 477–482.

6. Some of this information was previously published as Sterling, E. (2006, July 26). *Getting justice off its junk food diet.* Silver Spring, MD: The Criminal Justice Policy Foundation; http://cjpf.org/Getting_Justice_Off_Its_Junk_Food_Diet.pdf

7. *N.B.:* In 2001, Detective Brown went to federal prison for two years for lying under oath about his expertise in drug cases.

8. Evans, R. I. (1998). An historical perspective on effective prevention. In W. J. Bukoski & R. I. Evans (Eds.), *Cost-benefit/cost-effectiveness research on drug abuse prevention: Implications for programming and policy.* National Institute on Drug Abuse Research monograph series no. 176, NIH publication no. 98-4021. Washington, DC: U.S. Government Printing Office; Foundation for a Drug Free World. Retrieved from http://www.drugfreeworld.org/contact/index.html (accessed May 15, 2008).

9. Popper, 1959.

10. Chambliss, W. J. (2001). *Power, politics, and crime.* Boulder, CO: Westview.

11. Neuman, W. L. (2000). *Social research methods: Qualitative and quantitative.* Toronto: Allyn & Bacon.

12. Kubrin, C. E. (2003). Structural covariates of homicide rates: Does type of homicide matter? *Journal of Research in Crime and Delinquency, 40,* 139–170.

13. Neuman, 2000; Singleton, R., et al. (1999). *Approaches to social research.* New York: Oxford University Press.

14. Byrne, J. M., & Stowell, J. (2007). Examining the link between institutional and community *violence:*

Toward a new cultural paradigm. *Aggression and Violent Behavior, 12*(5), 552–563; Hayes, T. C., & Lee, M. R. (2005). The southern culture of honor and violent attitudes. *Sociological Spectrum, 25*(5), 593–617; Wolfgang, M., & Ferracuti, F. (1967). *The subculture of violence: Towards an integrated theory in criminology.* London: Tavistock.

15. Michalowski, R. J., & Kramer, R. C. (Eds.). (2006). *State-corporate crime: Wrongdoing at the intersection of business and government.* New Brunswick, NJ: Rutgers University Press; Sutherland, E. H. (1939). White collar criminality. *American Sociological Review, 5*, 1–18; Chambliss, W. J. (1979). *On the take: From petty crooks to presidents.* Bloomington and Indianapolis: Indiana University Press.

16. Reiman, J. (2009). *The rich get richer and the poor get prison* (9th ed.). Upper Saddle River, NJ: Prentice Hall.

17. Ibid., p. 82.

18. Popper, 1959.

19. Neuman, 2000; Singleton et al., 1999.

20. Chambliss, 1979.

21. Ferrell, J. (1996). *Crimes of style: Urban graffiti and the politics of criminality.* New York: Northeastern University Press.

22. Campbell, L. (2008). European street gangs and troublesome youth groups. *British Journal of Criminology, 48*(1), 116–118; Tita, G. E., Cohen, J., & Engberg, J. (2005). An ecological study of the location of gang "set space." *Social Problems, 52*(2), 272–299; Rodriguez, L. J. (1993). *Always running: La vida loca: Gang days in L.A.* Willimantic, CT: Curbstone; Jankowski, M. S. (1991). *Island in the street: Gangs and American urban society.* Berkeley: University of California Press.

23. Herzog, S. (2008). The lenient social and legal response to trafficking in women: An empirical analysis of public perceptions. *Journal of Contemporary Criminal Justice, 24*(3), 314–333; Maher, M. (1994, March 21). A change of place. *Barron's,* 33–38.

24. Hamm, M. (2002). *In bad company.* Boston: Northeastern University Press; Chambliss, 1979.

25. Chambliss, W. J. (1973). The Saints and the Roughnecks. *Society, 11*(1), 24–31.

26. Ibid.; Chambliss, 1979.

27. Chambliss, 1979.

28. Polman, H., Orobio de Castro, B., & van Aken, M. A. G. (2008). Experimental study of the differential effects of playing versus watching violent video games on children's aggressive behavior. *Aggressive Behavior, 34*, 256–264.

29. Linz, D. G. (1989). Exposure to sexually explicit materials and attitudes toward rape: A comparison of study results. *Journal of Sex Research, 26,* 50–84; Linz, D. G., Donnerstein, E., & Adams, S. M. (1989). Physical desensitization and judgments about female victims of violence. *Human Communication Research, 15,* 509–522.

30. Erikson, K. T. (1966). *Wayward Puritans.* New York: Macmillan; Thompson, E. P. (1975). *Whigs and hunters: The origin of the Black Act.* London: Alan Lane; Chambliss, W. J. (1964). A sociological analysis of the law of vagrancy. *Social Problems, 12,* 67–77.

31. Foucault, M. (1979). *Discipline and punish: The birth of the prison.* New York: Random House; Foucault, M. (1980). *The history of sexuality.* New York: Random House.

32. Babbie, E. (2004). *The basics of social research.* Belmont, CA: Wadsworth.

33. Ibid.

34. Ibid.

35. Hagan, F. E. (2003). *Research methods in criminal justice and criminology* (6th ed.). New York: Allyn & Bacon.

36. Ibid.

37. Academy of Criminal Justice Sciences. (2000, March 21). *Code of ethics.* Retrieved from http://www.acjs.org/pubs/167_671_2922.cfm

38. Hass, A. Y. (n.d.). *Re-arrest research study: Final report.* Court Services and Offender Supervision Agency, Community Supervision Services. Washington, DC.

39. Sherman, L., & Strang, H. (2004). Experimental ethnography: The marriage of qualitative and quantitative research. *Annals (AAPSS),* 595.

40. Sherman, L., & Strang, H. (2005). Randomized trials in restorative justice in the United Kingdom. *AEC Newsletter,* 1.

41. Ibid.

Chapter 5

1. King, H., & Chambliss, W. J. (2004). *Harry King: A professional thief's journey.* Bloomington, IN: iUniverse.

2. Ibid., p. 4.

3. Matsueda, R., Kreager, D., & Huizinga, D. (2006). Deterring delinquents: A rational choice model of theft and violence. *American Sociological Review, 71,* 95–122.

4. Chambliss, W. J. (1988). *Exploring criminology.* New York: Macmillan.

5. Huff, R. C. (2008). Historical explanations of crime. In R. D. Crutchfield, C. E. Kubrin, G. S. Bridges, & J. G. Weis (Eds.), *Crime readings* (3rd ed.). Newbury Park, CA: Sage.

6. Beales, D. E. (2005). *Enlightenment and reform in 18th-century Europe.* New York: Tauris.

7. Vold, G., Bernard, T., & Snipes, J. (2002). *Theoretical criminology* (5th ed.). New York: Oxford University Press.

8. Learn more about Beccaria at http://www.crimetheory.com/Archive/Beccaria/index.html

9. Reynolds, M. O. (2000). Certainty of punishment equals less crime. *Human Events.* Retrieved from http://findarticles.com/p/articles/mi_qa3827/is_200012/ai_n8928760/pg_1?tag=artBody;col1 on (accessed June 25, 2008); Mendes, S. M. (2004, February 1). Certainty, severity, and their relative deterrent effects: Questioning the implications of the role of risk in criminal deterrence policy. *Policy Studies Journal.* Retrieved from http://goliath.ecnext.com/coms2/gi_0199-45161/Certainty-severity-and-their-relative.html

10. Bentham, J. (1967). *A fragment on government and an introduction to the principle of morals and legislation.* W. Harrison (Ed.). Oxford: Basil Blackwell.

11. Ibid.

12. Tyler, C. (2004). A foundation of chaff? A critique of Bentham's metaphysics, 1813–16. *British Journal of the History of Philosophy, 12,* 685–703.

13. Kateb, G. (2007). *Punishment and the spirit of democracy. Why we punish: The foundations of our concept of punishment: An article from* Social Research. Farmington Hills, MI: Gale Group.

14. Trochim, W. (2006). Positivism and post-positivism. *Research Methods Knowledge Base.* Retrieved from http://www.socialresearchmethods.net/kb/positvsm.php

15. Clarke, R. V., & Cornish, D. B. (2000). Rational choice. In R. Paternoster & R. Bachman (Eds.), *Explaining crimes and criminals: Essays in contemporary criminological theory.* Los Angeles: Roxbury.

16. Piquero, A., Piquero, A. R., & Tibbetts, S. G. (Eds.). (2002). *Rational choice and criminal behavior: Recent research and future challenges.* New York: Routledge.

17. Green, S. L. (2002). *Rational choice theory: An overview.* Baylor University Faculty Development Seminar on Rational Choice Theory.

18. Cornish, D., & Clarke, R. V. (1987). Understanding crime displacement: An application of rational choice theory. *Criminology, 25,* 4.

19. LaFree, G., & Birkbeck, C. (1991). The neglected situation: A cross-national study of the situational characteristics of crime. *Criminology, 29,* 1.

20. Clarke, R. V. (1995). *Situational crime prevention: Everybody's business.* Paper presented at the Seventeenth National Conference of the Australian Crime Prevention Council, November, Adelaide and Burra, South Australia.

21. Cornish, D. B., & Clarke, R. V. (2003). Opportunities, precipitators, and criminal decisions: A reply to Whortley's critique on situational crime prevention. *Crime Prevention Studies, 16,* 41–96.

22. Pezzin, L. (1995). Earnings prospects, matching effects, and the decision to terminate a criminal career. *Journal of Quantitative Criminology, 11,* 29–50.

23. Treambly, P., & Morselli, C. (2000). Patterns in criminal achievement: Wilson and Abrahams revisited. *Criminology, 38,* 633–660.

24. Angell, J. (2006, May 15). Confessions of an Ivy League callgirl. *Boston Magazine.* Retrieved from http://www.bostonmagazine.com/articles/confessions_of_an_ivy_league_callgirl/

25. Cherbonneau, M., & Cope, H. (2006). Drive it like you stole it: Auto theft and the illusion of normalcy. *British Journal of Criminology, 46,* 193–211; Jacobs, B. (1996). Crack dealers' apprehension avoidance techniques: A case of restrictive deterrence. *Justice Quarterly, 13,* 359–381.

26. Learn more about this case by visiting http://www.idxinc.com/counterfeit.htm

27. Beauregard, E., D. Rossmo, D. K., & Proulx, J. (2007). A descriptive model of the hunting process of serial sex offenders: A rational choice perspective. *Journal of Family Violence, 22,* 449–463; Andresen, M. A. (2006). Crime measures and the spatial analysis of criminal activity. *British Journal of Criminology, 46,* 258–285.

28. Cohen L. E., & Felson, M. (1979). Social change and crime rate trends: A routine activities approach. *American Sociological Review, 44*(4), 389–406.

29. Tewksbury, R., & Mustaine, E. E. (2006). Where to find sex offenders: An examination of residential locations and neighborhood conditions. *Criminal Justice Studies, 19*(1), 61–75.

30. Cass, A. I. (2007). Routine activities and sexual assault: An examination of individual and school level factors. *Violence and Victims, 22*(3), 350–366.

31. Cornish & Clarke, 2003.

32. Felson, R., & Messner, S. (1996). To kill or not to kill: Lethal outcomes in injurious attacks. *Criminology, 34,* 519–545.

33. *Homicide: Behavioral aspects–victim/offender relationships.* (2009). Retrieved from http://law.jrank.org/pages/1322/Homicide-Behavioral-Aspects-Victim-offender-relationships.html; Decker, S. (1996). Deviant homicide: A new look at the role of motives and victim–offender relationships. *Journal of Research in Crime and Delinquency, 33,* 427–449.

34. Felson & Messner, 1996.

35. Macer, J., Baker, A., & Moynihan, C. (2008, December 1). Criticism and confusion in aftermath of Burress incident. *New York Times*. Retrieved from http://www.nytimes.com/2008/12/02/sports/football/02burress.html?_r=1&scp=1&sq=plaxico&st=cse

36. Abused wife cleared of husband's murder. (2006, March 3). *Sydney Morning Herald*. Retrieved from http://www.smh.com.au/news/National/Abused-wife-cleared-of-husbands-murder/2006/03/03/1141191843495.html

37. Moriarty, L., & Williams, J. E. (1996). Examining the relationship between routine activities theory and social disorganization: An analysis of property crime Victimization. *American Journal of Criminal Justice, 21*(1), 43–59.

38. Tunnell, K. D. (2002). The impulsiveness and routinization of decision-making. In A. Piquero, A. R. Piquero, & S. G. Tibbetts (Eds.), *Rational choice and criminal behavior: Recent research and ruture challenges*. New York: Routledge.

39. Exum, L. (2002). The application and robustness of the rational choice perspective in the study of intoxication and angry intentions to aggression. *Criminology, 40*(4).

40. Brantingham, P., Brantingham, P., & Taylor, W. (2005). Situational crime prevention as a key component in embedded crime prevention. *Canadian Journal of Criminology and Criminal Justice, 47*, 271–292.

41. Clarke, R. V. (2005). Seven misconceptions of situational crime prevention. In N. Tilley (Ed.), *Handbook of crime prevention and community safety*. Devon, England: Willan.

42. *Twenty-five techniques of situational prevention.* (2009). Center for Problem Oriented Policing, Community Oriented Policing Services, U.S. Department of Justice. Retrieved from http://www.popcenter.org/25techniques/

43. Cornish & Clarke, 2003; Clarke, R. V., & Eck, J. (2003). *Become a problem-solving crime analyst*. London: Jill Dando Institute of Crime Science, University College London. Retrieved from http://www.jdi.ucl.ac.uk/publications/other_publications/55steps

44. Cullen, F. T., Pratt, T. C., Miceli, S. L., & Moon, M. M. (2002). Dangerous liaison? Rational choice theory as the basis for correctional intervention. In A. Piquero, A. R. Piquero, & S. G. Tibbetts (Eds.), *Rational choice and criminal behavior: Recent research and future challenges*. New York: Routledge.

45. Van den Haag, E. (1982). The criminal law as a threat system. *Journal of Criminal Law and Criminology, 73*, 709–785.

46. Pogarsky, G. (2002). Identifying deterrable offenders: Implications for deterrence. *Justice Quarterly, 19*, 431–452.

47. McCarthy, B. (2002). New economics of sociological criminology. *Annual Review of Sociology, 28*, 417–442.

48. Information retrieved from the Maricopa County Sheriff's Department website at http://www.mcso.org/index.php?a=GetModule&mn=Sheriff_Bio (accessed June 20, 2008).

49. Schembri, A. J. (n.d.). *Scared Straight programs: Jails and detention tours*. Florida Department of Juvenile Justice. Retrieved from http://www.djj.state.fl.us/Research/Scared_Straight_Booklet_Version.pdf (accessed June 20, 2008).

50. Pratt, T. C., Cullen, F. T., Blevins, K. R., Daigle, L. E., & Madensen, T. D. (2006). The empirical status of deterrence theory: A meta-analysis. In F. T. Cullen, J. P. Wright, & K. R. Blevins (Eds.), *Taking stock: The status of criminological theory* (Vol. 15). New Brunswick, NJ: Transaction.

51. Nagin, D., & Pogarsky, G. (2001). Integrating celerity, impulsivity, and extralegal sanction threats into a model of general deterrence: Theory and evidence. *Criminology, 39*, 865–892.

52. Matsueda, Kreager, & Huizinga, 2006.

53. Netter, B. (2005). Avoiding the shameful backlash: Social repercussions for the increased use of alternative sanctions. *Journal of Criminal Law and Criminology*. Retrieved from http://goliath.ecnext.com/coms2/summary_0199-5374233_ITM; Grasmick, H., & Bursik, R. (1990). Conscience, significant others, and rational choices: Extending the deterrence model. *Law and Society Review, 24*, 837–861.

54. *Crime issues: Causes and prevention?* (2001). National Center for Policy Analysis, Dallas. Retrieved from http://www.ncpa.org/

55. Aitken, C., Moore, D., Higgs, P., Kelsall, J., & Kerger, M. (2002). The impact of a police crackdown on a street drug scene: Evidence from the street. *International Journal of Drug Policy, 13*, 189–198.

Chapter 6

1. Flajole, P. (2008, November 6). The twinkie defense revisited. *The Santa Clara*. Retrieved from http://media.www.thesantaclara.com/media/storage/paper946/news/2008/11/06/Scene/Twinkie.Defense.Revisited-3529122.shtml

2. Ellis, L. (2005). A theory explaining biological correlates of criminality. *European Journal of Criminology, 2*(3), 287–315.

3. Garpenstrand, H., Longato-Stadler, E., Klinteberg, B., Grigorenko, E., Damberg, M., Oreland, L., & Hallman, J. (2002). Low platelet monoamine oxidase activity in Swedish imprisoned criminal offenders. *European Neuropsychopharmacology, 12,* 135–40.

4. Eensoo, D., Harro, M., Pullmann, H., Allik, J., & Harro, J. (2007). Association of traffic behavior with personality and platelet monoamine oxidase activity in schoolchildren. *Journal of Adolescent Health, 40,* 311–317.

5. Physical attractiveness and criminal behavior. (2004). *Encyclopedia of criminology.* Retrieved from http://cw.routledge.com/ref/criminology/physical.html

6. *The founder of phrenology: Franz Joseph Gall.* Retrieved from http://www.phrenology.com/franzjosephgall.html (accessed December 9, 2008).

7. Ibid.

8. *The complete work of Charles Darwin online.* (2002). Retrieved from http://darwin-online.org.uk/

9. Lombroso, C. (1911/1972). Introduction. In C. Lombroso & G. Lombroso-Ferrero, *Criminal man according to the classification of Cesare Lombroso.* Montclair, NJ: Patterson Smith.

10. Beirne, P. (1988). Heredity versus environment: A reconsideration of Goring's "The English Convict." *British Journal of Criminology, 28,* 315–339.

11. Rafter, N. (2004). Ernest A. Hooton and the biological tradition in American criminology. *Criminology, 42*(3), 735.

12. Sheldon, W. (1949). *Varieties of delinquent youth.* New York: Harper and Brothers.

13. Glueck, S., & Glueck, E. (1950). *Unraveling juvenile delinquency.* New York: Commonwealth Fund.

14. Ellis, 2005.

15. Pinella-Fernando, G. (2008). Brain foods: The effects of nutrients on brain function. *Nature Reviews: Neuroscience, 9,* 568–578; Breakey, J. (1997). The role of diet and behavior in childhood. *Journal of Pediatric Child Health, 33,* 190–194.

16. Konofal, E., Cortese, S., Lecendreux, M., Arnulf, I., & Mouren, M. C. (2005). Effectiveness of iron supplementation in a young child with attention-deficit/hyperactivity disorder. *Pediatrics, 116,* 732–734.

17. Van de Weyer, C. (2006). *Changing diets, changing minds: How food affects mental well-being and behavior.* Sustain: The Alliance for Better Food and Farming. Retrieved from http://www.sustainweb.org/publications/

18. Richardson, A., & Montgomery, P. (2005). The Oxford-Durham study: A randomized controlled trial of dietary supplementation with fatty acids in children with developmental coordination disorder. *Pediatrics, 115*(1), 360–366.

19. Koester, S. (2007, January 28). Hypoglycemia may result in criminal behavior. *Associated Content.* Retrieved from http://www.associatedcontent.com/article/127978/hypoglycemia_may_result_in_criminal.html?page=1&cat=70

20. Blaylock, R. (2008). Nutrition and behavior. Retrieved from http://1phil4everyill.wordpress.com/2008/11/20/dr-russell-blaylock-nutrition-and-behavior/

21. Virkkunen, M. (2009). Reactive hypoglycemic tendency among habitually violent offenders. *Nutrition Reviews Supplement, 44,* 94–103.

22. Ellis, 2005.

23. Van Goozen, S., Matthys, W., Cohen-Kettenis, P., Thijssen, J., & Van Engeland, H. (1998). Adrenal androgens and aggression in conduct disorder pre-pubertal boys and normal controls. *Biological Psychiatry, 43,*156–158.

24. Dalton, K. (1971). *The premenstrual syndrome.* Springfield, IL: Thomas.

25. Easteal, E. (n.d.). *Premenstrual syndrome in the courtroom.* Retrieved from http://www.aic.gov.au/publications/previous%20series/proceedings/1-27/~/media/publications/proceedings/16/easteal2.ashx (accessed December 12, 2008)

26. Bellinger, D. C. (2004). Lead. *Pediatrics, 113*(1), 1016–1022; Needleman, H., McFarland, C., Ness, R., Fienberg, S., & Tobin, M. (2002). Bone lead levels in adjudicated delinquents: A case control study. *Neurotoxicology and Teratology, 24,* 711–717.

27. Lersch, K. (2008, May 20). Scholar studies link between crime and exposure to environmental contaminants. *USF Polytechnic.* Retrieved from http://www.poly.usf.edu/News/20080520-Crime-Environment.xml

28. Dietrich, K., Ris, M. D., Hornung, R., Wessel, S. Lanphear, B., Ho, M., & Rae, R. (2008). Association of prenatal and childhood blood lead concentrations with criminal arrests in early adulthood. *PLoS Med., 5*(5), e115.

29. Hoffman, J. (2007). Idea lab: Criminal element. *New York Times.* Retrieved from http://www.nytimes.com/2007/10/21/magazine/21wwln-idealab-t.html (accessed January 25, 2009).

30. Marcus, S. (2007). Lead toxicity. *eMedicine.* Retrieved from http://emedicine.medscape.com/article/815399-overview (accessed January 25, 2009).

31. Reyes, J. (2007, October). Environmental policy as social policy? The impact of childhood lead exposure on crime," *B.E. Journal of Economic Analysis and Policy, 7,* 1 (Contributions).

32. Walker, S. (2006). *Sense and nonsense about crime and drugs: A policy guide* (6th ed.). Belmont, CA: Wadsworth.

33. Pallone, N., & Hennessy, J. (1998). Brain dysfunction and criminal violence. *Society, 35,* 21–27.

34. Raine, A., & Yang, Y. (2006). Neural foundations to moral reasoning and antisocial behavior. *Social Cognitive and Affective Neuroscience, 1*(3), 203–213.

35. Barker, E., Seguin, J., White, H. R., Bates, M., Lacourse, E., Carbonneau, R., & Tremblay, R. (2007). Developmental trajectories of male physical violence and theft. *Archives of General Psychiatry, 64*(5), 592–599.

36. Tancredi, L. (2005). *Hardwired behavior: What neuroscience reveals about morality.* London: Cambridge University Press.

37. Johnston, E. (2006). Serotonin. Retrieved from http://bpd.about.com/od/bpdglossary/g/Serotonin.htm (accessed January 23, 2009).

38. Valzelli, L. (1973). The "isolation syndrome" in mice. *Psychopharmacologia, 31,* 305–320.

39. Sloan, F. (2007). Lack of serotonin leading violent, aggressive behavior. *Journal of Young Investigators.* Retrieved from http://www.jyi.org/news/nb.php?id=1335 (accessed January 18, 2009).

40. Bartol, C. R., & Bartol, A. M. (2008). *Introduction to forensic psychology: Research and application.* Thousand Oaks, CA: Sage.

41. Young, S., Smolen, A., Corley, R., Krauter, K., DeFries, J., Crowley, T., & Hewitt, J. (2002). Dopamine transporter polymorphism associated with externalizing behavior problems in children. *American Journal of Medical Genetics, 114,* 144–149.

42. Skondras, M., Markianos, M., Botsis, A., Bistolaki, E., & Christodoulou, G. (2004). Platelet monoamine oxidase activity and psychometric correlates in male violent offenders imprisoned for homicide or other violent acts. *European Archives of Psychiatry and Clinical Neuroscience, 254*(6), 380–386.

43. Hogg, W. F. (2008, July 26). Socially induced hyperactivity (SIH) in children. *Knol Beta.* Retrieved from http://knol.google.com/k/william-f-hogg-md/socially-induced-hyperactivity-sih-in/3ga0u5203tyhc/3#

44. Adler, L., & Florence, M. (2006). *Scattered minds: Hope and help for adults with ADHD.* London: Penguin.

45. Attention Deficit Hyperactivity Disorder (ADHD)—Cause. (2008, December 18). ADD and ADHD Health Center, webMD. Retrieved from http://www.webmd.com/add-adhd/tc/attention-deficit-hyperactivity-disorder-adhd-cause

46. High, C. (2007, April 6). ADHD and crime: Is your child at risk? *Associated Content.* Retrieved from http://www.associatedcontent.com/article/187737/adhd_and_crime_is_your_child_at_risk.html

47. Barkley, R., Fischer, M., Smallish, L., & Fletcher, K. (2004). Young adult follow-up of hyperactive children: Antisocial activities and drug use. *Journal of Child Psychology and Psychiatry, 45,* 195–211.

48. Estabrook, A. (1916). *The Jukes in 1915.* Washington, DC: Carnegie Institute.

49. Goddard, H. H. (1912). *The Kallikak family: A study in the heredity of feeblemindedness.* New York: Macmillan.

50. Rafter, N. H. (1997). *Creating born criminals.* Urbana: University of Illinois Press.

51. Curran, W. J. (1974). Sterilization of the poor: Judge Gesell's roadblock. *New England Journal of Medicine, 291,* 25–26. Retrieved from http://www.nejm.org/doi/full/10.1056/NEJM197407042910108

52. The information in this feature comes from these sources: Silliman, J., Fried, M. G., Ross, L., & Gutierrez, E. R. (2004). *Undivided rights: Women of color organize for reproductive justice.* Boston: South End; Ross, L. J. (2006). The color of choice: White supremacy and reproductive justice. In *Color of violence: The INCITE! anthology.* Boston: South End; Roberts, D. (2000, April). Black women and the pill. *Family Planning Perspective, 32*(2). Retrieved from http://www.guttmacher.org/pubs/journals/3209200.html

53. Lange, J. (1930). *Crime as destiny.* New York: Charles Boni.

54. Qun, P. (2003). The relationship of suicide risk to family history of suicide and psychiatric disorders. *Psychiatric Times, 20.*

55. Larsson, H., Tuvblad, C., Rijsdijk, F. V., Andershed, H., Grann, M., & Lichtenstein, P. (2007). A common genetic factor explains the association between psychopathic personality and antisocial behavior. *Psychological Medicine, 37,* 15–26; Scourfield, J., Van den Bree, M., Martin, N., & McGuffin, P. (2004). Conduct problems in children and adolescents: A twin study. *Archives of General Psychiatry, 61,* 489–496.

56. Viding, E., Blair, J. Moffitt, T., & Plomin, R. (2005). Evidence for substantial genetic risk for psychopathy in 7-year-olds. *Journal of Child Psychology and Psychiatry, 46,* 592–597.

57. Lyons, M. J. (2007). A twin study of self-reported criminal behavior. In G. R. Brock & J. A. Goode (Eds.), *Genetics of criminal and anti-social behavior.* Published online at http://www3.interscience.wiley.com/cgi-bin/bookhome/114298845/

58. Hutchings, B., & Mednick, S. A. (1977). Criminality in adoptees and their adoptive and biological parents: A pilot study. In S. A. Mednick & K. O. Christiansen (Eds.), *Biosocial bases of criminal behavior.* New York: Garner.

59. Tehrani, J., & Mednick, S. (2000). Genetic factors and criminal behavior. *Federal Probation, 64,* 24–28.

60. Jacobs, P. A., Brunton, M., & Melville, M. (1965). Aggressive behavior, mental sub-normality and the XYY male. *Nature, 208,* 1351.

61. A summary of studies can be found in Katz, J., & Chambliss, W. J. (1995). Biology and crime. In J. F. Sheley (Ed.), *Criminology.* Belmont, CA: Wadsworth.

62. Appelbaum, P. (2005). Law & psychiatry: Behavioral genetics and the punishment of crime. *Psychiatric Services, 56,* 25–27.

63. Hussein, S., & Sarwar, M. (2005). Biological oriented theories of criminality: Explanation and criticism. *Pakistan Journal of Social Sciences, 3*(5), 741–750.

64. Rafter, N. (2008). *The criminal brain: Understanding biological theories of crime.* New York: NYU Press.

65. Hunter, R. D., & Dantzer. M. L. (2005). *Crime and criminality: Causes and consequences.* New York: Criminal Justice Press.

66. Akers, R. L., & Sellers, C. S. (2004). *Criminological theories: Introduction, evaluation, and application.* Los Angeles: Roxbury.

67. Rafter, 2008.

68. Pinker, S. (2002). *The blank slate: The modern denial of human nature.* New York: Viking.

69. Wright, J. P., Tibbetts, S. G., & Daigle, L. E. (2008). *Criminals in the making: Criminality across the life-course.* Thousand Oaks, CA: Sage.

70. Lanier, M. M., & Henry, S. 2004. *Essential criminology.* Boulder, CO: Westview.

71. Hattie, J., Marsh, H. W., Neill, J. T., & Richards, G. E. (1997). Adventure education and Outward Bound: Out-of-class experiences that have a lasting effect. *Review of Educational Research, 67,* 43–87; Outward Bound at-risk youth expeditions. (2009). Retrieved from http://www.outwardbound.org/ and http://www.outwardbound.org/index.cfm/do/are.program_outcomes

72. Neill, J. T. (2002). *Meta-analytic research on the outcomes of outdoor education.* Paper presented at the 6th Biennial Coalition for Education in the Outdoors Research Symposium, Bradford Woods, IN, January. Retrieved from http://www.wilderdom.com/research/researchoutcomesmeta-analytic.htm

Chapter 7

1. Groth, N., Burgess, A., & Holmstrom, L. (1977). Rape: Power, anger, and sexuality. *American Journal of Psychiatry, 134,* 1239–1243; Anderson, W. P., Kunce, J. T., & Rich, B. (1979). Sex offenders: Three personality types. *Journal of Clinical Psychology, 35,* 671–676.

2. Douglas, J. E., Burgess, A. W., Burgess, A. G., & Ressler, R. K. (2006). *Crime classification manual: A standard system for investigating and classifying violent crimes* (2nd ed.). San Francisco: Jossey-Bass.

3. Pardue, A., & Arrigo, B. A. (2008). Power, anger, and sadistic rapists: Toward a differentiated model of offender personality. *International Journal of Offender Therapy and Comparative Criminology, 52*(4), 378–400.

4. Chua-Eoan, H. (2009). Crimes of the century: The top 25. *Times.com.* Retrieved from http://www.time.com/time/2007/crimes/16.html

5. Bartol, C. R. (2005). *Criminal behavior: A psychological approach.* Upper Saddle River, NJ: Prentice Hall.

6. Bettencourt, B. A., Talley, A., Benjamin, A. J., & Valentine, J. (2006). Personality and aggressive behavior under provoking and neutral conditions: A meta-analytic review. *Psychological Bulletin, 132*(5), 751–777.

7. Cleckley, H. (1982). *The mask of sanity* (Rev. ed.). St. Louis, MO: Mosby.

8. Harve, H., & Yuille, J. C. (2007). *The psychopath: Theory, research and practice.* Mahwah, NJ: Erlbaum.

9. Lilienfeld, S. O., & Arkowitz. H. (2007, December). What "psychopath" really means. *Scientific American.*

10. Copley, J. (2008). Causes of psychopathy. *Suite101.com.* Retrieved from http://personalitydisorders.suite101.com/article.cfm/causes_of_psychopathy

11. Kosson, D. S., Suchy, Y., Mayer, A. R., & Libby, J. (2002). Facial affect recognition in criminal psychopaths. *Emotion, 2*(4), 398–411.

12. Weber, S., Habel, U., Amnuts, K., & Schnider, F. (2008). Structural brain abnormalities in psychopaths—A review. *Behavioral Sciences and the Law, 26*(1), 7–28.

13. *Diagnostic and statistical manual of mental disorders* (4th ed.). (2000). Washington, DC: American Psychiatric Association.

14. Mayo Foundation for Medical Education and Research. (2009). *Antisocial personality disorder.* Retrieved from http://www.mayoclinic.com/health/antisocial-personality-disorder/DS00829

15. Fazel, S., & Danesh, J. (2002). Serious mental disorder in 23,000 prisoners: A systematic review of 62 surveys. *Lancet, 359*(9306), 545–550.

16. *Freud: Conflict and culture.* (2009). Library of Congress, online exhibit. Retrieved from http://www.loc.gov/exhibits/freud/

17. Timeline: Austrian cellar case. (2009). *BBC News Online.* Retrieved from http://news.bbc.co.uk/2/hi/europe/7370208.stm; Mitchell, J. (2008, May 7). Josef, Rosemarie, and Elizabeth Fritzl: The sadist, the silent, and the survivor. *Blogcritics Culture.* Retrieved from http://blogcritics.org/archives/2008/05/07/1329462.php; Paterson, T. (2009, March 17). Trial begins with shocking account of crimes that appalled the world. *The Independent.* Retrieved from http://www.independent.co.uk/news/world/europe/herr-fritzl-can-you-just-answer-one-thing-ndash-why-1646511.html

18. Ibid.

19. Stone, M. (2002). Review of "the neurotic character." *North American Society of Adlerian Psychology Newsletter,* March–April.

20. What is psychosis? (2006). *Fact Sheet 1.* Early Psychosis Prevention and Intervention Center. Retrieved from http://www.sharc.org.au/uploads/file/Fact1_WhatIsPsychosis.pdf

21. Darton, K., & Sharman, J. (2009). *Understanding psychotic experiences.* London: Mind Publications.

22. Busko, M. (2007). Childhood psychiatric disorders predict 1 path to young-adult crime. *Malaysian Psychiatric Association.* Retrieved from http://www.psychiatry-malaysia.org/article.php?aid=725

23. Copeland, W. E., Miller-Johnson, S., Keeler, G., Angold, A., & Costello, E. J. (2007). Childhood psychiatric disorders and young adult crime: A prospective, population-based study. *American Journal of Psychiatry, 164,* 1668–1675.

24. Baillargeon, J., Binswanger, I. A., Penn, J. V., Williams, B. A., & Murray, O. J. (2008). Psychiatric disorders and repeat incarcerations: The revolving prison door. *American Journal of Psychiatry.* doi: 10.1176/ 10.1176/appi.ajp.2008.08030416.

25. Silver, E. (2000). Extending social disorganization theory: A multi-level approach to the study of violence among persons with mental illness. *Criminology, 38,* 1043–1074.

26. Sellers, C., Sullivan, C., Veysey, B., & Shane, J. (2005). Responding to persons with mental illnesses: Police perspectives on specialized and traditional practices. *Behavioral Sciences and the Law, 23,* 647–657.

27. Pajares, F. (2002). *Overview of social cognitive theory and of self-efficacy.* Retrieved from http://www.emory.edu/EDUCATION/mfp/eff.html

28. Ward, D., Stafford, M., & Gray, L. (2006). Rational choice, deterrence, and theoretical integration. *Journal of Applied Social Psychology, 36,* 571–581.

29. Marziano, V., Ward, T., Beech, A., & Pattison, P. (2006). Identification of five fundamental implicit theories underlying cognitive distortions in child abusers: A preliminary study. *Psychology, Crime and Law, 12,* 97–105.

30. Cohen, L. J., & Galynker, I. (2009). Psychopathology and personality traits of pedophiles. *Psychiatric Times, 26*(6).

31. Maletzky, B. M., & Steinhauser, C. (2002). A 25-year follow-up of cognitive/behavioral therapy with 7,275 sexual offenders. *Behavior Modification, 26*(2), 123–147.

32. Marx, B. P., Miranda Jr., B., & Meyerson, L. A. (1999). Cognitive-behavioral treatment for rapists: Can we do better? *Clinical Psychology Review, 19*(7), 875–894; Maletzky, B. M. (2003). A serial rapist treated with behavioral and cognitive techniques and followed for 12 years. *Clinical Case Studies, 2*(2), 127–153.

33. Watson, J. B. (2004). *Behaviorism* (4th ed.). New Brunswick, NJ: Transaction.

34. Bandura, A. (1971). *Psychological modeling: Conflicting theories.* New Brunswick, NJ: Transaction.

35. Bushman, B. J., & Anderson, C. A. (2001). Media violence and the American public. *American Psychologist, 56*(6/7), 477–489.

36. Henry J. Kaiser Family Foundation. (2006). *TV violence key facts.* Retrieved from http://www.education.com/reference/article/Ref_TV_Violence_Key/

37. Entertainment Software Rating Board. (2009). *Game ratings and descriptor guide.* Retrieved from http://www.esrb.org/ratings/ratings_guide.jsp

38. Federal Communications Commission. (2003). V-chip: Viewing television responsibly. (2003). Retrieved from http://www.fcc.gov/vchip/; Federal Communications Commission. (2007). Violent programming and its impact on children. Retrieved from http://hraunfoss.fcc.gov/edocs_public/attachmatch/FCC-07-50A1.pdf

39. Myers, J. E. B. (2005). *Myers on evidence in child, domestic and elder abuse cases.* Frederick, MD: Aspen.

40. Hittle, S. (2009). Cycle of abuse can be seen in families. *LJWorld.com.* Retrieved from http://www2.ljworld.com/news/2009/apr/06/cycle-abuse-can-be-seen-families/?city_local

41. Anderson, C. A., Gentile, D. A., & Buckley, K. E. (2007). *Violent video game effects on children and adolescents.* New York: Oxford University Press.

42. Youth who killed girl by imitating wrestling moves is offered plea bargain; may be set free. (2004, January). *Jet.* Farmington, MI: Johnson, Gale Group.

43. Johnson, J. G., Cohen, P., Smailes, E. M., Kasen, S., & Brook, J. S. (2002, March). Television viewing and aggressive behavior during adolescence and adulthood. *Science, 295,* 2468–2471.

44. Salkind, N. J. (2004). *An introduction to theories of human development.* Thousand Oaks, CA: Sage.

45. Hasking, P. A. (2007). Reinforcement sensitivity, coping and delinquent behavior in adolescents. *Journal of Adolescence, 30*(5), 739–749.

46. Letha, A. (2007). *Human behavior in the social environment from an African-American perspective.* New York: Hawthorne.

47. Carnagey, N. L., & Anderson, C. A. (2005). The effects of reward and punishment in violent video games on aggressive affect, cognition and behavior. *Psychological Science, 16*(11), 882–889.

48. Goring, C. (1913). *The English convict: A statistical study.* London: HMSO.

49. Santrock, J. W. (2008). Concept of intelligence. In J. W. Santrock, *A topical approach to life-span development.* New York: McGraw-Hill.

50. Hirschi, T., & Hindelang, M. J. (1977). Intelligence and delinquency: A revisionist review. *American Sociological Review, 42,* 571–587.

51. Herrnstein, R. J., & Murray, C. (1994). *The bell curve: Intelligence and class structure in American life.* New York: Free Press.

52. Hawkins, D. F. (2005). Black and white homicide differentials: Alternatives to an inadequate theory. In S. L. Gabbidon & H. T. Greene (Eds.), *Race, crime and justice: A reader.* New York: Routledge.

53. Hagan, J., Krivo, L. J., & Peterson, R. D. (2006). *The many colors of crime: Inequalities of race, ethnicity, and crime in America.* New York: NYU Press.

54. O'Malley, S. (2005). *Are you there alone? The unspeakable crime of Andrea Yates.* New York: Simon & Schuster, Pocket Star.

55. Teo, T. (2005). *The critique of psychology.* New York: Springer.

56. Liebling, A., & Maruna, S. (2005). *The effects of imprisonment.* Portland, OR: Willan.

57. Elliott, A. (2002). *Psychoanalytic theory: An introduction.* Durham, NC: Duke University Press.

58. Pressley, M., & McCormick, C. B. (2007). *Child and adolescent development for educators.* New York: Guilford.

59. Bennett, S., Farrington, D. P., & Huesmann, L. R. (2005). Explaining gender differences in crime and violence: The importance of social cognitive skills. *Aggression and Violent Behavior, 10*(3), 263–288.

60. Burgess, R. L., & MacDonald, K. (2005). *Evolutionary perspectives on human development.* Thousand Oaks, CA: Sage.

61. Halicks, R. (2004, May 9). Iraqi prisoner abuse: People will do what they're told. *Atlanta Journal-Constitution,* p. 1E.

62. Hersh, S. (2004). Torture at Abu Ghraib. *New Yorker.* Retrieved from http://www.newyorker.com/archive/2004/05/10/040510fa_fact

63. Powers, R. (2009). United States military enlistment standards. Retrieved from http://usmilitary.about.com/od/joiningthemilitary/a/enlstandards.htm

64. Di Nuovo, S. (n.d.). Criminal and/or psychopathological deviance: Overlapping areas and the role of psychological assessment. Retrieved from http://www.forensicpsychology.it/numero%20001/art_dinuovo_inglese.htm (accessed April 27, 2009).

65. Huesmann, L. R., Eron, L. D., & Dubow, E. (2006). Childhood predictors of adult criminality: Are all risk factors reflected in childhood aggressiveness? *Criminal Behavior and Mental Health, 12*(3), 185–208.

66. Conduct problems prevention research group. 2002. Evaluation of the first 3 years of the fast track prevention trial with children at high risk for adolescent conduct problems. *Journal of Abnormal Child Psychology, 30,* 19–35.

67. Leschied, A., Chiodo, D., Nowicki, E., & Rodger, S. (2008). Childhood predictors of adult criminality: A meta-analysis drawn from the prospective longitudinal literature. *Canadian Journal of Criminology and Criminal Justice,* July.

68. Andrews, D. A., & Bonta, J. (2007). *The psychology of criminal conduct* (3rd ed.). Cincinnati: Anderson.

69. Farrington, D. P., & Welsh, B. C. (2007). *Saving children from a life of crime: Early risk factors and effective interventions.* London: Oxford University Press.

70. Barkley, R. A., Fischer, M., Smallish, L., & Fletcher, K. (2004). Young adult follow-up of hyperactive children: Antisocial activities and drug use. *Journal of Child Psychology & Psychiatry & Allied Disciplines, 45,* 195–211.

71. Bartol, C. R., & Bartol, A. B. (2004). *Criminal behavior: A psychosocial approach* (7th ed.). Englewood Cliffs, NJ: Prentice Hall.

72. Listwan, S., Sperber, K., Spruance, L., & Van Voorhis, P. (2004). High anxiety offenders in correctional settings: It's time for another look. *Federal Probation 68*(1), 43–50.

73. Davis, J. E. (2005). *Accounts of innocence: Sexual abuse, trauma, and the self.* Chicago: University of Chicago Press.

74. Foster, S. L., & Crain, M. M. (2002). Social skills and problem solving training. In T. Patterson (Ed.), *Comprehensive handbook of psychotherapy* (Vol. 2). New York: Wiley.

75. Dombeck, M., & Wells-Moran, J. (2009). Applying learning principles to thought: Cognitive restructuring. *MentalHelp.net.* Retrieved from http://www.mentalhelp.net/poc/view_doc.php?type=doc&id=9746&cn=353

76. Beck, E., Britto, S., & Andrews, A. (2007). *In the shadow of death: Restorative justice and death row families.* New York: Oxford University Press.

77. Little, G. L. (2005). Meta-analysis of moral reconation therapy: Recidivism results from probation and parole implementations. *Cognitive-Behavioral Treatment Review, 14,* 14–16.

78. Tremblay, R., Nagin, D., Séguin, J., Zoccolillo, M., Zelazo, P., Boivin, M., Perusse, D., & Japel, C. (2005). The early development of physical aggression in children. *Policy Brief-01.* Canadian Research Institute for Social Policy.

79. Aversion therapy treatment. (2009). Schick Shadel Hospital. Retrieved from http://www.schickshadel.com/programs/aversion_therapy_treatment.php

80. Lester, D., Braswell, M., & Van Voorhis, P. (2004). Radical behavioral interventions. In *Correctional counseling and rehabilitation.* Cincinnati: Anderson.

81. Abbas, A., Hoffman, N., Howard, R., & Spetzler, C. (2007, August). Teaching decision skills to troubled teens. Article reprinted from *ORMS Today.*

Chapter 8

1. Gottfried, M. H. (2009, May 12). "Melee" outside Frogtown bar was a gang fight, police say; beating victim identified. *St. Paul Pioneer Press.*

2. Blumstein, A., & Rosenfeld, R. (2008). Factors contributing to U.S. crime trends. *Understanding Crime Trends: Workshop Report.* Washington, DC: National Academies Press.

3. U.S. Department of Health and Human Services. (2001). *Youth violence: A report of the surgeon general.* Washington, DC: Author. Retrieved from http://www.surgeongeneral.gov/library/youthviolence/toc.html

4. Ritzer, G. (2007). *Sociological theories.* New York: McGraw-Hill.

5. Durkheim, E. (n.d.). *The sociology professor.* Retrieved from http://www.sociologyprofessor.com/socialtheorists/emiledurkheim.php (accessed June 4, 2009).

6. Elwell, F. W. (2003). *The sociology of Emile Durkheim.* Retrieved from http://www.faculty.rsu.edu/~felwell/Theorists/Durkheim/index.htm

7. Hawkins, D. F. (2009). *Violent crime: Assessing race and ethnic differences.* Cambridge, England: Cambridge University Press.

8. Einstadter, W., & Henry, S. (2006). *Criminological theory: An analysis of underlying assumptions.* Lanham, MD: Rowman & Littlefield.

9. Chambliss, W. J. (2001). *Power, politics, and crime.* Boulder, CO: Westview.

10. Summerfield, M. (2006). Social structure theory and crime. *Associated Content.* Retrieved from http://www.associatedcontent.com/article/16267/social_structure_theory_and_crime_pg2.html?cat=17

11. Calvó-Armengol, A., & Zenou, Y. (2004). Social networks and crime decisions: The role of social structure in facilitating delinquent behavior. *International Economic Review, 45*(3), 939–958.

12. Anderson, E. (2009). *Against the wall: Poor, young, black, and male (the city in the twenty-first century).* Philadelphia: University of Pennsylvania Press.

13. Williams, K. (2007). *Neighborhoods and crime: An examination of social disorganization and extra-community crime in St. Louis communities.* Paper presented at the annual meeting of the American Society of Criminology, Atlanta, November 14.

14. Park, R., & Burgess, E. (1925). *The city.* Chicago: University of Chicago Press.

15. Brown, N. (2009). Robert Park and Ernest Burgess: Urban ecology studies, 1925. *Center for Spatially Integrated Social Science.* Retrieved from http://www.csiss.org/classics/content/26

16. Shaw, C. R., & McKay, H. D. (1942). *Juvenile delinquency in urban areas.* Chicago: University of Chicago Press.

17. Squires, G., & Kubrin, C. (2005). Privileged places: Race, uneven development and the geography of opportunity in urban America. *Urban Studies, 42,* 47–68.

18. Sampson, R. J., & Raudenbush, S. W. (2001, February). Disorder in urban neighborhoods—Does it lead to crime? *Research in Brief.* Washington, DC: National Institute of Justice, Office of Justice Programs, U.S. Department of Justice.

19. Skogan, W. G. (2001, September). *Public involvement: Community policing in Chicago.* Washington, DC: National Institute of Justice, Office of Justice Programs, U.S. Department of Justice.

20. Sampson & Raudenbush, 2001.

21. Byrne, J., & Sampson, R. (1985). *The social ecology of crime.* New York: Springer Verlag.

22. Wortley, R., & Mazerolle, L. (2008). *Environmental criminology and crime analysis.* UK: Willan.

23. Andresen, M. A. (2006). Crime measures and the spatial analysis of criminal activity. *British Journal of Criminology, 46*(2), 258–285.

24. Xu, Y., Fiedler, M. L., & Flaming, K. H. (2005). Discovering the impact of community policing: The broken windows thesis, collective efficacy, and citizens' judgment. *Journal of Research in Crime and Delinquency, 42*(2), 147–186.

25. Bartol, C. R., & Bartol, A. M. (2006). *Current perspectives in forensic psychology and criminal justice.* Thousand Oaks, CA: Sage.

26. Merton, R. K. (1938). Social structure and anomie. *American Sociological Review, 3*(5), 672–682.

27. Merton, R. K. (1996). On social structure and science: In P. Sztompka (Ed.), *Essays by Robert K. Merton.* Chicago: University of Chicago Press.

28. Ibid.; see also Merton, 1938.

29. Messner, S., & Rosenfeld, R. (2002). Crime and the American dream. In S. Cote (Ed.), *Criminological theories: Bridging the past to the future.* Thousand Oaks, CA: Sage.

30. Musgrave, J. (2008, December 12). Madoff's arrest in billion-dollar fraud case shocks Palm Beach investors. *Palm Beach Post.* Retrieved from http://www.palmbeachpost.com/localnews/content/local_news/epaper/2008/12/12/1212madoff.html

31. Creswell, J., & Thomas, L. (2009, January 24). The talented Mr. Madoff. *New York Times.* Retrieved from http://www.nytimes.com/2009/01/25/business/25bernie.html?em; McCool, G., & Honan, E. (2009, March 13). Madoff to appeal bail; net worth revealed. *Reuters.* Retrieved from http://www.reuters.com/article/managementIssues/idUSN1343149520090313

32. Agnew, R. (1992). Foundation for a general strain theory of crime and delinquency. *Criminology, 30*(1), 47–87.

33. Agnew, R. (2001). Building on the foundation of general strain theory: Specifying the types of strain most likely to lead to crime and delinquency. *Journal of Research in Crime and Delinquency, 38,* 319–361.

34. McCord, J., & Ensminger, M. E. (2003). Racial discrimination and violence: A longitudinal perspective. In D. F. Hawkins (Ed.), *Violent crime: Race and ethnic differences* (pp. 319–330). Cambridge, England: Cambridge University Press.

35. Wong, P. T. P., Wong, L. C. J., & Lonner, W. J. (2006). *Handbook of multicultural perspectives on stress and coping.* New York: Springer.

36. Sellin, T. (1938). *Culture conflict and crime.* New York: Social Science Research Council.

37. Najam, A., & Mughal, O. (2008, August 30). *Jahalat:* There is no honor in murder; criminality is not culture. *All Things Pakistan.* Retrieved from http://pakistaniat.com/2008/08/30/honor-honour-killing-pakistan/; Islam: Five women buried alive in "honor killing." (2008, August 19). *Atlas Shrugs.* Retrieved from http://atlasshrugs2000.typepad.com/atlas_shrugs/2008/08/islam-women-bur.html

38. Case study: Honor killings and blood feuds. (2008). *Gendercide Watch.* Retrieved from http://www.gendercide.org/case_honour.html

39. Hassan, Y. (1999, March 25). The fate of Pakistani women. *New York Times.* Retrieved from http://www.nytimes.com/1999/03/25/opinion/25iht-edhass.2.t.html

40. Miller, W. B. (1958). Lower class culture as a generating milieu of gang delinquency. *Journal of Social Issues, 14,* 5–19.

41. Anderson, E. (2003). *A place on the corner: A study of black street corner men* (2nd ed.). Chicago: University of Chicago Press.

42. Cohen, A. (1955). *Delinquent boys.* New York: Free Press.

43. Ibid.

44. Ferracuti, F., & Wolfgang, M. (1967). *The subculture of violence: Toward an integrated theory of criminology.* London: Tavistock.

45. Wolfgang, M. E. (1958). *Patterns in criminal homicide.* Philadelphia: University of Pennsylvania Press.

46. Ibid.; see also Cohen, 1955.

47. Dur, R. (2006). Status-seeking in violent subcultures and the double dividend of zero-tolerance. *Tinbergen Institute Discussion Papers* 06-005/1.

48. Cloward, R. A., & Ohlin, L. E. (1960). *Delinquency and opportunity: A theory of delinquent gangs.* Glencoe, IL: Free Press.

49. Mears, D. P., Scott, M., & Bhali, A. (2007). Opportunity theory and agricultural crime victimization. *Rural Sociology, 72,* 151–184.

50. Ibid.; see also Wolfgang, 1958.

51. John F. Kennedy: Remarks upon signing the Juvenile Delinquency and Youth Offenses Control Act. (2009). *The American Presidency Project.* Retrieved from http://www.presidency.ucsb.edu/ws/index.php?pid=8347

52. Vinovskis, M. A. (2005). *The birth of Head Start: Preschool education policies in the Kennedy and Johnson administrations.* Chicago: University of Chicago Press.

53. Sykes, G., & Matza, D. (1957). Techniques of neutralization: A theory of delinquency. *American Sociological Review, 22*(6), 664–670.

54. Matza, D., & Sykes, G. (1961). Juvenile delinquency and subterranean values. *American Sociological Review, 26*(5), 712–719.

55. Matza, D. (1964). *Delinquency and drift.* New York: Wiley.

56. Finley, L. L. (2007). *Encyclopedia of juvenile violence.* Westport, CT: Greenwood.

57. Decker, S. H., & Weerman, F. M. (Eds.). (2006). *European street gangs and troublesome youth groups.* Lanham, MD: AltaMira/Rowman & Littlefield.

58. Thornberry, T. P., Krohn, M. D., Smith, C. A., & Tobin, K. (2003). *Gangs and delinquency in developmental perspective.* Cambridge, England: Cambridge University Press.

59. Costello, B. J. (2000). Techniques of neutralization and self-esteem: A critical test of social control and neutralization theory. *Deviant Behavior, 21*(4), 301–329.

60. Pressner, L. (2003). Remorse and neutralization among violent male offenders. *Justice Quarterly, 20*(4), 801–825.

61. Wacquant, L. J. D., & Howe, J. (2007). *Urban outcasts: A comparative sociology of advanced marginality.* Cambridge, England: Polity.

62. Weitzer, R. J., & Tuch, S. A. (2005). Racially biased policing: Determinants of citizen perception. *Social Forces, 83*(3), 1009–1030.

63. Smith, M. R., & Alpert, J. P. (2007). Explaining police bias. *Criminal Justice and Behavior, 34*(10), 1262–1283.

64. Wareham, J., Cochran, J. K., Dembo, R., & Sellers, C. S. (2005). Community, strain, and delinquency: A test of a multi-level model of general strain theory. *Western Criminology Review, 6*(1), 117–133.

65. Moon, B., & Blurton, D. (2008). *General strain theory and delinquency: Focusing on the influences of strain characteristics.* Paper presented at the annual meeting of the American Society of Criminology, Royal York, Toronto, September 10.

66. Kornhauser, R. (1978). *Social sources of delinquency* (p. 29). Chicago: University of Chicago Press.

67. Kalkhoff, W. (2002). Delinquency and violence as affect-control: Reviving the subcultural approach in criminology. *Electronic Journal of Sociology* (special issue on affect control theory), *6*(3).

68. Elrod, P., & Ryder, R. S. (2005). *Juvenile justice: A social, historical, and legal perspective.* Sudbury, MA: Jones and Bartlett.

69. About Chicago Area Project. (n.d.). *Chicago Are Project.* Retrieved from http://www.chicagoareaproject.org/about.html (accessed June 16, 2009).

70. President Lyndon B. Johnson's Annual Message to the Congress on the State of the Union. (1964, January 8). Lyndon Baines Johnson Library and Museum. Retrieved from http://www.lbjlib.utexas.edu/johnson/archives.hom/speeches.hom/640108.asp

71. Lewis, O. (1998). The culture of poverty. *Society, 35*(2), 7.

72. *Weed & Seed.* (n.d.). National Institute of Justice, Office of Justice Programs, U.S. Department of Justice. Retrieved from http://www.ojp.usdoj.gov/ccdo/ws/welcome.html (accessed June 17, 2009).

73. *Weed and Seed performance measures: Analyzing and improving data resources.* (2006). Community Capacity Development Office, National Institute of Justice, Office of Justice Programs, U.S. Department of Justice. Retrieved from http://www.weedandseed.info/docs/studies_other/jrsa-performance-measures-final.pdf

74. Weisburd, D., Lum, C., & Yang, S.-M. (2004). *The criminal careers of places—A longitudinal study.* University of Maryland.

Chapter 9

1. Akers, R. L., & Silverman, A. (2004). Toward a social learning model of violence and terrorism. In M. A. Zahn, H. H. Brownstein, & S. L. Jackson (Eds.), *Violence: From theory to research.* Cincinnati: LexisNexis-Anderson.

2. Ibid.

3. Chambliss, W. J. (1988). *Exploring criminology.* New York: Macmillan.

4. Mohanty, J., Keokse, G., & Sales, E. (2006). Family cultural socialization, ethnic identity, and self-esteem: Web-based survey of international adult adoptees. *Journal of Ethnic and Cultural Diversity in Social Work, 15,* 153–172; Arnett, J. J. (1995). Adolescents' uses of media for self-socialization. *Journal of Youth and Adolescence, 24,* 519–533.

5. Long, T. E., & Hadden, J. K. (1985). A re-conception of socialization. *Sociological Theory, 3,* 39–49.

6. Arnon, S., Shamai, S., & Ilatov, Z. (2008). Socialization agents and activities of young adolescents. *Adolescence, 43,* 373–397.

7. Sutherland, E. (1939). *Principles of psychology* (3rd ed.). New York: Lippincott.

8. Ibid., p. 6.

9. Sutherland, E., & Cressey, D. (1970). *Criminology* (8th ed.). Philadelphia: Lippincott.

10. Hektner, J., August, G., & Realmuto, G. (2003). Effects of pairing aggressive and nonaggressive children in strategic peer affiliation. *Journal of Abnormal Child Psychology, 31,* 399–412.

11. Vowell, P., & Chen, J. (2004). Predicting academic misconduct: A comparative test for sociological explanations. *Sociological Inquiry, 74*, 226–249.

12. Thornberry, T., Freeman-Gallant, A., Lizotte, A., Krohn, M., & Smith, C. (2003). Linked lives: The intergenerational transmission of antisocial behavior. *Journal of Abnormal Child Psychology, 31*,171–184.

13. Hochstetler, A., Copes, H., & Delisi, M. (2002). Differential association in group and solo offending. *Journal of Criminal Justice, 30*, 559–566.

14. Burgess, R., & Akers, R. (1966). A differential association-reinforcement theory of criminal behavior. *Social Problems, 14*, 363–383.

15. Zaghlawan, H., Ostrosky, M. M., & Al-khateeb. J. M. (2007). Decreasing the inattentive behavior of Jordanian children: A group experiment. *Education and Treatment of Children, 30*, 49–64.

16. Hirschi, T. (1969). *Causes of delinquency.* Berkeley: University of California Press.

17. Glaser, D. (1960). Differential association and criminological prediction. *Social Problems, 8*, 6–14.

18. Ibid.

19. Tittle, C. R. (2000). *The nature of crime: Continuity and change.* Washington, DC: National Institute of Justice.

20. Reckless, W. C. (1967). *The crime problem* (4th ed.). New York: Appleton-Century-Crofts.

21. Ibid.

22. Vito, G. F., Maahs, J. R., & Holmes, R. M. (2006). *Criminology: Theory, research, and policy* (2nd ed.). Sudbury, MA: Jones and Bartlett.

23. Ibid.

24. Reckless, 1967.

25. Ibid.

26. Ibid.

27. Vito, Maahs, & Holmes, 2006; Reckless, 1967.

28. Hirschi, 1969.

29. Chriss, J. J. (2007). The functions of the social bond. *Sociological Quarterly, 48*, 689–712.

30. Ibid.

31. Garnier, H., & Stein, J. (2002). An 18-year model of family and peer effects on adolescence drug use and delinquency. *Journal of Youth and Adolescence, 31*, 45–56.

32. Maguin, E., & Loeber, R. (2003). Academic performance and delinquency. *Justice Review, 28*, 254–277.

33. Zaff, J., Moore, K., Papillo, A. R., & Williams, S. (2003). Implications of extracurricular activity participation during adolescence on positive outcome. *Journal of Adolescent Research, 18*, 599–631.

34. Hammond, T., & Emler, N. (2007). Attitudes, values, and moral reasoning as predictors of delinquency. *British Journal of Developmental Psychology, 25*, 169–183; Regnerus, M. (2003). Moral communities and adolescent delinquency: Religious contexts and community social control. *Sociological Quarterly, 44*, 523–554.

35. Behind the Enron scandal. (2002). *TIME.* http://www.time.com/time/2002/enron

36. Enron's Fastow gets six-year term. (2006, September 26). *BBC News.* http://news.bbc.co.uk/2/hi/business/5380394.stm.

37. Janus, E. S. (2004). The preventive state, terrorists, and sexual predators: Countering the threat of a new outsider jurisprudence. *Criminal Law Bulletin, 40*, 596–598.

38. Winick, B. J. (1998). Sex offender law in the 1990s: A therapeutic jurisprudence analysis. *Psychology, Public Policy, and Law, 4*, 505–570.

39. Becker, H. (1963). *Outsiders: Studies in the sociology of deviance.* New York: Free Press.

40. Ibid.

41. Schrag, C. (1971). *Crime and justice: American style* (pp. 90–92). Rockville, MD: National Institutes of Mental Health, U.S. Government Printing Office.

42. Becker, 1963.

43. Lemert, E. M. (1951). *Social pathology: A systematic approach to the theory of sociopathic behavior.* New York: McGraw-Hill.

44. Ibid.

45. Ibid.

46. Siegel, L. J. (2005). *Criminology* (9th ed.). Belmont, CA: Thomson Wadsworth.

47. Newburn, T. (2007). *Criminology.* UK: Willan.

48. Andersen, M. L., & Taylor, H. F. (2006). *Sociology: Understanding a diverse society.* Belmont, CA: Thomson Wadsworth.

49. Theories of deviance. (n.d.). Retrieved from http://fasnafan.tripod.com/theoriesofdeviance.pdf (accessed July 24, 2008); Martin, R., Mutchnick, R. J., & Austin, W. T. (1990). *Criminological thought: Pioneers past and present.* New York: Macmillan.

50. Chambliss, W. J. (1973). The Saints and the Roughnecks. *Society, 11*(1), 24–31.

51. Bauldry, S. (2006). *Positive support: Mentoring and depression among high-risk youth.* Washington, DC: Office of Juvenile Justice and Delinquency Prevention, U.S. Department of Justice.

52. Blank, S., & Davie, F. (2004). *Faith in their futures: The youth and congregations in partnership program of the Kings County.* New York: District Attorney's Office, National Faith-Based Field Report Series.

53. Ibid.

54. Goldstein, A., Hamm, K., & Schumacher, R. (2007). Supporting growth and development of babies in child care: What does the research say? Retrieved from http://www.clasp.org/admin/site/publications/files/0365.pdf

55. Bynum, J. E., & Thompson, W. E. (1996). The family and juvenile delinquency. *Juvenile Delinquency, 3,* 430.

56. Galaway, B., & Hudson, J. (1990). *Restorative justice: International perspectives.* Monsey, NY: Criminal Justice Press.

57. Columbine High School. (n.d.). *CNN online.* Retrieved from http://topics.cnn.com/topics/columbine_high_school

58. Ibid.

59. Ibid.

60. Ibid.

61. Ibid.

62. Dwyer, K., & Osher, D. (2000). *Safeguarding our children: An action guide.* Washington, DC: U.S. Departments of Education and Justice, American Institutes for Research; see also the Center for Effective Collaboration and Practice website at http://cecp.air.org/guide/actionguide/Action_Guide.asp

Chapter 10

1. Gray, M. (2009, July 14). The L.A. riots:15 years after Rodney King. *Time.* Retrieved from http://www.time.com/time/specials/2007/la_riot/article/0,28804,1614117_1614084_1614831,00.html

2. Charting the hours of chaos. (2002, April 29). *LA Times.* Retrieved from http://articles.latimes.com/2002/apr/29/local/me-replay29

3. Cannon, L. (1999). *Official negligence: How Rodney King and the riots changed Los Angeles and the LAPD.* New York: Basic Books.

4. Weitzer, R., & Tuch, S. (2002). Perceptions of racial profiling: Race, class and personal experience. *Criminology, 40,* 435–456.

5. Bazley, T., Lersch, K., Mieczkowski, T., & Reynolds, K. (2009). *Police on patrol: Neighborhood characteristics and variations in use of force.* Paper presented at the annual meeting of the American Society of Criminology, Royal York, Toronto.

6. Terrill, W., & Reisig, M. D. (2003). Neighborhood context and police use of force. *Journal of Research in Crime and Delinquency, 40*(3), 291–321.

7. Chambliss, W. J., & Seidman, R. (1971). *Law, order, and power.* Reading, MA: Addison-Wesley.

8. Hamid, M. (2001). *Moth smoke.* New York: Picador.

9. Birua, V. (2007). Crime and social control in Pakistani society. *Journal of Criminal Justice and Popular Culture, 14*(2), 227–236.

10. Chambliss, W. J. (1988). *Exploring criminology.* New York: Macmillan.

11. Ibid.

12. Holmes, D., Hughes, K., & Julian, R. (2003). *Australian sociology: A changing society.* Australia: Pearson Education.

13. Vold, G. (1958). *Theoretical criminology.* New York: Oxford University Press.

14. Ibid., p. 204.

15. Turk, A. (1969). *Criminality and the legal order* (p. xii). New York: Rand McNally.

16. Deflan, M. (2007). Sociological theories of law. In D. S. Clark (Ed.), *Encyclopedia of law and society: American and global perspectives.* Thousand Oaks, CA: Sage.

17. Sellin, T. (1938). *Culture, conflict and crime.* New York: Social Science Research Council.

18. Russell, S. (2002). The continuing relevance of Marxism to critical criminology. *Critical Criminology, 11,* 113–135.

19. Blundenden, A. (2004). *Marx/Engels selected works* (Vol. 1). Moscow, Russia: Progress Publishers.

20. Marx, K. (1887/2008). *Capital (Das Kapital).* Kindle ed. Misbach Enterprises.

21. Tucker, R. C. (1978). *The Marx-Engels reader* (2nd ed.). New York: Norton.

22. Marx, K., & Engels, F. (1887/1993). Crime and primitive accumulation. In D. F. Greenberg (Ed.), *Crime and capitalism: Readings in Marxist criminology.* Philadelphia: Temple University Press.

23. Engels, F. (1887/1993). The demoralization of the English working class. In D. F. Greenberg (Ed.), *Crime and capitalism: Readings in Marxist criminology.* Philadelphia: Temple University Press.

24. Bonger, W. (1916). *Criminality and economic conditions.* Boston: Little, Brown.

25. Gordon, B. (2009). Egoism and capitalism vs. altruism and communism. *The Atlas Society.* Retrieved from http://www.atlassociety.org/egoism-and-capitalism-vs-altruism-and-communism

26. Ibid.; see also Bonger, 1916.

27. Lynch, M. J., & Michalowski, R. (2006). *Primer in radical criminology: Critical perspectives on crime, power, and identity* (4th ed.). Monsey, NY: Criminal Justice Press.

28. Chambliss, W. J. (1993). On lawmaking. In W. J. Chambliss & M. S. Zatz (Eds.), *Making law:*

The state, the law, and structural contradictions. Bloomington: Indiana University Press.

29. For two articles on whether or not the crime-prevention policy behind Megan's Law is effective, see Welchans, S. (2005). Megan's Law: Evaluations of sexual offender registries. *Criminal Justice Policy Review, 16*(2), 123–140; Zgoba, K., Dalessandro, M., Veysey, B., & Witt, P. (2008). *Megan's Law: Assessing the practical and monetary efficacy.* Retrieved from http://www.ncjrs.gov/pdffiles1/nij/grants/225370.pdf

30. Chambliss, W. J., & Seidman, R. T. (1971). *Law, order, and power.* Reading, MA: Addison-Wesley.

31. Chambliss, W. J. (1978). Toward a political economy of crime. In C. Reasons & R. Rich (Eds.), *The sociology of law.* Toronto: Butterworth.

32. Chambliss, W. J. (1964). A sociological *analysis* of the law of vagrancy. *Social Problems, 12,* 67–77.

33. Chambliss, W. J. (2001). *Power, politics, and crime.* Oxford, England: Westview.

34. Reiman, J. (2009). *The rich get richer and the poor get prison* (9th ed.). Upper Saddle River, NJ: Prentice Hall.

35. Miller, L. (2006). *Interest groups and the Pennsylvania criminal law.* Paper presented at the annual meeting of the Law and Society Association, July 6, Baltimore, MD.

36. Young, J. (1986). The failure of criminology: The need for a radical realism. In R. Matthews & J. Young (Eds.), *Confronting crime.* Beverly Hills, CA: Sage.

37. Lea, J. (2002). *Crime and modernity: Continuities in left realist criminology.* London: Sage.

38. Tyler, T. R., & Huo, Y. J. (2002). *Trust in the law: Encouraging public cooperation with the police and court.* New York: Russell Sage Foundation.

39. Community policing defined. (2009). Office of Community Oriented Policing Services. U.S. Department of Justice, Washington, DC. Retrieved from http://www.cops.usdoj.gov/RIC/ResourceDetail.aspx?RID=513

40. Ahlin, E., Beckman, K., Gibbs, J., Gugino, M., & Varriale, J. (2007). *Trends in research on community policing 2000–2004: A review of the published literature.* Paper presented at the annual meeting of the American Society of Criminology, Atlanta, GA; Lurigio, A., & Rosenbaum, D. (1994). Community policing. *Crime and Delinquency, 40*(3); Skogan, W. G., & Steiner, L. (2004). *Community policing in Chicago, year 10: An evaluation of Chicago's alternative policing strategy.* Illinois Criminal Justice Information Authority. Retrieved from http://www.northwestern.edu/ipr/publications/policing_papers/Yr10-CAPSeval.pdf

41. Reiman, 2009.

42. Chambliss, 2001; Johnson, R. M. A. (2007). Racial bias in the criminal justice system and why we should care. *Criminal Justice* (Winter); Lynch, M., Patterson, E. B., & Childs, C. (2008). *Racial divide: Racial and ethnic bias in the criminal justice system.* Monsey, NY: Criminal Justice Press.

43. Pepinsky, H., & Quinney, R. (1991). *Criminology as peacemaking.* Bloomington: Indiana University Press.

44. Chesney-Lind, M. (2004). Beyond bad girls: Feminist perspectives on female offending. In C. Sumner (Ed.), *The Blackwell companion in criminology.* Oxford: Blackwell.

45. Hunnicutt, G., & Broidy, L. M. (2004). Liberation and economic marginalization: A reformulation and test of competing models. *Journal of Research in Crime and Delinquency, 41,* 130–155.

46. Chesney-Lind, M., & Pasko, L. (2004). *The female offender: Girls, women, and crime.* Thousand Oaks, CA: Sage.

47. Messerschmidt, J. W. (1986). *Capitalism, Patriarchy, and Crime: Toward a Socialist Feminist Criminology.* Totowa, NJ: Rowman & Littlefield.

48. Radical Women. (2001). *The Radical Women manifesto: Socialist feminist theory, program organization, and organizational structure.* Seattle: Red Letter Press.

49. Simpson, S. S. (2006). Caste, class, and violent crime: Explaining difference in female offending. *Criminology, 29*(1), 115–135.

50. Britton, D. M. (2003). Feminism in criminology: Engendering the outlaw. In M. Chesney-Lind & L. Pasko (Eds.), *Girls, women, and crime: Selected readings.* Thousand Oaks, CA: Sage.

51. Adler, F. (1975). *Sisters in crime: The rise of the new female criminal.* New York: McGraw-Hill.

52. Butterfield, F. (2003, December 29). Women find a new arena for equality: Prison. *New York Times,* p. A9.

53. Schwendinger, J. R., & Schwendinger, H. (1983). *Rape and inequality.* Newbury Park, CA: Sage.

54. Hunnicutt, G. (2009). Varieties of patriarchy and violence against women: Resurrecting patriarchy as a theoretical tool. *Violence Against Women, 15*(5), 553–573.

55. Miller, J. (2008). *Getting played: African American girls, urban inequality, and gendered violence.* New York: New York University Press.

56. Chesney-Lind & Pasko, 2004.

57. Siegel, J. A., & Williams, L. M. (2003). The relationship between child sexual abuse and female delinquency and crime: A prospective study. *Journal of Research in Crime and Delinquency, 40*(1), 71–94.

58. Garcia, C. A., & Lane, J. (2010). Looking in the rearview mirror: What incarcerated women think girls need from the system. *Feminist Criminology, 5*(3), 227–243.

59. Adler, 1975.

60. Simon, R. J. (1975). *Women and crime.* Lexington, MA: Lexington Books.

61. Daigle, L. E., Cullen, F. T., & Wright, J. P. (2007). Gender differences in the predictors of juvenile delinquency: Assessing the generality-specificity debate. *Youth Violence and Juvenile Justice, 5*(3), 254–286.

62. Miller, J., & Decker, S. H. (2001). Young women and gang violence: Gender, street offending, and violent victimization in gangs. *Justice Quarterly, 18,* 115–140; quote on p. 127.

63. Hagan, J. (1989). *Structural criminology.* New Brunswick, NJ: Rutgers University Press.

64. Blackwell, B. S. (2000). Perceived sanction threats, gender, and crime: A test and elaboration of power-control theory. *Criminology, 38,* 439–488.

65. Einstadter, W. J., & Henry, S. (2006). *Criminological theory: An analysis of underlying assumptions.* Lanham, MD: Rowman & Littlefield.

66. Daly, K. (2006). Feminist thinking about crime and justice. In S. Henry & M. Lanier (Eds.), *The essential criminology reader.* Boulder, CO: Westview.

67. Klockers, C. B. (1979). The contemporary crises of Marxist criminology. *Criminology, 16,* 477–515.

68. Akers, R. L., & Sellers, C. S. (2004). *Criminological theories: Introduction, evaluation, and application.* Los Angeles: Roxbury.

69. Balfour, G. (2006). Re-imagining a feminist criminology. *Canadian Journal of Criminology and Criminal Justice, 48*(5), 732–752.

70. Simpson, S. S., & Herz, D. C. (2006). Gender, crime and criminal justice. In J. S. Chafetz (Ed.), *Handbook of the sociology of gender.* New York: Springer.

71. Daly, K., & Chesney-Lind, M. (2002). Feminism and criminology. In S. Cote (Ed.), *Criminological theories: Bridging the past to the future.* Thousand Oaks, CA: Sage.

72. Kovandzic, T., & Vieraitis, L. (2006). The effect of county-level prison population growth on crime rates. *Criminology and Public Policy, 5,* 213–244.

73. Taylor, M. L. (2001). *The executed God: The way of the cross in lockdown America.* Minneapolis, MN: Fortress.

74. Dorne, C. K. (2008). *Restorative justice in the United States.* Upper Saddle River, NJ: Pearson/Prentice Hall.

75. Burkemper Jr., T. B., Balsam, N., & Yeh, M. (2007). Restorative justice in Missouri's juvenile system. *Journal of the Missouri Bar,* May–June.

76. What is restorative justice? (n.d.). *Centre for Restorative Justice.* Retrieved from http://www.sfu.ca/crj/introrj.html (accessed September 1, 2009).

77. Bazemore, G., & Schiff, M. (2005). *Juvenile justice reform and restorative justice: Building theory and policy from practice.* Portland, OR: Willan.

78. Bonta, J., Wallace-Capretta, S. , Rooney, J., & McAnoy, K. (2002). An outcome evaluation of a restorative justice alternative to incarceration. *Contemporary Justice Review, 5,* 319–338.

Chapter 11

1. DeVita, A. (2007, September 11). *Domestic violence no more.* Retrieved from http://domesticviolencenomore.com/2007/09/11/domestic-violence-cases.aspx

2. *How widespread is intimate partner violence?* (2007, October 24). National Institute of Justice, Office of Justice Programs, U.S. Department of Justice. Retrieved from http://www.ojp.gov/nij/topics/crime/intimate-partner-violence/extent.htm

3. Tjaden, P., & Thoennes, N. (2000). *Full report of the prevalence, incidence, and consequences of violence against women.* Washington, DC: National Institute of Justice, Office of Justice Programs, U.S. Department of Justice.

4. Schewe, P., Riger, S., Howard, A., Staggs, S. L., & Mason, G. E. (2006). Factors associated with domestic violence and sexual assault victimization. *Journal of Family Violence, 21*(7), 469–475.

5. Campbell, J. C., Webster, D., Koziol-McLain, J., Block, C. R., Campbell, D., Curry, M. A., Gary, F., McFarlane, J., Sachs, C., Sharps, P., Ulrich, Y., & Wilt, S. A. (2003). *Assessing risk factors for intimate partner homicide.* Washington, DC: National Institute of Justice, Office of Justice Programs, U.S. Department of Justice, National Criminal Justice Reference Service.

6. Denise Amber Lee missing since January 17, 2008 from North Port Florida . . . abducted by Michael Lee King. (2007). *Scared Monkeys Missing Persons Site.* Retrieved from http://missingexploited.com/2008/01/19/denise-amber-lee-missing-since-january-17-2008-from-north-port-fl-abducted-by-michael-lee-king/

7. Van Derbeken, J. (2008, October 1). Murder verdict in case that "shook up" S.F. Retrieved from http://www.sfgate.com/cgi-bin/article.cgi?f=/c/a/2008/10/01/BAAA138OQS.DTL

8. Hannon, L. (2004). Race, victim precipitated homicide, and the subculture of violence thesis. *Social Science Journal, 41*(1), 115–121; Wolfgang, M., & Ferracuti, F. (1982). *The subculture of violence: Towards an integrated theory in criminology.* Beverly Hills, CA: Sage.

9. WSMV Nashville. (2006). Police say Opry Mills shooting involved rival gangs. Retrieved from http://www.wsmv.com/news/9524371/detail.html

10. Cohen, A. K. (1955). *Delinquent boys: The culture of the gang.* Glencoe, IL: Free Press.

11. Anderson, E. (1999). *Code of the street: Decency, violence and the moral life of the inner city.* New York: Norton.

12. Jankowski, M. S. (1991). *Islands in the streets.* Berkeley and Los Angeles: University of California Press.

13. Administrator Flores reflects on 6 years of progress in juvenile justice. (2009). *OJJDP News at a Glance,* January/February. Retrieved from http://www.ncjrs.gov/html/ojjdp/news_at_glance/225359/pfv.html; Rosenfeld, R. (2008). *Understanding homicide and aggravated assault.* Presentation at the Conference on the Causes and Responses to Violence, Arizona State University; New program supports community anti-gang efforts. (2003). *OJJDP News at a Glance,* September/October. Retrieved from http://www.ncjrs.gov/html/ojjdp/news_at_glance/201826//; Harries, K. D. (1997). *Serious violence: Patterns of homicide and assault in America.* Springfield, IL: Thomas.

14. Athens, L. (2005). Violent encounters, violent engagements, skirmishes, and tiffs. *Journal of Contemporary Ethnography, 34*(6), 631–678.

15. Smith, D., & Parker, R. N. (1980). Types of homicide and variation in regional rates. *Social Forces, 59,* 136–147.

16. Miethe, T. D., & Drass, K. A. (1999). Exploring the social context of instrumental and expressive homicides: An application of qualitative comparative analysis. *Journal of Quantitative Criminology, 15,* 3.

17. Salfati, C. G., & Taylor, P. (2006). Differentiating sexual violence: A comparison of sexual homicide and rape. *Psychology, Crime, and Law, 12,* 107–126.

18. Miller, M., Azrael, D., & Hemenway, D. (2007). Homicide victimization of Americans in relation to household firearm ownership, by age and gender. *Social Science and Medicine, 64,* 656–664.

19. Hepburn, L., & Hemenway, D. (2004). Firearm availability and homicide: A review of the literature. *Aggression and Violent Behavior: A Review Journal, 9,* 417–440.

20. Hepburn, L., Miller, M., Azrael, D., & Hemenway, D. (2007). The US gun stock: results from the 2004 National Firearms Survey. *Injury Prevention, 13,* 15–19.

21. Povey, D., Coleman, K., Kaiza, P., & Roe, S. (2009). Homicides, firearm offences, and intimate violence 2007/08. *Home Office Statistical Bulletin.* Retrieved from http://www.homeoffice.gov.uk/rds/pdfs09/hosb0209.pdf (accessed January 30, 2009).

22. The U.S. compared to other nations. (2003). Centers for Disease Control, Special Committee on Gun Violence. Retrieved from http://www.abanet.org/gunviol/factsaboutgunviolence/uscompared.shtml (accessed January 30, 2009).

23. Hemenway, D., Shinoda-Tagawa, T., & Miller, M. (2002). Firearm availability and female homicide victimization rates across 25 populous high-income countries. *Journal of the American Medical Women's Association, 57,* 100–104; Hepburn & Hemenway, Firearm availability and homicide; Miller, M., Azrael, D., & Hemenway, D. (2002). Household firearm ownership levels and homicide rates across U.S. regions and states, 1988–1997. *American Journal of Public Health, 92,* 1988–1993; Miller, Azrael, & Hemenway, Homicide victimization of Americans; Squires, P. (2000). *Gun culture or gun control? Firearms, violence and society.* New York: Routledge.

24. Fox, J. A., & Levin, J. (1998). Multiple homicide: Patterns of serial and mass murder. *Crime and Justice: A Review of Research, 23,* 407–455.

25. Egger, S. A. (2002). *Killers among us.* Upper Saddle River, NJ: Prentice Hall.

26. Ferguson, C., White, D., Cherry, S., Lorenz, M., & Bhimani, Z. (2003). Defining and classifying serial murder in the context of perpetrator motivation. *Journal of Criminal Justice, 31,* 287–293.

27. Hickey, E. W. (2005). *Serial murderers and their victims.* Belmont, CA: Wadsworth.

28. Fleming, T. (1996). *Serial and mass murder: Theory, research, and policy.* Toronto: Canadian Scholars Press.

29. Fox, J. A., & Levin, J. (1996). *Overkill: Mass murder and serial killing exposed.* New York: Plenum.

30. Fox, J. A., Levin, J., & Quinet, K. (2005). *The will to kill: Making sense of senseless murder.* New Jersey: Allyn & Bacon.

31. Garbarino, J. (1999). *Lost boys: Why our sons turn violent and how we can save them.* New York: Free Press.

32. Harries, K. (1989). Homicide and assault: A comparative analysis of attributes in Dallas neighborhoods, 1981–1985. *Professional Geographer, 41,* 29–38.

33. Miethe, T. D., McCorkle, R. C., & Listwan, S. (2006). *Crime profiles: The anatomy of dangerous persons, places, and situations.* Los Angeles: Roxbury.

34. Ibid.

35. *Stalking victimization in the United States.* (2009). Washington, DC: Bureau of Justice Statistics, U.S. Department of Justice.

36. Riedel, M., & Przybylski, R. K. (1993). Stranger murders and assault: A study of a neglected form of stranger violence. In A. V. Wilson (Ed.), *Homicide: The victim/offender connection.* Cincinnati: Anderson.

37. Straus, M. A. (1990). The National Family Violence Surveys. In M. A. Straus & R. K. Gelles (Eds.), *Physical violence in American families: Risk factors and adaptations to violence in 8,145 families.* New Brunswick, NJ: Transaction.

38. Straus, M. A., & Gelles, R. J. (1988). How violent are American families? Estimates from the National Family Violence Research and other studies. In G. Hotaling (Ed.), *New directions in family violence research.* Newbury Park, CA: Sage.

39. Humphreys, C., Mullender, A., Thiara, R., & Skamballis, A. (2006). "Talking to my mum": Developing communication between mothers and children in the aftermath of domestic violence. *Journal of Social Work, 6,* 53–63.

40. Dobash, R. E., & Dobash, R. P. (1992). *Women, violence, and social change.* London: Routledge.

41. Watts, C., & Zimmerman, C. (2002). Violence against women: Global scope and magnitude. *Lancet, 359,* 1232–1237.

42. Walker, L. E. (1979). *The battered woman.* New York: Harper & Row.

43. Definition of child maltreatment. (n.d.). *U. S. Department of Health and Human Services, Centers for Disease Control and Prevention.* Retrieved from http://www.cdc.gov/ncipc/dvp/cmp/CMP-def.htm (accessed January 16, 2009).

44. Child Welfare Information Gateway. (2007). U.S. Department of Health and Human Services, Administration for Children & Families. Retrieved from http://www.childwelfare.gov/

45. Smith, M. G., & Fond, R. (2004). *The children of neglect.* New York: Brunner-Routledge.

46. Botash, A. S. (2008, July 2). Pediatrics: Child sexual abuse. WebMD. Retrieved from http://emedicine.medscape.com/article/800770-overview

47. Glaser, D. (2002). Emotional abuse and neglect (psychological maltreatment): A conceptual framework. *Child Abuse & Neglect, 26,* 697–714.

48. Child maltreatment 2006. (n.d.). U.S. Department of Health and Human Services, Administration for Children and Families. Retrieved from http://www.acf.hhs.gov/programs/cb/pubs/cm06/summary.htm (accessed January 6, 2009).

49. Miethe, McCorkle, & Listwan, 2006.

50. Spohn, C. C., Beichner, D., & Davis-Frenzel, E. (2001). Prosecutorial justifications for sexual assault case rejection. *Social Problems, 48,* 206–235.

51. Monroe, L., Kinney, L., Weist, M., Dafeamekpor, D. S., Dantzler, J., & Reyonlds, M. (2005). The experience of sexual assault: Findings from a statewide victim needs assessment. *Journal of Interpersonal Violence, 20,* 767–776.

52. The FAQ: Rape shield laws. (2007). National Center for Victims of Crime. Retrieved from http://www.ncvc.org/ncvc/main.aspx?dbID=DB_FAQ:RapeShieldLaws927; Spohn, C., & Horney, J. (1992). *Rape law reform: A grassroots revolution and its impact.* New York: Plenum.

53. Wyatt, K. (2008, May 13). Anonymous rape tests are going nationwide: New law may help traumatized women seek justice later. *ABC News.* Retrieved from http://abcnews.go.com/Health/story?id=4847901&page=1

54. Acquaintance rape. (2008). National Center for Victims of Crime. Retrieved from http://www.ncvc.org/ncvc/main.aspx?dbName=DocumentViewer&DocumentID=32306

55. Koss, M. P., Gidycz, C. J., & Wisniewski, N. (1987). The scope of rape: Sexual aggression and victimization in a national sample of students in higher education. *Journal of Consulting and Clinical Psychology, 55,* 162–170.

56. Fisher, B. S., Cullen, F. T., & Turner, M. G. (2000). *The sexual victimization of college women.* Washington, DC: National Institute of Justice and Bureau of Justice Statistics, U.S. Department of Justice.

57. Rohypnol. (2003, February). Fact sheet: Drug policy information clearinghouse. Executive Office of the President, Office of National Drug Control Policy. Retrieved from http://dvusd.org/assets/pdfs/rohypnol.pdf

58. Sanday, P. R. (2007). *Fraternity gang rape.* New York: New York University Press.

59. Armstrong, E., Hamilton, L., & Sweeney, B. (2005, August 12). *Hooking up and party rape: The social organization of gender and sexuality at a large research university.* Paper presented at the annual meeting of the American Sociological Association, Philadelphia.

60. Schwartz, M., & DeKeseredy, W. (1997). *Sexual assault on the college campus: The role of male peer support.* Thousand Oaks, CA: Sage.

61. Bergen, R. K. (2005). Studying wife rape: Reflections on the past, present and future. *Violence Against Women, 10,* 1407–1416.

62. Bennice, J., & Resick, P. (2003). Marital rape: History, research and practice. *Trauma, Violence and Abuse, 4,* 228–246.

63. Sanday, P. R. (2007). *Fraternity gang rape.* New York: New York University Press.

64. Ullman, S. (2008, December 12). *Comparing gang and individual rape incident characteristics in a large sample of urban women.* Paper presented at the annual meeting of the American Society of Criminology, Royal York, Toronto.

65. Vetten, L., & Haffajee, S. (2005). Gang rape: A study in inner-city Johannesburg. *SA Crime Quarterly,* 12.

66. Sampson, R. (2003). *Acquaintance rape of college students.* Washington, DC: U.S. Department of Justice, Office of Community Oriented Policing Services (COPS). Retrieved from http://www.cops.usdoj.gov/pdf/e03021472.pdf

67. Sawyer, R. G., Thompson, E. E., & Chicorelli, A. M. (2002). Rape myth acceptance among intercollegiate student athletes. *American Journal of Health Studies,* Winter; Brown, T. J., Sumner, K. E., & Nocera, R. (2002). Understanding sexual aggression against women: An examination of the role of men's athletic participation and related variables. *Journal of Interpersonal Violence, 17*(9), 937–952.

68. Koss, Gidycz, & Wisniewski, 1987.

69. McMahon, S. (2004). *Student-athletes, rape-supportive culture, and social change.* New Jersey: Department of Sexual Assault Services and Crime Victim Assistance, Rutgers, the State University of New Jersey.

70. Girshick, L. (2002). *Woman to woman sexual violence: Does she call it rape?* Boston: Northeastern University Press.

71. Scarce, M. (2002). *Male on male rape: The hidden toll of stigma and shame.* Cambridge, MA: Da Capo.

72. Ibid.

73. Groth, N. (1979). *Men who rape: The psychology of the offender.* New York: Plenum.

74. Hazelwood, R. R., & Burgess, A. N. (1995). *Practical aspects of rape investigation: A multidisciplinary approach.* New York: CRC Press.

75. Stevens, D. J. (1999). *Inside the mind of a serial rapist.* San Francisco: Austin and Winfield.

76. Ryan, K. (2004). Further evidence for a cognitive component of rape. *Aggression and Violent Behavior, 9*(6), 579–604.

77. Johansson-Love, J., & Greer, J. H. (2003). Investigation of attitude change in a rape prevention programme. *Journal of Interpersonal Violence, 18*(1), 84–99.

78. Miethe, McCorkle, & Listwan, 2006.

79. Federal Bureau of Investigation. (2007, June). *Crime in the United States, 2006.* Washington, DC: U.S. Department of Justice.

80. Ibid.

81. *National crime victimization survey, 2005.* (2006). Washington, DC: Bureau of Justice Statistics, U.S. Department of Justice.

82. Erickson, R. (2003). *Teenage robbers: How and why they rob.* San Diego: Athena Research Corporation.

83. Weisel, D. L. (2007). Bank robbery. Problem-oriented guides for police. *Problem-specific guides series 48.* Washington, DC: U.S. Department of Justice, Office of Community Oriented Policing Services.

84. Willis, K. (2006). Armed robbery: Who commits it and why? *Trends and Issues in Crime and Criminal Justice,* 348.

85. Miethe, McCorkle, & Listwan, 2006.

86. Matthews, R. (2002). *Armed robbery.* Portland, OR: Willan.

87. Wright, R. T., & Decker, S. H. (1997). *Armed robbers in action: Stickups and street culture.* Boston: Northeastern University Press.

88. Miller, J. (1998). Up it up: Gender and the accomplishment of street robbery. *Criminology, 1,* 37–66.

89. Di Tella, R., Galiani, S., & Schargrodsky, E. (2003). Crime inequality: When victims adapt. Retrieved from http://www.sedici.unlp.edu.ar?id=ARG-UNLP-ART-0000000201

90. Willis, 2006.

91. Feeney, F. (1986). Robbers as decision-makers. In D. B. Cornish & R. V. Clarke, *The reasoning criminal: Rational choice perspectives in offending* (pp. 53–71). New York: Springer-Verlag.

92. Jacobs, B. A., & Wright, R. (2006). Street justice: Retaliation in the criminal underworld. *British Journal of Sociology, 58,* 506–507.

93. Jacobs, B. A., & Wright, R. (2008). Moralistic street robbery. *Crime and Delinquency, 54*(4), 511–531.

94. Federal Bureau of Investigation. (2006). *Hate crime statistics.* Washington, DC: Author.

95. Herek, G. M., Cogan, J. C., & Gillis, J. R. (2002). Victim experiences in hate crimes based on sexual orientation. *Journal of Social Issues, 58,* 319–341.

96. Boeckmann, R. B., & Liew, J. (2002). Speech: Asian American students' justice judgments and psychological responses. *Journal of Social Issues, 58,* 363–381.

97. Public favors expansion of hate crime law to include sexual orientation. (2007, May 17).

Retrieved from http://www.gallup.com/poll/27613/Public-Favors-Expansion-Hate-Crime-Law-Include-Sexual-Orientation.aspx

Chapter 12

1. Miethe, T., McCorkle, R. C., & Listwan, S. H. (2006). *Crime profiles: The anatomy of dangerous persons, places, and situations.* Los Angeles: Roxbury.

2. Shover, N. (1996). *Great pretenders: Pursuits and careers of persistent thieves.* Boulder, CO: Westview.

3. King, H., & Chambliss, W. J. (2004). *Harry King: A professional thief's journey.* Bloomington, IN: iUniverse.

4. Jacobs, B. A., & Wright, R. (2006). Stick up: Street culture and offender motivation. *Criminology, 37*(1), 149–171.

5. King & Chambliss, 2004.

6. Greenberg, M. S., & Beach, S. R. (2004). Property crime victims' decision to notify the police: Social, cognitive, and affective determinations. *Law and Behavior Journal, 28,* 2; Fleisher, M. S. (1995). *Beggars and thieves: Lives of urban street criminals.* Madison: University of Wisconsin Press.

7. Federal Bureau of Investigation. (2004). *Uniform crime report handbook.* Washington, DC: U.S. Department of Justice.

8. Clark, D. S. (2007). *Encyclopedia of law and society: American and global prospectives, 3,* 1478–1479; LaFave, W. R., & Scott, A. W. (1972). *Handbook on criminal law.* St. Paul, MN: West.

9. FBI, *Uniform crime report handbook,* 2004.

10. *Criminal victimization in the United States, 2006.* (2008). National Crime Victimization Survey, Bureau of Justice Statistics, U.S. Department of Justice. Retrieved from http://bjs.ojp.usdoj.gov/content/pub/pdf/cvus06.pdf

11. Visser, M. S., Harbaugh, W. T., & Mocan, N. H. (2006). An experimental test of criminal behavior among juveniles and young adults. *National Bureau of Economic Research,* NBER Working Papers 12507; Cornish, D., & Clarke, R. V. (Eds.). (1986). *The reasoning criminal.* New York: Springer-Verlag.

12. McKay, M. J. (2002, November 7). Addicted: Shoplifting for thrills. *CBS News.com/48 Hours Mystery.* Retrieved from http://www.cbsnews.com/stories/2002/10/17/48hours/main525948.shtml; Dolan, A. (2007, October 12). Hunt for millionaire shoplifter who made £1,000 a day from forged till receipts. *Mail Online.* Retrieved from http://www.dailymail.co.uk/news/article-487277/Hunt-millionaire-shoplifter-1-000-day-forged-till-receipts.html

13. Howsen, R. M., & Jerrell, S. B. (2009). Some determinants of property crime: Economic factors influence criminal behavior but cannot completely explain the syndrome. *American Journal of Economics and Sociology, 46*(4), 445–457; Shover, N., & Honaker, D. (1992). The socially bounded decision making of persistent property offenders. *Howard Journal, 31,* 4.

14. Dabney, D., Hollinger, R., & Dugan, L. (2004). Who actually steals? A study of covertly observed shoplifters. *Justice Quarterly, 21*(4), 106–136.

15. National Association for Shoplifting Prevention. (2006). *Shoplifting Statistics.* Retrieved from http://www.shopliftingprevention.org/WhatNASPOffers/NRC/PublicEducStats.htm; Klemke, L. W., & Egger, S. A. (1992). *The sociology of shoplifting: Boosters and snitches today.* Westport, CT: Praeger.

16. What do people shoplift? (2005, November 28). *BBC News.* Retrieved from http://news.bbc.co.uk/2/hi/uk_news/magazine/4477596.stm; Cameron, M. O. (1964). *The booster and the snitch: Department store shoplifting.* Glencoe, NY: Free Press.

17. Berlin, P. (2006). Why do shoplifters steal? *National Association for Shoplifting Prevention.* Retrieved from http://www.shopliftingprevention.org/whatnaspoffers/nrc.htm; Klemke & Egger, 1992.

18. Kivivouri, J. (1998). Delinquent phases: The case of temporally intensified shoplifting behavior. *British Journal of Criminology, 38,* 663–680.

19. Robertson, D. (2007, December 26). Every credit card purchase leaves consumers at risk. *The Times.* Retrieved from http://www.timesonline.co.uk/tol/money/consumer_affairs/article3095536.ece.

20. Hoffman, S. (2009, January 21). Heartland data breach could leave 100 million accounts exposed. *CRN/ChannelWeb.* Retrieved from http://www.crn.com/security/212901821;jsessionid=1OM234F2QQZDOQSNDLOSKHSCJUNN2JVN

21. Sidden, K., & Simmons, D. (2005, October 1). How to control the technology that causes payment fraud. *American City & County.* Retrieved from http://americancityandcounty.com/mag/government_banking_security/

22. Check fraud prevention. (2008). *National Check Fraud Center.* Retrieved from http://www.ckfraud.org/ckfraud.html

23. Embezzlement. (2010). *Cornell University Law School, Legal Information Institute.* Retrieved from http://topics.law.cornell.edu/wex/embezzlement

24. Schwartz, L. B., & Kahan, D. M. (2009). Theft—False pretenses and fraud. Retrieved from http://www.law.jrank.org/pages/2190/Theft-False-pretenses-fraud.html

25. Prentice, R. A. (1993). Anatomy of a fraud: Inside the finances of the PTL ministries, *American Business Law Journal, 31*(3), 519–534.

26. The "Nigerian" scam: Costly compassion. (2003, July). Federal Trade Commission. Retrieved from http://www.ftc.gov/bcp/edu/pubs/consumer/alerts/alt117.shtm

27. Scammers with religion reporting on the latest frauds, scams, fake lotteries, spams, and hoaxes. (2009). *Consumer Fraud Reporting.* Retrieved from http://www.consumerfraudreporting.org/AFFreligion.php

28. Shapiro, D. M. (2010). The Angola lonely hearts club. *Biloxi Confidential.* Retrieved from http://www.trutv.com/library/crime/notorious_murders/classics/dd_biloxi_confidential/11.html

29. What is a Ponzi scheme? (n.d.). U.S. Securities and Exchange Commission. Retrieved from http://www.sec.gov/answers/ponzi.htm (accessed August10, 2010).

30. Warrell, H. (2007, June 12). Four jailed after £1m fraud. *Third Sector Online.* Retrieved from http://www.thirdsector.co.uk/news/Article/663705/four-jailed-1m-fraud/

31. New developments in Travolta extortion case. (2009, January 29). *FoxNews.com.* Retrieved from http://www.foxnews.com/story/0,2933,484904,00.html

32. Wood, S. (2009, April 30). 87-month term in insurance scam. *Philly.com.* Retrieved from http://articles.philly.com/keyword/insurance-fraud/recent/3

33. Schultz, J. (2009, April 23). Detectives bust major fencing operation. *PalmBeachPost.com.* Retrieved from http://findarticles.com/p/news-articles/palm-beach-post/mi_8163/is_20090423/detectives-bust-major-fencing-operation/ai_n52015356/

34. NRF says online auctions drawing amateurs into organized retail crime. (2008, September 22). *National Retail Federation.* Retrieved from http://www.nrf.com/modules.php?name=News&op=viewlive&sp_id=572

35. Steffensmeier, D., & Ulmer, J. (2005). *Confessions of a dying thief: Understanding criminal careers and illegal enterprise.* Piscataway, NJ: Transaction-Aldine.

36. Federal Bureau of Investigation. (2008). *Crime in the United States, 2007.* U.S. Department of Justice. Retrieved from http://www2.fbi.gov/ucr/cius2007/data/table_01.html

37. Frederickson, A. (2007, February 9). Gender, social networks, and residential burglary. *Associated Content.* Retrieved from http://www.associatedcontent.com/article/139878/gender_social_networks_and_residential_pg2.html?cat=4

38. Mullins, C. W., & Wright, R. (2003). Gender, social networks, and residential burglary. *Criminology, 41*(3), 813–840.

39. *2009 safety and security reporting manual.* (2009). Retrieved from http://www.ntdprogram.gov/ntdprogram/pubs/safetyRM/2009/pdf/2009_S&S_Monthly_Summary_Report_form_S&S-50.pdf

40. Koppel, H. (1987). *Lifetime likelihood of victimization.* Washington, DC: Bureau of Justice Statistics, U.S. Department of Justice.

41. *Property crime rates: Key facts at a glance.* (2011). Bureau of Justice Statistics, National Institute of Justice, Office of Justice Programs, U.S. Department of Justice. Retrieved from http://bjs.ojp.usdoj.gov/content/glance/house2.cfm

42. National crime victimization survey resource guide. (2010). *National Archive of Criminal Justice Data.* Retrieved from http://www.icpsr.umich.edu/NACJD/NCVS/

43. Police recorded crime. (2010). *UK Home Office.* Retrieved from http://www.homeoffice.gov.uk/rds/recordedcrime1.html

44. *World Factbook 2002.* Retrieved from http://www.faqs.org/docs/factbook/print/uk.html

45. The Prolific and Other Priority Offenders Strategy. *Home Office Crime Reduction,* 2008. Retrieved from http://www.crimereduction.homeoffice.gov.uk/ppo/ppominisite01.htm

46. Lo, C. C., Kim, Y. S., & Cheng, T. C. (2008). Offense specialization of arrestees. *Crime and Delinquency, 54*(3), 341–365.

47. Maguire, M. (1982). *Burglary in a dwelling.* London: Heinemann.

48. Artinfo. (2008, August 7). U.K. crime family convicted and sentenced for £82.5 million art burglaries. *ArtInfo.com.* Retrieved from http://www.artinfo.com/news/story/28262/uk-crime-family-convicted-and-sentenced-for-825-million-art-burglaries/

49. Cromwell, P., & Olson, J. N. (2004). *Breaking and entering: Burglars on burglary.* Belmont, CA: Wadsworth.

50. Vaughn, M. G., DeLisi, M., Beaver, K. M., & Howard, M. O. (2008). Toward a quantitative typology of burglars: A latent profile analysis of career offenders. *Journal of Forensic Sciences, 53*(6), 1387–1392; Tunnell, K. D. (1992). *Choosing crime: The criminal calculus of property offenders.* Chicago: Nelson-Hall.

51. Samaha, J. (2005). *Criminal justice.* Belmont, CA: Wadsworth; Cromwell, P., Olson, J. N., & Avary, D. W. (1992). *Breaking and entering: An ethnographic analysis of burglary.* Newbury Park, CA: Sage.

52. Vaughn et al., 2008; Wright, R., & Decker, S. (1996). *Burglars on the job: Streetlife and residential break-ins.* Boston: Northeastern University Press.

53. Cromwell, P., & Olson, J. N. (2004). *Breaking and entering: Burglars on burglary.* Belmont, CA: Wadsworth.

54. Decker, S., Wright, R., & Logie, R. (2006). Perceptual deterrence among active residential burglars. *Criminology, 31*(1), 135–147.

55. Pyle, R. (2009, January 27). Teen: Breaking in while people slept a thrill. *Avalanche-Journal.* Retrieved from http://www.lubbockonline.com/stories/012709/loc_381901271.shtml

56. Sanders, B. (2005). *Youth crime and youth culture in the inner city.* New York: Routledge.

57. Yao, T. (2007, November 13). *An examination of routine activities in urban residential burglary.* Paper presented at the annual meeting of the American Society of Criminology, Atlanta. Retrieved from http://www.allacademic.com/meta/p201461_index.html; Clarke, R. V., & Felson, M. (1993). *Routine activity and rational choice: Advances in criminological theory* (Vol. 5). New Brunswick, NJ: Transaction.

58. Padovano, D. (2008, September 29). Arrest made in dorm burglary case. *Syracuse.Com.* Retrieved from http://www.syracuse.com/news/index.ssf/2008/09/arrest_made_in_dorm_burglary_c.html

59. Robinson, M. B., & Robinson, C. E. (1997). Environmental characteristics associated with residential burglaries of student apartment complexes. *Environment and Behavior, 29*(5), 657–675.

60. Brantingham, P. L., & Brantingham, P. J. (1993). Environment, routine, and situation: Toward a pattern theory of crime. In R. V. Clarke & M. Felson (Eds.), *Routine activities and rational choice: Advances in criminological theory* (Vol. 5). New Brunswick, NJ: Transaction.

61. Atlas, R. (Ed.). (2008). 21st century security and CPTED: Designing for critical infrastructure protection and crime prevention. New York: Taylor & Francis.

62. Motor vehicle theft. (2004). *Crime in the United States, 2004.* Federal Bureau of Investigation, U.S. Department of Justice. Retrieved from http://www2.fbi.gov/ucr/cius_04/offenses_reported/property_crime/motor_vehicle_theft.html

63. *Criminal victimization in the United States, 2006.* (2008). National Crime Victimization Survey, Bureau of Justice Statistics, U.S. Department of Justice. Retrieved from http://bjs.ojp.usdoj.gov/content/pub/pdf/cvus06.pdf

64. Zickefoose, S. (2009). Bait cars put major dent into Calgary auto theft. *Canada.com.* Retrieved from http://www2.canada.com/cars/story.html?id=1370129; Harlow, C. W. (1988). *Motor vehicle theft.* Washington, DC: Bureau of Justice Statistics, U.S. Department of Justice.

65. Miethe, McCorkle, & Listwan, 2006.

66. Kellett, S., & Gross, H. (2006). Addicted to joyriding? An exploration of young offenders' accounts of their car crime. *Psychology, Crime and Law, 12*(1), 39–60.

67. Gottfredson, M., & Hirschi, T. (1990). *A general theory of crime.* Stanford, CA: Stanford University Press.

68. Stauffer, E., & Bonfanti, M. S. (2006). *Forensic investigation of stolen-recovered and other crime-related vehicles.* Oxford: Academic Press.

69. Miethe, McCorkle, & Listwan, 2006.

70. De Vries, L. (2007, August 2). N.J. cops bust high-end car theft ring. Luxury vehicles were to be shipped to Europe, Mideast, West Africa; some had been carjacked. *CBSNews.com.* Retrieved from http://www.cbsnews.com/stories/2007/08/02/national/main3126238.shtml?source=RSSattr=HOME_3126238; Blake, K. (1995). What you should know about car theft. *Consumer's Research,* October, 23–27.

71. Miethe, McCorkle, & Listwan, 2006.

72. Ibid.

73. FBI, *Crime in the United States, 2007,* 2008.

74. Brownlee, K. (2000). Ignoring juvenile arson is like playing with fire. *Claims, 48,* 3.

75. FBI, *Crime in the United States, 2007,* 2008.

76. *Fire and arson scene evidence: A guide for public safety personnel.* (2000). Technical Working Group on Fire/Arson Scene Investigation. Retrieved from http://www.ncjrs.gov/pdffiles1/nij/181584.pdf

77. Federal Bureau of Investigation (2008). *Crime in the United States, 2007: Arson.* Bureau of Justice Statistics, U.S. Department of Justice. Retrieved from http://www2.fbi.gov/ucr/cius2007/offenses/property_crime/arson.html

78. Morgan, C. S. (1953). Preventing arson. *Journal of Criminal Law, Criminology, and Police Science, 44*(2), 258–261.

79. *Fire and arson scene evidence,* 2000.

80. Firefighter accused of arson caught on tape. (2008, November 14). *ABC 7 News.* Retrieved from http://www.wjla.com/news/stories/1108/569981.html

81. Underwriting. (1996). *American Re-Insurance Company, Claims Division.* In *Motive, means, and opportunity: A guide to fire investigation.* Retrieved

from http://www.interfire.org/res_file/mmo4b.asp; Arson: Behavioral and economic aspects—Arson for profit. (2008). *Net Industries.* Retrieved from http://law.jrank.org/pages/530/Arson-Behavioral-Economic-Aspects-Arson-profit.html

82. Fighting insurance fraud. (2011). *Safeco Insurance.* Retrieved from http://www.safeco.com/insurance-101/consumer-tips/fighting-insurance-fraud

83. Steck-Flynn, K. (2009). Arson investigation. *Crime & Clues.* Retrieved from http://www.crimeand-clues.com/index.php/crime-scene-investigation/40-crime-scene-processing/96-arson-investigation

84. Dittmann, M. (2004). Types of fire-setters. *Monitor on Psychology, 35*(7), 42.

85. Juvenile fire setter intervention program. (2008). Retrieved from http://www.ci.weatherford.tx.us/index.asp?NID=818

86. Slavkin, M. L., & Fineman, K. (2000). What every professional who works with adolescents needs to know about firesetters. *Adolescence,* Winter.

87. Riding, T., Swann, C., & Swann, B. (2005). *The handbook of forensic learning disabilities.* Oxford: Radcliffe Medical.

88. Arson: Behavioral and economic aspects—Offender types. (2011). *Net Industries.* Retrieved from http://law.jrank.org/pages/529/Arson-Behavioral-Economic-Aspects-Offender-types.html

89. Williams, D. L. (2005). *Understanding the arsonist: From assessment to confession.* Tucson, AZ: Judges and Lawyers Publishing.

90. Martinez, B. (2002). *Multiple fire setters: The process of tracking and identification.* Tulsa, OK: PennWell Books.

91. Reed, P. (2009). Torch my ride: Arson for hire. *Edmunds.com.* Retrieved from http://www.edmunds.com/advice/insurance/articles/115584/article.html

Chapter 13

1. Bowden, M. (2001). *Killing Pablo: The hunt for the world's greatest outlaw.* New York: Atlantic Monthly Press.

2. Rojas, C., & Meltzer, J. (2005). *Elusive peace: International, national, and local dimensions of conflict in Colombia.* New York: Palgrave Macmillan.

3. What's wrong with the drug war? Mandatory minimum sentences. (2009). *Drug Policy Alliance Network.* Retrieved from http://www.drugpolicy.org/drugwar/mandatorymin/

4. Caulkins, J. P., Reuter, P., Iguchi, M. Y., & Chiesa, J. (2005). *How goes the war on drugs? An assessment of U.S. drug problems and policy.* Santa Monica, CA: Drug Policy Research Center, RAND.

5. Meier, R. F., & Geis, G. (2007). *The Roxbury series in crime, justice, and law.* London: Oxford University Press.

6. Dombrink, J., & Hillyard, D. (2007). *Sin no more: From abortion to stem cells: Understanding crime, law, and morality in America.* New York: New York University Press.

7. Cohen, M. R., & Cohen, F. S. (2008). *Readings in jurisprudence and legal philosophy* (Vol. II). Frederick, MD: Beard Books.

8. Parloff, R. (2009, September 18). How marijuana became legal: Medical marijuana is giving activists a chance to show how a legitimized pot business can work. Is the end of prohibition upon us? *CNNMoney.com/Fortune.* Retrieved from http://money.cnn.com/2009/09/11/magazines/fortune/medical_marijuana_legalizing.fortune/index.htm

9. National Organization for the Reform of Marijuana Laws. (2009). Retrieved from http://norml.org/index.cfm?Group_ID=3376

10. Abrams, D. I., Jay, C. A., Shade, S. B., Vizoso, H., Reda, H., Press, S., Kelly, M. E., Rowbotham, M. C., & Peterson, K. L. (2007). Cannabis in painful HIV-associated sensory neuropathy: A randomized placebo-controlled trial. *Neurology, 68,* 515–521.

11. Becker, H. (1963). *Outsiders: Studies in the sociology of deviance.* New York: Macmillan.

12. Gellner, E. (2000). Trust, cohesion, and the social order. In D. Gambetta (Ed.). *Trust: Making and breaking cooperative relations.* Oxford: Oxford University Press.

13. *National survey on drug use and health: National findings.* (2007). Washington, DC: Department of Health and Human Services.

14. The science of drug abuse and addiction. (2009). *National Institute on Drug Abuse, National Institutes of Health.* Retrieved from http://drugabuse.gov/index.html

15. Burke, P., O'Sullivan, J., & Vaughan, B. (2005). Adolescent substance use: Brief interventions by emergency care providers. *Pediatric Emergency Care, 21*(11), 770–776.

16. Nutt, D., King, L., Saulbury, W., & Blakemore, C. (2007). Development of a rational scale to assess the harm of drugs of potential misuse. *Lancet, 369*(9566), 1047–1053.

17. Board on Behavioral, Cognitive, and Sensory Sciences and Education (BCSSE). (2004). New treatments for addiction: Behavioral, ethical, legal, and social questions. *National Academies Press,* 7–8, 140.

18. Everitt, B., Belin, D., Economidou, D., Pelloux, Y., Dalley, J. W., & Robbins, T. W. (2008). *Neural mechanisms underlying the vulnerability to develop compulsive drug-seeking habits and addiction.* Cambridge, England: Department of Experimental Psychology, Behavioral and Clinical Neuroscience Institute, The Royal Society, University of Cambridge.

19. Zhang, X., Mi, J., Wetsel, W., Davidson, C., Xiong, X., Chen, Q., Ellinwood, E. E., & Lee, T. H. (2006). Pl3 kinase is involved in cocaine behavioral sensitization and its reversal with brain area specificity. *Biochemical and Biophysical Research Communications, 340*(4), 1144–1150.

20. Bickel, W., Miller, M., Yi, R., Kowal, B., Lindquist, D., & Pitcock, J. (2007). Behavioral and neuroeconomics of drug addiction: Competing neural systems and temporal discounting processes. *Drug and Alcohol Dependence, 90S,* S85–S91.

21. Miethe, T. D., McCorkle, R. C., & Listwan. S. J. (2006). *Crime profiles: The anatomy of dangerous persons, places, and situations.* Los Angeles: Roxbury.

22. Becker, H. C. (2008). Alcohol dependence, withdrawal, and relapse. *Alcohol Research and Health, 31*(4).

23. Dangerous drugs and drug abuse in the news. (2010, June 21). CDC survey finds 1 in 5 high school students abuse prescription drugs. *Drugdanger.com.* Retrieved from http://www.drugdanger.com/NEWS/2010/20100607-CDC_Survey.htm

24. Hagan, F. E. (2010). *Crime types and criminals.* Thousand Oaks, CA: Sage.

25. Inciardi, J., & McElrath, K. (Eds.). (2007). *The American drug scene: An anthology.* New York: Oxford University Press.

26. Effects of long-term marijuana use. (2008). *DrugRehab.com.* Retrieved from http://www.drug-rehab.com/long-term-marijuana-use.htm

27. Johnston, L. D., Bachman, J. G., & O'Malley, P. M. (2010). *Monitoring the Future: Questionnaire responses from the nation's high school seniors, 2009.* Ann Arbor, MI: Institute for Social Research.

28. National Center on Addiction and Substance Abuse. (2003). *Teen tipplers: America's Under age drinking epidemic.* New York: Author.

29. Mulvey, E. P., Odgers, C., Skeem, J., Gardner, W., Schubert, C., & Lidz, C. (2006). Substance use and community violence: A test of the relation at the daily level. *Journal of Consulting and Clinical Psychology, 74,* 743–754; Hoaken, P. N S., & Stewart, S. H. (2003). Drugs of abuse and the elicitation of human aggressive behavior. *Addictive Behaviors, 28,* 1533–1554.

30. *National survey on youth violence and illicit drug use.* (2006). Substance Abuse and Mental Health Administration. Retrieved from http://www.oas.samhsa.gov/2k6/youthViolence/youthViolence.htm

31. *Illicit drug use among persons arrested for serious crimes.* (2005, December 16). Substance Abuse and Mental Health Services Administration. Retrieved from http://www.oas.samhsa.gov/2k5/arrests/arrests.htm

32. The connection between drug abuse and crime is well known. (2009, July 22). *National Institute on Drug Abuse.* Retrieved from http://www.drugabuse.gov/PODAT_CJ/introduction/

33. Friedmann, P. D., Taxman, F. S., & Henderson, C. E. (2007). Evidence-based treatment practices for drug-involved adults in the criminal justice system. *Journal of Substance Abuse Treatment, 32,* 267– 277.

34. Knight, K., & Farabee, D. (2007). *Treating addicted offenders: A continuum of effective practices.* Kingston, NJ: Civic Research Institute.

35. Sullivan, J. P., & Elkus, A. (2008). Mexico's criminal insurgency. *Small Wars Journal,* August.

36. Helson, G. D. (2004, July 14). [Interview]. Supervisory Special Agent, U.S. Drug Enforcement Administration, San Diego, CA.

37. Vungkhanching, M., Sher, K., Jackson, K.,& Parra, G. (2004). Relation of attachment style to family history of alcoholism and alcohol use disorders in early adulthood. *Drug and Alcohol Dependence, 75,* 47–54.

38. Elkins, I., King, S., McGue, M., & Iacono, W. (2006). Personality traits and the development of nicotine, alcohol, and illicit drug disorders: Prospective links from adolescence to young adulthood. *Journal of Abnormal Psychology, 115,* 26–39.

39. Watt, T. T. (2004). Race/ethnic differences in alcohol abuse among youth: An examination of risk taking attitudes as a mediating factor. *Journal of Ethnicity in Substance Abuse, 3*(3), 33–47.

40. Lindsey, R. L., Weist, M. D., Smith-Lebeau,L., Rosner, L., Dixon, L. B., & Pruitt, D. D. (2004). Significance of self-reported drug or alcohol use among inner-city teenagers. *Psychiatric Services, 55,* 824–826.

41. Leinwand, D. (2007, March 15). College drug use, binge drinking rise. *USA Today.* Retrieved from http://www.usatoday.com/news/nation/2007-03-15-college-drug-use_N.htm

42. Iversen, L. (2005). Long-term effects of exposure to cannabis. *Current Opinion in Pharmacology, 5*(1), 69–72; also, see Facts on cannabis and

alcohol. (n.d.). *SaferChoice.org*. Retrieved from http://www.saferchoice.org/content/view/24/53/ (accessed January 12, 2010).

43. Majority of Americans support legalizing marijuana. (2009, December 9). *Angus Reid Public Opinion*. Retrieved from http://www.visioncritical.com/wpcontent/uploads/2009/12/2009.12.09_Drugs_US.pdf

44. Nadelmann, E. (2003). The U.S. is addicted to war on drugs. *Globe and Mail*.

45. Drug legalization: Myths and misconceptions. (n.d.). *Schaffer Library of Drug Policy*. Retrieved from http://druglibrary.org/SCHAFFER/debate/myths/myths1.htm (accessed January 12, 2010).

46. McVay, D. A. (2008). *Drug war facts* (6th ed.). Canada: Common Sense for Drug Policy.

47. Bertram, E., Blachman, M., Sharpe, K., & Andreas, P. (1996). *Drug war politics: The price of denial*. Berkeley: University of California Press.

48. Copeman, M. (2003). Drug supply and drug abuse. *Canadian Medical Association Journal, 168*(9), 1113; Drug abuse and addiction. (2008, September 17). *National Institute on Drug Abuse*. Retrieved from http://www.drugabuse.gov/scienceofaddiction/addiction.html

49. Kreek, M. J., Nielsen, D. A., Butelman, E. R., & LaForge, S. (2005). Genetic influences on impulsivity, risk taking, stress responsivity, and vulnerability to drug abuse and addiction. *Neurobiology of Addiction, 8*(11).

50. National Drug Control Strategy: 2009 Annual Report. (2009). Retrieved from www.whitehousedrugpolicy.gov/publications/policy/ndcs09/2009ndcs.pdf

51. Levinson, D. (2002). *Encyclopedia of crime and punishment*. Thousand Oaks, CA: Sage.

52. Federal Bureau of Investigation. (2009). *Crime in the United States, 2008*. Washington, DC: U.S. Department of Justice.

53. Weber, K. (2008, March 27). Prostitution trends. *kulr8.com*. Retrieved from http://www.kulr8.com/news/local/17074691.html

54. Hakim, D., & Rashbaum, W. K. (2008, March 10). Spitzer is linked to prostitution ring. *New York Times,* A1.

55. N.Y. governor apologizes after prostitution link. (2008, March 10). *msnbc.com*. Retrieved from http://www.msnbc.msn.com/id/23561606/

56. Sterk, C. E. (2000). *Tricking and tripping: Prostitution in the era of AIDS*. New York: Social Change Press.

57. Sex-tourism operation nets three. (2009, September 1). *CNN.com/crime*. Retrieved from http://www.cnn.com/2009/CRIME/08/31/cambodia.sex.tourism/

58. Sterk, C. E. (2000). Female crack users and their sexual relationships: The role of sex-for-crack exchanges. *Journal of Sex Research, 37*(4).

59. Edwards, J. M., Halpern, C. T., & Wechsberg, W. M. (2006). Correlates of exchanging sex for drugs or money among women who use crack cocaine. *AIDS Education and Prevention, 18,* 420–429.

60. Sharpe, T. T. (2005). *Behind the eight ball: Sex for crack cocaine exchange and poor black women*. Binghamton, NY: Haworth.

61. Norton-Hawk, M. (2004). Comparison of pimp and non-pimp controlled women. *Violence Against Women, 10*(2), 189–194.

62. Flowers, B. (2001). *Runaway kids and teenage prostitution*. Westport, CT: Praeger.

63. Dalla, R. (2006). *Exposing the "pretty woman" myth*. Portland, OR: Book News.

64. Agnes, F. (2008). The bar dancer and the trafficked migrant. In G. Letherby et al., *Sex as Crime*. Portland, OR: Willan.

65. Rabiroff, J., & Hae-Rym, H. (2009, September 9). "Juicy bars" said to be havens for prostitution aimed at U.S. military. *Stars and Stripes,* Pacific ed.

66. Sarup, K., & Anzia, L. (2008). Virginity for sale: The dark world of forced teen prostitution. *Women News Network*. Retrieved from http://www.alternet.org/rights/111358/virginity_for_sale:_the_dark_world_of_forced_teenprostitution/

67. Batstone, D. (2007). *Not for sale: The return of the global slave trade—and how we can fight it*. New York: HarperOne.

68. Hwang, S.-L., & Bedford, O. (2003). Precursors and pathways to adolescent prostitution in Taiwan. *Journal of Sex Research,* May.

69. Vito, G. F., Maahs, J. R., & Holmes, R. M. (2007). *Criminology: Theory, research, and policy*. Sudbury, MA: Jones and Bartlett.

70. Leichtentritt, R. D., & Davidson-Arad, B. (2004). Adolescent and young adult male-to-female transsexuals: Pathways to prostitution. *British Journal of Social Work, 34,* 349–374.

71. Kramer, L., & Berg, E. (2003). A survival analysis of timing of entry into prostitution: The differential impact of race, educational level, and childhood/adolescent risk factors. *Sociological Inquiry, 73,* 511–529.

72. Abramovich, E. (2005). Childhood sexual abuse as a risk factor for subsequent involvement in sex work: A review of empirical findings. *Journal of Psychology & Human Sexuality, 1,* 131–146.

73. Brown, J., Cohen, P., Chen, H. Smailes, E., & Johnson, J. (2004). Sexual trajectories of abused

and neglected youths. *Journal of Developmental and Behavioral Pediatrics, 25,* 77–83.

74. Miner, M., Flitter, J., & Robinson, B. (2006). Association of sexual re-victimization with sexuality and psychological function. *Journal of Interpersonal Violence, 21,* 503–524.

75. Sex for sale: Confessions of a client. (2008, October 11). *Today.msnbc.com.* Retrieved from http://www.msnbc.msn.com/id/27651436/

76. Should prostitution be illegal? (2009). *ProCon. Org.* Retrieved from http://prostitution.procon.org/viewanswers.asp?questionID=001315

77. Farley, M. (2007). *Prostitution and trafficking in Nevada: Making the connections.* San Francisco: Prostitution Research and Education.

78. Ramos, N. (2008). Prosecuting Johns. *Newsweek. com.* Retrieved from http://www.newsweek.com/id/168395

79. Novak, B. D. (2009). Freeing Jane: The right to privacy and the world's oldest profession. *Berkeley Electronic Press.* Retrieved from http://works.bepress.com/benjamin_novak/1/

80. Albert, A. (2002). *Brothel: Mustang Ranch and its women.* New York: Random House.

81. Justice Stewart in *Jacobellis v. Ohio,* 378 U.S. 184 (1964).

82. Davies, S. (2009, January 17). Kids face porn charges over "sexting." *NineMSN.com.* Retrieved from http://news.ninemsn.com.au/article.aspx?id=719928

83. Hughes, D. R. (2001). How pornography harms children. *ProtectKids.com.* Retrieved from http://www.protectkids.com/effects/harms.htm

84. Ferraro, M. M., Eoghan, C., & McGrath, M. (2005). *Investigating child exploitation and pornography: The Internet, the law, and forensic science.* San Diego: Academic.

85. Wells, M., Finkelhor, D., Wolak, J., & Mitchell, K. (2007). Defining child pornography: Law enforcement dilemmas in investigations of Internet child pornography possession. *Police Practice and Research, 8*(3), 269–282.

86. Callanan, C. (2007). 2007 Global Internet Trend Report. Retrieved from http://www.docstoc.com/docs/10715839/Inhope—Global-Internet-trends-2007

87. *Miller v. California,* 413 U.S. 15 (1973).

88. *Roth v. United States,* 354 U.S. 476 (1957).

89. *Miller v. California,* 413 U.S. 15 (1973).

90. *Pope v. Illinois,* 481 U.S. 497 (1987).

91. Hargrave, A. M., & Livingstone, S. (2009). *Harm and offence in media content: A review of the evidence.* Chicago: University of Chicago Press.

92. Boyle, K. (2000). The pornography debates: Beyond cause and effect. *Women's Studies International Forum, 23*(2), 187–195.

93. Hayes, M. (2008). Social and behavioral science research on the impact of pornography. *AgainstPornography.org.* Retrieved from https://againstpornography.org/socialsciencestudies.html

94. Burns, R. J. (2002). Male Internet pornography: consumers' perception of women and endorsement of traditional female gender roles. Austin: University of Texas, Department of Communication Studies.

95. Jensen, R. (2004). Pornography and sexual violence. *National Resource Center on Domestic Violence.* Retrieved from http://www.nrcdv.org/

96. Nisbet, M. C. (2009, June 7). The effects of pornography on perceptions of women & sexual violence. *Scienceblogs.com.* Retrieved from http://science-blogs.com/framingscience/2009/06/effects_of_pornography_on_perc.php; Bergen, R. K., & Bogle, K. A. (2000). Exploring the connection between pornography and sexual violence. *Violence and Victims, 15*(3), 227–234.

97. Jensen, R. (2008, October 20). The cruel boredom of pornography. *Countercurrents.org.* Retrieved from http://www.countercurrents.org/jensen201008.htm

98. Malamuth, N., Addison, T., & Koss, M. (2000). Pornography and sexual aggression: Are there reliable effects and can we understand them? *Annual Review of Sex Research, 11,* 26–91; Seto, M. C., Maric, A., & Barbaree, H. E. (2001). The role of pornography in the etiology of sexual aggression. *Aggression and Violent Behavior, 6,* 35–53.

99. Vega, V., & Malamuth, N. M. (2007). Predicting sexual aggression: The role of pornography in the context of general and specific risk factors. *Aggressive Behavior, 33,* 104–117.

100. *New York v. Ferber,* 458 U.S. 747 (1982).

101. Werhan, K. (2004). *Freedom of speech: A reference guide to the United States Constitution.* Westport, CT: Praeger.

102. Mota, S. A. (2002). The U.S. Supreme Court addresses the Child Pornography Prevention Act and Child Online Protection Act in Ashcroft v. Free Speech Coalition and Ashcroft v. American Civil Liberties Union. *Federal Communications Law Journal 55,* 85–98.

103. Obscene, indecent, and profane broadcasts. (2008). Federal Communications Commission, Consumer and Governmental Affairs Bureau. Retrieved from http://www.fcc.gov/cgb/consumerfacts/obscene.html

Chapter 14

1. Cook, D. (2009, 13). November Former Rep. William Jefferson sentenced to 13 years in prison. Retrieved from http://www.csmonitor.com/USA/Politics/2009/1113/former-rep-william-jefferson-sentenced-to-13-years-in-prison

2. Thompson, D. F. (1995). *Ethics in Congress: From individual to institutional corruption.* Washington, DC: Brookings Institute.

3. Erickson, M. M., & Hills, R. M. (2007). *Research on corruption and its control: The state of the art.* Washington, DC: International Bank for Reconstruction and Development, World Bank.

4. Sutherland, E. H. (1949). *White collar crime.* New York: Dryden.

5. Shover, N., & Hochstetler, A. (2006). *Choosing white collar crime.* New York: Cambridge University Press.

6. Miethe, T. D., McCorkle, R. C., & Listwan, S. J. (2006). *Crime profiles: The anatomy of dangerous persons, places, and situations.* New York: Roxbury.

7. Clinard, M. B., & Yeager, P. C. (2005). *Corporate crime.* Somerset, NJ: Transaction.

8. Crack down on corporate crime. (2003, March 16). *CitizenWorks.org.* Retrieved from http://www.citizenworks.org/corp/reforms.php

9. Beacham, L. G. (2006, February 7). Mining deaths a wake-up call to preserve civil justice. *Commondreams.org.* http://www.commondreams.org/views06/0207-24.htm

10. OSH Act of 1970. (2004, January 1). Occupational Safety and Health Administration, U.S. Department of Labor. Retrieved from http://www.osha.gov/pls/oshaweb/owadisp.show_document?p_table=OSHACT&p_id=2743

11. *Workplace injuries and Illnesses—2008.* (2009, October 29). Washington, DC: Bureau of Labor Statistics, U.S. Department of Labor.

12. Kennedy, Jr., R. F. (2004). *Crimes against nature.* New York: HarperCollins.

13. White, R. (2003). Environmental issues and the criminological imagination. *Theoretical Criminology, 7*(4), 483–506.

14. Natural resource management. (2009). Retrieved from http://www.pactworld.org/cs/natural_resource_management

15. Social science in natural resource management. (n.d.). U.S. Geological Survey, U.S. Department of the Interior. Retrieved from http://www.fort.usgs.gov/resources/spotlight/prairiedogs/pdog_socialscience.asp (accessed December 2, 2009).

16. *Waste research strategy.* (1999, February). Washington, DC: U.S. Environmental Protection Agency, Office of Research and Development.

17. FDA issues warning for Plavix, Prilosec users. (2009, November 18). *wibw.com.* Retrieved from http://www.wibw.com/toyourhealth/headlines/70429472.html

18. Gobert, J., & Punch, M. (2003). *Rethinking corporate crime.* New York: Cambridge University Press.

19. Friedrichs, D. O. (2002). Occupational crime, occupational deviance, and workplace crime: Sorting out the difference. *Criminal Justice, 2,* 243–256.

20. Internet security. (2009). Bank of New York Mellon Corporation. Retrieved from http://www.bnymellon.com/security/index.html

21. Vashista, A., Johnson, D., & Choudhury, M. (2005). Securities fraud. *American Criminal Law Review, 42,* 877–942.

22. Winslow, E. (2003). *Blind faith: Our misplaced trust in the stock market.* San Francisco: Berrett-Koehler.

23. SEC surpasses $2 billion in fair fund distributions in 2009. (2009, November 25). U.S. Securities and Exchange Commission. Retrieved from http://www.sec.gov/news/press/2009/2009-254.htm

24. Rosenbaum, S., Lopez, N., & Stifler, S. (2009). *Health insurance fraud: An overview.* Washington, DC: School of Public Health & Health Services, Department of Health Policy, George Washington University.

25. New analysis examines fraud in both private and public health insurance markets. (2009, June 26). *PharmacyChoice.com.* Retrieved from http://www.pharmacychoice.com/news/article.cfm?Article_ID=421093

26. Ledue, C. (2009, October 20). Pharmaceutical companies to pay $124M over Medicaid fraud charges. *HealthCareFinanceNews.com.* Retrieved from http://www.healthcarefinancenews.com/news/pharmaceutical-companies-pay-124m-over-medicaid-fraud-charges

27. Corum, D. (2008, November 24)[[check]]. Fraud and buildup add 13 to 18 percent in excess payments to auto injury claims. Malvern, PA: Insurance Research Council.

28. 26 U.S.C. § 7201 18 U.S.C. § 3571.

29. Articulated and clarified in *Spies v. United States,* 317 U.S. 492 (1943), and *United States v. Carlson,* 8 U.S.C. 1324a (2000).

30. Chambliss, W. J. (2001). *Power, politics, and crime.* Boulder, CO: Westview.

31. Cole, C. (2010, March 8). Closing coal plant a numbers game. *Azdailysun.com.* Retrieved from http://

azdailysun.com/news/local/article_4da48786-38c9-5fba-a8f7-209b3cf4604f.html

32. Pasternak, J. (2006, November 21). Navajos' desert cleanup no more than a mirage. *Los Angeles Times.* Retrieved from http://articles.latimes.com/2006/nov/21/nation/na-navajo21

33. President Obama repeals "Bennett Freeze" law. (2009, May 9). *nhonews.com.* Retrieved from http://navajohopiobserver.com/main.asp?Search=1&ArticleID=11493&SectionID=1&SubSectionID=1&S=1

34. Sampson, Z. C. (2008, November 12). Appeals court clears way for Rep. Jefferson trial. *RealClearPolitics.com.* Retrieved from http://www.realclearpolitics.com/news/ap/us_news/2008/Nov/12/appeals_court_clears_way_for_rep__jefferson_trial.html

35. Green, P., & Ward, T. (2004). *State crime: Governments, violence, and corruption.* London: Pluto.

36. Wrage, A. A. (2007). *Bribery and extortion: Undermining business, governments, and security.* Westport, CT: Praeger Security International.

37. Pavkovic, S. (2009, April 17). Jury convicts former Sen. Joseph Coniglio of extortion and mail fraud. *nj.com.* Retrieved from http://www.nj.com/news/index.ssf/2009/04/former_state_senator_convicted.html

38. Becker, K. (n.d.). *Genocide and ethnic cleansing.* Model United Nations Far West, 50th Session Issues. Retrieved from http://www.munfw.org/archive/50th/4th1.htm

39. Convention on the Prevention and Punishment of the Crime of Genocide. (1948, December 9). Article III. Retrieved from http://daccess-dds-ny.un.org/doc/RESOLUTION/GEN/NR0/044/31/IMG/NR004431.pdf?OpenElement

40. United Nations Secretary Kofi Annan's action plan to prevent genocide. (2004, April 7). United Nations Documents on Genocide Prevention. *PreventGenocide.org.* Retrieved from http://www.preventgenocide.org/prevent/UNdocs/#actionplan

41. Cohen, S. (2002). Human rights and crimes of the state: The culture of denial. In E. McLaughlin, J. Muncie, & G. Hughes (Eds.), *Criminological perspectives* (2nd ed.). London: Sage.

42. Markusen, E. (2002). Path to genocide studies. In S. L. Jacobs & S. Totten. *Pioneers of Genocide Studies.* New Brunswick, NJ: Transaction; Chalk, F., & Jonassohn, K. (1990). *The history and sociology of genocide: Analyses and case studies.* New Haven, CT: Yale University Press.

43. Dallaire, R. (2004). *Shake hands with the devil: The failure of humanity in Rwanda.* New York: Da Capo.

44. Rwanda: How the genocide happened. (2008, December 18). *BBC News.* Retrieved from http://news.bbc.co.uk/2/hi/africa/1288230.stm

45. *Rwanda: The preventable genocide.* (2000, July 7). *Council on Foreign Relations.* Retrieved from http://www.cfr.org/rwanda/rwanda-preventable-genocide/p15629

46. Niarchos, C. N. (1995). Women, war, and rape: Challenges facing the international tribunal for the former Yugoslavia. *Human Rights Quarterly, 17,* 649–690.

47. Smith-Spark, L. (2004, December 8). How did rape become a weapon of war? *GlobalPolicy.org.* Retrieved from http://www.globalpolicy.org/component/content/article/163/28294.html

48. Thomas, D. Q., & Ralph, R. E. (1994). Rape in war: Challenging the tradition of impunity. *SAIS Review,* Winter–Spring.

49. *Federal republic of Yugoslavia, Country reports on human rights practices.* (2001, February 23). U.S. Department of State. Retrieved from http://www.state.gov/g/drl/rls/hrrpt/2000/eur/865.htm

50. Amnesty International. (2004). Retrieved from www.amnesty.org (accessed December 18, 2009).

51. Rape as military strategy. (2009, March 16). Panel discussion, Women's Studies, Research Center, Brandeis University, Waltham, MA.

52. Siegel, D., Van de Bunt, H., & Zaitch, D. (Eds.). (2003). *Global organized crime: Trends and developments.* Boston: Kluwer Academic.

53. Glenny, M. (2008). *McMafia: A journey through the global criminal underworld.* New York: Knopf.

54. *Results of a pilot survey of forty selected organized criminal groups in sixteen countries.* (2002, September 2002). Global Program Against Transnational Organized Crime, United Nations Office on Drugs and Crime.

55. Lyman, M. D., & Potter, G. W. (2004). *Organized crime.* Upper Saddle River, NJ: Pearson/Prentice Hall.

56. Witwer, D. (2008). *Corruption and reform in the Teamsters Union.* Champlain: University of Illinois Press.

57. United Nations Office on Drugs and Crime. (2002, September). Results of a pilot survey or forty selected organized criminal groups in sixteen countries. Retrieved from http://www.unodc.org/pdf/crime/publications/Pilot_survey.pdf

58. Shaw, M. (2005). Drug trafficking and the development of organized crime in post-Taliban Afghanistan. Retrieved from http://siteresources.worldbank.org/SOUTHASIAEXT/Resources/Publications/448813-1164651372704/UNDC_Ch7.pdf

59. Rubin, B. (2004). *Road to ruin: Afghanistan's booming opium industry.* Center for American Progress and Center on International Cooperation, New York University.

60. McFeeley, R. (2001). Enterprise theory of investigation. *FBI Law Enforcement Bulletin, 70*(5), 19–26.

61. Lambert, K. A. (2009, October 8). RICO class action controversy continues. *Litigation News.* Retrieved from http://www.abanet.org/litigation/litigation-news/top_stories/class-action-rico-williams.html

Chapter 15

1. Omar Hassan al-Bashir. (2009, March 4). *New York Times.* Retrieved from http://topics.nytimes.com/topics/reference/timestopics/people/b/omar_hassan_al_bashir/index.html

2. Aas, K. F. (2007). *Globalization and crime.* Newbury Park, CA: Sage.

3. Barak, G. (2001). Crime and crime control in an age of globalization: A theoretical dissection. *Critical Criminology, 10*(1), 57–72.

4. Sheptycki, J., & Wardek, A. (Eds.). (2005). *Transnational and criminology.* London: Glass House.

5. Reichel, P. (2005). *Handbook of transnational crime and justice.* Newbury Park, CA: Sage.

6. Howard, G. J., Newman, G., & Pridemore, W. A. (2000). Theory, method, and data in comparative criminology. In D. Duffee (Ed.), *Criminal justice 2000: Measurement and analysis of criminal justice.* Washington, DC: National Institute of Justice.

7. Myamba, F. (2009, October 26). *Cross–national comparative criminological/victimological research: Methodological barriers and future directions.* Paper presented at the annual meeting of the American Society of Criminology, Royal York, Toronto. Retrieved from http://www.allacademic.com/meta/p34851_index.html

8. *About INTERPOL.* (2010, January 29). Retrieved from http://www.interpol.int/public/icpo/default.asp

9. *United Nations surveys on crime trends and the operations of criminal justice systems (CTS).* (2010). United Nations Office on Drugs and Crime, Vienna, Austria. Retrieved from http://www.unodc.org/unodc/en/data-and-analysis/United-Nations-Surveys-on-Crime-Trends-and-the-Operations-of-Criminal-Justice-Systems.html

10. Van Dijk, J., Van Kesteren, J., & Smit, P. (2007). *Criminal victimization in international perspective: Key findings from the 2004–2005 ICVS and EU ICS.* This report was produced in cooperation with the United Nations Office on Drugs and Crime (UNODC) and the United Nations Interregional Crime and Justice Research Institute (UNICRI).

11. Zhuo, Y., Messner, S. F., & Zhang, L. (2008). Criminal victimization in contemporary China: A review of the evidence and challenges for future research. *Crime, Law, and Social Change, 50*(3), 197–209.

12. Thompson, R. B, Fields, C. B., & Barker. T. (2009). *Comparative and international criminal justice.* Upper Saddle, NJ: Prentice Hall.

13. Ouimet, M. (1999). Crime in Canada and in the United States: A comparative analysis. *Canadian Review of Sociology and Anthropology, 36*(3), 389–408.

14. Belli, R. (2006, November 1). *To prosecute or not to prosecute? A comparative study of prosecutorial discretion at the national and level.* Paper presented at the annual meeting of the American Society of Criminology, Los Angeles.

15. Lenning, E., & Brightman, S. (2009). Oil, rape, and state crime in Nigeria. *Critical Criminology, 17,* 35–48.

16. Chen, X. (2002). Social control in China: Applications of the labeling theory and the reintegrative shaming theory. *International Journal of Offender Therapy and Comparative Criminology, 46,* 45–63.

17. LaFree, G., Morris, N. A., & Dugan, L. (2009). Cross-national patterns of terrorism comparing trajectories for total, attributed and fatal attacks, 1970–2006. *British Journal of Criminology.* doi:10.1093/bjc/azp066.

18. Chen, Social control in China, 2002.

19. Murphy, K., & Harris, N. (2007). Shaming, shame, and recidivism: A test of reintegrative shaming theory in the white-collar crime context. *British Journal of Criminology.* doi:10.1093/Bjc/Azm037

20. Chen, Social control in China, 2002; Chen, X. (2002). Community and policing strategies: A Chinese approach to crime control. *Policing and Society, 12*(1), 1–13.

21. Fromme, R., & Schwein, R. (2007). Operation smokescreen: A successful interagency collaboration. *FBI Law Enforcement Bulletin, 76*(12), 20–25.

22. Shaw, M. (2007). *Comparative approaches to urban crime prevention focusing on youth.* Montreal, Canada: International Center for the Prevention of Crime.

23. *International report on crime prevention and community safety: Trends and perspectives.* (2008). International Center for the Prevention of Crime. Montreal, Canada.

24. Roslycky, L. L. (2009). Organized transnational crime in the Black Sea region: A geopolitical dilemma? *Trends in Organized Crime, 12*(1), 21–29; Piazza, J. A. (2008). Incubators of terror: Do failed and failing states promote transnational terrorism? *International Studies Quarterly, 52*(3), 469–488.

25. Aldrich, R. J. (2009). US–European intelligence co-operation on counter-terrorism: Low politics and compulsion. *British Journal of Politics & International Relations, 11*(1), 122–139.

26. CBP, ICE release annual report on counterfeit goods seized. (2009, January 8). *CBP.gov.* Retrieved from http://www.customs.gov/xp/cgov/newsroom/news_releases/archives/2009_news_releases/january_2009/01082009.xml

27. Database on international intellectual property. (2010, April 23). *Interpol.int.* Retrieved from http://www.interpol.int/Public/FinancialCrime/IntellectualProperty/DIIP/Default.asp

28. *Report to the president and Congress on coordination of intellectual property enforcement and protection.* (2008). United States National Intellectual Property Law Enforcement Coordination Council. (2008). Retrieved from http://counterfeiting.unicri.it/docs/US NIPLECC_Report_and_Appendices_Final.pdf

29. Nykodym, N., Taylor, R., & Vilela, J. (2005). Criminal profiling and insider cyber crime. *Computer Law & Security Report,* 408–414.

30. Sanger, D. E., & Markoff, J. (2009, May 29). Obama outlines coordinated cyber-security plan. New York Times. Retrieved from http://www.nytimes.com/2009/05/30/us/politics/30cyber.html?_r=1&scp=1&sq=obama%20cybersecurity&st=cse

31. Jackson, W. (2009, May 29). Obama action plan calls for cybersecurity coordinator. *Federal Computer Week.* Retrieved from http://fcw.com/articles/2009/05/29/obama-cybersecurity-strategy.aspx

32. *International crime threat assessment.* (2000). This global assessment was prepared by a U.S. government interagency working group in support of and pursuant to the president's International Crime Control Strategy. Representatives from the following agencies, services, and departments participated in the drafting of this document: Central Intelligence Agency; Federal Bureau of Investigation; Drug Enforcement Administration; U.S. Customs Service; U.S. Secret Service; Financial Crimes Enforcement Network; National Drug Intelligence Center; the Departments of State, Treasury, Justice, and Transportation; Office of National Drug Control Policy; and the National Security Council.

33. *United Nations surveys on crime trends,* 2010.

34. Lasseter, T. (2009, May 11). Afghan drug trade thrives with help, and neglect, of officials. *Rawa News/McClatchy Newspapers.* Retrieved from http://www.rawa.org/temp/runews/2009/05/11/afghan-drug-trade-thrives-with-help-and-neglect-of-officials.html

35. Risen, J., & Landler, M. (2009, August 26). Accused of drug ties, Afghan official worries U.S. *New York Times.* Retrieved from http://www.nytimes.com/2009/08/27/world/asia/27kabul.html

36. Addis, C. L., & Katzman, K. (2009, May 18). *Middle East elections 2009: Lebanon, Iran, Afghanistan, and Iraq.* CRS Report for Congress. Retrieved from http://www.fas.org/sgp/crs/mideast/R40586.pdf

37. What is human trafficking? (2010). Global Initiative to Fight Human Trafficking, United Nations Office on Drugs and Crime. Retrieved from http://www.ungift.org/knowledgehub/en/about/human-trafficking.html

38. *Trafficking in persons report 2009.* U.S. Department of State. Retrieved from http://www.state.gov/g/tip/rls/tiprpt/2009/

39. Bliss, K. E. (2009, September 24). *Trafficking in the Mesoamerica corridor: A threat to regional and human security.* Center for Strategic and International Studies. Retrieved from http://csis.org/event/trafficking-mesoamerican-corridor-threat-regional-and-human-security

40. *United Nations convention against transnational organized crime and its protocols.* (2010). United Nations Office on Drugs and Crime. Retrieved from http://www.unodc.org/unodc/en/treaties/CTOC/index.html

41. Ibid.

42. Curtis, G. E., & Karacan, T. (2002). *The nexus among terrorists, narcotics traffickers, weapons proliferators, and organized crime networks in western Europe.* Washington, DC: Federal Research Division, Library of Congress.

43. Ruby, C. L. (2002). The definition of terrorism. *Analyses of Social Issues and Public Policy,* 9–14.

44. Ackerman, G. A. (2008, April 2). Testimony before the Senate Committee on Homeland Security and Governmental Affairs. Nuclear terrorism: Assessing the threat to the homeland. Retrieved from http://hsgac.senate.gov/public/index.cfm?FuseAction=Hearings.Hearing&Hearing_ID=42449878-5e68-4eef-978d-8e671fed2ab0

45. May, L. (2006). Humanity, international crime, and the rights of defendants. *Ethics & International Affairs, 20*(3), 373–382.

46. *Draft code of crimes against the peace and security of mankind.* (2005). United Nations. *Yearbook of the International Law Commission, 1996,* vol. II (Part Two). Retrieved from http://untreaty.un.org/ilc/summaries/7_4.htm

47. Tavakoli, N. (2009). A crime that offends the conscience of humanity: A proposal to reclassify trafficking in women as an international crime. *International Criminal Law Review, 9*(1), 77–98.

48. United States Secret Service's Operation Rolling Stone nets multiple arrests: Ongoing undercover operation targets cyber fraudsters. (2006, March 28). U.S. Department of Homeland Security, United States Secret Service. Retrieved from http://www.scribd.com/doc/1220551/US-Treasury-pub0906

49. *Identity theft research review.* (2010). National Institute of Justice, Office of Justice Programs, U.S. Department of Justice. Retrieved from http://www.ojp.usdoj.gov/nij/topics/crime/id-theft/welcome.htm

50. Grabosky, P. (2007). The Internet, technology, and organized vrime. *Asian Journal of Criminology, 2*(2).

51. Byrne, J. M., & Rebovich, D. J. (2007). *The new technology of crime, law, and social control.* Monsey, NY: Criminal Justice Press.

52. Wall, D. (2007). *Cybercrime.* Manchester, UK: Replica.

53. Men jailed for inciting terrorism on the Internet: A combined 24 years and a recommendation to deport. (2007, July 9). *The Register.* Retrieved from http://www.theregister.co.uk/2007/07/09/internet_terror_incitement_sentence/

54. *Terrorism Act 2006, Chapter 11.* (2006). Retrieved from http://www.legislation.gov.uk/ukpga/2006/11/pdfs/ukpga_20060011_en.pdf (accessed April 22, 2010).

55. Davis, B. R. (2006). Ending the cyber jihad: Combating terrorist exploitation Of the Internet with the rule of law and improved tools for cyber governance. Retrieved from commlaw.cua.edu/res/docs/articles/v15/davis.pdf

56. *Law enforcement analytic standards.* (2004, November). International Association of Law Enforcement Intelligence Analysts. U.S. Department of Justice. Retrieved from http://www.it.ojp.gov/documents/law_enforcement_analytic_standards.pdf

57. Korneev, D. O., Bogdanov, L. Y., & Nalivkin, A. V. (2004). Passive millimeter wave imaging system with white noise illumination for concealed weapons detection. doi: 10.1109/ICIMW.2004.1422305

58. Sex offender residency restrictions: How mapping can inform policy. (2008, July). *In Short, Toward Criminal Justice Solutions.* National Institute of Justice, Office of Justice Programs, U.S. Department of Justice. Retrieved from www.ncjrs.gov/pdffiles1/nij/222759.pdf

59. Chajewski, M., & Calkins-Mercado, C. (2007). *A geo-spatial analysis of sex offender residency restrictions in the state of New Jersey.* New York: John Jay College of Criminal Justice; Grubesic, T. H., Murray, A. T., & Mack, E. A. (2007). Geographic exclusion: Spatial analysis for evaluating the implications of Megan's Law. *Social Science Computer Review, 25*(2),143–162.

60. Presidential Decision Directive 42 (PDD-42). (1998, June). *International Crime Control Strategy.* Retrieved from http://www.fas.org/irp/offdocs/iccs/iccsi.html (accessed February 22, 2010).

61. President Bill Clinton, Speech at the United Nations, October 22, 1995.

62. Nuth, M. S. (2008). Taking advantage of new technologies: For and against crime. *Computer Law & Security Report, 24*(5), 437–446.

63. Wagley, J. R. (2006, March 20). *Transnational organized crime: Principal threats and U.S. responses.* Washington, DC: CRS Report for Congress, Library of Congress.

Chapter 16

1. Bluestein, G. (2010, February 17). Alabama professor in slayings shot victims methodically, survivor says. Associated Press. *Diverse.* Retrieved from http://diverseeducation.com/article/13547/

2. Barak, G. (2003). Revisionist history, visionary criminology, and needs-based justice. *Contemporary Justice Review, 5*(3), 217–225.

3. Kaplan, M. B. (2008). Hate crime and the privatization of political responsibility: Protecting queer citizens in the United States? *Liverpool Law Review, 29*(1), 37–50.

4. Reiman, J. (2009). *The rich get richer and the poor get prison* (9th ed.). Upper Saddle River, NJ: Prentice Hall.

5. Anderson, G. S. (2007). *Biological influences on criminal behavior.* Boca Raton, Florida: Taylor and Francis Group.

6. Jones, C. M. (2005). *Genetic and environmental influences on criminal behavior.* Retrieved from http://www.personalityresearch.org/papers/jones.html

7. Akers, R. L. (2009). *Social learning and social structure: A general theory of crime and deviance.* New Brunswick, NJ: Transaction.

8. Crosswhite, J. M, & Kerpelman, J. L. (2009). Coercion theory, self-control, and social information processing: Understanding potential mediators for how parents influence deviant behaviors. *Deviant Behavior, 30*(6), 611–646.

9. Friedrichs, D. O. (2010). *Trusted criminals: White collar crime in contemporary society.* Belmont, CA: Wadsworth.

10. Greene, R., & Kropf, N. (2009). *Human behavior theory: A diversity framework.* New Brunswick, NJ: Transaction.

11. Agnew, R. (1999). A general strain theory of community differences in crime rates. *Journal of Research in Crime and Delinquency, 36*(2), 123–155.

12. Henry, S. (2009). School violence beyond Columbine: A complex problem in need of an interdisciplinary analysis. *American Behavioral Scientist, 52*(9), 1246–1265.

13. Wells, L. E. (2010). Explaining crime in the year 2010. In J. Klofas & S Stojkovic (Eds.), *Crime and justice in the year 2010.* Florence, KY: Wadsworth.

14. Brown, S. (2006). The criminology of hybrids: Rethinking crime and law in technosocial networks. *Theoretical Criminology, 10*(2), 223–244.

15. Colvin, M. (2000). *Crime and coercion: An integrated theory of chronic criminality.* New York: St. Martin's.

16. Chen, X. (2002). Social control in China: Applications of the labeling theory and the reintegrative shaming theory. *International Journal of Offender Therapy and Comparative Criminology, 46,* 45–63.

17. Pollock, J. M. (2004). *Prisons and prison life: Costs and consequences over the years.* Los Angeles: Roxbury.

18. France, A., & Crow, I. (2005). Using the "risk factor paradigm" in prevention: Lessons from the evaluation of communities that care. *Children and Society, 19*(2), 172–184.

19. Haines, K., & Case, S. (2008). The rhetoric and reality of the "risk factor prevention paradigm" approach to preventing and reducing youth offending. *Youth Justice, 8*(1), 5–20.

20. Pugh, G. (2007). Policies in the UK to promote the well-being of children and young people. In A. France & R. Homel (Eds.), *Pathways and crime prevention: Theory, policy and practice.* UK: Willan.

21. Hawkins, D., Brown, E., Oesterle, S., Arthur, M. W., Abbot, R. D., & Catalano, R. F. (2008). Early effects of communities that care on targeted risks and initiation of delinquent behavior and substance abuse. *Journal of Adolescent Health, 43,* 15–22.

22. France, A., & Homel, R. (2006). Societal access routes and developmental pathways: Putting social structure and young people's voices into the analysis pathways into and out of crime. *Australian and New Zealand of Criminology, 39*(3), 287–294.

23. Manning, M., Homel, R., & Smith, C. (2010). A meta-analysis of the effects of early developmental prevention programs in at-risk populations on non-health outcomes in adolescence. *Children and Youth Services Review, 32,* 506–519.

24. Homel, R., Freiberg, K., & Branch, S. (2007). Pathways to a better quality of life for children and families through smarter social systems. *The Brisbane Line,* May.

25. Prevention and developmental pathways. (n.d.). Key Centre for Ethics, Law, Justice and Governance, Griffith University. Retrieved from http://www.griffith.edu.au/humanities-languages-criminology/key-centre-ethics-law-justice-governance/research/prevention-developmental-pathways

26. France, A., Freiberg, K., & Homel, R. (2010). Beyond risk factors: Towards a holistic prevention paradigm for children and young people. *British Journal of Social Work.* doi:10.1093/bjsw/bcq010

27. Haines & Case, 2008.

28. Morris, K., Barnes, M. (2008). Prevention and social exclusion: New understandings for policy and practice. *British Journal of Social Work, 38,* 1194–1211.

29. Society for Prevention Research. (2007). *Standards of evidence: Criteria for efficacy, effectiveness, and dissemination.* Falls Church, VA: Author.

30. Chafouleas, S. M., & Whitcomb, M. (2004). Integrating home, school, and community resources: Evaluation of a district-wide prevention program. *Reclaiming Children and Youth, 12*(4), 203–209.

31. Forman, J. (2004). Community policing and youth as assets. *Journal of Criminal Law and Criminology, 95*(1), 1–48.

32. Walker, L. (2009). Modified restorative circles: A reintegration group planning process that promotes desistance. *Contemporary Justice Review, 12*(4), 419–431.

33. Buchner, B., Bobb, M. J., Root, O., & Barge, M. (2008). *Evaluation of a pilot community policing program: The Pasadena Policy-Community Mediation and Dialog Program.* Washington, DC: Office of Community Oriented Policing Services, U.S. Department of Justice.

34. Braga, A. A. (2005). Hot spots policing and crime prevention: A systematic review of randomized controlled trials. *Journal of Experimental Criminology, 1*(170), 317–342.

35. McDevitt, J. (2008). *Promoting cooperative strategies to reduce racial profiling.* Washington, DC: Office of Community Oriented Policing Services, U.S. Department of Justice.

36. Velez, M. B., Krivo, L. J., & Peterson, R. D. (2003). Structural inequality and homicide: An assessment of the black-white gap in killings. *Criminology, 41*(3), 645–672.

CREDITS

Photo Credits

Chapter 1 p. 2, © Karim Shamsi-Basha/ The Image Works; p. 4T, ©TANNEN MAURY/epa/Corbis; p. 4B, Getty Images; p. 6, ©Ted Soqui/Sygma/Corbis; p. 7B, © Jack Kurtz/The Image Works; p. 9, © LACY ATKINS/ San Francisco Chronicle/Corbis; p. 10, David Sacks/ Getty Images; p. 13L, Royalty-Free/CORBIS; p. 13R, DON EMMERT/AFP/Getty Images; p. 14, Used with permission of the Orlando Sentinel, © 2012. Photo: George Skene; p. 16, Courtesy of the Ventura County Sheriff's Department.

Chapter 2 p. 24, © Jack Kurtz/The Image Works; p. 26, Bettmann/Corbis; p. 28, HIP/Art Resource; p. 31, © Radius Images/Corbis; p. 33, © LARRY DOWNING/ Reuters/Corbis; p. 34, Musee de la Tapisserie, Bayeux, France/ Bridgeman; p. 35, The Granger Collection; p. 37, © Bettmann/Corbis; p. 42, Russell Lee/Corbis; p. 43, Bettmann/Corbis; p. 44, ©Topham/The Image Works.

Chapter 3 p. 48, Scott Olson/Getty Images; p. 50, © Jeff Tuttle/epa/Corbis; p. 57, The Topeka Capital Journal, Thad Allton/AP Images; p. 60, © Banana-Stock/PunchStock; p. 63, © BananaStock/PunchStock; p. 66, Andersen Ross/Getty Images; p. 68R, Polly Klaas Foundation/AP Images; p. 68L, Ben Margot/AP Images.

Chapter 4 p. 78, Thinkstock Images/ Getty Images; p. 80, William Fernando Martinez/AP Images; p. 84, Patrick Bennett/Corbis; p. 87, Photo courtesy of NSOR; p. 90, Hugh Patrick Brown/Sygma/Corbis; p. 91, Courtesy of Albert Bandura; p. 97, Courtesy of Philip Zimbardo.

Chapter 5 p. 102, © DEA Picture Library/Art Resource, NY; p. 104, Dana Hoff/Brand X Pictures/ Getty Images; p. 105, © Scala/Art Resource; p. 106L, © Lebrecht/The Image Works; p. 106M, The Art Archive/Musée du Château de Versailles/Dagli Orti; p. 106R, The Art Archive/Musée du Château de Versailles/Dagli Orti; p. 107, THE KOBAL COLLECTION/ WARNER BROS./GORDON, MELINDA SUE; p. 109, Aaron Roeth Photography; p. 110, Walt Zeboski/AP Images; p. 111, PETER DaSILVA/epa/ Corbis; p. 114, Spencer Platt/Getty Images; p. 117, Jonathan Drake/ Reuters/Corbis; p. 118, FBI/AP Images; p. 119, Charlie Riedel/AP Images.

Chapter 6 p. 124, VICTOR HABBICK VISIONS/ Getty Images; p. 126, © John Storey/San Francisco Chronicle/Corbis; p. 128, © Mary Evans Picture Library /The Image Works; p. 129, © Print Collector/HIP/The Image Works; p. 132, Peter Essick/Aurora Photos; p. 134, ©WDCN/Univ. College London/Photo Researchers, Inc.; p. 135L, © Hans Berggren/Naturbild/ Corbis; p. 135R, ©Trevor Snapp/Corbis; p. 136, © Photodisc/PunchStock; p. 140T, Jack Hollingsworth/Getty Images; p. 140B, Photolibrary.

Chapter 7 p. 148, © St Petersburg Times/Keri Wiginton/The Image Works; p. 150, © Curt Borgwardt/ Sygma/Corbis; p. 152, © Bettmann/Corbis; p. 153, © David M. Grossman/The Image Works; p. 155, © Ho/Reuters/Corbis; p. 156, © Pima County Sheriff's Dept. via The Arizona Republic/AP Images; p. 158, © Roy McMahon/Corbis; p. 160, © LWA-Dann Tardif/ Corbis; p. 162, Ethan Miller/Getty Images; p. 163T, Clarissa Leahy/Getty Images; p. 163B, © Stockbyte/ PunchStock; p. 166, © Mike Stewart/Sygma/Corbis.

Chapter 8 p. 174, Leon Neal/AFP/Getty Images; p. 176B, Courtesy of Google Maps; p. 176T, Courtesy of St. Paul Police Department; p. 177, © Debbie Noda/ ZUMA Press/Corbis; p. 179, © Noah Addis/Corbis; p. 180, © Syracuse/J.Berry/The Post-Standard/ The Image Works; p. 183, © Car Culture/ Corbis; p. 186, © David Grossman/The Image Works; p. 189, Paul Bereswill/ Getty Images; p. 192, PhotoLink/Getty Images.

Chapter 9 p. 198, Ellen Denuto/Getty Images; p. 200, Kevin Higley, File/AP Images; p. 202, © Bob Daemmrich/The Image Works; p. 205, © BananaStock/ PunchStock; p. 207, © BananaStock/PunchStock; p. 208, © PhotoAlto/PunchStock; p. 209T, John Bryson/Time & Life Pictures/Getty Images; p. 209B, Merced Sun-Star, Marci Stenberg/AP Images; p. 217, Alison Wright/Corbis.

Chapter 10 p. 224, Stock Montage/Getty Images; p. 226, Peter Turnley/Corbis; p. 229, Bill Hudson/AP Images; p. 230, © Paul Chinn/San Francisco Chronicle/ Corbis; p. 231, © Mary Evans Picture Library/The Image Works; p. 233B, © Andrew Fox/Corbis; p. 233T, © Stockbyte/PunchStock; p. 236, AP Images; p. 239, © Lawrence Manning/Corbis; p. 240, Photodisc/Getty Images; p. 241, Comstock/Getty Images; p. 244, © CARLOS JAVIER ORTIZ/epa/Corbis.

Chapter 11 p. 250, © Image Source/Corbis; p. 252, © Dan McCoy Rainbow/Science Faction/Corbis; p. 253, Charles Rex Arbogast/AP Images; p. 260, AP Images; p. 265, ©TOBIAS SCHWARZ/Reuters/

Text and Figure Credits

Chapter 2 Table 2.1, p. 27: Reprinted with permission of ProCon.org.

Chapter 3 Figure 3.1, p. 52: Reproduced by permission from UNICRI (United Nations Interregional Crime & Justice Research Institute), 2000 International Crime Victimization Study Codebook, p. 38; Table 3.6, p. 67: Reprinted with permission of Monitoring the Future.

Chapter 4 Box 4.1, p. 82: Eric Sterling, "Making the War on Drugs." Some of this information was previously published in *Getting Justice Off Its Junk Food Diet* by Eric Sterling. The Criminal Justice Policy Foundation, Silver Spring, Maryland, July 26, 2006. N.B.: In 2001, Detective Brown went to federal prison for two years for lying under oath about his expertise in drug cases; Table 4.1, p. 83: Reprinted with permission of Monitoring the Future; Table 4.5, p. 97: Academy of Criminal Justice Sciences, Code of Ethics, III. Ethical Standards, March 21, 2000. Reprinted with permission.

Chapter 6 Figure 6.3, p. 138: By Henry Herbert Goddard, 1912, *The Kallikak Family: A Study in the Heredity of Feeble-Mindedness,* New York: The Macmillan Company.

Chapter 8 Figure 8.1, p. 180: Reproduced by permission of crimetheory.com.

Chapter 9 p. 202: FAMILY CIRCUS @ BILL KEANE, INC. KING FEATURES SYNDICATE; p. 215: William Chambliss, "The Saints and the Roughnecks." Reprinted with permission of the author.

Chapter 10 Figure 10.3, p. 237: Reproduced by permission from The Student Room, http://www. thestudentroom.co.uk/wiki/Revision:AQA_Sociology_ A2_-_Crime_and_Deviance_-_Left_Realist_Criminology, Section 4; Figure 10.4, p. 242: William Chambliss, "Conflicts, Contradictions, Dilemmas and Resolutions," *British Journal of Law and Society,* 1979, 2:153, Wiley-Blackwell Publisher.

Chapter 11 p. 258: Figure "Global Firearm Deaths." Reprinted by permission of Small Arms/Firearms Education and Research Network (SAFER-Net); p. 259: Figure "Gun Deaths per 100,000 Population." Reprinted by permission of Small Arms/Firearms Education and Research Network (SAFER-Net); p. 274: Hate Map, www.splcenter.org/get-informed/hate-map. Used by permission of Southern Poverty Law Center.

Chapter 12 Table 12.1, p. 286: "Theft Surveys." www.hayesinternational.com/thft_srvys.html. Copyright © 2008 by Jack L. Hayes International. Used by permission of Jack L. Hayes International.

Chapter 13 Figure 13.1, p. 314: Reprinted with permission of Monitoring the Future; Figure 13.2, p. 316: 2008 Monitoring the Future (MTF) study, special tabulations for combined 8th-, 10th-, and 12th-graders (December 2008); Table 13.2, p. 317: National Survey on Drug Use and Health. Office of Applied Studies, Substance Abuse and Mental Health Data Archive (SAMHDA), *Illicit Drug Use Among Persons Arrested for Serious Crimes,* NSDUH Report, 16 December 2005; Figure 13.3, p. 319: Courtesy of The Effective National Drug Control Strategy, prepared by the Network of Reform Groups in consultation with the National Coalition for Effective Drug Policies. www. csdp.org/edcs/edcs.htm.

Chapter 15 p. 359: "Homicide and Serial Sex Crimes" Flyer, originally published Lyon, France, November 25–26 2008 Crimes Conference. Reprinted with permission of INTERPOL.

NAME INDEX

SUBJECT INDEX

Page references in **bold** refer to definitions. Page references followed by an "*f*" or "*t*" refer to figures or tables, respectively.